The PDMA Handbook
of New Product
Development

The PDMA Handbook of New Product Development

Milton D. Rosenau, Jr.
Rosenau Consulting Company

Abbie Griffin
University of Chicago

George A. Castellion
SSC Associates

Ned F. Anschuetz
DDB Needham Worldwide

John Wiley & Sons, Inc.
New York • Chichester • Brisbane • Toronto • Singapore

Copyright © 1996 by the PDMA (Product Development and Management Association)
Published by John Wiley & Sons, Inc.

Library of Congress Cataloging in Publication Data:
The PDMA handbook of new product development / Milton D. Rosenau, Jr.
    p.   cm.
    Includes index.
    ISBN 0-471-14189-5
    1. New products—United States—Management—Handbooks, manuals,
etc. 2. Product management—United States—Handbooks, manuals, etc.
3. Marketing—United States—Handbooks, manuals, etc. 4. Design,
Industrial—United States—Handbooks, manuals, etc. I. Rosenau,
Milton, D., 1931–   II. Product Development & Management
Association.
HF5415.153.p35   1996
658.5′75—dc20   96-33743

Contents

PART FOUR   FINISHING THE JOB

PART FIVE   PDMA'S BEST PRACTICES RESEARCH

Foreword

Twenty years ago, when the Product Development & Management Association was being formed, the profession of product development was in its infancy. Materials to help practitioners learn were scarce. During the last two decades knowledge of the field has grown. The PDMA has played an important role in that growth as it pursued its mission of disseminating information on best practices via conferences, workshops, research studies, and publications.

The *PDMA Handbook of New Product Development* is an addition to PDMA's portfolio of information products. Each chapter of this book was written by product development professionals who are at the leading edge of knowledge in their respective areas of new product expertise. We are proud to present it to you.

PDMA's handbook has value for anyone involved in product development. Together the thirty chapters present a complete picture of the knowledge needed for effective product development. Foundation concepts such as identifying customer needs, using multifunctional teams, and having an appropriate development process are covered. So are important issues emerging in the field, such as process ownership, pipeline management, metrics, and product architecture. Experienced professionals can learn from the authors' leading-edge thinking and practice.

The champion of this project was Milton D. ("Mickey") Rosenau, Jr., and PDMA owes him a great debt for his unremitting efforts on its behalf. Additional thanks are due to the three senior editors, Ned Anschuetz, George Castellion, and Abbie Griffin, for their contributions to its development and ultimate success. Using a team approach and parallel processing, they achieved a fast cycle time. We believe that this new handbook will be an important reference standard for new product development professionals.

I hope you will find the *PDMA Handbook of New Product Development* a valuable source of practical and immediate knowledge and that you will keep it close at hand.

Albert L. Page
President (1994–1995)
Product Development & Management Association

Chicago, Illinois
December 1995

Dr. Page is a Professor of Marketing at the University of Illinois Chicago. He earned the MBA and Ph.D. degrees in marketing from Northwestern University. His research and teaching interests span the fields of product development, industrial marketing, and services marketing. He has published over 25 papers on these topics, including five articles in The Journal of Product Innovation Management. *He has also been a consultant to corporate and nonprofit clients on many occasions. Dr. Page is a long-time member of the PDMA and has held several offices within the association. He is now the Past-President.*

The PDMA would like your feedback on the following questions:

- What are your suggestions for additions to the next edition?

- What should be deleted in the next edition?

- What would you like to contribute to the next edition?

Send feedback to:

Editor, PDMA Handbook of New Product Development
401 North Michigan Avenue
Chicago, IL 60611-4267
Phone: (312) 527-6644
Fax: (312) 527-6729

Please include your name, address, phone, and fax number.

Introduction

WHO THIS BOOK IS FOR

This book is a unique resource covering many *practical* aspects of product development and is written for *everyone* who is involved in the development of new products and services:

- Novices and less experienced practitioners will find basic information on critical elements in new product and service development.
- Experienced practitioners and experts will find a useful source for information about aspects of the field that are outside their area of expertise.
- Academics will find authoritative practical material to support their executive education and extension programs.

There is important, current information for you whether you are primarily developing goods (assembled or nonassembled) or services that are intended for either consumer or business-to-business markets. No book can make a complex process simple, but this book should provide every reader with immediately useful information.

THE BOOK'S APPROACH

We have deliberately aimed this handbook at the basic or less experienced level, since even experienced practitioners will find helpful guidance outside their expertise. For example, a marketing expert can gain some basic insight to manufacturing issues, or a technologist can obtain guidance about market research.

USEFUL AND UNIQUE FEATURES OF THIS BOOK

Each chapter was written by experts who were chosen to convey *practical* contemporary knowledge. Many authors are widely recognized service providers, some authors are themselves practitioners employed by America's leading corporations, and some authors are academics selected because their research or teaching exposes them to effective current corporate practices. The goal has been to provide authoritative information about today's best practices in product development.

We have deliberately aimed for short chapters, which was quite a challenge for expert authors. Many of these might have written a book on their subject matter. Each chapter also contains references to mostly very current sources of additional information. This format provides you with what you immediately have to know and steers you toward more resources if you want or need further guidance on a particular topic.

Software can play a useful role in product development (as in many other fields). We have an appendix that summarizes the generic software that you may find helpful; we deliberately avoided mention of specific products because of rapid obsolescence. In addition, the handbook provides an extensive glossary of the important terms in the field.

The handbook also contains a complete index of all the articles, abstracts, and book reviews that have been published in the *Journal of Product Innovation Management*. This journal is the leading source of new knowledge in the field of product development. This appendix provides the first source of this consolidated information.

HOW THIS BOOK IS ORGANIZED

We have organized the handbook chapters in four sections that correspond to the development sequence:

1. Before you get started
2. Getting started
3. Doing the development
4. Finishing the job

The next section is a report on the second Product Development & Management Association (PDMA)–sponsored best practice research project, which was completed in 1995. You can learn what practices companies have found most effective from this. Hopefully, your company will adopt these proven approaches.

Following this we have the three appendices:

A. A summary of software tools
B. An extensive glossary
C. The complete index of everything that has been published through the end of 1995 in PDMA's *Journal of Product Innovation Management*, which is the premier source of emerging knowledge.

ACKNOWLEDGMENTS

This has been—in common with other PDMA projects—an all-volunteer activity. All the authors volunteered their time and talent, often taking personal time to complete their contribution despite already full professional calendars. We hope you are pleased with their work. Each contribution was reviewed anonymously by another expert and by the chief editor or the cognizant senior editor. The ultimate responsibility for chapter content ultimately lies with each author, but the editors wish to thank the expert reviewers who also gave generously of their time:

William Ausura
Edward J. Bartkus
Phyllis A. Britnell
Sergio Burani
Michael M. Cone
Jim Crimmins
William Herbein
Rick Knoll
Stephen Krzeminski
William B. Lee
Rick Lightburn
Thomas MacAvoy
C. Lee Meadows
Patricia W. Meyers

John J. Moran
Duane Niedert
Kumar Nochur
Marvin L. Patterson
Paul G. Phillips
William Riggs
Marcia Rorke
Barry Siadat
Stephen M. Somemeyer
Jack Thatcher
Bill Torregrossa
Johnnie P. Walker
W. Martin Watson

We also appreciate the help of C. Merle Crawford in arranging for the partial use of the glossary from his well-regarded text, *New Products Management*. Merle has been the driving force behind much of what PDMA set out to do when it was founded, and this handbook would never have come into being if he had not stimulated the PDMA's formation and growth.

Finally, we appreciate the support that our publisher, John Wiley & Sons, has provided. Robert J. Argentieri and his able assistant, Minna Panfilli, have provided timely counsel and have shepherded a multiauthored manuscript through the editorial process.

Chief Editor:
Milton D. Rosenau, Jr., CMC
Rosenau Consulting Company

Senior Editors:
Abbie Griffin   George Castellion   Ned Anschuetz
University of Chicago   SSC Associates   DDB Needham Worldwide

December 1995

Milton D. Rosenau, Jr., *Rosenau Consulting Company*

A Certified Management Consultant, he heads Rosenau Consulting Company, which he founded in 1978. This company, which has twice been named as one of the 100 leading management consulting firms in the United States, is a specialized management consulting firm helping clients move profitable new product ideas to market quickly. Clients are primarily major corporations, including many Fortune 500 corporations, that manufacture high-technology industrial products. His personal background includes successful new product development for industrial and consumer markets as well as commercial diversification from technology developed on government contract programs. He is the President of the Product Development & Management Association.

Abbie Griffin, *University of Chicago, GSB*

Dr. Griffin is an Associate Professor with a joint appointment in the Marketing and Operations Management departments. Her research focuses on measuring and improving the process of new product development, including the marketing techniques associated with developing new products. She has published articles on product development in Marketing Science, Sloan Management Review, *and the* Journal of Product Innovation Management. *Prior to becoming an academic, she worked in product development at Corning Glass Works, was a consultant with Booz, Allen and Hamilton and started her career as an engineer at Polaroid Corporation. Her personal background includes a passion for quilting.*

George A. Castellion, *SSC Associates*

George Castellion is a management consultant in new product development providing services to clients in R&D-intensive industries. He specializes in working with client firms in the uncertain, complex, and conflictual world at the front end of a new product development process, the fuzzy front end. Dr. Castellion established SSC Associates after a practitioner career as an inventor, as manager of R&D groups, and in several line positions in marketing. He is founding Director of the PDMA's Frontier Dialogues on the Fuzzy Front End and on New Product Teams, and is the PDMA's VP for Association Development.

Ned Anschuetz, *DDB Needham Worldwide*

Ned is a Senior Vice President at DDB Needham Worldwide, a major advertising agency where he has worked since 1979. He is a Group Director of Strategic Planning and Research as well as Research Director for the agency's new products group. He has been an active member of the Product Development and Management Association and the American Marketing Association. Ned has broad experience in concept development and evaluation for a wide range of new consumer products and services developed in partnership with major national advertisers.

About the Product Development & Management Association (PDMA)

The PDMA is a nonprofit professional organization dedicated to serving people with an interest in new products. Professionals, executive managers, and academics in the field recognize the PDMA as the global leader in communicating knowledge and tools for the benefit of people and organizations that develop new products and services. Growing at 20 percent a year, the PDMA today stands at over 2000 members representing business people and academics from all sectors of the economy in over 20 countries.

The development of new products or services involves an integrated set of unique activities. The PDMA is the only organization that addresses this challenge by providing:

- Conferences and meetings
- Publications
- Awards
- Sponsored research

PDMA's membership is unique in several ways. It represents the best new-products professionals from the most widely admired and accomplished new products companies in the world, from the largest to the smallest, and from capital goods to high technology to package goods to services of all kinds. PDMA's members include the field's foremost academics and service providers. Whereas most other professional associations are vertical organizations specializing in one industry or one function, PDMA's membership is horizontal and multifunctional, the current state of the new product field. This unique characteristic allows PDMA to address innovation management issues in the same way as multifunctional new product development teams do in practice.

PDMA fills an information void in the business world. Practitioners turn to PDMA to find the answers they cannot get anywhere else. Through PDMA's national and international meetings, its local area chapter meetings, its publications, audio and visual tapes, awards programs, research programs, workshops, and in-depth discussion meetings, PDMA offers members the opportunity to learn about the strategies, processes, and organizational issues that are involved in product development. Members usually describe PDMA's greatest value to them as being the networking opportunities it offers. The membership directory is the only place in the world where you can gain access to 2000 new product professionals.

CONFERENCES AND MEETINGS

Annual International Conference. At the annual PDMA International Conference, executives and academics from organizations that are leaders in innovation present cutting-edge ideas, research, and case studies. Basic and advanced workshops offer effective training for managers at all levels of experience.

Jointly sponsored conferences. In addition to the annual conference, PDMA jointly sponsors several meetings throughout the year, focusing on important new product issues.

Local chapter meetings. With ten regional chapters throughout the country, PDMA currently sponsors over 30 local meetings annually, offering an excellent opportunity for local involvement and exchange of ideas.

Frontier Dialogues. The Frontier Dialogue meetings offer a venue for a small number of experienced participants to think creatively and exchange ideas about significant developments in new product innovation. The Dialogues provide secluded settings, experienced facilitators, and confidentiality to stimulate fresh insights that participants find most useful in their professional lives. Sponsoring organizations have included Becton Dickinson, Corning, Dow Chemical, Eli Lilly, Eastman Chemical, Polaroid, Rohm & Haas, Procter & Gamble, Johnson & Johnson, 3-M, and Hewlett-Packard.

PUBLICATIONS

Journal of Product Innovation Management. The *Journal of Product Innovation Management,* published six times a year, brings its readers the theory and practice that will enable them to operate at the cutting edge of effective management practice. The *Journal* takes a multifunctional, multidisciplinary, international approach to the issues of innovation, and draws on the work of authors from all over the world. Contents include articles by practitioners and academics, abstracts of relevant articles published elsewhere, and book reviews.

Visions. PDMA's quarterly newsletter, *Visions,* offers views from practitioners on new product development and updates members on chapter news, regional meetings, and upcoming events.

Membership Directory. PDMA's *Membership Directory* is published annually with updated additions published in *Visions.*

AWARDS

Crawford Fellows. The PDMA confers honorary recognition to select individuals who have made unique contributions to advancing the field of new product development. This honor is named after the founder of the PDMA, Professor C. Merle Crawford.

Outstanding Corporate Innovator Award. The only program of its kind, the Outstanding Corporate Innovator Award recognizes leading companies that have consistently sustained growth through innovation over a period of at least five years. Recipients receive their awards and present their successful innovation programs at PDMA's Annual International Conference. Recent recipients have included Bausch & Lomb, Chrysler, Welsh Allyn, Nabisco, Hewlett-Packard, Mariott, Harris Corporation, Merck, Apple Computer, Eli Lilly, Nordic Track, Safety Kleen, Fluke, Senco Products, and Pepsi.

Dissertation. The PDMA supports academic research through an annual dissertation competition. Current doctoral students compete for a $5000 grant to support their dissertation research. The winners report their results at PDMA's Annual International Conference. Through this competition, PDMA attracts beginning scholars into the field of product development.

SPONSORED RESEARCH

PDMA supports innovation directly by investing in research such as its *Best Practices Study,* a survey of new product practices by a large number of companies, and its *Salary Survey,* which provides a benchmark for assessing compensation in the field. PDMA also supports other important research projects which further development of knowledge in the field.

Membership and Further Information

To obtain membership or other information about the PDMA, please call the PDMA International office at (800) 232-5241.

PART ONE

BEFORE YOU GET STARTED

A bad beginning makes a bad ending.
—EURIPIDES, GREEK PLAYWRIGHT, 438 B.C.

Uncertainty, complexity, and conflict prevail in the "fuzzy front end" of new product development. Seasoned new product developers sense the key issues *before* they becomes issues. High leverage goes hand in hand with many actions that can be taken in the front end to resolve these issues. This section sets the stage for action.

Frequently, appropriate action is ignored even though decisions made in the fuzzy front end have high financial impact. Some of this neglect is due to pressure on the new-products people to get moving. Some reluctance to commit is because management tools such as schedules and budgets, effective in other functional areas of the firm, work differently in the new product arena. Some comes from a reluctance to deal, right from the start, with the gritty realities of "soft issues" such as political behavior and the composition of new product teams.

1 NEW PRODUCTS

What Separates the Winners from the Losers
Robert G. Cooper

1.1. INTRODUCTION

New products are critical to the success of modern corporations. Facing increasing competition at home and abroad, rapidly evolving technologies, changing customer needs, and shorter product life cycles, a steady steam of successful new products is fundamental to business success.

What are the keys to new product success? What separates winners from losers? The answers to these questions are central to successful new product management: They provide insight for managing new product projects (e.g., are certain practices strongly linked to success?) and they provide clues to new product selection (what are the telltale signs of a winner?). In this chapter we report findings from myriad studies of what makes new products winners.

These success factors can be divided roughly into two groups:

> Of the two sets of critical success factors, new product process factors have by far the greatest impact.

1. *Process factors:* factors that capture the nature of the new product process and

the project is undertaken. These factors are often controllable.

2. *Selection factors:* factors that describe the new product project and its situation. These tend to be outside the control of the project leader, team, or management but are useful in project selection.

Of the two sets, process factors, presented first, have by far the stronger impact on success.

1.2. CRITICAL SUCCESS FACTORS: PROCESS-RELATED

1. A Unique, Superior Product

Superior and differentiated products—those that deliver unique benefits and superior value to the customer—are the key to success and new product profitability. Their success rates are reported to be three to five times higher than those of copycat, reactive, and ho-hum products with few clearly differentiated characteristics. (Note that a "customer" buys the product; a "user" uses the product; the two are not necessarily the same, although we often use the terms interchangeably.)

That differentiated, superior products are the key to success should come as no surprise to product innovators. Apparently, however, that has not been obvious to everyone: Study after study shows that "reactive products" and "me-too" offerings are the rule rather than the exception in many firms' new product efforts; and the majority fail!

What do these superior products with unique customer or user benefits have in common? The winning products:

- Feature good value for the customer's money, reduce the customer's total costs (high value in use), and boast excellent price and performance characteristics.
- Provide excellent relative product quality relative to competitors' products and in terms of how the user measures quality.
- Are superior to competing products in terms of meeting users' needs, offer unique features not available on competitive products, or solve a problem that the customer has with a competitive product.
- Offer product benefits or attributes easily perceived as useful by the customer, and benefits that are highly visible.

A point of distinction: *Benefits* are what customers or users value and pay money for; by contrast, *attributes* are product features, functionality, and performance—the things that engineers and designers build into products. Often benefits and attributes are connected, but sometimes the designers get it wrong, so that added product features and performance do not yield additional benefits for customers and users.

The management implications are clear:

- The four ingredients of a superior product noted above provide a useful checklist of questions in assessing the odds of success of a proposed new product project. They logically become top-priority questions in a project screening checklist.
- These ingredients become challenges to the project team to build into the new product design. Note that the definition of what is unique and superior must be based on an in-depth understanding of customer or user needs, wants, problems, likes, and dislikes. This leads to success factor 2 below.

What about competitive advantage gained via elements other than product advantage? These include brand name or company reputation, superior marketing communications (advertising and promotion), a superb sales force or distribution channel, superior technical support and tech service,

New Product Process Success Factors

1. *Developing a superior, differentiated product, with unique benefits and superior value to the customer or user*
2. *Having a strong market orientation throughout the process*
3. *Undertaking the predevelopment homework upfront*
4. *Getting sharp, early product definition before development begins*
5. *Quality execution—completeness, consistency, proficiency—of activities in the new product process*
6. *Having the correct organization structure: multifunctional, empowered teams*
7. *Providing for sharp project selection decisions, leading to focus*
8. *Having a well-planned, well-resourced launch*
9. *The correct role for top management: specifying new product strategy and providing the needed resources*
10. *Achieving speed to market, but with quality of execution*
11. *Having a multistage disciplined new product game plan*

Project Selection Success Factors

12. *Having a unique, superior product (this item is in both factor lists)*
13. *The product–market environment:*
    - *Market attractiveness*
    - *Competitive situation (minor impact)*
    - *Stage of product life cycle*
14. *Synergy and familiarity*

> *The impact of product superiority far outweighs other elements of the marketing mix in determining success.*

or simply product availability. The limited evidence available suggests that the impact of nonproduct advantage pales in comparison to the impact of product advantage—less than half the effect. The message is evident: By all means, strive for advantage via nonproduct elements—every advantage helps! But don't pin your hopes on these elements alone: Whenever you hear yourself saying "Our company's reputation, brand name, or sales force will make this product a winner," be on guard.

2. A Strong Market Orientation: Market Driven, Customer Focused

A thorough understanding of customers' needs and wants, the competitive situation, and the nature of the market is an essential component of new product success. This tenet is supported by virtually every study of product success factors. Conversely, failure to adopt a strong market orientation in product innovation, unwillingness to undertake the needed market assessments, and leaving the customer out of product development spell disaster; these are the culprits found in almost every study of why new products fail.

A provocative finding of recent studies is that not only does a strong customer focus improve success rates and profitability, but it also leads to reduced time to market. Contrary to myth, taking a little extra time to execute marketing actions in a high-quality fashion does not add extra time. Rather, it pays off, not only with higher success rates, but in terms of staying on schedule and achieving better time efficiency.

Sadly, a strong market orientation is missing in the majority of firms' new product projects. Detailed market studies are frequently omitted—in more than 75 percent of projects, according to one investigation. Further, marketing activities are the weakest-rated activities of the entire new product process, rated much lower than corresponding technological actions. Moreover, relatively few resources and little money are spent on marketing actions (except for the launch), accounting for less than 20 percent of the total project.

A market orientation must prevail throughout the entire new product project:

- *Idea generation.* Devote more resources to market-oriented idea generation activities, such as focus groups with customers and market research to determine customers' generic needs. Use the sales force actively to solicit ideas from customers and to develop relationships with innovative or lead users.

- *Design of the product.* Often, market research, when done at all, is done too late, after the product design has already been decided, simply as an after-the-fact check. Market research must be used as an input to the design decisions and serve as a guide to the project team before they charge into design of the new product. Determine customer or user needs at the outset, starting with a user needs-and-wants study, followed by a competitive product analysis.
- *Throughout the entire project.* Customer input should not stop upon completion of predevelopment market studies. Seeking customer input, and testing concepts or designs with the user, are very much iterative processes. Keep bringing the customer into the process to view facets of the product via a series of concept tests, rapid prototype development and tests, and customers trials and test marketing, verifying all assumptions about the winning design. Leave nothing to chance.

Even in the case of technology-driven new products (where the ideas came from technical or laboratory sources), the likelihood of success is greatly enhanced if customer and marketplace inputs are built into the project soon after its inception.

3. Predevelopment Work: The Homework

Homework is critical to winning. Countless studies reveal that the steps that precede actual design and development of a product make the difference between winning and losing. Successful firms spend about twice as much time and money on these vital up-front activities:

> *Undertaking the homework and getting sharp product definition before development are closely linked and, together, are vital to new product success and shorter times to market.*

- Initial screening: the decision to get into the project (the idea screen)
- Preliminary market assessment: the first, quick market study
- Preliminary technical assessment: the first, quick technical appraisal of the project
- The detailed market study or marketing research (described above)
- The business and financial analysis just before the decision to "go to development" (building the business case)

Surprisingly, most firms confess to serious weaknesses in the up-front or predevelopment steps of their new product process. Pitifully small amounts of time and money are devoted to these critical steps: only about 7 percent of dollars and 16 percent of effort. "More homework means longer development times" is a frequently voiced complaint. This is a valid concern, but experience has shown that homework pays for itself in reduced development times as well as improved success rates:

1. All the evidence points to a much higher likelihood of product failure if the homework is omitted. So the choice is between a slightly longer project or much increased odds of failure.
2. Better project definition, the result of sound homework, actually speeds up the development process. One of the major causes of time slippages is poorly defined projects as they enter the development stage: vague targets and moving goalposts.
3. Given the inevitable product design evolution that occurs during the life of a project, the time to make the majority of these design improvements or changes is not as the product is moving out of development and into production. More homework upfront anticipates these changes and encourages them to occur earlier in the process rather than later, when they are more costly.

Again the message is obvious. Don't skimp on the homework! If you find yourself making the case that "we don't have time for the homework," you're heading for trouble. You're wrong on two counts: first, cutting out the homework drives your success rate way down; and second, cutting out homework to save time today will cost you in wasted time tomorrow. It's a "penny wise, pound foolish" way to save time. Make it a rule: No significant project should move into the development stage without the five actions described above having been completed, and done in a high-quality way.

4. Sharp, Early Product Definition

Sharp, early product definition is one result of solid up-front work. How well the project is defined prior to entering the development stage is a major success factor that will have positive effects on both profitability and reduced time to market. Some companies undertake excellent product and project definition before the door is opened to a full development program. This definition includes:

1. Specification of the target market: exactly who the intended users are.
2. Description of the product concept and the benefits to be delivered.
3. Delineation of the positioning strategy.

4. A list of the product's features, attributes, requirements, and specifications (prioritized: "must have" versus "would like to have").

Unless these four items are clearly defined, written down, and agreed to by all parties prior to entering the development stage, the project faces tough times downstream: The odds of failure have just skyrocketed by a factor of 3. Here's why:

- Building a definition step into the new product process forces more attention on the up-front or predevelopment activities, a key success factor. Note that merely doing the homework, however, does not necessarily guarantee sharp product definition.
- The definition serves as a communication tool and guide. All-party agreement or "buy in" means that each functional area involved in the project has a clear and consistent definition of what the product and project are, and is committed to it.
- This definition also provides a clear set of objectives for the development stage of the project and the development team members: The goalposts are defined and clearly visible.

5. Quality of Execution

More emphasis is needed on completeness, consistency, and quality of execution in the new product process. Certain key activities—how well they are executed, and whether they are done at all—are strongly tied to profitability and reduction in time to market. Particularly pivotal activities include the vital homework actions outlined above (factor 3) and market-related activities (factor 2). But proficiency of most activities in the new product process affects outcomes, with successful project teams consistently doing a better quality job across many tasks.

There is a *quality crisis*, however, in product innovation. Investigations reveal that the typical new product project is characterized by serious errors of omission and commission:

> There is a quality-of-execution crisis in the new product process: Things don't happen as they should, when they should, and sometimes don't happen at all!

- Pivotal activities that are widely believed to be central to success are often omitted altogether. For example, more than half of all projects typically leave out detailed market studies and a test market (trial sell).
- Quality of execution ratings of important activities are also typically low. In postmortems on projects, teams typically rate themselves as "mediocre" in terms of how good a job they did on these vital activities.

New product success is thus very much within the hands of the men and women leading and working on projects. The best way to double the success rate of new products and at the same time reduce development time is to strive for significant improvements in the way the innovation process unfolds. The solution that some firms have adopted is to treat product innovation as a process: They use a formal product delivery process, and they build into this process quality assurance approaches. For example, they introduce checkpoints and metrics into the process that focus on quality of execution, ensuring that every play in the game plan is executed competently, and they design quality into their game plan by making mandatory certain vital actions that are often omitted, yet are central to success.

6. The Correct Organizational Structure and Climate

Product innovation is very much a team effort! Do a postmortem on any bungled new product project and invariably you'll find each functional area doing its own piece of the project, with very little communication between players and functions—a fiefdom mentality; and no real commitment of players to the project—that is, inadequate personnel resources devoted to the project, with players having numerous other functional tasks under way at the same time. Many studies concur that good organizational design is strongly linked to success and reduced time to market.

> *Organize around an empowered, multifunctional team—a key to success and reduced time to market.*

Product development must be run as a multidisciplinary, multifunctional effort. Good organizational design means projects:

- That are organized as a multifunctional team with members from research and development (R&D), engineering, marketing and sales, operations, and so on (as opposed to each function doing its own part independently).
- Where the team is a "true" team (where team members are not just representatives of their respective functions, there to protect their "functional turf").
- Where the team is dedicated and focused (i.e., devotes a large percentage of its time to this project, as opposed to spread over many projects).
- Where the team members are in constant contact with each other via frequent but short meetings, interactions, project updates, and even co-location.
- Where the team is accountable for the entire project from beginning to end (as opposed to accountability for only one stage of the project).
- Where there is a strong project leader who leads and drives the project.

- Where top management is committed to (and strongly supports) the project (e.g., via an executive sponsor).

While the ingredients of good organizational design should be familiar, surprisingly many firms have yet to get the message.

A second organizational success ingredient is climate and culture. A positive climate is one that supports and encourages intrapreneurs and risk-taking behavior; where new product successes are rewarded and recognized (and failures not punished); where team efforts are recognized rather than individuals; where senior managers refrain from "micromanaging" projects and second-guessing team members; and where resources are made available for creative people to work on their own "unofficial projects" (e.g., via free time or bootstrapping funds). Idea submission schemes (where employees are encouraged to submit new product ideas) and open project review meetings (where the entire project team participates) are other facets of a positive climate.

7. Focus and Sharp Project Selection Decisions

Most companies suffer from too many projects and not enough resources to mount an effective or timely effort on each. This stems from a lack of adequate project evaluation and prioritization, with negative results:

1. Scarce and valuable resources are wasted on poor projects.
2. Truly meritorious projects do not receive the resources they should. The result is that good projects are starved for resources and move at a crawl.

The desire to weed out bad projects coupled with the need to focus limited resources on the best projects means that tough "go or kill" and prioritization decisions must be made. This results in sharper focus, higher success rates, and shorter times to market. Project evaluations, however, are consistently cited as weakly handled or nonexistent: Decisions involve the wrong people from the wrong functions (no functional alignment); no consistent criteria are used to screen or rank projects; or there is simply no will to kill projects at all—projects are allowed to get a life of their own.

What some companies have done is to redesign their new product processes: They have built in decision points in the form of tough gates and have created a funneling process that weeds out the poor projects. At gate reviews, senior management rigorously

> *Build tough go or kill decision points into the new product process to yield a funneling effect: Mediocre projects are killed, and resources are focused on the good projects.*

scrutinizes projects and make go/kill and prioritization decisions. Effective decisions rely on solid criteria, however. Fortunately, new product success is fairly predicable, and certain project characteristics consistently separate winners from losers. These characteristics can and should be used as criteria for project selection and prioritization. Three important success factors are product superiority (above), synergy, and market attractiveness (below). These three factors, and the list of items that comprise them, should be an integral part of firms' screening and project evaluation decisions, along with various financial attractiveness and strategic fit criteria.

8. Planning and Resourcing the Launch

Emerson once said, "build a better mousetrap and the world will beat a path to your door"; the problem is that Emerson was a poet, not a businessman. Not only must the product be a superior one, but it must also be launched, marketed, and supported in a proficient manner. A well-structured launch is strongly linked to new product profitability. The message is this: Don't assume that good products sell themselves; and don't treat the launch as an afterthought. Just because the launch is the last step in the process, never underestimate its importance. Plan for the launch early in the project (some companies require a preliminary launch plan to be delivered as part of the "business case" before the development stage even begins); and be sure to allocate sufficient resources to the launch.

9. The Role of Top Management

Top management's role in product development is as a facilitator—to set the stage—not to be an actor front and center. Here is top management's role:

- To provide the necessary product development resources, and to keep the commitment. Availability of needed resources—R&D or product development budgets and people—has been found to be a strong driver of new product performance at the business unit level. Often, the failure to execute at a high level is the direct result of insufficient resources—not enough money, people, or time.
- Management must also decide on and articulate a new product strategy for the business, something that is often notably missing. Having a new product strategy is also strongly connected to the business unit's new product performance. Here, an effective new product strategy means defined new product goals (e.g., percentage of the business's sales to be derived from new products in the next year), goals that are clearly linked to total business goals; delineated arenas of focus (e.g., product types, markets, and technologies where the business unit intends to concentrate its new product

efforts); and strategies with a longer-term orientation that are visible to everyone in the business.

By contrast, senior management micromanaging of projects or electing to push favorite projects has a negative impact. For example, projects strongly supported by senior management—so-called "pet projects"—are no more successful in the marketplace than other projects despite the added support.

10. Speed—But Not at the Expense of Quality of Execution

Speed is the new competitive weapon. Speed yields competitive advantage: to be first on the market; it means less likelihood that the market or competitive situation has changed; and it results in a quicker realization of profits. So the goal of reducing the development cycle time is admirable. A word of caution, here, however: Speed is only an interim objective; the ultimate goal is profitability. While studies reveal that speed and profitability are connected, the relationship is anything but one to one. Further, there is a dark side to speed: Often the methods used to reduce development time yield precisely the opposite effect and in many cases are very costly because they are at odds with sound management practices. The objective remains successful products, not a series of fast failures. Additionally, an overemphasis on speed has led to trivialization of product development in some firms: too many product modifications and line extensions and not enough real new products.

Some of the ways that project teams have reduced time to market have been highlighted above. Other methods include:

- *Parallel processing.* The relay-race approach to product development is antiquated. Given today's time pressures, a more appropriate model is a rugby game: Activities are undertaken in parallel (rather than sequentially) with team members constantly interacting with each other. Time compression is the result.
- *Flowcharting.* Here the team maps out its entire project from beginning to end in flowchart format. Then team members focus on trying to reduce the time of each element or task in the process. Often, reductions by as much as 50 percent have been achieved.
- *A time line and discipline.* Most project teams use computer software to plan their projects in a critical path or Gantt chart format. Numerous software time-line packages now exist. The rules are simple: Practice disciple; the time line is sacred; and resources can be added but deadlines never relaxed. This type of discipline, driven by a demanding time-line, cuts time to market dramatically.

11. A Multistage, Disciplined New Product Game Plan

A game plan or systematic new product process—a *stage-gate system*—is the solution to which many firms have turned to overcome the deficiencies that plague their new product programs. Companies have reengineered their new product processes and have tried to build in the critical success factors outlined above (the stage-gate process is outlined in [1]). Stage-gate systems are simply road maps or templates for driving new products from idea to launch, successfully and efficiently. These systems break the innovation process into stages, each stage comprising multiple concurrent, multifunctional activities or actions (a team approach is mandatory). Gates are the quality control checkpoints in the process, opening the door for the project to proceed to the next stage. Gates are where the tough go/kill decisions are made: Gates typically specify deliverables (what must be delivered by the team to a given gate), criteria for go (upon which the go/kill and prioritization decisions are based), and outputs (an action plan for the next stage, and resources approved).

> *Leading companies have adopted stage-gate processes, a system developed by the author, to provide a road map from idea to launch, and to drive new product products to market effectively and on time.*

   The payoffs of such processes have been widely reported: improved teamwork, less recycling and rework, improved success rates, earlier detection of failures, a better launch, and even shorter cycle times (by about 30 percent).

1.3. CRITICAL SUCCESS FACTORS: SELECTION-RELATED

The next three factors describe the new product project and its setting. Unlike the ones above, which are process-related, the factors that follow are less controllable by the project team. They tend to be more useful then as project selection criteria.

12. The Market Environment

Pick attractive markets! This sounds a bit like saying "buy low and sell high." Except in new products, the choice is much more apparent—that is, there are evident market characteristics to look for, characteristics that more often result in success. Here are the ingredients of an attractive market situation:

- The market is a large one, and the product type represents an essential one for the customer.

- The market is growing quickly.
- There is a positive economic climate in the market for the new product.
- The market demand for this type of product is stable over time (as opposed to cyclical and unstable).
- Potential customers in the market are innovative adopters, amenable to trying new products.
- Potential customers are relatively price insensitive.
- Potential customers themselves are very profitable.

Note that few of these characteristics on their own are highly predictive of success, but when taken together, they are more strongly linked to performance. The implications for management are evident: Create an "index of market attractiveness," perhaps using the seven characteristics cited above, and use this index in scoring or rating your projects in your project prioritization decisions.

The *competitive situation* is the second facet of the market environment. Numerous studies reveal that the competitive situation has surprisingly little impact on new product outcomes: Products win and lose despite the competitive situation; new products are not that much less successful when aimed at markets characterized by many and strong competitors, competitors who would defend their positions, ag-

> *New products succeed not so much because of their external environment, but because of what project teams and leaders do—success is not situationally determined but is the result of positive actions.*

gressive competitors who compete on the basis of price, low barriers to entry, and customers who are loyal to competitors.

A final market descriptor is the *stage of the product life cycle* of the product market at which the new product is aimed. New products seem to do best in product markets that are in the early growth and growth phases of the life cycle, and to do worst at either end of the life cycle: in mature markets and in markets in the introductory phase. The two growth phases demonstrate almost twofold success rates to those of the mature and introductory phases.

While the effects of these three marketplace characteristics are evident, they are not nearly as strong as the other success factors cited above. One message is that new products succeed not so much because of their external environment but because of what project teams and leaders do: that success is not situationally determined but is the result of positive actions by the team and team leader.

13. Synergy and Familiarity

"Attack from a position of strength" may be an old adage, but it certainly applies to the launch of new products. Where new product synergy with the base business is lacking, new products fare poorly on average. *Synergy* is a familiar term, but exactly what does it translate into in the context of new products? Synergy means having a strong fit between the needs of the new product project and the resources, competencies, and experience of the firm in terms of:

- R&D resources (e.g., ideally the new product should leverage or build from internal and existing technical competencies).
- Marketing, selling (sales force), and distribution (channel) resources.
- Manufacturing or operations capabilities and resources.
- Technical support and customer service resources.
- Market research and market intelligence resources.
- Management capabilities.

These six synergy ingredients become obvious checklist items in a scoring or rating model to help prioritize new product projects. If your synergy score is low, there must be compelling reasons to proceed with the project. Synergy is not essential, but it certainly improves the odds of winning.

> **Synergy and familiarity become important criteria in project selection.**

Familiarity is a concept parallel to that of synergy. Some new product projects take the company into unfamiliar territory: a product category new to the firm; new customers and unfamiliar needs served; unfamiliar technology; new sales force, channels, and servicing requirements; or an unfamiliar manufacturing process. Sadly, the firm often pays the price: step-out projects tend to fail, so beware of the unknown! The encouraging news is that the negative impact here is not as strong as for most factors. New and unfamiliar territory certainly results in lower success rates and profitability on average, but the rates are not dramatically lower.

The message is this: Sometimes it is necessary to venture into new and unfamiliar markets, technologies, or manufacturing processes. Do so with caution, and be aware that success rates will suffer; but note that the odds of disaster are not so high as to prevent making the move altogether.

1.4. FACTORS WITH LIMITED OR UNEXPECTED EFFECTS

Several factors, thought to affect performance directly, have unexpected effects:

1. *Order of entry.* Does first to market win? That is, is the first product of its type in a market necessarily more successful? The evidence is mixed; indeed, there is no strong or consistent evidence that first-in products are

more successful, except where the next-ranked product is a parity or "me to" product. There do seem to be some tendencies, however, with pioneer products having a slight edge. The message is that it is better to be "best in" than "first in."

2. *Innovativeness.* A myth exists that highly innovative products are much more risky, whereas more ordinary new products—modi-

> There is a U-shaped relationship between product innovativeness and success.

fications, tweaks, extensions—are more successful. The myth is only partly true. Indeed, new products low on the innovativeness scale are very successful: a solid success rate and good profitability on average. But so are the truly innovative new products! It is the ones in between where performance falls off and which suffer higher failure rates—the moderately innovative products. In short, there is a U-shaped relationship between innovativeness and success.

3. *Nature of benefits offered.* Are there any magic customer benefits—benefits that more often lead to success than others? The answer appears to be "no," with a few exceptions. The only customer benefit that has a consistently negative impact on performance is "low price"; that is, where the competitive advantage of the new product is based on price alone, success rates drop. By contrast, the benefit "good value for money" yields positive results.

Sources of the Critical Success Factors

The keys to new product success outlined in this chapter are based on numerous research studies into why new products succeed, why they fail, and comparisons of winners and losers. Many of these investigations have been reported over the years in the PDMA journal, the Journal of Product Innovation Management. *Perhaps the most revealing of these studies have been the large-sample, quantitative studies of successful versus unsuccessful new products (for an excellent review, see [2]). They began with Project SAPPHO in the early 1970s, followed by the NewProd series of studies, the Stanford Innovation Project, and more recently, studies in countries outside North America and Europe. This long tradition of research has enabled us to pinpoint the critical success factors—those that separate winners from losers, which are outlined in this chapter. See also [1].*

1.5. SUMMARY

Generating a continuous stream of new product successes is an elusive goal. But the quest goes on, because the goal is so important to corporate success. This chapter has provided an overview of some of the key drivers of new product performance, and hence insights into how to win with new products.

REFERENCES

1. Cooper, R. G. *Winning at New Products: Accelerating the Process from Idea to Launch*. Reading, MA: Addison-Wesley, 1993.
2. Montoya-Weiss, M. M. and Calantone, R., Determinants of new product performance: a review and meta-analysis. *Journal of Product Innovation Management* 11(5): 397–417 (November 1994).

Robert G. Cooper
McMaster University

Cooper is the Lawson Marden Chaired Professor of Industrial Marketing and Technology Management at the Michael De Groote School of Business, McMaster University. He is also Professor of Marketing at the university, and Director of Research of the Canadian Industrial Innovation Centre, Waterloo, Canada. He is a leading scholar, researcher, and consultant in the field of new product management, and has published over 75 articles and books on the topic. Cooper is the developer of the stage-gate method for managing new product projects, and creator of the NewProd diagnostic model.

SEVEN STEPS TO STRATEGIC NEW PRODUCT DEVELOPMENT

2

Bob Gill, Beebe Nelson, and Steve Spring

Strategy without product planning is empty; product
planning without strategy is blind.
— *with apologies to Immanuel Kant*

2.1. INTRODUCTION: WHAT IS STRATEGIC NEW PRODUCT DEVELOPMENT?

Strategic new product development (SNPD) is the link between corporate strategic planning and the product development process. It allows product planning to be tied to corporate strategic directions, so that new products deliver what is needed to accomplish corporate strategy. The seven steps to strategic new product development are in reality surrounded by two others. Step zero is the setting of corporate strategy, and step eight is the product development process itself. This chapter assumes that in your corporation there is a process for setting corporate strategy; the new product development process is the subject of many of the other chapters in this handbook. Lack of a formal business strategy does not mean that product planning cannot be accomplished, but without it the product plan is likely to be beset by corporate indecision, sometimes known as "strategy of the month."

Strategic new product development is also the "other side" of product development reviews. Without a clear process for making decisions about which product ideas will be resourced and supported, the development process is often plagued by corporate indecision, which takes the form both of committing to too many projects at the same time and of stopping or changing projects that are under way. The time for corporate involvement in the product development process is early, before resources are committed and when strategic decisions are being made about how best to proceed. Once the decision has been made to proceed, new product teams need to be supported by clear commitment and adequate resourcing.

The seven steps to strategic new product development that we outline (see Table 2.1) start with deciding what new product development must accomplish for the corporation's overall strategic objectives (step one: setting new product delivery targets); next, we recommend that you develop an understanding of the current conditions affecting new product development in a form that is accessible to decision makers and actionable (step two: gathering strategic information, and step three: mapping the strategic geography), and determine how decisions will be made to narrow down to specific choices (step four: creating a list of new product options, and step five: setting criteria). Once this is accomplished, what remains is to select what will be done (step six: creating the portfolio) and to make sure that it happens while monitoring changes that might affect projects in the portfolio (step seven: managing the portfolio).

> *Where do we want to go (step one)? Where are we now (steps two and three)? How will we narrow down to the best choices for getting where we want to go (steps four and five)? How will we get it done (steps six and seven)?*

Strategic new product development allows project decision making to be done in the context of a portfolio of projects rather than project by project. One result of such strategic new product planning is a portfolio of products and product ideas that is aligned with corporate goals and achievable within set resources. When management fails to make a portfolio plan, they fail to identify and act on opportunities, lack confidence that they have selected the right product mix, and tend to be reactive in their decision making. Teams

TABLE 2.1   Seven Steps to Strategic New Product Development

Step one:	setting new product development targets
Step two:	gathering strategic information
Step three:	mapping the strategic geography
Step four:	creating a list of new product options
Step five:	setting criteria
Step six:	creating the portfolio
Step seven:	managing the portfolio

bear the brunt of changing priorities, shifting resources, and short-term firefighting, and as a consequence, the development process is delayed unnecessarily and those who actually do the work to bring new products to market are frustrated and demoralized. (See [2], especially Chapter 4, "The Aggregate Project Plan," for a discussion of the benefits of strategic new product development as well as suggestions for how to proceed to implement SNPD.)

2.2. STEP ONE: SETTING NEW PRODUCT DEVELOPMENT TARGETS

> *Product development portfolio: the collection of new product concepts that are within our ability to develop, are most attractive to our customers, and deliver short- and long-term corporate objectives, spreading risk and diversifying investments.*

The company's business plan should provide insight on the company mission, key strategic objectives, and what role new products are to play in corporate growth. Strategic new product planning aims to accomplish certain strategic objectives, including specific financial or market share targets, with certain specified resources. Although these objectives and resource targets may change as the plan develops, if the targets are not clearly set, the planning effort becomes a vague, empty, and directionless exercise.

The company's business objectives can be accomplished through a number of routes. New advertising and sales initiatives, changes in distribution channels, new market identification, extension of existing product lines, and acquisitions and mergers will all contribute, along with new products, to achieving the corporation's goals.

Many corporations set clear targets for new product contribution to corporate goals. For example,

1. An industrial products firm whose goal is to be in the forefront of innovation: 15 percent of sales from products introduced in the last five years; three new patents each year.
2. A large consumer goods firm with a strategy of pursuing topline growth: 30 percent of sales from products that are less than three years old.
3. A midsize computer company, whose key focus is bottom-line profitability: 50 percent of new products from existing platforms; 20 percent of sales from products new to the market within the past five years.
4. A chemicals company seeking to develop new businesses: 20 percent of sales from products introduced in the past three years with a 1:5 ratio of breakthrough products to derivatives.

5. A communications firm whose strategic goal is geographic expansion: 15 percent of sales from products introduced in the past three years; 25 percent of new product sales revenues from regions new to company; 25 percent of new products tailored to meet specified needs of regions new to company.

3M, for example, sets a target of 25 percent of profits earned from products developed within the last five years—and exceeds the target! Other targets might be the growth of a market in a particular region, increase in market share, blocking of a key competitor, or introduction of a new technology. The more specific and measurable these targets, the more the corporation will be able to take seriously the objective of delivering on them.

Setting new product targets must be done in the context of deciding what resources can and will be allocated to accomplishing these objectives. In the short term, these objectives should be developed considering financial resources available as well as person and process resources. What design or marketing skills will be available? What manufacturing capabilities can the corporation afford to devote to new product development and production? What portion of the advertising effort can and should go to new products? In the long term, decision makers must take into account the company's capacities and competencies. A product target that is not clearly tied to a resourcing plan is only wishful thinking.

The output at the end of step one is a clearly worded target expressing what new products will contribute to the overall business goals.

2.3. STEP TWO: GATHERING STRATEGIC INFORMATION

2.3.1. Strategic Elements

Strategic new product planning continues with the three C's of marketing strategy, which is to gather information about what is going on in the external and internal environment in three domains: the customer, the competition, and the capabilities of the company. In the *customer domain*, you need to pull together information about the markets you will play in and the needs and wants of primary customers both for today and in the future. This information will be key in deciding on the relative importance of competitor and capability information, since the entire process must be focused on an understanding of current and future customer needs in order to generate plans that can succeed in the marketplace.

In looking at the *competitive environment* it is important to understand who the primary competitors are, what technologies they employ, how they compete with your products today, what is likely for the future, and what might cause customers to switch to other alternatives.

Information about *company capabilities* will identify the areas in which the company is especially strong today, and areas that could be strengthened to improve competitive position. The capabilities that should be investigated include technology, manufacturing processes, and marketing capabilities, including distribution channels.

2.3.2. Sources of Information

Much of the information you need for strategic new product development planning already exists in the company. Internal published documents, such as formal documented three- to five-year business plans and manufacturing and technology strategies, will supply information that provides a context for strategic thinking. Corporate databases may contain relevant information, and market research reports are likely to contain market segmentation and customer needs information. Customer service or sales databases often have relevant customer information as well.

Gathering the existing information begins the process of engaging key people in the development of a new product strategy, creating buy-in for the process and the outcomes. Information is often seen as the property of functional areas, and functional leaders may thwart efforts to compile and collate "their" information. It is essential to begin to overcome these institutional barriers by bringing representatives from functional areas into the process early. This early multifunctional participation lays the groundwork for multifunctional cooperation throughout the product development process, which is key to new product development success at all stages.

In most companies, the issue is not where to find information, but how to compile it, how to make it comparable, and how to keep it updated. Strategic new product development begins a process of organizational learning in which the corporation's store of information is brought together and rendered in a format that makes it useful and comparable. In beginning the process of strategic new product development, it is important to realize that the building of a corporate knowledge base is an effort that will take place over years and pay off over years. Begin where you can, with a commitment to upgrading, adding, and expanding. This process can be tied to ongoing efforts in your company to create a corporate "data warehouse," a common repository of information accessible to anyone in the company who has need of it.

Gathering information can be an overwhelming task at the beginning. It is helpful to set boundaries on the process by asking yourself what the output will be at the end of this year's planning process. What will you be presenting? What decisions will need to be made? Even though you have to specify the outcome in advance of knowing exactly what you will find, this will help you to decide where to look for relevant information.

> *The output at the end of step two is a compilation of current information that gives a picture of the customer, the competition, and corporate capacities.*

2.4. STEP THREE: MAPPING THE STRATEGIC GEOGRAPHY

Once information has been gathered, the challenge is to display it in such a way as to provide a framework for the planning process. Mapping formats, which allow diverse information to be displayed in two- and three-dimensional matrices, enable planners to consider how circumstances in one domain might affect circumstances in another, and multiple mapping techniques and formats permit planners to sort data and consider potential impact. Be flexible in the approach and experiment with various methods, and remember that mapping provides scenarios for decision making and not the solution itself. What is essential is that the mapping formats bring together decision makers and stakeholders to generate scenarios based on current information.

The tools that are useful in mapping the strategic geography are chiefly matrices and grids that allow you to sort one kind of information against another to discover where your strengths and weaknesses lie (Table 2.2). These matrices provide nearly endless templates for checking hypotheses: Where does our existing technology stand in terms of customer needs? Which markets are already addressed by our competition? How do our existing products meet needs in our primary markets? and so on. Matrices allow decision makers to pose their questions and get answers that are discussible and shared. In this process people's pet theories or special ideas about customers, competition, and capabilities have to stand the test of open dialogue.

The output of this process will be a map of the opportunities (see [3] for examples of such maps). This includes where your company has strengths that others don't have, where your technology could be exploited to meet customer needs in new ways, where competitors are likely to be unable to develop in promising new markets to which you have an entry. It also includes where you clearly should not be competing, because you don't have the technology, or the market is already saturated by your competitor, or customer needs are not strong in that area. To learn what you should not be doing can be as useful as learning

TABLE 2.2   Matrix Scoring Model[a]

		Product		
		A	**B**	**C**
Criteria	**Weight**	**S × W = T**	**S × W = T**	**S × W = T**
Economic criteria	2	5 × 2 = 10	2 × 2 = 4	6 × 2 = 12
Investment				
Risk				
Profit				
Customer needs criteria	4	7 × 4 = 28	3 × 4 = 12	6 × 4 = 24
Strong customer appeal				
Target segment size				
Segment growth rate				
Distribution channels				
Manufacturing criteria	1	3 × 1 = 3	1 × 1 = 1	9 × 1 = 9
Easily produced				
Fit with capabilities				
Few service problems				
Technology	3	9 × 3 = 27	4 × 3 = 12	10 × 3 = 30
Fit with present technology				
Level of new technology				
Total score		**68**	**29**	**75**

(Total score = the sum of weight x score for each product)

[a] T, total score; S, scoring scale: very good = 10, poor = 1; W, pre-assigned weight of criteria.

what you should. You will also find holes, places that look like opportunities but which have not been developed either by you or by the competition. Part of the planning process will be deciding how much new opportunity you can afford to pursue. One way of capturing the opportunities is by plotting these against a time line (Figure 2.1). This "event map" becomes the backdrop for new product decision making. A set of "gap analyses" (Figure 2.2) allows you to set targets against current or likely situations to see what would need to be added to produce a desired result.

2.5. STEP FOUR: CREATING A LIST OF NEW PRODUCT OPTIONS

> *The output of this process will be a map of the opportunities.*

Once the corporation has set its goals for new product development and mapped its strategic geography, it must develop a list of new product ideas and options. This should be a *complete* list of all the new product options available to the corporation to ensure that decision makers can select from all available options. It may be necessary to go to several sources and look through formal published

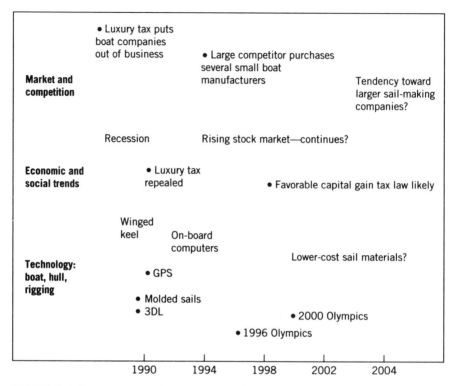

FIGURE 2.1 An event map shows past and future sailing trends to help our hypothetical company, Springsails Inc., pinpoint product opportunities by linking events and trends from different domains.

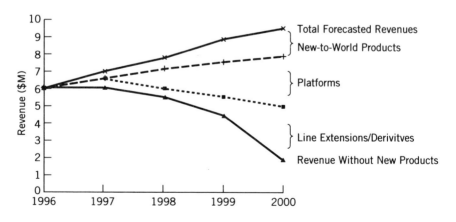

FIGURE 2.2 New product gap analysis: five-year company new product growth plan.

lists as well as informal sources to get this information in one place. Some companies list all projects, not just new product options, so that they can make decisions from among all the possible ways in which corporate dollars can be spent, putting new products up against reengineering projects, improvement projects, and so on.

For the list of new product options to be useful for decision making, it is important to lay out all the options in a standard format. This standard format should be short, simple, realistic, and easy to use, and at the same time it must provide enough information to allow the decision makers to make reasonable decisions about each option. Specific information for each option might include a concept overview, goals and objectives, key milestones and decision points, required resources and costs, and the current status of the concept or program. Options will be at different stages in the development process, and the level of information available for each option will be a best guess for this stage of the product's development. Listing projects on a one-page template like the one shown in Figure 2.3 provides for comparability in the decision-making process.

2.6. STEP FIVE: SETTING CRITERIA

> *At the end of step four the output is a complete list of all new product options in easily comparable format.*

At this point, knowing what new products need to contribute to corporate goals, what resources can be allocated to achieving these goals, what options are available, and what opportunities appear as a result of strategic mapping, it is appropriate to create criteria for the corporate new product portfolio. There are two kinds of criteria that will be applied in the new product planning process. One includes threshold, or hurdle, criteria, and the other we might call portfolio criteria. The threshold criteria include measures such as return on investment (ROI), net present value (NPV), or economic value added (EVA), or simple risk–return measures. If any product fails to meet specified criteria, it should not be chosen. However, it is important to set and measure these criteria judiciously. Frequently, in portfolio thinking, an idea that could not stand on its own two feet with respect to these measures is quite feasible when considered in the context of related projects. This may be true of platform projects, or projects that expand capacities in technology, manufacturing, or marketing. Threshold criteria are important, but their application must take into account an option's relationship to other options or to strategic initiatives. Which threshold criteria to use, and how many, will differ from company to company, but in general you should choose those that give high comparability between options (such as NPV), and as few as possible.

Program Manager: Date:

Product Description:

Target Market:

Updates and Concerns
Key Program Assumptions:
Major Open Issues:

Program Financial History						
	Date	Program Cost	Revenues	ROI	NPV	BET
Feasibility						
Last Quarter						
	1995	1996	1997	1998	1999	2000
Sales Volume						
Price						
Cost						
EVA						
Product Development						
Manufacturing Development						
Inception						
Other						
Total Product Cost						

Program Schedule

	Low	Medium	High
Strategic Fit			
Customer Value			
Corporate Growth Potential			
Competitive Advantage			
Corporate Risk			

FIGURE 2.3 Example of template for sample record form.

The second kind of criteria, portfolio criteria, set the balance of newness to market, newness of technology, short versus long term, and high versus low risk (see [2]). They are derived from the opportunity maps, which have identified what opportunities can be filled, and the key to these criteria is balance. Portfolio criteria allow you to avoid putting all your eggs in one basket by detailing how many baskets there are and setting guidelines for how many eggs should end up in each of them.

When used in the context of strategic new product planning, both threshold and portfolio criteria shift attention from the question "which product should I choose?" to the question, "which set of options best fulfills the company's need for products over the next five to ten years?"

> **Threshold criteria** *provide minimum acceptable performance targets.* **Portfolio criteria** *allow a business to create balance and diversity.*

> *At the end of this step, the output is a set of both threshold and portfolio criteria that decision makers have agreed to use in selecting the new product portfolio.*

2.7. STEP SIX: CREATING THE PORTFOLIO

The process for developing the portfolio is a decision-making process in which the terms of analysis allow one to compare and contrast possible new products, and to decide which to include and which to reject based on the criteria developed for achieving new product goals. In some companies the process of new product planning is handled in a fairly random fashion. When a company is growing fast, often its decision-making process is to develop everything it can and eliminate products that do not perform. As a company's growth slows, however, some more formal planning process becomes necessary, and many companies move to a linear process. At one end of the spectrum of linear processes we have the product plans that were jotted down on the back of an envelope. At the other end are complex voting processes that invite in stakeholders from functional areas and regions. What these processes have in common is that they compare product to product and result in a prioritized list. The processes that we advocate here involve iterative matrixed displays of information which move decision making from linear to strategic, from implicit to explicit, and from individual to collaborative.

There are two things that are needed to be successful in developing the new product portfolio from this point. One is the participation of relevant people, and the other is the use of appropriate tools for analysis and decision making.

The two things are not independent. The better the tools, the more credibility the process will have and the easier it will be to create participation. The corporation's culture will often hold back the new product planning effort. A good planning process will begin to reveal what has been overlooked in the past and so can be seen as a threat by a lot of people. A good process also prevents people from jumping to solutions, and may be seen as overly long and laborious by people who are used to the back-of-the-envelope method. Good processes also build in criteria that shift the decision making from idiosyncratic and political to collaborative and objective, so that old power bases are threatened. The planning process asks people to look not at their own corner of success but at the success of the entire enterprise, and this point of view is not an easy or automatic one to take. The more your company has participated in programs that encourage big-picture thinking, problem surfacing, collaborative thinking and working, continuous improvement, and focus on the customer, the more the culture will be ready for good new product planning processes.

The decision-making process at this point requires a set of tools that will help people compare and contrast a lot of different information while engaging in discussions that result in collaborative decision making. A number of tools help groups function in this way, and some of these are described below. The important thing to remember in using these tools is that they are designed to display incomplete information, to get people to surface and discuss their assumptions, to point in the direction of needed additional information, and to result in specific further actions (such as finding more information, clarifying points, etc.) or in collaborative decisions. They are not methods for extracting the "correct" answers; they are, when used correctly, tools for generating consensus.

Tools that prove useful in creating the portfolio include Q-sorts, nominal group process, Delphi processes, and consensor processes. These tools include opportunities for participants to make individual decisions, by voting or ranking, which are then brought to group discussion. In this way the final decisions are shaped by individual and group input and consensus can be built. (See [1] for good descriptions of selection processes.)

Q-Sorts

Q-sorting is a method for assigning criteria to various items. To do a Q-sort you need index cards or stick-on notes. Write one item or project on each note and sort the cards into stacks: high conformance to the criterion versus low conformance. Then sort the high stack into high and medium, and the low stack into medium and low. At this point you have three stacks: high, medium, and low. These three stacks can be sorted again into very high, high, medium, low, and very low. Finally, you can review the stacks to be sure they are satisfactory. The Q-sort can be repeated with any number of criteria and the results fed in to a matrix such as the one in Table 2.3.

The Q-sort can be used in nominal group processes when groups are trying to come to consensus. Each group member completes a Q-sort on his or her own. The results are then shared with the group, and discussion allows members to share opinions and exchange data. Individuals then resort their cards, and the results are again shared and discussed. This process can be repeated until consensus and closure are achieved, usually no more than three times.

Other methods that are useful with nominal group processes are multipicks, in which individuals vote to retain or eliminate various items; and opinion surveys in which individual opinions are tallied beforehand (sometimes anonymously) and discussed in the group. All of these methods share a format which allows both solitary reflection and group discussion, and a structured process which moves the group towards consensus.

2.8. STEP SEVEN: MANAGING THE PORTFOLIO

At the end of step six, the output is a portfolio *of new product options that fulfills the new product target, addresses key concerns in the customer and competitor domains, maintains and grows corporate capacities, and can be developed within set budget limits.*

Once the portfolio has been developed, what do we have? In the first place, as we have already stressed, we have a "best fit," not a "right answer." If the process has been successful, we have consensus and buy-in from the people who are the decision makers and stakeholders. We have specific product ideas that we have decided to put into the new product pipeline, and these product ideas will be resourced with money, skilled personnel, and other functional resources. We have also decided which product ideas should be killed and which incubated. New product development teams can go forward full steam with the full support of corporate officers and the assurance that needed resources will be available. Strategic new product planning puts real velocity in the new product development process.

As a result of new product planning, we also have identified customer needs that should be further assessed, technology directions that could be explored based on unmet customer needs, and market directions and opportunities to

TABLE 2.3 Matrix Scoring Model[a]

	Product		
Criteria	A	B	C
Economic criteria	5	2	6
Investment			
Risk			
Profit			
Customer needs criteria	7	3	6
Strong customer appeal			
Target segment size			
Segment growth rate			
Distribution channels			
Manufacturing criteria	3	1	9
Easily produced			
Fit with capabilities			
Few service problems			
Technology	9	4	10
Fit with present technology			
Level of new technology			

[a] Scoring scale: very good = 10, poor = 1.

explore. A good planning process yields a portfolio of products to be fed into the new product pipeline, and it also focuses the efforts of marketing, R&D, and new product teams in the earliest stages of the product development process.

A good planning process builds confidence, consensus, and commitment to the new product plan, allowing the corporation to identify and pursue opportunities intentionally at the fuzzy front end and to support existing product development with singlemindedness. It allows for an optimal product mix that will use resources and exploit opportunities synergistically.

> *The key results of a good strategic new product development process are confidence (we looked at the important information), consensus (the right people were there), and commitment (the new product decisions are like contracts between the new product development teams and management and are not broken easily or capriciously).*

2.9. SUMMARY

The introduction of strategic new product development amounts to a profound change in the culture of most companies. In some companies, strategic planning is already done in a way that creates direction for business units, functional organizations, and teams. In these companies, applying strategic new product development will ensure that business planning drives the new product development process, and the transition should not be a difficult one. In others, however, the whole notion of closely linking strategic planning to day-to-day tactical operations does not exist, and in these companies strategic new product development will challenge political turf and deeply held assumptions. In these companies it is important to begin the process, understanding that the effort will be iterative and additive. If some linking is accomplished in the first year between corporate strategy and new product planning, and if planners are beginning to understand that new product planning needs a new way of thinking and a whole new set of practices, you have done well and have a foundation to build on in the second year.

Strategic new product development is not a one-time effort. The process we have outlined provides a basis of accessible strategic information and ways of making new product decisions that can be built on in the future. Some best practice companies have a new product planning process that is virtually continuous; we recommend an annual planning process with quarterly reviews. By implementing a continuous process the company will be able to anticipate and respond to market or other changes in a planned way that continues to optimize new product strategy without placing its development teams at the whim of changing strategies.

ACKNOWLEDGMENTS

The authors are grateful to PDMA members from Black & Decker, Corning, DuPont, Kodak, and New Pig who graciously agreed to be interviewed as we prepared this chapter, and to the strategic product planning organization in the Photographic Imaging Business Unit at Polaroid Corporation, with whom we have developed and tested these ideas.

REFERENCES

1. Sounder, W. E. and Mandakovic, T. R&D project selection models. *Research Management* (July–August 1986).
2. Wheelwright, S. C. and Clark, K. B. *Revolutionizing Product Development: Quantum Leaps in Speed, Efficiency, and Quality.* New York: Free Press, 1992.
3. Willyard, C. W. and McClees, C. W. Motorola's technology roadmap process. *Harvard Business Review*, pp. 13–19 (1987).

Bob Gill
Polaroid Corporation

Bob Gill is Process Owner for new product planning and delivery in Polaroid's Photographic Imaging business unit. His current role includes stewardship of the front end of the development process, implementation of the review process, and process improvement based on learning from within and outside the company. Bob has held assignments in research, product development, manufacturing, service, and logistics prior to his current assignment.

Beebe Nelson
Adams Hill Associates

A consultant and educator, Nelson works with individuals, groups, teams, and organizations to increase effectiveness of team and business processes, chiefly in the area of new product development. She holds a masters in counseling and a doctorate in philosophy from Harvard University and is a member of the faculty of the Critical and Creative Thinking Program and of the Philosophy Department at the University of Massachusetts at Boston. She lives in Gloucester, Massachusetts.

Steve Spring
Productivity Associates

Steve Spring is the President of Productivity Associates, a professional services organization that works with individuals and organizations to improve and maintain productivity. He has more than ten years' experience as a consultant, educator, and manager. His consulting focus has been on establishing and improving new product development processes and on researching industry practices in new product innovation. Steve is an experienced and expert sailor.

MARKET ANALYSIS AND SEGMENTATION ISSUES FOR NEW CONSUMER PRODUCTS

3

Robert E. Davis

3.1. INTRODUCTION

In many consumer goods companies, the initial market analysis clarifies exactly how the new product will benefit the company and the consumer. It justifies the commitment of resources, and lays out the risks associated with the project. It asks for management agreement that the new product is worth pursuing. Clearly more is involved than simply calculating the project's expected profit or determining that the market is a promising one or even that the product fits in perfectly with the corporate mission. True, all of these factors are important considerations, but none on its own is enough to give the project a green light.

There are four key factors that should be addressed in an initial market analysis, all of which taken together form the basis for making a decision to commit significant resources. The first factor is an obvious one: Does it fit within the overall mission of the company? The other three factors are business synergy, market attractiveness, and consumer need. This chapter only touches on business synergy and market attractiveness. Its emphasis is on identifying consumer needs and then assessing the business potential of products that meet the need.

3.2. BUSINESS SYNERGY

This factor focuses on a company's ability to exploit successfully opportunities in the market. It is a composite factor, consisting of answers to the following kinds of questions:

1. If the market is one that is new to the company, are its management skills, talents, and experience applicable, or will it have to learn a new business?
2. In this market, can the company build on its technological strengths to gain a product advantage, or will it have to acquire and learn new technology?
3. Does the market fit with the company's manufacturing strengths and facilities, or will significant new capital investment be required to enter the market?
4. Is there marketing synergy? Can the company make use of its existing sales force and trade relationships, or will new channels have to be developed?

There are many examples of failures that have been attributed to a poor fit between a company's core competencies and a new and unfamiliar market into which the company attempted to enter.

- Fruit of the Loom, a garment manufacturer that enjoys high name recognition for its underwear, introduced Fruit of the Loom laundry detergent in 1977. It failed and was discontinued in 1981. Observers at the time felt that it failed mainly because the garment manufacturer did not understand the laundry detergent business.
- Procter & Gamble tried to enter the carbonated beverage market when it acquired the Orange Crush business. P&G never understood the role of independent bottlers in that market and eventually withdrew from it.

The issue is the basic relationship between the old business and the new. Can the collective wisdom, talents, skills, and resources of the company be transferred directly to the new market? If not, it is a market that probably should be avoided.

3.3. MARKET ATTRACTIVENESS

This is also a composite factor that looks at the fundamentals of the market and the nature of the competition in it. It boils down to answers to a series of questions, such as:

1. Is the market a large one?
2. Has it been growing over the past few years?
3. Are there many competitors in this market?
4. Who are the competitors?
5. Is there a dominant competitor?
6. What is the pricing of the leading competitors?

7. What is their cost structure?
8. What are their sales, advertising, and promotion strategies and practices?
9. How have they reacted in the past to new competitors?
10. What are their technologies, and are they protected?

A simple procedure can be used to assess the attractiveness of markets very early on [1,4]. It consists of three steps:

1. *List and weigh the selection factors for the company.* Talk to management to identify the important factors. The list then becomes a checklist for assessing the relative attractiveness of markets. A factor may be considered so important that it must be satisfied before a market can be considered. For example, management may be decide that the threshold market size is $75 million.
2. *Rate each market on each factor.* There are a great many rating scales and schemes that can be used. One approach might be to try a few alternative rating scales. In most cases, some markets will always be rejected and others will always pass.
3. *Calculate the weighted sum of the ratings for each market.* Those with relatively high ratings receive further attention, and those with low ratings are rejected.

Most consumer markets are difficult to enter. They tend to be fragmented with many competitors in them (e.g., shampoo), or they are dominated by relatively few competitors who are fiercely competitive (e.g., disposable diapers). Nonetheless, it is possible to find a successful new product opportunity in every consumer market. This almost always requires a significant innovation that is superior to existing products in some way or fulfills a previously unmet or unrecognized consumer need.

Failure to find a competitive product advantage can result in disaster, as Procter & Gamble found when it entered the orange juice market with Citrus Hill. The company thought that it had a technology that would deliver a consumer-noticeable product advantage. It never materialized. The result was that Citrus Hill was more or less a parity product in a very large market with formidable competitors. Citrus Hill was eventually discontinued after P&G lost hundreds of millions of dollars.

3.4. CONSUMER NEED

Consumer need is a key factor that looks at the opportunity in the market from a consumer standpoint. The key question is: Have we identified a new product opportunity that will arouse enough consumer interest to generate the sales needed for an acceptable rate of return? Spending money to develop ideas coming largely from within the company and later learning that consumers are unwilling to pay for them is an unnecessary waste of scarce resources that companies can no longer afford.

The ability to identify strong new product ideas seems to come, in part, from having a profound understanding of consumer needs, wants, and preferences. High-level creativity is crucially dependent on having a large amount of well-organized knowledge. Before the fruits of real creativity can be reaped, a buildup of knowledge must occur. The point is not, of course, that having extensive knowledge in itself guarantees high-level creativity.

Don't count on consumers to tell you how to solve their problems. They can only tell you that they have a problem or a need. Most often, they don't even recognize a need until they are told about it. Consumers tend to think in terms of very minor improvements—a kind of polishing, if you will—of the products they are accustomed to using. Development efforts that are tailored to what consumers think they want are almost bound to work on minor improvements that have little economic value when realized because too many others have made the same improvements at the same time. The big ideas fulfill needs or desires that the consumer perhaps has not yet perceived, but which the consumer will regard as important once recognized. This is a creative process and one that is elusive and difficult to formalize. The one thing that can be said is that there is almost universal agreement that a successful new product comes out of the marriage of consumer need and technical capability.

3.5. UNDERSTANDING THE CONSUMER

There are a great number of market research techniques that can be used for understanding the consumer. The key questions are:

- *Consumer needs and hierarchy of needs*. Which needs are critical? Which are secondary? How well are these needs currently being met?
- *Habits and practices*. How do consumers use the products? Who? Under what circumstances? What other products are involved? What in-store products influence purchase?
- *Consumer perceptions of products*. How do consumers perceive current products relative to meeting their needs?
- *Product "signals"*. How does the consumer know the product is working? Physical/sensory signals?

- *Emotional reasons.* Do consumers use the product for emotional as well as practical reasons?

Market research techniques generally fall into one of two types: "soft" qualitative approaches such as group interviews and more rigorous and projectable quantitative studies. The qualitative approaches have an allure because they tend to be inexpensive, fast, and easy to design and execute. In reality, they offer mixed blessings and should be used carefully and very selectively.

It is important always to remember that market research only provides information about the consumers' present world. This applies to both qualitative and quantitative approaches. How likely is it that they will be used to identify attributes not present in existing products of the type being studied, much less a complete list of all relevant attributes? Neither contains an effective mechanism to encourage this outcome. The point is that market research provides only some of the material upon which the search for strong new ideas is based.

3.5.1. Qualitative Research Techniques

Used properly, qualitative approaches can be valuable in turning up clues, ideas, or hypotheses that are stimulating to the creative juices. However, qualitative research studies have significant limitations. They frequently use very small numbers of respondents who are not truly representative of any group of consumers beyond themselves; they are subject to manipulation by a moderator or a dominant personality in a focus-group setting; they can register different impressions with viewers; and so on. Qualitative interviews are useful only in specific and limited situations. In general, these approaches should be viewed as a first step in exploring issues that should later be quantified by research which is projectable to the whole population.

Focus Group Interview

The most frequently used method of qualitative research, a focus group, is a discussion among six to ten consumers about a topic. The group is usually led by a trained moderator. The consumers in the group have some common characteristics (i.e., age, occupation, users of product, nonusers, etc.) that relate to the topic. The basic assumption is that the process of group dynamics will generate more useful information than other types of qualitative research.

- *Open-ended interaction.* Participants have the opportunity to react to each other's responses. Respondents can answer questions in their own words rather than being forced to give yes/no, multiple-choice, or numerical answers.

- *Stimulation.* Participants not only react to each other's comments, but also stimulate each other, creating synergy that can have a multiplying effect. This is created by group support, new ideas, challenge, and the excitement of group interaction.
- *Surfacing of roles.* Group dynamics provide insights into how peer pressure plays a role in the overall acceptance of an idea, concept, or product. The focus group provides an environment in which the participants can influence and be influenced by others, just as they do in real life.

One-on-One or In-Depth Interview

A one-on-one or in-depth interview is a type of qualitative research in which a consumer is interviewed in person on an individual basis for an extended period of time. The objective is to learn the consumer's habits, attitudes, and motivations.

A one-on-one usually uses a free-flowing question outline or guide. The outline is developed much like one used for a focus group interview; the outline defines the key topic areas to be covered but gives the interviewer a great deal of latitude to pursue other topics that come up during the interview. The characteristics of one-on-one or in-depth interviews are:

- *Flexibility.* Each interview is a separate situation, so its content can vary and different approaches can be experimented with more easily than in other types of interviews.
- *Anonymity.* If the subject to be discussed is sensitive, this approach may be more appealing than a focus group environment. A respondent may be more likely to talk with only the interviewer present and reveal intimate or personal information about his or her life and share feelings and emotions.
- *Purity.* The responses do not become biased by group dynamics and peer pressure. Role playing is minimized and thoughts can be expressed with less pressure to say only those things that are considered socially acceptable.
- *Depth of information.* Generally more in-depth information can be obtained because of the concentration of time with one person.
- *Mobility.* One-on-ones can be done almost anywhere.

In-Home Visits

Home visits are another qualitative tool for gaining consumer insights. Home visits allow for intimate interactions with consumers in their own environment where purchase and repurchase decisions are constantly being made. It allows a unique opportunity to tap into the consumers' experiences and thought processes as the product is being used.

Home visits often provide insights that may be elusive in other situations. In focus groups or one-on-one interviews, for example, consumers have to recall and describe situations, problems, or habits. The listener must carefully visualize what is described. When you are in a consumer's home, you see firsthand exactly what is done and can ask "why" about things that consumers may be doing subconsciously and therefore would never articulate in a focus group. Like any qualitative research, learning from home visits should be validated via quantitative research if important decisions are involved. Home visits involve a small base of households that might not be representative of the general population.

3.5.2. Quantitative Research Techniques

In general, quantitative research studies are done among relatively large samples of respondents selected to be representative of and projectable to a larger population. Typically, the respondents number from a hundred upward to thousands, depending on the specific requirements of the research. Quantitative studies take much longer than qualitative approaches and tend to cost a lot more. They are definitive in accepting or rejecting hypotheses that emerge from preliminary qualitative work. They provide the solid basis for true consumer understanding.

Brand Image Research

Brand image research is used to determine (1) which attributes are most important to consumers, (2) the image that consumers have of all key brands in the market relative to those attributes, and (3) which attributes tend to be most predictive of overall brand opinion. Consumers are asked to rate the importance of attributes. This is typically measured using a rating scale from "very important" to "not at all important." After completing the importance ratings, respondents are asked to rate competing brands on each attribute. Information is also collected about usage and purchase of the brands. It is important to note that the larger a brand's dominance in the market, the greater the expected value on all the ratings for that brand. Therefore, it is important to look at results among users of each brand as well as total consumers.

Segmentation Research

Segments are an identifiable group of consumers with common requirements or characteristics. Research conducted for segmentation analysis generally includes questioning on a broad range of marketing and product topics, plus life-style and demographic questioning. Sophisticated analytic tools are used to examine patterns of responses to key questions to identify groups of consumers who have very consistent responses with the group, yet responses that are very different from those of the other groups. Based on this analysis, consumers are grouped into segments.

- *Need-based segments*. Research that produces segments based on products or psychological needs is most likely to identify opportunities for new brands in a category, flankers or line extensions, and established brand repositioning. Need segmentation analysis can focus either on attribute importance data or on brand rating data. Brand rating data have the advantage that needs currently met by all or most brands do not drive differences between segments. On the other hand, segmentation based on brand ratings may fail to identify segmented needs which are not met by any brand in a category. Segmentation based on attribute importance has the advantage of identifying whether consumers do have different sets of needs on all attributes regardless of how they are met by existing brands.
- *Behavior-based segments*. Segmentation based on behavioral characteristics such as brands used and tasks performed, degree of loyalty, and so on, can identify important marketing opportunities, but application is more limited to line extension opportunities. As examples, segmentation based on tasks can identify particular ones where there is little competition currently or where brands being used for a particular task are not well suited for that purpose.
- *Descriptive segments*. Segmentation based on descriptive characteristics such as demographics, life-styles, and so on, can be important in considering tactical adjustments to specific elements of marketing programs but should not be used to address strategic issues or product issues. Differences in demographics or life-styles may not be linked to differences in consumer needs and therefore may not identify meaningful opportunities for new items or repositioning of established brands.

Conjoint Analysis

Conjoint analysis is based on a model of consumer behavior that underlies nearly all of conventional research techniques. The model states that a brand, product, or concept can be considered as a bundle of attributes, or attribute levels, each of which makes some contribution to overall consumer acceptability. Individual consumers may want different mixes of these attribute levels. Each consumer will be more likely to buy an existing brand, or to try a new brand, if it comes closer to his or her desired "mix" than other available alternatives.

Conjoint analysis uses standard principles of experimental design to estimate the contributions to overall choice behavior of many different attribute-level changes, all in the same study. By asking respondent preference between a relatively small number of pairs of hypothetical products (attribute-level bundles), conjoint analysis estimates their individual-level propensity to choose any hypothetical product over any other such product or group of products encompassed by the conjoint analysis.

3.6. CHARACTERISTICS OF SUCCESSFUL NEW CONSUMER PRODUCTS

In general, ideas for successful new consumer products have one or more of the following characteristics [2]:

1. They offer entirely new benefits not offered by existing products.
2. They offer a new secondary benefit in addition to the new key product benefit.
3. They make comparative claims versus competition.
4. They eliminate an important negative in existing products in the market.
5. They offer a higher-quality product than is currently available in the market.
6. They tap into current/emerging trends in society.
7. They offer a price advantage versus currently available alternatives.

If a feasible product opportunity with one of these characteristics has been identified, the indicated action flowing from the market analysis may be positive if the market is judged as attractive and their is a reasonable degree of business synergy. Parity or "me-too" products, especially in most highly competitive consumer markets, are a formula for failure.

3.7. HOW MANY CONSUMERS ARE INTERESTED IN THE NEW PRODUCT?

The next step is to test the ideas among consumers to get a reading on how many of them have an interest in actually buying the product, one of the key questions that must be addressed by an analysis. What is tested is commonly known as a "concept." Ideally, one would like to have a concept as close as possible to the final one that will be presented to the consumer in advertisements or in-store. The further removed the concept description is from the final presentation, the harder it is to translate any intention to buy responses into marketplace acceptance figures. However, at this early stage it is unrealistic to think of testing anything but a fairly basic presentation. A simple word description of the product's attributes and benefits will suffice for most products.

The most common method of measuring consumer interest in a new consumer product concept is to do a test among consumers who are shown a concept and then asked to express their interest in buying. The major premise of a concept test is that consumers' reactions to a concept are good indicators of their likely future behavior in the marketplace. Many studies have confirmed the validity of the relationship between purchase intention scales and subsequent consumer behavior in the marketplace [2]. A five-point purchase interest scale ("definitely would buy," "probably would buy," "might or might not buy," "probably would not buy," "definitely would not buy") is most often used.

The purchase interest scale is used to estimate how many consumers are interested enough to buy the new product described by the concept under perfect conditions (100 percent) of consumer awareness and retail distribution. There are many weighting schemes, most of which give the "top box" the highest weight by far. The result is an estimate of what is called the "interested universe," which is then adjusted downward by the expected consumer awareness and retail distribution that the company thinks that it can achieve.

$$\text{Consumer trial} = \text{interested universe} \times \text{consumer awareness} \times \text{retail distribution}$$

This is a very simple approach for estimating how many consumers are likely to try the new product and like it well enough to adopt it—one that will yield only a "ballpark" forecast. Other models are available commercially that use more sophisticated approaches and are more accurate. But they are generally time consuming, costly, and require reasonably accurate estimates of introductory marketing variables. Such models are appropriate in the later stages of development when more precise estimates are feasible.

3.8. UNDERSTANDING CONSUMER BUYING BEHAVIOR

The next question concerns itself with the rate at which consumers who adopt the new product will buy it. The good news is that consumer buying behavior is both regular and predictable in competitive markets. Competitive brands tend to differ mainly in how many buyers they have rather than in how loyal those buyers are. But insofar as they do differ in loyalty, small brands generally attract less loyalty among their buyers than large brands do among theirs. This phenomenon is called *double jeopardy*. The reverse, a small brand having few but exceptionally loyal buyers, has seldom if ever been reported. The regularity and predictability of consumer buying behavior is strongly and increasingly supported by empirical evidence [3]. It appears to hold true whenever competitive items differ in their popularity.

Table 3.1 shows the average purchase frequencies of 14 leading U.S. brands of laundry detergent. The number of households that bought each brand in a year—the annual penetration—varies from 25 percent to 1 percent. In contrast, both the repeat purchase rate and the number of times on average that each brand's buyers bought it in the year vary much less, but also tend to be lower for brands with fewer buyers. The remarkable feature of these data is that the deviations are quite small given how much the brands differ in their formulas, branding, advertising, pricing, packaging, distribution, and so on.

New Brand Targets.   Double jeopardy provides important information for planning new products. Suppose that a company is launching a new brand into the detergent market with an annual sales target of a 2 percent share, or 24 purchases per 100 households. This could be made up of 24 percent buying the new brand once a year or 1 percent buying it 24 times, or anything in between. These alternatives have very different implications. The results in Table 3.1 show that it would have to be purchased by roughly 8 percent of households on average 3 times (or more precisely, by some 9 percent buying on average about 2.7 times). There can be variations, but it cannot be 1 percent buying 24 times nor 24 percent buying once. For anything like that to happen, the new brand would

TABLE 3.1   Shares, Penetrations, Repeat, and Purchase Frequencies: Laundry Detergents[a]

Brand	Market Share (%)	Household Penetration (%)	Repeat Purchase[b] (%)	Purchase Frequency (number) #
Tide	25	54	71	4.4
Wisk	10	29	62	3.4
Bold	8	27	58	2.9
Era	6	22	55	2.7
Cheer	5	19	55	2.7
A&H	5	16	57	3.0
All	5	19	53	2.5
Fab	5	18	55	2.7
Oxydol	4	12	55	2.8
Solo	2	9	50	2.4
Gain	2	9	50	2.4
Ajax	2	9	50	2.4
Rinso	2	6	53	2.7
Dash	1	4	54	2.8

[a] According to data from IRI, 1985.
[b] Fitted percent repeat purchase (negative binomial distribution).

have to differ more radically from all existing brands in the market than they differ from each other.

Niche Brands. Niche brands are thought of as being bought relatively often by relatively few people. This notion raises issues of the definition of market segments. However, within any market that actually includes some nonniche brands, a very heavily bought small brand would be a departure from double jeopardy. Such a situation is possible if the brand's properties uniquely fit its particular users. Because the general trend would be in the opposite direction, such cases ought to stand out as significant exceptions. A small brand having few but exceptionally loyal buyers has seldom, if ever, been reported. Most niche brands are just brands with small shares of the market that appeal to a small group of consumers or for certain usage occasions. They are not bought, however, exceptionally often by their buyers.

A market analysis should consider that consumer markets almost always show a regular pattern whereby smaller brands tend to attract somewhat less loyalty, with deviations that are mostly small.

3.9. PUTTING IT ALL TOGETHER: HYPOTHETICAL EXAMPLE

Suppose that a consumer packaged goods company is assessing the potential of several markets, including glass cleaners. It is a logical extension of what the company is selling now and is seen as a very good fit with the company's existing capabilities. It is a large market dominated by a single competitor that is judged to be sleepy and vulnerable. The idea for the product is vague—almost no creative thinking has been done. The ingredients of a potentially successful new consumer product are missing.

A cross-functional team consisting of marketing and product development people is put together to do a preliminary market study and analysis of unrecognized and unmet consumer needs in the market. It takes the form of focus group interviews and in-home observational visits. The group interviews suggest that cleaning, ease of use, lack of streaking, and odor are the prime purchase motivators in the market. The product of the leading competitor is rated highly on all of these key attributes. The in-home observations also show very clearly that it takes several rolls of paper towels to clean all the windows in a house, more than the cost or the cleaner itself. Several hands are required to clean a window: one to hold the roll of towels, one to hold the cleaner, one to wipe the window, and sometimes one to hold onto the ladder. Not surprisingly, consumers appear to hate the task.

The team meets to discuss these findings and to develop creative product solutions. Because all team members had taken part in the research, all of them were looking for solutions to real problems. Among the technically feasible ideas that emerged, the following were taken into small-scale concept testing.

1. A powder-like cleaner that can be sprayed on directly and that can be wiped off easily without soaking the towel
2. A disposable nonwoven cloth impregnated with a cleaning agent
3. A new spray that not only cleans but repels dirt, reducing the need for frequent cleaning

The team decided to proceed directly to concept testing because the ideas were so unique for this market—each of them appeared to introduce a new dimension.

The concept test commissioned by the team was very short and focused, designed to measure consumer interest and little else. This meant that it was relatively inexpensive and very fast. Focus group interviews were conducted concurrently to provide diagnostics to supplement the quantitative concept test. The analysis of the concept test yielded the results shown in Table 3.2. Of the three concepts that were tested, only the powder cleaner appeared to have the potential of achieving the sales and share required for an attractive investment. The cross-functional team made the projections a key part of their analysis to recommend the glass cleaner market. The market analysis recognized, however, the risk associated with this small market. Further development would continue only as long as consumer research indicated strong acceptance of both concept and product, at the $2.75 premium pricing.

This illustration is designed to make the point that a market analysis to assess the potential of a new product should go well beyond merely looking at the

TABLE 3.2 Concept Test and Sales Forecast for Three Glass Cleaners

	Spray	Nonwoven cloth	Powder Cleaner
Interested universe (from concept test)[a]	17.1%	19.8%	27.5%
Price per unit tested in concept test	$1.95	$2.75	$2.75
Number of U.S. households		100,000,000	
Expected retail distribution		75%	
Expected consumer awareness		50%	
Above average repeat rate		50%	
Annual purchase occasions[b]		1.6 times	
Projected year 1 retail sales (millions)	$9.9	$16.3	$22.6
Projected share of market	11%	17%	24%

[a] Calculated by weighting the 5-point purchase intent scale (0.9, 0.255, 0.05, 0.005, 0.0).
[b] Estimated from household purchase panel data from IRI and Nielsen.

traditional factors of business synergy and market attractiveness. Successful entry into any new market depends very much on a company's ability to develop new products that fulfill consumer needs in a better way. If a company is unable to meet the challenge of gaining competitive superiority, their chances of achieving success are slim. In the hypothetical glass cleaner example, the development team took the extra step of doing a rather limited investigation of consumer needs and frustrations that helped them identify problems that had a product solution within the company's technical capability. They then tested their new product concepts among consumers to better define the real market opportunity. Only one of the concepts, the powder-like cleaner, exceeded the minimum business requirements of the company. The product was judged to be technically feasible and could be manufactured by a supplier, requiring no capital investment. The decision was made to proceed to the next stage of development.

3.10. SUMMARY

Market analysis is a complex and sequential process that is crucial if a company is to enjoy a high new product success rate. It boils down to a detailed examination of a product category to ensure that it is one that will reward the company. It allows the company to direct resources at markets and products of greatest potential while avoiding those of high risk and low return.

The first step looks at the basic fundamentals of the market and whether there is synergy between it and the company's capabilities. Selection factors such as match to the company's resource base, market size, market growth, and market competitiveness are identified and differentially weighted as to their relative importance. An overall evaluation is made and a decision is made to go to the next step.

The next step involves identifying a product opportunity. It requires learning about consumers and making the creative leap that results in an innovative and technically feasible product—one that is clearly better than existing products in some way—an entirely new benefit, superior performance, higher quality, or lower price with performance equal to competition.

The final step is a quantitative one where the product idea or concept is tested to see how many consumers have an interest in buying the product. The results of the concept study are translated into forecasts of likely sales and profitability. Only markets and products that meet or exceed the company's financial requirements are taken to the next step in the development process.

REFERENCES

1. Cooper, Robert G. The NewProd system: the industry experience. *Journal of Product Innovation Management* 9:113–127 (1992).

2. Davis, Robert E. From experience: the role of market research in the development of new consumer products. *Journal of Product Innovation Management* 10:309–317 (1993).
3. Uncles, M. D., Hammond, K. A., Ehrenberg, A. S. C., and Davis, R. E. A replication study of two brand-loyalty measures. *European Journal of Operational Research* 76:375–384 (1994).
4. Urban, Glen L. and Hauser, John R. *Design and Marketing of New Products.* Englewood Cliffs, NJ: Prentice Hall, 1993.

Robert E. Davis

Market Facts, Inc.

Robert E. Davis is a Vice President of Market Facts, Inc. where he helps clients evaluate new products through the use of market research and forecasting models. Before joining Market Facts, Mr. Davis was Procter & Gamble's Market Research Manager for new products. He has been involved in new product work since 1968 when he worked as the market research manager on the first simulated test markets ever conducted to evaluate the sales potential of new products. He is regarded as an authority on new product market research throughout the world. He has given new product seminars to management, marketing, and product development people in the United States, Canada, Mexico, Venezuela, Hong Kong, China, Japan, Spain, and Switzerland.

MARKET ANALYSIS AND SEGMENTATION ISSUES FOR NEW BUSINESS-TO-BUSINESS PRODUCTS

4.

Edith Wilson

4.1. INTRODUCTION

Business-to-business markets differ importantly from consumer markets, which is first explored by posing and answering two questions. Because you must segment any business-to-business market, three ways to do that are described. Next, the critical challenge of helping your customer make money is covered. Finally, five other issues that must be considered are discussed.

4.2. TWO QUESTIONS TO DISTINGUISH MARKET TYPES

1. What does it mean to be in a business-to-business market rather than a consumer market?

Many companies find themselves selling to other businesses rather than to end consumers. The breadth of this type of customer class is vast, ranging from original equipment manufacturers (OEMs) to customers who utilize major pieces of capital equipment in their firms' infrastructure and processes. There are no hard delineators as to what constitutes a business-to-business product as compared to a consumer product. Until recently, high-technology products were more likely to be business-to-business products than low-technology products.

However, the sale of personal computers in superstores has changed that differentiation. A simple differentiation is to ask whether or not you can identify your customers' firms and the applications in which they use your products. If the answer is yes, your organization is probably in a business-to-business market; if it is no, you are probably in a consumer market.

2. Is there much difference between being in a business-to-business market or a consumer market?

There is not much difference between the two types of markets except that it may be easier to understand the true preferences and needs of the customers and users in the business-to-business market. This is because the number of customers are usually much smaller and there are target people to speak to about the nature of the problems that the customer is trying to solve. For example, if you are trying to sell large computer systems to multinational banks, it is fairly straightforward to determine that there are a number of people involved in the purchase, use, and support of banks' financial computer systems. With some hard work, identifying who all of these people are and interviewing them in preparing your product definition is feasible within a reasonably sized budget. In juxtaposition, consumer markets usually include huge numbers of end customers and a number of marketing channels distributing the products. Statistical sampling methods are necessary for this type of market, since it is impractical to interview everyone.

> *Business-to-business markets are often characterized by having a small set of customers.*

4.3. THREE WAYS TO SEGMENT A MARKET

Segmentation of the market is the initial step. There are a variety of ways to slice and dice the marketplace, and if this is the first attempt at making a segmentation model, doing the exercise in a number of ways will be very insightful as to which is the right way for your organization.

4.3.1. Geography

One of the easiest methods to segment a marketplace is by geography. In segmenting the market this way, insight into the geographic distribution of the market will be gained. There is merit in associating the geographic distribution

	Number of Sales per Year
Tokyo	240
Shanghai	110
Taipei	30
Bangkok	10

FIGURE 4.1 Sales in Asia. The sales locations are marked by stars, showing the close proximity of the various regions.

information with the size of the target businesses to which you hope to sell. For example, if you are researching the sales of computer equipment into large banks, you would first identify what a large bank is. In this situation we could decide that it is banks that have more than $1 billion of assets. Next, you will research where these banks are located in both you home country and internationally. See Figure 4.1 for how to look at these data in both tabular and graphic formats. With the data collected about location, clustering of the marketplace will be possible and will provide insight into where the probable markets for your products will be. This will be useful when you are planning distribution and support systems.

4.3.2. Size and Growth

Another method of segmentation is to look at the size of target businesses and their growth rates (Table 4.1). In continuing the banking example, collect infor-

TABLE 4.1   Sales in Asia: Size and Growth of Markets

	1996 Sales	1997 Sales	1998 Sales	1999 Sales
Tokyo[a]	240	220	230	210
Shanghai	110	220	380	500
Taipei	30	100	200	600
Bangkok	10	50	150	400

[a] It is notable that the growth rate in Tokyo is flat, whereas the other three regions are booming.

mation on each bank's size and growth rate. This will show you what is growing and what is not, but this is just the tip of the iceberg. Your team will need to identify the underlying causes of these changes.

4.3.3. Benefit Base

A most useful segmentation method is to look at the benefits that your product could provide and then to analyze the size of these markets. This method results in identification of the many ways that a product is and could be used. In this type of segmentation, a computer company would look at the market as a computer market that conducts numerical analyses. From this perspective, the market now includes not only banks but stock brokerage firms, store, hospitals, and utility companies, to name a few. Computer companies that use this perspective will identify themselves as a financial solution provider, not a provider of banking solutions.

> *Business-to-business markets may be segmented by geography, size or growth rates, or benefits delivered.*

Caution still needs to be taken to disaggregate the market into the least common denominators. This is done by looking for the commonalties between the market subsegments and for the differences. Table 4.2 illustrates the principles.

4.4. THE KEY IS UNDERSTANDING USERS' AND CUSTOMERS' NEEDS

If you take the premise that all users and customers believe that their needs are unique and require a customized solution, your business will quickly become a service business. Companies that are enormously successful acknowledge this

TABLE 4.2   Sales in Asia: Market Comparisons[a]

	Tokyo 4	Shanghai 1	Taipei 2	Bangkok 3
Custom features	A	B	C	D
Similar subsystems	I	I	F	F
Common base	Base	Base	Base	Base

[a] In the model, by market segment, the similarities and differences are noted and compared to the market attractiveness. In order to build a product for the most attractive market, Shanghai, the product must have the base, and attributes I and B; for the second most attractive market, Taipei, the product must have the base and attributes F and C.

customer desire, yet are able to capitalize on the similarity of the needs to provide customers the capacity to differentiate themselves through the use of their products. It is critical to understand that you must analyze the market to develop a successful product. This is unfortunately not a completely straightforward task, as a variety of market analysis methods are required to identify the intricacies of the various aspects of the users' and customers' needs.

4.4.1. Step One: Generating the User and Customer Chain

> *It is critical to understand how your product will help your target customer make money.*

The goal of this step is to record the user and customer chain for the segment of the market that you are targeting. In Figure 4.2 a generic chain is depicted. It is interesting to note that the marketing channel portion of the chain can take on a number of different forms, depending on the business, yet for most business-to-business products, some form of distribution representative or direct sales force is used to generate orders. This is in stark contrast to consumer products, which rely heavily on a distribution network that often includes many layers of relationships and product transfers.

The primary purpose of generating a user and customer chain is to outline who each of the key parties is in the target market segment, to identify the needs of each party, and to highlight how users and customers make their purchase decision. The second reason for outlining the chain is to analyze whether or not this model is the same for all customers and users or if there are differences that indicate a fragmented or nonhomogeneous market segment. If you discover a fragmented market situation, further segmentation may be necessary.

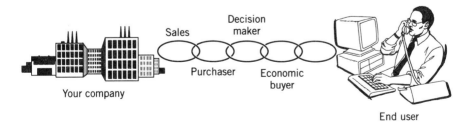

FIGURE 4.2 User and customer chain. In the model, each link of the chain needs to be identified and assigned to the person or people who embody that role at your target customers. The needs of each of these links then need to be identified. Caution should be taken not to oversimplify this chain, because there are probably more rather than fewer people whose inputs you will need.

4.4.2. Step Two: Identifying Each User's and Customer's Problems

Within the chain of users and customers, identification of each of their needs is the first step. This can be very difficult, since many of these people may not be people with whom anyone in your firm has contact. The starting point, after creating the user and customer chain, is to examine each link's key problems and motivations to purchase and use your product. Many methods are available to do this, but it is useful first to develop a picture of what the key problems are. Two methods are very useful in doing preliminary analyses: customer visits and focus groups. A third method, shadowing, can also be used.

In customer visits, it is key to visit a range of customers within a target segment and to first conduct visits with the full range of users and customers [5–7]. Of particular importance is to speak to customers who currently purchase your products, as well as to customers to whom you tried to sell your products in the past but lost the deal, and to customers who are unaware of your product line or company. Using this methodology and cataloging which group they fall into will allow you to complete a table similar to Table 4.3. If the market is large, visiting at least ten customers [2] is necessary to assure statistical projection, and if the total market is smaller than ten, visiting all the companies should be sought.

The second method, focus groups [1,3,4], allows the team to query a small set of customers in a detailed fashion. This discussion is led by an outside facilitator and is viewed and videotaped by the team from behind a one-way mirror. The benefits of focus groups are that the customers do not know which company is asking the questions and that a dialogue is generated between customers from a number of different companies. Additional benefits include having a video of customers that a wide cross section of company people can view later. The down-

TABLE 4.3 Types of Customers[a]

Customer	Current	Bid but Lost Deal	New
Tokyo 1	$2M	$4M	$8M
Tokyo 2	$1M	$0M	$1M
Shanghai 1	$0.5M	$2M	$0M
Shanghai 2	$2M	$1M	$0.5M
Shanghai 3	$4M	$2M	$8M
Taipei 1	■	■	■
Taipei 2	■	■	■
Taipei 3	■	■	■
Bangkok 1	■	■	■
Bangkok 2	■	■	■
Bangkok 3	■	■	■

[a] In this table, the significance of conducting research not only on current customers but also on old, lost, and new customers is shown. This is particularly necessary when your product does not command the most market share.

side is that the focus group's success is very dependent on the skills of the facilitator and the selection of the participants. One major risk is that one participant can dominate a session, and team's key questions do not get addressed or answered.

A third method, shadowing the customer, is used by many companies and does not rely on a formal meeting but on members of the selling company's staff spending several hours to days with a customer in the section of their operation where your product is used. For example, a medical products group might spend several weeks "shadowing" when they are conducting market research for a new patient monitoring system product. Here, a team including engineering, support, and manufacturing personnel might spend a week in a major medical school hospital observing how patient monitoring equipment is used in the operating, recovery, and intensive care unit rooms to identify what spoken and unspoken needs of the customer are currently unmet. This method is attractive because it allows a team to hypothesize and test what product attributes would truly create value for the customer by identifying unspoken needs.

In summary, you should employ whichever method will provide you answers to the questions:

> *Customer visits, focus groups, and shadowing are three ways to identify user and customer problems.*

1. What currently makes the customer successful?
2. What will be necessary for them to be successful in the future?
3. How does this company make money?

If you do not have answers to these questions, it will be very difficult to identify how your company's products can be attractive to their company.

4.5. FIVE OTHER ISSUES IN GAINING PRODUCT ACCEPTANCE

Assuming that you have answered these questions satisfactorily and plan to develop a new business-to-business product, there are five other issues to consider.

4.5.1. The Gatekeeper

After examining your qualitative data, you still need to identify who the gatekeeper is and what the gatekeeper's motivations and needs are. The reason for this is that most purchasing decisions rely on satisfying this person, although, often, this is a person who the sales team has not even identified. In many business-to-business transactions, only high- and low-level customers and users are known, but there are several middle-level managers who wield significant amounts of power through their ability to influence the purchasing decisions. Typical gatekeepers include R&D, manufacturing, quality, support, and finance managers. In large organizations, the gatekeepers can be at a level below this.

4.5.2. Why Asking "What Do You Need?" Does Not Work

Customers think they know what they need but usually do not. This bold statement illustrates that sellers of equipment need to be very wary of what their customers tell them. Savvy companies have learned that customers are very influenced by what the last supplier told them, by how you ask your questions, and by prototypes. At the heart of these difficulties is that the customer may be speculating about solutions to their problems while never sharing their strategies and fundamental business problems with you. The reason that knowledge about their business strategies and difficulties is so valuable is that you can then use this knowledge to select the pivotal differentiators that your product needs to embody.

For example, if you are selling semiconductor processing equipment, there are only about 25 large customers in the world that can be large-volume purchasers of your equipment. When you visit these customers, they will exaggerate their need for high-performance testing and spend lots of time on the details of the specifications that you need to provide to meet their product needs. This information is just the tip of the iceberg. As you spend more time with them, you will discover that they can make money only if they are very fast at identifying bugs within their product while it is still in development. Then they must be able to scale down the test set and use a subset of these test procedures in manufacturing. This sounds simple, but the design of a test instrument that allows an R&D engineer easy access to the fullest range of tests and that allows an inexpensive manufacturing "go or no-go" test has been impossible in the past. Thus the company that can achieve a simple transition from R&D into manufacturing has a compelling product to offer because it will improve the purchasing company's ability to get their chip products out to the market quickly and cost-effectively.

You must have an intimate understanding of the prospective customer's situation.

4.5.3. Are the Needs Beyond the Scope of Features? Hard Versus Soft Needs

Depending on the positioning of your product on an S-curve, you will notice that the needs are hard versus soft. Low-range products on Figure 4.3 are usually

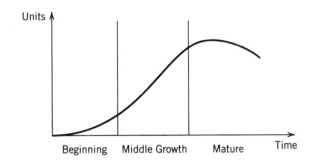

FIGURE 4.3 S curve. In the model, at the beginning of the life cycle, it is necessary to demonstrate the viability of the product by designing adequate performance into the product. In the middle phase, cost becomes an issue, and in the mature and declining period, softer factors become an issue.

differentiated by features because the market is still rather insensitive to price since few real competitors exist. As the product type matures and moves into the midrange of the S-curve, cost becomes more of a delineator between competitors, and finally, when the product is in the mature or declining phase, "softer" attributes are necessary to differentiate products. These softer attributes include channel, service, relationship, and support. Each of these makes it easier for the purchaser to interact with your company as a supplier. For example, imagine that your customer is a multinational manufacturer of computers that designs the computers in California but manufacturers them in China, and you are hoping that they will purchase disk drives from you. A winning strategy of soft need fulfillment could be: (1) meet their specification and price objectives, and (2) provide local manufacturing and support of disk drives in China (since they know that if there are difficulties, the time and language differences of working with a non-China-based company could spell disaster for their company).

4.5.4. The Role of Relationships

Another ripe area for differentiation is in the area of relationships and trust. Companies that supply other companies can gain an advantage here because more and more companies around the world are being driven to meeting various ISO9000 standards and other quality objectives, which means that they need to have very dependable suppliers. It is well worth the effort to document your processes and achieve high standards in the quality of the products that you ship because you can sell this as a means of making your customer more successful. It may seem that this is not a critical step in achieving a sound relationship with your customers, but it will enhance your relationship if you are consistently there and able to supply them with sufficient supplies of good products. Additionally, many corporations are trying to have fewer vendors and have active projects to encourage the use of a set of preferred suppliers who are known to be depend-able providers of products.

4.5.5. What About the Competition: "How Do They Affect the Needs of the Customer?"

Competition will almost always be present. There are two exceptions: at the beginning and at the end of the S-curve. In the first case, a market is being formed and competition is from alternative solution sets and will not become direct unless customers perceive value from the solution you are providing and competitors can emulate your solution. At the end of the cycle, many competitors will exit from the market, because there is insufficient money to be made or for a variety of reasons it is not sound for them to remain in that line of business. Between these extremes there is competition and it will always influence your target customers. It is extremely important to recognize that competition ad-vances the expectations of your customers and that you should always be in a position to project what your competition will be offering at the time you are targeting market release. By these means you should be able to assure that you product will be sufficiently competitive for you to command the revenues and profits you need for your business to thrive.

4.6. SUMMARY

Business-to-business marketing has many attributes similar to those of consumer marketing but can be easier if you are willing to invest the time to conduct research on your chain of users and customers. Identification of customers' key needs and motivations is necessary to differentiate your products. Caution should be taken not to underestimate the power of identifying the underlying process by which your customers make money, so that you can position your product to aid them in that pursuit.

REFERENCES

1. Calder, Bobby J. Focus groups and the nature of qualitative marketing research. *Journal of Marketing Research* 14:353–364 (August 1977).
2. Griffin, Abbie. Functionally integrating new product development. Doctoral thesis, MIT Sloan School of Management, Cambridge, MA, 1989.
3. Krueger, Richard A. *Focus Groups: A Practical Guide for Applied Research.* Newbury Park, CA: Sage Publications, 1988.
4. Morgan, David L. *Focus Groups as Qualitative Research.* Newbury Park, CA: Sage Publications, 1988.

5. Wilson, Edith. Product definition factors for successful designs. Thesis, Department of Mechanical Engineering, Stanford University, Stanford, CA, December 1990.
6. Wilson, Edith. Product definition: assorted techniques and their marketplace impact. *Proceedings of the IEEE International Engineering Management Conference*, 1990.
7. Wilson, Edith. Improving market success rates through better product definition. *World Class Design to Manufacture Journal* 1(4):13–15 (1994).

Edith Wilson
Hewlett-Packard Company

Edith Wilson has been with Hewlett-Packard since 1980 and has held a variety of positions. These include being an engineer, a project manager, an R&D section manager, and corporate manager of product definition and prospecting for new business. Her business assignments have taken her from California to Bristol, England and to the Far East. She has also contributed to the academic world in the capacities of being an Associate Fellow at the University of Sussex in England to her current position as Senior Lecturer at Stanford University's School of Engineering. Her other activities include renovating historic buildings and travel. The author lives in Palo Alto, California with her husband and daughter.

OPTIMIZING PRODUCT DEVELOPMENT
5 THROUGH PIPELINE MANAGEMENT
John R. Harris and
Jonathan C. McKay

5.1. INTRODUCTION

Today, many companies have upgraded their product development process, yet a perception often exists that the process has not yet optimized—development output is far from being maximized, connections between strategic plans and actual deployment or resources are nebulous, and the organization still lacks the flexibility to respond to changes rapidly. Recent publications have pointed to the need to better manage the aggregate of development projects [2, pp. 38–40; 7] but do not provide specifics, treating the issue as more of a call to action. Traditional portfolio management approaches [3, pp. 163–203; 4; 5, pp. 75–84] help in determining the best mix of products, but do not balance this mix from a resource and skill perspective. Additionally, portfolio management does not address the ongoing management of project and functional staffing, portfolio trade-offs, and cross-project interaction.

In the course of helping over 140 technology-based companies worldwide upgrade their development process, our company has encountered this same issue—something was missing that dynamically integrates product strategy, project management, and functional management. What is missing is a continual process to optimize the development pipeline: the cross-project management of all development-related activities such as new product development, product support, technology development, process improvements, and so on. Traditionally, emphasis in improving the product development process has focused on improving project management (high-performance teams, integrated development methodology, empowering stage-gate or phase reviews, and enabling tools [1]), but has not specifically addressed cross-project management issues. Usually, the connection between strategy, project management, and functional management is limited to the annual budgeting process—a holdover from the functional orientation of the past—which is inadequate for a high-performance product development process.

While many principles described in this article are analogs to factory management, there are major differences. Unlike a factory with stable, characterized processes and standard equipment and personnel, product development projects have inherent uncertainty and instability, and individuals participating in development each have a unique combination of skills, experience, motivation, and attitude. These factors frustrate attempts simply to apply factory management principles to the product development pipeline. The only solution is a unique process that provides continual adjustments concurrently over multiple time horizons. The goal of this chapter is to introduce the pipeline management framework, the process elements, and implementation considerations.

5.2. PIPELINE MANAGEMENT FRAMEWORK

Many companies are missing a process that integrates product strategy, project management, and functional management. This often unrecognized yet critical process—pipeline management—is introduced in this chapter.

Having a pipeline management capability allows companies continually to optimize their product development performance, which is a powerful competitive advantage. Examples of the impact of pipeline management are listed below and are in sharp contrast to the situation that most companies face:

- Strategic and financial plans are based on realistic development skills, and capabilities and detailed plans are in place to address deficient areas.
- Functional budgets are aligned with project needs and strategic plans.
- Bottlenecks are eliminated so that all projects proceed rapidly through development.
- Firefighting is minimized as proactive, cross-project trade-offs are made continuously.

- Decisions made on all projects and in every function are coordinated based on aligned priorities.
- Ripple effects on projects due to external changes or development problems are smoothly resolved.
- Time to market is reduced significantly across the board because projects are staffed for success.

Pipeline management is based on the three-gear mechanism diagrammed in Figure 5.1 linking product strategy with project management and functional management. Overall priorities flow from product strategy and drive project and functional management. Project and functional management provides staffing and capability information to assure realistic product strategy. All three gears must be in place and synchronized to avoid each function and each project attempting to optimize its own area, leading to suboptimal overall product development performance.

Each gear of pipeline management has a distinct contribution. The strategic gear sets balanced priorities among the numerous opportunities and adjusts the organization's skill sets to deliver the products. The project gear fine-tunes resource deployment smoothly for projects during ramp up, ramp down, and midcourse adjustments. The functional gear helps functional managers make continual adjustments to maximize the flow through their area in accordance with overall development priorities.

The speed of the gears in Figure 5.1 is governed by marketplace volatility, rate of technology change, typical development cycle times, and so on. In most cases the gear speeds do not correspond to the cadence of how most companies operate—the annual planning and budgeting cycle. For example, a major PC

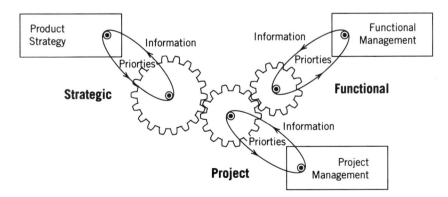

FIGURE 5.1 Three gears of pipeline management. Copyright © 1995 Pittiglio Rabin Todd & McGrath; reproduced by permission.

modem manufacturer faces a market where new PCs are introduced every six months and has responded by adjusting its pipeline strategically every six months, tactically every two weeks, and functionally on a daily basis. Contrast this with a leading pharmaceutical company, which faces a development cycle of more than a decade and accordingly adjusts its pipeline strategically every few years, projectwise on an annual basis, and functionally every quarter.

5.2.1. Strategic Pipeline Management

All companies appear to have a semblance of strategic pipeline management through the annual planning and budgeting cycle; however, significant deficiencies exist that prevent senior management from providing true leadership for the pipeline. Typically, budgets are set by each function, independent of other functions except for overall reconciliation of the bottom line. Consequently, the objectives for each function are unique and misaligned across the company, especially in the area of product development. For example, a common misalignment has R&D committed to developing a vast array of new products, while manufacturing is focused on cost reduction. These groups are destined to work against each other in many situations because they are following their respective functional objectives! Another issue with the annual planning process is that unrealistic product development strategies are often formulated in the absence of a fact-based understanding of the organization's development capabilities and capacity across all functions, leading to disappointment when the plans cannot be realized.

In contrast, strategic pipeline management results in tight linkages between product strategies and organizational capabilities and capacities. From the lower levels of pipeline management, information bubbles up that validates the achievability of product development strategies. As a result, difficult trade-offs can be accomplished to set overall pipeline priorities. (*Note*: Strategic balance is based on balancing the portfolio of development projects along many dimensions, such as focus versus diversification, short versus long term, high versus low risk, extending existing platforms versus development of new platforms, and so on. Each class of projects has a unique set of financial return targets appropriate to its risk-and-return profile and strategic fit [6, pp. 232–258].)

In the course of achieving strategic balance, transitory and chronic overloads can be identified and dealt with appropriately. During this exercise many companies realize that their development-related resources are far out of balance across the functional areas because the focus on building staff for product development is usually on highly visible dedicated groups (typically, R&D) while support groups (such as product management, manufacturing, and purchasing) are overlooked. A statement by the general manager at a major telecommunications equipment company illustrates this fallacy: "If I can hire another person, of course it will be a design engineer because I want more new products!" This same division had cut back overhead, decimating the purchasing group. Since purchasing could no longer adequately support product development, the design engineers were forced to take time from development to select vendors. The design engineers were extremely inefficient at working with vendors and their inexperience resulted in rampant material cost, delivery, and quality problems that threw the organization into crisis. Without the correct staffing ratios between functional areas involved in product development, overall performance is severely compromised.

In areas of strategic importance where resource gaps exist, long-term, actionable plans can be put in place to build the organization, or a proactive search can begin to identify and qualify suitable partners or subcontractors. This is very different from the standard budgetary approach, which is based on incremental changes from the prior year (that reinforces the status quo) and delays needed organizational shifts until full-blown restructuring is necessary.

With an overall view of the pipeline, functional objectives can then be aligned so that the organization is motivated to work together, as opposed to the traditional functional managers' incentives to optimize performance in their area, frequently to the detriment of overall performance. Since the budgeting process is one of the last bastions of true functional orientation left in many companies, this cross-functional, pipeline-based objective alignment represents a dramatic change, calling into question many basic measures of functional performance.

Finally, strategic pipeline management sets empowerment boundaries for project and functional management so that adjustments in resources and schedules are made in accordance with strategic priorities. In both cases, the situations that would cause conflict with strategic objectives are escalated to senior management since these issues will affect strategic plans.

5.2.2. Project Pipeline Management

> *Strategic pipeline management focuses on achieving strategic balance, which entails setting priorities among numerous opportunities and adjusting the organization's skill sets to deliver the products.*

Project pipeline management is the most overlooked of the three gears. This results in lack of flexibility and significant inefficiency in product development. Functions and projects are viewed discretely, not in aggregate. Rarely do functional managers gather to discuss improving the flow of projects through their collective functions. In most companies functional managers focus exclusively on their area, with only occasional contact with an upstream or downstream function to resolve a specific problem. Compounding this problem are overly empowered product development teams that can ignore what may be good for the business in favor of their particular project. For example, at a struggling computer company, team leaders on longer-term projects refused to lend software engineers temporarily to the team trying to launch a next-generation machine that was necessary to keep the company afloat.

The purpose of project pipeline management is to optimize the pipeline continually to achieve the maximum possible throughput. These proactive adjustments are in accordance with strategic pipeline priorities and include ramping-up and ramping-down project teams, and compensating for the inevitable glitches in product development. All activities that require resources across all development-related functions are considered, including new product development, technology development, and support activities that are often underestimated (e.g., marketing support, manufacturing troubleshooting, and sustaining engineering). Additionally, broad initiatives such as implementing new systems and improving the development process must be accounted for.

Project pipeline management is based on allocating effective development capacity between hard and soft commitments. Effective development capacity is based on the real level of resources available in each functional area after subtracting for vacation, administration, training, recruiting, and so on (often overlooked, these activities can represent a large portion of available time). Hard commitments are those that are linked directly to strategic goals where commitments have already been made. Examples include projects that are in the latter phases of development (after specification and planning are complete) and activities that require immediate resolution in support of production or field problems. Soft commitments are those that have some flexibility and include projects in early phases of development before specification and planning are complete and improvement activities that can be delayed and modified.

Figure 5.2 provides an example of effectively loading the development pipeline. In the current period the aggregate project requirements add to the effective capacity to account for everyone's activities. In future periods the level of hard commitments drops as projects are completed, although a floor always remains to deal with support activities. Meanwhile the level of soft commitments rises because of their inherent flexibility to be delayed, canceled, or rescoped. In the distant future combined requirements drop because new ideas, not yet defined, will appear. The ratio of hard versus soft commitments is a strategic choice, based primarily on industry considerations. For example, an automotive parts supplier has only hard commitments because it must agree contractually to deliver new parts on a specific schedule at the initiation of a project because the entire car platform schedule hinges on hundreds of suppliers delivering precisely

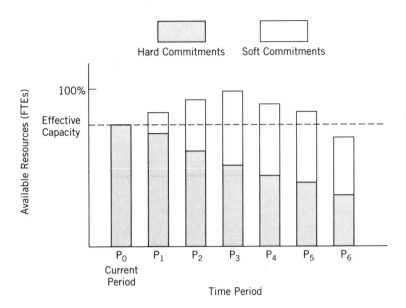

FIGURE 5.2 Balancing effective capacity against commitments. Copyright © 1995 Pittiglio Rabin Todd & McGrath; reproduced by permission.

on schedule. In contrast, a pharmaceutical company will have an immense level of soft commitments because of the high failure rate of new chemical entities as they progress through a sequence of increasingly rigorous clinical trials.

Project pipeline management requires tight integration with the product development process. However, for pipeline management to work, adjustments have to be made to the workings of empowered, cross-functional teams and stage-gate or phase reviews. The underlying issue is the natural tendency of organizations moving to teams is to swing the pendulum too far toward team autonomy. Companies that manage their pipeline effectively evaluate their projects in the context of the overall business and realize that, at times, they may have to compensate for staff changes on projects for the good of the company (this is not viewed as disempowering but rather, as responsible business management). Stage-gate or phase reviews also have to be modified to take into account strategic pipeline priorities and the resource availability across all functions. In a well-functioning stage-gate or phase review process, projects are not added to the pipeline until resources are available to staff them adequately.

Effective project pipeline management is achieved by fine-tuning resource deployment for projects during ramp up, ramp down, and midcourse adjustments.

5.2.3. Functional Pipeline Management

Functional managers have always been responsible for handling the flow of projects through their area. However, the traditional approach leads to poor overall performance as each functional manager attempts to optimize his or her functional area based on that area's specific objectives. With strategic pipeline management aligning priorities across the organization and functional managers participating in project pipeline management, many of these problems are addressed. However, the role of the functional manager takes on a new level of responsibility, in addition to assuring functional excellence.

Pipeline management places realistic, though challenging demands on each functional manager (as opposed to typical unrealistic demands) but requires a different orientation to managing the area, emphasizing building long-term capabilities and capacities to handle the projects coming down the pipeline. Having people simply work harder and longer is only a short-term solution, appropriate for temporary surges in workload. For pipeline management to work, functional managers have to shift from being reactive to anticipating requirements and addressing bottleneck issues before they occur: identifying other functional areas that have transferrable skills that could be borrowed; cross-training personnel within the function to handle multiple jobs; beginning hiring cycles with sufficient lead time for recruiting, hiring, and training; modifying the organization to leverage experience so that temporaries can be used; planning for outsourcing non-core competencies with sufficient lead time to identify, screen, and certify the contractors; and instituting longer-term efficiency improvements.

The type of proactive activities that a manager performs depends on where the function falls on the spectrum from dedicated to shared, as shown in Figure 5.3. At one extreme, dedicated functions are focused exclusively on projects, such as a design team focused on a next generation semiconductor design. At the other extreme are shared groups that are inundated with demands from many areas, such as a manufacturing engineering group trying to support multiple development teams, troubleshoot on the factory floor, work with vendors, and so on. For dedicated groups the challenge is to staff a project correctly or to recommend that the project be delayed, rescoped, or canceled. For shared groups the challenge is determining how to get out of the victim mode by creating an effective early warning system so that overloads can be identified and communicated to the upstream groups that place demands, so that overloads can be avoided.

> *Pipeline management has three distinct facets: strategic, project, and functional. To capture all of the benefits of pipeline management these facets must be in place and synchronized.*

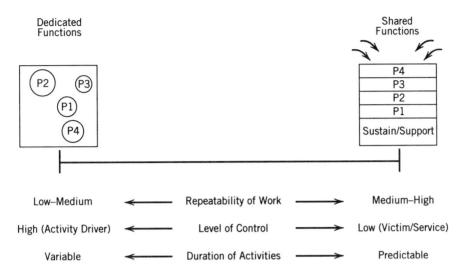

FIGURE 5.3 Spectrum of functional activities. Copyright © 1995 Pittiglio Rabin Todd & McGrath; reproduced by permission.

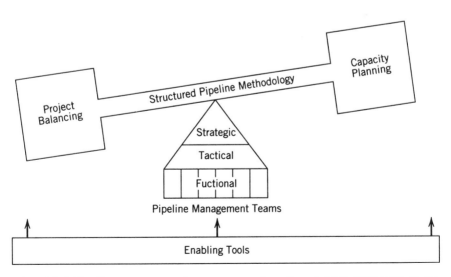

FIGURE 5.4 Pipeline management process overview. Copyright © 1995 Pittiglio Rabin Todd & McGrath; reproduced by permission.

5.3. THE PIPELINE MANAGEMENT PROCESS

Product development is rife with technical and market unknowns. Therefore, pipeline management must be a dynamic process to enable continuous optimization. Pipeline management is not black magic. It can be designed, implemented, and improved continuously based on best practices. The pipeline management process has three elements, as shown in Figure 5.4: pipeline management teams, a structured methodology, and enabling tools that must be integrated into a company's product development process. The descriptions of the elements below are purposely genericized since the actual application to each company will be unique depending on company size, organization structure, development cycle times, and levels of technical and market uncertainty.

5.3.1. Pipeline Management Teams

Pipeline management decision making is based on resolution of problems to optimize development performance at the lowest level possible. Each level of pipeline management has specific empowerment boundaries set by the next-higher level. If functional managers cannot resolve a pipeline problem within their area, they escalate the problem to the project level (and participate in the decision making). Problems that cannot be resolved at the project level are escalated to the strategic level.

At the strategic level, the pipeline management team is the management body that owns the strategic planning process. However, they are using pipeline management to help them link their strategy to project loading and functional budgeting. The project pipeline management team(s) are made up of the managers who oversee development through stage gates or phase reviews. In smaller organizations one pipeline team may span both the strategic and project levels.

The skills and attitude required to resolve pipeline issues represent a dramatic shift from the way that most managers currently operate. Most managers respond to pipeline problems reactively and discretely to resolve conflicts within their area. Contrast that to the role of a member of a team who proactively addresses global pipeline problems in a public, cross-functional forum. Even the roles of individual functional managers must change substantially (as described in Section 5.2).

Pipeline issues being resolved by teams is also a challenge because all development-related resource areas must be represented. Often, this group will be quite large and thus needs to be condensed, which entails creating effective two-way communication channels to the groups not directly represented. Even holding a team meeting can be difficult, due to the travel schedules of many managers.

5.3.2. Structured Pipeline Methodology

Since pipeline management is the intricate balancing of multiple projects across multiple functions, the methodology used must be standardized or pipeline management is impossible. The methodology has two facets: project balancing and capacity planning. As described earlier, project balancing entails selecting the best mix of projects along many dimensions such that overall strategic goals can be achieved. The result of this exercise must be refined into distinct priorities across development spending categories (e.g., new product development, technology development, product support, etc.) and between specific development projects. This level of rigor often reveals major strategic direction problems, as evidenced by a major equipment manufacturing firm, where it was realized that most of their projects were risky and long term, putting the entire business at risk in the short term.

Capacity planning is a forward-looking activity that monitors the skill sets and effective resource capacity of an organization. Both resource commitments and available resource capacity must be assessed on a regular basis, consistently across the organization. Since pipeline management is fact driven, data integrity, which is very difficult to achieve in this area, is critical. The three most common data inaccuracies are highly motivated project teams underestimating the resources required to complete a project, functional managers trying to protect their turf by padding resource requirements, and general inconsistency in estimating resources across functional areas. Over the long term, resource accuracy and consistency can be achieved only by tracking historical product development performance.

5.3.3. Enabling Tools

Since pipeline management is so complex, due to the number of projects and sheer volume of data that must be analyzed and interpreted, two categories of tools are necessary: decision assistance and data handling. Decision-assistance tools are required to analyze data at a high level and to perform trade-offs systematically without losing sight of priorities or getting bogged down in details. Data-handling tools are needed to deal with the vast amount of information needed to analyze project priorities, understand resource and skill set loads, and perform pipeline analysis.

Although automation is useful, the answer is not always in the use of a complex, fully integrated computer system. For example, an advanced materials company had an information system designed and installed so that it had a detailed skills profile on every person and their staffing on projects projected for the next year. With this system the company felt they would be able to determine instantly the optimal staff for any project and thus optimize their pipeline. In reality the system was rarely used and eventually was shelved. They found they could not allocate people solely on their skill profile because it ignored many other intangible factors (such as attitude, energy level, and motivation) that made people very different from one another. The system's complexity was so daunting that no one had the time to use it. There was no cross-functional forum of managers to do trade-offs and compromises. The company learned a costly lesson that a data-handling tool can only enable pipeline management, not supplant it.

5.4. IMPLEMENTATION CONSIDERATIONS

The pipeline management process has three elements: pipeline management teams, a structured methodology, and enabling tools. The implementation of each of these elements will be unique depending on company size, organization structure, development cycle times, and levels of technical and market uncertainty.

A car hurtles down a highway in heavy traffic. Suddenly the driver realizes that he is on the wrong path and needs to change direction. The exit ramp is upon him—he'll have to swerve to make it. Will he miss the exit? Will he try for it and make it, or will he have an accident? Why didn't he realize he was going in the wrong direction earlier? Wasn't he paying attention to the road signs? What will he change so that this situation won't occur again?

The story above describes how many companies manage their development pipeline—reacting when it's too late and risking disaster. Compounding this problem is the fact that the competitive highway is getting faster and more crowded, and the leadership path has more turns and sharper curves than ever before. In this environment, implementing a pipeline management process will soon become a competitive necessity. Pipeline management is implemented in two stages: alignment followed by process implementation.

Pipeline alignment, the balancing of project demand with resource supply, is best described through a case study. A large medical equipment company faced a major problem: Products were not getting out the door and market share was slipping. Upon completing a rapid diagnostic, it became clear that their major problem was a severely overloaded development pipeline. Alignment began by identifying all of the projects under development, which surprisingly turned out to be over 80—three times what everyone expected (this is a common occurrence where no one is aware of all the projects under way across all functions). Next, the resources required for each project were forecasted and verified—very difficult to do in a company without an effective project planning methodology. In parallel, the senior management team worked to analyze their portfolio and determine the proper strategic balance, which led to the shocking realization that the bulk of their development projects were short term but their top corporate objective was growth to curtail market-share loss. Finally, the pipeline was balanced through a series of very difficult working sessions with the senior management team, and the development organization was shifted to focus on a few major, high-impact projects. At the conclusion of the alignment effort, the president commented that he had "traded in 80 turtles for 35 racehorses."

Many organizations have gone through a traumatic alignment only to find themselves in the same chaotic situation a short time later. Although there is tremendous value in this first step, an on-going pipeline management process must be put in place to fix the underlying problems.

Since pipeline management is predicated on product development discipline and predictability, solid planning, and talented and adaptable core team leaders, a well-functioning project management process must already be in place (high-performance teams, integrated development methodology, empowering stage-gate or phase reviews, and enabling tools). In fact, in many companies the need for a pipeline management process becomes apparent only after the basic development process has been improved.

Pipeline management can be quite challenging to implement because it is a completely new concept for most organizations and cuts across all functions and all levels of management. The changes include a cultural shift toward true teamwork at all levels of management, skills improvement to handle the unique demands of pipeline management, procedural modifications to the planning and budgeting process, implementation of new systems, integration with the product development process, and potential modifications to the organization. Obviously with so much at stake and the effort involved in implementation, the cost of miscues is high.

5.5. SUMMARY

Product development in many organizations is undergoing massive transformation. As much of the traditional "technology development" is being scaled down or removed from the product development process, and the process itself has been improved, development is becoming much more predictable. Just as manufacturing was once an artform and has evolved to a sophisticated, managed process, product development is transforming from an unstructured activity into a competitive weapon—but something is missing to complete this transition. The missing element is pipeline management, which continually optimizes product development performance from the strategic, project, and functional perspective.

The pipeline management process consists of cross-functional management teams, a structured methodology, and enabling tools. Although implementation is difficult, the payoff is immense and can vault companies far ahead of their competition.

REFERENCES

1. Anthony, Michael T., McGrath, Michael E., and Shapiro, Amram R. *Achieving Product and Cycle-Time Excellence*. Newton, MA: Butterworth-Heinemann, 1991.
2. Clark, Kim B. and Wheelwright, Steven C. *Leading Product Development*. New York: Free Press, 1995, pp. 38–40.
3. Cooper, Robert G. *Winning at New Products: Accelerating the Process from Idea to Launch*, 2nd ed. Reading, MA: Addison-Wesley, 1993, pp. 163–203.
4. Corso, Mariano, De Maio, Adriano and Verganti, Roberto. A multi-project management framework for new product development. *European Journal of Operation Research* 78:178–191 (1994).
5. Gruenwald, George. Goals—deciding where to go. In: *New Product Development*. Lincolnwood, IL: NTC Business Books, 1992, pp. 75–84.
6. McGrath, Michael E. *Product Strategy for High-Technology Companies*. Burr Ridge, IL: Irwin Professional Publishing, 1995, pp. 232–258.
7. Reinertsen, Donald G. and Smith, Preston G. Capacity planning and resource allocation. In: *Developing Products in Half the Time*. New York, Van Nostrand Reinhold, 1991.

John R. Harris
Pittiglio Rabin Todd & McGrath (PRTM)

John is a principal in the Rosemont, IL office of PRTM. He has led many previous engagements in product development, with a majority of his work in the computer industry. Prior to joining PRTM, John spent six years at Texas Instruments. As a branch manager, John had responsible for a computer systems engineering group working on computer operating systems. John has authored many articles on product development and is a co-author of the revised edition of PRTM's PACE® book. John holds a degree in Computer Science from University of Kansas and an MBA from the University of Texas in Austin.

Jonathan C. McKay
Pittiglio Rabin Todd & McGrath

Jon is a director in the Rosemont, IL office of PRTM, an international, results-oriented management consulting firm to technology-based companies. He has implemented Product And Cycle-time Excellence® (PACE®), a continually updated architecture of development best practices, at many of PRTM's 140+ PACE clients. Prior to consulting, he spent several years with Bell Helicopter Textron and Scientific Atlanta's Broadband division in test engineering and marketing. He has a B.S. in Aerospace Engineering and Computer Science from Pennsylvania State University and an MBA from the Harvard Business School.

CHOOSING A DEVELOPMENT PROCESS THAT'S RIGHT FOR YOUR COMPANY

6

Milton D. Rosenau, Jr.

6.1. INTRODUCTION

A new product development (NPD) process defines and describes the normal means by which a company can repetitively convert embryonic ideas into salable products or services. Such a process identifies the required steps and resources and should focus the attention of senior management on the status of product development projects at appropriate times. Properly executed, the NPD process will also encourage continuous improvement.

In the next section we describe an overall framework for a process. After that comes a description of the commonly employed stage-gate process. This is followed by a discussion of some tools to help customize a stage-gate process to your firm's situation. Then other processes are covered. Finally, we cover problems that you may encounter and some ways to deal with these.

6.2. OVERALL FRAMEWORK FOR ORGANIZING NPD PROCESSES

Time and quality urgency obsoletes the sequential functional "baton passing" (or "relay race") process, which suffers from a lack of coordination and communication. In this historical approach, one function (e.g., the marketing department) does whatever it feels is desirable to advance a new product idea, then passes the information baton on to another function (e.g., the engineering department or software development). The process then continues with a baton pass when engineering drawings or software specifications are tossed "over the wall" to the manufacturing or operations department for production. This was—and, where still practiced, is—slow, creatively suboptimal, and error prone. It inevitably exacerbates functional dissension.

Today, we recognize the quality and time-to-market benefits of an orderly NPD process that incorporates multifunctional teamwork in many activities. Multifunctional activities may take longer than they did in the traditional relay race, but improved goal clarity and teamwork usually result in faster time to market by reducing subsequent redesign and rework. The total orderly process is really comprised of two parts: A front-end idea generation and sorting process (often called the *fuzzy front end*); and the NPD process itself. Figure 6.1 illustrates a way to screen raw ideas during the fuzzy front end [12, pp. 43–60], and Figure 6.2 illustrates generically the steps by which plausible ideas may be developed into salable goods or services. (Some practitioners prefer to include the concept study activity shown in Figure 6.2 within the fuzzy front end rather than in the NPD process; since this is somewhat of a gray area, either delineation is acceptable if commonly understood in a company.)

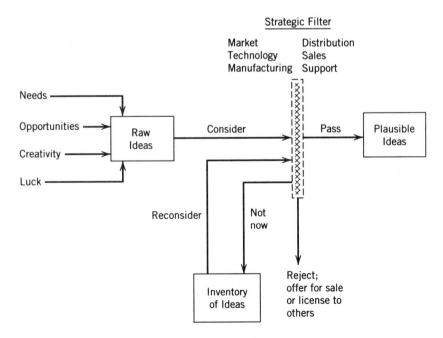

FIGURE 6.1 Idea generation and sorting in the fuzzy front end.

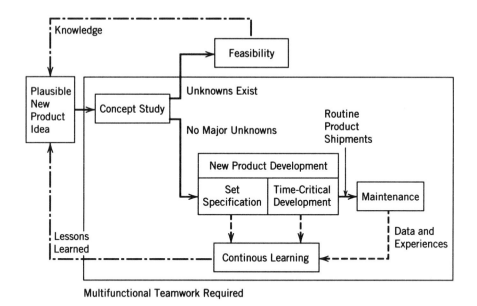

Multifunctional Teamwork Required

FIGURE 6.2 Key activities in an NPD process.

6.2.1. Where We Start the NPD Process

The first NPD activity is idea generation, which involves separating "the chaff from the wheat." Although some sources of raw ideas are shown in Figure 6. 1, this subject is dealt with more fully in Chapter 12. These ideas must be judged against the company's strategic plan, after which some are rejected, some are set aside or put into an idea inventory for later reconsideration, and some are judged to be plausible now for potential development.

The NPD process that we deal with in this chapter starts with a plausible idea, which is subjected to frequent evaluations in each stage to preclude introduction of a new product or service that will fail in the market. These evaluations are necessarily largely qualitative (i.e., subjective) in the earlier stages (hard data are not yet available) and become more quantitative (i.e., objective, if meaningful data are employed) in later stages [4].

The rest of the NPD process describes all the tasks required to achieve routine, timely, trouble-free manufacturing and delivery of a product or service. While the details will differ in each company, you should expect to incorporate five additional key activities, as

Following idea creation, a complete NPD process will include five activities: concept study, feasibility investigations, development of the new product or service, maintenance, and continuous learning.

shown in Figure 6.2: A concept study activity, a feasibility activity, a staged NPD activity, a maintenance activity, and a continuous learning activity. Your process should somehow organize these activities to satisfy your market requirements, consistent with your company culture.

There are two other important elements in an effective and fast NPD process: a time-to-market that is realistic for the NPD specification and resources that will be available, and the use of a multifunctional team. These activities and elements are discussed in the following sections.

6.2.2. Five Key New Product Development Activities

Concept Study

Any NPD process starts with a plausible new product idea or concept, which may come from any source. The concept must be examined closely enough to determine if there are substantial unknowns about the market, the technology, or the production process. Some examples of unknowns are:

- *Market unknown.* The proposed new product is to be a very low-price modification of something you now sell, intended for third-world markets to which you do not now sell.
- *Technology unknown.* You wish to introduce a highly sensitive diagnostic blood test for a particular disease but do not know of any existing physical of chemical reactions with adequate sensitivity and reliability.
- *Production process unknown.* You wish to incorporate newly developed plastics as covers for your product, but have never used plastics.

> **If there are major unknowns about the market, the technology, or the production process, you will be unable to prepare a realistic NPD schedule.**

If there are substantial unknowns such as these, you are not ready for NPD; rather, you must engage in a feasibility activity [9, pp. 9 and 12]. If you start a NPD project while there are still major unknowns, its scope, schedule, and outcome will be unpredictable; and you may incur substantial expense while frustrating the development team.

Feasibility

The objective of a feasibility effort is the rapid and economical production of knowledge as to how to resolve or overcome unknowns or to clarify the nature of any limitations. Subsequent events (e.g., a competitor going out of business, a new technology breakthrough, or new production capabilities) may remove the limitation, in which case NPD can begin. Or you may develop your own knowledge during a feasibility effort. As illustrations, based on the three previous examples, you can remove the market unknown through third-world market research, the technology unknown by laboratory research and development, and the production process unknown by small-scale production experimentation with plastics process technology.

New Product Development

If there are no major unknowns, either initially as perceived during the concept study or after a feasibility effort, you can start NPD. This activity is commonly divided into several stages (discussed in detail in Section 6.3). The first of these NPD stages should include all the work to set a firm specification, which is the detailed description of what you intend to produce to satisfy the targeted market requirement. As such, it includes objectively testable particulars defining what the product has to do to be acceptable. In the case of inherently subjective elements (e.g., style, taste, aroma, etc.), the means by which these will be judged must be detailed explicitly.

NPD may also require the development of production processes and tests to assure reliable product assembly and delivery. This is one of the important reasons why multifunctional teams should be involved, so these essential undertakings are carried out as close to concurrently as practical. In some cases, very minor alterations of the product itself can greatly simplify its production and test. This is also true for user support features such as built-in diagnostics.

Maintenance

Assuming that the development is ultimately successful, product shipments (or service availabilities) are begun. At this time, maintenance support activity is required to some extent. All new products and services have some initial problems, which may be reduced (but, regrettably, probably never totally eliminated) if the company has a superior quality program. A common example is that many users have unanticipated compatibility problems with hardware and software that require time to understand and fix.

While the level of maintenance activity should decline with time, the demands for help from users (and even your company's manufacturing or operations function) are immediate and compelling. Such firefighting demands intrude on the resources that might otherwise be working on the next model or another NPD effort [9, p. 15], so your NPD process must make allowance for this reality.

Continuous Learning

The final activity shown in Figure 6.2 is continuous learning, both during and at the end of the NPD process [9, pp. 186–187]. Unfortunately, this is the activity most frequently omitted by companies, but offers great benefits in terms of continuous NPD process improvement [13, pp. 300–310]. First, an objective examination of how a NPD project is progressing may permit process changes to simplify its remaining steps and those required on subsequent projects. Second, information may be developed to permit an improvement to the product being developed or its schedule.

Input to the continuous learning activity *during* the NPD activity is important, as illustrated in Figure 6.2. If postproject appraisals are conducted long after much of the critical work is done, many of the key people are no longer accessible and the memories of those who are available have been tempered by later events. Thus a really effective continuous learning activity will include data collection at frequent intervals during the entire NPD process.

Continuous learning should be an ongoing NPD activity.

6.2.3. Two Additional New Product Development Process Considerations

Multifunctional Teamwork

Figure 6.2 also indicates that multifunctional teamwork is required for all but the ideation and feasibility activities. It can be helpful in those activities as well but is really crucial in the other four activities. Using multifunctional teams will allow you to solve all product development problems simultaneously. This is in contrast to the traditional way, where each functional department solved only a partial set of problems. They subsequently passed this partial solution on to the next department to solve its own set of problems, which they did while inadvertently creating new problems for other functional departments.

Critical Three-Parameter Trade-off

A NPD process helps your firm bring commercially successful new products to market in a way that is timely for your industry and market, now and in the future. Shortening product life cycles in many industries encourage—or, in some cases, demand—the development of new products sooner than ever before. A substantial literature has developed to describe the issues and propose approaches to shorten time to market [1, 3, 5, 7, 9, 11–13]. A NPD process should encourage the use of realistic estimates of time to market and also aid product line planning.

Realistic time estimates depend on understanding the difficulty of achieving the proposed specifications and the effectiveness of the resources assigned to the product development effort. Figure 6.3 depicts the nature of the

> *Time to market depends on the specification's difficulty and the effectiveness of the resources (human and physical) that are dedicated to the effort.*

relationships among specification difficulty, resource effectiveness, and time-to-market. While the illustration is simple, the implications are subtle. (In fact, many companies suffer from "new product gridlock," where there are too many NPD efforts and, consequently, all efforts lack adequate resources and none are completed on schedule. See Chapter 5.)

As an example of the three-parameter trade-off, a given NPD project may be started with sufficient resources, but its progress will suffer if some of the human resources are distracted by other assignments (e.g., urgent maintenance firefighting) or some of the physical resources (e.g., a pilot plant) are tied up by other commitments when they are required. Thus the resources actually applied to the effort are less effective than planned, resulting in a longer development schedule than intended. In addition, specifications that seemed sensible when

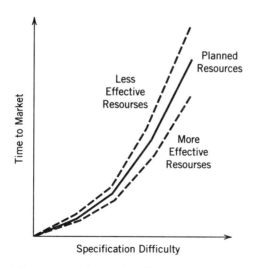

FIGURE 6.3 Critical three-parameter trade-off.

the NPD project began are sometimes changed because the marketing function wants to react to some competitive situation or the technologists want to incorporate a novel, exciting technology. Again, time to market is longer than desired [10].

The important implication of this three-parameter trade-off is that your NPD process must recognize the interrelationship and establish the NPD schedule only after product specifications are agreed to (and ideally, "cast in concrete") and resources are identified and committed. Senior management must thereafter assure that the resources remain allocated and undistracted, or the NPD team must advise cognizant senior management of the impact of any resource change.

6.3. STAGE-GATE PROCESSES USED IN NEW PRODUCT DEVELOPMENT ACTIVITY

Figure 6.4 depicts a general stage-gate process. Table 6.1 lists nonproprietary stages used by five companies, aligned with generic stages you might consider using. It is unclear if the illustrated alignment is appropriate without knowing much more about which tasks the five companies actually carry out in their stages. Nevertheless, these stage names do indicate the kind of work commonly included in sequential stages.

The stages are portrayed in a straight line in Figure 6.4 and in a vertical column in Table 6.1. The picture is more complicated in Figure 6.2 to emphasize the critical branch point (after concept study) and the two information feedback loops (feasibility and continuous learning). In many cases, feasibility activities do not lead to either NPD or commercialization, and continuous learning should be an ongoing activity.

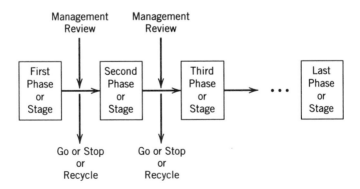

FIGURE 6.4 Generic stage-gate process.

TABLE 6.1 Examples of Stages Used by Five Companies

Stage	Xerox	CalComp	Exxon Chemicals	Ivac	Keithley
Get an idea	Pre-concept		Idea		Concept
Prove that it works	Concept		Preliminary assessment	Aggregate plan and advanced development Preliminary design	Study
Determine who will pay for it		Market requirement specification	Assessment		Definition
Develop and test it	Design demonstration	Design Engineering model Prototype System verification Manufacturing verification	Development	Detail design Prototype iteration, test, and evaluation	Design prototype
Scale it up	Production		Validation	Pilot production	Pilot
Launch it	Launch	Production	Commercial launch	Production	Introduction
Support it	Maintenance	End of life (obsolete)			
Figure out how to do it again, better			Postlaunch review		Postmortem

> *Each company must tailor its stage-gate process to its market and culture.*

Stage-gate process use is very common because it is orderly and encourages management oversight at various appropriate times during the NPD process [1, pp. 93–162 and 205–253]. When well designed and adhered to, a stage-gate process assures appropriate participation by senior management when it is truly useful, especially at points where there is an incremental jump in risk or cost. During each stage, a group of tasks or activities are carried out. When these tasks are complete, a management review is conducted. If the work is satisfactory and the business case is still persuasive, the next stage would normally be authorized; however, in a well-managed stage-gate process where project priorities are clearly identified by management, a given NPD effort might be stopped (temporarily or otherwise) to free resources for a higher-priority effort. The opportunity to avoid new product gridlock due to insufficient resources for the next stage is one important potential benefit of a stage-gate review.

> *A NPD project that is meeting all of its milestones may be stopped merely to allocate certain resources to a higher-priority effort.*

In some cases, the result of a stage's work is not sufficiently promising to justify continuing the effort. In this situation, the developers may be told to go back and repeat some tasks in the expectation that more work and time will overcome the problems. In other cases, the NPD project will be canceled; hopefully, the results to date will be documented for future reference, reactivation should conditions change, or sale to another company.

Although some people object to the stage-gate process because it seems slow, its speed depends primarily on how it is implemented and the three-parameter trade-off (discussed above). Two keys to stage-gate speed are that the stages be as short as possible and that there be no dead time between stages (e.g., due to waiting for a management decision).

Another objection is that it appears to be restrictive. Although it is perhaps not as useful for a new-to-the-world NPD effort (because it is normally unclear

> *You should normally use some form of a stage-gate NPD process that includes and promotes multifunctional teamwork while stressing speed.*

what actually has to be done to succeed), a stage-gate process can help developers focus this creativity on those tasks that need to be done—not on trying to figure out what tasks must be done.

6.4. SOME TOOLS TO CUSTOMIZE A GENERIC PROCESS TO YOUR FIRM'S NEEDS

There are many "tricks of the trade" that can facilitate a NPD process. Three key tools are described briefly: flexible gates, a coordination matrix, and responsibility matrix.

6.4.1. Flexible Gates

> *Permissive and permeable gates can shorten time-to-market.*

The normal assumption is a stage-gate process, whether fast or slow, is that gates are rigid. This means that all the prior stage's work and deliverables must be complete before the next stage can begin. As illustrated in Figure 6.5 two other kinds of gates are possible: permissive and permeable. A permissive gate is one where work in a subsequent stage may begin even though some (noncritical) work in a prior stage is not yet complete. A permeable gate is one where some work in a subsequent stage is authorized (e.g., most commonly the initiation of long-lead activities) before a substantial amount of work in the prior stage is completed. When a permeable gate is authorized, it is done so as a calculated risk to save calendar time and must not be taken as an early authorization to carry out more work in the subsequent stage, nor is it a justification to assure that the subsequent stage will ever be authorized.

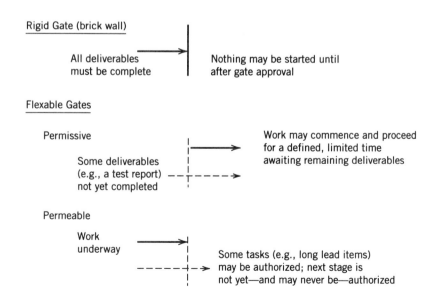

FIGURE 6.5 Three kinds of gates.

6.4.2. Coordination Matrix

A coordination matrix, similar to that used by Keithley Instruments (a winner of the PDMA's Outstanding Corporate Innovator award), can clarify which functional department has lead responsibility for each task or activity in each stage. Figure 6.6 is a general representation of this kind of matrix. Such a matrix may also identify the stage goal (below the stage's name in Figure 6.6), the stage deliverables (i.e., "gateway requirements"), and at the top, shows who is responsible for each gate approval. In practice, the approval boxes may be drawn at different levels to signify the management level required; also, some gate approvals may be the responsibility of the multifunctional team itself or the NPD project manager.

The activities that are listed at the bottom ideally include every task that must be done. These might come from a complete critical path schedule for the NPD effort. If each new product is similar to others, a generic critical path schedule (see below) template can be constructed. If products are varied, the generic critical path schedule and coordination matrix can be constructed for a modestly complex NPD effort; simpler efforts would then merely omit those tasks that are not required.

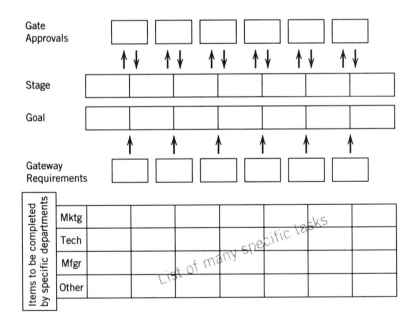

FIGURE 6.6 Generic coordination matrix.

6.4.3. Responsibility Matrix

A responsibility matrix, similar to that used by Xerox and others, can be used in conjunction with a coordination matrix or a critical path schedule to clarify the specific involvement of each functional department in each task or activity in each stage. Table 6.2 is a general representation of this kind of matrix.

6.5. OTHER PROCESSES

There are three other processes used in varying degrees by companies to augment (or, sometimes, supplant) a stage-gate process. These are quality function deployment (QFD), new product rugby, and the use of project management tools and techniques. These are described briefly in the following sections.

6.5.1. Quality Function Deployment

QFD is a systematic process that ties *what* the market requires to *how* it will be accomplished in the NPD effort. Its use is therefore most valuable during the portion of the NPD activity in which a multifunctional team agrees on the specification and makes their production process implementation choices, and it is an important mechanism to promote multifunctional teamwork [2]. QFD captures the "voice of the customer" and deploys it throughout the NPD activity [9, pp. 63–67 and 225–237]. Its full use involves many matrices and a vast amount of detail, and it is more common to use only the first matrix, called the "house of quality."

6.5.2. New Product Rugby

New product rugby is a term to describe the process in which stages are partially or heavily over-

> *QFD is a valuable device to promote multifunctional teamwork while deciding how the new product or service will be arranged to satisfy what the market requires.*

TABLE 6.2 Generic Responsibility Matrix

Function	Task[a]					
	1	2	3	4	5	. . .
A	C	C	C	A	A	
B	I	A	C	I		
C	A	O	C	I		
D		C	A	C		
E		I	C	O	C	
⋮						

[a] A, accountable; C, concurrence required; I, input required; O, optional input.

lapped rather than sequential with crisp demarcation between a stage and its successor [6]. The objective is to shorten time-to-market. The analogy to the sport is derived from the passage of the rugby ball from one player to another as they both proceed toward the goal. New product rugby is most common in Japanese companies, where it is practiced in all industrial sectors, but most frequently in the automobile industry. It is not unlike the use of permeable or permissive gates, although in general the amount of stage work that is overlapped would be greater for those using rugby.

6.5.3. Simple Project Management Tools and Techniques

There is a vast literature on project (or program) management, some of which is directly applicable to NPD [9] or similar projects [8] (i.e., not aerospace or construction projects). Effective project management requires much more than the simple use of the ubiquitous microcomputer software. It is concerned with defining the project's goal, planning all the work to reach the goal, leading the project and support teams, monitoring progress (or lack thereof), and seeing to it that the project is completed in a satisfactory way. Project management software can help organize tasks, but it does not get the tasks done.

The overwhelming value of the software is to provide:

Using project management software is helpful but not sufficient.

1. A time-based critical path schedule that clearly indicates when and how each required task is linked to predecessors and successors [9, pp. 88–104].
2. Resources dedicated to each task, which determines the task's duration.
3. A resource requirement histogram that clearly shows when and the amount of each specific resource that is required [9, pp. 105–112], which can highlight resource conflicts or inadequacies that preclude meeting the schedule.

These three project management tools are valuable—frequently essential—for completing a NPD schedule in a timely way.

6.6. PROBLEMS TO AVOID

When you establish your NPD process, whatever its form, there are six problems for which you should be alert:

1. Performing a discounted cash flow analysis [9, pp. 209–224] at early stages, which is a waste of time since the numbers are merely wild guesses

that are prone to an advocate's favorable exaggeration. *Solution*: Use simple estimates of sales, profits, and development expense until the specification is set.

2. Allowing specifications to change without clear notice and appropriate management review during development. *Solution*: Freeze the specification prior to initiating time-critical development and change it only by reverting to the management review at which it was approved.

3. Starting NPD with major unknowns (e.g., unproven new technology so that you must try to invent on schedule). *Solution*: Initiate a feasibility effort if there are major unknowns about the market, technology, or process.

4. Making a NPD project schedule that presumes there will be no firefighting maintenance interruptions. *Solution*: Dedicate resources to a separate maintenance function that insulates developers or schedule NPD projects on the assumption that the development team will only be available part time (sadly, perhaps only 50 to 75 percent) for NPD work.

5. Allowing waste (dead) time between stages. *Solution*: At the start of each stage, schedule the end of stage review and get it on everyone's calendar; if someone must miss the review, insist that they send an empowered replacement.

6. Allowing stages to be longer than absolutely required. *Solution*: Use project management software to perform a detailed examination of the schedule versus resource trade-off and bring the results to cognizant managers.

6.7. SUMMARY

A complete new product development process is helpful—perhaps essential—for all but new-to-the-world products and services. It will include six activities: idea creation, concept study, feasibility investigations, development of the new product or service, maintenance, and continuous learning. Normally, the NPD activity will be subdivided into discrete stages, which may or may not be overlapped. The specific composition of the stages is chosen to be most useful to each company. The systematic use of the process minimizes the overcommitment of finite resources, thus increasing the probability of completing each development effort on schedule.

REFERENCES

1. Cooper, Robert G. *Winning at New Products: Accelerating the Process from Idea to Launch*, 2nd ed. Reading, MA: Addison-Wesley, 1993.

2. Griffin, Abbie. Evaluating QFD's use in U.S. firms as a process for developing products. *Journal of Product Innovation Management* 9:171–187 (March 1992).

3. McGrath, Michael E., Anthony, Michael T., and Shapiro, Amram R. *Product Development: Success Through Product and Cycle-Time Excellence.* Stoneham, MA: Butterworth-Heinemann (Reed Publishing), 1992.

4. McGrath, Rita G. and MacMillan, Ian C. Discovery-driven planning. *Harvard Business Review,* p. 44ff (July–August 1995).

5. Meyer, Christopher. *Fast Cycle Time: How to Align Purpose, Strategy, and Structure for Speed.* New York: Free Press, 1993.

6. Nonaka, I. and Takeuchi, H. *The Knowledge-Creating Company: How Japanese Companies Create the Dynamics of Innovation.* New York: Oxford University Press, 1995, p. 78.

7. Rosenau, Milton D., Jr. *Faster New Product Development: Getting the Right Product to Market Quickly.* New York: Amacom, 1990.

8. Rosenau, Milton D., Jr. *Successful Project Management,* 2nd ed. New York: Van Nostrand Reinhold, 1991.

9. Rosenau, Milton D., Jr. and Moran, John J. *Managing the Development of New Products: Achieving Speed and Quality Simultaneously Through Multifunctional Teamwork.* New York: Van Nostrand Reinhold, 1993.

10. Rosenau, Milton D., Jr. New product specification trade-offs. *Visions,* pp. 11–12 (April 1994).

11. Rosenthal, Stephen R. *Effective Product Design and Development: How to Cut Lead Time and Increase Customer Satisfaction.* Homewood, IL: Business One Irwin, 1992.

12. Smith, Preston G. and Reinertsen, Donald G. *Developing Products in Half the Time.* New York: Van Nostrand Reinhold, 1991.

13. Wheelwright, Steven C. and Clark, Kim B. *Revolutionizing Product Development: Quantum Leaps in Speed, Efficiency, and Quality.* New York: Free Press, 1992.

IMPLEMENTING A
7 PRODUCT
DEVELOPMENT PROCESS
Paul J. O'Connor

7.1 PROCESS USE PRECEDES BENEFITS

Research on effective product development (NPD) shows that as complexity of projects increases, a cross-functional approach is better than a functional hand off approach, [5,7]. When put into an organizational process, cross-functional NPD increases both speed-to-market and effectiveness [2]. Yet a tension exists between performing NPD and performing day-to-day business operations. A typical sales force receives rewards upon achieving aggressive sales quotas, not by soliciting customer information for use in developing new products. Manufacturing operations usually streamline themselves to speed production and eliminate inventory, not to conduct unforeseen pilot production runs. NPD, by its very nature, injects new activities into the organization—often inharmonious with the standard practices of functional departments.

One solution to overcoming this common tension is to establish an NPD process that enables cross-functional work while retaining the functional structure that carries out day-to-day practices. As pointed out in Chapter 6, a stage-gate framework is a commonly used work-flow and decision-making process that does just this. The detailed design of a stage-gate framework for NPD is only of partial value to the firm. The critical challenge is in establishing cross-organizational use. As trivial as it sounds, a firm must first use the NPD process fully before it can accrue the desired benefits of speed, efficiency, and strategic impact.

Implementing an effective NPD process does not happen quickly and effortlessly. Evidence suggests that some organizations have taken five to seven years to put their process in place [6]. Toyota, as an example, took seven years during the 1970s to implement their full quality function development (QFD)° development process [3]. While such implementation practices might have been acceptable in the past, they are not acceptable in today's fast-paced, competitive environment. How an organization goes about setting up its new product process has become just as important as what the process is.

> *The key challenge of implementation is gaining rapid acceptance and use of the NPD process across all parts of the firm.*

7.2 A CLOSER VIEW OF THE ISSUES

A generic stage-gate framework is described in Chapter 6. Details of the framework, however, differ from organization to organization. It is from these details that key challenges to implementation arise. A closer look at the nuances of one stage-gate framework, particularly its front end as seen in Figure 7.1, helps illuminate some of the issues confronted when setting it up. The process in this case begins with customer need or product concept identification activities, often referred to as the *fuzzy front end*. A champion or advocate of the idea presents the concept for a first review. Here, a team of managers evaluates its impact on the business. Based on their judgment, concepts terminate that do not fit the business unit mission or NPD strategy. Note the implication to establishing the process: The team of managers must have a common understanding of both mission and NPD strategy. For this to be so, top management must commit to and clearly articulate both. Failure to achieve such commitment during implementation makes the decision point less definitive and undermines the effectiveness of the framework.

Proceeding into the framework we see that concepts requiring fundamental technology research separate from product development and proceed to a technology development process. Similarly, line extensions and incremental improvements to existing products circumvent the front end of the stage-gate framework and go to full development. The remaining NPD concepts proceed through the full process. Thus criteria are needed that discern the nature of potential projects.

°QFD for Toyota is a full NPD process from concept through launch, not the first house of quality that most Western organizations have embraced.

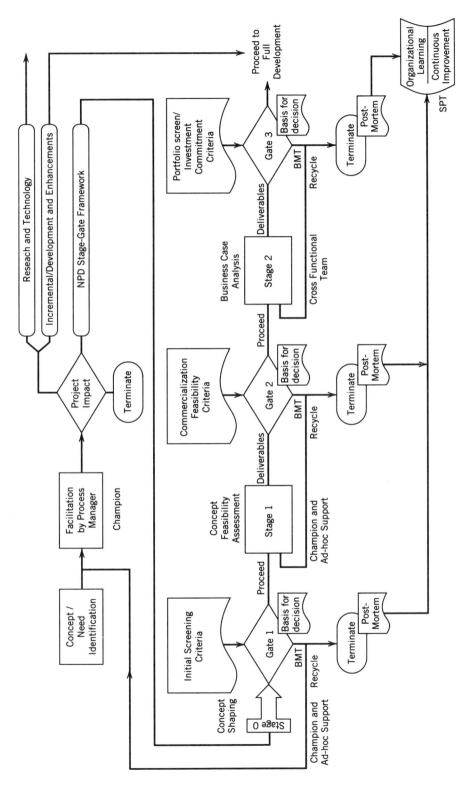

FIGURE 7.1 Front end of a stage-gate framework.

Because such decisions can be political (due to notions of control of projects or burden from projects), this is a sensitive point for implementation. Some issues that surface might include: What makes a line extension different from a new product? How will projects not in the front end of the NPD pipeline get funds and personnel? Will such projects take resources away from full NPD projects? Does any one person's opinion influence such decisions more than anyone else's?

Next in the framework, the concept champion guides the project into the NPD process. The champion's first tasks are to shape the concept and generate information that helps overcome the initial screening criteria use at the first gate. Management gatekeepers in this organization are called the *business management team* (BMT). Several challenges arise by creating these work and decision-making activities. For example: Who is on the BMT? Who creates or changes criteria? Where do champions come from? Why will everybody do these activities now (and into the future) if they have never done them before?

Assuming that implementation efforts resolve some of the key early issues, the framework begins to open somewhat. Upon passing the first set of criteria, a concept champion will receive the resources needed to conduct feasibility assessment. Working with ad hoc support, the champion then seeks to deliver information that surpasses the requirements for the next gate. If successful, the concept moves on as a full NPD project, with a cross-functional team assigned to it. Once again, implementation efforts confront new issues: What is an ad hoc group, and how does it form? Does the champion continue to lead the project? What happens to the concept upon termination? Do champions and the ad hoc group receive rewards for their performance?

During stage 2 of this case, the cross-functional team might work on activities such as QFD, competitive analysis, specification delineation, life-cycle costing, market forecasting, and developing pro forma cash flows. If the BMT judges the output of their work sufficient to pass gate 3 criteria, the project will proceed to full development and launch. Yet implementation issues pervade. For example: *Is the BMT comprised of the same members at later gates? What about when the organization restructures? On how many projects can a person serve as a team member? When is the full portfolio of projects reviewed? Who assigns whom to which project? Do some projects receive a higher priority than others?*

All of the issues suggested above merely skim the surface and serve to underscore the challenges of customizing the framework to an organization. More important, though, the scope and shear number of issues suggest a critical need for their resolution during design and roll-out of the framework. Waiting to encounter issues during use might seem the quickest path to setting up a new work flow. Doing so, however, is assuredly the slowest path to accruing the desired benefits.

7.3. WHAT GETS IMPLEMENTED

> *The best time to recognize implementation issues is during design, not during use.*

There are three basic components to any stage-gate framework: the decision-making process (gates), the work-flow process (stages), and supporting systems and practices. Understanding these components is necessary to effective implementation of the full framework for NPD.

7.3.1. The Decision-Making Process

A key element of a stage-gate framework is its ability to manage risk: the risk of individual projects and the aggregate risk of the portfolio of projects in the NPD pipeline. The framework does this by requiring go/no-go/recycle decisions at project milestone gates. Investment of resources increases as projects proceed through each gate. The justification of such investments also needs alignment with business unit strategy. Thus, successful implementation requires setting up a decision-making process that (1) uses specific criteria, (2) aligns itself with a business unit's strategy, (3) evaluates the risk of a project by itself and within the NPD portfolio, and (4) causes management to allocate resources in a timely manner.

The first organizations that implemented stage-gate processes typically emphasized the risk management of only a single project at a time. Those making decisions at a gate review meeting were only senior enough in the organization to allocate resources for the next stage. In keeping with standard risk management techniques, the first stages required fewer resources or less investment than the latter stages. Thus gate keepers early in the process were notably less senior than gate keepers later in the process. Although this seemed to make sense, two flaws became apparent. First, top management tended to second-guess earlier decisions, forcing the project to recycle. Second, single-project (monadic) screening of new concepts passed without consideration of their full impact on the NPD portfolio. Fortunately, the solution is simple: Involve top management at early gates, when they have the greatest impact on single projects and the full portfolio of projects [8].

7.3.2. Cross-Functional Work Flow

> *Top-management participation at early gate reviews is critical for achieving an effective stage-gate framework.*

Collaborative work across functions is a basic component of a stage-gate framework. Just as the decision making should align with strategy, the actual work on an NPD project (stages) should align with the decision process. The central question for designing and implementing work flow is: What activities will deliver the information or insight needed to overcome the decision criteria hurdles at the next gate?

The activities within stages differ from process to process. Similarly, activities within a stage of a process may differ from project to project. A well-designed work flow is a guideline for NPD teams, not a command to conduct specific steps. For example, the process for a consumer-packaged-goods company may show a concept test in the first stage of activity. Yet a method of generating the concept may have been used that negates much of the risk that the concept test was intended to help avoid. In such a case, skipping the activity seems sensible. The goal for the team is to pass the gate criteria, not to conduct unnecessary, predetermined tasks.

Stages should facilitate the work of NPD teams, not bog them down with unnecessary tasks.

7.3.3. Organizational Systems and Practices

Every organization has systems or practices that, either intentionally or unintentionally, support or hinder NPD. For example, accounting methods may exist that ensure proper budgeting and cost allocation practices for day-to-day business but not for opportunistic new product development activities. Similarly, a manager may conduct performance evaluations and not be aware of subordinates' collaborative contributions to cross-functional NPD teams. In such cases, the systems work against the desired NPD process. Following are some organizational systems and practices that can affect an organization's ability to accrue benefits from a newly established NPD process.

- Accounting methods
- Enterprise information systems
- Compensation practices
- Planning cycles
- Capital budgeting
- Training and development

- Communication systems
- Organizational learning
- Expense budgeting
- Career planning
- Communication systems
- TQM practices

Accelerate NPD process implementation by following a simple rule: Remove hindering systems and practices before establishing new driving forces. Consider the consequences of doing the opposite. Suppose that you institute $1 million bonus (driving force) for a team should its project be launched on time. But the organization may also have in place exceedingly rigid and time-consuming total quality management (TQM) practices (hindering force). Driven by the reward, the team will probably do everything it can to get around the TQM practices. What will the risk be to quality or the voice of the customer? Will there be negative fallout on other TQM activities or NPD projects? A better approach is to streamline the TQM practices for increased speed before setting up the bonus.

7.4. THE IMPORTANCE OF HOW THINGS ARE IMPLEMENTED

> *Focus on changing systems and practices that slow NPD before setting up new systems and practices aimed at speeding NPD.*

Typically, business units within corporations implement their own stage-gate framework. Alignment with a common strategy is nearly impossible at a corporate level. Each of the corporation's business units has its own mission and, accordingly, needs its own decision-making, work-flow, and support systems. Perhaps, more important, each business unit must accept and use it's NPD process for its own purposes. Corporate staffs, however, do help in supporting implementation and improvement. For example, Dow Chemical, Procter & Gamble, and Polaroid each have a central group that provides support to business unit efforts. These central groups provide internal consulting, facilitation, and secondary information to their business units.

As mentioned previously, full implementation requires alignment of strategy, decision-making, work-flow, and support systems. Gaining this alignment requires

> *An NPD process needs to be customized for each organization and its strategy.*

the participation of the entire organization. Because of the magnitude and visibility of the task, mistakes can be quite serious. Implementation can slow significantly if key personnel or entire departments shun the initiative. The challenge of gaining acceptance and use of the desired process is always a formidable organizational change task.

Similar to other major change initiatives, the speed of NPD process implementation is dependent on several factors. Perhaps the most important, though, is the total commitment and serious involvement of the business unit's top management. The desire and willingness of the organization to change come from this commitment. Involvement also causes a dialogue that helps form a political alliance among the business unit's top functional leaders toward all gate criteria. This greatly helps alignment of the entire initiative.

7.5. POTENTIAL IMPEDIMENTS TO FULL IMPLEMENTATION

Some managers perceive a stage-gate process as time consuming and rigid [4]. These perceptions can be damaging to gaining acceptance of the NPD process. Flexibility and speed must be a central theme of the process. Design the work flow to encourage concurrent and cross-functional activities within each project. Build paths where teams, upon consensus of top management, can skip activities. Also, craft the gate criteria such that they are fluid over time, changing in response to opportunities and possible shifts in strategy.

Perceptions about the process are also important. Many companies position their stage-gate framework with names that avoid the rigid connotation of "stage-gate." Reynolds Metals Consumer Product calls their process "FIRST" (Fast Innovation Requires Strategy and Teamwork), Eaton Engine Components calls its process "PROPEL" (Phase Review of Products for Eaton Leadership), and SC Johnson and Sons' Professional Division has embraced "ATOM" (Accelerate to Market). The purpose of these names is to position the process as fast and flexible to the internal user, facilitating easier acceptance and use.

Position the process as fast and flexible. Make sure that the design matches the promise.

7.6. CHANGE: FROM CURRENT STATE TO DESIRED NPD PROCESS

Perhaps the toughest issues to deal with in getting a fast stage-gate framework set up are those that are people oriented. The initiative challenges the vested interests of some managers because it requires them to conduct work or make decisions differently. Naturally, there is often reluctance to do this. Organizational behavior experts use a common model for dealing with such change issues [1]. As Figure 7.2 shows, the challenge is in moving from a current state to a desired state.

People need motivation or inducement to progress from the current state of product development to the fast stage-gate framework. For people to change the way they do work, they must believe that the change is worth the effort. The change equation shows one way of looking at this:

Change will occur when

$$P_{cs} + G_{s-g} > COC_{econ, psy}$$

where

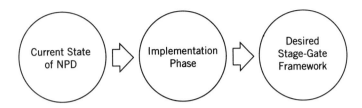

FIGURE 7.2 Transition model for change management.

P_{cs} = perceived pain of the current means of product development

G_{s-g} = perceived gain from the desired stage-gate process

$COC_{econ,\ psy}$ = perceived cost of change, both economic and psychological

Movement toward a fast stage-gate process happens when the organization perceives the equation as true. Organizations whose top managers perceive themselves as very successful in their business often have the most challenging implementations. Why should they change if, for example, earnings are at an all-time high? The pain is not apparent. The answer lies in showing the future consequences of the current state.

7.7. BEGINNINGS: ANALYZE THE OLD AND ENVISION THE NEW

The key task for implementation advocates is to work the change equation continually throughout the initiative. They need to make sure that the pain plus the gain continually remains greater than the perceived cost of change. This requires constantly gathering, analyzing, and disseminating both information and perceptions related to each of the three contributing factors in the change equation.

Begin by having a cross-functional design team detail and analyze the current state (or pain) of product development within the organization. Do this by reviewing

> *Work the change equation to sustain progress throughout your implementation.*

a half dozen or so past NPD projects. For each project, it is helpful to map the flows of work, decisions, and communication across functions. Some of the details that can be quite revealing include time delays, how decisions were (or were not) made, the project's interface (or lack thereof) with the market, and the degree of success or failure of the projects.

Next, couple these findings of the current state with a close look at best (desired) practices. Start by conducting literature research. Polaroid Corporation, for example, publishes an annual document for internal distribution that summarizes such secondary research. PDMA's Best Practices Study [6], along with the *PDMA Handbook of Product Development* and its annotated bibliography of recent books, may also contribute to this effort.

Benchmarking activities are a strong complement to a literature review. Be sure to involve top managers in benchmarking activities and seek comparison with at least five or six noncompetitive organizations. Such external benchmarking should focus on the hows, whys, and consequences of decision-making, workflow, and subsystems.

Using a cross-functional group to debrief and analyze all of the findings is also essential. Their goal is to present the insights to top management so as to make a compelling case to proceed with implementation. This can be accomplished by articulating the pain of the current situation, the potential gain of the desired process, and the best course forward for implementing.

7.8. PARTICIPATIVE DESIGN LEADS TO ACCEPTANCE AND USAGE

A common mistake made by many organizations is separating the jobs of process design and implementation. It is better to think of design as part of implementation. Handing an already designed process to an organization and asking everyone to use it is asking for problems. It is like injecting a foreign organism into one's body: The immune system will retaliate.

During implementation, it is easier to accept and use what one creates than to appreciate what someone else creates for you. Thus a key principle to implementation is that those who will be using a component of the NPD process should design that component. Project doers on NPD teams should design the work flow. The business unit's top management should create the gate criteria and design the decision flow. The controllers of the systems (usually direct reports to top management) should design or redesign the support systems. A full implementation initiative, therefore, has three different work groups. Integrating the work of all three implementation work groups calls for periodic meetings of all participants. An implementation manager then coordinates (not instructs) the three work groups. Table 7.1 shows the contributors and their responsibilities.

Top management involvement is a key to participative design. Their role is to build consensus among themselves and articulate the specific criteria for each gate to the entire organization. Start this effort by conducting a workout session with them on strategy, constraints, and new product objectives. Be sure to use a

TABLE 7.1   Implementation Contributors and Responsibilities

Contributor	Who	Responsibility
Business Management Team (BMT)	Top business unit leader and top functional managers	Creates and uses gate criteria Ongoing responsibility as gatekeepers and portfolio managers
Work-flow design team (WFDT)	NPD project contributors representing all needed functions	Design work flow that aligns with decision criteria
Systems and practices team (SPT)	Direct reports to top functional managers, overseers of current systems and practices	Identify and mitigate hindering systems and practices Ongoing responsibility for process improvement
Process implementation manager	Manager well respected throughout the organization, adept at NPD, and has good influence and communication skills	Coordinate all implementation activities

competent and independent facilitator to avoid poor dialogue. The output of the session is a list of "must pass" and "should pass" criteria for evaluating projects, divided among the different gates. Throughout implementation, top management should then amend, alter, or otherwise mold the criteria. The goal is to match and focus (align) the stages of work flow and create a means to manage the risk of the portfolio of projects. Once crafted, the criteria for each gate become a critical document, shared with the entire organization.

Participative design also ensures that the new process matches the current culture of the business unit. The result is that the change that people must make re-

> *Those who will be using a component of the framework should design that component.*

mains within the norms of the organization, helping to increase the desirability of accepting and using the fast stage-gate framework.

7.9. DESIGNING IMPROVEMENT INTO THE PROCESS

The framework should also provide a means to improve the organization's overall NPD effort. There are several sources of insights that help. Figure 7.1 shows how all gates have a "basis for decision" document as outputs. Similarly, terminations of projects call for postmortem summaries. The documentation of activities and projects provides a rich source of data. Over time, analysis of the accumulated documents will indicate recurring challenges or problems. Metrics of projects and the process provide another source of valuable data. Following are some potential metrics that the organization may want to track.

- Time to react (to knowledge of opportunity or threat)
- Cycle time to launch
- Slippage from schedule
- Number of programs completing process (to launch)
- Financial returns on programs
- Cycle time in each phase
- Cycle time to break even
- Number of programs stopped
- Core team turnover
- Participation in stage-gate process (person-years per function)

Ownership of the process is a key aspect to its continuous improvement. Without ownership, responsibility will wane and effectiveness of the process will dissipate. Often, the individual manager, assigned as the stage-gate process manager or coordinator, assumes full responsibility. Yet making a person singularly responsible for the improved effectiveness of the process is self-defeating. Strategy, systems, and practices are usually "owned" by other mangers or by functional departments. A better approach is to share ownership and responsibility across functions, at the top of the business unit. One way to do this is to assign improvement responsibility to the systems and practices team (comprised of direct reports to top functional managers) as well as to the process manager. This team then reports at regular intervals to the BMT on process metrics, hindrances, and improvement activities. Should investment in process improvement or new tools be warranted, the BMT can allocate resources immediately to do so.

Build continuing improvement into the NPD process.

7.10. SUMMARY

Gaining acceptance and use of a new product development process is a significant change management challenge. It requires aligning the process with strategy, involving contributors from across the organization, and positioning the process appropriately. A sound, well-implemented process is worth the work, delivering both speed and effectiveness to a business unit's NPD efforts.

REFERENCES

1. Beckhard, R. and Harris, R. *Organizational Transitions: Managing Complex Change.* Reading, MA: Addison-Wesley, 1987.

2. Cooper, R. G. *Winning at New Products: Accelerating the Process from Idea to Launch*. Reading, MA: Addison-Wesley, 1993.
3. Eureka, W. E. *Introduction to QFD: Collection of Presentations and Case Studies*. Detroit, MI: American Supplier Institute, January 1987.
4. Kleinschmidt, E. and Cooper, R. G. *Formal Processes for Managing New Products: The Industry Experience*. McMaster University, Hamilton, Ontario, Canada, 1991.
5. Larson, E. and Gobeli, D. Organizing for product development projects. *Journal of Product Innovation Management* 5:118 (1988).
6. O'Connor, P. Implementing a stage-gate process: a multi-company perspective. *Journal of Product Innovation Management* 11:183–200 (1994).
7. Page, A. Assessing new product development and performance: establishing crucial norms. *Journal of Product Innovation Management* 10:273–290 (1993).
8. Wheelwright, S. and Clark, K. *Revolutionizing Product Development: Quantum Leaps in Speed, Efficiency and Quality*. New York: Free Press, 1992.

Paul J. O'Connor
The Adept Group

He has influenced and guided the product development efforts of consumer and industrial companies in North America and Europe. His dedicated interest to new product development includes resolving real issues related to implementing processes, conducting project and portfolio evaluations, as well as inducing creativity, teamwork, and leadership. Mr. O'Connor developed and pioneered the use of NewProd, a statistical software model of critical factors influencing success or failure of new products, for project portfolio analysis, team building, and project tracking. He is President of the Adept Group located in Jacksonville, Florida and a past president of the Product Development and Management Association.

POLITICAL BEHAVIOR IN
8 THE PRODUCT DEVELOPMENT PROCESS

Stephen K. Markham
Patricia J. Holahan

8.1. INTRODUCTION

Getting approval for product development activities is not just a rational exercise of informing others that a project is important; rather, it is a long process of generating support. Product development professionals not only have to be proficient in specific disciplines, including marketing, project management, and team building—they must also be adept at political maneuvers.

This chapter will help people in the product development function cope with political activity at the company level by focusing on the relationships of the product development function with management and other departments. The product development function may comprise an entire department, formal multifunctional teams, ad hoc teams, or just a person with an idea. The political activity associated with each of these product development organizations is similar. One must always convince other people of the value of specific product development efforts so that the necessary resources and assistance will be obtained.

The first objective of this chapter is to discuss forms of political behavior in the product development process. The second objective is to introduce a model of political behavior that not only explains why there is political behavior but also how political strength can be developed. The final objective is to discuss team and individual influence strategies to assist product development professionals to contribute to the firm in a positive way.

8.2. POLITICAL ACTIVITY IN PRODUCT DEVELOPMENT

The terms *power, influence,* and *political activity* often conjure up negative images of force and manipulation. In its worst manifestation these perceptions are correct. Most people in product development have seen cases in which superior projects and people fall victim to the political machinery of the corporation. A major cause of frustration among product development professionals is that they often have considerable foresight but little power to act on what they see.

Contrary to the idea that politics is always a mechanism for unfair and unjust allocations of resources, however, politics may serve a useful function within the organization. It is by exercising power and influence that an organization aligns itself with the environment. Product development personnel in many firms make liberal use of political activity to the benefit of their firms.

Common mechanisms for exercising power are the champion, the product development team, and the use of product development processes such as the stage-gate process. Recognizing that successful new products are scarce, champions influence management and others by convincing them that their project has an attractive payoff for the organization. Champions also promote their projects as critical to the organization across a number of dimensions, such as filling a neglected market niche, leading the competition in time to market or product specifications, and having strategic advantages. Champions also argue that devoting resources to their project reduces the uncertainty of future technological or product advances. Research has found champions able to protect projects from termination, gain additional resources for their project, and help project performance [3]. Champions clearly are immersed in political activities.

Champions do no work alone; multifunctional teams are needed to support the champion and to take on the work of the project. Team members often are intensely engaged in supporting the project, but protecting and promoting a project requires not only commitment and dedication, but also appropriate political activity. Team members must be able to secure needed information and resources and to gain acceptance and support for their project. Team members do this by engaging in boundary-spanning activities, which include seeking support and acceptance, bargaining with other units, selling the project to others, protecting the project from criticism, and so on [1].

Political activity surrounds product development decisions because they involve the flow of resources, control, and growth. As a decision-making tool, the stage-gate process is a focal point of political activity. Shepherding a project from one stage to the next involves a high degree of political activity on the part of the champion, the sponsor, and the team. The team must convince management that the project has met the gate requirements. This often has to be done in the presence of those who would like to see the project terminated. Getting approval for the next gate is not just a matter of presenting information but often includes generating support from various people in the organization.

Not only is the stage-gate process an arena for political behavior, it is also a political tool. Controlling the product development process is a form of political behavior. Product development shares control of the process with management. Although management makes the decisions, product development personnel provide the information and help set the criteria. In approving and supporting a stage-gate process (or any other product development process), management effectively transfers control (power) of product decisions to an agreed upon set of criteria devised by people involved in product development. Not only is this a major focus of political activity, but it is a significant transfer of power to product development.

Product development has also devised other programs to commit management to a course of action defined by predetermined sets of criteria. These kinds of programs include: developmental shoot-outs, skunkworks, critical factors selection, and so on. It is asking a lot for management to commit to a course of action not yet specified. One has to have great power to hold management to this kind of arrangement.

Having power is not without costs. It takes time and energy to exercise control; therefore, there must be a significant advantage to having power. Having power allows product development to react to the business environment in ways that, hopefully, are good for the entire organization. Power also allows one to help set the agenda and keep product development issues before the organization. In this way product development helps define problems facing the company. This is critical, since organizations often look inward and neglect examining the competitive environment until it is too late. Having power also means putting allies in strong positions to ensure the necessary resources to implement the agenda.

8.3. STRATEGIC CONTINGENCIES MODEL OF POLITICAL BEHAVIOR

The strategic contingencies model of power and influence identifies issues, activities, and resources that are critical for organizations to achieve their goals [5]. The model has two parts. The first part explains why some activities in organizations are highly political in nature; the second part explains how and why a specific subunit such as product development accrues political power in the organization.

8.3.1. Level of Political Activity

According to the strategic contingencies model, several conditions give rise to political behavior in organizations (see Figure 8.1) [5]. Each of these conditions is discussed below. From this discussion it will become clear that several of these conditions are characteristic of the product development process.

1. *Goal differences*. Functional areas such as marketing and production may not share the same objective as the product development team. Differences in priorities and resource allocations between departments are common. Thus conflict may arise as each group vies to meet its respective goals.
2. *Scarce resources*. All organizations are constrained by a finite set of resources such as money, technology, expertise, and so on. Product development activities will of necessity compete with the functional areas for resources.
3. *Interdependency*. When departments depend on each other for material, expert, or information resources, they become dependent on each other. This dependency creates conflict as each group tries to develop dominance over the others. Each department will try to make other departments dependent on it.
4. *Ambiguity*. Product development is risky, since outcomes are never certain. Projected market share, revenues, performance, and profits often are merely a best guess. In this ambiguous circumstance, defining the problem becomes a contest of opinions. In the absence of objective information, each group will try to define the problem the firm must solve. By

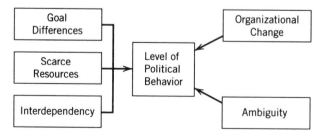

FIGURE 8.1 Predictors of political behavior.

defining the problem, each department attempts to reduce ambiguity in a way that is advantageous to its own department.

5. *Organizational Change.* Although not directly related to product development, downsizing, reengineering, turnarounds, mergers, acquisitions, relocations, and automation all call into question established power structures. Change realigns the organization with the environment, creating new areas of importance and eliminating established areas. Thus each group will try to become central in solving organizational problems.

The more prevalent each of these conditions, the more political activity there will be. If other departments do not feel that product development is critical, there will be more resistance and political activity. Similarly, the more other departments have to share resources or be dependent on product development, the more political activity one can expect. In addition, ambiguous changing conditions give rise to political activity as each department attempts to secure resources for itself. There is little doubt that the product development setting in many organizations is ripe for political behavior.

8.3.2. Level of Product Development Power

Knowing why political activity arises is essential in assessing the political reality of product development. Nevertheless, the reasons why political activity arises do not tell us how much political power product development has or how to generate more. The second part of the strategic contingency model explains how product development can develop political power in the organization [5,6].

The strategic contingencies model states that power accrues to departments that address strategic issues or critical problems for the firm. If a department (1) helps the firm cope with uncertainly, (2) obtains scarce resources for the firm, (3) is depended on by other departments or is central to the firm, and (4) is nonsubstitutable, that department will accrue power (see Figure 8.2). For ex-

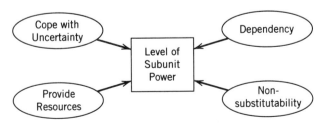

FIGURE 8.2 Strategic contingencies that determine subunit power.

ample, in fast-paced high-technology industries, time to market is likely to be a strategic contingency for the firm that helps provide scarce resources (revenue). Departments that help deliver products to market fast will accrue power.

Below are some observations about each of these contingencies. Note that these observations may not be true for your company. The point is that analysis and recommendations need to be made for your company; there are no "silver bullets" here, only approaches.

1. *Cope with uncertainty.* Major sources of uncertainty in organizations today include technological advances, competitor actions, and shifting customer demand. In many firms product development plays a major role in dealing with these uncertainties.

   In the short run, product development may be viewed as a cause of uncertainty, since it usually has a number of projects, any one of which may fail. Remind management that new products will account for greater revenues in the future [4] and that product development programs rather than individual projects must be funded.

   New products also have strategic implications for market positioning and competition. Short-term perspectives often focus inward, which greatly increases uncertainty because of neglecting competitive market information. Supply others with market intelligence about rapid changes and developments in the market. Offer recommendations about how product development faces market challenges rather than how a new technology can be researched.

2. *Provide scarce resources.* To the extent that product development provides scarce resources to the firm, it will accrue power. Although others may argue that product development uses resources, new products will account for an ever-larger portion of revenues. It should be argued that product development is a source of resources, not just an expense. Companies may be forced to cut costs for reasons such as increased competition, a declining market, a potential merger, to look good on the quarterly report, or to fight a falling stock price.

   In addition to producing revenue-generating products, product development should be efficient and cost-effective. Also, accounting practices should reflect the cost and revenues associated with each project so that the financial contribution of product development is not lost. Product development needs to portray itself as a profit center rather than a cost center. This might be done by keeping track of the overall figure for gross profit from new products minus the cost of product development.

3. *Dependency.* Product development will accrue power to the extent that the firm or other departments within the firm depend on product inno-

vations. There are many reasons why a department may depend on product development, such as bringing new products to market quickly, or supplying inputs for other departments, such a new products for marketing to sell or for operations to produce.

To understand how other departments depend on product development, one must recognize critical issues facing the organization and how product development addresses those issues. For example, national and international competition have increased the rate of product introductions. Competitive threats are based on both new technologies that provide for new product platforms that have price and performance advantages and on market research that provides increasing customization for different market segments. As product development becomes recognized as the resource to cope with these issues, the firm becomes dependent on product development.

4. *Nonsubstitutability*. To the extent that product innovation is important and cannot be undertaken in other departments, power will accrue to product development. To a large extent, the capacity to work multifunctionally helps product development maintain its unique position.

Providing information about competitors' product offerings is a way that product development builds credibility. Explain that shortened product life cycles mean shorter revenue streams. In financial terms, explain how future revenue streams will depend more and more on new products. Explain in market and strategic terms the necessity to be first to the customer. Explain the advantage of retaining or gaining a competitive position for add-on sales and services. Raising these issues helps others to recognize the critical need for an appropriate level of product development.

The environment often determines what is critical for a given company. These critical contingencies take many forms: high-quality products, timely delivery, low costs, supplier retention, efficient distribution, good industrial relations, regulatory issues, and availability of capital, to name a few. Any one of these issues may be critical for your company. Since product development is only one of many "voices" in an organization, it must convince management and other departments that it deals with uncertainty, delivers scarce resources, and can handle critical problems. In any given firm, product development may not be seen as the most critical subunit, which is why product development has varying degrees of power in different companies. This has significant implications for assessing the level of power that product development has as well as how to generate more influence.

In summary, product development must determine what is important for the firm and what it can do to assist the firm. The observant reader will probably respond, "but that is what I am doing already." The point here is not to change any intentions but rather to be sensitive about how things get done in the organization by understanding what is important to decision makers. Engaging in political behavior does not necessarily mean that one is engaging in any form of dishonest or manipulative behavior. Quite the opposite. The more open and honest one is at framing issues in terms of critical problems, the more effective one will be in influencing others.

8.4. INFLUENCING OTHERS

In this section we examine two methods of influencing others. First we look at how product development teams cope with political activity by dividing political tasks between members. Then we examine personal influence tactics.

8.4.1. Teams and Political Influence

When we think about influence techniques, we usually focus on personal influence tactics, which we discuss in the following section. In product development, however, we must also think of influence techniques as team activities. Ancona and Caldwell [1] empirically derived a list of external team activities and found they fell into four categories, each of which they represent as a team member role. As a list of team activities, this conceptualization of roles and responsibilities is especially pertinent to the discussion of political activity in product development. Table 8.1 details these roles and responsibilities. Note that most of the activities are political in nature. Each team must have someone accepting these informal role responsibilities, or the project is disadvantaged. Table 8.1 should be used as a checklist of political activities for team leaders to assure that the team will be able to cope with its political environment. If a project team is considering how to organize its political efforts, this list is a good place to start.

8.4.2. Individual Influence Tactics

Not only must product development prepare teams for political activity, but it must help individuals develop skills to influence others. How actually to influence others, however, is a persistent, difficult question. Although there are many anecdotal methods offered as influence techniques, David Kipnis and his colleagues [2] have developed an empirically derived list of influence tactics. In addition, Kipnis has determined which tactics work best in attempting to influence superiors and subordinates. Table 8.2 summarizes his findings.

The most used tactic is reasoning; it is also the most successful. This suggests that a straightforward, open approach probably should be the foundation of all

TABLE 8.1   Boundary Spanning Roles and Responsibilities in Product Development

Ambassador: protect and persuade
- Absorb outside pressure for the team
- Protect team from extra work and requests
- Persuade others of team importance
- "Talk up" the team
- Acquire resources
- Assess support and opposition to the project
- Gather information about company strategy that is useful to team

Task coordinator: coordinate and negotiate with outsiders
- Resolve design problems
- Coordinate tasks with external groups
- Procure needed assistance from other groups
- Negotiate with others on delivery dates
- Review product design with outsiders

Scout: Scanning competitor, market, and technology developments
- Scan in and out of form for marketing ideas
- Collect technical information from outside the firm
- Find out what competing firms are doing with similar projects

Guard: avoid releasing information
- Keep news about team secret until appropriate
- Avoid releasing information to protect the team's image or project
- Control the release of information to present the profile wanted

Source: Adapted from [1].

attempts to influence. Coalition building relies on the influence of other people to bring pressure on the influence target. Although generally successful, this may cause resentment if someone feels that he or she is being forced to comply. Ingratiating must be used cautiously. Pandering or patronizing people could result in resistance rather than assistance. On the other hand, developing goodwill can be a sincere and mutually beneficial situation. Like reason, bargaining is straightforward, yet the person agrees because of the exchange, not because he

TABLE 8.2   Influence Tactics and Their Applications

Tactic	Behavior	Application
Reason	Use facts to develop a logical argument	Sup and Sub
Coalition	Mobilize other people in organization	Sup and Sub
Ingratiation	Impression management and use goodwill	Sup and Sub
Bargaining	Negotiate to exchange benefits and favors	Sup
Assertiveness	Take a direct and forceful approach	Sub
Higher authority	Gain support from higher levels	Neither
Sanctions	Use rewards and punishments	Neither

[a] Sup, use with superiors; Sub, use with subordinates.

or she believes that the request is the best action to take. Assertiveness may be used with subordinates, but it is a dangerous tactic with superiors. Using higher-ups in the organization brings direct pressure from the person's superior to comply with a request. Such tactics are seldom appreciated and may result in active resistance in other areas. Like the use of higher authority and assertion, the use of sanctions has negative connotations and could be counterproductive in the long run. Gaining support for product development activities is a long-term prospect, and forcing someone to do something may not be in the best interests of product development in the long run.

8.5. SUMMARY

Since product development decisions usually represent change for an organization, political activity almost always will surround product decisions. Product development personnel therefore engage in a great deal of political behavior, such as championing, stage-gate processes, and using teams. By helping the organization align with the environment, product development can make a strong contribution to the organization. To do this, however, product development professionals must learn to help the organization cope with uncertainty, gather scarce resources, and solve critical problems. In this way, product development helps define the agenda and influence the organizational mission and objectives.

Departments that are persuasive at convincing top management that they are the most important in terms of dealing with critical problems are the most likely to get needed resources. If the most persuasive subunits are indeed dealing with critical issues, political activity is positive. Unfortunately, the political process that helps a firm align itself with the environment is the same political process that can misdirect resources. Helping the product development function to exercise influence to help the firm is what this chapter is all about.

REFERENCES

1. Ancona, D. G. and Caldwell, D. Beyond boundary spanning: managing external dependence in product development teams. *Journal of High Technology Management Research* 1(2): 116–135 (1990).
2. Kipnis, D. and Schmidt, S. *Profile of Organizational Influence Strategies.* San Diego: University of Associates, 1982.
3. Markham, S. K., Green, S. G., and Basu, R. Champions and antagonists: relationships with R&D project characteristics and management. *Journal of Engineering and Technology Management* 8: 217–242 (1991).

4. Page, A. L. Assessing new product development practices and performance: establishing crucial norms. *Journal of Product Innovation Management* 10(4): 273–290 (1993).
5. Pfeffer, J. *Power in Organizations.* Boston: Pitman, 1981.
6. Salancik, G. R. and Pfeffer, J. Who gets power—and how they hold on to it: a strategic-contingency model of power. *Organizational Dynamics* (Winter 1977).

Stephen K. Markham
North Carolina State University

Stephen Markham holds a Ph.D. in Organizational Behavior from Purdue University and an MBA from the University California, Irvine. Presently he is an Assistant Professor of Management at North Carolina State University (NCSU), where he teaches course in leadership, technology management, and managerial effectiveness. Dr. Markham's research focuses on roles that people take in product/process development teams. He also conducts research on product development processes. Dr. Markham is co-director of the Technology, Education and Commercialization (TEC) program at NCSU. The TEC program seeks to commercialize technology through the cooperative efforts of university, private, and government agencies.

Patricia J. Holahan
Stevens Institute of Technology

Patricia Holahan holds a Ph.D. in Organizational Behavior from Purdue University. Presently, she is an Assistant Professor of Management at Stevens Institute of Technology, where she teaches graduate courses in the management of technology, and organizational design and theory. Dr. Holahan also holds an appointment as a Senior Research Associate with the Stevens Alliance for Technology Management, where she conducts research on the management of multifunctional teams and advises corporate sponsors on issues related to the transfer of management technologies. Dr. Holahan also works as a consultant to several major corporations, advising them on issues related to team-based work designs, and team reward and recognition systems.

FACTORS AFFECTING
9 MULTIFUNCTIONAL TEAM
EFFECTIVENESS

Patricia J. Holahan
Stephen K. Markham

If new products and processes are to be developed
rapidly and efficiently, the firm must develop the
capability to achieve integration across the functions in a
timely and efficient way.

—Clark and Wheelwright, 1993

9.1. INTRODUCTION

Product development (PD) professionals have recognized for some time now that
when product development is accompanied by highly integrated activity across
the functions, lower development costs, shorter development times, and higher
product quality result. Unfortunately, many PD professionals have also come to
realize that achieving highly integrated activity through the use of multifunctional
project teams is frequently more attractive in theory than in practice. Many factors have been found to reduce the effectiveness of these project teams. This
chapter focuses on these factors and discusses how multifunctional PD teams
might function more effectively.

In this chapter we propose that three sets of factors are required if timely
and efficient multifunctional teamwork is to occur. A model of these three factors
is shown in Figure 9.1. The first set of factors has to do with how the PD process
is structured. If multifunctional teamwork is to occur, it must be designed into

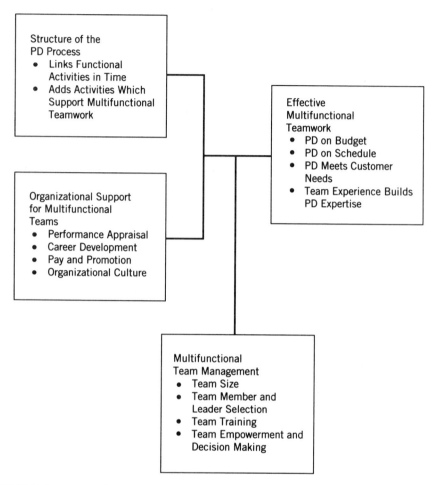

FIGURE 9.1 Determinants of effective multifunctional teamwork.

the PD process. Product development processes designed without this goal in mind do not provide the proper framework for teamwork to occur. The second set of factors relates to the extent to which the organization values and supports multifunctional teamwork. If the organizational infrastructure does not offer the necessary supports for multifunctional teamwork, then again, it is unlikely that successful multifunctional integration will be achieved. Finally, those who comprise the PD team and the ability of the team's leader to manage the team process have been found important determinants of effective multifunctional integration.

In this chapter we examine these three sets of factors that underlie effective multifunctional teamwork. We begin by discussing the structure of the PD process. We then examine organizational contexts that support and promote effective multifunctional integration. The final section of the chapter covers issues related to management of the team itself.

9.2. STRUCTURING THE PRODUCT DEVELOPMENT PROCESS

The structure of the product development process largely determines whether multifunctional teamwork can occur. If effective multifunctional integration is to occur, the product development process cannot be structured simply as a sequential process where one functional area hands off outputs to the next. Nor can the development process be structured as a set of parallel activities, where each functional area works independently of the others but development activities are carried out concurrently. Rather, *each* stage of development must contain an *integrated set of activities*, where key inputs are provided by each of the functional areas, and outputs are a result of a highly integrated problem-solving process. According to Clark and Wheelwright, effective multifunctional teamwork starts with a product development process that links in time the activities of the functions and adds activities that support multifunctional interaction [1].

Therefore, if the PD process is to set the stage for effective multifunctional teamwork, the design of the process must include each of the functions having an important role in each of the stages of development. For example, manufacturing must be actively involved in proposing concepts and investigating them at the earliest stage of development. Similarly, engineering must build very early prototypes to support marketing's desire to better understand customer needs and wants. One effect of these changes on product development is to pull forward in time the activity and involvement of the downstream functions. Linking the activities of the functional areas in time, however, is not enough; activities that support multifunctional *interaction* must be *added* to the process [1]. For instance, Clark and Wheelwright note, engineers may be required to *participate with* marketing in interacting with customers. Manufacturing may be required to do process development during the concept development stage *in collaboration with* design engineers [1].

Stage-gate systems may be one vehicle for linking the activities of the functional areas in time and adding activities that support multifunctional interaction. In a stage-gate system the product development process is divided into a predetermined set of stages or activities. Gates or formal go/no go decision points are then built into the process and control the entrance to each successive stage. When the activities to be performed at each stage are designed to be an integrated set of activities requiring multifunctional involvement and the gate criteria require highly integrated decision making, (i.e., joint, multifunctional involvement) a foundation for multifunctional teamwork is laid. Structuring the development process in this way enables multifunctional teamwork, but it is not a sufficient condition for achieving integration across the functions. In subsequent sections of this chapter we discuss the other conditions that are necessary for achieving effective integration across the functions.

In summary, the structure of the new product development process largely determines whether teamwork can occur. Product development processes that are structured sequentially or that require only concurrent activities within the functional areas do not engage team behavior. If a foundation for multifunctional integration is to be laid, the product development process must:

- Link in time the activities of the functions.
- Add activities that require multifunctional collaboration.

9.3. ORGANIZATIONAL SUPPORT FOR MULTIFUNCTIONAL TEAMS

A recent major study of work teams found that nearly 80% of the respondents named organizational barriers as the major roadblock to effective teamwork [5]. Traditional organizational structures and management processes often work against efficient and effective multifunctional integration. The fact that multifunctional project teams must work horizontally and most organizations are designed vertically creates conditions ripe for competition, conflict, and role ambiguity. Teamwork is further thwarted by human resource systems that are designed to recognize, promote, and reward individual (versus team) achievement. In this section we discuss several of the organizational factors that pose the biggest barriers to effective multifunctional teamwork (see Figure 9.1) and suggest strategies for overcoming them.

9.3.1. Performance Appraisal

Performance appraisal is an important means for obtaining credit for work on a multifunctional team. Unfortunately, in many instances assessment of a team members's performance on a multifunctional project team is missing from the formal performance evaluation process, and team members' contributions to the project team go unrecognized and unrewarded. The message that employees receive is that teamwork is not valued by the organization, and their commitment to the team suffers. Often, this error in the design of the performance appraisal system is a result of the fact that multifunctional project teams take people out of their departments where department managers do not actually see or in many cases know how they perform—yet the department manager remains the sole evaluator of the person's performance.

If employees' contributions to the outcomes of their team assignments are to "count"—be factored in when it comes to pay, promotion, and assignment decisions—changes in the organization's performance appraisal process are needed. First, the performance appraisal process must include an evaluation of the employees' contributions to the team outcome. One means of doing this is to develop a process by which feedback from the team leader and team members is included in the formal evaluation process. Second, this feedback can be weighted in proportion to the percentage of time the employee was dedicated to the team when deriving the final performance rating. For example, if during the last rating period, the employee allocated 100 percent of his or her time to the project team, the team's feedback would count for 100 percent of the performance rating.

If multifunctional teamwork is to be taken seriously, the performance appraisal system must be redesigned to include an evaluation of the team member's behavior. Moreover, systems designed to incorporate feedback from multiple raters whereby team leaders and team members provide feedback for performance appraisal purposes are needed.

9.3.2. Career Development

Product development processes that rely on multifunctional integration require a broader set of skills than those required by sequential, functionally oriented development processes. For example, an effective marketer must not only be knowledgeable about customer needs, market research technologies, and marketing strategy, but must also have an appreciation of product design and manufacturing capabilities. The specialist in some ways must also become a generalist. Accordingly, if the organization is to have a ready pool of knowledgeable and well-trained talent, multifunctional skills must be developed. Cross-training and lateral career paths are ways of developing multifunctional skills.

Cross-Training

One of the prime requirements for effective multifunctional interaction is for team members to have an understanding and appreciation of the contributions to be made from the other functional areas. This includes understanding their technical skills and methods as well as their attitudes and values [8]. When the marketer has a sense of what wearing the engineering hat feels like, and vice versa, multifunctional communication and understanding are aided. Interdisciplinary training and education of this type not only aid in breaking down barriers to multifunctional communication, but enable team members to know enough about the other areas to ask the right questions and evaluate answers received.

Job rotation is another way to cross-train and can be an effective means of building trust and respect among team members. Often, problems related to a lack of trust or respect are minimized when team members truly understand the nature of the work, processes, and constraints under which their functional counterparts operate. Rotating engineers throughout their careers or transferring design engineers to the factory floor during ramp-up are practices used by several organizations to cross-train [6].

Lateral Career Paths

Finally, more emphasis needs to be placed on lateral career paths. Organizations in which the only acceptable career paths emphasize depth of experience and functional expertise do not create a reservoir of multifunctional skills. More attention needs to be given to career paths that reward people for acquiring multiple skills and broadening their knowledge base. This type of experience is critically important not only for team members, but also for effective team leaders. The value the organization places on developing a broader base of skills can be made explicit through criteria included in the performance appraisal and promotion policies.

9.3.3. Promotion and Pay

If highly integrated multifunctional teamwork and cooperation are truly goals of the organization, these must be reflected in the promotion and pay policies. That is, team leaders, team members, and functional managers must be rewarded for multifunctional cooperation. Many experts approach the issue of rewards from the vantage of how to reward project teams for their efforts. Although rewarding teams is a part of the problem, we argue that the matter of rewards and multifunctional integration is one that applies to the design of the organization's reward system as a whole. This view is consistent with that of Coombs and Gomez-Mejia, who note that "perhaps the single most important factor contributing to the relative integration of functional areas is the way rewards are allocated across different units. The compensation system . . . can send powerful signals to the employees as to the organization's goals. If different signals are sent to the various functions, it would seem logical that coordination would suffer" [2, p. 45].

Coombs and Gomez-Mejia make several suggestions regarding compensation design to achieve multifunctional integration. They recommend including cooperation between the functional areas as an explicit factor in the performance appraisals for general managers, functional managers, and project and team leaders. This practice communicates that the organization values multifunctional cooperation and collaboration. Coombs and Gomez-Mejia also suggest making rewards (promotion, pay increases, etc.) contingent on performance measures that reflect the *combined efforts* of all the functional areas. For example, rather than using function-specific performance criteria such as patents granted or production levels, they suggest using profitability measures for a given product as the basis for distributing compensation dollars across functions. If you want highly integrated multifunctional activity, you must measure and reward performance that is the result of the desired behavior.

Promotion is another powerful way to reward teamwork and multifunctional collaboration. Promotion sends clear messages to others in the organization regarding what is valued and rewarded. When promotions are announced throughout the organization and it is made explicit that the promotion was contingent on the person's skills as a team player as well as technical skills, the link between teamwork and rewards becomes firmly established.

9.3.4. Organizational Culture

We have discussed several of the formal organizational systems that can be designed to support multifunctional teamwork. However, it is also important that senior management build a culture in which multifunctional teamwork can thrive. The following excerpt from Bob Hershock at 3M describes the challenges that management faces in attempting to establish a culture that supports the use of multifunctional product development teams.

> When we first contemplated [multifunctional teams], we were fully aware that our organizational policies and our management styles weren't set up to handle the special needs of teams . . . . The organization had to see the team's needs as a priority and to respond quickly. This represented a major policy change for management. Now, instead of the team serving the needs of management, the organization would serve its new internal customer—the team. Division managers and directors had to change their roles. Formerly they had acted in the traditional roles of controllers and delegators. Now they had to become enablers, going out of their way to help the [teams] accomplish their goals [3, pp. 96–97].

Effecting large-scale cultural change (i.e., large-scale change in roles and responsibilities, and the values by which the organization operates) is not an easy task. Although changes in the organization's performance appraisal, career development, and reward systems can serve to institutionalize an organization's values, these changes need to be supported by top management." Organizational values need to be clearly communicated throughout the organization, and senior management must be a model multifunctional team if the values and attitudes needed for effective multifunctional integration are to become firmly established in the organization. Employees engage in behavior they believe will be rewarded and pattern their behavior after senior people in the organization they respect and admire. When they observe senior managers actively engaging in multifunctional collaboration, empowering their direct reports and treating one another with respect and trust, a foundation for team behavior and multifunctional collaboration is laid at lower levels in the organization.

In summary, multifunctional product development teams are often faced with an organization that has rewards, norms, systems, and structures that reinforce traditional ways of managing. Multifunctional PD teams need to be supported by organizational systems designed for teams and multifunctional collaboration rather than for individuals and functions (or fiefdoms). Accordingly, the organization's performance appraisal, career development, and reward systems should be examined to determine changes needed to support multifunctional integration. Similarly, a culture (i.e., the attitudes and values) that supports teamwork must be communicated and modeled if effective multifunctional integration is to be achieved.

9.4. MANAGING THE TEAM

The preceding sections of this chapter dealt with the need to design the product development process to engage teamwork and the need to design the organizational context to support multifunctional teamwork. These activities establish the required infrastructure for integrated multifunctional activity to occur. However, how the product development team is managed is also important for achieving effective multifunctional teamwork (see Figure 9.1). In this section, managing the product development team is discussed. Topics covered include team size, team leader and member selection, team training, and issues related to empowerment and decision making in multifunctional product development teams.

9.4.1. Team Size

The old adage, "small is beautiful," still holds when it comes to product development teams. Numerous examples of the advantages of small versus large teams are documented in the practitioner and research literatures. If we think of what makes for an effective team, the reasons for this finding become obvious. Effective teams are those wherein members have a collective goal and feel mutually accountable for the team results. Moreover, there exists an atmosphere of openness and trust whereby differing viewpoints are readily shared and conflicts managed with candor and mutual respect. These dynamics are difficult to establish in any team and become increasingly more difficult to achieve as team size increases. Katzenbach and Smith correctly note: "Large numbers of people have difficulty interacting constructively . . . much less doing real work. Ten people are far more likely than fifty . . . to work through their individual, functional, and hierarchical differences toward a common plan and to hold themselves jointly accountable for the results" [4, p. 114]. Parker notes that as team size increases, decreases are witnessed in team productivity and in team member accountability, participation, and trust [7].

Product development requires inputs from many groups, hence the tendency for team size to be large. The question then becomes how we keep the team small (8 to 12 members) when the task requires the work of several functions and subfunctions. Two approaches can be applied to multifunctional PD teams to keep team size small [7]. The first is the use of a core team. The core team approach requires that representatives be selected from each of the functions critical to the product development effort. These team members become the central coordinating and decision-making body. Clark and Wheelwright note: "Individually, core team members represent their functions and provide leadership for their function's inputs to the project. Collectively, they constitute a management team that works under the direction of the . . . project manager and takes responsibility for managing the overall development effort" [1, p. 539].

Another approach to keeping the team size small is to break the large team up into subgroups or subcommittees. Each subcommittee has a leader and is responsible for coordinating and managing a specific domain of activity. The leaders of the subcommittees meet regularly to provide the needed overall project planning and coordination. Periodic meetings among all the members of the subcommittees may also be held.

9.4.2. Selecting Team Leaders and Team Members

You cannot have effective teamwork without effective team members and team leadership. Accordingly, selecting team members and team leaders with the knowledge, skills, and abilities to optimize the team process becomes critically important. What, then, are the characteristics of team leaders and members that are especially relevant to multifunctional teams?

Selecting Team Leaders

Parker describes the job of the multifunctional team leader accordingly: "Leaders of multifunctional teams must manage a diverse group of people who often have a wide variety of backgrounds, training and interests. In addition to people management skills, a team leader must be able to follow the often highly technical nature of a team's work. Frequently he or she must accomplish this without the authority that is usually associated with a leadership position in a functional organization" [7, p. 54]. From this description we can derive three sets of skills and knowledges or competencies needed by multifunctional team leaders. These competencies include interpersonal, technical, and political skills.

Interpersonal Skill. With regard to interpersonal skills the team leader must have a sensitivity to the needs of the team's members, an awareness of the group's interactions, and the ability to create an atmosphere of openness, respect, and trust within the team. Parker calls the leader's ability to understand and facilitate the human dynamics of the team—positive process leadership [7]. Process leadership entails skills such as establishing norms for openness, candor, and respect among the teams members, facilitating constructive conflict resolution, managing group discussions to ensure equal participation, and helping the group reach decisions through consensus building. The objective here is not a comprehensive listing of the skills involved in effective process leadership, but rather, an awareness that one of the criteria for effective team leadership is the extent to which the leader possesses strong interpersonal skills.

Technical Skill. The team's leader must have sufficient expertise across disciplines to see the big picture, anticipate problems, and guide the structuring of the team's activities. Thus, breadth of the team leader's technical expertise and experience with the product development process is critical.

Political Skill. Leaders of multifunctional product development teams often work with little or ambiguous authority over the resources (e.g., funding, equipment, technology, information, personnel) needed to accomplish their task. Acquiring sufficient resources frequently involves influencing people outside the team's boundaries (e.g., senior managers, functional heads). Moreover, the uncertain nature of the outcomes of the product development task itself often necessitates that the team leader garner ongoing organizational support for the project. Because of these circumstances the leader's political skills are important to the team's overall success. That is, because team leaders often lack legitimate power or authority, their political skills (i.e., ability to influence others through persuasive communications, listening, negotiating, constructive conflict resolution, and maintaining open relationships with key players external to the team) become a critical resource to the team.

Selecting Team Members

Team members must be both technically proficient and good team players. Being a good team player encompasses possessing a well-developed toolkit of interpersonal skills as well as the attitudes and values that support teamwork and integrated problem solving.

Team Player Skills.   Like team leaders, the team's members need to have good interpersonal skills. Team members need to be skilled in communications, conflict resolution, and group problem-solving and decision-making techniques. Equally important are the attitudes and values the team players bring to the table. If team members do not have healthy respect for one another and the contributions each of the disciplines has to make toward achieving the collective goal, respect and openness will not prevail. Moreover, if the team's members think of their roles only in terms of their discrete contributions, the value of teamwork and potential for integrated problem solving is lost. For example, if the design engineer sees his or her work as a completed design and the manufacturing engineer sees his or her role in terms of a well-designed manufacturing process, the value of teamwork is lost. Unless the team members see their goal as delivering a high-quality product that satisfies customer needs, is producible at a commercially feasible price, and available for the targeted market introduction, and unless they are willing to be held collectively accountable for this goal, the value of working together as a team is compromised.

Technical Skill.   There is no substitute for good technical experts. When there is insufficient expertise on the team, decision making and problem solving will be suboptimal. Thus team members need to be expert in their relevant disciplines. However, when team members have multifunctional experience (i.e., breadth as well as depth of experience), decision-making and problem-solving processes are aided. As noted earlier, breadth of experience may be the result of formal education or training, job rotation, or lateral career moves.

9.4.3. Team Training

Training for multifunctional teams needs to be focused on the skills and attitudes needed for integrated problem solving and effective multifunctional teamwork. With this in mind, it is not enough for the team's members to be trained in communication, conflict resolution, group problem solving, and decision-making methods. Nor is it sufficient for the leader to be skilled in positive process leadership and meeting management techniques. Rather, the team's ability to work together effectively and efficiently will depend on the attitudes the team members hold about each other and teamwork itself.

Stereotypes, professional hierarchies (created by differences in levels of training, professional status, and financial rewards received), and our culture's emphasis on individual achievement all work against effective multifunctional teamwork in our contemporary organizations. Professionals do not come together naturally with the attitudes, sense of mutual respect and trust, and feelings of shared responsibility which are critical to achieving effective multifunctional teamwork. Therefore, it is increasingly recognized that the organization's investment in training team members and leaders in, not only the tools and techniques of teamwork, but also the attitudes that underlie their ability to work together effectively is money well spent.

Team building is a specific form of team training and can facilitate the team's development. Team building usually consists of the entire team going through a structured set of activities together to learn more about their specific patterns of interaction (e.g., patterns of dialogue, conflict management, decision processes, etc.). Team building can be useful in helping team members better understand how their personal preferences and biases get in the way of the team's process and in identifying barriers to integrated problem solving. Team building has been used both proactively (i.e., to get the team off to a good start) and reactively (i.e., to help the team eliminate destructive patterns of interacting and establish norms that reinforce effective teamwork). The optimal strategy may be to have the team participate in team building at the start of their work together and then provide the opportunity for process consultation on an ongoing basis.

9.4.4. Team Empowerment and Decision Making

Empowerment is at the very heart of the rationale for using multifunctional teams—it provides the mechanism by which communication and problem solving occur across the functions, with authority derived from an appropriate knowledge base rather than from organizational rank. What, then, are the critical conditions and leader behaviors that facilitate empowerment?

Conditions for Empowerment

For the product development team to be empowered certain conditions must exist. First, the team must be given the authority to make decisions that affect their work. Second, the team must be given the resources needed to carry out their work and implement their decisions. Third, the team must be held collectively accountable for the outcomes of their work. Fourth, the team must be rewarded based on the outcomes of their work. Finally, if multifunctional teams are to be truly empowered they must be supported by an organizational culture where managers are willing to work collaboratively: sharing control, decision making, and organizational power in an effort to optimize organizational performance. Without this supportive environment, empowerment cannot be realized.

Leading Empowered Teams

Setting goals, assigning roles, planning, making decisions, holding meetings, communicating, exercising control, and monitoring and providing performance feedback are all activities in which multifunctional product development teams engage. Shonk has proposed a leadership continuum that depicts how a team leader's behavior changes with respect to these activities as the level of team autonomy or empowerment increases [9]. An abbreviated version of Shonk's leadership continuum is presented in Table 9.1. This continuum proposes that fully empowered teams require a different style of leadership than moderately empowered teams. As teams are able to function at higher and higher levels of empowerment, the leadership role changes from one of a team leader to that of a team boundary manager. Shonk's distinction between a team leader and a team boundary manager is based on the extent to which the leadership role is internally versus externally focused. Team leaders are actively involved in helping the teams set goals, assign roles and responsibilities, execute planning processes, and so on

TABLE 9.1   Team Leadership Continuum

	Moderate	Team empowerment	High
Activity	**Team Leader**		**Team Boundary Manager**
Goal setting	Team, with leader, sets team goals.		Team sets team goals. Boundary manager ensures fit with larger organization.
Assigning roles	Shared responsibility. Leader provides some direction and facilitates teamwork.		Team has responsibility within defined limits. Leader manages boundary and is a resource to the team.
Planning	Team plans with leader.		Team plans. Boundary manager coordinates plans with other units.
Decision making	Shared responsibility. Leader provides some direction and facilitates teamwork.		Team decides within defined limits.
Meeting	Team and leader jointly set agenda and meet. Team leader leads.		Team sets agenda and meets without boundary manager. Manager is a resource.
Communications	Team responsibility. All team members and leader in the communications loop.		Team keeps boundary manager informed. Manager communicates with groups outside the team.
Control	Team and leader exercise control.		Team exercises control. Boundary manager kept informed.
Performance feedback	Team and leader assess team's performance.		Team assesses team's performance. Boundary manager provides input.

Source: Adapted from J. Shonk, *Team-Based Organizations: Developing a Successful Team Environment*, Business One Irwin, Homewood, Illinois, © 1992.

TABLE 9.2 Achieving Effective Multifunctional Teamwork

Factor	Item	Criteria	Agreement[a]
Structure of the PD process	PD process links in time functional activities.	Each of the functional areas has an important role in each stage of product development.	1 2 3 4 5
	PD process incorporates activities that support multifunctional teamwork.	Each stage of the PD process requires intense multifunctional interaction and problem solving.	1 2 3 4 5
		Where stage-gate processes are used, gate criteria assess development from an integrated, multifunctional perspective.	1 2 3 4 5
Organizational support for multifunctional teams	Performance appraisal system	Cooperation with other functional areas is incorporated as a factor in the performance appraisal of team leaders, project managers, and general managers.	1 2 3 4 5
		Contribution to PD team is measured as part of each person's performance appraisal.	1 2 3 4 5
	Career development	Opportunities exist within the organization for cross-training (e.g., formal education/training in other disciplines, job rotation).	1 2 3 4 5
		The organization values breadth as well as depth of experience, and this is reflected in promotion and pay policies.	1 2 3 4 5
	Pay and promotion	Pay and promotion policies are designed to reward multifunctional cooperation and persons who are effective team players.	1 2 3 4 5
		The organization employs performance measures that reflect the combined efforts of all the functional areas (e.g., profitability for a specific product).	1 2 3 4 5
		Some portion of each person's rewards are contingent on the team's performance (i.e., extent to which the team achieved its collective goal).	1 2 3 4 5
	Organizational culture	Senior managers visibly display attitudes and behavior that communicate/demonstrate support for multifunctional teamwork.	1 2 3 4 5

Multifunctional team management	Team size	Core multifunctional PD team is small (8 to 12 core members).	1 2 3 4 5
	Team leader/member selection	Leader has the breadth of technical know-how needed to understand the big picture and to coordinate the inputs from a diverse set of players.	1 2 3 4 5
		Leader has sufficient process skills to manage the participation and involvement of all team members.	1 2 3 4 5
		Leader has the ability to influence key stakeholders external to the team.	1 2 3 4 5
		Team's collective technical expertise has sufficient depth and breadth to accomplish PD task.	1 2 3 4 5
		Team members possess the necessary interpersonal skills to facilitate open dialogue, effective conflict resolution, and member participation in problem solving and decision making.	1 2 3 4 5
		Team members value teamwork and demonstrate a healthy respect for their fellow teammates.	1 2 3 4 5
	Team training	Team training develops the attitudes and values necessary for effective teamwork as well as the requisite interpersonal skills.	1 2 3 4 5
		Team building is available to assist intact teams with their development.	1 2 3 4 5
	Team empowerment and decision making	The team has the authority to make and carry out key decisions.	1 2 3 4 5
		Team has access to the resources needed to carry out its mission.	1 2 3 4 5
		Team is held accountable for the outcomes of its work.	1 2 3 4 5
		Team is rewarded on the outcomes of its work.	1 2 3 4 5
		Team is supported by an organizational culture in which power and decision making are shared and collaboration is valued and rewarded.	1 2 3 4 5

[a] 1, Disagree strongly; 2, disagree somewhat; 3, neither disagree nor agree; 4, agree somewhat; 5, agree strongly.

(see Table 9.1). Team boundary managers, by contrast, delegate these activities to the team itself—spending the greatest portion of their time managing the interfaces between the team and other stakeholders with whom the team is interdependent (e.g., other organizational units, suppliers, customers, etc.).

9.5. ACHIEVING EFFECTIVE MULTIFUNCTIONAL TEAMWORK

In this chapter we have discussed three requirements for achieving effective multifunctional teamwork: structuring the product development process to engage teamwork, designing the organizational context to support multifunctional teamwork, and effectively managing the team process (see Figure 9.1). Each of these conditions is necessary to achieve timely and efficient multifunctional integration in product development activities. Assessing the extent to which conditions in your organization meet these requirements is a useful way of diagnosing problem areas that may be hindering effective multifunctional integration. A checklist to assist you in making this evaluation is provided in Table 9.2, where each of the three requirements and related criteria are listed. By reviewing the list of criteria and indicating the extent to which these criteria are met in your organization, you should have a fairly comprehensive assessment of what you do well and what changes may be needed to achieve higher levels of effectiveness in working with multifunctional product development teams.

REFERENCES

1. Clark, K. B. and Wheelwright, S. C. *Managing New Product and Process Development*. New York: Free Press, 1993.
2. Coombs, G. and Gomez-Mejia, L. R. Cross-functional pay strategies in high-technology firms. *Compensation and Benefits Review* 15:40–48 (1994).
3. Hershock, R. J., Cowman, C. D., and Peters, D. From experience: action teams that work. *Journal of Product Innovation Management* 11:95–104 (1994).
4. Katzenbach, J. R. and Smith, D. K. The discipline of teams. *Harvard Business Review* 71(2): 111–120 (March–April 1993).
5. Leimbach, M. P. *Meeting the Corporate Challenge*. Eden Prairie, MN: Wilson Learning Corporation, 1992.
6. Nevens, T. M., Summe, G. L., and Uttal, B. Commercializing technology; what the best companies do. *Harvard Business Review*, pp. 154–163 (May–June 1990).
7. Parker, G. M. *Cross-Functional Teams: Working with Allies, Enemies and Other Strangers*. San Francisco: Jossey-Bass, 1994.
8. Pearson, P. H. The interdisciplinary team process, or the professionals Tower of Babel. *Developmental Medicine and Child Neurology*, pp. 390–395 (June 1983).
9. Shonk, J. *Team-Based Organizations: Developing a Successful Team Environment*. Homewood, IL: Business One Irwin, 1992.

Patricia J. Holahan
Stevens Institute of Technology

Patricia Holahan holds a Ph.D. in Organizational Behavior from Purdue University. Presently, she is an Assistant Professor of Management at Stevens Institute of Technology, where she teaches graduate courses in the management of technology, and organizational design and theory. Dr. Holahan also holds an appointment as a Senior Research Associate with the Stevens Alliance for Technology Management, where she conducts research on the management of multifunctional teams and advises corporate sponsors on issues related to the transfer of management technologies. Dr. Holahan also works as a consultant to several major corporations, advising them on issues related to team-based work designs, and team reward and recognition systems.

Stephen K. Markham
North Carolina State University

Stephen Markham holds a Ph.D. in Organizational Behavior from Purdue University and an MBA from the University California, Irvine. Presently he is an Assistant Professor of Management at North Carolina State University (NCSU), where he teaches course in leadership, technology management, and managerial effectiveness. Dr. Markham's research focuses on roles that people take in product/process development teams. He also conducts research on product development processes. Dr. Markham is co-director of the Technology, Education and Commercialization (TEC) program at NCSU. The TEC program seeks to commercialize technology through the cooperative efforts of university, private, and government agencies.

PART TWO

GETTING STARTED

*Most people miss opportunity when they
see it, because it comes wearing
coveralls and looks like work.*

—THOMAS EDISON, INVENTOR AND ENTREPRENEUR, 1900

Most new product ideas fail to translate into profitable products, a common cause being inadequate sales. Learning too late that potential customers are unlikely to buy a new product misuses scarce innovation and marketing resources.

New-products people learn to listen to the voice of the customer. They are aware that "top-down" market research, performed in the library or on-line, establishes only that a market exists or is emerging. "Bottom-up" research, interviewing a number of the new product's potential customers, can establish who the customer is, what the customer wants, and how the customer wants to receive it. Only then can a realistic assessment be made of the product's key features and initial sales. Only then can a determination be made of how a product aligns with a firm's capabilities and willingness to bring it to market.

10 DEVELOPING A STRATEGY AND PLAN FOR A NEW PRODUCT

Douglas G. Boike and Jeffrey L. Staley

10.1. INTRODUCTION

In launching a new product development project, the need for a comprehensive strategy and plan is clear. Consensus and clear communication are necessary. Numerous details regarding the product plan must be described. A process must be established for developing these plans.

10.2. NEED FOR STRATEGY AND PLAN

Part One of this book has provided advice on establishing the necessary foundation for new product development success. The overall corporate strategy context has been set. Segmentation of the market has been established. A portfolio of product needs has been identified. A product development process has been agreed to. Finally, a basic approach to teams and their management has been set. The details of establishing a strategy and plan for an individual new product development effort must now be addressed. This introductory chapter and subsequent chapters in Part Two explore this challenge.

10.2.1. Establishing a Consensus

One of the key objectives for establishing a formal plan and strategy for a new product project is to achieve consensus on all of the key inputs required for success. Research has repeatedly shown that poorly defined or conflicting goals and objectives drive a large portion of new product delays and failures. Figure 10.1 illustrates a competitive analysis of new product development performance, highlighting a typical result that 40 to 50 percent of product delays and failures can be attributable to poor and unclear product strategy and definition [1,4,6]. Forcing an early resolution of many confounding problems of market needs, specifications, resource requirements, schedule, and key milestones prevents significant rework and quality problems later.

10.2.2. Providing a Clear Communication and Plan of Record

As research presented in Table 10.1 illustrates, the related confounding problem facing product development is communicating clearly the needs, requirements, resources, and plans for a new product effort—in essence, internalizing the strategy [1,2,4,6]. This communication must take multiple forms, (e.g., written, verbal, electronic); however, a well-documented plan and specification must serve as the foundation. In summary, the establishment and communication of a clear plan and strategy for a new product development project is a key requisite for success.

Strategies and plans for new product projects must reflect consensus and should be communicated clearly.

10.3. KEY ELEMENTS OF A COMPREHENSIVE STRATEGY AND PLAN

A comprehensive strategy and plan must address a wide range of inputs, assumptions, plans, and resource requirements. In the following paragraphs we describe the most common elements found in new product plans. More detail on developing these critical plan elements is provided in subsequent chapters in this section.

10.3.1. Statement of Customer Needs

All successful new product development efforts must be rooted in a clear understanding of the customer needs to be addressed. Figure 10.2 summarizes the results of further research on best practices wherein "customer connection" and

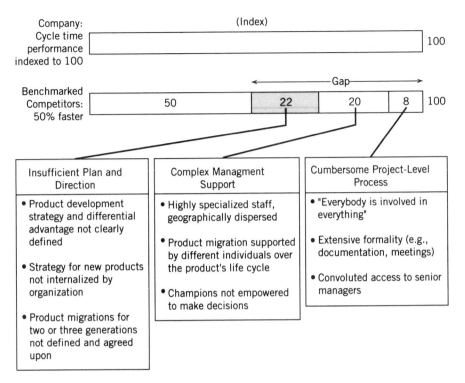

FIGURE 10.1 Drivers of new product delays and failures: typical example from competitive analysis.

TABLE 10.1 Key Attributes of Successful New Product Development: Results From a Comparative Study of Over 200 Companies (Percents)

Attribute	Evidence of Systematic Practice	
	More Successful Firms	Less Successful Firms
Clear, well-communicated strategy for new products	52	18
Team leadership and champions	48	18
Top-management access	48	27
Clear responsibility and empowerment for teams	48	32
Rewards and recognition for innovators	43	27
Skills and diversity in place	39	23
Communication (both formal and informal) networks supported	35	27

1. Use a Commonly Agreed to, Customer-Centered, and Disciplined
Approach for Executing Individual Product Development Projects

3. Set the New Product
Development Agenda,
Managing the Portfolio of
Projects, and the
Process in Aggregate

2. Cultivate a Supportive
Organization and
Infrastructure for New
Product Development

FIGURE 10.2 Best practices in new product development: further results from a comparative study of over 200 companies.

"early definition of customer value" were found to be two of the most distinguishing practices separating high-performing companies from low-performing companies [1–3]. At the onset of a new product development project, the statement of needs can be coalesced from a range of sources, including focus group research, customer advisory panels, key customer interviews, and competitive product analysis. The findings must be summarized clearly and in documented form to provide a plan of record for the entire product development team. Table 10.2 presents an example of such a statement for a common household product. As can be seen, the statement of needs must be from a uniquely customer-oriented viewpoint.

**TABLE 10.2 Example Statement of
Customer Needs for a
Better Can Opener**

- Small, compact
- Attractive, modern styling
- Solid base—difficult to tip over
- Easy to attach can and engage cutter
- Fast
- Does not spill can contents
- No sharp edges on cut
- Priced less than $25
- Easy to disassemble and clean parts
- Attractive new package
- Brand name

10.3.2. Market Conditions and Response

> Successful new product projects must be rooted in a clear understanding of customer needs.

To evaluate properly the potential success and failure of a new product development effort, an understanding of the probable market and competitive environment is required. This understanding could include many of the following factors:

Market Conditions

- Potential market size and growth
- Likely pricing
- Trends in customer needs
- Likely new product features and attributes
- Anticipated market share to be achieved

Competitive Profile

- Competitive product and service offerings
- Current and future pricing
- Current market shares
- Likely new product introductions and timing
- Market perception

This understanding is critical to the management of risk and financial return associated with a new product development effort.

> *Market conditions and response must be anticipated.*

10.3.3. Product Attributes and Specifications

Subsequent chapters in this part of the book outline numerous methods for "concepting" new products. The net result of much of this effort must be the description and specification of the new product attributes, features, and performance. This description should reflect clear connection to the customer, market, and competitive needs outlined in the preceding two sections. This description should also outline the product in sufficient detail for designers, manufacturing, and marketing team members to begin work on their respective elements of work. A common document generated at this point would be a product specification. A typical product specification might include all or some of the following elements [6]:

- *Performance:* product's primary operating characteristics
- *Features:* supplementary characteristics of a product
- *Reliability:* probability of product failing over time (e.g., mean time between failure)
- *Durability:* measure of product life (to replacement)
- *Serviceability:* ease of repair (e.g., downtime, mean time to repair)
- *Aesthetics:* the look, feel, sound, and so on, of a product
- *Packaging:* the requirements for packing, labeling, and handling
- *Perceived quality:* subjective reputation of a product, which includes aspects such as ease of use and product integrity
- *Cost:* various elements of cost such as manufacturing cost and service cost

A sample of such a specification for the common household product is shown in Table 10.3. This exhibit illustrates the more in-depth rigor required in a product specification.

> *The documentation of new product attributes, features, and specifications is an important reference for a new product project.*

10.3.4. Development Schedule and Milestones

The next level of understanding required is the agreement to a development schedule and series of milestones for the new product development effort. The proposed schedule and milestones should be based on the agreed product development process to be used. The schedule and milestones should

TABLE 10.3   Example Product Specification for a Better Can Opener

Performance
- Will open full range of U.S. market cans
- Will open can in 5 seconds or less
- Separates can top from can

Features
- Fits in two-thirds space of current generation products
- Easy-action can insertion and removal
- Captures both lid and can for easy removal
- Automatically sharpens during use

Reliability
- Estimated one miscut in 100

Durability
- All mechanical and electrical components projected to 10-year life under normal usage

Serviceability
- All critical parts can be disassembled for cleaning
- Can be serviced at company service depot in less than 15 minutes

Aesthetics
- New ergonomic styling concept

Packaging
- Box size 6- by 12-inch
- New lightweight package design and packing material
- Attractive labelling and graphics
- Industry standard bar code

Perceived quality
- Rugged design
- Quiet
- Easy-to-clean parts and stain-free finish

Cost
- Manufactured cost less than $10
- Service and warranty cost less than $1.50

be realistic based on the resources available and past performance of the development organization. At the same time, however, the schedule and milestones should reflect the competitive realities of the marketplace. Gaps between required performances and schedule and likely potential outcome should be resolved at the onset of a new program rather than at a point too late to develop contingency plans. The agreed-to development schedule and milestones should be documented in a suitable format. Traditional techniques include PERT and Gantt charts [6]. More innovative techniques include the use of software-based planning and tracking tools [5]. Later charts in this book outline the steps required in establishing a development schedule and a set of milestones.

> *Key milestones and schedules must be established*

10.3.5. Resource Requirement and Phasing

A companion element to successful new product development effort planning is the identification and provision of required resources. These resources needs must reflect the scope of work agreed to in the specification, the timing and sequence of key phase activities, and the breadth of functional skills required for success. Past history and programs may provide a suitable reference for developing these resource plans. Integration of this specific project with all other ongoing efforts must also take place to ensure that sufficient resources are in place to execute the entire portfolio of programs. The resultant resource plans must include the following elements:

- Type of resource (functional or industry area of specialty)
- Timing for availability
- Level of effort
- Expected reporting relationship

As with realistic schedules and milestones, the availability of needed resources is a crucial determinant of success in a new product development effort [1–4,6].

Plans must be established for all forms of resources required for the project.

10.3.6. Product Financials

Every successful product development effort must in the end be rooted in sound business and financial success. At the onset of a new product effort, these financials must be estimated and validated against corporate standards and funds availability. Several of the key measures that should be estimated include the following:

- Development cost (e.g., hours, capital)
- Prototype and pilot costs
- Manufacturing costs: tooling and scaleup, in addition to ongoing manufacturing cost
- Related costs (e.g., advertising, packaging, promotion)
- Pricing
- Anticipated sales (e.g., units, revenue)
- Payback measures (e.g., return on investment, profit contribution, anticipated margin)

Each company has its own measures; however, it is important that these be examined at the onset of a new product effort.

10.3.7. Key Interfaces: Both Internal and External

> *Financials must be analyzed and assessed relative to corporate measures and funds availability.*

Finally, a sound strategy and plan for a new product development effort must acknowledge and reflect all the key interfaces required for success. A sample of these internal and external interfaces include the following:

Internal Interfaces

- Research and development
- Other product programs
- Field sales and marketing organization
- International divisions
- Administrative support functions (e.g., human resources, management information systems, finance)

External Interfaces

- Key suppliers and vendors
- Distributors and sales partners
- Key customers
- Alliance and joint venture partners
- Relevant regulatory organizations

Integration of these interfaces into a sound product plan should include the nature of the interface, the performance or action required, the expected timing, and the key point of contact.

10.4. DEVELOPING THE STRATEGY AND PLAN

> *Both internal and external interfaces must be identified and confirmed.*

With an understanding of the key elements of a successful plan, it is important to anticipate the required steps to develop such a plan.

10.4.1. Key Participants

The key participants in developing a new product plan should represent all of the key functions required for success. In addition, this team should be considered the core team for the subsequent development effort. As such, most best practice companies ensure that the team consists of the following specialties:

- Sales and marketing
- Development and design
- Manufacturing
- Procurement (if significant content outsourced)
- Service (if significant value add provided by service)

A team leader must be established at the onset whose role is to facilitate, guide, and lead the team through the consensus building and documentation activities required.

10.4.2. Potential Approaches

The development of a plan for a new product development effort can be completed in a number of ways. The process chosen should reflect the needs and practices of a company, its processes and markets. The range of options include:

- *Annual or semiannual planning cycles:* a process established on a calendar or fiscal year basis
- *Market- or competitive need–driven processes:* a process that is initiated upon the identification of a market or competitive need
- *Bottom-up idea or concept-driven process:* a process that is driven by or a new product conceptualization
- *End of product life cycle:* a process that is initiated by the end of life of an existing product

Regardless of which process is used, it is important that associated processes such as financial and resource planning run in parallel to ensure that sufficient resources are made available.

The development of a plan and strategy can be one of the first responsibilities of a new product core team.

10.5. DOCUMENTING THE RESULT

As described at the onset of this chapter, an established consensus and clear communication are the key objectives sought in new product planning. Documenting the consensus for subsequent communication and reference is therefore critical.

10.5.1. Key Documents

The most commonly used document employed for this purpose is a *product plan.* This product plan can take a number of forms: either a short one- or two-page summary such as that illustrated in Table 10.4 for the common household product or a more lengthy multipage document. An alternative would be to employ the short summary document in combination with more detailed documents or references to specifications, development, and resource schedules.

10.5.2. Media Choices

Most common today are electronic forms of documentation. The choice of format should reflect tools in use currently at a company. Efforts should be made to maintain the plan in a continuously updated form, with sufficient access to all affected parties and a release control mechanism in place (e.g., Release x.y)

TABLE 10.4   Example Product Plan for a Better Can Opener

Customer needs
- Small, compact, attractive styling
- Easy-to-use, solid
- Easy to clean
- Does not spill contents
- Priced less than $25

Key product attributes
- Will open full range of U.S. cans in 5 seconds or less
- Separates and captures both can and top
- Fits in two-thirds current space
- One miscut per 100
- Ten-year life
- Fifteen-minute service time
- Ergonomic design
- Quiet
- Easy-to-clean

Product financials
- $950,000 development cost
- $350,000 tooling and capital
- $8.75 manufacturing cost
- $1.38 service cost
- 10.9% rate of return

Market and competition
- Meet competition x product at $1.50 lower suggested retail
- Gain 3% market share
- Penetrate two leading discount chains

Development schedule

	Phase	Completion date
0	Customer needs	February
I	Product concept	April
II	Product design	June
III	Prototype validation	August
IV	Manufacturing scaleup	September
V	Product release	October

Resource requirements

Person-weeks	Phase
10	Marketing/product manager
25	Design engineering
15	Computer-aided design
10	Manufacturing engineering
10	Quality and test engineering

Key interfaces
- Advertising campaign launch: U.S., September; Canada, October
- Transfer to European market in April

> *Product development plans must be fully documented and should be kept under release control.*

10.6. SUMMARY

An effective strategy and plan for a new product will address all of the key elements of detail necessary to conduct a successful project. It will be documented in both summary form with a product plan as well as in more detail through documents such as specifications, development schedules, and resource plans. The development of this plan and strategy can often be viewed as one of the first official responsibilities of a core developmental team. Well-documented and clearly communicated plans and strategies have repeatedly been found to be essential to new product success.

REFERENCES

1. Deck, M. High performance new product development. Presentation at the Conference Board Executive Forum, New York, 1994.
2. Deck, M. and Staley, J. High performance new product development. Conference Presentation at the Institute for International Research and Product Development and Management Association, Arlington, VA and London, 1995.
3. Deck, M. Why the best companies keep winning the new products race. *R&D*, pp. 4LS–5LS (November 1994).
4. Gertz, D. and Baptista, J. *Grow to Be Great.* New York: Free Press, 1995.
5. Rosenau, M. and Moran, J. *Managing the Development of New Products.* New York: Van Nostrand Reinhold, 1993.
6. Rosenthal, S. *Effective Product Design and Development.* Homewood, IL: Business One Irwin, 1992.

Douglas G. Boike
Mercer Management Consulting

Dr. Boike is a Vice President of Mercer Management Consulting and specializes in technology-intensive industries and organizations. A recognized expert in manufacturing systems, product design practice, and technology strategy, he was worked widely in the automotive, electronics, and industrial equipment industries. Prior to joining Mercer, Dr. Boike held senior positions at Booz-Allen & Hamilton and Xerox Corporation. Dr. Boike received a B.A. in physics from Kalamazoo College, a M.E. in Engineering Management from Rochester Institute of Technology, and a Ph.D. in Engineering Science from Thayer School, Dartmouth College. He is President of the Chicago Chapter of the PDMA.

Jeffrey L. Staley
Mercer Management Consulting

Mr. Staley is a Principal of Mercer Management Consulting and focuses on new product development and technology development issues in the computer, automotive, and industrial equipment industries. Mr. Staley has held senior positions at Hewlett-Packard, Digital Equipment Corporations, and Arthur D. Little. He received a B.S. and M.S. degree in mechanical engineering from Purdue University as well as an S.M. in management science from MIT's Sloan School of Management. Mr. Staley is the author of numerous articles and is a member of the AMA's R&D Council and the National Technology Transfer Council.

11 OBTAINING CUSTOMER NEEDS FOR PRODUCT DEVELOPMENT
Abbie Griffin

11.1. SHOULD YOU IGNORE CONSUMERS OR NOT?

There is great controversy in recent business publications as to whether firms should actively involve customers in the process of product development or whether customers and their input should be ignored. Those who claim that customers should be ignored argue that customers and potential product users cannot tell firms exactly what they want. Thus there is little or no use in talking to customers. Product developers on their own can best determine what products will be successful.

An alternative possibility is that product developers have been asking customers the wrong questions. We have been asking them for information which they cannot provide to us. Thus, rather than totally ignoring customers, perhaps we can improve the products we develop by changing the types of information we seek from customers to that which they can provide to us. This chapter defines the kinds of information that customers can supply to firms that will aid in producing better products and outlines three techniques for obtaining an in-depth knowledge of consumer and potential user needs.

11.1.1. Why Your Company Must Understand Consumer Needs in Depth

Products and services that don't solve peoples' problems, or don't solve them at a competitive cost, fail. Apple Computer discovered this expensively with the

153

Newton MessagePad personal digital assistant (PDA). Newton evolved out of research's technology development efforts to eliminate the keyboard and allow "hand-entry" computer inputs. Conceived as a hand-held, pen-based, electronic, digitized notepad, the Newton's function was to "capture, organize and communicate ideas and data" without requiring keyboard data entry. Potential users were not asked about the problems they have capturing, organizing, and using information prior to development. Apple management leaped to define Newton's form and features without first understanding how customers currently solved information-capturing problems and what unsolved issues remained [2]. Apple found that $800 bought a lot of pens, Post-it notes™, notepaper, calendars, and even electronic address books. Newton did not solve people's remaining needs surrounding information use in a cost-effective way. Newton sales were dismal.

The most successful product development efforts match a set of fully understood customer problems with a cost-competitive solution to those problems. Success can thus be obtained through two paths. By one path the firm first captures a complete understanding of the complex set of needs surrounding a problem for which a set of consumers would like a better solution and then they develop a product or service that solves the set of problems. Alternatively, firms can develop products that do new things or have new features and then see if they solve enough of a set of problems for people to buy at the price the firm can afford to charge. Apple developed Newton using the second path.

> *The most successful new products match a set of fully understood customer problems with a cost-competitive solution to those problems.*

On the one hand, by ignoring customers, firms risk wasting money developing solutions to problems that do not exist, or for which potential consumers already have an adequate solution, given the cost. On the other hand, interacting with and talking to customers truly can be misleading if we ask them for information which they inherently are not able to provide.

11.1.2. Information Consumers Cannot Provide

Consumers cannot tell firms exactly what products to develop. Consumers cannot provide the details of exactly what the future blockbuster product for your firm looks like, the features it should have, or the technologies it should contain. If you find someone who can—hire that person! They are doing the job your development team should be doing. That is, they have the technical capability to translate their needs into yet-to-be-developed technologies and forecast the features that will advantageously deliver those needs some number of years in the future.

Consumers also cannot provide reliable information about anything with which they are not personally familiar or have experienced. By definition, consumers are not familiar with a new product a firm may be thinking of developing and will not provide reliable information when asked to react to a concept or prototype. They will, of course, provide answers to questions (most people want very much to be helpful). In reacting to product concepts without experiencing them, some consumers may try to imagine how they think they really will feel. Others will just tell us what they think we want to hear. When we ask them to tell us what someone else wants or needs, or how they will react to something, consumers will freely hypothesize. However, information derived from unknowledgeable consumers is at best inaccurate and at worst is an irrelevant fantasy. To act upon it is extremely risky.

11.1.3. Information Consumers Can Provide

Consumers can provide reliable information about the things with which they are familiar and knowledgeable or which they directly have experienced. A consumer can provide the subset of the needs information that is relevant to them in an overall area of consumer problems. They can provide the problems and needs *they* have. They can indicate the products and features they currently use to meet their needs, where these products fall short of solving their problems and, where they excel. The only way that a full set of consumer needs for a product area can be obtained is by coming to understand a number of consumers, each of whom contributes a piece of the needs information.

11.2. BASIC PRINCIPLES FOR OBTAINING CONSUMER NEEDS

Current customers and potential users can provide reliable information about the problems and needs they experience, those that are relevant to them. For each person, this is a subset of the full set of information needed for effective product development.

The objective of this chapter is to define and present techniques for obtaining the qualitative consumer needs necessary to start product development. These needs can be used for quantitative market research later in the project (see Chapters 14 and 15). More important, this information provides the detailed understanding of the functional nuances to the development team that will dictate the engineering trade-offs they make during product development. The techniques presented focus on producing rich, detailed, context-specific information and ensuring that this information is transferred completely to those who need it, the development team.

11.2.1. Defining Consumer Needs

Consumer needs are the problems that a product or service solves and the functions it performs. They describe what products let you do, not how they let you do it. For example, many businesspeople have a need to "be able to do any work I want, wherever I am."

Features deliver the solutions to peoples' problems. Features are the ways in which products function. A portable PC delivers a partial solution to being able to work wherever I want. So does taking a secretary and all one's paper files on a trip, but although this was a preferred solution for some in past eras, this is not a particularly feasible solution today.

Consumers have general problems for which they need a solution and which relate to the overall product function. For example, a portable PC must "let me see what I'm working on as I am working." The current feature delivering the solution to this need is a screen—some are active matrix, some passive matrix, and some are backlit.

Consumers also have very specific needs or aspects of the overall function that a successful product must also solve. Most detailed needs are specific to the particular contexts in which the product is used. Portable PCs are used in many different venues. Some of the detailed needs include "letting me see what I'm working on" "in my office," "in a darkened airplane," "in the artificial light of the airport waiting lounge," and my personal favorite "in bright sunlight next to the hotel pool." Different kinds of screens deliver better against each of these detailed needs.

Consumer problems are generally very complex, and frequently different needs conflict. At the same time I want to be able to see my work in all those different venues, I also want to be able to shove the device into my briefcase so that I can easily carry it with me wherever I go. Therefore, providing multiple screens is not a useful solution for me. The development team thus needs to have a good understanding of the relative importance of all the contexts and ways in which their products will be used, misused, and abused to select the most appropriate feature sets for their product. It is first uncovering and understanding and then delivering against these detailed needs that differentiates between product successes and failures.

No product is perfect. Each product is a compromise, delivering only partially against a complex set of consumer needs for any problem area. Products consist of sets of features that deliver extremely well against some needs, adequately against others, and do not deliver against others at all. As new technologies and features are developed by different firms, product compromises shift across the set of consumer needs. Because of both technology and competitor evolution, consumer needs tend to be far more stable than features. Providing product development teams with a rich understanding of the complex and detailed consumer needs and problems prepares them to select the best technology and feature set compromises in the future to continue delivering successful products for the firm.

11.2.2. From Whom to Obtain Needs

> *Understanding features leads to today's dominant products; understanding needs leads to tomorrow's dominant products.*

Only the people involved with the details of how a problem affects day to day—the way they perform their job or live their life—can provide you with their needs. And only the people who interact with, use, or are affected by the operating of a particular product can provide you with the details of how that product excels at and fails to solve their problems. A purchasing agent cannot identify the logistical and physical problems that a grocery clerk has operating a point-of-sales scanner system. Nor can they help you understand the difficulty of the procedure the general manager of the grocery store must go through to produce a daily income statement or rectify the store's inventory position at the end of the month with the software associated with the scanner system. In the same vein, a mother cannot provide adequate information about the athletic support her son needs for playing baseball, nor can she even provide concrete details about the feminine hygiene needs of her newly adolescent daughter. The details of consumer needs and problems must be gathered directly from the people who have them.

Special Considerations in Business-to-Business Markets

Gathering detailed information generally is more difficult in business-to-business markets because most products affect multiple groups of people. Because no one can provide accurate information about something they don't actually experience, several different groups must be investigated to obtain complete information about the detailed issues surrounding a function [3]. Grocery store general managers only partially understand the consumer needs of their clerks. They have general information, but not the details that will help firms differentiate between acceptable and superior products. The need to investigate multiple groups' needs increases the cost and effort associated with obtaining good, complete product development market research for business-to-business markets.

11.3. TECHNIQUES FOR DEEPLY UNDERSTANDING CONSUMER NEEDS

Firms can obtain detailed understanding of customer needs through three techniques (see Table 11.1);

TABLE 11.1   Summary of Needs Obtaining Techniques

Needs Uncovering Technique	Information Obtained	Major Benefits	Major Drawbacks
Be a user	Tacit knowledge Feature trade-off impacts on product function	Knowledge depth Generates irrefutable belief in identified needs	Hard to transfer knowledge to others Time and expense
Watch users critically	Process knowledge Tacit knowledge	Learn customer language Find unarticulated needs	Time and expense Must translate observations to words
Interview users for needs	Large volumes of details Context-specific needs	Speed of information collection Information breadth	Cannot elicit reliable tacit and process needs "Marketing's job"

- Be an involved consumer with those needs and problems.
- Critically observe and live with consumers who have those needs.
- Talk to consumers with needs.

> *Different techniques for understanding needs produce different kinds of information. No one technique is sufficient to produce a full understanding of customer and potential user needs.*

11.3.1. Be an Involved Consumer of Your Own and Competitor's Goods and Services

What to Do and Keys to Success

An enormous amount of consumer needs knowledge and understanding can be gained by putting every development team member in situations where they are actively involved consumers with the problems your firm is trying to solve. Also, when your firm already has a product commercialized in a particular functional area, encourage team members to use your products routinely and all competitive products in "everyday" as well as "extraordinary" situations.

At one company both men and women work on the product development team for a feminine hygiene pad product. Teams at this company are known for the lengths to which they go to try to fully understand and identify with consumer problems. The entire team personally tests the group's and competitors' current and new products. Male team members have worn pads underneath armpits and in shoes to test chafing and smell-elimination characteristics. They have also worn these pads in the anatomically appropriate area, with and without having doused the pads with liquid to simulate various normal-use conditions.

Team members at another firm in the point-of-sales scanner system market work full shifts as checkout clerks several days a year in different kinds of local stores. Stores readily agree to assign the development people shifts because they do not have to compensate them and because they hope to get improved products. By working full shifts, development personnel learn about shift startup and close-out, the effects of different payment modes, breakage, and fatigue, and are exposed to a random day's worth of the strange things that can happen in a checkout line that can affect the operator and the system. Operating a system in a laboratory setting just does not provide the same breadth of interaction experience.

While routine continual personal gathering of consumer information is not feasible for all product areas, with a little imagination it is possible to do far more than many firms encourage development teams to do.

What Kind of Information Is Obtained

Having employees become actively involved consumers is the best way, sometimes the only way, to transfer "tacit" information into the product development team. Tacit information is knowledge someone has but cannot or does not articulate. It is the intuitive aspect of the knowledge a person has about their needs. Becoming a routine customer for all the various products in the category may also be the most efficient way to drive home to development teams the trade-offs firms have made in their products and the effects trade-off decisions have had on product function.

GM misses out on inexpensively imbuing employees with a great deal of competitive and daily ownership information by some of its policies. GM requires that any employee traveling on business for the firm and renting a car must rent a GM car. Development team members miss out on great opportunities to see inexpensively how other firms' design differences affect performance. In addition, GM provides managers with new cars and then assumes responsibility for maintaining those cars. Because of this policy, senior people at GM may lose an appreciation for how having to maintain a car over time causes problems for consumers.

Codicils

Although this is a good technique to bring rich data into the product development team, it is only one of several techniques that should be used, because of several inherent problems:

- The firm must learn how to transfer one person's experience and knowledge to others. A means of codifying experiences must be found.

- If experiences are not well documented, retaining personal knowledge becomes a critical problem if in your organization team members frequently shift product areas or end markets or leave the firm.
- Project management must take steps to ensure that individuals do not think that their own needs are representative of the market. They will differ from the "average" consumer in unexpected ways.
- Encouraging team members to be a customer takes time, money, and personal effort. Obtaining cooperation from team members requires management support and example.

> *By actively using products, developers are exposed to needs that are "tacit" and difficult to extract verbally from customers.*

11.3.2. Critically Observe and Live with Consumers

What to Do

Product developers who cannot become consumers may be able to live with their customers, observing and questioning them as they solve a set of consumer problems. Developers of new medical devices for doctors usually cannot act as doctors and personally test devices in patient situations. However, they can observe operations, even videotape them, and then debrief doctors about what happened and why they took particular actions later, with or without viewing the videotape simultaneously.

Sometimes observation of consumers in their natural settings leads directly to new products or features [4]. Development team members at Chrysler observed that many pickup truck owners had built holders for 32-ounce drinks into their cabs, so the 1995 Ram truck comes with cupholders appropriate for 32-ounce drinks. In other instances, observation only points out the problem, and the team must still determine whether the problem is specific to that person or applies across the entire target market, and if so, develop an appropriate solution. Another Chrysler engineer had watched the difficulty his petite wife had wrestling children's car seats around the family minivan. It took him several years to convince the firm that his leap to a solution—integrating children's car seats into the car's seating system—would solve a major problem for a large number of consumers. It did.

Keys to Success

Critical observation, rather than just casual viewing, is a major key to obtaining information by watching consumers. Critical observation involves questioning why someone is performing each action rather than just accepting what they are doing.

The best results are achieved when team members spend significant time with enough different consumers to be exposed to the full breadth of problems that people encounter. They must spend enough time observing consumers to uncover both "normal" and "abnormal" operating conditions. In addition, using team members from different functions is important because people with different training and expertise "see" and pay attention to different things.

What Kind of Information Is Obtained

Living with consumers is an effective way to identify tacit information and learn consumer language. It is also the most effective means for gathering work-flow or process-related information. These consumer needs are particularly important for firms marketing products to other firms. Products and services they develop must fit into the work flows of those firms, which means that the work flows must be understood fully. Even when questioned in detail, people frequently forget steps in a process or skip over them. Although forgotten or unimportant to the consumer, these steps may be crucial to product design trade-offs.

Codicils

Observing and living with consumers is not especially efficient. Its inherent problems:

> **When new products must fit into work flows or customer processes, critically observing customers is crucial to effective development.**

- Gathering information broadly requires significant team member time and expense. Actions unfold slowly in real time.
- Observation or even unobtrusive videotaping may change people's behavior such that "natural" actions are not captured.
- The team again has to turn actions into words, reliably capturing consumer needs.

11.3.3. Talk to Consumers to Get Needs Information

What to Do

By talking to customers, development teams can gather consumer needs relatively faster and more efficiently than by emulating or observing consumers. A structured, in-depth probing, one-on-one, situational interview technique called voice of the customer (VOC) can uncover both general and more detailed needs of consumers [1,5]. This method differs significantly from standard focus group qualitative techniques in the way questions are asked. Rather than asking consumers "What do you want" directly (as happens in focus groups), VOC uses an indirect method of discovering wants and needs by leading consumers through the ways they currently find and use products and services to fulfill particular needs.

VOC interviews investigate needs from a functional rather than a product-based point of view. For example, one study asked consumers about the various ways they transported food they had prepared at home to another place and stored it for some period of time before later consuming it. This is the general function that picnic baskets, coolers, and ice chests fulfill. Asking about the function rather than a product yields information about many different and unexpected products that consumers use to perform this function, including knapsacks, luggage, and grocery store bags with handles. Detailed probing draws out the specific features, drawbacks, and benefits of each product. Most important is delving into why various features of the products are good and bad. What problem does each of these features solve, and at the same time, does a particular feature cause any other problems? Probing the why uncovers the needs.

One advantage of interviewing is that many different use situations can be investigated in a short period of time, including a range of both "normal" and "abnormal" situations. Each different use situation provides information about additional dimensions of functional performance that a consumer expects. A good way to get started is to ask each consumer to tell about the last time they used a product that fulfilled the function. The food transporter study began: "Please tell me about the most recent time you prepared food in your home, to be shared by you and others, then took the food outside your home and ate it somewhere else later." By asking consumers to relate what they did, why they did that, what worked well and did not work well about what they did, both detailed and general consumer needs are obtained indirectly.

After a consumer relates his or her most recent experience, the consumer is asked about the specifics of how they fulfilled the function in a series of other potential use situations. These use situations are constructed by the team to attempt to cover all the performance dimensions within which consumers will expect the product to function. For example, consumers were asked about the last time they took food with them:

- On a car trip
- To a football or baseball game
- On a bike trip
- Canoeing or fishing
- To the beach

- On a romantic picnic
- Hiking or backpacking

They were also asked to relate the most disastrous and marvelous times they ever took food with them. Although no consumer had experienced all situations, the food transporting and storing needs resulting from each situation were fully uncovered by the time 20 people had been interviewed [1].

Keys to Success

Although VOC is not difficult, it approaches gathering needs differently than do traditional focus groups or other qualitative market

> *Buried in the stories that consumers relate about specific use instances are the nuggets of detailed needs which a superior product must deliver.*

rch techniques. It results in a much larger list of far more detailed and context- or situation-specific consumer needs, because the objective is to obtain a level of detail that enables teams to make engineering trade-offs during product development. There are several keys to being successful in obtaining the voice of the consumer.

It is critical to ask consumers about functions (what they want to do), not features (how it is done), because only by understanding functional needs can teams make the appropriate trade-offs in technologies and features as they become feasible in the future. It is continual probing as to "why" something is wanted or works well that gets to underlying needs.

A second key is that the voice of the consumer only covers reality. If someone has never been on a romantic picnic, they cannot be asked about what they would like in this situation because what they would relate is fantasy.

The final key to success is to ask detailed questions about specific use instances. General questions produce general needs. General needs are not as useful in designing products as are the details of problems. Consumers are very capable of providing an excruciating level of detail when they are asked to relate the story of specific situations that occurred in the last year.

What Kind of Information Is Obtained

Both the details of consumer problems as well as the more general functional needs are obtained with VOC. Through indirect questioning, consumer needs that relate to technical design aspects can be obtained, even from nontechnical consumers. For example, by relating how their car behaves in various driving situations (flooring the accelerator at a stop sign, traveling at city speeds around 35 mph, and traveling at interstate speeds), senior citizens can provide information that determines the gear ratios governing the speeds at which an automatic transmission shifts gears, even though they may have no idea how their transmission works.

Codicils

- The development team obtains a better understanding of a full set of detailed needs if the team interviews consumers rather than outsourcing it to a market research group.
- Some consumers are completely inarticulate. Getting conversation out of them is like pulling teeth. It always seems that one of the first two consumers the team interviews will be inarticulate.
- Extreme care must be taken to maintain the words of the consumer and not immediately translate one problem into a solution before understanding the full set of needs.
- Tacit and process-related needs may not be complete.

11.4. PRACTICAL ASPECTS OF GATHERING CONSUMER NEEDS

Regardless of which technique is used to gather consumer needs, the development team will be interacting with consumers, which always involves some risk. By structuring and planning the interactions carefully, firms can increase the probability that both the team and consumer will benefit. This will increase the likelihood that a particular consumer will agree to work with the firm in the future.

11.4.1. How Best to Work with Consumers

The most basic principle behind working with consumers is that they should be involved only so that the firm can learn from them. If they are involved for any other reason, say to provide an excuse to delay decisions about a project, the firm is probably wasting its money. If product features are defined first, consumer needs gathered to "prove" they have specified the "right" product, they are also wasting money. Gathering customer needs makes sense only if the task is completed before the product is specified.

Consumers will be most willing to interact with the development team if they see how they can benefit. For most household markets, that generally means that consumers receive money for interviews or observation periods. Development teams investigating business-to-business markets may find that they can provide benefit to consumers by helping them gain an understanding of their own end customers. Gathering customer needs proceeds more smoothly when the interaction becomes a two-way conversation rather than a grilling.

Most firms have a portfolio of products that they have already commercialized. If the product development team collects consumer needs themselves rather than contracting with a market research firm to gather the data anonymously, most or all of the consumers interviewed will be familiar with at least some of their current product line. Some consumers, especially in business-to-business markets, may spend the first 10 to 15 minutes of an interview venting their anger and frustration at current products. The team needs to be careful not to get defensive during this tirade but to listen to what the consumers say and try to find out why these items bother them. Once consumers understand that the team is talking to them to try to serve them better in the future by developing better products, and once they have vented their immediate anger they generally calm down and gladly answer questions.

11.4.2. Pitfalls to Avoid When Interacting with Consumers

There are several pitfalls to avoid when gathering information from consumers. The first is that the team is not there to sell anything to the consumer, even if a salesperson is on the interview team. They are strictly on a fact-finding mission. Selling will both use up the limited time you can schedule with each consumer and erode their willingness to interact.

The second pitfall to avoid is not talking to enough consumers to obtain a complete set of needs. Only observing one firm's business processes or only substituting your firm's people as surrogates for actual consumers or only interviewing one consumer is almost more dangerous as not interacting with any consumers. No one consumer provides a full set of consumer needs for any product area. Research has demonstrated that extensive interaction with about 20 consumers is required to obtain about 90 percent of consumer needs [1].

Finally, several steps must be taken to ensure that the results the team has obtained are used. Information that does not affect the product development effort has wasted the time and energy of the team as well as the firm's money. Results are more likely to be used when the information users were involved in the data gathering. Both technical specialists and managers find the data more believable if they assisted in collecting the information. Data that are in a usable form are also more likely to be used in the development. Data that are buried in a report are less likely to be used than those which are pasted all over the walls of the development area. Reminders of what was learned can never hurt.

11.5. SUMMARY

No one technique will provide easily all the consumer needs that product development seeks. Tacit needs are best conveyed by being a consumer. Process-related needs are best identified by critical observation of consumers. In-depth interviewing is the most efficient means to obtain masses of detailed needs, but may not provide the tacit and process-related information. Unfortunately, few projects can afford the time and expense of fully implementing all these processes. When personnel are fairly stable, management may be able to implement an ongoing customer-need-generating process which works to provide product developers continuously with consumer interactions. Otherwise, it is best for development teams to use the most appropriate consumer-need-generating technique(s), given the informational requirements, budget, and time frame for their project.

REFERENCES

1. Griffin, Abbie and Hauser, John R. The voice of the customer. *Marketing Science* 12(1):1–27 (1993).
2. Kounalakis, Markos. *Defying Gravity: The Making of Newton.* Hillsboro, OR: Beyond Words Publishing, 1993.
3. MacQuarrie, Edward F. The customer visit: qualitative research for business-to-business marketers. *Marketing Research*, pp. 15–28 (March 1991).
4. Urban, Glen L. and von Hippel, Eric. Lead user analyses for the development of new industrial products. *Management Science* 34:569–582 (1988).
5. Zaltman, Gerald and Higgie, Robin A. Seeing the voice of the customer: the Zaltman elicitation technique. *Working Paper 93-114.* Cambridge, MA: Marketing Science Institute, 1993.

Abbie Griffin
University of Chicago, GSB

Dr. Griffin is an Associate Professor with a joint appointment in the Marketing and Operations Management departments. Her research focuses on measuring and improving the process of new product development, including the marketing techniques associated with developing new products. She has published articles on product development in Marketing Science, Sloan Management Review, *and the* Journal of Product Innovation Management. *Prior to becoming an academic, she worked in product development at Corning Glass Works, was a consultant with Booz, Allen and Hamilton and started her career as an engineer at Polaroid Corporation. Her personal background includes a passion for quilting.*

12 TECHNIQUES AND TOOLS TO GENERATE BREAKTHROUGH NEW PRODUCT IDEAS

Gerald Haman

12.1. INTRODUCTION

If you want to develop a breakthrough new product, you first need to generate a high volume of creative ideas. That was the strategy advertising executive Alex Osborn used when he first developed the brainstorming technique in 1941. Since then, a wide array of techniques and tools have been designed to generate new product ideas. These new resources have emerged from creativity and innovation training that, according to *Training* magazine's annual surveys [3], grew about 1000 percent during the past decade. A key reason for this training growth has been a need for creative ideas to fill the new-products pipeline. That pipeline can be filled by using techniques and tools to open the faucets that control people's imagination. Consider this chapter to be a quick training on creative idea generation. First, you will be introduced to the advantages of using techniques and tools. Second, you will learn techniques and tools (including computer software) to expand and focus the creative minds of you and others. Experience has shown that these methods can be used by individuals and groups in all phases of the new product development process from strategy development to implementation planning.

12.2. ADVANTAGES OF TECHNIQUES AND TOOLS

Why should you use techniques and tools in idea generation? Because of benefits gained by exercising your imagination in the following ways:

Think "Outside of the Box"

Breakthrough new products result from thinking "outside of the box" and searching through your mind and other people's heads for new insights. Techniques and tools help you think outside the box to make new and interesting connections and help you think creatively.

Work Through the New 3Rs

Years ago, the American educational system promoted the 3 Rs (reading, writing, and arithmetic). When it comes to generating new product ideas, there is another set of 3 Rs—record, recall, and reconstruct. Breakthrough new product ideas occur when you work through the new 3 Rs, as shown in Figure 12.1. The 3 Rs are the fundamental stages most creative minds go through when generating new product ideas. Think of your brain as a knowledge bank where you can fill it with deposits of new product ideas. Working through the 3 Rs is like managing a bank account to maximize your return on ideas (ROI). The first R, record, involves making deposits of potential product ideas in the knowledge bank. The second R, recall, is the stage when you make "withdrawals" from your bank. Your ability to recall those ideas depends on your memory and skill in recording during the first stage. Reconstruct, the third R, involves taking the ideas that you recalled or withdrew in stage 2 and reconstructing or reinvesting them in new combinations, configurations, or formulations. It is during this third reconstruction stage where you "yield the dividends" of the ideas in your knowledge bank and experience a high ROI. In essence, most techniques and tools, when used properly, can help develop new product ideas by facilitating your ability to record, recall, and reconstruct ideas.

Move Through the M—Curve

After participating in hundreds of brainstorming sessions, it was evident that one could visually diagram the typical volume of ideas that a group generated over

FIGURE 12.1 The new 3Rs: record, recall & reconstruct.

time. The diagram for most sessions resembled the two arches from the letter M, like the Golden Arches from McDonald's restaurants. The M—Curve is a illustration of the volume of ideas generated over a given amount of time. Figure 12.2 shows the volume of ideas on the vertical axis and the amount of time it takes to generate those ideas on the horizontal axis. Research showed that most of the ideas generating during arch 1 were old ideas, while the new ideas occurred in arch 2. Most important, the breakthrough ideas typically occurred near the end of arch 2, at the end of the session. This does not mean you can skip arch 1 and go to arch 2. The ideas generated during arch 1 are important because they provide the basis to "reconstruct" new ideas in arch 2. Most people stop after arch 1 because they run out of time or are frustrated with generating just "old" ideas they may have thought about before. To maximize your productivity while in arch 1, it is helpful to use a traditional technique such as brainstorming to help you "record" and "recall" many of the old ideas. As time moves on and you move onto arch 2, it is useful to use new tools and techniques to facilitate thinking about the old ideas in new ways.

To develop breakthrough new product ideas, you should move through both arches of the M-Curve's golden arches. The obvious question is: How do you do it? There are two parts to answer. First, you must select an effective combination of techniques and tools described in this chapter. Second, you should allow sufficient time to move through arches 1 and 2. Most people greatly underestimate how much time they should spend on a session.

Think on the Verge of Possibilities

Breakthrough new product ideas are the result of thinking on the edge or the "verge" of new possibilities. Effective idea generation includes devoting time to both divergent and convergent thinking. Divergent thinking occurs when you expand thinking to record and recall a high volume of new or interesting ideas.

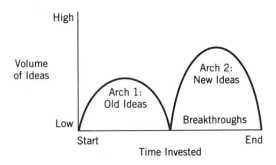

FIGURE 12.2 The M-curve of idea generation (the golden arches).

This is typically followed by convergent thinking, which focuses thinking to evaluate and prioritize ideas. In other words, divergent thinking helps fill the new-products pipeline with potential concepts, while convergent thinking helps you funnel the high volume of ideas into a small group or single idea that could yield a significant ROI.

12.3. DIVERGENT TECHNIQUES

Divergent thinking is often associated with the most common idea generation technique, brainstorming. The following guidelines should be considered when leading brainstorming sessions or any of the more than 100 possible techniques [2, pp. 132–207].

Divergent thinking guidelines for brainstorming include: (1) avoid judging or evaluating ideas; (2) record a high volume of ideas; (3) build on other ideas; and (4) seek new and interesting combinations of ideas.

12.3.1. Idea Links

Idea Links™ is a technique that provides methods for producing breakthrough and out-of-the-box ideas. Your goal is to go out on the verge or edge of possibilities, beyond brainstorming, and generate ideas by linking thoughts with seemingly unrelated stimuli such as key words. Idea Links categorize such stimulating key words as people, places, or things. Ideas Link directions are as follows:

1. Define your problem as a question. *Example*: In what ways might you develop a new cereal product that appeals to children?
2. Select an Idea Link word or phrase from the lists of people, places, or things. Table 12.1 provides a brief list of potential Idea Link words and phrases. You may add your own items to the lists by recalling people, places, and things that have plenty of unique and interesting connections. *Example*: Select Michael Jordan from the Idea Link People list.
3. Record a list of ideas associated (Link Connection) with the selected Idea Link. Set a quota to encourage you to generate a high quantity and wide variety of associations. *Example*: When considering Michael Jordan, you might think of basketball, Olympics, Dream Team, Chicago, flying, Nike shoes.
4. Choose one Link Connection and brainstorm ideas about its potential relationships to the problem defined as a question. *Example*: Basketball may

Table 12.1   Idea Links™: People, Places, and Things

People	Places	Things
1. Abraham Lincoln	Buckingham Palace	Aspirin
2. Albert Einstein	Disney World	Automobile
3. Andy Warhol	Egyptian pyramids	Baseball
4. Bill Clinton	Eiffel Tower	Candle
5. Bill Gates	Empire State Building	Chopsticks
6. Cleopatra	Gas station	Clock
7. David Letterman	Grand Canyon	Color crayon
8. Elizabeth Taylor	Great Wall of China	Compact disk
9. Elvis Presley	Hawaii	Flower
10. Georgia O'Keefe	Hollywood	Hamburger
11. Helen Keller	Hospital	Hammer
12. Hulk Hogan	Las Vegas strip	Light bulb
13. Jesse Jackson	Moscow	Map
14. Joe DiMaggio	Niagara Falls	Money
15. Madame Curie	North Dakota	Paint brush
16. Madonna	Oceans	Pencil
17. Mahatma Gandhi	Outer space	Phonebook
18. Marilyn Monroe	Parthenon	Photograph
19. Michael Jackson	Restaurants	Pizza
20. Michael Jordan	Rocky Mountains	Poker chip
21. O.J. Simpson	Rome	Shoe
22. Oprah Winfrey	Sistine Chapel	Sponge
23. Princess Diana	The Smithsonian	Telephone
24. Robin Hood	Tokyo	Television
25. Thomas Edison	Washington, D.C.	Toilet paper

prompt you to think of round balls and a round-rimmed hoop, which triggers the idea of a cereal shaped like basketball rims with fruit-flavored ball-shaped nuggets.

5. Repeat step 4 until time runs out or you have discussed all the Link Connection's relationships to the problem. *Example*: Flying may make you think of rocketing to outer space and seeing the planets and stars, which triggers the idea of a cereal called Galaxy that is shaped like planets and stars and has out-of-this-world flavors.

12.3.2. Idea Exchange

The Idea Exchange™, sometimes called Brainwriting, provides a structure for building on different ideas in a quiet, nonjudgmental setting that encourages reflection. During this technique, participants do not talk to each other but instead, record their ideas on blank paper. Directions are as follows:

1. Distribute a blank paper to each person and put an extra sheet in the middle of a table or area.

2. Review the brainstorming and divergent thinking guidelines (described earlier in this article).

3. Write the problem or a question on top of the blank sheet.

4. Record three ideas and then exchange it for another paper in the middle of the table.

5. Review the ideas recorded by other people on the worksheet and then add three more new ideas that come to mind or that were prompted by other people's ideas.

6. Repeat steps 4 and 5 until the time is up or the sheets are filled with ideas.

The Idea Exchange is a great alternative to traditional brainstorming because it gives people who are uncomfortable talking in front of a group an avenue to share their ideas and helps them avoid being intimidated by highly creative people who dominate the discussions. Additionally, the flow of ideas is not inhibited by the facilitator's ability to record ideas, as the ideas are already recorded on the individual papers, making it easier to compile the ideas in a follow-up report.

12.4. CONVERGENT TECHNIQUES

After diverging, convergent thinking is needed to evaluate and prioritize ideas. This requires a more analytical, logical, and left-brained approach, which can be a big adjustment after the right-brained divergent thinking. Whereas divergent thinking involved going "outside of the box," convergent thinking often involves going back "inside" the box to analyze ideas and make decisions. Convergent thinking techniques involve organizing thoughts in ways that help you compare and evaluate ideas. In this section you will learn how to use stoplight voting, thought organizers, and a matrix converger to foster convergent thinking.

> *Guidelines for convergent techniques include: (1) identify positive aspects of ideas first; (2) follow a deliberate system or plan for evaluation; (3) consider unique and interesting ideas; and (4) keep on track.*

12.4.1. Stoplight Voting

Stoplight voting fosters convergent thinking by giving participants a quick method for voting on their preferences. The following steps will help you apply this technique:

1. Display a list of previously generated ideas on wall or flip charts.
2. Distribute green self-adhesive dots (one dot for every 10 ideas that are listed) to each participant.
3. Evaluate ideas by having participants stick green dots next to the ideas they prefer. Green dots will be used to mark ideas they want to "go" forward with and pursue. If they strongly support an idea, they can put several or all of their green dots next to it.
4. Count the total number of votes for each idea. Ideas with the highest number of green "go" dots warrant further discussion and development.

Option: Distribute one or more "red" dots to each participate. Give them the option to put a red dot next to ideas that they want to "stop" or that they do not support.

12.4.2. Thought Organizers

Thought organizers are tools to help you categorize information about your ideas into groups that can be more easily compared or evaluated. Thought organizers are based on acronyms called SWOT, ALOU, and LCO:

SWOT

- Strengths
- Weaknesses
- Opportunities
- Threats

ALOU

- Advantages
- Limitations
- Opportunities
- Unique features

LCO

- Likes
- Concerns
- Opportunities

Directions for using thought organizers as follows:

1. Create a list of ideas to be considered.
2. Draw lines to create four quadrants on a blank paper or flip chart. Select a thought organizer (SWOT, ALOU, or LCO) and write the categories (i.e, strengths, weaknesses, etc.) in each quadrant (LCO needs will use only three).
3. Record one idea from the list at the top of paper or flip chart and record the reactions to each category word in the related quadrant.
4. Repeat step 3 (one page or chart per idea) until your time is up or all of the stimulus have been used and the ideas have all been recorded.
5. Compare the responses for each idea and then rank the ideas based on analysis.
6. Discuss output with group to ensure that the technique generated results that they find accurate.

12.4.3. Matrix Converger

One of the most efficient ways to converge is to use a matrix converger that allows you to compare ideas according to selected criteria. Convergent thinking requires analytical left-brained methods that are sometimes quantitative or numerical. A matrix helps you synthesize data into key concepts with numbered ratings. Figure 12.3 is an example of a matrix converger that is an ideal tool for synthesizing large amounts of information into one document.

Follow these directions when using a matrix converger:

1. Generate and prioritize a list of evaluation criteria.
2. Create a list of ideas to be considered.
3. Record criteria on the upper section of each column in the matrix.
4. List potential ideas on left areas of the rows.
5. Rate each idea by assigning points for each criteria on a scale of 0 to 5 (0, poor; 5, excellent).
6. Total the points for each idea.
7. Prioritize or rank the ideas based on scores.

12.5. COMPUTER TOOLS: IDEA GENERATION SOFTWARE

The computer revolution has affected the idea generation process. Over a dozen software programs [1, pp. 180–226] have been developed during the past decade

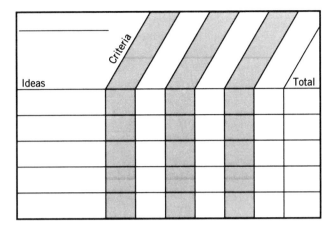

FIGURE 12.3 Matrix converger.

and have brought us into the age of computer-enhanced creativity. Researchers have been able to computerize the creative process and speed up the new product development process. This software will help you record, recall, and reconstruct ideas that are stored in your brain's bank of knowledge. Two of the most effective programs are IdeaFisher and MindLink Problem Solver.

12.5.1. IdeaFisher

The IdeaFisher was developed by Marsh Fisher, a founder of Century 21 Real Estate. IdeaFisher contains over 700,000 ideas and 6000 questions that are ideal for people who do not have access to the ideas of others. You simply type an idea or concept into the IdeaBank and it will generate up to several hundred associations. The Question Bank has several modules that are specifically designed for developing ideas for new or improved products, names, advertisements, and promotional materials. IdeaFisher has become a secret weapon for many new product consultants. There are several versions of the software, including IdeaFisher Pro and the Writer's Edge.

12.5.2. MindLink Problem Solver

MindLink is based on the popular new product development techniques pioneered by Synectics. Special exercises help you overcome mental blocks by using thought-provoking graphics, literature, humor, and word associations. The latest version includes the Thought Warehouse for creating a database of your new product ideas. MindLink's Guided Problem Solving section makes it easy for you to work through a proven method used in new product development. You can even exercise your creative brain by using the "Gym" for a mental workout.

12.6. SUMMARY

The techniques and tools described in this chapter can help you fill your new-products pipeline with creative ideas. They were designed to help you think "outside of the box" and be more effective at recording, recalling, and reconstructing ideas. By using divergent techniques and allowing enough time to move through the second arch of the M-curve, you can fill that pipeline by generating a high volume of ideas. Then use the convergent techniques and you will be more likely to end up with at least one breakthrough new product idea.

You have a golden opportunity to learn more. This chapter introduced just a few techniques and tools from a potential selection of hundreds of different options. Invest the time to learn more about creativity and innovation by reading a books or articles, listening to tapes, and attending training seminars. Your investment in learning about creative thinking will yield a significant return on ideas and ensure a continuous flow of successful new products.

REFERENCES

1. Parnes, S. *Sourcebook for Creative Problem Solving*. Buffalo, NY: Creative Education Foundation Press, 1992.
2. VanGundy, A. *Idea Power*. New York: Amacom, 1992.
3. Zemke, R. Annual training industry survey. *Training*, Lakewood Publications, Minneapolis, MN, October editions from 1985 to 1995.

Gerald Haman
Creative Solutions International

Gerald Haman is president of Chicago-based Creative Solutions International (CSI). Prior to founding CSI, worked for Procter & Gamble and Arthur Andersen. Haman's diverse background also includes experience as a university instructor, award-winning inventor, and concert producer for Grammy award-winning musicians. He has created solutions and resources that have been used by customers in over 100 Fortune 500 corporations and in 17 countries. Haman's creativity tools and expertise have been recognized in over 50 publications including Fortune, Success, and U.S. News & World Report. He has received numerous awards for his creative ventures including recognition by the United States Congress and participated the Presidential thinktank conference on The Future of The American Workforce.

CLASSIFICATION OF SOURCES OF NEW PRODUCT IDEAS

13

Ronald T. Lonsdale
Noel M. Noël, and
Stanley F. Stasch

13.1. INTRODUCTION

Successful new product introductions can assure a company's long-term prosperity, and the company's logical starting point in thinking about new products should be the generation of new product ideas. However, idea generation is a very chancy process. The majority of ideas turn out not to make sense. Drucker has noted that "innovative ideas are like frogs' eggs; of a thousand hatched, only one or two survive to maturity." [4]

Idea generation for new products should not be left to chance or accident. "The objective of all idea-generating activities is to guarantee that the company does not leave the exploration stage of new-product development to chance. New product gestation has to be a *planned function* [3, p. 339]. This chapter presents a classification scheme to help managers plan their new product activities and think about the many conceivable sources and origins of new product ideas.

13.2. CLASSIFICATION OF SOURCES OF NEW PRODUCT IDEAS

This chapter presents a classification of sources of new product ideas according to (1) the source of the idea, and (2) the "other necessary or supportive factors" present in association with the idea source [1;2, p. 81]. This classification scheme has 10 major categories, which are divided into the 22 subcategories shown in Table 13.1.

13.2.1. Laboratory Sources

Obviously, many ideas for new products begin in a laboratory setting. Laboratory-based sources of new product ideas seem to fall into at least three subcategories: those based on product research, those focused on process technology research, and those discovered accidentally in the laboratory.

1. Basic Research on "Product"

Both consumer and industrial companies develop new products based on research in their laboratories. Procter & Gamble scientists spent more than four decades developing the fat substitute Olestra. Reportedly this new product will take the calories and cholesterol out of such products as potato chips and ice cream.

Hewlett-Packard researchers noted that the reflectometers used by telephone companies to locate faults in their fiber optics systems were very time consuming to operate. It took Hewlett-Packard several years to develop its award-winning reflectometer, which operated a hundred times faster than existing competitive products.

A number of American universities are financing new companies to exploit the discoveries made in their laboratories by faculty members. Since Congress recently passed a law giving universities greater rights to profit from federally funded research findings, universities have been establishing venture-capital funds and technology-development companies.

2. Basic Research on Processing Technology

Some new products can be commercialized only after basic research has led to improved or new processing technology. Johnson & Johnson developed a patented processing technology which allowed them to use highly absorbent peat moss in a new line of very thin sanitary napkins. After Warner-Lambert developed a method of testing whether containers on its production lines were airtight, they attempted to commercialize the new device.

3. Accidental Discovery

Sometimes research done in a laboratory leads to a discovery that is accidental, in the sense that it is useful but different from what was hoped for from the

TABLE 13.1   Classification Scheme Showing Observed New Products

A. Laboratory sources
1. Basic research on product
   - P & G's Olestra
   - HP's reflectometer
   - Kodak's electric camera
   - Dry-air heat treatment
2. Basic research on processing technology
   - J&J's peat moss technology
   - WL's air-tightness tester
3. Accidental discovery
   - Upjohn's Rogaine
   - Molded steel

B. Management sources
1. "Just got the idea"
   - Federal Express
   - MicroFridge
   - PC Flowers
   - Swizzle sticks
   - Weber grill
   - CanUp
   - Elevator car top safety device
2. Organizational encouragement
   - General Electric
   - Xerox
   - Steelcase
3. Corporate "think tank" environment
   - Xerox
   - Steelcase

C. Company situation
1. Desire to break into a new market
   - AT&T's credit card
   - Clorox-branded detergents
2. Desire to improve market position
   - Gillette's Sensor
   - J&J's peat moss sanitary napkin
   - Xerox
   - Steelcase
3. Desire to regain market leadership
   - Nike's Air Jordan
   - Reebok's Pump
4. Desire to remain a viable competitor
   - Kodak's electronic camera
   - Xerox
   - Steelcase
5. Company in a "difficult situation"
   - Marvin windows

D. Distribution sources
1. Changing Patterns
   - PC Flowers
2. Distributor suggestions
   - Generic cigarettes

E. Supplier sources
1. Supplier offering new ingredient
   - NutraSweet's Simplesse

F. Consumer sources
1. Listening to consumers
   - GE
   - Warner Lambert toilet bowl cleaner
   - White Castle frozen hamburgers
   - Marriott Corporation
2. Dissatisfied consumers
   - Swizzle sticks
   - Weber grill
   - Dry-air heat treatment
   - My Own Meals

G. Marketplace sources
1. Identifying an unsatisfied need
   - CanUp
   - Elevator car top safety device
   - HP's reflectometer
   - Upjohn's Rogaine
   - MicroFridge
   - Swizzle sticks
   - Weber grill
   - Dry-air heat treatment
   - My Own Meals
   - Lifeline
2. Changing behavior
   - My Own Meals
   - Hair test for drug use
3. Accidental discovery
   - My Own Meals
   - Lifeline

H. Foreign sources
1. New products suggested by foreign products
   - Hershey's Symphony
   - C-P's Fabuloso
   - *National Sports Daily*

I. Government regulations
1. Regulation and deregulation
   - CFC's
   - Federal Express

J. Military and space programs
1. Adapting technology
   - GPS System

research. Such accidental discoveries can lead to new consumer and industrial products.

Upjohn's well-known hair restoration product, Rogaine, is one such discovery. The company was experimenting with a drug to combat high blood pressure, a high-dosage tablet containing Minoxidil. Eighty percent of the men and women taking the experimental drug were surprised when hair started growing on their head and sometimes on their arms, backs, and cheeks.

New industrial products can also result from accidental discovery. A Stanford metallurgical professor came upon a remarkable discovery while developing a high-performance steel for the government. He found that he could make a normally brittle high-carbon steel behave like warm fudge at about half the metal's normal melting point and that it had the added strength of forged steel after it had cooled. With this new type of steel, it would be possible in a single step to mold complex gears and other machine parts that normally require extensive machining.

13.2.2. Management Sources

Managers can be the sources of new product ideas by coming up with the ideas themselves. Management can also institute an organizational structure that encourages new-product ideas, or they can organize something akin to "corporate think tanks."

1. "Just Got the Idea"

Apparently many new products result because the managers "just got the idea." Perhaps the best-known example is Federal Express, conceived by the founder Frederick Smith, who was convinced there was a market for a small-package overnight air delivery service. A more recent example is Robert Bennett's desire to start a business involving any product that allowed him to use his sales and marketing abilities to the maximum. He founded MicroFridge, Inc., which markets and distributes a miniaturized combination refrigerator–freezer–microwave oven designed for lodgings with limited electrical wiring facilities. His patented switching device limits electric power to only one of the appliance's three functions at a time, so it can be plugged into ordinary household outlets without blowing fuses. The appliance was targeted to college dormitories and budget motels.

2. Organizational Encouragement

Because researchers at the General Electric Company are supposed to get their ideas accepted by other departments and divisions, the company's management uses a variety of organizational tactics to encourage cross-pollination of new-product ideas among technology groups.

To foster close, informal contacts between researchers in different disciplines, the company organizes or sponsors art exhibits, concerts, and activities such as choral groups and a regular Friday evening beer and pretzel party. Meetings or talks about new developments or technologies are widely publicized to encourage interdisciplinary work, and the R&D director insists that researchers vary their tablemates in the cafeteria. These efforts have proven to be very successful at General Electric.

Instead of pushing marketers to come up with ideas and then asking scientists to make them work, the company increasingly gives researchers wide berth to imagine and invent—and then shop the invention around GE's divisions. The results have been most fruitful. GE and its scientist-salesmen regularly manage to transfer technology from the laboratory to the market, a transition that frequently baffles American business. Of 250 technology projects that GE undertook between 1982 and 1986, an internal study done by Booz Allen found that 150 produced major applications. The average for U.S. industry was 1 in 10 [7].

3. Corporate "Think Tank" Environments

Xerox and Steelcase are two of a number of corporations reportedly creating corporate "think tank" environments to get their researchers, designers, and engineers to think about ideas that might help the company's new product development. Because these people are removed from the day-to-day pressures of routine business matters, it is believed they are more likely to come up with new-product ideas that ordinarily would not have occurred to them.

Xerox recently announced a new machine that combines high-speed copying, printing, scanning, facsimile, and computing capabilities in a single unit. The machine had its origin at Xerox's California research center, where "the project started as a labor of love for a tiny team of Xerox engineers, marketers, and futurists who had been directed to come up with technologies that would supplant traditional copiers before competitors beat them to the punch" [6].

The main reason that Steelcase recently constructed its corporate development center was the desire to create a light, airy environment to stimulate creativity and innovation. The large structure has outside terraces where people can work, and inside are one-person think tanks (called "caves"). Other unusual features include coffee stations that stand among blackboards where researchers can diagram ideas for others to see and comment on. According to an official who guided the center's conceptual design: "We're trying to anticipate the needs of the office of the future. We want to understand better what people will need to become more effective in their jobs. The bottom line for us is whether we produce better products" [9].

13.2.3. Company Situation

A company's current situation in its industry may stimulate or force it to search out new product ideas. Real-world examples suggest five types of company situations that encourage such searching: the company's current markets offer few growth opportunities, the company is trying to strengthen its competitive situation or improve its market position, the company desires to regain the position of leadership it once held, the company wishes to remain competitive in a certain market, and the company is in a difficult or desperate situation.

1. Desire to Break into a New Market

When a company's market enters the maturity phase or experiences strong new competitors, the company often begins looking for new product ideas. AT&T's move into the credit-card business probably resulted from the increased competitive pressure on its core businesses of long-distance services and telecommunications equipment.

Because the Clorox Company dominated the liquid chlorine bleach market, its earnings were heavily reliant on bleach profits. To reduce its reliance on a single product line, the company introduced Clorox-branded detergent products, which attempted to leverage on its storage existing brand franchise to give it an entry into a much larger market.

2. Desire to Improve Market Position

The desire for an improved position in a market can stimulate a firm to look for new product ideas. The Gillette Company obtained a majority of its operating income from the shaving market, which showed signs of becoming a low-margin commodity business because of the growing popularity of disposable razors and the decline of high-margin razor-and-blade systems, such as Trac II and Atra. To counter this market trend, the company used its many resources to concentrate on products with a technological edge that could command a premium price. The result was its highly successful Sensor shaving system, introduced in January 1990.

3. Desire to Regain Market Leadership

With some companies, the position of leadership is a point of pride. If threatened, such companies aggressively direct bold efforts to search out new-product ideas that might help them regain their leadership position. When Nike lost its leadership position to Reebok in the mid-1980s, the company quickly launched new products, especially its very popular Air Jordan shoe. When Nike regained the leadership position in 1989, Reebok aggressively counterresponded with a new basketball shoe—the "Pump"—which had an inflation device to provide a snugger fit. Introduced in time for the 1989 Christmas season, the Pump enjoyed great success through the winter and the following spring.

4. Desire to Remain a Viable Competitor

The Eastman Kodak Company has dominated the photographic film market ever since the birth of modern picture taking. However, if the future brings cameras that take pictures electronically, without film of any kind, the film industry may fade into oblivion. Such developments could lead to the demise of the Eastman Kodak Company if it does not prepare itself to play an important role in this rapidly changing market. Kodak has already announced several new products involving electronic photography, a hybrid of film and electronic photography. Consumers can take pictures as they always have, but they will have a new option—prints can be stored on a compact disk, which permits the images to be viewed on either a television set or a computer.

5. Company in a "Difficult Situation"

Occasionally, a company may find itself in a difficult situation due to competitive or market conditions which result in declining sales and excess or unused capacity. When a company is facing an uncertain future, management may be motivated to search for new-product ideas in the hope that they will reverse the company's downward trend.

The Marvin Company had been in the lumber business for many years. When an economic turndown left its employees with little to do, the company turned to making window frames. At the time, window frames were essentially a commodity business, with hundreds of little companies across the nation producing windows of standard sizes and shapes. Marvin decided not to compete against them, but rather, to concentrate on a wide line of customized, made-to-order, high-quality, weather-resistant windows. The company offers a wide variety of windows produced to meet a builder's or architect's specifications. According to the vice-president of marketing, this successful new product line results from the following strategy: "The whole idea is to offer so much we never have to say no to an inquiry" [5].

13.2.4. Distribution Sources

An idea for a new product may start when a firm notices some changing trends or patterns in distribution, or when a distributor suggests a new product.

1. Changing Patterns

Two businessmen became intrigued with the electronic marketing system called Prodigy, developed by IBM and Sears. They believed that the new electronic marketing method opened up opportunities for new businesses, new products, and new services. They started PC Flowers, which used the Prodigy electronic marketing system to allow customers to order flowers with their personal computer. Through the Prodigy system, customers gained access to the FTD network of floral shops, which provided worldwide delivery. Customers selected from drawings of some two dozen floral arrangements displayed on their PC monitor. The Prodigy system then sends the orders to the PC Flowers' computer system. Clearly, PC Flowers could exist only after the new electronic marketing system was already in place.

2. Distributor Suggestions

Sometimes a distributor may be looking for additional products to fill out a line. If a search reveals that no one supplies the desired product, the distributor may approach a manufacturer with suggestions regarding a possible new product. Topco, Inc., a cooperative that distributes a wide range of generic products to grocery stores, wanted to include generic cigarettes in its product line but found no such product available. Topco approached Liggett Group Inc., the smallest of the six big U.S. tobacco companies and asked the company to produce generic cigarettes which Topco would then sell at a discount under a generic label or store labels.

13.2.5. Supplier Sources

1. Supplier Offering New Ingredient

Today's technology-oriented industries are producing various electronic components, food ingredients, genetic materials, and so on, which other manufacturers might use within some new product yet to be developed. The firms that develop such components sometimes contact these manufacturers and provide information and assistance on how their offerings might be used in the manufacturers' products. They even help them to develop and launch new products. According to the president of NutraSweets' Simplesse Company, which produces the fat substitute Simplesse, the company "is working with several manufacturers to launch new products containing Simplesse as soon as the FDA allows it" [8].

13.2.6. Consumer Sources

Consumers are good sources of new product ideas in two ways. One, consumers let companies know about their likes and dislikes in regard to products. Also, consumers can be so dissatisfied with the available products that they take it upon themselves to design a better product.

1. Listening to Consumers

More and more companies have an "800" telephone number for customers who wish to ask a question or express a complaint. Such telephone calls can be a source of ideas on how current products can be improved. Sometimes callers even suggest a new product. As a result of such calls, General Electric made modifications to one of its clothes dryers, and Warner-Lambert received suggestions for developing its Efferdent dentures cleanser into a product that removes tough toilet bowl stains.

Taking a cue from its customers, White Castle discovered that some of its customers were taking burgers home to put into the freezer, so it started freezing its little square hamburgers and selling them through grocery stores.

The Marriott Corporation, which is in the lodging and food service businesses, undertakes considerable consumer research on room design and taste testing. Listening to customers has been a tradition at Marriott Corporation since its founder, J. Willard Marriott, believed strongly that one of the keys to success was giving customers good service. This belief translated into the practice of managers talking directly with customers, a practice that continues to this day.

2. Dissatisfied Consumers

Consumers dissatisfied with current products may be motivated to come up with improved versions. Dissatisfied consumers might possibly be one of the best sources for new-product ideas. Reportedly, the now common cocktail swizzle stick started with a dissatisfied consumer after the repeal of prohibition. The Weber grill, an outdoor cooking appliance which seems to be a feature of almost every patio and backyard in the United States, was also the creation of a dissatisfied consumer.

Ken Davidson was dissatisfied with standard whirlpool treatments for his son's tennis elbow. The whirlpool could not provide enough heat because people cannot tolerate very hot water for even a short time. Knowing that human beings can stand hotter temperatures if the heat is dry rather than wet, Davidson developed a dry-air heat-treatment device which became widely accepted by physical therapists.

13.2.7. Marketplace Sources

There are three ways that the marketplace itself can be a source of new product ideas: the marketplace identifies a need that is not being satisfied; changes in the marketplace or in its behavior suggest ideas; someone accidentally discovers that the marketplace is interested in a certain new product.

1. Identifying an Unsatisfied Need

James Cosgrove saw that one market trend was toward smaller housing units in increasingly crowded cities. This, along with the trend toward more convenience packaging, was creating a storage space problem in many kitchens. He designed CanUp, a patented space-saving device for storing standard-sized food cans on a plastic rack mounted to the underside of kitchen cabinet shelves. The racks allow consumers to store cans in space that previously had been unusable.

The Guardian Elevator Company, a small company that maintained and repaired elevators in high-rise buildings, noted that it was getting more calls for unusual elevator repairs. It was increasingly being asked to repair elevators damaged by teenagers who managed to ride on the roofs of the elevators instead of inside them. In addition to the increased maintenance costs, building owners were concerned about unnecessary elevator downtime and liability claims in the event of accidents. The Guardian Company designed the Elevator Car Top Intrusion Device, which shuts off the elevator while sounding a loud alarm whenever an infrared beam detects tampering by someone trying to get onto the elevator roof.

2. Changing Behavior

The widespread acceptance of microwave ovens in the first half of the 1980s spawned more new frozen-food products that were microwaveable. The rapid growth of VCRs during the second half of the 1980s has contributed to consumers' eating out less often and buying more "take out" food to eat at home.

Because the 1980s was also a decade of increased drug consumption, many employers began testing their employees for drug usage. The standard test involved urine analysis, but this test could identify drug use only if it had occurred within the last few days. Werner Baumgartner invented a process that produced a person's drug-use profile over the previous three months: the drugs enter the bloodstream, and traces are left behind in the protein that makes up hair. Neither washing, dyeing, or bleaching will remove the evidence of drug usage. Baumgartner's hair test is therefore much more likely to identify a drug user than the standard urine analysis test.

3. Accidental Discovery

Sometimes the marketplace helps someone to accidentally discover an idea for a new product. Some event or encounter in the marketplace might suggest an idea that results in a successful new product.

Because Mary Anne Jackson was a working mother, she felt guilty about not spending more time with her baby. In an attempt to assuage these feelings, she spent much of her weekend cooking a week's supply of nutritionally balanced meals that would then be doled out to her daughter by the baby-sitter. Soon, many other working mothers wanted information about the meals she was cooking, so she began thinking about marketing a line of nutritious, easy-to-prepare meals for children. She launched her product line, My Own Meals, in Chicago in 1988.

Ray Tannatta was both a professional fireman and a licensed plumber who invented Lifeline, a device that could keep people from suffocating if they were trapped in a smoke-filled hotel room. Rooms equipped with Lifeline allow a trapped person to breath filtered air through the building's plumbing system until the person is rescued or the smoke dissipates. Tannatta's inspiration to invent the device came from a tragedy at a high-rise apartment fire he was fighting: a hotel occupant suffocated close to the sink that could have saved him.

13.2.8. Foreign Sources

1. New Products Suggested by Foreign Products

Products in foreign countries can be the basis for a product introduced into the United States. A foreigner coming to the United States might notice the absence in this country of a product that is in widespread use in his or her native land and may see an opportunity to introduce the product as a new one.

Hershey Foods introduced a milk chocolate bar, Symphony, modeled after a creamier and smoother-tasting chocolate bar marketed in Europe. The Colgate-Palmolive Company reportedly considered introducing into the United States its Fabuloso household cleanser. Because Latin American women were attracted to the brand's pleasant fragrance and lighter cleaning formula, Colgate believed Hispanic women in the United States would also use the product.

The idea for the now defunct *National Sports Daily*, a nationwide sports newspaper, started with a foreigner. Emilio Azcarrago, a Mexican citizen, believed such a newspaper would be successful in the United States because most other countries were able to support a daily national sports newspaper.

13.2.9. Government Regulations

1. Regulation and Deregulation Changes the Environment

Business and environmental changes can occur from new laws being passed or old laws being repealed, new proclamations being made by government agencies, or the regulation or deregulation of certain industries. Such changes in regulation often encourage people and companies to think about new product ideas.

It is common knowledge that new airlines came into existence because of airline deregulation. Federal Express Company was able to introduce its "Overnight Letter" service when the Postal Service changed its regulations. More recently, the DuPont Company introduced a family of air conditioner and refrigerator coolants to replace the ozone-depleting chlorofluorocarbon coolants (called CFCs) used in the past. The new coolants currently are more expensive than CFCs, but as new government taxes are imposed on CFCs, the new coolants will become less costly. The government tax imposed on CFCs clearly encouraged industry to seek out a new product to replace them.

13.2.10. Military and Space Programs

1. Adapting Military or Space Technology

Over the last 50 years federal administrators have made substantial research expenditures for military and space needs. Often these expenditures are for programs that can suggest new product ideas for civilian or commercial usage. The U.S. military has a network of satellites called GPS, global positioning systems. Any motor vehicle or boat that can receive and interpret signals from GPS can pinpoint its exact location on earth. Now available on the market, such receivers are the direct result of the government's work on geographic positioning systems.

Large commercial airline manufacturers estimate that between 500 and 1500 supersonic jumbo jets could be sold annually by the year 2005 if the industry could come up with an acceptable supersonic jet engine. The industry is capable of building an engine that can propel a jumbo jet at speeds three times the speed of sound using technology that has already been developed for military jets. However, that technology must first be modified to make it more cost-effective and environmentally responsible.

13.3. MANAGERIAL IMPLICATIONS AND SUGGESTIONS

Two managerial implications follow from these findings. First, the generation of new product ideas is a chancy matter, but the procedure for coming up with new product ideas should not be left to chance. Since the sources of new product ideas are rather well identified in Table 13.1, managers can begin to think about the generation of new product ideas in a more orderly and systematic manner.

It should be noted that idea generation can be more complex than a single-factor phenomenon. Some new products appear to have their origins in a number of sources or factors. For example, in Table 13.1, "My Own Meals" is listed under four subcategories (F2, G1, G2, G3), the dry-air heat treatment device is listed under three subcategories (A1, F2, G1), and several items (e.g., H-P's reflectometer and PC Flowers) appear under two subcategories.

Second, the classification scheme can also help managers re-design their organizations to make them more effective in identifying

> *Tune your organization to capture new product ideas.*

and capturing new product ideas. In the past, the company responsibility for product idea generation has often been assigned to specific departments, such as R&D or marketing. However, the various categories in Table 13.1 suggest that a number of other groups should participate in this responsibility as well. In the remaining discussion we present ten suggestions that managers can use to help make their firms more effective when searching among the sources of new product ideas presented in Table 13.1.

1. If your firm does not have its own R&D laboratory, it should consider giving support to one or more independent research labs doing the kinds of R&D that is applicable to your firm's business. The firm should also search out the possible existence of scientific newsletters dealing with topics related to the firm's business.

2. Management should look into the kind of things that can provide organizational encouragement which might cause employees to come up with new product ideas. Suggestion boxes, lunches that bring together two or more previously unacquainted employees, beer and pretzel new product idea parties, and so on, are only a few of the things that might be tried.

3. Table 13.1 lists five subcategories of company situations which might lead to new product ideas. The firms can make available training and reminder sessions to those managers and marketing personnel who have some responsibility toward the five company situations listed in the table.

4. Regarding distribution sources of new product ideas, marketing and sales personnel should be regularly reminded to be in contact with distributors about new product ideas, and to report immediately all actual or rumored new product introductions by competitors. Training sessions on this responsibility can be scheduled regularly to help emphasize its importance and improve its effectiveness.

5. Employees with responsibility related to the firms' suppliers—mostly purchasing, management, and R&D personnel—should receive guidance on how to query supplier personnel about any of their current and future developments that might in some way suggest an idea for a new product.

6. Consumers are the most important source of new product ideas. To exploit this source, the firm should have its marketing research personnel regularly carry out projects designed to capture consumer "dissatisfactions" that lead to new product ideas. Sales and marketing personnel should also be encouraged to be in contact with consumers for this purpose. If the firm does not have its own marketing research activity, it might consider a partnership arrangement with an independent marketing research firm.

7. The marketplace can also be a good source of new-product ideas. Sales and marketing personnel who are in touch with customers and potential customers—especially dissatisfied ones—have the best opportunity to identify new product ideas from this source. They should be encouraged and trained to do so. The other ideas noted in suggestion 6 are also appropriate here.

8. All management, marketing, and sales personnel—and the company's distributors, as well—who have contact with foreign sources can be trained and encouraged to look for and report new product ideas gained from foreign sources.

9. Regarding changes in regulation and deregulation that may suggest new product ideas, a company can ask lawyers or its legal counsel to inform it of regulatory changes that might affect the company's products or markets. It might also be possible to subscribe to one or more newsletters that provide information about regulation changes.

10. To monitor new product ideas originating in space and military programs, the firm may wish to make contact with appropriate persons in their state and national governments. Often, their elected representatives can be helpful in providing direction. Occasionally, one or more of the trade associations to which the firm belongs might provide a useful direction.

REFERENCES

1. Crawford, M. The dual-drive concept of product innovation. *Business Horizons*, pp. 32–38 (May–June 1991).
2. Crawford, M. *New Products Management*. Homewood, IL: Irwin, 1991.
3. Davis, K. *Marketing Management*. New York: Wiley, 1985.
4. Drucker, Peter F. The innovative company. *Wall Street Journal*, February 26, 1982, p. 18.
5. Harris, J. The window frame as fashion item. *Forbes*, April 30, 1990, pp. 125–130.
6. Hooper, L. Xerox tries to shed its has-been image with big new machine. *Wall Street Journal*, September 20, 1990, pp. A1, A6.
7. Naj, A. GE's latest invention: a way to move ideas from lab to market. *Wall Street Journal*, June 14, 1990, pp. A1, A9.
8. NutraSweet changes marketing plan for Simplesse fat substitute. *Marketing News*, March 18, 1991, pp. 6, 17.
9. Witcher, G. Steelcase hopes innovation flourishes under pyramid. *Wall Street Journal*, May 26, 1989, pp. B1, B4.

Ronald T. Lonsdale
Loyola University of Chicago

Ronald T. Lonsdale is currently an Associate Professor of Marketing in the Graduate School of Business at Loyola University of Chicago. He earned his Ph.D. from Purdue University. His research interests include new product development and marketing in Latin American countries. He has articles published in several journals and proceedings.

Noel M. Noël
Indiana University-Northwest

Noel Mark Noël (a.k.a. Lavenka) is an Associate Professor of Sales and Marketing at Indiana University and President of Brandmetrics, Inc. based in Chicago, Illinois. His primary research and business interests include the measurement of consumer perceptions of product quality and new product development in the food products industry. Directly related publications can be viewed in the Journal of Food Science, *the* Journal of Food Products Marketing, Psychology and Marketing, *and* Marketing Research: A Magazine of Management Applications.

Stanley F. Stasch
Loyola University of Chicago

Stanley F. Stasch has been the Charles H. Kellstadt Professor of marketing at Loyola University since 1977. For the 14 years prior to 1977 he was on the faculty of the Graduate School of Management at Northwestern University. He earned his Ph.D. at Northwestern University, and has authored numerous articles and textbooks.

14 EVALUATING IDEAS AND CONCEPTS FOR NEW CONSUMER PRODUCTS
Ned F. Anschuetz

14.1. INTRODUCTION

Creating a new product is a learning process. Someone generates an idea for a new product, expresses the idea as clearly as possible so that it can be communicated to other members of the team, to management, and to the consumer. The team tests the idea by observing interest by consumers, and then goes back to the drawing board to refine the idea or develop a new one. Evaluating ideas and concepts in new products involves clear communication of the idea and accurate reading of the response. This chapter focuses on these two issues.

14.2. THE MANY PURPOSES OF IDEA AND CONCEPT EVALUATION

The purpose of idea and concept evaluation will change as development proceeds from early screening, to concept refinement, and finally to estimating sales potential of a more finished concept. Figure 14.1 shows the new product attrition rate [4, p. 284]. In the typical company, informal screening reduces a set of 100 new product ideas to about 27 that actually move forward to formal testing. After formal testing, about 12 will be introduced into market. In the ultimate evaluation, marketplace acceptance of the new product, about 9 will be commercially

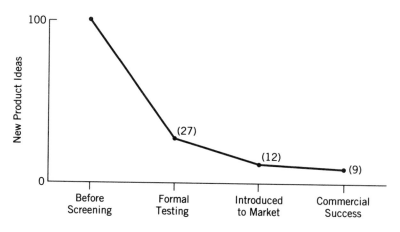

FIGURE 14.1 New product attrition rate.

successful. Evaluation is a process of focusing on the ideas with highest potential and learning how to make them into successful new products.

14.2.1. Early Evaluation: Selecting Ideas to Develop

The output from idea-generating sessions and external scanning of the marketplace may be a very large number of rough, undeveloped ideas. Some preliminary evaluation must be made to reduce the list to a smaller, more manageable number of ideas to develop further. At this early stage, judgmental evaluation by members of a multifunctional new product team is valuable. Team members with different expertise will provide a balanced view of the merits of the idea on a predetermined set of criteria such as fit with the company's new product strategy, fit with corporate resources, and so on.

14.2.2. Midcourse Evaluation: Improving the Idea

As an idea is taken forward, it is important to get feedback from consumers on how to improve it. Rather than being concerned with a go/no go decision, the intent is to learn how best to optimize the idea; if a poorly developed idea is evaluated, research will not provide a very useful picture of its real potential. Developing the concept requires answering many of the questions a good journalist would ask. Who is interested in the product? Why are they interested—what benefits appeal most to them, and what detracts most from the appeal? When, where, how, and how much might they use the product? What competitive products would this replace? [1] Answering these questions through concept research will define the new product concept and will provide the context to help communicate the idea more clearly to both consumers and management as development progresses.

14.2.3. Late-Concept Evaluation: Estimating Sales Potential

Toward the end of the concept development stage, the idea may be evaluated for sales potential. At this point, there is usually a much smaller number of new product ideas, and the concepts that express them are designed to be as similar as possible to what consumers will be exposed to in the marketplace. Marketing inputs such as advertising support, distribution expectations, promotional events and timing, relative price, and so on, are combined to offer a realistic picture of what the business results of the idea may be. In this kind of research, consumers rate their interest in buying the product after seeing a concept, often a rough commercial, and then are given a prototype of the product to try. Reactions to the concept are used to estimate trial interest, and reactions to the product itself are used to estimate probable repeat sales.

14.3. JUDGMENTAL SCREENING OF NEW PRODUCT IDEAS

If a large number of new product ideas has been generated from ideation and marketplace scanning, the first step is to reduce this to a smaller number of high-potential projects. Here, a major consideration is management's judgment of how well the idea fits with the overall new product strategy of the company, technical resources, investment expectations, and so on. This internal screening of ideas is done prior to obtaining external consumer feedback. [1, pp. 132–137]. In reducing the number of ideas, it is often useful simply to establish a checklist of the elements of the new product strategy and to evaluate each idea against the strategy. Doing this will usually winnow out many good ideas that are just off strategy, and other smaller ideas that address one narrow element of the strategy. Table 14.1 illustrates a sample of criteria that can be used to build a checklist for initial judgmental screening.

   In doing judgmental screening, it is often a good idea to collect judgments from all members of the cross-functional team as well as from management. Isolating areas of disagreement among team members can prove helpful in uncovering insights about the project. If, for example, members of the team have different views on the cost of manufacturing a specific new product, clarifying that issue will help the team make better judgments about that as well as related product ideas.

TABLE 14.1   Sample Judgmental Screening Criteria

Strategic screens
- Fit with corporate mission and strategy
- Familiarity to company
- Market competitiveness
- Market size and expected growth

Consumer screens
- Importance of consumer need addressed
- Consumer benefit delivered
- Product superiority
- Perceived value for the money

Product development screens
- Fit with corporate technical capabilities
- Degree of technical difficulty
- Time to market
- Competitors' ability to follow
- Estimated development costs

Package development screens
- Fit with corporate packaging capabilities
- Degree of packaging difficulty
- Status of packaging
- Time to market
- Competitors' ability to follow
- Estimated package development costs

Manufacturing screens
- Availability of existing manufacturing capabilities
- Need to outsource or develop additional facilities
- Availability of raw materials
- Estimated unit or capital costs

Regulatory and legal screens
- Ability to protect from quick competitive response
- Estimated timing for regulatory approval (e.g., FDA)
- Anticipated regulatory issues

> *Use judgmental ratings from team members to reduce a large number of ideas to a more manageable number.*

14.4. TRANSLATING NEW PRODUCT IDEAS INTO CONCEPTS

Once the list of potential ideas has been narrowed, the challenge is to translate ideas into concepts that communicate the idea to consumers as clearly as possible. Unless consumers understand the product idea clearly, any evaluation of their reactions to it will be impossible to read with any confidence.

14.4.1. How to Write Concepts for Concept Tests

As in any form of communication, new product ideas should be expressed in language, tone, and visuals that are familiar and understandable to consumers. The amount of detail in a new product concept will vary by the purpose of the research. Very early product ideas may consist of simple written descriptions and line drawings of the new product. Generally, as much information is included as is possible for clarity. The purpose of consumer research at this stage is usually to determine the level of interest in the entire bundle of product features to decide whether to proceed with development. The concept will often consist of a simple standard description of the product that will include its major benefits, features, package size, and price. A simple line drawing may accompany the description. [5]

As the product is developed further, concept tests may be done to estimate initial trial levels. For this kind of work, some practitioners believe that the concept should

> **Write concepts from the consumers' point of view. What's in it for them?**

be similar in tone and style to what consumers will see in the market. The concept may resemble a rough print ad for the new product with an interesting headline focusing on the key consumer benefit, convincing support for the benefit, attractive graphics, and copy with style and personality.

Perhaps the most important consideration is that all the concepts in a test be *rendered in the same format* so that they can be compared fairly with one another and with norms. If a concept with the quality of a color print ad and advertising copy receives greater purchase interest than one with a simple line drawing and unexciting copy, one won't know whether it's the idea or the style that has captured the interest of consumers. Holding the format constant helps differentiate ideas from style.

14.4.2. Preparing Concepts for Consumer Durables and Services

The ideas for consumer packaged goods above hold true for consumer durables and services as well, with important variations. Consumer durables may require mockups at some point to help consumers understand important design considerations. For durables, the trial-generating power of the new product idea is especially important since repeat purchase is not a major consideration. In addition, the price value of different product features becomes much more important for design considerations.

Preparing a concept for a consumer service such as a new credit card or bank service can be as simple as that for other consumer products or may require some additional ingenuity. Since it is intangible, a service may be made more concrete by videotaping a dramatization of it. In evaluating the potential for a new bank, for example, a videotape may clearly communicate customer service in a way that other forms cannot. Once again, the only rule is that the concept be as clear as possible to the intended audience.

Consumer durables and services also lend themselves to a particular kind of concept evaluation that is very useful for improving a new product idea: concept optimization. In this kind of work, the new product concept is broken up into bundles of attributes that may affect consumer choice. A new telephone, for example, may come in three different sizes, two different colors, with three different communication features, and four different price points. By offering consumers choices among different combinations of product features, managers can learn not only which concepts have the greatest acceptance, but the relative importance of the different features in consumer choice. The relative importance weights, or utilities, can be used to design product concepts that optimize the appeal of a bundle of features for the price consumers are willing to pay. Concept optimization, sometimes called conjoint or trade-off analysis, is offered by many leading marketing research firms. Preparing concepts for this kind of research requires analyzing the components of the new product ideas that are controllable by management.

14.5. TESTING CONSUMER RESPONSE TO NEW PRODUCT CONCEPTS

There are standard ways of testing new product ideas that have been written into clear concepts. The basic idea is to get a fair reading of consumer interest in trying and using the product. This usually is done first qualitatively with a few consumers and then quantitatively with a larger sample to permit better generalization of the findings.

14.5.1. Qualitative Exploration of Ideas and Concepts

The first step in getting consumer feedback about an idea is usually a discussion with a small number of consumers, either individually or in small groups of 4 to 10 consumers. This kind of research is called qualitative because the reactions of such a small number of consumers are not at all projectable or generalizable to a larger sample—one cannot get a sense for the percent of consumers interested in the idea or estimates of likely trial, but one can get a sense for how some consumers think about and talk about the new product idea. Qualitative research can be particularly helpful in understanding how to write a concept for further testing with a larger number of consumers.

During a typical focus group discussion, a moderator will ask many of the same questions that could be asked in a larger survey but will be able to probe reactions in more detail. Typical questions in qualitative research will focus on reasons for or barriers to purchase interest, likes and dislikes, clarity of the words or idea, feelings about when, where, how, and how often they would use such a product, who else in the family might also use it, how they would improve the idea, and so on. The results of such research are *not* projectable and should only be considered as ways of refining concepts prior to a more projectable study using a larger, more carefully drawn sample.

Some precautions about qualitative work are needed. Recruit a sample of your consumers, but don't try to get a representative sample—that is just not possible. Avoid pretending that qualitative research is really quantitative. Don't ask respondents to vote for their favorite idea and interpret the results using numbers—that misses the point of this kind of work altogether and can be very misleading. As tempting as it is, avoid evaluating new product ideas in qualitative research, since the probability of error is so great. If you rely on 20 or 30 consumers from one or two locations to kill an idea, to give a project life, or to determine its direction, you are looking for very expensive trouble.

14.5.2. Quantitative Concept Tests

> *Use qualitative research to get insights about consumer perceptions and language, but understand its limitations.*

Qualitative research is never sufficient for making important decisions about new product ideas. At some point it is necessary to survey a large sample of consumers to determine the level of purchase interest and areas of likes and dislikes of the concept. Surveys must be conducted in such a way that consumers are able to see the new product concept. This is usually done through mail surveys where consumers, often members of an ongoing research panel, receive a copy of the concepts through the mail and are asked to fill out a self-administered questionnaire about the new product idea. Another approach is to recruit consumers from shopping malls to participate in individual interviews in which they are exposed to the new product concepts and are asked similar questions.

The usefulness of quantitative research points out the critical consideration in designing it: making sure the right respondents are evaluating the product idea. A large representative sample is useful if one has no idea of who would have an interest in the product, since the results will help define the target audience. In the more usual case, however, new product managers will have some idea of who the product will appeal to and should be sure that respondents included in the research meet relevant category usage definitions.

> *Carefully construct the sample in quantitative research. Make sure that you are talking to relevant prospects.*

In addition to purchase interest, the survey should include several questions that will help understand who is interested, why they are interested, and how the idea could be improved. This "diagnostic" information will make the results useful to the project even if purchase interest is below expectations. Areas of questioning will include purchase interest, perceptions of how different the product is from what is currently available, and ratings of the appeal of specific product features. The survey should include questions to provide confirmation of basic assumptions in the new product strategy. If, for example, a new food product has been developed to address consumer concerns about better nutrition at breakfast, the survey should ask consumers about this concern. Purchase interest in the new product idea can then be analyzed by whether or not consumers have nutrition concerns at breakfast.

Sales estimating research uses inputs from the concept test along with marketing plan assumptions to form a sales estimate over the first year. The concept test provides an estimate of trial, a number that is usually derived from purchase interest scores that are adjusted from experience. For example, although 65 percent of consumers may say they are "definitely" or "probably" interested in buying the product if it becomes available in the future, the actual number who will actually try will probably be lower. Many concept testing services use norms from past experience in relevant categories to adjust purchase interest scores to obtain an estimate of likely trial. Along with an estimate of trial, a client will provide estimates of year 1 awareness due to advertising and promotion, distribution, trial generating promotion and sampling programs, and estimates of probable repeat purchasing based on product satisfaction and category norms. Marketing inputs along with trial estimates are entered into a mathematical model to estimate share levels at the end of year 1 [6, pp. 449–466]. Table 14.2 provides some practical tips to keep in mind when preparing concepts and conducting concept tests.

14.6. BENEFITS AND RISKS OF CONCEPT EVALUATION

14.6.1. Risks

There are several risks in the process of evaluating new product ideas that management needs to keep in mind. The two major evaluation errors are:

TABLE 14.2 Tips for Concept Testing

Tips for Communicating Consumer New Product Ideas	Tips for Reading Consumer Response
• Use consumer language. • Keep the idea simple, focused, and organized. • Be clear—from the consumer's point of view. • Be realistic—don't overpromise or oversell. • Focus on a major consumer benefit. • Differentiate the brand from the competition. • Keep all concepts that will be tested in the same format. • Use experienced professionals to prepare the concepts.	• Make sure that your respondents are in your target audience. • Include several diagnostic questions to understand why results come back as they do, and how to improve the idea. • Use qualitative research to explore language and ideas, to get hunches. • Understand the level of error associated with different types of evaluation. • Make sure the results are useful, whether or not consumers find the idea appealing. • Balance enthusiasm for the project with objectivity. • Use experienced research suppliers to provide early guidance on methodology.

1. *Identifying a new product idea as promising when, in fact, it is a loser.* A good evaluation system should eliminate a high percentage of losing ideas, leaving the most promising ones to invest in. If your company has had a track record of bringing more losers to market than the competition, you should examine your evaluation process to determine ways of reducing this error.

2. *Killing a good idea when, in fact, it could be a winner.* A good evaluation system should also avoid throwing out good ideas. This kind of error is generally less visible and given less attention by management than the previous one because the risks involve losing *potential* sales and profit rather than actual financial outlays. Lost opportunities, however, are real risks that ultimately lead to a weakened competitive position. If your company has introduced fewer good new product ideas in recent years than the competition, the source of this error should be determined and corrected.

Several factors contribute to both kinds of new product evaluation errors. The further removed from reality a concept or idea is, the less accurate a prediction about its ultimate success will be. Evaluations of ideas early in the process generally have very low predictive value. Similarly, errors are common in evaluating descriptions of very new products with which consumers have low familiarity or of new product ideas that require consumer experience to understand, such as a new food product or cosmetic fragrance. Of course, the truer the concept and product are to what is finally introduced into market, the greater the expense and the less useful evaluation is as an early way to allocate resources. Accuracy costs time and money.

The trade-off between accuracy of prediction and cost occurs at each stage of the evaluation process. Table 14.3 illustrates some of the options that face a manager. Early evaluation is usually quick, relatively inexpensive, and leaves room for a great deal of error. The chance of missing a good idea and of backing a poor idea are fairly high. Reducing error, however, costs time and money. Simulated and in-market tests offer great accuracy of prediction because the idea is communicated in a more finished commercial message and the product consumers respond to is very close, if not identical, to what will actually go to market.

A major source of error in evaluating new product ideas is more human than technical in nature. Human sources of error in evaluation [3] include:

- Predicting outcomes based on personal experience or observing a very limited set of cases. Using focus groups, for example, to make major product decisions is very risky and will result in large errors.
- Overoptimism that leads to overestimating sales potential and to maintaining momentum behind a project that should be modified or killed. An enthusiastic new product manager who will be rewarded for bringing a project to completion, and the new product to market, will be very motivated to keep a project alive, biasing assumptions critical to accurate evaluation.
- Fear of failure that leads to *over*researching an idea, reluctance to get behind it, and to reducing or pulling marketing support after launch if even slight problems arise. Exaggerated fear of failure leads to too many lost opportunities.

These and other biases that influence evaluation can be overcome partially by adhering to objective standards and by balancing the passion for a project with objective critical appraisal of its prospects.

14.6.2. Evaluation Versus Learning

Evaluating new product ideas and concepts is usually a business of winnowing out weak from strong ideas. But that is only part of the opportunity. Developing new products is a learning process that can convert weak ideas into strong ones. Evaluation should include rich diagnostics that provide clues as to what consumers find appealing or unappealing about an idea and how the new product concept can be improved. The process itself should enable the marketing manager to learn about the target audience, the product, the elements of the marketing

TABLE 14.3 Error and Cost Trade-offs in Idea Evaluation

Error	Concept	Product Rendering	Cost of Concept and Product	Type of Evaluation	Cost of Evaluation
Great	Simple written description	Simple line drawing	Low	Judgmental	Low
	More elaborate description	Rough drawing	Low	Qualitative exploration	Moderate
Moderate	Refined marketing copy, description	Photograph of product and package	Moderate/low	Quantitative concept test	Moderate
Moderate	Rough print ad, animatic	Prototype of product and package	Moderate/high	Concept and product test	Moderate to high
Lower	Finished commercial	Sample run	High	Simulated test market	High
Lowest	Finished campaign	Final production quality	High	In-market test	High

mix, the benefits that consumers desire, and so on. At the end of the process, whether or not a new product becomes successful, the manager and the company should be much smarter about the consumer in a way that will increase the odds for success in the future.

> *Use concept evaluation to learn something about consumers that will be useful in the future regardless of how the new product idea performs.*

REFERENCES

1. Cooper, R. G. *Winning at New Products: Accelerating the Process from Idea to Launch*, 2nd ed. Reading, MA: Addison-Wesley, 1993.
2. Gruenwald, G. *New Product Development*, 2nd ed. Lincolnwood, IL: NTC Business Books, 1992.
3. Mowen, J. C. and Gaeth, G. J. The evaluation stage in marketing decision making. *Journal of the Academy of Marketing Science* 20(2):177–187 (Spring 1992).
4. Page, A. L. Assessing new product development practices and performance: establishing crucial norms. *Journal of Product Innovation Management* 10:273–290 (September 1993).
5. Page, A. L. and Rosenbaum, H. F. Developing an effective concept testing program for consumer durables. *Journal of Product Innovation Management* 9:267–277 (December 1992).
6. Urban, G. L. and Hauser, J. R. *Design and Marketing of New Products* 2nd ed. Englewood Cliffs, NJ: Prentice Hall, 1993.

Ned Anschuetz
DDB Needham Worldwide

Ned is a Senior Vice President at DDB Needham Worldwide, a major advertising agency where he has worked since 1979. He is a Group Director of Strategic Planning and Research as well as Research Director for the agency's new products group. He has been an active member of the Product Development and Management Association and the American Marketing Association. Ned has broad experience in concept development and evaluation for a wide range of new consumer products and services developed in partnership with major national advertisers.

EVALUATING IDEAS AND CONCEPTS FOR NEW BUSINESS-TO-BUSINESS PRODUCTS

15

Ronald N. Paul

15.1. INTRODUCTION

This chapter deals with front-end screening and evaluation processes for business-to-business products. At this point, too, these products are often nonexistent, with features and benefits vaguely understood. References to these processes have thus come to be called the *fuzzy front end*. But before describing them, it is appropriate to discuss the nature of the business-to-business market.

15.2. BUSINESS-TO-BUSINESS DEFINED

By business-to-business we mean the universe of nonconsumer purchasing organizations listed as follows:

1. Product producers or manufacturers
2. Resellers, both retail and wholesale
3. Government, institutional and professional

Each of these categories is a potential direct purchaser of both goods and services. In the case of resellers (i.e., retailers and wholesalers), they are ultimately

influenced by their customers' acceptance of new products. Such customers include consumers in the case of retailers, and organizations in the case of wholesalers. As a result, in certain situations, the resellers' willingness to stock a new
product is critical to successful introductions, and their attitudes need to be
incorporated into an evaluation process.

Furthermore, the term *product* has a broad-based context. It not only includes specific physical products but also nontangible service ideas and concepts.
Issues involved in evaluating nontangible ideas may be more difficult to communicate, but the same processes apply. [3]

15.3. CHARACTERISTICS OF BUSINESS-TO-BUSINESS MARKETS

Evaluation methodologies of ideas and concepts for new business-to-business
products are similar to those of consumer products. However, there are five
major differences and they *do* affect the fuzzy-front-end process.

1. *Critical purchase decisions are made by one or more business entities rather
   than directly by the consumer.* Frequently, both wholesalers and retailers
   are involved in purchase decisions. This means that the viewpoints of both
   parties must be considered.
2. *Consumers play an indirect but often vital role.* While an organization may
   be the original purchaser, the ultimate user can be one or more individuals,
   and the element of consumer reaction becomes a major factor as well.
3. *Purchasing situations frequently involve both multiple buying influences
   and individuals.* In some cases, committees make final decisions, further
   complicating the sales process.
4. *Buyer concentration may affect the evaluation process.* The fewer the number of potential customers, the more important it is to have an evaluation
   by *key* market makers.
5. *Personal selling is usually of greater importance.* Business-to-business markets often have small customer bases and thus create closer relationships
   in the selling processes.

These characteristics will need to be remembered and considered, particularly during market research activities. The overall process is quite trade focused. Success is based on reaching the *right* people in the *right* organization
using the *right* methods.

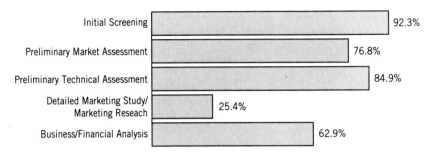

FIGURE 15.1 Frequency of new product process activities.

15.4. IMPORTANCE OF THE IDEA EVALUATION PROCESS

> *Business-to-business markets differ from consumer markets and meaningful market information is substantially more concentrated.*

The importance of fuzzy-front-end activities has been confirmed by a considerable amount of research. In a comprehensive study of 123 industrial firms and 252 case histories, the activities listed in Figure 15.1 preceded the actual product design and development [1]. This same research measured the importance by rating the proficiency of the activities for both successful and unsuccessful product launches, as shown in Figure 15.2.

Activity		Proficiency of Activities (0–10 rating)
Initial Screening	3.7	Failure
	6.3	Success
Preliminary Market Assessment	4.4	Failure
	5.9	Success
Preliminary Technical Assessment	5.2	Failure
	7.5	Success
Detailed Marketing Study/ Marketing Reaseach	4.7	Failure
	6.6	Success
Business/Financial Analysis	5.6	Failure
	6.9	Success

FIGURE 15.2 Proficiencies of activities: success versus failure.

A later study correlated new product results with the amount of time devoted both to front-end activities and to the product development, testing, and commercialization phases. Divided into "high" and "low" groups, based on mean scores for all these activities, the study compared 92 high-front-end companies with 90 low-front-end companies. The high-front-end companies spent 44 percent of their total development time on their front-end activities versus 22 percent for the low-front-end group. Study author A. L. Page's conclusions are:

> Spending more time on the front end of the new product development process, based on the results from this study, lowers the overall development time of a new product, increases the percentage of expenditures on new product development to products that will ultimately become successful, and creates a positive impact for the organization. Managers who emphasize the front end feel their programs are more successful and meet the company's corporate objectives [4].

> **The front end of development is critical for success.**

The importance of these activities to new product success thus suggests that initial activities be conducted competently.

15.5. OVERALL STEPS IN THE EVALUATION PROCESS

Although individual company practices differ, Figure 15.3 shows a summary of a typical evaluation process [2]. Step 1 is usually conducted on an internal basis and uses existing organizational knowledge. Depending on the ease of accomplishment and the nature of the idea, initial customer input should be received as early as possible and thus becomes part of step 2. It is within step 3 that it becomes important to obtain detailed marketplace concept evaluations, in addition to completing a sound business analysis.

15.5.1. Step 1: Internal Idea Screen

Regardless of the number of ideas or concepts generated in prior phases of the new product process, the need exists to eliminate those that will probably not be successful. While some judgmental risk exists in early screening, it is prudent to apply at least three major criteria to determine if an idea should be considered further. These criteria relate to answering the questions posed below.

1. *Does the proposed product fit within the company's strategic goals?* Is it consistent with the company's existing product portfolio? Does it fit within the company's distribution channel?

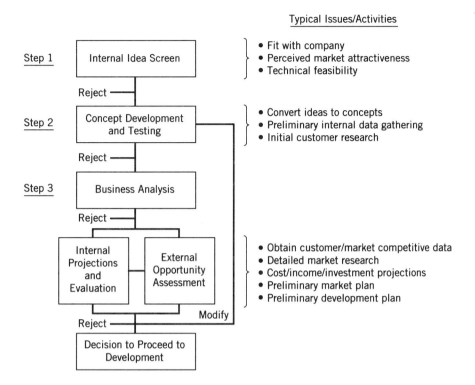

Typical Issues/Activities

Step 1 — Internal Idea Screen
- Fit with company
- Perceived market attractiveness
- Technical feasibility

Reject

Step 2 — Concept Development and Testing
- Convert ideas to concepts
- Preliminary internal data gathering
- Initial customer research

Reject

Step 3 — Business Analysis

Reject

Internal Projections and Evaluation   External Opportunity Assessment
- Obtain customer/market competitive data
- Detailed market research
- Cost/income/investment projections
- Preliminary market plan
- Preliminary development plan

Modify

Reject

Decision to Proceed to Development

FIGURE 15.3 Evaluating ideas and concepts: a three-step approach

2. *Does the product fit the company's core competencies?* Is the company technically qualified to pursue its development? Does it seem feasible to pursue in light of manufacturing capabilities? Or should the company use outside manufacturing resources?

3. *Does the product offer a meaningful customer advantage?* Will the product be able to compete with current and likely future competitive offerings?

Thus, issues relating to likely customer acceptance and competitive environment should also be considered during this first step.

> *Early objective assessment of the competitive situation and probable market acceptance is critical.*

However, in many cases, at this early stage, the external data used to help eliminate ideas are often unavailable. Extensive marketplace inputs, while vital, are more commonly employed after a judgmental screening, based primarily on internal data, has been completed.

The initial screening step is best accomplished by a management group that can bring experience and knowledge of company goals, strategies, and strengths to this early decision-making process. As such, representatives from all major functional areas should be involved.

Many ideas at this stage are easily eliminated. The process then continues with those deemed worthy of further evaluation. If a large number remain, a ranking, based on available internal data or knowledge, is done. A simple ranking form is provided in Table 15.1.

The major benefit of this approach is simplicity. Its weakness is that it is easy to manipulate the data by combining weight and rating numbers to obtain favorable results for preferred options. With a relatively small number of ideas, a ranking may be deferred until later or may not be used at all. In any event, at the end of this screening, the ideas left are ready to move onto step 2.

15.5.2. Step 2: Concept Development and Testing with External Customers

Development of a concept statement that provides a detailed description of the product, including features and benefits, begins the actions undertaken in step 2. If and when possible, performance and physical attributes such as speed, output, size, weight, and color should be included in the statement.

The concept statement then allows the ideas to be translated into terms a potential customer can understand. Sketches, mock-ups, or other visual or physical aids may also be appropriate to ensure understanding of the concept. (Examples of once-new products that would have been difficult to communicate without this step include such commonplace products as fax machines and voice mail.)

Another objective in step 2 is initial marketplace reaction. Only a limited number of potential customer inputs are generally obtained, and these reactions will lead either to further pursuit or to dropping of an idea. The product concepts, regardless of form, should be shown to prospective customers in a struc-

TABLE 15.1 Example of a New Product Idea Ranking Form

Factor	(1) Weight	(2) Rating 1 (Poor) → 5 (Excellent)	(1) × (2) Score
Strategic fit	20	5	100
Manufacturing fit	10	2	20
Sales force fit	10	3	30
Competitive environment	10	5	50
Investment level	10	2	20
Development risk	15	4	60
Market need	15	5	75
Total	100		355

tured setting such as a focus group environment, or presented individually. The major requirement is to obtain objective reactions. It is further recommended that during this concept presentation, the subject of product price also be researched.

In presenting concepts to prospective customers, the experience and objectivity of outside consultants or market research firms is often employed. If presented by the company, particularly the sales force, the possibility of bias exists.

> **Buyers and users should be shown sketches, models, or other concept renditions to gather objective reactions.**

Manufacturing, technical feasibility, and cost considerations—subjects that ultimately bear upon new product desirability—are often researched preliminarily at this juncture. This concurrent approach is an effective use of time. However, internal considerations can often be deferred until marketplace input is obtained. Obviously, not all products subjected to concept testing survive this step.

15.5.3. Step 3: Conducting the Business Analysis

This is the appropriate front-end time to conduct a more rigorous evaluation of those products surviving step 2. Here internal and external inputs are developed. Individual circumstances will dictate whether these evaluations are concurrent or sequential with data difficulty, costs, and time requirements governing the evaluation schedules. It should also be noted that until all external evaluations are completed, a final internal evaluation is not feasible.

15.6. EXTERNAL ASSESSMENT

Objectives for a typical external assessment are presented as follows:

- *Overall.* Describe the overall market (i.e., size, past and expected growth, segmentation, distribution channels, and key competitors).
- *Product specific.* How do potential users react to product concept(s)? What changes or modifications would improve the acceptance? How important are the perceived features and benefits? What are the critical design elements? How do potential users view the product's competition? What pricing is appropriate? What share of market might it capture?
- *Market specific.* Based on potential users' reactions, what segments or customers represent the target market(s)?

- *Competitive environment.* What competition will the product encounter? How might major competitors react?
- *Overall assessment.* How attractive an opportunity, from an external point of view, does this product represent? Should the company continue to evaluate?

Consultants or market research firms may conduct portions of that assessment for reasons akin to those reviewed in step 2. At a minimum, data on competitive activities or specific information requiring interviews with competitors are typically gathered by such outside agencies.

Two of the most important issues involved in an external assessment relate to (1) selecting respondents and (2) determining the methodology of obtaining input. For respondents, the practice is to include all those likely to influence a purchase decision. With business-to-business products, multiple individuals in customer organizations as well as those in the distribution channel represent typical purchasing prospects. It is also recommended that input from the internal sales organization be solicited.

With regard to methodology, the most workable techniques employed are telephone and personal interviews. Mail surveys are not viewed as appropriate tools because high nonresponse rates, particularly in many highly concentrated business-to-business markets, do not yield a significant proportion of targeted prospects.

15.7. INTERNAL ASSESSMENT OR EVALUATION

Internal assessment can best be thought of as obtaining all information needed to prepare a "mini" business plan. The external assessment will yield a significant portion of the information needed for this process. However, considerable effort is still required to gather and complete the necessary cost and investment analysis for an in-depth internal assessment. Financial measurement tools commonly used for the process include NPV (net present value) and IRR (internal rate of return). An outline example of a typical assessment is shown as follows:

> *A thorough internal assessment should focus the company's limited resources on prospective winners and defer investment in less promising development efforts.*

1. *Description of product.* What are the perceived user benefits, advantages over current products, etc.?
2. *Target customers or markets.* Who will the users be? What potential do they represent?

3. *Market opportunity assessment.* What were the results of the opportunity assessment? What issues remain to be resolved during prototype testing?
4. *Projected financial requirements.* How long will it take to develop the product? What will it cost to produce? What price will it command?
5. *Projected financial results.* What are the projected costs and benefits for the next five years? What are the risks? What is the projected return on investment? How does this compare to other alternatives?

With the completion of both assessments, physical product development can be initiated with confidence and the belief held that both its development and launch will be successful.

15.8. SUMMARY: BENEFITS AND RISKS

There are risks of eliminating a potentially successful product by using a rigorous screen and ranking process. However, the alternatives of pursuing products that are impossible to produce or to profitably market is equally unattractive. An equally important factor is the competitive nature of the market—being that early entrant may well be the best requirement for success.

The key is to achieve balance by considering cost, time, and risk associated with the internal evaluation process versus cost, time, and risk of marketing products too quickly. For example, if a product can be produced inexpensively in sample lots, little justification exists to invest in a formal front-end research process. If, on the other hand, a sizable investment in time-to-develop as well as millions of dollars are needed, the detailed evaluation is prudent.

No process yet developed guarantees new product success. As reviewed here, though, the evidence supports following a disciplined approach in the concept

> **Use an orderly, thorough, objective evaluation process to evaluate ideas and concepts.**

evaluation stage of the new product process.

REFERENCES

1. Cooper, R. G. and Kleinschmidt, E. J. An investigation in the new product process: steps, deficiencies, and impact. *Journal of Product Innovation Management* 3:71–85 (1985).
2. Crawford, C. M. *New Products Management*, 4th ed. Burr Ridge, IL: Richard D. Irwin, 1994.
3. Page, A. L. Assessing new product development practices and performance: establishing crucial norms. *Journal of Product Innovation Management* 10:273–290 (1993).
4. Page, A. L. and Stovall, J. S. Importance of the early stages in the new product development process. *1994 PDMA Proceedings.*

Ronald N. Paul
TECHNOMIC, INC.

Ronald N. Paul is president of TECHNOMIC, INC., a marketing and management consulting firm whose clients include many of America's largest and most prestigious companies. Active primarily in the food industry, TECHNOMIC's services include strategic planning, competitive analysis, new product concepts and planning, and trade and consumer market research. He is currently an officer of PDMA, a Certified Management Consultant, a former director of the Institute of Management Consultants, and has been a frequent speaker at industry, security analyst, and professional meetings. He has authored numerous articles for Harvard Business Review, Business Marketing, and Sales and Marketing Management.

16 PRODUCT ARCHITECTURE
David Cutherell

16.1. INTRODUCTION

The translation of market needs to product design is one of the major challenges in introducing new products. Establishing a product architecture bridges the gap between identifying customer needs and creating a product design. A good product architecture will translate the customer needs effectively and also assist the product manager in organizing the design and development of the product. In this chapter we cover what is needed to develop a product architecture and describe some of the things that must be considered during that development. The methods discussed in this chapter can be applied to any product, no matter how complex. The only thing that varies is how many times the cycle has to be repeated.

16.2. PRODUCT ARCHITECTURE

Developing a product architecture is the act of transforming a product function into a product form. It is a very important aspect of developing a product:

- Architecture affects the performance of the product.
- Architecture influences how the product can be changed once it is in production.

- Architecture determines the variety of the products that you can offer to your customer.
- Architecture can reduce the time it takes to develop new products.
- Architecture determines how the development of a product is managed.
- Architecture determines the ease with which a product can be serviced.

To understand this process one should start out by looking at the product from two perspectives [7, pp. 129–150]. The first is to look at the *function* of a product; the second is to look at the *components* of a product. For example, the function of a screwdriver is to turn screws, and it is usually made up of two physical components, the handle and the blade.

> **Effective product architecture assures that a product's components permit it to perform its required functions efficiently.**

Furthermore, the function of the product can be broken down into a number of *functional elements*. Functional elements are the individual operations that a product performs. These functional elements are usually expressed in schematic form to understand in greater detail how the product operates. This creates a language for the product that is functionally driven. This then allows brainstorming to occur around each functional element to determine how that function will be accomplished. Some of the functional elements of an inkjet printer are: store paper, store ink, deliver ink to paper, increment paper, and process print information. Each of these functions say what the functions are but not how the function is accomplished.

The components of the product can be thought of as *physical* elements. These physical elements are the parts and subassemblies that implement the function of the product. These physical elements become more defined as the product is designed. Some physical elements depend upon the original product concept, and some of the physical elements are not defined until the detailed design phase. Each physical element usually has at least one function associated with it, and very often there are multiple functions associated with each physical element. Some of the physical elements of a printer are the chassis, the carriage, the printed circuit boards, motors, and paper trays. One example of a physical element that has multiple functions is the chassis. It not only supports the product, but also defines the aesthetics of the product and helps direct airflow through the printer to cool the electronics.

> **Chunks are composed of several physical elements.**

The physical elements of a product are usually arranged into major building blocks, called *chunks*. These are made up of a number of physical elements. The *architecture* of a product is the way in which the functional elements of a product are assigned to its physical chunks and by which the chunks interact. In other words, the architecture of the product is the way that the function of the product maps into the form (chunks) of the product.

16.2.1. Prerequisites to Developing a Good Architecture

There are a number of items that must be understood prior to developing a product architecture successfully. These items all lead to understanding the problem prior to trying to solve it.

- Have a clear understanding of the customer's needs. All aspects of a product's architecture must flow from the needs of the market for which the product is intended. Understanding these needs is the single most important aspect of developing a good architecture.
- Have a clear understanding of the constraints. A number of constraints are imposed on the architect that must be met. These can be cost, schedule, reliability, aesthetics, and/or environmental in nature.
- Have a clear understanding of the priorities. Since customer needs and constraints are often in conflict, it is important to understand their priorities. This allows proper selection of features and functions of the product.
- Develop a historical perspective. There are usually existing products that perform a part or all of the functions of the product being designed. Become familiar with the architecture of these products and know how well they meet customer needs while satisfying the constraints placed upon them.
- Know your own limitations. There will be times when the product architect does not have the adequate skill base or time to devote to solving the problem. At this point it is wise to seek help from a professional in the field.

16.2.2. Modular Versus Integral Architectures

The first basic type of architecture is a *modular architecture*. In a modular architecture the functional elements map directly to the physical elements. In other words, the chunks implement one (or very few) of the functional elements. Also, the interactions between the chunks are better defined (and in some cases they are subject of engineering standards). Since interactions are well defined it is often easy to make changes to one chunk without affecting another.

The other basic type of architecture is an *integral architecture*. In an integral architecture functional elements of the product are mapped into a single or a very small number of chunks. This usually leads to individual chunks having numerous functions. Also, the interactions among components can be significantly more complex. Since a change in one area affects other areas of the prod-

TABLE 16.1   Modular versus Integral Product Example

Swiss Army Knife	Carving Knife
Each blade has its own function.	There is only one blade.
There are blades for cutting, opening cans, opening bottles, driving screws, etc.	The blade is designed to slice and to keep a sharp edge for many cuts.
Each knife is made up of a combination of blades and handle pieces.	The blade and the handle are of integral construction.
There are knifes for general use, survival, fishing, and to attach to a keychain.	There are knives specifically designed for the home or commercial markets.

uct, understanding the interactions is important to identifying all the changes needed.

> **Product architectures may be modular or integral.**

Table 16.1 shows a comparison of two similar products, one being entirely modular and the other entirely integral.

16.2.3. Modular Versus Integral: Which Is Better?

There is no set answer to the question of which architecture is better. The real answer is, of course: *It depends.* Very few products are completely modular or integral. It is usually the case that the some level of modularity is employed, depending on the intent of the design. It can generally be stated that integral architectures are usually driven by performance or cost, whereas modular architecture is driven by product change, product variety, engineering standards, and product service requirements. The implications of each of these are covered in detail in the next section.

TABLE 16.2   Pros and Cons of a Modular Architecture

Pros of Modular Architectures	Cons of Modular Architectures
Modularity improves your ability to change the product once it is introduced.	Too much modularity can make products look too much alike.
Modularity improves the variety and the speed of introduction for new products.	Modularity makes it easier to for your competitors to imitate the design.
Modularity improves maintainability and serviceability of the product.	Modularity reduces product performance.
Modularity allows development tasks to be decoupled.	Modular designs are usually more expensive than integral designs.
Modularity permits testing of subsystems through their interfaces.	

Tables 16.2 and 16.3 show some of the pros and cons associated with each architecture. These show that there are trade-offs to be made when making this important decision.

> *One of the most important decisions made during the system-level design of a product is the degree of modularity that a product exhibits.*

16.3. METHODS FOR ESTABLISHING PRODUCT ARCHITECTURES

The general goal of a product is to fill customer needs. The goal of establishing the architecture of a product is to break down the product into smaller chunks that can be addressed by individual designers or design teams. The end result will be to create a rough geometric layout that can be used by the individual design teams during the design process. The process should also define the interfaces between the chunks and clarify the interactions at those interfaces. Since the definition of most products is best created using a number of people, the architecture of the product should be done by a multifunctional group. This will help ensure that the design of the product is in concert with the overall product strategy. Ulrich and Eppinger [7, pp. 129–150] have devised a four-step methodology to help accomplish this.

16.3.1. Step 1: Create a Schematic of the Product

The *schematic* of a product is a functional representation of that product [5, pp. 140–166]. The blocks represent the function, and the lines illustrate how the functions are connected. It is important to note that the function represents *what* the product does and not *how* it does it. In addition, there are different types of lines to represent whether the flow is a signal, a material transfer, or an energy transfer. It is not desirable to add too much detail at this point. A good rule of thumb is to have no more that 30 elements in the schematic. It is worth noting that the schematic is not unique. Therefore, several should be created to explore

TABLE 16.3 Pros and Cons of an Integral Architecture

Pros of Integral Architectures	Cons of Integral Architectures
Makes it harder for your competitor to copy your design	Hinders change of design in production
Allows tighter coupling of team with less interface	Reduces the variety of products than can be produced
Increases system performance	
Reduces system cost	

different alternatives. An example of a functional schematic is shown in Figure 16.1 (This schematic is based on Hewlett-Packard's HP1200C [1].)

16.3.2. Step 2: Cluster the Elements of the Schematic

The next step is to group the elements into chunks (these are also sometimes called modules or assemblies). Be sure to define the chunks so that the interactions between them are as simple as possible; the simpler the interactions, the

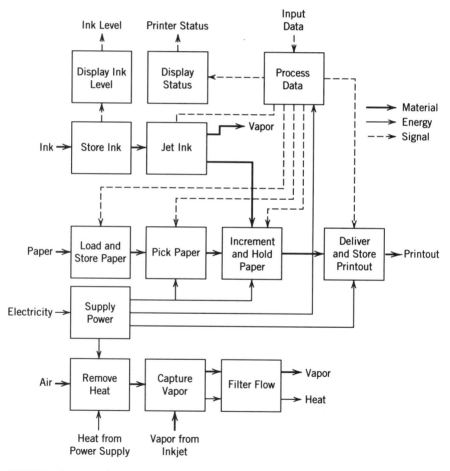

FIGURE 16.1 Functional schematic of a desktop inkjet printer.

better the architecture. There are a number of considerations to make at this time.

- What is the variety of the product needed If a large variety is needed, the chunks should be arranged so that they can be shared among products.

> **Chunks should have simple interactions with each other.**

- What is the capability of the manufacturer of the product? There might be certain processes of the manufacturer you will want to use. You might need to arrange the chunks to take advantage of these processes.
- Are there any areas that you see that the product will change? If there are certain areas that you anticipate change, you will want to make those into chunks.
- Are there any interface standards that must be adhered to? There might be internal or external interfaces between the chunks that you will want to adhere to to be compatible with products that are already developed.
- Are certain components going to share functions? There might be performance reasons or cost reasons that drive sharing of functionality among the components.

Figure 16.2 shows the clustered schematic of a desktop inkjet printer.

16.3.3. Step 3: Create a Rough Geometric Layout

The next step is to create a rough geometric layout. This step is often called conceptual design because the rough layout represents the first concept for the product. It is quite possible that this is being done in conjunction with the previous step, using somewhat of an iterative process. Often, the layout of the product will force the team to consider details of the geometric interfaces that are not seen in the preceding step. However, if you ignore the earlier step you will often overlook some concepts that will provide a better solution. As with the schematic, there are usually multiple configurations that the geometric layout can take. It is very useful at this point to explore as many of these configurations as possible. They can be examined and compared through analysis, models, simulations, or rapid prototyping. Figure 16.3 shows a rough geometric layout of the inkjet printer. Several different layouts for the paper path were considered prior to choosing the one shown.

16.3.4. Step 4: Define Interactions and Detail Performance Characteristics

Since each chunk is usually given to an individual or group, it is important to understand what happens between the chunks. The boundary between these

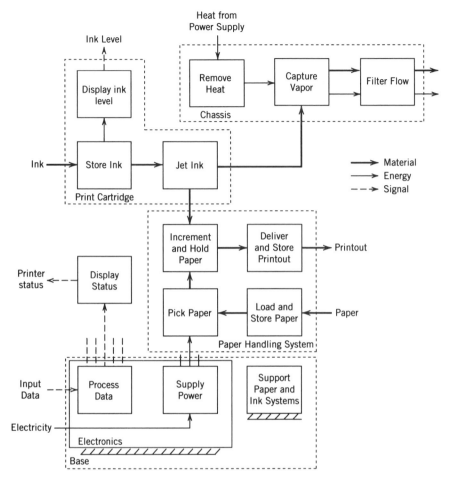

FIGURE 16.2 Clustered schematic of desktop inkjet printer.

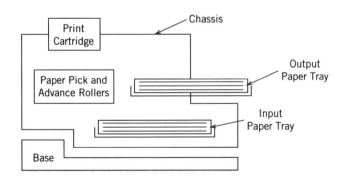

FIGURE 16.3 Rough geometric layout of a desktop inkjet printer.

chunks are called *interfaces,* and what flows across the interfaces are *interactions.* There are four basic types of interactions.

1. *Spatial interactions* are geometrical in nature.
2. *Energy interactions* usually are either electrical or thermal but can be other forms as well (such as laser and photovoltaic).
3. *Information interactions* can come in many forms, such as analog signals, digital signals, visual signals, and fiber optic signals.
4. *Material interactions* can also come in many forms, such as powder, liquid, solid, and gaseous.

Once the interactions are understood, the level to which a chunk must perform its functions is defined. The functional, performance, and interaction information, together with appropriate quality and design constraints, are used to build a detailed specification for that chunk. This information can be used to communicate among designers and can also be used by the manufacturing to create tests that will assure the quality of the product.

16.3.5. Representing the Product Architecture

A diagramming technique used to represent the architecture once it is defined is the system hierarchy diagram shown in Figure 16.4. At the top is the product,

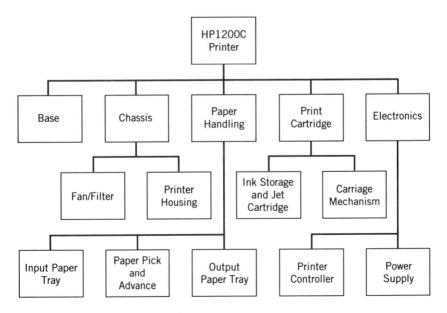

FIGURE 16.4 System hierarchy diagram.

below it at the next level are the chunks, and below that level are the physical elements of each chunk. It used as the basis for a work breakdown structure that in turn can be used to organize a project team around the product under development. This allows for team development around specific products along with proper allocation of budget and resources for each team.

> *A product development project work breakdown structure can be based on the architectural hierarchy of the product's chunks.*

> *The architecture of a product can best be represented using a system hierarchy diagram.*

16.3.6. Questions to Ask While Establishing Product Architecture

There are a number of questions that should be considered while establishing the product architecture. The implications of the answers to these questions are located in Section 16.5. Some questions that relate to product change:

- Which elements will require upgrading?
- Who will perform the upgrade?
- Which elements will be consumed?
- Will there be any add-on products?
- In what different environments will this product be used?
- Are there areas of the product that the user will want to change to increase its utility?

Some questions that relate to the variety of the product line:

- How many models do you plan to introduce based on the initial product?
- What additional user needs will those products satisfy?
- What is the product line strategy?

Some questions that relate to component standardization:

- What components does your firm use in large amounts?
- Which components are similar among the products that your company produces?
- Which existing components do you want to use in your new product?

Some questions that relate to product performance:

- What are the critical performance factors of a product?
- What are the competitors performance factors?
- Is performance more important that other considerations, such as variety and change?

16.4. PRODUCT FAMILIES AND PRODUCT ARCHITECTURES

16.4.1. Product Families

Platform Products

A *product family* is a set of products that is based on a common platform [2]. A *platform* encompasses the design and components shared by the set of products in a product family. This set of products have specific features and functions that are driven by different customer needs. Subsequent platforms are introduced as new technology, increased market knowledge, and manufacturing know-how become available.

In the automotive industry, automobiles are quite frequently based on a platform concept that will evolve over a number of years. The Chrysler Concord is a good example. Its "cab forward" design was a major improvement in space utilization for sedans and served as a basis for a number of other models, such as the Eagle Vision and Dodge Intrepid.

Derivative Products

Derivative products are the products that are designed around a platform product. Usually, the design of these products involve incremental improvements in either technology or customer needs. They often require little development and have minor impact on manufacturing processes.

There are three basic types of derivative products.

> *Effective product architecture provides an economical basis for derivative products.*

1. *Cost-reduced products* take the original product and reduce the cost of it either by removing features or by improving manufacturing efficiencies. This cost savings is then passed on to the customer.
2. *Product line extensions* take the basic product and add features without changing the price significantly.

3. *Enhanced products* are products that have added features that enhance the value of the product to the user. This is usually associated with a model of higher cost.

A really good example of a product with many derivative products is the Sony Walkman. In over ten years there were in excess of 200 Sony Walkman models based on just three platforms. Each model was designed for specific needs in specific global markets [4].

16.4.2. Product Families and Product Architecture

There are some far-reaching decisions made when mapping out the product family. These decisions can alter the design of the product significantly. Although this chapter is not meant to cover product family planning, here are just a few of the choices that are made that affect product architecture significantly.

- On what technologies are you basing the platform?
- What new products are going to be introduced based on the original product?
- What new features are going to be added or subtracted from the original platform to create these new products?
- Is there going to be a cost-reduced version of this product?
- How will the product be customized for different markets or distribution channels?
- What upgrades will be offered?
- Are components expected to be common with other platforms?

16.5. IMPLICATIONS OF CHOICE OF ARCHITECTURE

16.5.1. Product Development Management

The management of a product's development cycle is highly dependent on the architecture of the product. A well-defined product architecture with clearly allocated functions and well-defined interactions will be easy to organize and natural to manage. Degree of modularity will be a strong driver of the development cycle management [6]. Chunks of a modular product can generally be handed to "supplier-like" teams, whereas close team coordination is required throughout the process for integral architectures. Figure 16.5 shows other aspects of how the two approaches differ.

Concept Development → **System-Level Design** → **Detailed Design** → **Test and Refinement**

MODULAR APPROACH

Concept Development	System-Level Design	Detailed Design	Test and Refinement
Choose technological principles	Team leader uses architectural skills	Component design proceeds in parallel	Efforts focused on checking for unanticpated coupling and interaction
Set performance targets	Map functional elements to components	Monitor components relative to interface standards and performance targets	Required performance changes localized to a few components
	Define interface standards and protocols	Design performed by "supplier like" entities	
	Division of effort into specialist	Component testing can be done independently	

INTEGRAL APPROACH

Concept Development	System-Level Design	Detailed Design	Test and Refinement
Define features and variety	Team leader uses integration skills	Constant interaction required to evaluate performance and to manage implications of design changes	Effort focused on tuning the overall system
Choose architectural approach	Emphasis on system level performance	Component designers are all on the core team	Required performance changes propagate to many components
	Division of product into few integrated subsystems	Component tests must be done at same time	
	Assignment of subsystems to multi-disciplinary teams		

FIGURE 16.5 Differences in product development management according to architectural approach. Reprinted from *Research Policy* 24(3): 419–440, Karl T. Ulrich, The role of product architecture in the manufacturing firm, copyright 1995, with kind permission of Elsevier Science NL, Sara Burgerhartstraat 25, 1055 KV Amsterdam, The Netherlands.

It is important to note that different project management skills are needed for each approach. The modular approach needs more of a system architect type project manager who forces the definition of the components and their interfaces early in the project. The project manager is then responsible to enforce these interfaces and resolve conflict as necessary. The project manager for an integral approach needs to be very focused on the performance of the product and be technically capable of making the correct trade-off decisions needed to achieve that performance.

> *The selection of the new product development project manager should be based on a match of his or her characteristics and the choice of product architecture.*

The development associated with a product family is quite different from the development of a single product. Since product platforms can depend on significant development work in either technology or standardization of components, they should be the focus of an effort that is distinct and different from the subsequent introduction of derivative products. For example, in the 1970s Black & Decker spent a significant amount of resources developing the components that would go into their line of power tool products. After this effort was complete, they designed each line of power tools around these standard components. Another example of this is the Sony Walkman. They had technology development teams that created the innovations to make the Walkman smaller. The product teams then took this technology and incorporated it into the products that were designed to meet the needs of regional markets.

16.5.2. Product Change

The architecture of a product will determine how the product can *change*. Frequently, products undergo some change during the product life cycle. Since modularity creates interfaces that are well understood, one portion of the product can be changed without affecting the other portion of the product. This makes a strong argument to anticipate the areas where the product will change and design in modularity to those areas of change. There can be a number of inducements for change. See Table 16.4 for some specific ways that product change can come about.

16.5.3. Product Variety

The *variety* of a product is the number of products that can be designed into given product line. The product family usually presents the customer with a variety of choices to satisfy their individual needs. The degree of modularity of

TABLE 16.4 Product Change Inducements

Change	Example
Upgrades	Computer processors can be changed by plugging in new ones.
Adaptation to environment	Most products sold internationally must be able to accept a variety of voltages.
Consumable components	In the computer industry, printers have inkjet cartridges and tone cartridges.
Flexibility in Use	Photography enthusiasts will have a variety of 35mm lenses to attach to a single camera body.

a product determines the variety of products that can be offered in a single product line without creating custom designs for each product in that product line. A good example of product variety is the Swatch watch, through its use of component swapping modularity. To date, hundreds of different watches have been offered through this technique.

16.5.4. Product Performance

The *performance* of a product is how well the product achieves the functionality desired. Product performance is usually measured in such ways as efficiency, size, weight, and speed. For example, the heavier a car is, the less gas mileage it will get. Performance can usually be improved by implementing an integral product architecture. For example, a hand-held electronic calculator is meant to be small, light, and have a long battery life. With the exception of the batteries, very little of the product is modular and the product is optimized through the use of a very integral architecture.

16.5.5. Product Cost

It has been said that 80 percent of the cost of the product is determined in the early phases of design. This makes decisions made about product architecture very influential in the overall cost of the product. Integral architectures tend to be more complex and costly to design but can be less costly per unit to produce due to lower manufacturing overhead. More modular architectures tend to be simpler and less expensive to design but can result in more expensive products, due to increased overhead for manufacturing. Cost considerations dictate a careful trade-off between development cost and production cost. As a result, high-volume, low-cost products can typically withstand the higher development cost of an integral architecture. Some examples of high-volume products that are integral in nature are calculators, disposable razors, single-use cameras, and ballpoint pens.

16.5.6. Component Standardization

The use of the same component or chunk in a variety of products is called *component standardization*. Component standardization is driven by the modularity of the product. Component standardization has several benefits. Inventory is usually reduced because the number of parts to make a firms of products is reduced. Standard components that are manufactured by outside suppliers are usually produced at larger volumes and undergo greater reliability testing. Thus they have a higher reliability at a reduced cost. Standard components can also be produced to help speed development of a variety of products. The learning curve associated with that component can be applied toward new products, which ultimately reduces the development time needed.

16.5.7. Impact on Product Service

> *A modular architecture simplifies product service.*

The service of a product is the maintenance and repair of the product over its life cycle. There are elements of any product that wear or fail over time. When looking at the architecture of the product it is wise to anticipate those areas and make them modular. This allows either the user or the service person to diagnose and replace the failed item. Even better, if the item that fails is part of a consumable, it will be replaced in a regular fashion and will therefore be replaced prior to failure. Both laser and inkjet printers are good examples of this. The laser printer has a drum that is the weak spot of the design. This drum is usually incorporated into the toner cartridge so that it is replaced when the toner runs out. In an inkjet printer, the inkjet nozzles are the highest failure-rate item. The ink jets are part of the ink reservoir that is replaced periodically when the ink runs out. Thus in both cases the consumable is paired with the failure item to be a modular component that is replaced when the consumable runs out.

16.6. SUMMARY

Through the process of establishing a product architecture, the product manager creates the tie between customer needs and product design. Product architecture is the way in which the function of a product is mapped into the form of the product [9]. The architecture of a product dictates how the product is subdivided into smaller pieces, and it describes the interactions between these pieces.

The two basic types of architecture are modular and integral. The degree to which a product is modular or integral is an important decision. This decision affects the design of the product as well as how the product development effort is managed. The many implications of a product's architecture can also affect product change, product variety, component standardization, product performance, product cost, and product service.

There is a methodology to facilitate the definition of a product architecture. It is functionally driven and has four general steps: create a schematic of the product, cluster the elements of the schematic, create a rough geometric layout, and define the interfaces and identify the interactions.

ACKNOWLEDGEMENTS

Many people have helped contribute to this chapter. First and foremost, I would like to thank Karl Ulrich. Much of this chapter reflects his views and methods in product development. His support over the last few years has helped to bring my understanding of product architecture to a level that allowed me to write this chapter. I would like to thank the many people at DTM Corporation, especially Craig Wadham and Kris Grube. They helped me put many of the methods of this chapter into practice during the design and development of DTM's Sinterstation 2000™. I would like to thank my editor, Abbie Griffin, for her continuous support while writing this chapter. Finally, I would like to thank my wife for giving me time that I should be spending with her so that I could pursue this endeavor.

REFERENCES

1. Bockman, Kevin M. et al. HP DeskJet 1200C printer architecture. *Hewlett Packard Journal* 45(1): 55–66 (February 1994).
2. Meyer, Marc H. and Utterback, James M. The product family and the dynamics of core capability. *Sloan Management Review* 34(3):29–47 (Spring 1993).
3. Pine, B. Joseph, II. *Mass Customization: The New Frontier in Business Competition.* Boston: Harvard Business School Press, 1992.
4. Sanderson, Susan and Uzumeri, Vic. Managing product families: the Sony Walkman. *Working paper.* Troy, NY: Rensselaer Polytechnic Institute, 1992.
5. Ullman, David G. *The Mechanical Design Process.* New York: McGraw-Hill, 1992.
6. Ulrich, Karl T. The role of product architecture in the manufacturing firm. *Research Policy* 24(3): 419–440 (1995).
7. Ulrich, Karl T. and Eppinger, Steven D. *Product Design and Development.* New York: McGraw-Hill, 1995. pp. 129–150.
8. Ulrich, Karl T. and Tung, K. Fundamentals of product modularity. *Proceedings of the 1991 ASME Winter Annual Meeting Symposium,* Atlanta, GA, 1991.
9. Wheelwright, Steven C. and Clark, Kim B. *Revolutionizing Product Development: Quantum Leaps in Speed, Efficiency, and Quality.* New York: Free Press, 1992, pp. 57–85.

APPENDIX: TYPES OF MODULAR ARCHITECTURES

There are a variety of modular architectures to keep in mind when determining the architecture of a product [3, pp. 171–212; 8]. Figure 16.6 illustrates various kinds of modularity.

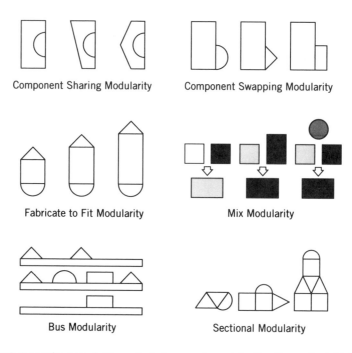

Component Sharing Modularity   Component Swapping Modularity

Fabricate to Fit Modularity   Mix Modularity

Bus Modularity   Sectional Modularity

FIGURE 16.6 Iconic description of six types of modularity. From Karl Ulrich and Karen Tung, Fundamentals of product modularity, *Proceedings of the 1991 ASME Winter Annual Meeting Symposium on Design and Manufacturing Integration.*

Component Sharing Modularity. Component sharing modularity is when the same component is used across many different products. This is often done to standardize components or to adhere to industry standards. This type of modularity can happen on a single product line or among products from a variety of companies. Black & Decker's line of power tools use many of the same motors, controls, and casings, which allows them to manufacture in bulk for economies of scale. A hard drive in a desktop computer is a good example of component sharing: The same hard drive can be used in many different computers.

Component Swapping Modularity. In component swapping modularity, different components are used with the same basic product. This is done to increase the variety of products that can be offered or to increase the flexibility in use. The Swatch watch is a good example of component swapping modularity. The basic watch is made up of hands, faces, movements, cases, and wristbands. New watches are created by swapping individual components to create new styles. Photographers also enjoy products with a large degree of swapping modularity. Cameras have the ability to swap lenses, flashes, cases, and straps.

Fabricate-to-fit Modularity. In fabricate-to-fit modularity, one or more of the components is variable in some way, such as size or shape. This is usually done to satisfy a customer need, such as for variable sizes. PVC piping is an example of fabricate-to-fit modularity. Each pipe can be cut to the length desired and then assembled with other standard components. Custom-fit bicycles are another example. Some companies produce bikes that are custom made to fit the person buying the bike.

Bus Modularity. In bus modularity, many different kinds of components can be attached to a common structure through a standard interface. This can be done for a variety of reasons, including offering greater product variety and allowing third-party development of add-on products. This type of modularity is seen in both the lighting and electronics industries. In track lighting, for example, a bus is attached to the wall and a variety of lights can be attached anywhere along the bus. There are a number of electronic bus structures in the computer industry. Two of the more common buses in the personal computer industry are NuBus and EISA.

Mix Modularity. In mix modularity, several standard components are mixed together to produce a new product. This is done primarily to offer a greater product variety. The paint industry is probably one of the most widely recognized examples of mix modularity. A huge variety of paint colors can be created with standard paint components. The food industry can serve as a very tasty example of mix modularity. Some restaurants create a huge variety of meals from some very standard and basic ingredients. Also, many of the packaged foods in grocery stores are simply reformulations of an existing product.

Sectional Modularity. In sectional modularity, sections of a product can be configured in a variety of ways through a standard interface. The product is then build up of a number of sections that can be configured to the needs of the customer. Office furniture is an example of sectional modularity. Work surfaces, drawers, and partitions are designed so that they can be assembled to fill any size room and can be customized to a number of different work areas.

David A. Cutherell
Design Edge

David Cutherell is Director of Business Development for Design Edge, a product development firm in Austin. There he is responsible for operations and development of new business opportunities. Prior to joining Design Edge, he worked at DTM Corporation and was responsible for the development of numerous generations of rapid prototyping equipment. He lectures at the University of Texas in both the School of Business and the School of Mechanical Engineering in product development subject matter. He has received a B.A. from Austin College, a B.S.M.E. from Texas A&M University, and a M.S.M.E. from the University of Texas at Austin.

17 HOW INDUSTRIAL DESIGN FITS INTO PRODUCT DEVELOPMENT

Walter Herbst

17.1. INTRODUCTION

Emotional response is a basis of all purchase decisions. Products are ultimately purchased because they either make us feel good, make us work better and more efficiently, or simply because we like them. Once over the hurdle of how one product may have greater attributes over another, the ultimate purchase decision is usually based on looks. If it looks right, it must be, at least that is the perception. But while appearance and style are important in the purchase decision of a product, there is more to this subject of design. The chapter begins with an overview, then covers key activities in more detail.

17.2. HOW INDUSTRIAL DESIGN FITS INTO PRODUCT DEVELOPMENT

"Industrial design is the professional service of creating and developing concepts and specifications that optimize the function, value, and appearance of products and systems for the mutual benefit of both user and manufacturer" (Industrial Designers Society of America, 1142 Walker Road, Great Falls, VA). We can use this formal definition as a beginning and review the skills of those people to better understand exactly what their backgrounds are and to make the definition of industrial design a little more personable.

> *Industrial design is the combination of aesthetics coupled with function and supported with a full understanding of materials and manufacturing processes.*

It's safe to say that all industrial designers are basically artists. That is, they can sketch and render concepts that readily communicate their ideas. Industrial designers are all basically creative *idea* people. If you give any one of them a problem, the industrial designer has the ability to *visualize* a solution. Having the ability to visualize also allows one to explore various three-dimensional options. So, with visualization capabilities, it's not unusual that a number of broad creative solutions to specific problems can be put on paper. Industrial designers are interested not only in how things look, but in how things work. While they are visualizing, they are also thinking about the operating mechanics of the product as well as thinking about the materials and processes required for the production of the product. The formal education they all share is an undergraduate degree in industrial design with courses that stress aesthetic design, human factors, mechanical engineering, materials and processes, and basic drawing and art classes. Their campus time is usually shared equally between the fine arts campus and the engineering campus.

Now that we've done a little review on the industrial designer and their skills, let's take that as a beginning and review in order *all* the tasks involved in the development process, for a quick summary of where and how industrial design (ID) fits (Table 17.1). We'll look at what the key activities of industrial design are for each of those tasks.

Rather than elaborate on the minor tasks with which ID is involved it is far more important that we review in detail those tasks where ID takes the lead role. Those areas include: preliminary concepts, design consolidation, and control drawings. It is also important to review ID's role in visual model development, as that area is critical in the design process even though the industrial designer is not responsible for getting the work done, but rather, assumes responsibility for the final work output.

17.2.1. Preliminary Concepts

Before actual concepts can begin a target opportunity is defined, usually with a basic *business opportunity plan* (BOP). The BOP defines trends, preferences, competition, general specifications (to include features, functions, and cost), and includes an initial business plan. Once completed, even casually, preliminary concept design can begin.

In beginning the design we find the level of creativity, in terms of total exploration, to be far greater if the expected solutions are not defined but remain ambiguous. It is far better to define the problem than to define the solution. An

TABLE 17.1 Key Industrial Design Activities

Task Definition	ID's Role	What ID Does at this Stage
Strategic planning	Core participant	Contributes from an experience point of view. Participates in recognizing overall design needs as well as material and process opportunities for capital planning and manufacturing cost targets.
Research	Minor participant	ID is involved principally as an observer for the interactive research tasks but has an opportunity to contribute to the questionnaire design for the research.
Preliminary concepts	Leads the effort	ID not only establishes the basic direction for the physical form of the product, but is a key player in exploring the attributes that will allow for a strategic competitive advantage. Materials and processes are also explored in this early concept task.
Concept research	Minor participant	ID is often an observer in order to interpret first hand the target markets' perceptions of the preliminary concepts.
Design consolidation	Leads the effort	Following research review, design changes and consolidations are developed by ID to maximize the potential of the final design direction.
Concept confirmation research	Minor participant	ID is an observer in order to understand, first hand, if the design consolidation effort met the target markets perceptions.
Control drawings	Leads the effort	These drawings are developed by ID to ensure the final nuances of the form. In developing the control drawings, the physical definitions of the product are delineated and include defining electromechanical components as overall volumes to confirm fit.
Visual model development	Minor participant	ID reviews the modelmakers' efforts and may not only make last-minute changes as the model develops, but takes responsibility for color, texture, finishes, and graphics. ID will also review the concurrent development of a "breadboard" proof-of-concept model to ensure that no surprises are brewing.
Market confirmation	Minor participant	This is ID's final chance to observe the end users, in final preference research. If there is a problem to the end user, in terms of the "looks like–feels like" of the product, it must be addressed now.
Preliminary engineering	Minor participant	ID acts in an advisory capacity to engineering as problems arise and if trade-offs have to be considered regarding the overall design.
Prototype development	Minor participant	ID oversees the prototypes and confirms overall forms, fits, finishes, and final graphics relative to the initial control drawings and the follow-up preliminary engineering.

TABLE 17.1   Key Industrial Design Activities (*Continued*)

Task Definition	ID's Role	What ID Does at this Stage
Final engineering	Minor participant	ID can be expected to make minor changes during the prototype exercise. These changes need to be transmitted and re-viewed with engineering. ID continues to maintain its position as an advisor as needed.
Tooling release	Core participant	ID plays an active role in final materials, final engraved textures, and final colorants. Tool-ing trade-off requests are not unusual, and as they relate to visual surfaces, ID plays an active role.

example of an ambiguous solution was in a project we received from a major writing instrument company. They had a very successful history with their liquid correction fluid. They recognized the user problem of having to cope with the combination of a bottle dispenser and dried-out or distorted brushes (Figure 17.1). Rather then defining the solution, only the problem was presented.

The final creative solution that went to market was a penlike product that dispensed the correction fluid through a spring-loaded ball-point-pen type of point. To help the usage and flow of the product, the dispensing pen was de-signed using a flexible material with a belly shape extending from the barrel. The belly was squeezed, the tip was placed on the word needing correction, and a thin white correction line was placed on the mistake easily and accurately (Figure

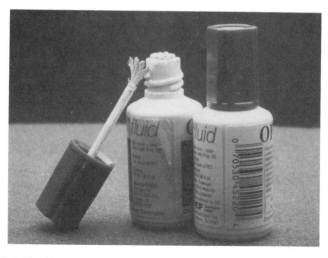

FIGURE 17.1 Liquid correction fluid: existing product.

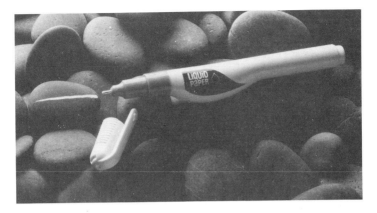

FIGURE 17.2 Dispensing pen solution.

17.2). A follow-up solution, which required two years of development, was a dispenser that laid down a very thin white tape over the mistake. The tape did not require a drying time, thus allowing the user the opportunity to make corrections quickly (Figure 17.3). Had the project greater definition relative to the solution, the final designs would not have been nearly as creative and probably would have been in the form of larger-necked bottles and finer brush applicators.

As an ongoing activity during the preliminary concepts task, it is also the industrial designer's responsibility to appreciate solutions required to achieve forecasted time to market needs, as well as forecasted manufactured costs. These

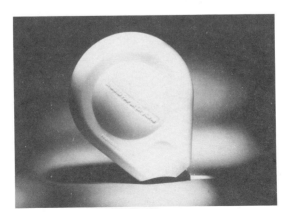

FIGURE 17.3 Tape dispenser follow-up solution.

efforts need to be addressed while paying attention to the manufacturing variables that will assure a quality product. It also needs to be mentioned that the
most successful creative solutions always include a multifunctional team. For the
concept design phase the team is always led by the industrial design group.

The tasks that assure the preliminary design concepts will be successful start
with a basic brainstorming session led by an industrial designer and includes
marketing and engineering. The purpose is do a brain dump. Throw every idea
on the table: the rational, the silly, the turn-it-upside thought—they all count.
All ideas are considered good ideas that can be amplified. Brainstorming culminates in a multitude of thumbnail ideations for review (Figure 17.4). Thumbnails are the most basic visual identification technique, usually consisting of very
rough pencil sketches, minimally amplified with colored Magic Markers. It is not

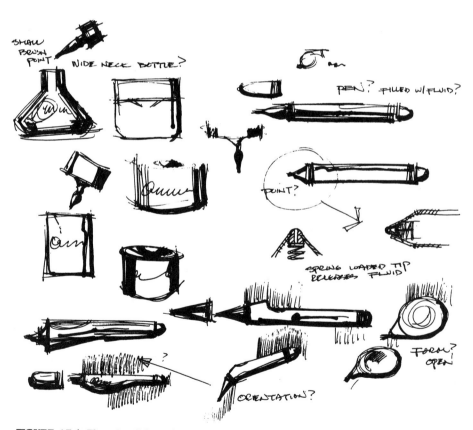

FIGURE 17.4 Thumbnail ideations.

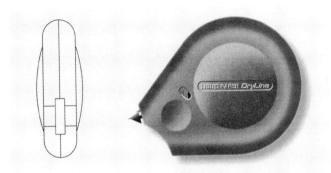

FIGURE 17.5 Realistic rendering using Photoshop computer technology.

unusual for 50 to 100 individual, very rough ideations, to be presented to the internal team. The core team then picks the sketches up, reviews each of them for form, human factors, and manufacturing process ideas and chooses those concepts that it believes have the best opportunity for success for continued development. The continued development is in the form of colored design renderings, colored sketches, or preliminary shape studies. The renderings can also be developed using computer technology, the most popular being MAC-generated Photoshop, which outputs photo-realistic renderings, or the more sophisticated, UNIX-based Alias (Figure 17.5).

Accompanying the design concepts are very preliminary, graphic cross sections of the product (Figure 17.6). These cross sections allow the industrial designer the opportunity to understand and communicate the manufacturing processes that will be required for completion of

> *Preliminary cross sections allow the designer to convey ideas to engineering regarding manufacturing processes.*

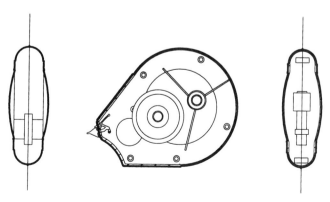

FIGURE 17.6 Cross sections.

the program. The sections, which help describe the manufacturing process, are critical in early discussions with other members of the team and are a great help in understanding the manufacturing variables of cycle time dealing with time, quality, and cost. At this early stage of design, it is relatively easy to convert a high-production, large-capital-budgeted, long tooling process, such as injection molding, to a lower-production, minimal-budget, short tooling process, such as extrusion, if the constraints demand it.

17.2.2. Design Consolidation

The design consolidation phase allows for a modification of a number of the original thumbnails to incorporate the comments that were reviewed in both research and in senior management reviews. It would be highly unlikely that one of the original design concepts would move ahead unchanged. Normally, there are design features on any one solution that can add significantly to another design, so a consolidation takes place. The consolidation presentation is a more sophisticated rendition of the design chosen. Details are elaborated and graphics are more detailed and include attention to both the functional graphics of control areas and to addressing decorative graphics. The decorative graphic aspect includes the branding of the product and use of the logo. Decorative graphics include model names as well as visual model numbers.

Since the design consolidation phase culminates in one of the last checks before enormous resources are spent in modeling, engineering, and prototyping, great attention must be paid to ensure that the final rendering absolutely represents the product. In most cases of consolidation, computer-generated renderings are supplied. These computer renderings are photo-realistically correct and include absolute details, including final graphics and textures. The renderings can also show the product in its true environment and can be developed with appropriate props. Studio lighting as well as specific spot lighting can be computer generated to emphasize various features.

The renderings should be of such a nature that they will be suitable for buyer review as well as for marketing collateral needs, including catalogue sheets. Because the final renderings are computer generated, the electronic databases can be used for the color separation and printing needs of marketing. This final consolidation of the design includes a more complete explanation of the materials and processes as well as reviewing the number of parts that will go into the housing of the product. The industrial designers' task is to include this detail into a more comprehensive sectioned view of the product. I don't want to confuse this exercise with engineering or even with control drawings. The sectioned views deal more with a simplistic representation of the final parts, as seen through a slice of the product rather than with the absolute engineering of the parts.

Although the industrial designer is more than competent in developing these initial manufacturing parameters, the multifunctional team is again brought into the picture for the conclusion of the design consolidation phase. This may include marketing, engineering, manufacturing, and purchasing. The ID group takes the lead in the review, which is not only for the purpose of sharing ideas, but in building consensus of the total design to include the recommendation of materials and processes to allow the program to proceed in an orderly manner. The entire team is necessary, as marketing needs to give a more comprehensive projection of annual volumes, engineering needs to confirm those critical path portions of the tooling program, and purchasing, in concert with engineering and ID, needs to review capital budgets and preliminary piece-part cost relative to all the processes available.

17.2.3. Control Drawings

The control drawing task becomes a critical element for continued development of the product. The drawings are the responsibility of

> *Control drawings are used by ID to transfer the absolute shape of the product to engineering.*

ID, as they delineate the absolute three-dimensional form of the product. It would be most unusual if the creator of the chosen design did not personally develop the control drawings to ensure design integrity. The drawings consist of defining all the piece parts that will make up the housing portion that is visible. These details will be developed as individual parts as well as assemblies, where the parts are actually put together to form the complete product. The reasons for the control drawings are threefold, the first being the fact that in all product development programs, visual models need to be built. For a modelmaker to build something, a set of plans must be developed. The control drawings are those plans.

The second reason is one of transference. Ultimately, the product requires complete engineering. Again, to assure absolute compliance with the aesthetics of the design, the engineering team needs an accurate data base from design. The control drawings represent that database. Included in the file are suggested assembly methods for the finished products, the final materials, colors, finishes, textures, and sourced components as required.

The third reason deals with the need to begin reviewing the design with the manufacturing and tooling resources. The control drawings attach enough details to the individual housing elements that review can now begin in earnest. If the design is such that either tooling or assembly is going to exceed original expectations, it is early enough in the process that changes can still be made without a great impact on time or overall development budgets.

When we talk about developing a database, we are referring to a CAD method of drawing (Figure 17.7). CAD is simply computer-assisted design. The computer-generated drawing is most often used as the transfer to engineering, as it is not only more accurate then drawing with a pencil and T-square and measuring with rulers, but far more efficient. The efficiency is not that it takes less time to develop the control drawing, but rather that it allows engineering to get a running start with an accurate database that is design sensitive. The ultimate engineering details *must* be CAD generated for greater accuracy, and starting with a database from ID simply reduces the time element.

17.2.4. Visual Model Development

ID is a minor participant in this task from the point of view of actually producing the work. However, the visual model development is so critical to the success of the design that an in-depth review of the exercise is important. Model development is given over to a small and very elite group of professionals that have been trained either as modelmakers (which is very rare), or as tool-and-die workers, or simply as craftsmen, who may have developed their skills totally on their own. The modelmakers are a rare breed, as they not only possess an excellent background in math but also must possess terrific creative skills in analyzing equipment available to produce desired shapes. They need to couple those skills with color sensitivity and extreme patience, as the finished model must be visually perfect (Figure 17.8). Computer skills have also become a major requirement in an area of modelmaking commonly recognized as rapid prototyping. Rapid prototyping takes all of the traditional required model-building skills and moves them up a notch by requiring complex computer transfer of information and reformulating databases to numerically controlled computer-assisted automated equipment.

The visual models can be identified from actual production parts only by virtue of the fact that they are normally perfect. It is not unusual for one to analyze a production part and find some flaw. The flaw may be in a mating part that varies ever so slightly. Or the flaw may be in a label application. And while those production flaws may be minor, the visual model should be perfect. The textures, finishes, shape, feel, weight, and color must be perfect for the development process to work at maximum efficiency.

ID's responsibility during this task is one of being the model champion, assuring that every incremental task is perfect, that each curve and detail is exactly as imagined and drawn. A good relationship between ID and the modelmaker is critical, as more often then not, minor changes will have to be made on the spot. Waiting for final completion of the finished model may be too time consuming if changes need to be made. As changes are made, ID has the re-

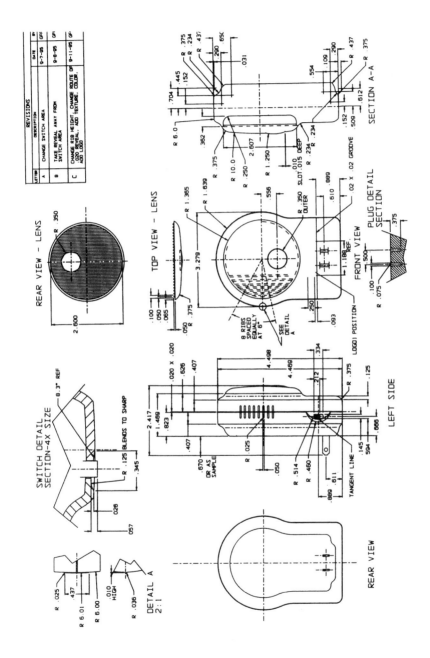

FIGURE 17.7 CAD database.

247

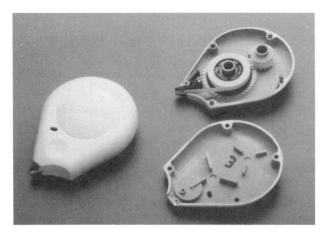

FIGURE 17.8 Finished visual model.

sponsibility of documenting them on the control drawings. Making visual changes without documentation will only lead to problems missed down the line in engineering and production.

The support tasks that ID will oversee start with the selection of appropriate materials for the project. What materials will replicate the production part best? How should a chrome-plated zinc casting for a faucet be replicated in the model shop? How about a knob that requires a soft touch? A number of decisions have to be made up front and ID plays a critical role. Remember, successful development relies on appropriate time, budget, and quality variables. ID takes that responsibility during the modelmaking process.

Following a review of material opportunities, ID must be present for the initial *roughing* out of the shape. Does it have to be tweaked; is it proceeding on an appropriate course; are the handles of the correct angle? Following that roughing-out activity, final finishing takes place. Even though a specific color may have been specified from a color chart, it may have to be changed based on any number of reasons. Perhaps the reflections are changing the color, or placing the product into a stimulated retail environment with artificial lighting isn't giving it the perception of quality that is desired. And what about the final texturing of the part? Is the original specification still appropriate? You can see that while ID does not actively fabricate the model, the role they play is critical for the success of the model.

So what happens to the model, and why is it so critical to the success of the product? Why can't required changes simply be noted so that the process can continue into the engineering phase? The answer to those questions is marketing driven. The model needs to be so perfect that marketing may use the product for preselling to buyers before proceeding with the costly steps of final engineering, tooling, and production. As part of that presell, marketing may use the model for catalogue development or trade show introduction. Remember, at this point the model is so perfect that a buyer can easily recognize the impact at retail and can start making commitments for the new product.

Modeling is also important for consumer reaction. After all, just because a buyer falls in love doesn't assure that the product will sell through. The marketing department will almost always do consumer testing with finished visual models. This is the last chance for confirmation before a very timely and costly development.

So, we've reviewed where ID fits into the role of product development and where it is most active, and why that activity is critical to the success of the product. Having noted that, I think it is also important to call out those areas to which ID can't contribute.

ID cannot make a positive contribution to a bad idea. It may try to stop the idea from happening, but it can't save a bad product

> *Industrial design can not make a positive contribution to a bad idea.*

concept that doesn't fit a marketing need. It also can't save poor quality. The Cadillac Alante was a lovely-looking car, but it took six years to solve all the quality issues, and by then the market had simply tired of the product. ID couldn't solve shampoo products labeled "Look of Buttermilk" or "Touch of Yogurt" with better packaging when all they promised with poor branding was a very bad hair day. ID surely couldn't solve Polaroid's Polavision instant movie camera when videotape technology was simply far better [1]. You just can't solve a bad idea or poor quality with industrial design, not even great design.

17.3. WORKING WITH INDUSTRIAL DESIGNERS

So, where do you start? Your own organization may have an ID department, but unless it is a very large organization, the chances of having an internal department are slim. The reason for that comes in the numbers. It normally takes five to ten engineers to support the efforts of one industrial designer. And if it doesn't actually take that multiplier of bodies, it does take that multiplier of time.

Consider the fact that good ID works better when working in a larger group and you can see why most domestic corporations do not have design departments. Fortunately, there are a large number of professional ID firms. When selecting a firm it is important that the members be associated with the International Conference of Industrial Designers (ICSID). In the United States the professional organization is the Industrial Designer's Society of America (IDSA). IDSA is in effect the licensing organization, much as AIA (American Institute of Architects) is to that profession, and you do want to work with a professional. Similar experience to your program is not necessarily important, as often, designers' greatest resources for your needs is their background in other areas, which may make a significantly greater impact, due to knowledge of other technologies.

Large consulting offices can normally dedicate a team of multifunctional professionals, while the smaller boutiques may view you as their most important client. The risk, of course, is that another *most important* client may also enter their lives. There is no correct answer to the question, "Should I go large or small"?

When interviewing ID firms, go to their facilities. Do they have the technologies that will support your engineers? Don't be afraid to bring your engineers along. After all, they'll be partners for a long time. Probably the most important part of the selection is simply the culture. Will they fit, and does the fit feel good? You're going to want a long-term relationship, as there is a learning curve, so go slowly in your selection. Go with your gut: If it feels right, it probably is. And don't worry, as their professional competence has already been confirmed by their peers and hopefully, by your due diligence.

REFERENCES

1. Power, Christopher et al. FLOPS: Too many products fail. Here's why—and how to do better. *Business Week*, August 16, 1993, p. 76ff.

Walter Herbst
Herbst LaZar Bell

Walter is one of the founders and CEO of Herbst LaZar Bell, a 33-year-old product development and design organization. The firm is one of the largest in the United States. He is a Faculty Fellow at Northwestern University's McCormick School of Engineering and also serves on the faculty of the Kellogg Graduate School of Management at Northwestern in their Marketing Department. Mr. Herbst holds over 30 patents in a broad range of products. The firm he founded is one of the leaders in the use of technology and in the practice of concurrent development.

18 TOOLS FOR QUANTITATIVE MARKET RESEARCH

Steven H. Cohen

18.1. INTRODUCTION

The use of qualitative research to understand buyers' feelings and motivations about new products and services has been explored in earlier chapters. In this chapter we review common research tools for quantifying this information and for developing forecasts of likely market acceptance.

18.2. CONDUCTING QUANTITATIVE RESEARCH

Quantitative market research involves using a structured methodology to collect data from a sample of current and/or potential customers and employing those data to generalize the results to a wider population. It typically involves a formal questionnaire, a controlled interviewing environment, tabulation of results, and statistical testing. Quantitative research answers many questions involving new product development.

- How large is the current market, and how much do they purchase?
- Who are our customers and our competitors' customers?
- Who are nonbuyers?
- What market segments exist, and what motivates them?

- What is awareness of my brand or company?
- What is our image?
- How satisfied are my customers?
- What factors influence satisfaction?
- How do potential buyers react to my new concept, package, communications, or name?

18.2.1. Quantitative Survey Research Comes in Different Packages

Quantitative surveys are distinguished by their data collection method. Mail, telephone, and in-person surveys have unique features that make each one more or less appropriate for new product research (see Table 18.1).

Mail surveys are the most cost-effective means of collecting data. Hundreds or thousands of surveys can be collected for the cost of typesetting, printing, and postage. Respectable response rates of 40 percent or more can be achieved with a well-laid-out survey, prenotification via a motivating letter, postcard follow-ups, second survey mailings, and the cautious use of incentives. The biggest influence on mail response is topic salience: An interesting topic will induce higher response. This no doubt biases results toward those most interested, but incentives and follow-up procedures can balance this tendency.

Mail surveys can be any length, but for longer surveys, a larger incentive is suggested. Moderately complex tasks such as ranking and choosing several desired features from a list can be done easily through the mail. Top-of-mind responses and probes are impossible in mail surveys since the interaction between an interviewer and the respondent is absent.

Mail surveys have disadvantages that limit their use. Printing, mailing, and collecting a sufficient number of responses can take several weeks. Security can also be an issue. When testing a new product's description and features, the loss of control over just who receives the survey and what they do with it could be a cause for concern. Nor does the researcher have control over who fills out the survey (the targeted executive or his or her secretary).

The most marketing research dollars are spent on telephone surveys. Telephone surveys are moderately expensive and involve relatively easy response tasks. Top-of-mind questions and open-ended probes are ubiquitous in telephone surveys. Security can be controlled in telephone surveys. The use of incentives, while rare, seems to be increasing, especially for those in hard-to-reach occupations or those with some rare characteristic.

The cost and time needed to complete a telephone survey depend on the number of interviews, the incidence of a qualified respondent, the length of the interview, the time of year, and the number of surveys to be completed. Good

TABLE 18.1 Comparison of Survey Methods

	Survey Method			
	Mail	**Telephone**	**In Person (Home or Office)**	**In Person (Intercepts)**
Use of incentives	Recommended	Not necessary except in rare cases	Recommended	Recommended
Cost per interview	Low	Depends on population to be reached	High	Moderate
Ability to use visuals and physical prototypes or to do taste tests	Visuals only	Not possible	Yes	Yes
Possible interview complexity	Few skip patterns; many complex question types possible	Complex skip patterns; many question types not possible	Both complex skip patterns and question types are possible	Both complex skip patterns and question types are possible
Awareness, open-ended questions, and probes	Not possible	Possible	Possible	Possible
Speed of response	Slow	Fast	Moderate	Moderate
Security	Low	High	Moderate	High
Survey length	Long surveys possible	Moderate length	Long surveys possible	Long surveys possible
Control over who responds	Low	High	High	High
Control over conduct of interviews	Low	High	Moderate	High

research practice demands that several attempts be made to each phone number, allowing the more mobile respondent to be reached. Supervision of interviews done in central facilities is excellent, as interviewers are constantly monitored and provided with feedback on their performance. Concerns about long surveys and premature interview terminations have prompted some firms to place limits on the length of telephone surveys, ruling that surveys will be no longer than 20 minutes.

> *The cost and time needed to complete a telephone survey depend on the number of interviews, the incidence of a qualified respondent, the length of the interview, the time of year, and the number of surveys to be completed.*

In-person surveys take manyforms, from shopping mall intercepts to trade shows, from prerecruited invitations to come to a central interviewing facility to in-home interviews. In-person interviewing is expensive, since, in most cases, monetary incentives must be used to gain the cooperation of an unbiased sample.

Completing surveys at a central location affords an unparalleled degree of control over the interviewing situation:

- Visuals and product prototypes can be shown; new products can be smelled, tasted, or manipulated.
- Probing, skip patterns, and top-of-mind questions can easily be asked.
- Complex stimuli and tasks such as rankings, simulated shopping situations, and watching test commercials are easily accomplished.

There are several disadvantages to in-person surveys. For intercept surveys, cooperation fees vary from nothing to $10 or more. For interviews recruited by telephone with an in-person follow-up, anywhere from $30 to more than $100 in cooperation fees will need to be paid to each respondent.

In-person surveys may yield a biased sample. Shopping mall intercepts may be biased toward those who shop and who shop more often at these types of locations. Intercepts at trade shows are biased toward trade show attendees. Prerecruited interviews may be biased toward those living or working nearby or to those willing to travel to the central interviewing site. In-home interviews may be biased toward those neighborhoods where interviewers are willing to work.

18.2.2. How to Calculate a Sample Size

Most practical discussions of how to calculate a sample size mention three possible methods. The statistical method uses a formula to choose the sample size. An agreed-upon statistical confidence level, an acceptable plus or minus range of error tolerated, and the expected variability in the results of a few key questions are key inputs. In most cases, a 90 or 95 percent level of confidence will be used along with a plus or minus range of error from 3 to 10 percent. The expected variability is estimated from prior surveys. In the absence of prior work, using 50 percent is the most conservative method.

Industry "rules of thumb" provide yet another method of selecting a sample size. Most marketing research companies should be able to provide commonly used sample sizes for satisfaction studies, new product concept tests, or awareness and image studies. Table 18.2 shows commonly used sample sizes for various types of studies.

In the cost-based method, you take a fixed survey budget, subtract all costs not associated with data collection, divide by the cost per interview, and "voilà!" the sample size appears. This method is poor since it uses neither statistical

TABLE 18.2   Typical Sample Sizes Used in Different Types of Marketing Research Studies

Study	Minimum Size	Typical Size (Range)
Market studies	500	1000–1500
Strategic studies	200	400–500
Test-market penetration studies	200	300–500
Concept/product tests	200	200–300/cell
Name test	100/name variant	200–300/cell
Package tests	100/package variant	200–300/cell
TV, radio commercial tests	150/commercial	200–300/commercial
Print ad tests	150/advertisement	200–300/commercial

Source: Adapted from [2].

concerns nor industry rules of thumb. This is probably the worst way to choose a sample size for research.

Three other size issues are worth noting. First, money is probably better spent on methods to increase response than on additional interviews. A response rate of 10 percent from a sample of 1000 without any procedures for increasing response will not yield results as valid or reliable as 100 interviews achieved via a 50 percent response rate from a sample of 200 that had multiple contacts, incentives to respond, and so on. Second, select a sample size based on the smallest subgroup that you expect to analyze. At a minimum, 75 to 100 respondents per sub-

> *Money is probably better spent on methods to increase response than on additional interviews.*

group is recommended. If you expect to analyze three subgroups (e.g., light, medium, and heavy buyers; young, middle, older ages), the final sample size should be around 300. Finally, do not confuse statistical significance with substantive significance. It is easy to find statistically significant results with large samples, yet it is also easy to find nonsignificant but interesting results with small samples. Let statistics guide your analysis, but keep your eye on the meaning of the results.

18.3 GUIDELINES FOR CONDUCTING SURVEY RESEARCH

A full list of do's and don'ts for surveys is best left for a textbook. However, a partial and irreverent list of favorites follows.

1. Importance ratings are notoriously easy to collect and difficult to interpret, since each rating is independent of the others and we ordinarily do not

ask respondents to distinguish among them. Avoid asking direct importance questions whenever possible.

2. They are respondents; therefore, they answer questions. Respondents will generally answer our questions, no matter how irrelevant or poorly phrased those questions are. Well-worded questions will be answered intelligently and must be salient to the respondent's situation.

3. Pretest, pretest, pretest. Even the best writer of surveys needs to pretest. Avoid jargon associated with your industry and phrase questions in simple terms.

4. Calculate a response rate. Know how many respondents terminated, refused, and completed your interview. It will help to frame your results and help you plan your next survey effort.

5. Ranking tasks are difficult. Although you would like to have concepts or features ranked, most people are incapable of reliably telling you much beyond their first or second favorites, or their least and second-least favorites. Avoid ranking if you can.

6. Build a database. Keep track of respondent answers across studies. Track the same questions across time and concept tests. Build institutional learning.

7. Don't use misplaced precision. Reporting a result as 4.127 on a scale of 1 to 5 is ridiculous.

8. All lists, including customer lists, are imperfect. Find the best list you can and use screening procedures to refine the list for the survey.

9. Use incentives whenever you can. Incentives can improve response rates and thereby the quality of your data and the results.

18.4. TYPES OF QUANTITATIVE MARKET RESEARCH

We now discuss several key methodologies appropriate to the new product development process. These include a method to understand the importance of product features and pricing (trade-off or conjoint analysis) and methods for forecasting market potential before introduction.

18.4.1. Trade-Off or Conjoint Analysis

For almost 20 years, trade-off or conjoint analysis has proven to be a versatile, easy-to-understand, yet difficult-to-implement tool of the marketing researcher.

Designing the Study

Conjoint analysis is a marketing research technique that *reveals the drivers of preference* by decomposing a respondent's overall rating of a product or service into weights attributable to each of the product's components. It is used for concept screening, pricing, product design, location siting, competitive analysis, segmentation, and distribution decisions [4,12].

When designing a conjoint study, the researcher first enumerates the key decision attributes or factors, such as product features, the price, or the brand name.

> *Conjoint analysis is a marketing research technique that reveals the drivers of preference.*

Next, the levels of each attribute are determined. Presence or absence of a feature has two levels, price might have three levels ($2.00, $2.50, and $3.00), and brand might have five levels, representing the major players in the category.

An experimental design is then used to create product or service descriptions, called profiles. The profiles are created so that the effect of each factor on preference can be statistically estimated net of the other factors of interest. Respondents are then asked to react to the profiles in some way, perhaps by ranking the profiles or rating them. The analysis of these data decomposes the respondents' reactions, allocating more weight or utility to those factors that drive high ratings.

An important first step in designing a conjoint study is to figure out how many profiles are necessary to show to respondents so that the feature utilities can be estimated. For example, if there are four decision attributes, each with three levels, there are $3^4 = 81$ possible product profiles. Clearly, no sane researcher would ask a respondent to provide 81 reactions.

How can we capture the important information from respondents, yet not overburden them? The magic of experimental design allows us to play a variation on the old television show "Name that Tune." In that show, contestants tried to guess the name of a mystery song given as few musical notes as possible. In market research a technique called fractional factorial design allows the researcher to present a small, selected number of profiles for evaluation, yet obtain estimates for the most salient influences. The marketing literature provides ready reference on designs for applied situations [4].

What Does the Respondent Do?

Most researchers will certainly agree with the imperative to ask reasonable questions and to present stimuli for response that are as realistic as possible. Early applications of conjoint analysis depended on ranking tasks to collect trade-offs. Respondents would rank order a set of product profiles from the most to least preferred. It has been proven that statistical analyses that treat ranks as if they are ratings yield comparable results. Most recent applied work has used ratings rather than ranking tasks.

Paired comparisons of product profiles are also used in conjoint studies. Respondents indicate their degree of preference between successive pairs of profiles. Commercially available software manipulates the preference decision between successive pairs with information from prior responses, so that the respondent's decision becomes harder and harder as each pair is encountered [7]. The presentation of pairs stops when the respondent is indifferent between the two profiles in that pair.

Recent conjoint work has utilized *discrete choices* as the respondent task [1,8]. In this case, respondents are shown several competitive product profiles that comprise their possible options. One of the choices may even be "none of the above." The respondent's task is to choose his or her most preferred product or service from the competitive set. As a much more realistic task for respondents, this technique has gained in popularity over the past few years.

Forecasts and Simulations

The final step of a conjoint study is to forecast the changes in respondent preferences or choice shares attributable to changes in the product's price, features, and so on. Several hypothetical or actual products are first "designed" using the features under study, and then the equations that embody the feature preferences are applied to these products to discover each one's overall utility or attractiveness. A market-share simulator is used to predict what buyers will do.

Brighter Future for Conjoint Analysis

Conjoint analysis is an evolving methodology that will continue to increase in usability and appeal. Computer programs are now becoming available that aid in designing efficient product profiles [5]. As modeling of choice has increased, we expect to see an increase in the use of conjoint analysis to estimate both choices and purchase volumes.

> *We expect to see an increase in the use of conjoint analysis to estimate both choices and purchase volumes.*

Growth in the use of "latent class" modeling of conjoint data is also likely [1]. These are techniques that segment respondents on the basis of the relationship between the response and the features. For example, a recent study investigating purchase intent for a new durable tested price, product features, and appearance. While aggregate results indicated that price was the dominant predictor of preference, the latent class approach uncovered a large group of people wholly driven by price and a smaller feature-oriented group that was much less price sensitive.

Future conjoint analysis work must investigate incorporating the effects of changes in the marketing mix on the study results. Conjoint forecasts tell us little about the trajectory of growth in new product share. Combining conjoint results with diffusion models (see below) can increase its usefulness.

In conclusion, we echo the words of Green and Srinivasan [4], who point out the danger associated with the ready availability of software for conjoint analysis. In the hands of the inexperienced user, conjoint analysis software may produce misleading results. However, for the experienced and savvy researcher, conjoint analysis is the premier tool for understanding what buyers want.

18.4.2. Forecasting Sales

Survey-based forecasting methods are an integral part of marketing research practice and provide important information and diagnostics to the new product team. We discuss the most powerful survey-based forecasting procedures: simulated test markets (STMs) and new product diffusion models.

Simulated Tests Markets

STMs are used to predict new product awareness, trial, repeat, volume, share, and profits and provide diagnostic information on consumer likes and dislikes. STMs meld consumer survey results with managerial inputs about planned advertising spending, pricing, and distribution. Undertaken prior to a test market, or in some cases in place of a test market, STMs supplement the gut feel of managers with a systematic conceptual framework and data collection procedure. STMs are often undertaken when the risks and costs of a full-blown test market are too great.

Steps in Implementing an STM Study

> *STMs are often undertaken when the risks and costs of a full-blown test market are too great.*

The STM begins with product information and marketing input from the new product or service developer. These inputs include product features, positioning, pricing, distribution, and so on. These are the managerial inputs that together with the subsequent survey results, form the basis of the forecast. Respondents are recruited using telephone calls or shopping mall intercepts. They then are engaged in an initial interview that typically involves a review of the respondent's knowledge, involvement, and use of products in the category.

Exposure to advertising for the product is followed by a purchase "experience." This experience can yield either stated purchase intent, an "actual" purchase using their own money, or a purchase with their cooperation incentive money. Diagnostic questions, including perceptions of value, likes and dislikes, uniqueness, and attribute ratings, follow the purchase experience.

When a product is available for further testing, a home-use period corresponding to an appropriate amount of time for the product category is followed by a call-back interview. During this interview, repeat purchase intentions are asked, as are additional diagnostic questions on satisfaction. Additional call-backs, or *sales waves*, may be employed. STMs typically take from 10 to 14 weeks to execute and employ samples of 400 or more.

Forecasting Sales Potential

If purchase intent is recorded, survey results are adjusted, typically downward, to compensate for overstatement of actual purchase. These "intent deflators" are heavily researched by academics and are closely guarded proprietary secrets of commercially available STM services. Usually, the survey results are compared to a proprietary database of past STMs to characterize the performance of the product tested.

STM Accuracy

Commercially available STM services share similar data collection and modeling procedures, accuracy claims, and strengths and weaknesses [9]. Commercial providers make strong claims for the accuracy of their services. Accuracy claims of ± 10 percent in more than 90 percent of the cases are not unusual. Few unbiased sources or academic articles that document the accuracy of commercial STMs exist, and none have been published in the past ten years or so; thus these claims must be taken with a grain of salt.

> **Few unbiased sources that document the accuracy of commercial STMs exist.**

Although commercial STM providers cannot point to unbiased evaluations of their forecasting accuracy, proving accuracy is a very difficult and time-consuming exercise. Consider what must happen to validate an STM forecast:

- Only those products introduced into the market can ever be validated. Products forecast to fail by an STM are rarely commercialized, so there is an inherent bias toward successful products.
- STMs forecast year one sales based on the year 1 marketing plan. Hence at least one year after the forecast was made using the STM, the client and STM provider must reconstruct the actual marketing plan to understand

how it would have affected the forecast had it been used instead of the forecast plan.

Urban and Katz [11] show that about half of the difference between actual sales and STM forecasts can be attributed to a difference between the in-market execution and the plan used in the forecast, rather than to any systematic errors in the STM procedure.

Ehrman and Shugan [3] point out that STMs are plagued by what they call *survivor's curse*. Actual sales will often disappoint, since only products with high forecasts on average will be introduced. This leads to what they call *prophet's fear*: the tendency of forecasters to be pessimistic in their forecasts, so that fewer products will be introduced and hence the accuracy of their forecasts cannot be tested.

They suggest several solutions. First, more experimentation and testing of different products offer more diagnostic information. Spending more money on new product tests decreases the uncertainty of the forecasts. Third, launching a new product in the absence of a good STM outcome is desirable—if for nothing else but to judge the value of the STM. Finally, lowering the critical value for a product launch will allow more products to be launched and will decrease survivor's curse.

STM Strengths Outweigh Weaknesses

The strengths of STMs far outweigh their shortcomings, ensuring their continued use in marketing and new product research. STMs significantly reduce risk and decrease long-term costs. By systematically weeding out losers, STMs are the most cost-effective means of judging the in-market success of new products. The information gained from an STM is more timely than that which would be available from a full-blown test market: three or four months versus six months to one year. Conducting an STM also allows a manufacturer to keep their new product hidden from competitors, something that cannot be done in a real test market.

The diagnostic information from an STM can optimize the marketing mix through better positioning, pricing, distribution, and product configuration. STMs increase managers' understanding of

> By weeding out losers systematically, STMs are the most cost-effective means of judging the in-market success of new products.

the new product process and increase their participation in new product planning. Finally, relative to other methods of new product forecasting that are not survey based, STMs are very accurate.

The inherent weaknesses of STMs still call for caution. The competitive environment is often ignored, although this is being addressed by new developments in STM technology. Since many STMs incorporate managerial judgment into the forecast, outcomes can be very inaccurate. Totally new products may not be amenable to STM testing since consumers will not have a good frame of reference. If the STM does not use an in-home test, problems in use that affect repeat purchase or after-use word of mouth cannot be determined. Finally, the entire question of trade response and the actual implementation of the marketing and product introduction plan is not addressed in an STM. If these are handled poorly, the STM forecast will be inaccurate.

Diffusion Models

Diffusion models, such as those illustrated in Figure 18.1, are used to describe the rate of diffusion of a new product over time through a social system [6]. Properly used, diffusion models can predict the future trajectory of sales and can help managers control this trajectory through prudent manipulation of the marketing mix. These models are typically used for first-purchase-only situations, usually durable goods or ongoing services, rather than for packaged goods or consumables that have trial and repeat components.

> *Diffusion models can predict the future trajectory of sales and can help managers control this trajectory through prudent manipulation of the marketing mix.*

In back-casting the sales of existing products, diffusion models fit sales histories very well. To judge the sales of new products, forecasting is a much trickier proposition, since no information is available for the forecast. Often, the sales histories of analogous products or other products in the line are used to help forecast the sales of the new product. Diffusion models can also incorporate survey data to forecast new product sales. Urban et al. [10] describe the use of a macroflow diffusion model to forecast the sales of a new automobile. In-market sales matched the model's forecasts quite well.

18.5. SUMMARY

Quantitative survey research plays an important role in new product testing. The knowledge to be gained, the testing of managerial assumptions, and the ability to simulate the outcomes of alternative courses of action make the techniques discussed in this chapter an invaluable part of the new product development process.

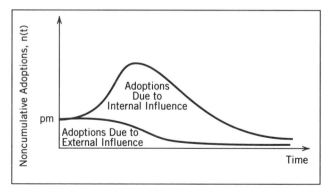

A. Adoptions Due to External and Internal Influences in the Bass Model

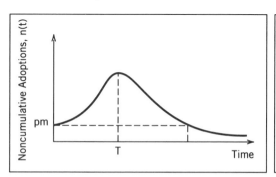
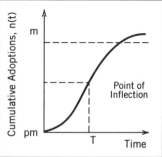

B. Analytical Structure of the Bass Model

FIGURE 18.1 Bass new product diffusion model. From Vijay Mahajan, Eitan Muller, and Frank Bass, New product diffusion models in marketing: a review and directions for research. *Journal of Marketing* 54(1)1-26 (January 1990).

REFERENCES

1. DeSarbo, Wayne, Ramaswamy, Venkatram, and Cohen, Steven H. Market segmentation with choice-based conjoint analysis. *Marketing Letters* 6(2):137–18 (March 1995).
2. Dillon, William, Madden, Thomas, and Firtle, Neil. *Marketing Research in a Marketing Environment*. Homewood, IL: Irwin, 1987.
3. Ehrman, Chaim M. and Shugan, Steven M. The forecaster's dilemma. *Marketing Science* 14(2): 123–147 (April 1995).
4. Green, Paul E. and Srinivasan, V. Conjoint analysis in marketing research: new developments and directions. *Journal of Marketing* 54(4):3–19 (October 1990).
5. Kuhfeld, Warren F., Tobias, Randall D., and Garratt, Mark. Efficient experimental design with marketing research applications. *Journal of Marketing Research* 31(4):545–557 (November 1994).
6. Mahajan, Vijay, Muller, Eitan, and Bass, Frank. New product diffusion models in marketing: a review and directions for research. *Journal of Marketing* 54(1):1–26 (January 1990).
7. Sawtooth Software. *Adaptive Conjoint Analysis*. Sun Valley, ID: Sawtooth Software, 1987.
8. Sawtooth Software. *The CBC System for Choice-Based Conjoint Analysis*. Sun Valley, ID: Sawtooth Software, 1993.

9. Shocker, Allan D. and Hall, William G. Pretest market models: a critical evaluation. *Journal of Product Innovation Management* 3:86–107 (June 1986).
10. Urban, Glen L., Hauser, John R., and Roberts, John H. Prelaunch forecasting of new automobiles: models and implementation. *Management Science* 36(4):401–421 (April 1990).
11. Urban, Glen L. and Katz, Gerald. Pre-test market models: validation and managerial implications. *Journal of Marketing Research* 20(3):221–234 (August 1983).
12. Wittink, Dick R. and Cattin, Phillipe. Commercial use of conjoint analysis: an update. *Journal of Marketing* 53(3):91–96 (July 1989).

Steven H. Cohen
Stratford Associates, Marketing Research & Decision Modeling, Inc.

Steve Cohen specializes in research design, analysis, and the application of marketing science tools to the solution of business problems. He has investigated the potential for new and existing products and services around the world. Steve has served clients in industries as diverse as financial services, computer hardware and software, consumer durables, business-to-business services and products, and telecommunications. Before founding Stratford Associates, Steve held senior positions in several marketing research and consulting organizations. He has been an Area Editor for Marketing Science, *has spoken at industry conferences, and has published in academic marketing journals.*

PART THREE

DOING THE DEVELOPMENT

Farming looks mighty easy when your plow is a pencil and you're a thousand miles from a cornfield.

—Dwight David Eisenhower, U.S. President, 1956

Product cost, product quality, and time-to-market issues in doing the development are highly dependent on the quality of the work done in the upstream phases. One way of improving performance on these issues is to overlap traditional tasks, moving away from doing them sequentially in relay-race fashion. Another is to work on key tasks simultaneously, using a multifunctional framework for interaction between functions during the new product development process.

An effective framework can take many forms, depending on the new product situation. Some situations reflect different new product options: product improvements, additions to product lines, new category entries, and new-to-the-world products. Others mirror the choices that a firm makes in balancing resources for ongoing operating concerns with those needed for integrating development. Still others flow from the nature of the industry in which the firm chooses to compete.

19 ASSEMBLED PRODUCT DEVELOPMENT
Robert Stoy

19.1. INTRODUCTION

Assembled products consist of components that can be hardware or software or consumables, or mixtures of all these components. Examples of hardware products are electric drills, hospital wheelchairs, or furniture products. Examples of software products are spreadsheet applications, games, or programming language products, although there is certainly some hardware associated with the distribution media. Consumable product examples are hair shampoo, chemicals, and automobile air filter cartridges. More complex products are systems such as laser printers or automobiles that use all of the different types of components interacting with one another.

19.2. CRITICAL SUCCESS FACTORS FOR ASSEMBLED PRODUCT DEVELOPMENT

It is essential to know the specific factors that will make the product successful in the market being served, and this implies that the customer, the market needs, and the company's strengths are well understood. There are several key success factors that help ensure an organization's success in developing assembled products:

- Knowledge of the specific functionality of the product being created: the features, benefits, and performance specifications.
- A thorough understanding of the technologies being used in the product: for example, injection molding plastic parts or object-oriented software languages or monoclonal antibody purification methods.
- Having people available who are skilled in the necessary technologies, either as employees, contractors, or consultants, as well as having the requisite manufacturing and distribution facilities.

19.3. MANAGING COMPLEXITY

Development projects can be complex if many skill disciplines are needed, or if people from multiple geographic sites are participating in development activities, or if many different suppliers of parts and subassemblies are used, or because the product demands a multiyear development cycle using a large team. For these complex projects, several important decisions should be made early in the development cycle.

A team organization strategy should be developed. If more than a dozen people are involved directly and full-time in the project, an organization consisting of a core team with subteams is probably necessary. Clear roles and responsibilities for all of these teams are necessary. Is a system architect or system subteam needed? If the product is technically complex, consisting of the interplay of various technology elements, a system architect or system development team may be needed. Sometimes, the project manager takes the role of system architect, but this is an overload of work on any but the smallest projects.

> *Ford Motor Company used a co-located team, Team Taurus, to develop the 1996 Taurus beginning in 1991 when the team was formed. A group of 150 engineers was located in one part of Ford's Design Center and they had a single, unifying goal expressed by a banner that said "Beat Accord," the best-selling Toyota product. Engineers were in offices alongside marketers, designers, and factory floor workers and all were dedicated to putting out only one product, the 1996 Taurus [4].*

What should be the involvement of senior management? If the project is significant to the organization's financial success, and the success of most large projects is certainly essential to future revenue plans, it is necessary to involve senior company management in the oversight of the project. This involvement should be during early development stages, when the influence of senior management provides the greatest leverage on results. Without the participation of management in the key decisions (they don't have to make the key decisions, just understand and support them), the will to support a complex project during the inevitable difficult times can dissipate. The project manager and the project team must communicate well and often with senior management. For smaller projects that are less complex, less visible, involving fewer people, and less critical to future revenue plans, there is certainly less need to consider all of the foregoing activities. However, there is one additional complexity for small projects that often makes their success problematic, and that is the necessity of sharing people with other projects. Senior management should make every effort to support the dedication of staff to a single project.

19.4. CREATING A PLAN FOR THE REST OF THE DEVELOPMENT PROCESS

19.4.1. Critical Staffing Decisions

As the development process begins, a plan for all of the activities during the development cycle, including the initial sale of the product to the customer, should be prepared and agreed to by the project team and by management. Figure 19.1 shows an overview of the major project activities from a design, build and test point of view. The project activity plan is sized to the project and its complexity. It is not uncommon to see this planning consume 20 percent of the project duration, although other development activities are usually proceeding in parallel with these planning activities.

Understanding critical staffing needs and bringing the right people onto the project team are among the earliest planning activities. Match the skills required on the project to the people available and see what skills are missing or inadequately represented. Develop a plan to secure the proper skills, whether by adding more people, hiring new people, or using consultants. If people with critical skills are not available, consider delaying the start of the project. Similar thoughts and cautions apply to the availability of critical physical resources, such as pilot manufacturing facilities or specialized development equipment.

19.4.2. Selecting Development Partners

Will all of the development work be done within the company, or will development partners be engaged? This is another of the earliest decisions necessary to make. It may be that another company has the better expertise in creating a hardware subassembly or a software program. Consider a licensing or original

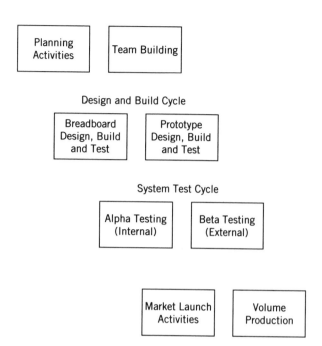

FIGURE 19.1 Design, build, and test cycle.

equipment manufacturing agreement with that company and involve them early in the design concepts [5]. They can probably help create a better product if brought in early when there is flexibility in changing the design concepts.

Management of the development partner is always a concern and should not be approached lightly. Using a single contact person from each organization is advisable to prevent miscommunication. Scheduled review meeting are important, particularly when the partner is not co-located with the development company. Contractual agreements, requirements documents and specifications, and delivery and service agreements are all important and need to be reviewed during the partnership. If there are multiple development partners, a team of people may need to be organized simply to work these issues.

It is important to agree upon strategies of make versus buy as early as possible because these strategies affect resources needed as well as development cycle time. Predicting project schedules is almost impossible without knowing whether certain components will be bought "as is" from existing suppliers or undergo development by the project team. Also, patent licensing and royalty payment schemes should be assessed and understood early in the planning process. These inevitably affect the eventual revenues from the product and can adversely alter the profitability of the product if not carefully managed.

19.4.3. Development Cycle Milestones

Only the smallest projects can get by without setting intermediate milestones prior to the shipment of the product. For projects that last more than a few months, set key milestones. Try not to let more than two months go by without a key milestone. The reasons for doing this are: helps project team see progress and keeps morale up with a sense of accomplishment; and helps the rest of the organization, especially senior management, see progress. Meeting these intermediate milestones is the key measure of judging whether the product ship date will be achieved. The objective is to find key, meaningful milestones, not simple publicity milestones.

19.4.4. Strategies for Concurrent Engineering

Since all assembled products have production operations as a sustaining endpoint, involvement of the manufacturing and customer service functions is critical to the product's success. While the project is being planned, it is possible to reduce cycle time to its minimum by conducting manufacturing and engineering activities in parallel [7]. On the surface, there appears to be more risk in this approach because manufacturing is asked to commit to expenditures and the use of resources before there is certainty that the engineering solution is fully correct and in its final form. However, the revenue from the cycle time gain that can be achieved is usually much greater than the potential of increasing expenses for materials or capital equipment. Large capital-intensive projects should use return-on-investment or internal rate-of-return calculations as an aid in assessing risk.

19.4.5. Recording the Plan with Software Tools

The development plan, with all its activities, should be recorded, preferably in a Gantt chart or network diagram format. For the simplest projects a short written list of events with dates is appropriate. For large complex projects, schedules of milestones for the entire project are needed along with more detailed schedules for the activities of the subteams. A number of software programs for various computer operating systems exist; some are suitable only for smaller projects, while others can accommodate the most complex projects. The values of using software are in the relative ease of updating the plan and in the ability to perform "what if" analyses on the effects of changing resources and modifying activity duration.

> *Software manufacturers usually have on-line forums as part of the commercial on-line service providers that are worth investigating. There are useful discussions of specific project management software applications as well as general discussions of value engineering, cost analysis, project management techniques, and upcoming seminars and meetings.*

19.4.6. Managing the Plan

The project manager is responsible for managing the development plan, and for some projects, the manager will personally update and control the schedule. For larger projects, this task of schedule updating is often delegated to one or more team members, although the project manager needs to have up-to-date knowledge of the status of scheduled tasks.

Schedule plans are often completed in the planning phase and then not updated until the product ships, at least in those organizations that are not contractually bound to maintain updated schedules. This approach shortchanges the project because it reduces the communication of critical activities among team members (interactive tasks start to fail) and does not provide for organization learning to improve the next project. At the very least, schedule updates should be done at agreed-upon major milestones. This can be built into the planning process and the schedule.

> *Schedules should be updated at major project milestones, at the very least.*

For large projects, the subteams should maintain their own detailed schedule of tasks and ensure that their schedule is connected to the overall project schedule, something that all of the larger project management software applications can easily do. The project manager will need to ensure that this activity takes place and that a common task structure is used by all the subteams.

19.5. DEVELOPMENT

19.5.1. Breadboards

Assembled products often involve the creation of breadboards, which are not to be confused with any devices constructed during the feasibility or research work that preceded development. The breadboard devices, which may be subassemblies or subsystems of the product, are created by the development group, not manufacturing, and are made to engineering documentation, not final manufacturing documentation. The documentation is often incomplete and may be little more than schematics or sketches.

Breadboards should have one thing in common—they exist to reduce design risk and are created to test specific, critical design components about which uncertainty exists. For example, breadboards may be created to show only the outward appearance of the product, or the thermal control of the product, or some particular mechanism that is critical to functionality, or some software control function. The testing of breadboard functionality is performed by the appropriate development team members, often with the designing staff participating in the effort if not leading the test effort. In larger projects, a test team may be in place to perform this work. Test protocols that address the specific functionality of the breadboards are needed and success is judged by the degree to which the protocols are completed successfully. It is frequently true that complete functional testing of a subassembly cannot be done because other product elements (or subsystems) are not yet in place.

Products with embedded software are notoriously difficult to test from the perspective of getting the software to work with the hardware. The hardware cannot be tested adequately without the software being completed and working, and the software cannot be tested without working hardware. One way to get the job done is to do incremental software and hardware development using several short iterative cycles. This approach is better than assuming that both hardware and software have been developed independently with no flaws and waiting until the end of a lengthy development cycle to test the system as a monolithic device.

The testing of this higher-integration-level system is left to later in the development cycle of most products, either at the prototype design level or the advanced manufacturing system design level. The key to success in breadboard construction and testing is to assess thoroughly those critical elements of the final product that are not well understood and which are essential to product performance, and then see that the breadboards address those elements.

19.5.2. Prototypes

The concept of prototypes has been in a state of flux for the past decade in the case of hardware design. The original definition of a prototype device was a complete system, with almost full functionality, built by the engineering development group to engineering documentation (not final manufacturing documentation). This prototype is able to carry out all important functions of the product and have most of the appearance features of the eventual product. This concept has changed as more manufacturing groups get involved early in the development process and as design for manufacturability has become more prevalent. Today, many companies have shortened development cycles by changing the prototyping process. There is great recognition that the prototype is so close to the final product that manufacturing and service groups must have a larger stake in the form that a prototype takes. Many prototypes are now built by manufacturing personnel to engineering documentation (made better by the use of newer computer-aided-design software) and with the help of the development staff. This improves manufacturing knowledge of the assembly process, the supplier's capabilities, and the testing needs of the product. All of this early knowledge contributes to a shorter cycle time to get the product into final production with fewer delays because of rework. Prototype software code is developed by the software designers and programmers, and early user testing or examination can result in significant reductions of cycle time.

If product prototypes are constructed (whatever the mixture of hardware, software, and consumable components), testing is centered around the performance of the subsystems as well as the entire system. Complex subsystems should be tested separately as much as possible prior to system integration. If the breadboards have adequately tested the key subsystems or components, the prototype testing can concentrate on the interaction issues that are inherent in a complex product. Prototype testing often involves more complex test protocols that deal with the system as a whole along with subsystem performance. The output of prototype testing should be a product configuration that meets the development team's product goals and requirements, and it should be possible to proceed from successful prototype to production startup. This happy result is usually achieved by a series of iterations between testing and redesign to correct flaws found.

Prototype evaluation is usually performed by the development group or by a special testing team consisting of development people familiar with the product. Further testing of prototypes can be done by special customers as long as they can tolerate the inevitable defects and operational failures of the prototype product. This early customer evaluation involvement is essential for the success of many software-dominant products.

Prototypes are related to the final product desired through the inclusion of all significant functionality and most of the appearance characteristics. The mistake that is often made is to try to proceed directly to production when some essential functionality (either in the product design or manufacturing process) has not yet been verified. Whatever is lacking might be included in a final prototype to be created by the development teams or might be a part of the advanced manufacturing devices to be built.

19.5.3. Advanced Manufacturing Models

When creating products with moderate- to high-volume production, it may be necessary to complete one or more advanced manufacturing models, assembled and tested by manufacturing personnel, to finalize some features found to be necessary as a result of prototype testing. There might also be manufacturing processes and suppliers that need to be further verified before a first production run, especially where there is substantial production startup cost involved. Also, there may be a need for models to submit to regulatory agencies for approval testing. All testing should be to final test specifications for manufacturing. Additional testing by development and manufacturing personnel to verify the performance of a subsystem or component in question is usually appropriate. For low-volume products, such as an electron-beam scanning microscope, advanced manufacturing models are rarely prepared; the prototypes are frequently modified until there is agreement that the product is ready for production.

19.6. DOCUMENTATION

The preparation of documentation associated with developing and selling a product can consume a surprisingly large portion of the resources and must be planned carefully as a critical part of the development project. Not only is engineering documentation needed for hardware components, but manufacturing assembly procedures, manufacturing test specifications and procedures, and quality control specifications and procedures are usually required. Any organization following the guidelines of ISO9000 will have to work with most or all of these documentation elements [2]. Software documentation on the design, structure, and testing of the code is needed and can consume up to 25 to 30 percent of the software resource time on a project.

A user guide or operator manual is normally required for assembled products, even if it is only a brief set of assembly and safety instructions for a child's toy. If the product can be serviced by field service engineers, either at the customer's site or at a repair center, a service manual should be

> *Preparing all required documentation can be a major and time-consuming undertaking. Do not be surprised to find that it consumes as much as 25 percent of the resource time for more complex products.*

created by the development team, led by the representative of the service function. It has become increasingly important to consider preparing these documents in languages in addition to English. In some industries and in several countries, native-language versions of manuals and product labeling are required, not simply nice to have. The trend is to include software screens in languages other than

English, making the software development process lengthier and more complex. Assuring that the translations are accurate can be costly and time consuming.

Engineering documentation, such as part, subassembly, and assembly drawings, whether in hard-copy or electronic format, is always necessary. Manufacturing must participate in deciding the appropriate content for manufacturing assembly and the part structure of the product. Assembly drawings are often required by the production assembly group, and certain kinds of computer-aided-design software make the creation of these drawings very easy because they are derived directly from the electronic models of the product.

Specifications for proper assembly of the product are usually required by the production function, and these documents are most often developed by the manufacturing staff. Manufacturing test specifications are a result of a cooperative effort between the design staff and the manufacturing staff. Quality control specifications, or final test specifications, are usually needed for a final manufacturing check of the product. This check may be done through the use of a sampling plan for high-volume products, or it may be done for all products if monthly unit production is low.

For those companies that are certified to be ISO9000 compliant, there are extensive requirements to ensure the operational validity of the design and manufacturing processes (2). For example, a company must demonstrate that it has a process for purchase of raw materials, that the process results in the purchase of materials that meet defined requirements, and that noncompliant materials cannot find their way into the product.

19.7. TESTING

Assembled product testing takes place not only after all manufacturing steps have occurred on the production floor, but during the entire development process as well [1]. The breadth and depth of testing during the development cycle depends on product complexity, the required degree of product safety and efficacy, and the amount of regulation that is applied to an industry. For example, the ISO9000 guidelines put considerable emphasis on testing in the development cycle as well as the manufacturing cycle. There may be several, iterative, cycles of designing and testing the product ideas, although these should be carefully planned to avoid unfocused work [8]. Each cycle should result in significant advances toward the final, desired product functionality. This is easier said than done, and much work must be done to assure a good testing effort with rapid build and test cycles.

19.7.1. Testing Strategies

One of the earliest tasks during the planning phase of a project is the definition of test strategy. In most projects, cycle time can be shortened by using a progressive testing strategy where verification testing takes place during all phases of development, not just at the completion of the project and prior to product shipment. Review and inspection of the design requirement and specification documents, especially for software-intensive projects, is a testing activity and can save considerable cycle time and reduce the need for test resources near the end of a project.

Subsystem and subassembly testing of prototype hardware is a useful way to decrease the redesign time that can occur during the prototype system integration activity. Computer simulation of circuit board designs, before a circuit board is built as a prototype device, saves expense and cycle time. Similar thoughts apply to other computer simulations, such as thermal analysis, stress analysis, fluid flow analysis, plastic molded part analysis, and dimensional tolerance analysis using computer-aided-design software.

System testing inevitably takes place in any complex product consisting of many parts that must work together as a whole [3]. The system-level testing comes after system integration activities. In those industries controlled by regulatory guidelines, a testing strategy is mandatory because the results of testing may be scrutinized by the regulating body, usually before a product can be delivered to a customer.

Testing strategies on the 777 were considered at program launch by the inclusion of flight test staff in the multifunctional design–build teams. Considerable simulation testing was done in parallel with aircraft development, and the payoff of this advanced testing was considerable. The team was able to get a head start on problems and able to work out solutions before actual flight testing took place. This resulted in 20 percent more flight test time per aircraft per month than was possible for earlier designs, such as the 757 and 767 [6].

19.7.2. Alpha Testing

This is testing of a product model that closely resembles the final product that will be manufactured and sold; it is often called system testing and usually takes place in-house. The product model being tested may be a late prototype device or an advanced manufacturing model. The testing is done by the developer of the product, although the testing can be carried out under contract by a testing organization. The purpose of the testing process is to ensure that all product performance requirements and design specifications have been met. The testing environment usually seeks to emulate the operating conditions that the product will be subjected to by the customer. For some products in some industries, the testing environment can closely match the customer's operating environment. In others, only a partial match can be achieved and additional testing is usually needed.

The test protocol for alpha testing should be developed, at least in outline form if not in final form, early in the development cycle when the product is going through the breadboard or prototype design phases. Every design requirement or specification should be testable or verifiable; otherwise, it serves no value to create the requirement.

The testing work is carried out by in-house staff, either people directly involved in the development effort or by a special testing group in the company that usually does not report directly to the project manager. The results of alpha testing either confirm that the product meets its requirements or show the areas where the product is deficient. One of the reasons that deficiencies arise, despite considerable earlier product testing, is that the alpha test environment usually does not employ the development technical designers to perform the testing. What is obvious to developers is usually not so obvious to alpha testers, so simple problems, such as label ambiguity, may quickly become apparent. This "closer to the customer" testing strategy often produces the need for small changes before the product is ready for required customer testing or production.

19.7.3. Beta Testing

Beta testing is performed by real users or customers, and in some cases, this testing must precede product shipment. For example, certain medical products need clinical trials or a period of use in a customer laboratory before being judged ready for shipment. This is not to be confused with marketing customer testing, where certain strategies regarding sale and marketing of the product are explored (e.g., publication of test results by market leaders to encourage purchase by other customers). The purpose of beta testing is to understand how the product performs in an end-user environment. For example, Microsoft distributed over 400,000 copies of its new operating system to software developers and end users before shipment of the final product. Products that are entirely new to the market should receive beta testing because there is no base of data on which to judge customer acceptance.

Test protocols are produced by the developing company and can range from rigorous (clinical trials of medical products) to nonexistent. In the first case, the developer closely monitors and follows up the beta test with in-house staff or, perhaps, contracted staff from a specialty testing company. In the second case the developer may simply contact the customer by phone after a few weeks and ask for opinions on the product.

It is critical that the customer performs the testing, not some company employee located at the customer's site. The test results, assuming that the beta tests are satisfactory, are used to provide supporting evidence that the product is ready to go into full production and be shipped for sale. In some regulated industries, the test results are provided to the regulating agencies as part of a submission for approval to ship the product.

19.7.4. Acceptance Testing

For some products (e.g., those in the defense industry and those created for other companies under contract) customer acceptance testing is necessary. The customer normally specifies the test conditions and the testing protocols as part of the contract with the developing organization. If the product passes, the customer essentially agrees that the product meets its specifications and also agrees to accept delivery.

19.7.5. Summary of Testing Pitfalls

- There exist untestable requirements. For example, if a product is required to perform to some specification at an ambient humidity of 5 percent and the company has no means to test at this level and does not normally bear the cost of outside test labs, the requirement is meaningless and should be changed. Also, the overworked term "user friendly" often shows up in a requirements document and is basically meaningless without more detailed specifications and measures.
- There is a lack of test strategy until late in the development cycle. It is better to plan the testing strategy early in the development cycle to be sure that all design requirements have been considered, such as the inclusion of test points on a circuit board.
- All testing is done at the end of the development cycle, just prior to manufacturing. This is a sure way to extend the development time and delay production because surprises will happen, which can easily be avoided by using an incremental test strategy.
- Independent testers and product evaluators are not used. No developers should be allowed to perform final testing of their own design. They are too close to the design and will miss obvious problems.
- New-to-market products don't plan to use beta (customer) testing. If the company is creating a product that is entirely new to the market, be sure

to get customer feedback as the design evolves and after alpha testing. Potential customers are the only unbiased source of criticism available.

- Early, negative test results are ignored in hope that the product will "naturally" improve during the development process. This is the "going to Abilene" paradigm and can be avoided only by honest and open evaluation of test results.

19.8. SUMMARY

This chapter has focused on some of the essential elements of the product development process for assembled products. After technical and market feasibility are confirmed, and after the customer requirements are understood, attention is turned to planning the rest of the development process. First comes the planning effort, where staffing decisions, make/buy decisions, and scheduling decisions are made. Product breadboards and prototypes are usually developed for assembled products and it is critical that their functional requirements be clearly understood and then tested in a rigorous fashion. Both internal system testing as well as external customer testing are needed for most products and strategies for these activities should be developed early in the development cycle to allow the designers to anticipate how their designs will be assessed prior to production.

REFERENCES

1. AT&T. *Design to Reduce Technical Risk*. New York: McGraw-Hill, 1993.
2. ISO9000:1994(E). Quality systems: model for quality assurance in design, development, production, installation and servicing. Geneva: International Organization for Standardization, 1994.
3. Kasser, J. *Applying Total Quality Management to Systems Engineering*, Boston: Artech House, 1995.
4. Kerwin, K. The shape of a new machine. *Business Week*, July 29, 1995, pp. 60–66.
5. Littler, D., Leverick, F., and Bruce, M. Factors affecting the process of collaborative product development: a study of UK manufacturers of information and communications technology products. *Journal of Product Innovation Management* 12(1):16–32 (1995).
6. Proctor, P. Early modeling helps speed 777 flight testing. *Aviation Week and Space Technology*, June 12, 1995, p. 124ff.
7. Turino, J. *Managing Concurrent Engineering: Buying Time to Market*. New York: Van Nostrand Reinhold, 1992.
8. Wheelwright, S. and Clark, K. *Revolutionizing Product Development: Quantum Leaps in Speed, Efficiency and Quality*. New York: Free Press, 1992.

Robert Stoy
Becton Dickinson

Dr. Stoy has developed products for the medical diagnostic industry for over 20 years, where he has been both a project manager and member of senior management. His experience includes project responsibility for a successful line of diagnostic instruments and implementation of structured product development processes at several companies. He is a member of his company's product management group and is the sponsor of several development programs. Early in this career Dr. Stoy contributed to research in the defense industry and taught at the University of Connecticut. He received his undergraduate and graduate degrees from the Georgia Institute of Technology.

20 NONASSEMBLED PRODUCT DEVELOPMENT
Trueman D. Parish and Lou E. Moore

20.1. FUNDAMENTALS

Identifying and satisfying market needs are the fundamentals of any product innovation. These fundamentals are the same for assembled products, nonassembled products, and services [2]. Once past the fundamentals, however, the similarities stop and nonassembled products take on a different look. This is where distinct constraints and opportunities are exposed.

20.2. WHAT IS A NONASSEMBLED PRODUCT? WHAT ARE ITS CHARACTERISTICS?

Nonassembled products are homogeneous materials typically produced in bulk. They may be packaged and sold in various size units. They are more often sold to intermediate users rather than the final end user. For example, most consumer nondurables, such as soaps, detergents, foods, and paper products, are manufactured by the tankcar or truckload. When the consumer purchases them, however, they are available in small retail packages.

Products of the materials and process industries, such as primary metals, chemicals, plastics, fuels, and many building materials, are nonassembled products and are often produced in large quantities. They are also often sold in bulk to fabrication and assembly industries. High capital investment, a process difficult to change, and a long product lifetime are typical characteristics of nonassembled products.

> *Nonassembled products differ significantly from assembled products, and are typically produced only by large firms.*

While software, services, and consumer durables do not possess the characteristics of nonassembled products, there are other assembled products that do. Disposable cameras and portable radios, for example, are mass produced in such highly automated industries that they take on many of these characteristics.

Special features of nonassembled product development place unique constraints on the innovation process and innovation strategy. At the same time they can lead to opportunities. These constraints include:

- High capital intensity
- Economy of scale
- Specialized equipment
- Specialized skills and competencies

20.2.1. High Capital Intensity

Industries that produce nonassembled products require large-quantity materials handling, packaging, and various processing steps. In general, this calls for a large amount of capital. That requirement generally prevents small firms from entering the business.

20.2.2. Economy of Scale

Closely related to the capital intensity are the economies of scale. That means a manufacturing plant capable of producing 10 million pounds of product per year may cost only four times as much to build as one producing 1 million pounds per year. These two elements, capital intensity and economies of scale, tend to reward market dominance, especially for radically new products. They also support Peter Drucker's innovation strategy, "fustest with the mostest," which was originally spoken by Confederate General Nathaniel Bedford Forrest. The interpretation of this quote is: "The key to success is to get there first with the most." Referring to DuPont's development of nylon, Drucker wrote, "When it came up with nylon, the first truly synthetic fiber, after 15 years of hard, frustrating research, DuPont at once mounted massive efforts, built huge plants, went into mass advertising—the company had never before had consumer products to advertise—and created the industry we now call plastics" [1].

Drucker also pointed out: "Enough of the internal DuPont documents of the time have been published to show that the top management people did aim at creating a new industry. They were far from convinced that Carothers (the father of nylon) and his research would succeed. But they knew that they would have founded something big and brand new in the event of success, and something that would go far beyond a single product or even beyond a single major product line." A small company could not have accomplished this feat.

20.2.3. Specialized Equipment

Not only is the equipment expensive for nonassembled products, it tends to be specialized. For example, in the plastics industry, a facility for manufacturing polyester plastics would be unable to produce polyolefin plastics even though these plastics might be indistinguishable to the average consumer.

20.2.4. Specialized Skills and Competencies

Manufacturing skills and know-how in these industries tend to be linked to the equipment. The ability to maximize quality and productivity from this equipment can be a substantial source of competitive advantage in these industries.

20.3. MODEL FOR INNOVATION OF NONASSEMBLED PRODUCTS

To show the impact of these constraints on nonassembled product innovation, a model used by a major chemical company is shown in Figure 20.1. The innovation model is shown in four components which are linked to each other and the market. Innovation begins and ends with the market, and boundaries between components are seamless and transparent. Similarly, the process is smooth and continuous. As indicated by the arrows, this is not a sequential, linear process. It is rather an interactive process where customer and market needs are considered early and validated and revalidated throughout the process. The characteristics of nonassembled innovation affect each of the four components and are explained in the following pages.

> *A firm requires a clear market need before justifying the large capital investment that is normally required to develop a nonassembled product.*

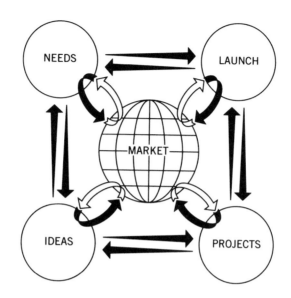

FIGURE 20.1 Eastman innovation process.

20.3.1. Needs

Because of their capital intensity, the specialized nature of equipment required for their production and their early position in the value chain, nonassembled products (especially radical new products) must have a large, well-defined market need. It is rarely economical to produce small quantities of products in nonassembled product industries. Consequently, a market failure has substantial costs. Drucker writes, "The strategy of being 'fustest with the mostest' has to hit right on target or it misses altogether. Or to vary the metaphor, being 'fustest with the mostest' is very much like a moon shot: a deviation of a fraction of a minute of arc and the missile disappears into outer space."

This model uses three steps in the needs process to avoid "disappearing into outer space": need identification, verification, and validation.

Need Identification

Identification is discovering an unmet market need for which a company might add value. Needs can be discovered in many ways. The most obvious is to listen to the customer. Sales, marketing, and technical people are trained to look for these opportunities and are given an easy route to communicate them to the right people within the company.

Other needs can be found in the pattern of customer complaints or requests for technical service. Still others can be found in structured studies of industry, society, or technology trends. For companies serving industrial customers, market needs can sometimes be found by studying the customer's customer. But no matter where the needs come from, it is very important to keep the person who submits it informed of its fate. In fact, it is equally important to build in positive reinforcement into the needs process.

Verification

Verification is the step where a shared understanding of the need is reached with the potential customer. This is the point where a quality function deployment (QFD) approach might be used. QFD is a structured method for clarifying customer requirements and identifying the work functions that will satisfy them. It ties requirements directly to design and production characteristics and limits the chance of omitting any important characteristics.

Validation

Validation is the step to determine the relative value of solving the need, to the customer and to the manufacturer. If any of these steps are excluded from the needs process, an element of surprise can enter the equation. By the time the project is complete, the customers' needs may well have changed and a lot of money will have been wasted. Market needs exist whether or not a solution can be envisioned. The premature search for a solution sometimes limits thinking. Therefore, a thorough understanding of the need must be obtained.

The characteristics of nonassembled innovation suggest that only needs with a fairly high dollar volume or profitability are likely to be attractive. This is especially true if the product requires a new manufacturing process. On the other hand, minor product modifications (e.g., a different molecular weight, flavor, or color) can often be produced in existing equipment and will serve existing markets. This advantage tends to drive nonassembled product development toward incremental improvements with only occasional, radically new products. The high capital intensity and economies of scale also reward products with rapid market penetration. For products serving industrial markets, the customers are often faced with high switching costs. The bigger the change required, the bigger the domino effect is down the line. Advantages at that point must outweigh the change and the cost, or incremental innovations will always win over radical change.

In the large companies where most nonassembled product innovation is done, there are usually many customer needs, making bookkeeping a nightmare. Information technology can be applied effectively to maintain a database of these needs. Such a database should contain relevant economic, technical, and market information, which will enable R&D functions as well as business organizations to respond effectively. With the database, the potential value of identified needs can be checked against the business strategies, and it also permits management to balance the portfolio effort.

20.3.2. Ideas

> *A multiplicity of customer need complicates the business of nonassembled product developers.*

Ideas are the DNA of everything that is worthwhile.

—*Marsh Fisher, Century 21 International*

After a need is identified, verified, and validated, it requires a solution. Though creativity plays a vital role throughout the innovation process, it is at this point where it plays its most important role. As John Kao, lecturer for Harvard Business School, says, some companies treat creativity "as an elective as opposed to a core part of the curriculum." The use of trained facilitators can be beneficial at this stage. They are experts to innovative problem-solving techniques and their objective is to help teams generate ideas that will result in new, unique, and unexpected solutions.

Selecting people with the appropriate skills is essential for success in the ideas stage. In the case of assembled products, product design engineers are critical. For nonassembled product development, process engineers often hold the key to finding creative ways to solve the customer need. Teams for generating solutions should include at least marketing, product, and process development people. It is especially important to avoid the trap of thinking that all creative solutions arise from R&D or product design. Ideation teams should be multifunctional and empowered to explore a variety of potential solutions for the need.

> *Creative process engineering is often critical.*

As this innovation model indicates, interaction with the market continues to be a critical factor. In the case of customer products, focus groups are sometimes used to test conceptual solutions to the need. In some cases, customer representatives may be included on the team that is devising the solution.

It is always important to avoid selection of one solution too early. Sufficient exploration of technical and economic feasibility should be done at the ideas stage before selecting the best idea to carry forward. This exploratory work often provides new ideas and refinement of initial solutions. However, once adequate exploration of ideas has been completed, the technical, economic, and market factors should be combined to select one solution to pursue to commercialization. Of course, there is always the possibility that no desirable cost-effective solution to the need can be found. In that case the need becomes inactive. In any event aggressive protection of any intellectual property developed and patented can be useful in building a wall of defense against competitors.

20.3.3. Projects

The projects stage is where the preferred solution is defined further. Since this usually involves substantial expense for scaleup and external sampling, the business case for further continuation of the project needs to be examined by the business management before proceeding. An innovation committee can approve and monitor each innovation project. The manager of the supporting business organization should chair this committee. This approach ensures a common understanding and buy in from all areas involved in supporting the project and helps identify and eliminate barriers. This committee can appoint an innovation team (and leader) with members from research, development, manufacturing, marketing, health, safety, environmental, and regulatory organizations to carry the project to completion. Teams should also include members from the original ideas team to help ensure continuity. The innovation project may require either part-time or full-time work, depending on the demands.

At the project stage, formal project management tools should be used to ensure timely and economical completion of the project. These tools can help the team leader coordinate the activities of the team and help ensure a common understanding of the objectives and tasks to be performed by the team.

Again, as Figure 20.1 shows, there is constant interaction with the market. This may range from market trials to telephone conver-

> *Project management tools are frequently required.*

sations with the expected customer. Feedback is essential to determine if the original need has been altered and to determine if the proposed solution will still satisfy the need.

During this stage, some experiments should be conducted to demonstrate the manufacturability of the product. This experimentation provides samples for market testing. In the heavily regulated process industries, a major part of the innovation project is obtaining approvals and permits, especially if the product is substantially new or requires new manufacturing facilities.

20.3.4. Product Launch

Finally, the product is launched. This is where the product is commercialized, the market is developed, the product is introduced, and sales are developed. (Market development actually begins early in the project, right from the beginning of identifying a need. See Chapter 15 for additional information.) Launch must include understanding the target customers, how to deliver the product, and how to introduce it.

> An innovation is a product so new and unique that buyers find the concept somewhat foreign. It does not yet have a place in buyers' lifestyles or business practices. Consequently, the market requires substantial education before buyers recognize a product's benefits and accept it as a legitimate way to satisfy their needs. The first automobiles, vacuum cleaners, and prepackaged convenience foods initially had to overcome considerable buyer apathy. The first business computers had to overcome skepticism bordering on hostility.
>
> ... Empirical studies indicate that demand does not begin to accelerate until the first two to five percent of potential buyers adopt the product. The attainment of those initial sales is often the hardest part of marketing a new innovation.
> —Thomas T. Nagle, Boston University School of Management

As with the innovation project efforts, a well-thought-out launch plan is a key to success. The product development plan and launch plan must be carefully linked to be sure that manufacturing capacity is available, regulatory approvals are completed on time, and intellectual property is protected. These issues must be coupled with market timing issues such as peak selling seasons for consumer goods and major trade shows in the industrial markets. Although these issues are important in all types of new product innovation, the high capital intensity for nonassembled products means that manufacturing requirements can become a dominant factor. If the new product is to be made in existing equipment, capacity availability and changeover time are critical issues. If a new plant must be built, one to three years may be required for design and construction.

> *Initial production can be a resource availability challenge.*

The complexity of this process will determine whether a major product launch effort is required. At one extreme are products requested by a single customer who has been a partner throughout the product development process. In this case, launch is only a continuation of the ongoing project work. At the other extreme a radically new and technically complex product might be introduced to a diverse group of customers. In this case an extensive product launch team would be needed to provide technical training to customers, technical services, advertising, and sales. For the more complicated products or those representing a major breakthrough, lead users, who are more aggressive, can occasionally be selected as the initial customers. This parallels the concept of early adopters in the consumer market.

Figure 20.1 shows that product launch does not end the innovation process. Often, as the new product is launched, the market acceptance suggests new needs for variants, and applications that were not envisioned in the original concept. This can lead back to the needs stage in a never-ending process for growth and renewal.

20.4. SUMMARY

Although new product development of nonassembled products seems to have many constraints, it also provides great opportunities for those in the industry. At one extreme, companies with large efficient plants and a high level of skills can generate a stream of incrementally improved products which provide good returns while discouraging new entrants. At the other extreme, companies in these industries occasionally produce bold new-product innovations, such as optical waveguides for telecommunications or plastic beverage bottles, which allow them to become leaders in the world marketplace.

REFERENCES

1. Drucker, P. *Innovation and Entrepreneurship.* New York: Harper & Row, 1985.
2. Utterback, J.M. *Mastering the Dynamics of Innovation.* Boston: Harvard Business School Press, 1994.

Trueman D. Parish
Eastman Chemical Company

Dr. Parish is a native of Cincinnati, Ohio. He received his B.S. degree from the University of Michigan, his M.S. degree from Massachusetts Institute of Technology, and his Ph.D. degree from Rice University in 1967. His major area of study was chemical engineering. His interests include the management of innovation and the use of information technology as an aid to innovation. Currently, he is involved in benchmarking the practices of highly innovative companies.

Lou E. Moore
Eastman Chemical Company

Lou E. Moore is a corporate innovation communications representative for Eastman Chemical Company. She was born in Erwin, Tennessee. She graduated from East Tennessee State University with a bachelor's degree in industrial technology in 1973. Moore came to Eastman in 1974 as an engineering technician and held a series of assignments before joining corporate communications in 1990. Moore is a member of the Industrial Research Institute's Communications Directors Network (chair, 1994–1995) and serves on the board of directors for CHILDREN of Tri-Cities. She is also a member of the Kappa Delta alumni association.

21 CONSUMER PACKAGED GOODS (BRANDED FOOD GOODS)
William S. Stinson, Jr.

21.1. INTRODUCTION

21.1.1. Importance of New Products

New products are still considered by many leaders in the food industry to be the life blood of the company. At the same time, high risk and high failure rates are often associated with new products. In the highly competitive global environment today, with resources shrinking and becoming more difficult to come by, it is critical to have the most efficient new product development process possible. We need to think in terms of reducing product development cycle time, (i.e., the length of time it takes to develop a new product from the time the idea is conceived until it is introduced into the marketplace)[1–4]. Equally important is quality by design, the building of quality and safety into the new product.

21.1.2. New Product Model

> It is critical to have the most efficient new product development process possible.

A model for a new product development process consists of the following elements:

1. Parallel and concurrent development activities
2. Multifunctional team work
3. Continuous and connected communications
4. Quality by design
5. Continuous feedback from the consumer

Each of these elements is important to success of the process. Everyone involved in the new-product process should understand the importance of each element and how it relates to his or her role in the process.

To reduce cycle time and to get the new product into the marketplace as fast as possible, it is essential to have as many development activities taking place concurrently or in parallel as possible. This requires considerable planning and coordinating among team members within product development as well as among the various support groups. High-priority issues need to be identified as early as possible and a team member or team members designated as responsible for the respective issues. Time lines to implementation for the various development activities need to be constructed and fit into the overall plan. The goal should be to reduce the opportunities for overall process conflicts and inefficiencies.

The model recognizes the need for a team approach to expediting the development process. This involves creating a team within product development to execute the early development work and then creating a larger team consisting of all the disciplines required to scale the product up to a feasible commercial process that culminates with the market introduction. Roles and responsibilities of the team members need to be defined. Management should provide an environment that empowers decision making by the team. The objective should be to build a high-performing team within a seamless organization.

Good communications is necessary for the successful execution of fast tracking the product development process. This begins with a clear understanding of the product specifications from marketing and ends with the successful ongoing maufacture of the new product on the plant production line. Good communications are frequent, timely, open, and candid. This allows for critical issues to be addressed at the right time in the development process.

Quality by design is a planning process that builds quality and safety into the new product and the new process. It does this by identifying and controlling risks, resources, requirements, responsibilities, and interrelationships. It should be started with prototype development and continue throughout the development process. Quality by design must be an ongoing process. It provides the mechanism to communicate accurate and timely information within the organization and among the team members.

Perhaps the most important element of the model is obtaining continuous feedback from the consumer and using this information to optimize the new product. It begins with the concept and concludes with a successful test market.

21.1.3. New Product Development Process: Flow Diagram

> *Everyone involved in the new product process should understand the importance of each element of the new product model and how they relate to their role.*

The flow of the new product development process is illustrated in Figure 21.1. It is segmented for discussion purposes into five development stages: concept, exploratory development stage, early development stage, intermediate development stage, and advanced development stage. This is an "ideal" model and should be tailored to each company's own specific needs.

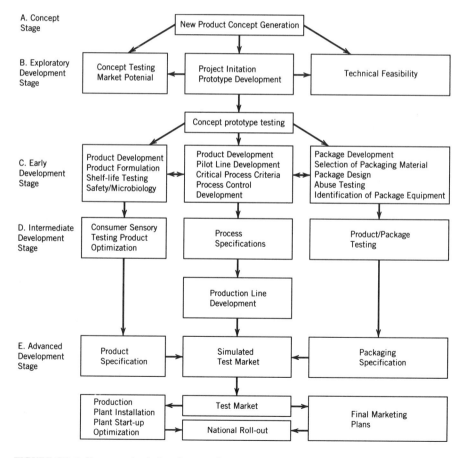

FIGURE 21.1 New product development process.

The concept stage and how it is developed lays the groundwork and foundation for the subsequent stages. It will not be discussed in this chapter, as it has received adequate attention in previous chapters.

21.2. EXPLORATORY DEVELOPMENT STAGE

21.2.1. New Product Development Request: Product Specifications

Marketing provides research and development product development with a request to develop a new product. Usually, this involves a meeting with the research and development product development vice-president. The request is accompanied by a product specification form (Figure 21.2) that spells out in detail the product attributes and parameters as perceived by marketing. The more detailed the characteristics desired: *product* (IV.A) section of the product specification form, the easier it is for product development to develop suitable prototypes and more accurately to assess feasibility. Of course, these characteristics will evolve and be changed and optimized as feedback is obtained from the consumer.

21.2.2. Feasibility

The research and development product development vice-president assigns a product development project leader to the request. Normally, the project leader then meets with the marketing representative to review and discuss the product specification form to make sure that it is clearly understood. This early dialogue assists in highlighting key attributes and measurement needs early in the process.

The first thing the project leader does before a full-blown development effort begins is to determine the feasibility of the new product request. He or she meets with all the people within the company who have the necessary expertise and experience to assist in assessing the feasibility. Often, this includes engineering, basic research, packaging, quality assurance, market research, and plant people. This is done by both one-on-one meetings and group meetings. An important consideration here is to identify any major problems that would make the project impossible. In addition, it is important to identify other major hurdles that would represent major challenges. After factoring all the inputs, including resources required, projected cost of development, and estimated time of development, a probability of feasibility is assigned. Since it is based on a multitude of inputs, the feasibility is assigned as low, moderate, or high, with a detailed report summarizing the rationale.

PRODUCT SPECIFICATION FORM

REQUESTED BY: _____

DATE: _____

I. PROJECT   Number: _____

                        Title: _____

II. OBJECTIVES   (Define consumer need, want, problem to be solved)

III. MARKET AND FINANCIAL ANALYSIS

    1. Market Size:

    2. Market Growth Rate:

    3. Major Segments:

    4. Competitive Brands:

    5. Sales Volume Expected:

       Dollar

       Tonnage

    6. Capital Investment Expected:

IV. CHARACTERISTICS DESIRED

    A. *Product* (Define in detail)

       1. Appearance:

       2. Taste:

       3. Texture:

       4. Competitive Uniqueness:

       5. Mode of Preservation (i.e., canned, frozen):

       6. Other:

    B. *Storage*

       1. Storage Conditions:

       2. Shelf-Life:

       3. Shelf-Life Relative to Competition:

    C. *Usage* (Describe primary use and any other occasions for use)

    D. *Packaging/Preparation*

       1. Servings (include number, and ways to serve):

       2. Packaging Features (include size):

       3. Methods of Preparation (i.e., oven, microwave, etc.):

V. **TIMETABLE**   *Date*   *Comments*   *Person Responsible*

Prototype Developed
and Shown with
Competitive Product:

Product Tested—Internal:

Product Tested—External:

Test Marketing:

National Rollout:

VI. **FACILITIES/LOCATION**

    1. Development and Testing:

    2. Full-Scale Production:

APPROVAL

_____

_____

FIGURE 21.2 Product specification form.

> *The first thing the project leader does before a full-blown development effort begins is to determine feasibility.*

21.3. EARLY DEVELOPMENT STAGE

21.3.1. Assign Product Development Team

Based on the feasibility, marketing decides whether to proceed to early development (prototype development) or to kill the concept. If the decision is to move forward with the concept, the product development project leader assigns a product development team to the prototype development. At this point, the team usually consists of the project leader, a food technologist and/or chef, and a technician.

21.3.2. Prototype Development

During the prototype development stage, product development and marketing meet frequently to evaluate and discuss the progress. Once an acceptable prototype(s) is developed, the next step is consumer testing. This is done by either using focus groups or central location testing (CLT). In both approaches, the consumers tested should represent the target market group. The focus group is a qualitative test, while the central location test is a quantitative test.

Prototypes are formulated to meet the characteristics desired, (section IV.A of the product specification form) without considering shelf-life, processing problems, functionality, and other issues that will be dealt with after the consumers' acceptability of the concept and prototype are established. An example of this might be a request by marketing to develop a canned spaghetti sauce that tastes like homemade Italian spaghetti sauce with the characteristics desired described in Figure 21.3. As mentioned previously, at this point little attention would be given to processing or costs of ingredients. The development team would begin the prototype development by doing an extensive investigation of spaghetti sauce

IV. Characteristic Desired
　　A. *Product* (Define in detail)
　　　　1. Appearance: rich, deep red color
　　　　2. Taste: "homemade" Italian spaghetti sauce
　　　　3. Texture: coarse and thick
　　　　4. Competitive Uniqueness: fresh "homemade" appearance and flavor
　　　　5. Mode of Preservation: glass jar
　　　　6. Other: Significant preference over leading spaghetti sauce in the marketplace

FIGURE 21.3 Portion of completed product specification form.

recipes that fit the broad criteria for homemade Italian spaghetti sauces. This might include visiting a number of Italian restaurants and tasting various spaghetti sauces. If any of these sauces seem on target, detailed notes would be taken, so the chef could then go back into the laboratory (kitchen) and duplicate the recipe. Also, reviewing cook books is a good starting point for prototype development. Quite often the chef, from his or her own experiences, can develop prototypes that meet the characteristics desired. Usually, a combination of these approaches leads to the development of several prototypes that meet the marketing request guidelines.

These would then be consumer tested to determine the feasibility of the concept and acceptability of the prototypes. Normally, it is better to have more than one prototype to consumer test as it provides more feedback for the product development team. The objectives are to determine if the concept has broad enough consumer appeal and if any of the prototypes delivers to the concept. If the consumer feedback is positive, the prototype selected represents the starting point for the development of the new product.

21.4. INTERMEDIATE DEVELOPMENT STAGE

> *During the early development stage, the feasibility of the concept is determined and prototypes are consumer tested.*

21.4.1. Activate Project and Assemble Project Team

After positive feedback is received from the consumer concept prototype test, the project is formally activated. The first step is to expand the product development team to a project team to include people from all the disciplines deemed necessary for optimization of the product and for development of a pilot-plant process. This includes, in addition to the original product development team, people from packaging development, engineering, microbiology, food safety and nutrition, and sensory analysis. Normally, the project leader who was assigned to the prototype development continues as the team leader for the project team.

21.4.2. Quality Design Meeting

Once the project team is established, a meeting should be scheduled to discuss the quality design of the product. This involves brainstorming all aspects of the project, including the concept, ingredients, process, product, packaging, distribution, shelf-life, and so one. It is helpful to have a checklist of critical items to facilitate the quality design meeting (Table 21.1). The purpose is to build quality and safety into the product.

Problems, issues, and opportunities are identified and recorded. The appropriate people on the team are assigned roles and responsibilities for follow up on specific issues. Meetings are scheduled as necessary and agreed upon by the team to review progress. At this time a preliminary timetable is developed that lays out all the key consumer testing anticipated along the development path, ending with a date for national introduction. The project team works closely with marketing so that the timetable is both realistic and timely.

The purpose of quality by design is to build quality and safety into the new product and new process.

21.4.3. Formula Development and Optimization

From this point, concurrent activities take place. Product development focuses on the formula, engineering begins putting together a pilot-plant process, and packaging development explores various packaging alternatives. While these activities are occurring concurrently, it is the project leader's responsibility to assure that all team members are communicating effectively. He or she needs to call the meetings and follow up with highlights of the meeting. An ideal approach to facilitating communications is to have all team members on a computer E-mail network.

Product development begins benchtop formula development using the characteristics desired information from the product specification form and feedback from the concept prototype consumer test for guidance. During this phase of development, base formulas are established and ingredients identified. Informal taste panel screenings of various formulas are held by sensory analysis to guide the development. At this point it is a good idea to initiate early shelf-life screening, to begin to determine formula tolerances, and to conduct a rough cost of the formula.

It is important to have regular up-date meetings with marketing to show product formulation progress and to get their input. After a product formulation is considered to be "on target," it is consumer tested to confirm. Usually, this is by way of a central location test. The consumers selected for the CLT should be representative of the target market. Questions asked, in addition to overall product acceptability, should be designed around the product characteristics desired so that the information received will aid product development in optimizing the formula.

TABLE 21.1 Checklist for Intermediate Development Stage

Activity	Disciplines Involved	Action/ Completed
Pilot-plant/co-manufacturer scale-up: a. Operations/equipment determined b. Verify secrecy agreements with equipment suppliers c. Complete process knowledge (yield, rework, waste disposal, etc.) d. Define critical control points e. Write process specs with flow diagram f. Identify sanitation process g. Update benchtop specs from pilot-plant testing h. Identify production site	Engineering, product development, microbiology, quality assurance, packaging development analytical, legal	
Raw materials supplier: a. Complete supplier information request form b. Sensitive materials specifications c. Draft physical, chemical, micro specs, and analytical test methods d. Define shipping, handling, storage, shelf-life requirements e. Identify potential alternative sources of supply f. Define materials-handling requirements	Purchasing/analytical, quality assurance, product development, microbiology, legal	
Microbiological: a. Complete abuse testing on finished product (in process materials, if necessary) b. Establish process control measures c. Determine specifications on ingredients and final product	Microbiology, product development, quality assurance	
Finished product: a. Optimize formula b. Shelf-life studies with pilot-plant c. Consumer testing (home use; preference) d. Draft specifications e. Determine physical and chemical specifications	Product development, microbiology, marketing, engineering, packaging, quality assurance, sensory	

TABLE 21.1 Checklist for Intermediate Development Stage (*Continued*)

Activity	Disciplines Involved	Action/ Completed
Packaging: a. Cost optimization b. Alternative sources c. Establish fill requirements d. Write specifications e. Approve label declarations	Packaging, engineering, product development, legal, quality assurance	
Financial: a. Final cost estimates completed for feasibility	Purchasing, product development, marketing, engineering	
Nutritional/safety: a. Submit final formula for nutritional estimates (calculated) b. Assess composition effect on health c. Complete evaluation of potential for foreign/ extraneous matter	Product development, food safety and nutrition, quality assurance, microbiology	
Patentability: a. Infringement search complete	Legal	
Methods approval: a. Determine accuracy of test procedures for in-process and final product b. Write up methods to use (i.e., solids, fat, moisture, etc.) c. Submit samples for testing and replication	Analytical, product development, microbiology, quality assurance	
Conduct consumer test	Marketing, product development	

> *During the optimization of a new product it is important to receive timely consumer feedback to keep on "target."*

21.4.4. Pilot-Plant Scale-Up

While product development is optimizing the formula, engineering begins to identify the processing requirements. This involves working closely with product development in the early stages at the benchtop to determine what equipment is required for scale-up to the pilot plant. Once the appropriate equipment is identified and debugged, testing in the pilot plant begins. At this point, product development continues to work closely with engineering as both formula and process parameters and tolerances need to be determined. Frequently, equipment and process modifications are required to produce the product successfully in the pilot-plant. Sometimes formula changes are necessary to adapt the product to the process. However, it is absolutely essential that the key quality attributes as confirmed by consumer testing are not altered by any of these changes. Formula changes should be triangle tested against a control by sensory analysis to confirm by means of trained panelists that no organoleptic differences can be detected.

A well-designed pilot-plant provides the project team with a small-scale production line to make the product for (1) shelf-life testing, (2) costing studies, (3) process controls and production specification development, (4) microbiological and safety testing, (5) nutritional analysis, and (6) consumer testing. An important benefit derived from the pilot line is that it facilitates engineering in the scale-up of the process for national commercial production.

21.4.5. Package Development

> *A well-designed pilot-plant facilitates the scale-up of the new process.*

Concurrent with the above-mentioned activities of product development and engineering, packaging development initiates the development of the package. This involves selection of the packaging material and design of the package. In today's competitive environment the package is almost as important as the product. Therefore, it is important to begin the package development as soon as the general attributes of the product are identified by product development. Criteria that need to be considered in developing the package include shelf-life, environment impact, appearance, and tamper evidence. Another important aspect in the package development process is selecting the packaging equipment and then running product and package tests on the equipment to identify any problem areas. After all the problems have been resolved, packaging specifications are written. This includes package material and package process specifications.

We now have a consumer "acceptable" formula with an "ideal" package that can be produced cost-effectively on a pilot-plant line. The next step is to take this finished product to a simulated test market with the idea of moving to commercialization. This could be a home use test (HUT) in six to eight cities across the United States in which the consumer uses the product as they would normally do at home. All consumer testing to this point has been either focus group or CLT testing, where the consumer has tasted the product but has not consumed it under normal everyday circumstances. The results of this consumer test will assess the viability of the new product in the marketplace.

> *In today's competitive environment, the package is almost as important as the product.*

21.5. ADVANCED DEVELOPMENT STAGE

21.5.1. Expand the Development Team: Quality Design

Once the new product is being consumer HUT tested and while awaiting test results, the development team needs to be expanded to facilitate the commercialization of the new product. We need to include manufacturing, division engineering, purchasing, process packaging, analytical, quality assurance, legal, and sales. Communications between all the functions and team members becomes even more important at this point as any missed date on the timetable from this point on could cause the date of the introduction of the new product to be missed.

It is now time for an expanded quality design meeting with all the functions included. At this meeting, all issues, problems, and opportunities relating to the product, package, and process are brainstormed, identified, and recorded. Here again a checklist that reflects items to be considered in the advanced development stage leading to commercialization is a very helpful tool (Table 21.2). The appropriate individuals are assigned roles and responsibilities for follow-up on specific issues. Meetings are scheduled as necessary to review progress. Normally, it is a good idea to meet weekly at this stage, to make sure that nothing slips between the cracks. Also, communication by E-mail on an as-needed basis to all team members is suggested.

The HUT provides a final check on the optimization of the product and the size of the market. If the HUT is positive, the next step would be a test market in 10 to 15 percent of the United States. The test market is the first time that actual sales of the new product occurs. The test market confirms all previous consumer testing and predicts the ongoing success of the new product.

> *At this stage communication between all functions and team members is very important, as any missed date could cause the introduction of the new product to be delayed.*

21.5.2. Site Selection for Market Test Production and National Production

Once marketing makes the decision to move forward to a HUT,

TABLE 21.2 Checklist for Advanced Development Stage

Activity	Disciplines Involved	Action/ Completed
Finalize all issues from intermediate development by plant runs: a. Build database b. Complete formal micro/ nutritional shelf-life studies/consumer tests on plant products c. Conduct nutrient analysis (production lots) d. Compare product/ process knowledge from pilot-plant, benchtop, and plant e. Based on plant runs, reiterate previous stage, if necessary	Product development, microbiology, sensory, marketing, quality assurance, engineering, food safety and nutrition	
Capital project team	Engineering, product development	
Installation	Engineering, product development, division engineering, plant	
Startup	Engineering, product development, division engineering, plant	
Confirm all plant specifications a. Formula b. Process c. Package d. QA specs e. Test methods for ingred./final product standards f. Operations manual g. Sanitation specifications	Product development, engineering, packaging, microbiology, plant, quality assurance, analytical	
Monitor production for six months and evaluate QC data	Product development quality assurance, marketing	

the pace and intensity of the product development process picks up. The locations for both test market and national production need to be decided. Will the pilot-plant line suffice for the test market, or does a co-manufacturer need to be involved? If the new product is truly unique, a co-manufacturer might not exist. Perhaps the pilot-plant line needs to be expanded to accommodate the test market.

Immediately after selecting the location for test market production, the location for national production must be determined. If production is going to be kept internal, the plant site best suited for the product needs to be determined. Some items to consider for site selection include workforce availability, similar products currently being manufactured, raw materials currently being used, and space available. Sometimes the most economical decision is to have a co-manufacturer produce the new product, at least in the short term. This often provides a much faster entry into the marketplace.

21.5.3. Production Line Development

After the location for the national production line has been decided, division engineering assumes responsibility for the design, layout, and installation of the line. The equipment needed for the processing line is determined. A capital project is written and submitted to senior management for approval. At this point, engineering, division engineering, and product development normally conduct test runs on all new equipment, either at the equipment manufacturer or in the pilot-plant, to verify that it meets the requirements for the process and new product. Lead times for the new equipment are established. A critical path is put together to lay out the timing for the delivery of the various components and construction elements involved in completing the installation of the processing line. Purchasing is intimately involved at this stage of the development process and takes responsibility for ordering equipment and assuring that deliveries are made on time. Ordering equipment is initiated once senior management and marketing give the okay to move to a national introduction.

> *A critical path is put together to lay out the timing for the delivery and installation of the processing line.*

21.5.4. Finalization of Product, Packaging, and Processing Specifications

Quality assurance becomes more involved during the finalization stage. Raw material and processing specifications need to be written. Sensitive ingredients, both microbiologically and quality related, need to be identified and recommendations made for their proper handling and storage. Analytical and microbiological testing of ingredients, intermediate processed materials, and finished product need to be identified and the appropriate equipment specified for testing. Shipping, handling, storage, and shelf-life requirements need to be defined.

Purchasing becomes involved in locating raw material and packaging suppliers. Potential ingredient supply problems are reviewed. Alternative suppliers are identified. Contracts are prepared to ensure that quantities and pricing are protected. Any problem areas are discussed with marketing and product development.

A test market usually lasts 1 to 1½ years. During this time, the final steps of the new product development process are implemented. Any final optimization of the product or package are made. All formula, package, process, and quality assurance specifications are finalized. An operations manual is written. Shelf-life studies are completed and pull dates established. Nutritional analysis are confirmed so that labeling can reflect accurately the nutritional profile of the product. Final marketing plans are developed. Although national production equipment is ordered after the decision of national introduction is made, long-lead-time equipment can be ordered prior to this decision, based on approval of senior management with the understanding that cancellation clauses are built into the contract.

21.5.5. Plant Installation and Startup

During the test market, any final optimization of product or package are made.

The last steps in the product development process are plant installation and plant startup. Division engineering and manufacturing are responsible for these operations. Product development and quality assurance also have key roles in the startup since they monitor and assure that the new product being made on the national production line has the same attributes and quality as the product tested in the earlier stages of consumer testing. With the completion of these steps, the product is ready for national rollout.

21.6. SUMMARY

The development of new products is a complex and involved process that can be divided into five stages: (1) concept, (2) exploratory, (3) early development,

(4) intermediate development, and (5) advanced development. In addition, there are five important elements of the new product development process that need to be understood and followed in order to maximize the chances for success: (1) concurrent development activities, (2) multifunctional teamwork, (3) continuous and connected communications, (4) quality by design, and (5) continuous feedback from the consumer. The process flow presented in this chapter is an "ideal model" and should be tailored to each company's specific needs.

REFERENCES

1. Himmelfarb, Philip A. New product development. *Today's Chemist at Work*, pp. 56–57 (April 1993).
2. Mancini, L. Operation crunch time: speeding new products to market. *Food Engineering*, pp. 54–58 (July 1993).
3. Millson, Murray R., Raj, S.P., and Wilemon, David. A survey of major approaches for accelerating new product development. *Journal of Product Innovation Management* 9:53–69 (March 1992).
4. Rosenau, Milton D., Jr. *Faster New Product Development*. New York: Amacom, 1990.

William S. Stinson, Jr.
Florida Department of Citrus

Currently Scientific Research Director, Processed Products, for the Florida Department of Citrus at Lake Alfred, Florida. He has a distinguished record of directing and executing successful new product programs at Hershey Foods and Celestial Seasonings. He has directed the development of several $100 million dollar products in his career. Dr. Stinson has a Ph.D. in Food Technology from Ohio State University and a MBA in Management from Xavier University, Cincinnati, Ohio. He currently is Chairman of the Research & Development Associates for Military Food and Packaging Systems, Inc. Dr. Stinson is an active member of the Institute of Food Technologists.

22 SERVICE DEVELOPMENT
Craig A. Terrill and
Arthur G. Middlebrooks

22.1. INTRODUCTION

Service development shares several common themes with product development, particularly the need for a systematic development process that starts with customer problems and needs. In addition, service development more closely mirrors product development for services that have a strong product component (e.g., fast food and retail distribution), or services that are "mechanized" and provide an intangible output (e.g., utility services, phone services, automatic teller services).

However, service development on the whole has several unique attributes that demand a different approach to the development process and offer new opportunities for innovation vis-à-vis product development. For example, the manufacturing process of product development is replaced by the service operations or "delivery" process that creates the customer's experience. Therefore, the service delivery process must be developed, tested and refined directly with customers. In particular, customers play a role in the service delivery process itself, which makes the development of the customer interface, service delivery environment and recovery procedures extremely critical. This chapter outlines the unique aspects of service development and key issues to address for increasing the effectiveness of service development efforts.

22.2. WHY SERVICE DEVELOPMENT IS DIFFERENT

The word *services* is one of the most widely applied, although seemingly generic, terms in business today. Misperceptions about what constitutes a service, let alone a new service, causes many service development efforts to be misfocused and less effective in their objective to create valued and competitive offerings. The five unique-to-services "disconnects" most often experienced by new service developers are:

1. Services are intangible experiences.
2. Service customers want individualized experiences.
3. Services also yield strategic benefits for customers.
4. Services are produced and delivered simultaneously.
5. Service quality is imperative, yet highly variable.

Services differ significantly from tangible products.

22.2.1. Intangible Experiences

The first disconnect relates to thinking and talking about services as products. They are *not* products! Just to be sure, next time you go to the doctor, try to put the doctor's analysis of your x-rays into your car's trunk. Or, ask you insurance company if you can visit its warehouse containing the inventory of policies. Or after you spend three hours and $50 at the ballpark, try to explain to someone what you have pocketed as a result. You can't—because services are more experiential in nature than tangible products. Developing new services requires a different approach, or at least a modified approach, than that used for new product development.

22.2.2. Individualized Experiences

The second disconnect is referenced in Webster's dictionary (Second Edition, unabridged, 1954) by defining service first as "the occupation, condition or status of a servant," and second as "performance of labor for the benefit of another, or at another's command." Services, by definition, means doing something for someone, not mass producing a product for the nonintimate "everyone." The challenge for new service developers is addressing this objective for individualized services as well as the objective for cost-effectiveness and economies of scale. In particular, new service developers that have significant operational infrastructures, such as hotels, financial institutions, utilities, and transportation companies, get caught in this "one size fits all" death trap.

22.2.3. Strategic Benefits

The third disconnect relates to thinking of service *only* as enhancements to the perceived "real" product or offering. For example, when Pizza Hut delivers its pizza, most assume that this is merely an ancillary service to its business of producing pizza. While ancillary services are important to create, they are tactical and represent only part of the potential spectrum of services that could be developed. Breakthroughs, by contrast, generally come from the more strategic new services that relate to the core business of the enterprise and provide unique benefits to customers. Domino's Pizza took this view when it innovated a pizza delivery business by placing the primary emphasis on the service of delivery. More and more product companies have begun recognizing the latent competitive weapon they have in offering strategic services. This is exactly what Lexus has accomplished in the United States, with a new service approach consisting of a company-owned dealership network and many service features that customers perceive to be competitively differentiated. The point for new service developers, then, is to consider both tactical and strategic services.

22.2.4. Simultaneous Production and Delivery

A fourth disconnect is the lack of understanding that a "service factory" exists where services are produced, often with the customer "working the production line." A new service concept is, in fact, the designed experience. This means that developers must design and plan for all the people interactions. These interactions collectively become the service experience. The service experience is literally built at each step in the delivery "chain," which includes customer-to-front-line employee exchanges, customer-to-back-line employee responses, and customer-to-customer interactions.

22.2.5. Quality Variability

The fifth disconnect arises because of the variability of quality. New service developers often do not take into account the fact that service quality begins with customer expectations, and that these expectations are not constant. In product development, after the appropriate amount of research, specifications relative to functionality can be rigidly set, upon which all future development efforts may focus. But, it is much more difficult to establish a common service experience. For example, how can a group of clients of a law firm collectively articulate what they want, let alone how they will collectively judge the quality of the service experience they receive? This difficulty simply cannot be ignored in new service development. It must be dealt with, because it is well known that the quality of

> *The customer's attitude about a service depends on how he or she was treated by the person who delivered the service.*

a new service must be extremely high at the time of launch [1]. To be effective in the development phase of new services, the unique nature of services requires developers to adopt approaches different from those of their product-developing peers.

22.3. CUSTOMER-INVOLVED SERVICE DEVELOPMENT

Like the word *services,* the term *customer-driven* causes glazed eyes for seasoned marketers, who believe that this is a well-ingrained "given" in all business endeavors. This is not true in service development! In a 1993 study of product and service developers, lack of understanding of market needs was the leading reason cited for new product and service failure [3].

Neglecting to bring customer opinion into the process is particularly destructive for new service developers, who must, themselves, become disciples of the market and zealots of solving customer problems. A "customer-involved" new service development process can help and is one that structures significant and specific customer involvement into the process. Pursuit of a customer-involved process enables developers to be close to the market and customer requirements. It also helps address the unique-to-services disconnects discussed earlier.

Simply defined, a customer-involved development process establishes customers as integrated partners or team members during all steps, from problem identification to postlaunch. The first step to implementing this approach is to determine what customer-involved insights and feedback would have the greatest impact. Based on our experience, the following seven purposes seem most appropriate:

1. Confirming requirements for the service, the customer interface, customer support services, and billing system requirements
2. Assessing points of value
3. Testing delivery experience
4. Propelling rapid learning and concept iterations
5. Identifying the variability in points of quality
6. Analyzing the impact in customers' processes
7. Customizing alternative approaches

In addition to determining what areas are most appropriate for in-depth insights and feedback, developers should carefully consider how to involve customers. This involvement could range from arm's length, "we're helping each other out" arrangements, to contractually bound, "there is something tangible in this for both of us" agreements. The total number of customers involved is another consideration and can range from a few to hundreds. A third consideration pertains to how extensively customers are involved. This level of involvement could range from response to survey questions to regular face-to-face meetings with the development team.

Combining these variables depends on the specific situation. The purpose and approach for integrating customer input into the development process will usually be driven by the following:

> *It is important to involve prospective customers in service development.*

- The kind of service customer, consumer, or business, and the level of their involvement in the service delivery
- The degree of newness of the new service
- The market dynamics of category size, window of opportunity, competitive uniqueness, and customer value impact
- The degree of intangibility and protectability of the new service

A rule of thumb is to configure customer involvement such that depth of insight is obtained to ensure "proof of value" for each customer, and breadth of coverage is attained to ensure "proof of concept" for the broader target market.

22.4. CUSTOMIZING THE SERVICE DEVELOPMENT PROCESS

The starting premise for any successful new service development program is the existence of a new services strategy. The new services strategy should be aligned with and prioritized by the organization's business strategy. The actual development process comes next, supporting the adage "form follows function" (in this case strategy). The linkage of development process to new product and service strategy to business strategy was first introduced in the late 1980s [3] and has now become a common, although not easily implemented objective for most new product and service managers. In similar linkage fashion, the development process must be customized for each new service objective to take into account factors such as the degree of newness, degree of customer involvement during development, and the level of investment.

The necessity of having a formal new service development process is usually self-evident and routinely discussed. Yet more than half of the new *service* developers responding to a 1995 study [4] indicated that no formal process is followed at their organizations. This compares to a much smaller number of new product developers, who responded that no formal process exists at their companies. This greater lack of adherence by service developers to one formal process may come from their intuitive desire for flexibility due to the unique nature of new services.

Figure 22.1 portrays a ten-step new service development process adopted from earlier writings [5] that can form the base process for most service organizations. Johnson and Scheuing point out that "few service firms are adequately prepared to meet the new challenges of developing a steady stream of service innovations." These authors have developed several models for new service development that call for a large dose of customer involvement during all steps of the development process [2]. The point here is not to debate what are the right steps in the process, but to emphasize the need for having a formalized, step-by-step process that is then customized. The benefits of customizing the process often show up in more rapid development times, greater protection of the new service, leverageable customer references at introduction, and faster experiential learning for quick enhancements and future adaptations.

> *The development of a new service is best accomplished with an orderly, staged process.*

At its core, customizing the process is simply adjusting the type and degree of rigor based on the situation. It *never* means skipping steps in the process! The fol-

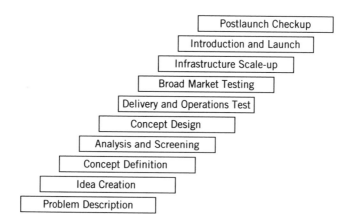

FIGURE 22.1 New service development process. From Craig A. Terrill and Arthur G. Middlebrooks, Kuczmarski & Associates, Inc., 1995.

lowing two primary factors determine "when" to customize the new service development process:

1. The degree of newness of the new service, categorized as new to the world, new to the company, new combinations or solutions, new service-line extensions, new enhancements or features, and new technologies and approaches for cost improvement.
2. The level of investment, which indicates the degree of risk and strategic expectations of the new service under development.

Once it is determined when customization should occur, there are seven essential "how" elements that should be reviewed for possible modification of the rigor applied:

1. Breadth and pervasiveness of research
2. Depth of analysis
3. Detail of documentation
4. Definition of what is to be launched
5. Complexity of decision-making process
6. Amount of operational, delivery and customer testing
7. Time needed for each step

Figure 22.2 shows the relationship between the customizing "when" factors and "how" elements. In general, when a truly new service is being developed, with significant investments in infrastructure and delivery, the development team's mission should be "go slower and get it right." If the opposite is true, the axiom "go faster and get it out" should guide the process.

22.5. CRITICAL ISSUES OF SERVICE DEVELOPMENT

Although much effort and literature has been devoted to identifying ways to improve the effectiveness, efficiency, time to market, and success rates of new product development, the unique issues and needs of new service development have received far less attention [7]. As described previously, the service development process has unique complexities and requirements because:

- Services tend to be intangible experiences, making them difficult to describe or test with customers until they are experienced.
- The role of the customer in the process is different—customers are intimately involved in service delivery.

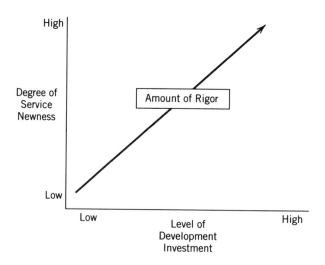

FIGURE 22.2 Customizing the service development process. From Craig A. Terrill and Arthur G. Middlebrooks, Kuczmarski & Associates, Inc., 1995.

- Service development must plan for the role of employees in service delivery. Employees are typically vital to delivering a consistently favorable service experience, yet individual discretion and service customization may result in variability of service quality.

As a result, five key issues emerge that must be addressed for effective service development:

1. Reversing the customer search approach
2. Mapping the service process
3. Building quality and planning for recovery
4. Innovating services
5. Planning for delivery during service development

22.5.1. Reversing the Customer Research Approach

Market research and new service development often operate like oil and vinegar. When properly integrated, they produce an experience to savor. But more often than not, they repel one another, with market research being severely restricted. A low level of market research during development can be attributed to two things: concerns over the results of completing new services research and inappropriate new service research methodology.

One of the biggest concerns of new service developers is the validity of market feedback that occurs so far in advance of introduction when a truly new concept is being developed. Services tend to have shorter life cycles than products, which means that at the time of introduction, the market's requirements may have already shifted into the next phase of evolution. A second concern is establishing market requirements that are too broad and targeted only for a mass market, which can result in undifferentiated services. Most often new services should be developed for a mass customization environment by creating platforms, systems, and delivery capabilities that enable the mass "production" of individually customized services. A third concern of new service developers is having their new concept stolen by a competitor during development.

In many companies, the traditional new product development market research methodology captures input from the market at two points in the development process.

> *Because it is hard to erect a barrier to competition, services often have short life cycles.*

The first point, which comes after the ideation step, is for refining and validating the customer requirements of the brainstormed concepts. The second is during the step where a complete business plan is developed and research is used for estimating market size, competitive share, ballpark pricing parameters, and the like. When visualized, the traditional methodology looks like a funnel that permits broad market inputs during the early steps in development and then permits more specific feedback later in the process, primarily on "product marketing" issues. Market research for service development, however, needs input from customers and a methodology that takes into account the experiential and customer intimate nature of services.

To address these concerns and shortcomings, new service developers should consider implementing a "reverse customer research" approach. It is the reverse of the traditional product approach because it starts with more narrow customer feedback and then receives broad-based market research as the new concept is being finalized. This reverse approach also allows for the increased level of customer intimacy during research that is essential for creating intangible services.

The proposed methodology for service development can simply be applied in four phases. The first phase would be exploratory research, with targeted customers considered "experts" or leading-edge thinkers. Insights regarding customers' "solvable" problems should be carried from one interview to the next. The second phase would be highly focused, in-depth research with a selected group of customers. It could also include the core customers that may previously have been established as development partners. For example, some companies use a customer advisory board of leading-edge thinkers to assist in service development.

To build the mandatory business case, the third phase would take inputs from the selected group and extrapolate them to estimate broad market characteristics. The fourth phase would feature vital broad-based research that is conducted to determine the total market's buying and satisfaction factors. This research should be conducted three months prior to introduction and should include testing the service delivery experience, as well as the expected benefits, with all the targeted market segments.

> *A service process map is invaluable for understanding its definition and delivery.*

22.5.2. Mapping Service Processes

Because services tend to be "performances" that may vary in their delivery, an outline of the service delivery process can aid in the effort to achieve consistent quality. A service process map graphically demonstrates the sequential flow of activities and interactions between the customer, front-line employees, support employees, and enabling company assets [2,6,8]. The primary goals of service process maps are to:

- Demonstrate the service delivery process from the customer's point of view, and define the customer's involvement.
- Define all the components and interactions involved in service delivery to ensure that each adds value.
- Identify critical areas where service delivery may break down, so that contingency and recovery plans can be developed.

Figure 22.3 illustrates the key components of a service process map. To create a service process map, start by identifying and sequencing all interactions between the customer and front-line company employees. These interactions may be in person or by phone, and involve direct contact between the customer and company. Next, map the physical operations of the service that are invisible to customers—the interactions between front-line company employees and support employees. Finally, indicate employee interactions with enabling assets required to support the process, such as important equipment, vehicles, and information databases.

For a new service, an initial service process map should be created that conveys a simple understanding of the entire service delivery system. Several alternative maps may be appropriate to describe different ways that the service might be defined or delivered. The customer interface portion of each alternative can then be tested with customers to determine the optimal service definition

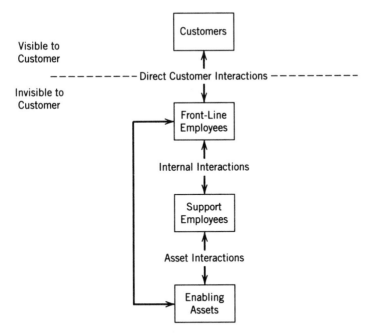

FIGURE 22.3 Service process map. From Craig A. Terrill and Arthur G. Middle-brooks, Kuczmarski & Associates, Inc., 1995.

and delivery approach. Finally, subsequent maps may be developed to demonstrate greater detail by outlining specific activities for critical areas of the process, such as hand-offs and points of customer interaction. Figure 22.4 illustrates a sample overview service process map for a typical restaurant experience.

22.5.3. Building Quality and Planning for Recovery

Unlike new products, most services must be developed with the assumption that delivery will fail. The variability of environmental conditions, customer expectations, employee responses, and the like are too numerous to "engineer" out of the service process entirely. Thus, the key to success is to instill quality up-front, then anticipate potential service failures and plan ahead for recovery.

The service process maps discussed in Section 22.5.2 can be useful for identifying potential points of failure in service delivery. With this knowledge, the process can be refined and contingencies developed to avoid failures. The most likely conditions for service delivery failure include the following:

- Successful delivery of the service is contingent upon elements outside the company's control (e.g., the weather, responsiveness of outside suppliers).

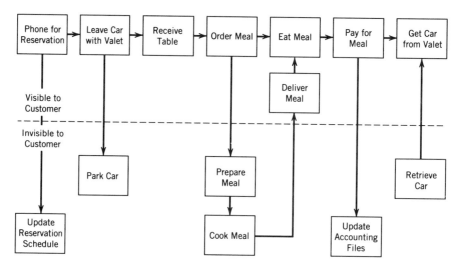

FIGURE 22.4 Service process map: restaurant experience. From Craig A. Terrill and Arthur G. Middlebrooks, Kuczmarski & Associates, Inc., 1995.

- Critical equipment malfunctions or internal communications are temporarily broken (e.g., due to information system problems).
- Demand exceeds the capacity to handle all customers or deliver the expected quality of service to all customers.
- Customers have a nonstandard service request.
- Customers are dissatisfied with some aspect of the service.

Service quality can be built into new services up-front to reduce the chance of failure. Specifically, this involves applying a three-step approach:

1. Assess the points of customer involvement in each step of the service delivery process, and ensure that each step is appropriate to and valued by the target customers. Too often, companies create service processes that optimize their own internal operations without paying enough attention to the customer's involvement during the process.
2. Identify and eliminate process steps that do not add value to the customer's experience. Every step of the process should be examined and fine-tuned to deliver the desired customer benefits and promised level of service.
3. Identify potential operational bottlenecks, and simplify internal interactions, activities, and policies where possible. If processes and procedures become too complex or are designed without adequate attention to customer needs, quality problems surface.

Despite careful design, service failures will inevitably happen due to the many variable and uncontrollable circumstances that can occur. Therefore, recovery policies and procedures should be developed and employees trained to respond appropriately to the most likely service delivery failures. For example, restaurant managers usually have full authority to cancel the bill for a customer's meal if any issues about the food or dining experience arise.

22.5.4. Innovating Services

> *The prompt resolution of a customer complaint or disappointment is critical to assure a reputation for high quality.*

Like product innovation, service innovation comes in different degrees of "newness"—new to the world, new to the company, line extensions, and the like. But compared to new products, services can typically be duplicated by competitors in less time and with less capital investment. As a result, a continuous stream of innovation is necessary to keep services from rapidly becoming undifferentiated commodities.

To avoid rapid duplication and "commoditization" of services, companies can continuously innovate in five important ways:

1. *Positioning innovation.* Develop a unique service or company identity that focuses on a target set of customers and uniquely differentiates the service/company from competitive offerings. For example, the restaurant chain Boston Market recently repositioned itself as providing "home-cooked meals" rather than competing directly against fast-food companies.
2. *Process innovation.* Eliminate or add steps in a service process, to differentiate the service from competitive offerings. Process innovation results in either decreasing or increasing the service complexity [8]. For example, many hotel and rental car companies have eliminated steps in their check-in and check-out processes to address the need to reduce time and customer dissatisfaction with these activities. Information technology is often key to changing the innovating process, supporting billing, supporting database marketing, and enabling mass customized experiences.
3. *Service offering innovation.* Create a unique set of benefits and features by bundling/repackaging existing services, adding new benefits to current services, or creating totally new service offerings. For example, several automotive repair chains have repackaged their oil change service to include a lifetime oil change, thereby locking customers in for future services.
4. *People innovation.* Increase or reduce employee discretion in delivering service to customers, thereby either increasing standardization or increas-

ing customization of the delivery [8]. People innovation can also involve changing the skills mix of customer-contact employees in order to deliver greater value to customers. For example, Walt Disney theme parks give employees a great deal of discretion to exceed customer expectations.

5. *Communications innovation*. Brand a service offering and/or use unique communication approaches to distinguish an offering. For example, the consulting firm CSC/Index created the term *reengineering* to describe its cost-reduction service, communicated it creatively through seminars, articles, and books, and developed a unique identity for its service. "Tangibilizing" the service experience is a key requirement in service development, and one that innovative communications can address directly.

Innovation is critical to ongoing service differentiation. Therefore, service innovation should not only focus on creating a balanced portfolio of new service offerings, but also on incorporating one or more of the five dimensions of service innovation.

22.5.5. Planning for Delivery During Service Development

Service delivery and support employees are a critical consideration for service development because (a) they have discretion in ensuring successful delivery, (b) the production and delivery occur at the point of employee–customer interface, and (c) the customer is typically involved with employees as part of the service experience. Therefore, service delivery employees must be considered and planned for actively as part of the development process.

Specifically, companies should consider four employee areas when developing services:

1. *Selection and systems*. Consistent, high-quality service delivery requires hiring the right people, and motivating and compensating them in alignment with customer needs and expectations. In addition, the physical evidence surrounding employees—such as employees' work style, expected behaviors, appearance, and uniforms—should reinforce and not conflict with the service's positioning. For example, Southwest Airlines hires flight attendants who are willing and able to deliver a pleasant, uplifting experience, thus supporting the desired delivery.

> *The people with whom a customer interacts must be well trained.*

2. *Skills*. Employee training is particularly critical for successful service delivery. Consistency in providing services

requires substantial training of customer-contact employees, as well as systems and procedures that make it easy to replicate the desired experience. For most services, four types of skills and knowledge are required:

- Knowledge of the service offering, how it works, its benefits and features
- An ability to identify individual customer requirements, and determine the appropriate service(s)
- An ability to customize a service, to some degree, to meet individual customer needs
- Knowledge of how to recovery from service failures

3. *Service customization.* Integral to the service development process is determining the degree of employees discretion and service customization required. If service customization and/or employees discretion must be high, employee requirements become more complex in terms of skill sets, training needs, communications, and recovery.

4. *Safety nets.* As discussed previously, employee guidelines, recovery procedures, and backup systems should be developed to address the inevitable service failures.

In summary, the service development process must "start with the end in mind" by incorporating employee delivery issues from the very beginning.

22.6. SUMMARY

Service development is different from product development. Successful companies incorporate the three C's of service development:

- *Customers* are actively involved throughout the process, frequently as development partners.
- *Concurrent development* of the service concept and the delivery process occurs because the process is the customer experience.
- *Customization* of the service development process enables a balance of risk and speed to market.

In addition, successful new service developers give extra consideration and attention to the five critical service development issues: reverse market research, service process mapping, service quality and recovery, continuous innovation, and planning for service delivery.

REFERENCES

1. Bitner, M. Managing the evidence of service. In: *The Service Quality Handbook*. New York: Amacom, 1993.

2. Johnson, E., and Scheuing, E. A proposed model for new service development. Journal of Service Marketing. (Spring 1989).

3. Kuczmarski & Associates, Inc. *Winning New Products and Services for the 1990s*®. Chicago: Kuczmarski & Associates, Inc., 1993.

4. Kuczmarski & Associates, Inc. *Winning New Products and Services for the 1990s*®. Chicago: Kuczmarski & Associates, Inc., 1995.

5. Kuczmarski, Thomas D. *Managing New Products*, (2nd ed.) Englewood Cliffs, NJ: Prentice Hall, 1992.

6. Shostak, G. Lynn. Service positioning through structural change. *Journal of Marketing* (January 1987).

7. Terrill, Craig A. The ten commandments of new service development. *Management Review* (February 1992).

8. Vecchiotti, R. I., and Terrill, Craig A. The challenge of new service introduction. In: *The AMA Management Handbook*, 3rd ed. New York: Amacom, 1994, pp. 15.27–15.32.

Craig A. Terrill
Kuczmarski & Associates, Inc.

Craig Terrill is a Partner with Kuczmarski & Associates, an innovation management consulting firm headquartered in Chicago, Illinois. Mr. Terrill is a nationally recognized expert in services marketing, innovation and growth strategies, and helps service organizations grow profitably through new service development and marketing strategies. Mr. Terrill is an adjunct professor of services marketing and marketing channels at the J.L. Kellogg Graduate School of Management at Northwestern University. In addition, his recent book on service industry innovation and differentiation strategies will be published in 1997.

Arthur G. Middlebrooks
Kuczmarski & Associates, Inc.

Art Middlebrooks is a Principal with Kuczmarski & Associates. Mr. Middlebrooks specializes in helping high-technology and service companies grow profitably through new product and service development, differentiation, and effective marketing strategies. In addition, Mr. Middlebrooks is an adjunct professor of services marketing at the University of Chicago Graduate School of Business and a guest lecturer in marketing and new products at the J.L. Kellogg Graduate School of Management.

MANUFACTURING
23 PROCESS PLANNING AND DEVELOPMENT
Philip E. Quigley

23.1. INTRODUCTION

The need to do effective material and operations planning is critical in the new product development process. Starting production on a new product is a critical challenge for operations management. Consider the following, which may be required:

1. Working with suppliers to ensure both the quality of the new parts, compliance with cost goals, and the ability of the supplier to meet production schedules.
2. Introduction or modification of manufacturing process, including machinery, test and inspection equipment, and training of workers.
3. The planning and timing issues of ramping one product down and another up in a plant.
4. Increasing capacity in a plant to meet new production schedules due to the forecasts for a new product.

These planning requirements are large and complex. Tools must be used that will minimize effort, yet ensure planning effectiveness. A materials requirements planning (MRP) system is a valuable tool in this process, but MRP needs a bill of materials (BOM) from which to plan. However, at the start of the new product process, there is no design, so how can MRP be used? The answer is to use a preliminary bill of materials (PBOM). What's the difference? The definition of a bill of materials is:

> *Bill of materials*: A listing of all the subassemblies, intermediate parts, and raw materials that go into a parent assembly showing the quantity of each required to make an assembly [3, p. 811].

This definition states that all the parts and subassemblies are known. But what if, as in the start of a new design, you don't know? You start by making an educated guess or forecasting. What you have is a preliminary bill of materials (PBOM; sometimes called an imaginary BOM) that is subject to change as you do more design work. How preliminary? This depends on the product and situation. You may know a lot about a product because it is based on another existing product, or you may be starting from scratch. The definition of the PBOM is:

> *Preliminary bill of materials*: (1) A forecasted listing of all the subassemblies, intermediate parts, and raw material that go into a parent assembly, showing the quantity of each required to make an assembly. (2) A forecasted listing of all the engineering design, process and tool design, and customer input that is required to design the assembly.

The PBOM now allows the new product team to use the MRP system to do planning. The MRP system can also be used to plan and schedule engineering design and tool design.

> *The PBOM is an educated guess or forecast of what parts will be needed in a new product. It won't be perfect, but it is good enough to start planning with.*

23.2. DEVELOPMENT AND MAINTENANCE OF PRELIMINARY BILL OF MATERIAL

Development of PBOM is done a four-step process (Figure 23.1).

1. *Assembly structure overview.* The production planner and responsible design and manufacturing engineers lay out an assembly or manufacturing tree of the product. At this time, assemblies and subassemblies are laid out. This gives a picture of the basic structure of the product. See Figure 23.2, which shows that there is an unknown [to be determined (TBD)] power supply needing further design, but other areas are understood more clearly.

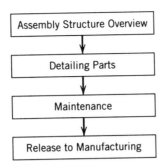

FIGURE 23.1 Preliminary bill of materials process.

2. *Detailing parts.* The production planner and responsible design and manufacturing engineers then work on each assembly and identify, as far as
   practical, the parts going into each assembly. Where parts are known or
   cannot be detailed, the part type *unknown* is used.

   Examples:
   - A power supply is needed but analysis and a decision is needed. The
     PBOM would say "Unknown Power Supply—TBD" (see Figure 23.3).
   - The basic design of a part has been complete but needs finishing
     details. The complete assembly would be "Unknown Cover,
     Machined—TBD" but the purchased casting could be called out (see
     Figure 23.4)

   The purpose of the PBOM is to call out as much as possible and indicate
   where further design is needed.

3. *Maintenance of the preliminary bill of material.* As the design process
   continues, further details will be known and can be put into the PBOM.

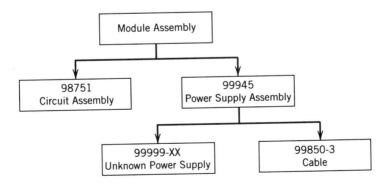

FIGURE 23.2 Assembly structure overview.

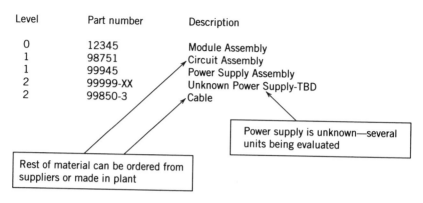

FIGURE 23.3 Indented preliminary bill of materials.

It is critical that the PBOM be updated on a continuing basis. The procedure for change should allow a responsible planner or engineer to change the PBOM without a formal sign-off or bureaucratic control.

4. *Formal release of the preliminary bill of material.* The engineering design is complete so the design is signed off as complete and ready for manufacture. Design changes are still expected but will now go through a formal approval process [4, Chap. 10] Attention must be paid to the MRP system being used and the BOM module. The system must allow quick changes of the PBOM and allow one person to change and edit the BOM quickly. If this isn't done, maintenance of the PBOM will be time consuming, and in the crisis atmosphere of a new product project it will not be done.

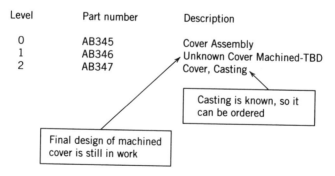

FIGURE 23.4 Machine cover assembly.

23.3. MATERIAL PLANNING WITH THE PRELIMINARY BILL OF MATERIAL

> *Maintenance of the PBOM must be done, and it must be easy to do.*

When a PBOM is developed and the data are loaded into the MRP system, a production plan can be loaded for the new product. MRP can then be run and a detailed materials plan can then be generated. The materials organization now has some preliminary planning numbers. These data can be used to:

1. Review requirements with suppliers for discussions on schedules and the ability of suppliers to meet requirements.
2. Alternative schedules can be loaded and requirements generated to do "what-if" analysis on the inventory impact of the new product. For example, the effect on existing product lines and the risk of obsolete inventory can be studied.
3. Advanced planning can be done when new materials or technology are specified. The purchasing department will have time to identify and meet with potential suppliers.

It is important to realize that the data is being used for advanced planning purposes only. The requirements are preliminary—purchase orders are not being issued. Letters of intent may be issued or quotes requested. The main purpose of the data is to help identify potential problem areas—suppliers who cannot meet a schedule, or identification of inventory problems with the introduction of the new product [2, Chap. 10].

Example: When the PBOM from Figure 23.3 is loaded into the MRP system, the requirements for the unknown power supply are

> *Problems are to be identified so that they can be fixed.*

identified. Suppliers can be called in to discuss requirements. Engineers can talk about possible units to use, and when the decision is made on which power supply to use, a supplier can be chosen quickly.

23.4. PRODUCTION AND CAPACITY PLANNING USING THE PRELIMINARY BILL OF MATERIAL

After the PBOM is developed, routers, or a list of detailed manufacturing operations, can be completed (see Figure 23.5). A this time the router is prelimi-

Part number: AB346

Operation	Description	Time
010	Issue Material	10 minutes
020	Drilling	120 minutes
030	Boring	30 minutes
040	Paint	90 minutes
050	Inspect	15 minutes
060	Stock	

FIGURE 23.5 Routing for machined cover preliminary.

nary, a best guess at what will be required to do the job. But it is good enough to start analyzing the load on the factory. It is good enough because it is based on previous experience with similar parts. The key is having the right people together to give the estimate. Now rough-cut and detailed capacity planning reports can be run from the proposed production schedule. These reports will allow the following planning to be done:

1. Analysis of the labor needed: additions, reductions, or changes in skill mix.
2. Analysis of machinery and equipment needed.
3. Layout of the facility can be modeled with the data generated from both the production schedule and capacity reports.
4. Adavanced modeling will allow overloaded manufacturing areas to be identified and corrected before production begins.

The key is to identify problem areas in the process on an ongoing basis. The goal is to have a smooth transition into full production. Nothing frustrates management and customers more than a hot new product that no one can get [3, Chaps. 9 and 11].

> **Remember, the goal is a smooth transition to production.**

Example: The final configuration of the machine cover from Figure 23.3 is not known, but an estimate of 10 hours of machining is put together based on the history of previous design. This estimate allows engineers to do an analysis of the impact of the hours in manufacturing.

23.5. USE OF THE PRELIMINARY BILL OF MATERIAL TO PLAN AND SCHEDULE ENGINEERING

One of the major challenges facing management in the new product development process is managing the load on engineering so that realistic design schedules can be developed and executed. Typically, management has overcommitted engineering resources and the result is constant shuffling and reprioritizing of people (see Chapter 5). Another term is *firefighting* [2, Chap. 4].

The PBOM can be a tool to proper planning of engineering efforts. The router is expanded to identify engineering effort. The MRP system can then be used to develop schedules and show load on critical engineering areas. The following steps are used:

1. Review the PBOM and identify areas where engineering design is needed.
2. Add engineering design release to the PBOM as the lowest-level item.
3. Create a router showing the basic engineering steps needed to complete the design.

Figure 23.6 shows a PBOM with engineering callout. The key concept here is doing a capacity plan of engineering and then deliberately assigning engineering resources to priority projects. This is a change for many organizations and takes a lot of effort to make it happen, but the benefits are enormous. This process can be used to identify high-risk areas in the design. Once identified, alternative designs can be analyzed using the PBOM approach [2, Chap. 10]

23.6. USE OF THE PBOM TO PLAN AND SCHEDULE TOOL AND PROCESS DESIGN

> *Engineering is a resource with finite limits—it must be managed.*

The PBOM now has assembly structure, detail part callout, and engineering design. The next areas to be added to the PBOM are process design and tool requirements. The steps in this process are as follow:

Level	Part number	Description
0	AB345	Cover Assembly
1	AB346	Cover Machined
1	AB347-1	Casting
2	AB346-Eng	Engineering Design
2	AB346-Tool	Tool Design

Engineering and tool design have been added to PBOM

FIGURE 23.6 Machine cover assembly adding design to bill of material.

1. Review the PBOM and identify where new tooling or manufacturing processes will have to be implemented.
2. Add the tooling or process development requirements to the PBOM.
3. Create routers for completing the tool design and fabrication and the process implementation.

Figure 23.7 shows a PBOM and routers for tooling.

The next step is using the MRP process to plan and schedule the tooling and process development. Capacity planning of the design and fabrication areas can be done. Status of effort can be done quickly and cheaply using the system. The key here is identifying critical areas or bottlenecks that could affect the overall project schedule. Judgment must be used on how much detail to be put into the PBOM. You should only put major tool or process requirements on the system. You must balance the work necessary to load and maintain the PBOM with the benefit it gives you [1, Chap. 10].

23.7. USE OF THE PRELIMINARY BILL OF MATERIALS FOR COSTING PURPOSES

The PBOM is ready to have cost data loaded into it. Data could include estimated purchase part costs, estimated direct labor cost, and estimated times for processes (e.g., heat treating, testing, etc.). Reports can be run showing total projected costs for a product that can be used to evaluate designs and propose alternatives if cost goals are not being met [4, Chap. 9]. A key activity here is maintenance of the PBOM and willingness to change it when necessary. Accuracy is an issue—the numbers won't be perfect. They are ballpark numbers in the beginning. They will get more accurate as the design matures.

23.8. CASE STUDY

An offshore oil tool company and its need to design and produce offshore drilling equipment quickly is a good example of the use of the PBOM. This example is

Operation	Description	Time
010	Engineering Review	4 Hours
020	Preliminary Design	12 Hours
030	Operations Design Review	2 Hours
040	Final Modification	2 Hours
050	Design Release	

FIGURE 23.7 Tool design router.

a real one where the author was the production control manager and MRP implementation project manager. The company built equipment for the offshore oil industry. Products were used by drill ships and platforms to drill for oil.

The market was competitive, new technology was being introduced, and quality levels matched the nuclear industry in the areas of welding and valve operation. Highly critical was the necessity to meet a schedule. It was agreed that schedules for drill ships, drilling permits, and so on, could be affected if product was delivered late. An example (Figure 23.8) is a riser assembly, a 50-foot piece of pipe with box-and-pin machined assemblies that were welded to the end of the pipe. Auxiliary pipes ran along the side. A typical contract specified for 25 to 30 of these assemblies.

Old Way of Designing and Manufacturing

The old way of designing was simple. Talks were held with the customer and then engineering designed the system. Sometimes engineering realized that there were similarities to other designs, and from time to time drawings were copied. A design review and approval process was then carried out with the customer. The engineering department would put together a preliminary list of material and orders would be placed with suppliers.

Manufacturing would receive a complete set of drawings after the design was complete. BOMs would be developed, schedules loaded into the system, and MRP run to develop material requirements. Purchase orders and work orders would then be released. Problems with late design releases, incorrect material ordered by engineering, and problems in tooling were constantly being found. These problems were caused by customer design changes, engineering realizing that original designs were incorrect, or errors caused by engineering expediting work due to customer schedule changes.

New Way

After receipt of an order, engineering and production control reviewed the order and customer requirements. PBOMs were created for the riser assembly. It was

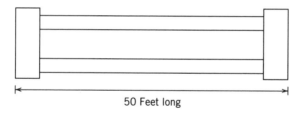

50 Feet long

FIGURE 23.8 Riser assembly. Generally, the size and type of pipe and the castings were known; the exact configuration of the final assembly was unknown.

discovered immediately that the design was similar to one that had been shipped to the same customer before. There were design modifications that became evident after the PBOMs were created. The following was found:

1. All of the critical long-lead material—pipe, castings, and fittings—could be ordered.
2. There were areas needing new design release.
3. New design could not move forward until the customer made some decisions as to their requirements.
4. The customer had two alternatives in mind and would authorize procuring material to support either design.

Based on the knowledge gained from the PBOMs, material was ordered, work was released to the factory, and the customer and engineering accelerated their analysis to finalize design.

The immediate impact was a saving of three months in the procurement cycle: Instead of waiting for prints and preliminary parts lists, orders were placed within a week of receipt of customer order. Another saving was in copying over existing BOMs. Hundreds of hours in engineering design were saved. A long-term effect of the use of a PBOM was in educating the engineering group and senior management on modular design. Key engineering efforts were scheduled using the PBOM approach, and management became aware of the effect of overloading the engineering group.

23.9. SUMMARY

The PBOM is a powerful tool in the new product or custom-design processes. It must be used with some thought and care by design teams. The PBOM takes work to develop and maintain, but the return on the investment is substantial.

REFERENCES

1. Berry, W., Vollman, T., and Whybark, C. *Master Production Scheduling*. Falls Church, VA: American Production and Inventory Control Society, 1983.
2. Clark, K. and Wheelright, S. *Managing New Product and Process Development*. New York: Free Press, 1993.
3. Fogarty, D., Blackstone, J., and Hoffman, T. *Production and Inventory Management*, 2nd ed. Cincinatti, OH: Southwestern, 1991.
4. Lunn, T. and Neff, S. A. *MRP: Integrating Material Requirements Planning and Modern Business*, New York: Irwin Professional Publishing, 1992.

Philip E. Quigley
AT&T Solutions

Before joining AT&T Solutions Mr. Quigley had management experience in manufacturing, where he has directed master scheduling, material and production planning, stockrooms, quality and cost improvement projects, new product teams, and systems implementations. Experience has been in the computer, oil tool, and aerospace industries. He is an active member of the Orange County chapter of APICS, where he has held various chapter management positions. He has developed and taught classes in quality, business process reengineering, operations management, and new product development in the MBA program at the University of La Verne.

24 ACCELERATING NEW PRODUCT DEVELOPMENT
Robert J. Meltzer

24.1. INTRODUCTION

Despite the dozens of tools available for managing projects, the complaint persists that every new product development (NPD) takes longer and costs more than first promised. The reasons for failing to maintain schedule integrity are more instructive than the rationalized reasons for success. Most failures can be ascribed to one or more of four causes:

1. The negotiated schedule was unrealistic at the start.
2. The project fell into any of a variety of pitfalls that can trap a project.
3. None of the means to speed a realistic schedule were used.
4. No method was in place to give early warning of schedule slip.

24.2. SCHEDULING: REALISM WITHOUT COERCION

It is not easy to withstand a high-level demand for instant new product. Data do not support the common wisdom that it pays to be first to enter the market unless it is assumed that later entries are of exactly comparable product. If later entries improve on first-entry products, as is to be expected, order of entry is inconsequential. This common wisdom creates marketing pressure to agree to unrealistic schedules. But unrealistic schedules can be as much the fault of development personnel, who tend to promise short delivery times because they have confidence. Despite pressure and overconfidence, it is possible to negotiate a realistic schedule to which all parties can agree without coercion.

24.2.1. Deliverables, Tasks, and Events

The final product, as introduced to the market, will always be comprised of a number of deliverables. A *deliverable* is an entity that is complete in the sense that it can be defined as if it were separate from the final product: manufactured separately, tested separately, and delivered separately. Some examples of a deliverable are subassemblies, software programs, and the operator's manual. To meet the schedule for market introduction, each deliverable must be available in accordance with an overall schedule of the kind that might be defined by a PERT chart or Gantt chart.

Each deliverable will be completed by performing *tasks*. Tasks make up a schedule devised for each deliverable. The completion of each task is marked by an *event*, a point in time. A task has duration, but an event does not. Schedule integrity can be lost if events and tasks are confused, as if the event had taken place when the task had only begun.

24.2.2. The "Garage Bill" Approach

When making a schedule for a new product development, we can take a lesson from a garage mechanic. You take your care in for a "minor" repair and are shocked to get a bill for $543.69. But the bill is unarguable because the total is made up of so many small items, each of which is individually defensible. The garage bill approach will include all the tasks necessary to complete the deliverable. It will result in a realistic schedule, difficult to argue with and likely to be close to reality. At General Electric they call the garage bill approach *process mapping*. No matter what it is called, every task, no matter how trivial it seems, must be written down. The cumulative time for omitting even "trivial" tasks can easily disrupt schedule integrity.

It is easy to make a detailed, believable schedule for a three-day task, not hard for a one-week task, difficult for a one-month task, and almost impossible for a three-month task. Therefore, insofar as possible, the duration of any one task should be limited to one week. There are other reasons to define each individual task so narrowly that it lasts no longer than a week:

- It is less likely that a necessary task will be omitted.
- There is early warning if a task is falling behind.

- Management has a reality-based sense of project status.
- The development team has a continuing sense of accomplishment.

24.3. PITFALLS IN THE ROAD TO RAPID NPD AND WHAT TO DO ABOUT THEM

24.3.1. "Everything's Been OK Up to Now"

Much of what people remember of the success of previous NPD efforts is romanticizing the past (Figure 24.1). The belief that our past has been successful makes invisible the internal inhibitors to rapid NPD. Only a humbling and often distasteful reexamination will discover how we could have done better. A fresh view requires us to recognize the avoidable errors that prevented making success even more successful.

24.3.2. Midstream Changes

Product development people constantly complain that NPD is delayed because the definition of the product changes during the course of development. The best preventive of the moving definition is a solid definition in the first place. The principal input to a solid definition comes from marketing and development personnel, with inputs from other members of the NPD team. Their task is to negotiate a product requirements document (PRD) [4].

Changes in definition during the project are minimized if a formal document to change a product requirement is mandated. The principle of the engineering change order (ECO) used to implement changes during production can be extended into the NPD arena as a development change order (DCO). This formalism does not prevent changes, but it does make everyone aware of what the

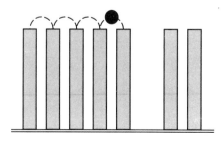

FIGURE 24.1 Everything's been a success so far.

consequences in development time and cost and in product cost will be. The very requirement that a development change order form must be filled out is something of a deterrent in itself.

24.3.3. "It's Gotta Be Perfect"

Even the most ordinary products fail of perfection, yet we buy them and use them with hardly a complaint. Consider just the imperfections of an ordinary coffee mug. It can't be stacked for storage. The coffee gets cold too fast. When inverted in a dishwasher the indentation in the bottom fills with water that will drip when the mug is removed.

> *The search for perfection is often nothing more than being scared.—John Fowles*

Perfection, if it is ever reached, comes by a series of relatively small incremental improvements. In general, no product reaches perfection before it is obsolete. It is better to be 90 percent right today than 95% right six months from now.

24.3.4. Too Many Projects

Limited resources is a frequent complaint of those involved in NPD. Available resources limit the number of NPDs that can be undertaken. But very often the number of NPDs for which market dates have been promised is too great for the NPD resources available. There is simple way to tell if there are too many projects for the resources available. It starts with chart of the kind everyone makes, like that shown in Table 24.1. The chart lists all the projects across the top and all the nonmanagement people down the left. Then the matrix is filled in, with each box containing the fraction of each person's time that will be de-

TABLE 24.1   Initial Development Department Manpower Loading

Person	Project						
	A	B	C	D	E	F	G
Abigail			0.3		0.2	0.5	
Barney				0.2			0.8
Clara	1.0						
Doug		0.5			0.5		
Erin			0.4				0.6
Frank		0.6	0.2				0.2

voted to each project, as shown in Table 24.1. If any box has a number less than 0.5, you have too many projects.

In the example shown, its clear that project A, project B, and project G are important enough to have at least full-time hours assigned to them. Abigail's time and Frank's time are diffused among three projects. It looks like projects C, D, and F should be killed or perhaps postponed.

With the elimination of these three projects, the resources of the development department, as shown in Table 24.2 are now concentrated on those projects that initially had the highest fraction of time assigned to them—assuming, of course, that the initial loading was in consequence of the importance of those projects. A concentration of forces on the projects of greatest importance substantially increases the likelihood that they will be completed on schedule.

24.3.5. Upper Management Interference

In development circles it is recognized that senior executives avoid personal time investment at the start of a new product development [7]. They have several unspoken reasons:

- It is unfamiliar territory for many executives.
- There is a high risk of being identified with what turns out to be a failure and little prospect of being credited with eventual success.
- There's great vagueness and uncertainty.

While neglecting participation at the start, executives will invest too much time at the end of the development when there is little opportunity to influence the outcome critically. They do it for a different set of reasons, also unspoken:

- Effort at the end has high visibility.
- There will be a perception created of instant result from executive action; the usual consequence of executive action at the end is some delay of product introduction.

TABLE 24.2   Readjusted Development Department Personnel Loading

	Project			
Person	A	B	E	G
Abigail			1.0	
Barney				1.0
Clara	1.0			
Doug		0.5	0.5	
Erin				1.0
Frank		1.0		

Another source of delay occurs when the president or the board of directors want to see a demonstration. This demand usually costs two extra weeks. But the delay is not the worst cost. Worse than the delay is a possibly false impression of progress that it can give. If management truly wants to know what is going on, take them to the development area to talk to the people who are doing the work. The best question they can ask is: "What is your greatest worry about what you are doing?" Almost always the answer they get will be an honest one.

24.3.6. Ocassional Pitfalls to Avoid

Letting the Boss Decide

"Kick it up to the management level" is certain to ensure delay because the senior manager cannot be expected to know the details of the issue suddenly thrust upon her and so must be brought up to speed. It is also an abrogation of responsibility.

"Manufacturing Will Find a Way"

Of course they will, but at what cost in time to market? The object is not to complete the NPD on time. The object is to get paying customers into the store. If the goods aren't there because of manufacturing problems, how can there be customers? "Throwing it over the wall" to manufacturing is but one example of a much broader problem, compartmentalization. Every company needs some Joshua out there constantly blowing down the walls.

Product Complexity

There is no successful complex product that has not had a successful simple antecedent. A complex system is one that has a number of subsystems, all of which must interact in the way intended—and only in that way. As the number of subsystems increases, the number of possible interactions that can have subtle but disastrous interactions increases very rapidly, as shown in Figure 24.2. The likelihood is high that some of the possible interactions will prove to be inimical to the intended performance of the system as a whole, resulting in extended development time.

Process Instead of Product

Development teams can get so caught up in some elaborate development process protocol that they lose sight of the goal: getting the product to the market quickly.

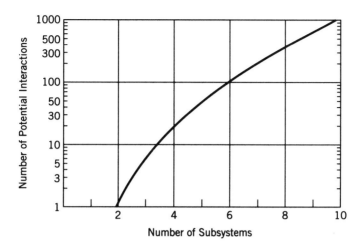

FIGURE 24.2 Number of possible system interactions.

24.4. ACCELERATING THE NPD PROCESS

24.4.1. Leverage Points in the NPD Process

The NPD process is like the process that starts and concludes any action. All such processes combine data with a knowledge base to reach a decision. An action follows the decision and the action produces a result. The desired result of the NPD process is a marketable product. Each of these points in the action process is a leverage point.

- Up-to-date data on customer needs and desires minimizes the need for *post hoc* market research.
- When the results of development process audits are part of the knowledge base, the next NPD is more likely than the last to proceed more rapidly.
- The NPD process is accelerated if the information validly needed for a go-ahead decision is available at the decision point. The implication is that the information needed is part of a NPD process definition.
- The action in NPD is project management. Accelerating the process implies that the tools for project management are available and used, that team membership and leadership are defined, and that senior management is behind the project ready to aid, but only when requested.

24.4.2. Tools for Leverage

Derivative New Product

Families.   Automobile engines constitute a family of product. The same basic engine can be changed to produce more horsepower or better mileage without the enormous time needed to develop a new engine and to change the very expensive tooling involved in producing the engine.

Platforms.   In a basic kitchen stove the structure becomes a platform upon which new products are created and differentiated by the addition of features and customer benefits.

Incremental Improvement.   To reach the market more quickly, all the potential of a breakthrough NPD need not be fulfilled at the time of initial market introduction. The best way to exploit a product that has broken through to new markets is to have in place a planned program for incremental improvement. The life of the breakthrough will be extended by the introduction of an improved replacement product before the market demands it.

Teams: Advantages and Hazards

An interfunctional team able to override bureaucratic impediments and "get the job done" is the best means we now have for accelerating NPD. Experience has shown that a team that is competently led and that understands the NPD process can deliver new product more quickly. But without competent leadership teams and without understanding of the process, NPD will take hardly less time than a project organized without teams.

Competent leadership for teams is always in short supply. Even competent leaders can be ignorant of the best practices for NPD. It can also happen that those outside the team, but whose services are required by the team, will feel they have been rejected as unfit to be part of an elite. A response of recalcitrance, abiding by bureaucratic rule and even surliness, can be the result.

Early Operator's Manual

An early operator's manual can accelerate NPD because:

- The manual defines the product in customer terms rather than in terms special to the industry.

- Writing the manual forces people to think through the details at the beginning rather than creating compromise paste-ons at the end.
- An operator's manual written with sufficient detail will define for software engineers what the inputs and outputs must be.

Contract Development

A persistent claim by all contract developers is that they can develop a product more rapidly than can the client's staff. A survey [5] among a group of contract developers gave several reasons:

- Contract organizations are smaller and less hierarchical, so decisions are made more quickly.
- Some contract developers claim that work goes faster because there are only senior people at work on the client's project. That will be expensive. Close senior supervision is what is needed.
- The use of contract development allows the client's R&D people to spend most of their NPD time using the company's core technologies through the early stages. The contractor is used for the development of core technologies into a product. No individual product may reach the market more rapidly, but there will be more new products as development of core technologies proceeds without diversion.

Whatever the validity of contract developer claims may be, they have made a sufficient impression that more product development is being outsourced today than ever before.

Rapid Prototyping Methods

A number of rapid prototyping methods have become available:

1. Stereo lithography
2. Selective laser sintering
3. Fused deposition modeling
4. Laminated object manufacture
5. Ballistic particle manufacturing
6. Photech
7. Low-pressure molding
8. Laser cutting
9. Adhesive assembly

In general, these methods will produce a part by using CAD data. The first six processes in the list are examples of additive rapid prototyping [1,6].

Concurrency

Concurrency as applied to NPD means that operations stages that would normally be sequential are carried out in parallel. The gates that open the way to a subsequent stage are generally lowered. The purpose of the gates in the stage/gate development process is to minimize the likelihood of error. Each gate that can be passed more easily increases the risk. In exchange for increased risk, the product can reach the market more quickly.

The U.S. Air Force first gave the name concurrency *to an NPD program that overlaps development, testing, and production. The General Accounting Office (GAO) report on the program is quoted here from an LA Times story. "Our reviews . . . have identified concurrency as one cause of cost, schedule, and performance problems in system acquisition programs. . . . The Pentagon is expecting to begin producing well before tests and design studies will have proven that the entire complex of hardware and soft-ware will work together."*

24.5. MONITORING AND MAINTAINING SCHEDULE INTEGRITY

24.5.1. Tools to Monitor the Schedule

Slip Rate: A Metric for the Accuracy of Schedule Prediction

Slip rate has been suggested as a metric of conformance to schedule [3]. Slip rate is defined as follows:

$$\text{slip rate} = \left(\frac{\text{planned schedule}}{\text{actual schedule}} - 1 \right) \times 100\%$$

The metric can be applied to the entire project, to individual deliverables, and down to the individual tasks that are the components of each deliverable. Slip rate is also a measure of NPD process improvement.

Graphing Progress

If there is an early warning system of potential late delivery, appropriate action can usually be taken to maintain schedule integrity. A graphic way to monitor schedule integrity is to use a chart like that of Figure 24.3 [3]. At each date along the horizontal axis the completion date for each deliverable is reestimated. Absolute schedule integrity is thus a horizontal line as shown for deliverable 1. World-class compliance to the schedule might be a line with a 10% slope, like that for deliverable 2 [3]. But deliverable 3 is in serious difficulty. Its slope is greater than the reality line, and unless there is immediate action (see section 24.5.3) there is a good chance that it will never be delivered.

24.5.2. Getting Out of Schedule Trouble

Even when all the stages of the NPD process have been well executed, there may still be loss of schedule integrity. The most common causes of schedule slip are outlined below.

Vendor Problems

There is a risk that a vendor, for reasons that seem legitimate to the vendor, may decide that the risk of disappointing you is more acceptable than taking the same risk with some other customer. Except when the vendor is also providing development services, the vendor will rarely have any detailed event schedule except for a delivery date. The only remedy is regular communication with the vendor.

Unanticipated Technical Problems

At the start of any NPD there will be some number of known technical issues that have to be resolved. The greatest hazard to schedule integrity does not come

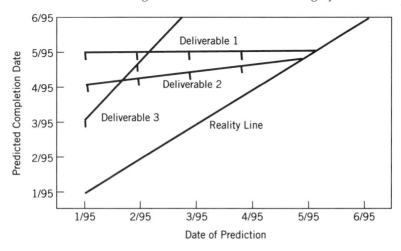

FIGURE 24.3 Schedule prediction.

from these but from technical surprises. To get out of the trouble, the first step is careful reconsideration of the troublesome requirement and the process that arrived at the requirement. But if reexamination shows that the requirement is valid, the tests for it are valid, and the tests are showing noncompliance, then at least two approaches are possible.

1. *Bring up the reserves.* This may be the time to bring in an expert or consultant, whether from inside the company or outside.
2. *Form a special-purpose team.* If one of the multitude of tasks becomes a problem, separate out a small group to solve that problem while the rest of the tasks move forward. Task segmentation allows nondependent tasks to move forward.

Catastrophe

Natural disasters and major accidents are a constant, if low-level, hazard. Companies without disaster-preparedness programs often go out of business.

Excess Optimism

Entrepreneurial people would not be able to raise the venture funds needed if they did not characterize their optimism as "realistic evaluation of the risks." An external evaluation can reduce the optimism but will never eliminate the risk inherent in any NPD.

Regulatory Issues

Hoping for the best with the regulatory agencies is all too common. Compliance always seems onerous. An FDA official has said, "All regulatory activities are the result of [somebody's] failure." Whether you agree or not, it is a point worth pondering.

24.6. HAZARDS TO ACCELERATING THE NPD PROCESS

The advantages of rapid new product development appear obvious. The potential problems engendered by an accelerated process are not so clearly seen, but there are several possible hazards [2].

1. *Rapid development favors small change projects.* Low-profit, trivial innovations can be developed quickly. In an accelerated development environ-

ment they tend to take precedence over products that are entirely new—products that create new markets and are more profitable.

2. *Error prevention procedures are weakened.* The purpose of the gates in the conventional NPD process is to minimize the likelihood of error. Each gate that can be passed more easily increases the chances for mistake.

3. *Teams can be effective—but also disruptive.* In the process of "getting the job done," there will be occasions when assistance is needed from those outside the team. On those occasions teams often experience noncooperation because those outside the team will have contributed without concomitant recognition. As yet, there is no generally acceptable system of rewards for team performance.

4. *Development stages respond unequally to acceleration.* It is easy to accelerate the testing of a product in the narrow environment of the company's quality assurance facilities. It is difficult to accelerate the discovery of product deficiencies as the result of the broader experience of customers using the product. The incidence of surprises in an accelerated development program will always be higher than those that have followed a conventional stage-gate process.

5. *Support services may not be supportive.* The people who work in those parts of the company not directly involved in NPD have worked under their own procedures with their own time frames. Their input to the accelerated NPD program may be necessary, but if the support services respond well to the team, it is probable that support to existing product will be disrupted.

24.7. SUMMARY

The means to achieve and maintain a realizable schedule are easy to state but not always easy to put into practice:

- A formal development process that can be formally altered to meet changed circumstances.
- A product requirements documents that is clear, complete, and unambiguous.
- Defined deliverables
  Start, duration, and precedence of each deliverable to be organized using conventional program management software.
  Defined tasks, each of short duration, that lead to the completion of each deliverable.

- A development change order (DCO) system that defines the change, the reason for the change, and the effect of the change on development time, development cost, and product cost.
- A means of monitoring the schedule (e.g., the plot shown in Figure 24.3) to provide early warning of a schedule slip.
- A generalized plan for recovering from schedule slip (see section 24.5.3)
- A mechanism to assure continuous improvement.

  A metric such as *slip rate* (section 24.5.1.).

  An audit of each development program and action to improve the process using audit information.

REFERENCES

1. Anonymous. Rapid prototyping technologies: a prelude to desktop manufacturing. *Medical Devices and Diagnostic Industry* (November 1994). See also *Proceedings of the International Conferences on Rapid Prototyping*, Management Development Center, University of Dayton, Dayton, OH.
2. Crawford, C. Merle. The hidden costs of accelerated product development. *Journal of Product Innovation Management* 9:188–199 (September 1992).
3. Mello, Sheila. Proactive use of metrics to manage development projects. Presentation at the 18th Annual International Conference of the Product Development and Management Association, Boston, 1994.
4. Meltzer, Robert J. *Biomedical and Clinical Instrumentation: Fast Tracking from Concept Through Production in a Regulated Environment.* Buffalo Grove, IL: Interpharm Press, 1993, p. 18.
5. Meltzer, Robert J. Avoiding the pitfalls of contract development. *Medical Devices and Diagnostic Industry* (June 1995).
6. Metelnick, J. Don't forget CNC in rapid prototyping. *Machine Design* (November 1994).
7. Wheelwright, Steven C. and Clark, Kim B. *Revolutionizing Product Development.* New York: Free Press, 1992, p. 33.

Robert J. Meltzer
The RJM Consultancy, Inc.

Principal of the RJM Consultancy, an international education and consulting company which, for over five years, has specialized in assisting organizations to accelerate their new product development process so as to bring more new products to the market more quickly. His personal background includes over 30 years' experience in the development of new products to meet the needs of scientific, consumer, and industrial markets. He shares his experience through lectures, articles, seminars, a newsletter, and consulting. He has chaired the Instrumentation Section of the NCCLS and is now U.S. editor of a refereed journal devoted to topics in biotechnology.

PART FOUR

FINISHING THE JOB

*Here is the answer . . . Give us the tools,
and we will finish the job.*

—Winston Churchill, English Prime Minister, 1941

Near-panic and disappointments prevail when finishing the job. Seasoned new product developers know that prelaunch and announcement tasks begin the final phase of development, not end it. Successful products need to move to mainstream customers, beyond the beachhead established with lead user and early adopter customers. This move, to early majority mainstream customers, is known as "crossing the chasm."

Launch control tools spot potential problems in securing a beachhead and crossing the chasm. They provide a structured way of deploying scarce resources. Finally, they help in deciding when to abandon a launch.

A critique of a product's development provides vital input for pinpointing causes of success or failure. It also helps fine-tune other finishing-the-job tools, such as metrics, process ownership, and reengineering of the process itself.

LAUNCHING A NEW BUSINESS-TO-BUSINESS PRODUCT

25

James D. Stryker

25.1. INTRODUCTION

"The project is complete. All that is left is to move the product into the marketplace." This traditional attitude has left too many outstanding product development efforts as either commercial failures or far less than what they could have accomplished. The inclusion of the launch stage (see Chapter 6) into the product development process is aimed at eliminating this problem by maximizing the impact of the new product effort once the product enters the market. A successful launch will require that the project team is sure that the physical product is defect free, that the required services surrounding the product are in place, that the logistics of moving the product into the market take place, that the actions required to sell the product effectively to the right targets begin, that the product's benefits are communicated, and that corrective actions are taken. The launch takes the new product out of its team-provided cocoon. It will have a major impact on how much profit the project will generate over the life of the product.

Profit Opportunity

Companies undertake a product development project because they anticipate that they will generate more profits over the life of the "new" product than by not undertaking the project. By focusing on the revenue stream over the life of the product, rather than limiting the project metrics to the time frame of the product development effort itself, the launch stage of the program becomes extremely important to the overall success of the project. This expanded definition of the time metric has become more popular in the last several years, led by firms such as Hewlett-Packard. Figure 25.1 shows the traditional project metric of "time to market" and the expanded measure of "time to objective." In this context, examples of a project objective could be a dollar amount of revenue, market share, or project payback period.

The total life of a product (as shown in Figure 25.2a) is determined by customer requirements, competitive offerings, changes in technology, and the inherent advantages offered by the product itself [6, pp. 558–565]. A month shortened from the projected time to market will add a month of full revenge generation to the product (Figure 25.2b). A focused and effective launch which shortens the time to objective by a month accomplishes the same aim (Figure 25.2c). Therefore, the ultimate revenue impact of condensing either the time to market or time to objective is the same.

Attempting to remove additional time from the design phase of a project involves high levels of risk during periods when design and technology uncertainty is greatest. On the other hand, good project discipline in defining market targets, competitive response, and customer requirements should have reduced the controllable risk associated with shortening the time after launch. If an organization has already made substantial improvements in their project time to market, they may find that reducing time to objective is an area of great opportunity.

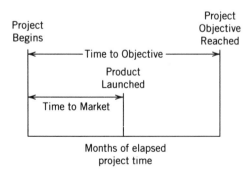

FIGURE 25.1 Time metric: new product development time to objective.

A. Nominal Effort

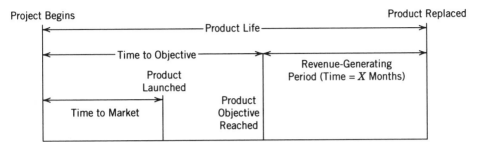

B. Shortened Time to Market

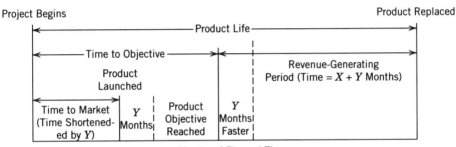

C. Shortened Time to Objective

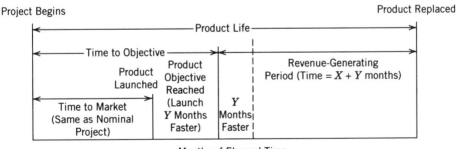

FIGURE 25.2 Revenue impact: faster new product development.

> *A fast, effective launch can generate as much incremental profits over the life of a new product as can shortening the actual development time.*

25.2. LAUNCH OVERVIEW

The launch *stage* in the product development process has the responsibility of commercializing the new product in the market. It usually begins after the new product has been produced. On the other hand, the process of preparing for the launch (launch *process*) begins on day one of the project and consists of five phased activities: planning, design, production of collateral material, implementation (the actual launch), and corrective action. These efforts are integral to the product development process and occur concurrently.

Launch *planning* is determined by the project's goals, target markets, and product advantage objectives developed at the project start. The *design* of the launch occurs as part of the "develop and test" stage of the development, when information is available on the product's actual performance and test market response. *Production* of launch collateral materials and other prelaunch activities are scheduled to be simultaneous with the scale-up stage's availability of product. The actual launch is the launch stage of the product development process; and corrective actions of the launch process are part of the post-launch review stage. Table 25.1 shows the relationship of launch activities to the project stages.

The launch process requires integration of both skills and personnel outside the project team. Therefore, many companies transfer launch responsibility to the product management or marketing departments [6, pp. 538–539]. However, the importance of the launch to the financial success of the project, and the integration of the launch activities into the overall project stages, support the requirement that the project team maintain responsibility for the launch.

Figure 25.3 illustrates a conceptual model of the elements in the first two launch phases of planning and designing a new product launch program. A successful new product must be designed to customer requirements and to make its sales and purchase process (to be initiated in the physical launch) as easy and self-evident as possible [2, p. 314]. Therefore, the initial project definition efforts in the "prove it works" stage becomes input to both the product design and the launch design. This includes the assessment of project goals, customer and product targets, and the internal–external environment (including competition). Once the product has been designed and customer field-trial response can be evaluated, the initial assessments must be reevaluated and the final plan designed. This launch design will integrate the assessments into a consistent theme and overall approach which defines a mission, including actions required, logistics, communication, and follow-up.

TABLE 25.1   Launch Activities

Project Stage	Input to Launch from Project Activities	Concurrent Launch Phases	Launch Phase: Sample Outcomes
Prove that it works	Project goals Target markets Target product competitive advantage	Planning	Target markets Approach Estimated cost
Develop and test	Target reassessment and revision New product performance Customer response field trial	Design	Detail plan All launch collateral material developed
Scale-up	Committed target dates	Production	Collateral material produced Preliminary training Initial positioning of inventory in channel
Launch	New product available	Actual launch	Sales process began Advertising began
Post launch review	Customer and channel reaction	Corrective actions	Targets revised Sales approach revised Product requirements modified

25.3. LAUNCH DESIGN: THE ASSESSMENT

The levers for design of a successful launch will be found in an assessment of the project's goals, targets, and environment.

> The new product team must design the product to meet both customer requirements and the sales-purchase process.

25.3.1. Goals

The starting point in developing the launch plan is a clear understanding of the magnitude of the task required of the project and therefore of the launch. The degree of change in market share, the number of new markets to be entered, the level of profit to be generated by the product, and the product life expectation are all key elements of the goal which have an impact on the magnitude

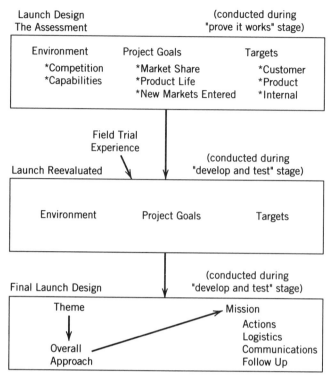

FIGURE 25.3 Launch design.

and speed of the launch. For example, if a project has an objective calling for doubling of market share in two years, significant momentum will be required to be generated through the launch.

A prime failure mode for a launch is the inadequate assignment of resources. This has often caused great products to take on the appearance of market duds. Frequently, the resources (including expense dollars) are contained in other functional departments and may be perceived to be outside the team's domain. Communication of the magnitude of the goal and the launch plan become the lever to make sure that these required resources are assigned. This communication needs to take place as the project is begun, integrated into the overall business's budgeting process, and reemphasized as the product and launch plans become finalized.

25.3.2. Environment

The launch must be designed to be successful in its own specific market–customer–organizational environment. Each product will exist in a different competitive situation, it must overcome a different set of customer and channel perceptions of the product and the firm, and it will have a different set of leverage points in its design, organization, and customer base.

The launch must be designed to overcome the existing market-share momentum of all competitors. The smaller the old product's market share, the greater the effort required to develop market recognition for the new product. The more visible the launch, the greater the probability of a competitive response. The response will depend on market acceptance of the new product and the competitors' capability to respond. Therefore, it is important both to develop a scenario analysis of the range of competitive responses and to design a response mechanism into the launch.

The plan must therefore answer the following questions:

- How will you overcome the competition's marketplace momentum?
- How will the competitor respond?
- How will you counter the competitor's reaction?

The marketplace (including the channel) will have preconceived notions of the product's use, performance, look, and the capabilities of the supplying company itself. If the product calls for a change in the customer's paradigm, the launch must focus considerable energy on overcoming the customer's expectation [3, p. 21]. If the market expects poor-quality goods from the firm, regardless of the specific facts surrounding the new product, the launch will have to take place directly into this negative environment. If previous experience has taught the sales force to avoid selling a new product until the bugs have been worked out, the launch must have a plan to overcome this hurdle or the product will languish on the warehouse shelf.

The plan must identify the positive and negative expectations of the channel and customers. In response, the launch must implement programs to overcome or blunt the negative impacts and to leverage the positive perceptions.

> *The launch must be designed to overcome sales force or market expectations that a new product will contain bugs; if not, their perceptions will result in sales avoiding selling and customers avoiding purchasing of the new product.*

25.3.3. Targets

There is an old industrial marketing rule that states: "To be effective, the marketing plan has to have something in it for everyone." Therefore, the launch must have elements aimed at the internal organization, channel, and customer. The launch plan must identify these key targets and then specify the level of effort and dollars to be allocated to each. It must identify the hurdles that must be overcome at each target, the actions to be implemented, and incentives (if any) to be offered.

Internal Organization

At launch, the obvious handoff occurs from the team to the company's sales force. From day one the launch plan and development process must have elements directed at influencing and strengthening the commitment of the sales force to the new product. The more the sales personnel know of the product, project targets, and project goals, the greater will be their commitment to making the launch work [2, p. 324]. The team must also identify all other internal functions that will have an impact on moving the new product into the market. For example, customer service representatives must be prepared to answer questions and deal with new product problems. Uninterrupted product supply is a requirement but is difficult because of the inherent uncertainty of initial demand patterns. Therefore, raising the involvement of the personnel responsible for managing the supply chain and material planning to a more personal level (resulting in commitment) may be important.

Channel

Success in moving the new product through an industrial channel will require that the channel make an investment in the product. Channel owners and managers may well have to invest their own cash in inventory of the new product. In addition, they will need to shift their personnel's time from other revenue-producing products to the new product. Therefore, for small and medium-sized distributors, the launch must start by targeting benefits for distribution management and ownership. At the next level, the distributor's sales personnel must be brought into the process as the front-line sales force. If the channel begins to encroach on consumer markets, the counterperson sales efforts must be targeted. In many markets the desk engineer or inside sales personnel have a tremendous impact on recommending product and brand selection to customers. If they are important, the launch program must make it easy for them to select the new product. The service department or independent service network must be prepared to handle new product repairs.

25.3.4. Customer Buying Process

Traditional marketing calls for targeting customer or market segments. The initial project definition identified these targets [1, pp. 267–268; 3, pp. 90–108]. However, this approach is too coarse for an effective launch. During the project's "voice of the customer" determination, the project team had to concentrate attention on particular individuals or functions at a customer. The launch must be similarly focused.

The most critical question for targeting the customer is: "Who has the determinant (final say) buying influence?" The determinant buying influence may not reside in the purchasing department; it may, for example, reside with the line foreman, test engineer, or repairperson. In many cases the determinant decision maker will seek advice from other members of the organization who are best termed the "vetoer", the "user," the "tryer," the "fixer." In some markets, what is critical is not getting the buyer to say "yes," but to be sure that the vetoer does not say "no." Several good examples of vetoers external to the use chain are a safety committee, legal department, or corporate influencer. In other markets, the use chain of user and fixer will have the veto power.

As ergonomics and self-directed work teams take on greater importance in today's workplace, the power of the actual user has increased proportionately. If one has to go through a trial period before a sale, or if repeat business is the key to success, the world-class new product is highly exposed to the whims of the user *making* the new product *not* work right. It is easy for the design team to be so enamored of the significant improvements contained in their new design that the launch ignores the importance of the resistance to change in the user groups.

> *In industrial markets it can be just as important to be sure that departments outside the traditional user do not veto the purchase as it is to have the buyer say "yes."*

A subset of the user is the tryer. The buyer may turn to a skeptic as a tryer to evaluate all new products. The skeptic will ensure that the status quo will be maintained unless the perceived benefits in the new product are overwhelmingly better.

In many ways the repairer is a user. He or she can have a substantial influence on the purchase decision and can make a durable product look like a child's toy. On the other hand, repairers are the first line in dealing with new product problems. If the launch can reach this target effectively, it can minimize customers' reactions to problems and buy time for the team to find resolution.

25.4. LAUNCH DESIGN: THE MISSION

The design of the launch requires the team to describe a theme and overall launch approach. With the theme and approach defined, the detail launch mission can then be developed. By structuring the launch mission under an overall theme and approach, the design team can avoid a cacophony of pet ideas and missed details. The theme allows the individual elements of the launch mission to reinforce each other. Once the theme and overall approach are defined, the four basic aims of the launch mission can be developed:

1. To meet effectively all of the logistic requirements of the organization and market.
2. To cause a number of individuals in different organizations to take action.
3. To transfer knowledge. It must create awareness of the product, and its features (communication).
4. To put in place the ability for fast feedback and corrective actions (follow-up).

25.4.1. Theme and Overall Launch Approach

The theme should communicate to all targets a vision of the new product's distinctive benefits and its positioning [1, p. 272]. The theme can be found in one or more of the following product definitions:

- Competitive positioning of the new product
- Position of the new product versus customer needs
- Position of the new product versus the rest of the company's product line
- Current market perception of the company and/or old product
- Key product or service benefits to the customer

The overall launch aproach summarizes how the new "physical" product and its surrounding benefits (packaging, warrantee, pre- and post-sale service, brand) will bring value to the customer at launch [1, pp. 269–272]. It will link the theme with the overall business strategy and capability, and describe how the customer will receive value beginning with the launch.

The decision on how the enterprise will bring value to the customer must be determined as part of the overall business strategy, not by the project. The determination of the competitive strategy focus of best cost, best product, or best total solution must be made clear at the project initiation and then clearly implemented in the overall launch approach [5, p. 29]. A test of the overall launch approach's effectiveness is to confirm:

- If it will cause the appropriate actions to take place at each launch target.
- If it will adequately reverse competitive momentum.

25.4.2. Logistics and Organizational Readiness

The launch must define and implement the material flow process from the business, through the channel, to the end customer. It must define the ordering process. For example, how will customers order: from whom and how much? How will the channel order: from whom and how much? It must determine where inventory will be stocked; in addition, it must determine the initial stocking levels of the new product, appropriate repair parts, price lists, and literature.

The logistics element of the launch must also deal with the uncertainties of new product demand patterns. Is demand outstripping product supply in the channel, or is inventory building up on distributors' shelves? In may companies distributor inventory status is either not available or takes too long to collect. In these cases the launch must incorporate actions to speed up acquisition of sales and inventory data. (An example of a solution for this is team sampling of selected distributors' sales data.)

Many teams have key suppliers included as team members [4, pp. 124–126]. Continuing supplier participation as a team member in the launch process, including frequent sales status reports, can shorten supplier response to erratic new product demand patterns. Implementation of this element is critical for the success of the launch. It is appropriate for the team to oversee the initial process of "filling the channel" to ensure that the appropriate material is available on schedule.

25.4.3. Who Has to Do What?

The launch has to cause internal personnel, personnel in the channel, and personnel at the customer to take action. For example, the sales force may have to take time from their selling activities to identify new target customers; the distributor will have to invest in new spare parts; the customer may have to load their purchasing database with new part numbers. Some of these actions may appear to be inconsequential, but all will be critical for the new product to develop recognition and fit into the normal sales–purchase–use continuum. A useful technique to develop an understanding of the actions required is for the design team to participate in a series of "a day in the life of" exercises. With participation of distributors, customers, and internal personnel, the team can develop a flow of the product's use and fulfillment processes in its daily life. Based on this series of flows, actions, hurdles, and customer moments of truth can be identified. Those activities and hurdles that have substantial impact on the customers' impression (moments of truth) of the product and company must be dealt with in the launch. These assessments should be conducted during the initial planning stage of the project, as it can assist in the product design definition.

A key check on the launch plan's robustness is confirmation that elements are directed to produce each of the action requirements. On the other hand, to assure the leanness of the program, one should review the plan for "orphan" activities, those that may look good but are not directed at the critical launch targets and action requirements.

The team must determine what will cause each action to be undertaken. Some activities, though, will be self-actuating. The organization or individual will see it to be in their best interest to take action (as long as the launch includes letting them know that an activity is required). In other cases the barrier is so significant that rewards or punishments are required. Table 25.2 illustrates the interrelationships of rewards and barriers at the various launch targets for the simple activity of ordering the new product.

It is critical that the specific needs of the channel have been incorporated in the project definition. The distributor will have to make investments in the new product. The launch must have elements that allow the channel to attain a return on this investment [1, pp. 296–297].

25.4.4. Knowledge Transfer: Communications

The key enabler to having people and organizations take action is knowledge. Transfer of new product knowledge from the team to the rest of the internal organization, the channel, and the customer includes not only awareness of the new product features, but also the process of selling, ordering, testing, and re-

TABLE 25.2 Sample Incentives for Action

	Internal	Channel	Customer
Action	Order product into distribution center.	Order product into warehouse for demo and sale.	Order product for use.
Barrier	None—just need to let system know of product and initial stock targets.	Risk that product will not sell. Lost profit by taking their sales force out of field for training on new product.	Satisfied with existing suppliers. Risk that they will be stuck with an underperforming product. Must load purchasing system.
Incentive	None.	Extra 5% discount. Inventory return privilege with no offsetting order.	Free one-month trial.

pairing the new product. This communication element of the launch includes training, advertising, and the sales processes.

What Are You Going to Tell Them?

To maximize the impact of the launch, all communication should have a consistent and supporting message tied to the theme. The theme can then become part of all literature, advertisement, and packaging. It becomes the basis for the sales force to develop a consistent approach for presenting the new product to target customers. Moreover, the reality of a sales presentation is that a customer will remember only three or four elements. The theme allows the team to focus the design of all sales presentations on the most effective benefits of the new product and its integrated service package. Without this discipline each salesperson will design his or her own approach, which can result in a rambling list of features.

Training may be required on how to sell, order, use, and repair the new product. This, too, should be derived from the theme. With the advent of CD ROMs and video, training can be accomplished quickly and inexpensively at all levels of the sales–channel–customer pipeline. However, this approach loses its personal content and contact. The training forum can be used as another form of selling, with considerable leverage to be gained from a personal touch. Even a brief 15-minute training session to introduce operators to the new product can go a long way toward eliminating initial skepticism and problems.

The team should have confirmed the product design with customers and the channel throughout the development process. The team now needs to confirm its theme and its launch program with partnered customers and distributors. A sampling of customers from key market segments who had not been involved in the product development process should be included. This confirmation of the launch should go beyond the typical, "Which advertisement format do you like?;" it should also test if the customer heard the theme message as it was intended, and whether this theme resonated sufficiently with the customer's value system to cause them to take action.

Who's Going to Tell Them?

The team must determine the most appropriate media to be used for each message and target audience. In some cases, the traditional trade paper and traditional channel salesperson will fit the new product's requirements to carry the message to the market. However, it is appropriate initially to question this conventional wisdom by comparing the themes, objectives, and hurdles that the new product must overcome against the objectives of current product communications. New products that seek to increase market share substantially or to open new markets may not be successful in using traditional communication approaches and investment levels. For example, a company that sells through industrial distribution might find a direct sales approach to be more effective in carrying a new product concept into a new market segment. The following list shows the broad range of industrial media mechanisms for carrying the message [1, p. 95].

- Direct sales
- Distributor sales
- Literature
- Videos
- CD ROMS
- Trade shows

- Inside sales
- Posters
- Giveaway
- Direct mail
- Tear pages
- Punch cards

- Demonstrations
- Newsletter
- Trade papers
- Sales aids
- Catalogs

The selection of which media to use can be accomplished by weighing the effectiveness of each media type in carrying the message to target audiences.

How Are You Going to Make Them Believe?

To change market-share momentum, the communication process must convey a sense of believability of the competitive advantage and urgency for action. Extravagant claims and vague hyperbola tend to be inappropriate in the industrial market. On the other hand, documents heavily laden with technical details are not read or may be too difficult to train a salesperson to present. The more a new product extends a customer's expectations, the more important it is that alternative credibility elements be added to the launch. Following are a number of credibility-enhancing approaches.

- Testimonials
- Demonstrations
- Extended warranties
- Third-party testing
- Industry listing (e.g., UL)
- Video comparisons

- Cutaway of new product
- Publish articles or books on new product
- Animation of new product operation
- Trials
- Word of mouth

25.4.5. Feedback and Corrective Action

Feedback is the area of the launch process that is most often ignored or understaffed. Success or failure frequently occurs from "little things that are often overlooked" [2, p. 314]. Traditional methods of communications from the customer tend to be designed to collect statistical information and are slow. The launch must incorporate feedback mechanisms to receive rapid information from the market on both the failures and the success of the product and support processes. Unexpected niche market successes may indicate an opportunity to redirect resources. Unexpectedly rapid market acceptance will call for fast production changes. The people and processes to take corrective action must be defined in the plan, and people assigned as part of the launch process. The team must be prepared to answer senior management's questions such as:

- Is the project on target for reaching its financial and market acceptance goals?
- Is the organization having difficulties in absorbing the product into its day-to-day activities?
- Is competition reacting, and how should we respond?

Field Problems

> *A formal review shortly after launch of the new products' results can lead to marketing or product improvements that will improve the program's success materially.*

In an industrial environment of zero defects, it is common for the team to assume that all is in order and, like the Maytag repairperson, to await a problem phone call. The reality is that there will be product problems that need immediate correction. The launch program must include a problem identification process which quickly focuses field problems into the team's hands. For example, use of an 800 number prominently displayed on the product for customers or distributors to call in problems or questions is one of the fastest ways to surface problems. Maintaining detailed records of customer and channel questions (as compared to problems) will reveal defects in the soft side of the introduction (poor instructions, bad applications, inadequate or misunderstood sales training, and poor labeling).

Field problems need to be resolved in a manner that leaves the customer delighted with both the product and the process of correction. If the customer is hassled or has to hassle to resolve a complaint, the system and people have failed. All personnel involved must view the error-correction process as an opportunity to gain new knowledge on how to improve the product and satisfy the customer. Within the scope of the total initial investment in the development and the long-term anticipated revenue stream, the corporate savings from invalidating marginal customer complaints during the launch phase is minuscule, and the benefit from delighting the customer is immense.

Other Opportunities

Regardless of the short-term program success, the team should view that they have at least missed the market requirements in some market segments. An aggressive effort to assess market acceptance will inevitably identify product enhancement opportunities. This will require additional formal customer assessment. The launch should include a program to revisit a select group of customers and possible customers shortly after introduction. The following questions provide a sample discussion agenda for post-launch interviews.

- Why did you buy or not buy the new product?
- What features do you like or dislike about the product?
- What were you disappointed to find had not been included in the new product?
- How did you find out about the new product?
- How has competition responded?
- On what applications did you try the new product?
- What were your anticipated benefits, and how has the product met them?
- Did you receive any unanticipated benefits?

The objective of these customer interviews is to determine if the launch conveyed the right feature benefit set; if the right communication vehicles were chosen for communication; whether the customer found an unanticipated benefit or use; whether the customer will provides a testimonial; whether there is an opportunity to tweak the product to improve the market response; whether the business should turn tail and withdraw the product.

25.5. AFTERMATH: GOOD LAUNCH OR THE BAD LAUNCH

In addition to the team survey of customers shortly after launch, an excellent continuous learning process should include reaction from both the internal organization and the sales channel. In a recent series of post-project surveys, a number of teams and sales organizations affected by new product development launches were asked to identify their view of elements of a good launch and elements that detracted from the success of a product at launch. In Table 25.3 we summarize these results.

There are a number of important messages in the results:

1. Good launch elements focus on making easier the organization's job in getting the new product to market. A good launch eliminates the hassle.

TABLE 25.3   Comparison of Good and Bad Launches

Good Launch	Bad Launch
Product on hand to ship	No product uniqueness versus competition
Full package of sales support collateral	Incomplete product offering
Full package of sales support collateral material:	No management focus on effort
	No market-customer targeting
Literature	Slow response to product flaws
Demonstration videos	Inappropriate or inadequate channel
Comparative competitive info	Inappropriate or inadequate internal organization
Technical support available	Inadequate resources
Incentives for the sales channel	
Training	

The internal organization is the first customer that the project team must satisfy.

2. Bad launch causes are much more strategic and are driven by an inadequate job by the team and management up front in the project. Unclear strategic purpose and competitive positioning show up immediately upon the product hitting the market. These errors are compounded by an inadequate allocation of resources assigned to get the task accomplished.

3. A bad launch heritage can be traced to management and the team viewing the development process as product centered and not on the multifunctional impact that the new product has on the *total* organization.

4. Bad launches come not from zero defects but from poor fixes. The sales organization and the industrial customer are surprisingly tolerant of a defect if they are acknowledged openly and fixed quickly. Responses based on "that's the first we have heard of that problem" only foster skepticism. Repeated attempts to fix a problem expose the problem to higher and higher levels in the customer's organization.

REFERENCES

1. Crawford, C. Merle. *New Products Management*, 4th ed. Burr Ridge, IL: Irwin, 1994.
2. Gruenwald, George. *New Product Development*, 2nd ed. Lincolnwood, IL: NTC Business Books, 1992.
3. Moore, G. A. *Crossing the Chasm.* New York: Harper, 1991.
4. Smith, Preston G. and Reinertsen, Donald G. *Developing Products in Half the Time.* New York: Van Nostrand Reinhold, 1991.
5. Treacy, M. and Wiersema, F. *The Discipline of Market Leaders.* Reading, MA: Addison-Wesley, 1991.
6. Urban, Glen L. and Hauser, John R. *Design and Marketing of New Products*, 2nd ed. Englewood Cliffs, NJ: Prentice Hall, 1993.

James D. Stryker
Ingersoll-Rand

Jim Stryker has new product and business development responsibility at Ingersoll-Rand, Production Equipment Group. As Director of Business Development, he is the process owner for product development, and provides leadership for all major product development teams. In his 25 years' experience, he has been responsible for corporate planning, corporate and group marketing, distributor management, and business unit management. His product development experience runs the gamut from project team leadership to operating responsibility for all development teams. He holds a B.S. degree from Stevens Institute of Technology and an MBA from Harvard Business School.

26 LAUNCHING A NEW CONSUMER PRODUCT
Brian D. Ottum

26.1. INTRODUCTION

Once a new product has been developed, it needs to be introduced into the market. This process goes by the very descriptive term *launch*. Other names for this process are commercialization and initial marketing. The ultimate purpose of the launch is to generate profits from the new product. The interim goals are to give the new product legitimacy, gain shelf space, and make the product a self-sustaining, "living" entity.

The launch of a new product is a key phase in the new product's life cycle. The launch occurs after new product development but before ongoing product management. Figure 26.1 shows the classic product life cycle and how the launch fits in. There are four stages of a product's life: innovation, growth, maturity, and decline. The launch is part of the late innovation stage, just before to just after the first sale dollars are generated [1].

26.1.1. Importance of the Launch

Companies work very hard to develop a new product. Whether or not it is a success in the market is determined largely by how well the launch is planned and executed. The new product can be unique,

> *You never get a second chance to make a first impression.*

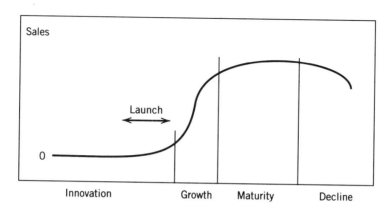

FIGURE 26.1 The launch is the early takeoff point of the product life cycle. Adapted with permission from C. Merle Crawford, *New Products Management*, 4th ed., Irwin, 1994.

superior, and potentially loved by customers but fail due to a poor launch. The product's positioning could be unappealing, the distribution insufficient, the advertising ineffective, or competitors too strong. All of these types of problems have caused new products to fail.

26.1.2. Preview of the Chapter

The remainder of this chapter covers the key components of the new product launch. Consumers come first (for good reason), then distribution (they're customers, too), then pricing, positioning, advertising and promotions, competitors, managing the key launch factors, and building in launch control. The chapter concludes with an example new product launch plan.

26.1.3. Special Note About Launching New Services

In this chapter, the term *product* is meant to cover both tangible products and services. Launching services is very similar to launching tangible products, but has unique challenges. Services are intangible, perishable, have simultaneous production and consumption, and have no inventory. The key differences in launching services versus products are [2]:

1. It is much more important to ensure that the production function is fully involved because they "create" the new service (e.g., launching a new debit card requires prior help of a bank's tellers, telephone customer service representatives, and marketing communications people).

2. The distribution of new services is often handled by company production employees, not by outside partners.

26.2. CONSUMER CONSIDERATIONS

As in the development stage, the consumer is the focus for most launch planning. If consumers do not need or like a product, it will fail. Similarly, if consumers don't hear about the new product, cannot get it, or don't perceive it as being unique or superior, the new product will fail. A properly designed launch capitalizes on the strengths that were built into the new product during development.

26.2.1. List of Questions to Ask Yourself

> The launch must be designed with the end user in mind.

When designing the new product launch with the customer in mind, a number of important questions need to be answered. These questions are usually asked in the prior development stage and the answers can be carried over. Table 26.1 presents this list of important questions and how the answers can be used to design a successful new product launch. The example new product in the table is a new snap-together, "no tools required" closet organizer with infinitely many assembly possibilities. It is sort of a "Closet LEGO-™rizer."

26.3. DISTRIBUTION CHANNEL

The distribution channel takes your new product from the point of production to where the consumer can buy it. Distribution channels can be "two step" (as in a lawn mower that gets sold to a wholesaler and then to a mass merchandise retailer), or "one step" (as in a fishing pole that is sold to hardware store), or "direct" (an exercise equipment maker with an 800-number for order fulfillment).

The distribution channel performs a critical role in the initial sales of a new product. They need to buy it, just like customers do. More important, they need to buy

> If those in the distribution channel don't buy the new product, no one else will.

it *before* consumers do. The distribution channel can make or break a new product launch. Just like the end user, the distribution channel needs to get excited about the new product.

TABLE 26.1   Consumer-Related Launch Questions to Ask Yourself

Question	Implications of the Answer	Closet Organizer Example
Who is the target audience?	This is the most critical element of the launch strategy. Everything builds off it. Be careful not to be too broad (or no one will buy the new product).	Male and female homeowners aged 30 to 50 who aren't normally "do it yourselfers."
What does the target audience think of the new product?	The most exciting features and benefits of the product need to be build into the advertising and promotions plan. The answer will also help sell the distribution channel on carrying it.	1. The love the fact that they can set it up in any configuration they want. 2. They love being able to change the setup easier later. 3. They like not having to measure or use any tools.
What are the key consumer segments, and why?	You need a thorough understanding of who you're going after. Rank order the segments to prioritize launch actions.	Men and women 30 to 40 with small children. They have recently acquired a lot more "stuff."
What is the typical buying process?	You need this information to decide where to sell the product, in what format, and how to advertise and promote the product.	High awareness of conventional closet organizers (both professionally installed and do-it-yourself). The vast majority buy right after moving.
Who are the major influences or specifiers in the buying decision?	These aren't end users but can exert a lot of influence on what gets bought. Think of them as consumers, too.	Home builders, architects, interior designers, and journalists (TV, magazine, trade journal, newspaper, etc.).
Where would consumers go looking to buy a new product like this?	Use this answer to decide which distribution channel to use.	Home centers, mass merchandisers, and hardware stores (in that order).
How much are consumers willing to pay for the new product?	Set the new product's price, taking into consideration distributor margins.	Suprisingly, 20% more than conventional "do-it-yourself" assembly units.
How many units do you expect to sell in the first year?	Set manufacturing targets and plan distribution logistics.	100,000 (roughly 2 for every 100 households that move during the year).

Distributors are growing in power in today's increasingly competitive environment. Grocery stores and other retailers are instituting "slotting fees" that must be paid by manufacturers before shelf space is granted for new products. "Superstores" are growing and dominating categories like never before (e.g., Wal-Mart, Toys 'R Us, and Home Depot). These trends make the distribution channel a powerful partner *and* customer in the new product launch.

26.3.1. Consumer Behavior and the Chosen Channel; They Must Match Up

It is absolutely critical to match up the distribution channel with your knowledge of how consumers shop for and buy current products. For example, if you were introducing a highly sophisticated mountain bike, you would not distribute it through mass merchandisers. Prior research during the development phase would have indicated that buyers of sophisticated mountain bikes typically shop the performance-oriented bicycle store, not mass merchandisers.

26.3.2. Existing Channel Versus New Channel

One of the toughest decisions faced by companies with new products to introduce is whether to stick with distribution channels they currently use for current products or to set up entirely new channels. This decision is so important because the choice of channel can make or break the new product. The pros for sticking with current channels include speed and low cost, increased loyalty, and familiarity. The biggest con for current channels is potential incompatibility with the new product. An entirely new channel can be tailored to the new product, but that takes time and money. Also, going with a new channel has the potential to alienate the company's existing channel.

Companies make this decision based on both financial and political factors. When everything appears equal, it is important to consider what's best for the consumer. A palatable decision can be a compromise: Introduce the new product with the existing channel, but require a certain amount of sales by a certain time. If sales targets cannot be met by the existing channel, bring on new channel partners later.

For either current or new partners, the best way to gain the distribution channel's support for the new product is to think of the channel as a customer. Seek to understand them, their situation, and preferences. Find out what motivates them. Use this understanding to craft an attractive offer that meets their needs as well as yours. The profit margin is usually the primary consideration, but other factors can help gain distribution support as well. These other factors might be preassembled displays for the new product, introductory signs, sales demonstration kits, or a multitude of other things.

26.4. POSITIONING

Positioning is the relationship the new product has to current products. The positioning statement is a short description of the new product that states succinctly why the consumer would want to buy it. The positioning emphasizes the uniqueness and superiority of the new product over current alternatives. The best positioning statements are very simple. "MTV Cops" was the initial idea for "Miami Vice," written on a cocktail napkin. "Mad Max on Water" was the positioning of the "Waterworld" movie. "German luxury with Japanese quality, reliability, and price" is a good description of what Toyota set out to make with Lexus.

Write a short description of the product.

26.4.1. How to Determine Positioning

The positioning of the new product is usually determined during the prior development stage. It is the job of the product launch to leverage and communicate the positioning to the target audience. If the positioning was not articulated earlier, it needs to be developed prior to launch. Consumer research (especially the perceptual mapping technique) is useful to determine the positioning of current products and how the new product may fit it.

26.4.2. Positioning Relative to Current Company and Competitive Products

When writing a positioning statement, it is important to consider both current company products and competitive products. The positioning statement needs to keep the new product distinct from the company's current products or they will be cannibalized by the new product. (This is acceptable only if the new product has higher margins or if the company plans to phase out the older products.) Competitive products need to form the basis for the positioning. You can emphasize that your new product is clearly superior, or that theirs is not as good as previously thought, or both.

26.5. PRICING

An entire chapter could be devoted just to the pricing of new products. Due to space limitations, only a few key concepts are covered here.

Few aspects of a new product launch get debated by companies as much as does the pricing strategy. This is because the decision is so important and often wide open. If you price the product too low, the company loses out on profits. Price the product too high and sales could suffer dramatically. Pricing current products is difficult but often a little easier than new products because there are usually more constraints. There is more history to draw upon and expectations (and requirements) of the market.

There are two main pricing strategies that work for both current and new products: skimming and penetration. A *skimming* strategy sets the initial price high, generating modest sales among the most motivated buyers. Price is slowly dropped over time, generating more and more sales among a larger population. A *penetration* strategy, on the other hand, is to price very competitively initially, to generate large initial sales.

If the new product is both unique and superior to those currently on the market, a skimming pricing strategy is smart. Pricing (and profits) can be kept high because consumers are willing to pay a premium. However, such a strategy could attract entrants to the market. If the new product is not unique among current products, a penetration strategy can be successful. The new product is priced aggressively, and large initial sales and market share are generated. Manufacturing costs tend to drop with increased volume, so the introducing company can be more profitable than new entrants. This strategy works well if the company wishes to have the dominant and most recognized brand.

Either of the skimming and penetration pricing strategies can work for new products. The key to using them is recognizing the relative superiority of the new product, competitors, and the company's long-term objectives. The traditional (and some say outmoded) method of pricing products is by their cost. Using this strategy, the company would project how much it would cost to produce the new product, add a traditional profit margin, and come up with the price.

Although cost is a crucial component of product profitability, it *should not* determine the price charged the consumer. A better way is *value-based pricing*. This strategy uses the value consumers place on the product as the guide for pricing. Value has little direct relationship to manufacturing cost. If a new product meets consumer needs better than does any current alternative, or allows consumers to do something they could not do before, they will value the product highly and would be willing to pay a high price for the product.

Establishing the value of the new product to consumers, or gauging their "willingness to pay,"

> **Price to capture value.**

is a key part of setting the new product's price. There are many consumer research techniques that help uncover this information, ranging from simple (interviews with target consumers) to highly sophisticated (conjoint or discrete choice experiments). In many situations, previous product testing will generate estimates of how much target consumers perceive the new product to be worth. The best way to make the pricing decision is to estimate the sales volume for each of several price points. Factoring in estimates of manufacturing and other costs, the company can choose the price that nets the highest level of profits.

26.6. ADVERTISEMENT AND PROMOTION

A big part of launching a new product is generating awareness, or "getting the word out." The company needs to let the target audience know that the new product is available, what it is, and why they should buy it. As in the rest of the launch plan, knowledge of the target consumer determines the tactics. "Getting the word out" is another term for marketing communications. The two main vehicles for marketing communications are advertisement and promotion. Advertising comprises paid announcements in various media: print (magazines and newspapers), broadcast (national and local TV and radio, cable TV), outdoor (billboards, buses), and other (direct mail or a "home page" on Internet's web). Promotions are both paid and unpaid product exposure in sponsorships, press releases, reviews, and store displays.

> *Tell the target audience about the new product.*

Obviously, the main content of the advertising and promotions is the positioning of the new product. What is its unique selling proposition? What do people think of current products, and how can you leverage this in launching the new one? Once you've developed something to say, it is very important to test it before using it. Do consumers play back the message you're trying to give them? Does the message excite them? Is the message believable and unique? An advertising and promotions launch plan needs to be "developed" just like the new product itself was.

Along with the content, the specific execution of the advertising and promotions plan needs to be determined. A few consumer questions help with this. Who is the target market? Which media are they paying attention to? Where do they typically hear about these types of products? What do they read, watch, and do with their free time?

After the content and outlet for the marketing communications has been determined, the company needs to decide how much to spend. "How much is enough?" is the key question. Here are some questions that need to be answered:

- How large a target audience are you trying to reach?
- Where are they?
- What do you need to tell them to get them to try the product?

- What is your forecast for awareness and trial? (Repeat for consumables.)
- What budget is available?
- What are your production schedule and capacity?
- What is the pricing strategy?

26.7. COMPETITORS

A product can be so new that there are no existing competitors and no need to consider their possible actions when designing the launch. Unfortunately, this is rarely the case [3]. There usually are similar products already on the market, made by companies that will react to the introduction of a new product. It is the job of the introducing company to incorporate likely competitive response into the new product's launch plan.

Competitive response to a new product can range from doing nothing, to dropping prices on existing products, to introducing

> **Build likely competitive response into the launch plan.**

similar products, and even to patent infringement lawsuits. A good indicator of possible competitive response is the importance of the competitor's current products to the competitor's overall financial health. Challenges to key product lines will not be ignored. On the other hand, many markets have room for niche products that are not threatening to the major players.

Another consideration in predicting competitive response is consumer perceptions of the new product versus those of current competitive products. If perceptions are similar, there is a greater threat to the competitor, and there is more likely to be a response. If the new product is perceived as clearly unique and superior to current products, competitive response may mean little. This is a position of strength.

A good new product launch plan builds likely competitive response into the general strategy. For example, a well-written positioning statement and resulting marketing communications can clearly make competitive products appear inferior. This takes away the opportunity to claim parity performance at a lower price, for example. In addition to the general strategy, the launch plan needs to have contingency plans for less likely competitive actions. For example, the company can be ready to offer coupons for the new product if competitors do so.

26.8. MANAGING THE LAUNCH

Everything discussed so far in this chapter has involved preparing and planning for the launch of the new product: understanding the target audience, setting up distribution, writing the positioning statement, setting pricing, designing advertising and promotions, and considering competitive actions. Not all of these factors are changeable. You must consider which of the factors you have control over and which you do not. Manage the first group to maximize sales of the new product. Understand how the other "preset" factors limit or dictate the launch. For example, a beverage company may develop a new flavor variation for an existing line of sparkling wines. The positioning and advertising and promotions plans can be written with a "clean sheet" of paper. Unfortunately, current company operations dictate the distributions and pricing plans.

> *Manage the launch factors you have control over—understand the impact of the rest.*

When it comes down to managing the launch, time and speed are important considerations. Again, if possible, knowledge of consumers should dictate the strategy. For example, is there seasonality to consumer purchasing behavior (e.g., toys, home computers, and the Christmas buying season?) Is there a particular time when your need the new product to be available to the market (e.g., for trade shows)? Consumer durables are usually more sensitive to timing than packaged goods, but not always.

The speed of the launch is also an important consideration. How fast will the product be introduced? How quickly can distribution be gained across the entire geography? What are the production and physical movement logistics constraints? Are there any regulatory or permission hurdles to overcome? Will the awareness-generating plan be made immediately national, or can it be phased in? Answering these questions can help get an accurate picture of how fast the launch can proceed.

26.9. BUILDING IN LAUNCH CONTROL

Just like every other complex project, the launch of a new consumer product seldom happens as planned. A good launch plan builds-in a monitoring of how well the launch is going and the ability to respond to problems that crop up.

> *Track the launch and make midcourse corrections.*

The process for developing launch control is simple. First, have the development team develop a list of negative events that have a significant probability of occurring. These can include problems such as stubbornly low target consumer awareness of the new product, low level of trial, distribution, problems, product quality problems, customer service snafus, and production holdups. The second step is to prioritize the list of potential problems

TABLE 26.2 Example New Product

Element of the New Product	Details
A new low-fat frozen dessert	An "ice cream novelty" in single servings made of ice cream, chocolate, caramel, nuts, and fruit.
Consumer behavior and perceptions	Adults currently do not buy many ice cream novelties unless they have children; they perceive these products as for kids only. They are increasingly fat-conscious and are currently buying low-fat ice creams and frozen yogurt. They're rather dissatisfied with the taste and excitement of current offerings.
Buying process	It is usually quite routine; they always buy the same set of products. They do not open the cooler door or pay attention to the ice cream novelty area.
Competitive products	A wide range are available, but few are low-fat, new and different, or targeted toward adults. Current adult-oriented novelties are high in fat.

TABLE 26.3 Example Launch Strategy

Launch Factor	Launch Objective	Launch Plan Details
Target audience	Adults, not children	Men and women aged 25 and over
Distribution	Make some minor adjustment but stay within current constraints.	Same as current products with a twist: Place product near frozen yogurts and low-fat ice creams in the freezer case.
Positioning	Make is distinct from current adult and child products.	A "guilt-free" dessert that makes adults feel like kids again.
Pricing	Penetration strategy: Price aggressively to get rapid trial and repeat sales.	Premium price over current child-oriented novelties, right in line with current high-fat adult novelties. Distribute 75-cents-off coupon in the Sunday papers.
Advertising	Reach health-conscious adults while keeping spending moderate	Print ads during launch in monthly general-interest and weekly news magazines. Test billboards in five cities.
Promotions	Maximize third-party mentions and recommendations to generate awareness.	Send product to food editors and nutritionists at magazines and major newspapers. Get review articles written. Get featured on food and health-related cable TV shows. Sponsor LPGA and men's professional tennis tournaments. Provide special signs to grocery stores.
Competitive response	Guard against competitors' repositioning their child-oriented products for adults.	Prepare advertising that emphasizes that this product was developed and designed for adults.
Launch control	Watch out for low awareness of the new product.	Conduct tracking studies of target market awareness and be ready to increase advertising spending.
Timing	Launch when seasonal demand ramps up.	Get full distribution by May 1; "drop" coupon in mid-May; start advertising in June; run promotions throughout spring and summer.
Speed	Go national as quickly as production capacity allows.	Go to major national retailers first, then fill in to cover 85% of all ice cream outlets.

by severity and probability. The third step is to decide which problems to worry about (usually, the ones with high severity and probability). The fourth step is to decide what to measure as an indicator of the possible problem (corresponding to the problem list above are consumer awareness, percentage of target audience who have tried the product, percentage of dealers carrying, customer satisfaction ratings, average number of rings before customer service people answer, and out-of-stocks). The fifth and last step is to design contingency launch plans for each problem.

26.10. EXAMPLE LAUNCH STRATEGY

Here is an example launch strategy for a new consumer packaged good, a low-fat dessert, that pulls together all the concepts presented in this chapter. The new product is described in Table 26.2, and its launch strategy is given in Table 26.3.

REFERENCES

1. Cooper, R. G. et al. What distinguishes the top performing new products in financial services. *Journal of Product Innovation Management* 11(4):281–299 (September 1994).
2. Crawford, C. M. *New Products Management,* 4th ed. Burr Ridge, IL: Irwin, 1994.
3. Redmond, W. H. An ecological perspective on new product failure: the effects of competitive overcrowding. *Journal of Product Innovation Management* 12(3):200–213 (June 1995.)

Brian D. Ottum
Ottum Research & Consulting

Brian has worked, studied, and taught in the new product development arena for over 13 years. He has a B.S. in Chemical Engineering, an MBA, a Ph.D. in a new product development, and is a member of Mensa. Brian worked in consumer research and international product development at the Procter & Gamble Company prior to earning his doctorate. He is president of Ottum Research & Consulting, an Ann Arbor, Michigan-based supplier of market research and new product development services. His firm focuses on the "fuzzy front end" of new product development: strategy, process, consumers, ideas and measurement. Brian is co-founder and President of PDMA's Great Lakes Chapter.

27 POSTLAUNCH EVALUATION FOR CONSUMER GOODS
David W. Olson

27.1. INTRODUCTION

After the long months (or in many cases, years) of development, having survived the perils of prelaunch consumer testing and the seemingly endless treacheries of internal politics, the product may finally be launched into the marketplace. In an ideal world, previous research will already have ensured that a genuine consumer need exists for the product (or service), and consumer testing will have proven that the new product delivers successfully on that need. In reality, though, even with the most thorough prelaunch research program, the marketer inevitably faces many more unknowns than knowns when he or she launches a new product. See Table 27.1. In this chapter we describe the process of designing a program to assess the new product's performance in the marketplace as soon as possible after launch, to tell the team and company management (1) how well the product is doing; and more important, (2) where its performance needs improvement if the sales prognosis is not good.

27.2. GOALS FOR POSTLAUNCH EVALUATION

In designing a program for evaluating the new product's performance following launch, there are several key overall goals to keep in mind.

TABLE 27.1 Typical "Knowns" Prelaunch Versus Postlaunch

Key Factor	Prior to Launch	After Launch
Target demographics and attitudes	×	
Actual user demographics and attitudes		×
Concept interest	×	
Immediate product acceptance	×	
Long-term purchase cycle/use-up rate		×
Name, packaging	×	
In-store visibility		×
Positioning/advertising	×	×
Cannibalization/source of volume		×
Pricing		×
Trade acceptance		×
Competitive response		×

27.2.1. The Right Performance Metrics

For everyone, the new product's *sales* will doubtless be the single most important measure of the brand's performance (although there are significant pitfalls; see Section 27.5.1). However, in addition to sales, the marketer will want to consider other measures of performance which are early leading indicators of likely sales performance (examples discussed in Section 27.5.2). What these other metrics might be depends very heavily on the specific product category involved. For example, in some cases, initial trade acceptance may be an absolutely crucial step toward success; in such cases the marketer should set specific goals for the number or percent of accounts accepting the new product and use this to gauge the new product's early performance. In other cases, sales may be direct from manufacturer (e.g., catalog sales), in which case, of course, trade acceptance is irrelevant.

> *The marketer must define the crucial measures of performance specific to this particular case, to guide postlaunch evaluation.*

27.2.2. Valid and Predictive Measures

Obviously, the marketer must try to ensure that the measures being obtained are reliable, valid, and predictive metrics of performance. *Reliability* refers to the measurement device itself, and whether its measures are stable or are subject to high degrees of random measurement error or fluctuation. If a measure is unreliable, it will show poor test-retest stability (i.e., if a new and independent reading is taken, it may show very different results from the first measurement). *Validity* and *predictivity* refer to whether the metrics themselves measure accurately what they purport to measure—in this case, new product success—and whether they can help predict future performance. Many new products are inappropriately evaluated using measures that are low in reliability and/or validity, which can give results that are either overly rosy and inflated, or unfairly and prematurely negative and damaging. Even sales audits, typically considered the "hardest" measure of success, can often be inaccurate if not collected in the proper way; the marketer must be continually vigilant on this score.

27.2.3. Speed of Reading Performance

There is clearly a strong desire for a *quick* read of the product's performance soon after it is launched, whether in the test market or nationally. However, the earlier the attempt to read the product's performance, the more difficult it is to get an accurate and valid assessment of longer-term performance. Early buyers are not necessarily reflective of the important larger mainstream mass of consumers, and it takes time for products to get incorporated into buyer purchase repertoires. For this reason, using consumer response models (Section 27.3) becomes an essential tool for the new product marketer, as they provide a means to use early consumer response data to project longer-term (i.e., first year) sales.

27.2.4. Actionable Diagnostics

The postlaunch evaluation program should be designed to provide a *clear* indication of where the product is performing well—aspects of the marketing program to leave alone—*as well as clear signals of the problem areas that need improvement*. Fortunately, methods exist to provide such clear learning (e.g., diary or scanner panels, telephone surveys, customer response cards, etc.); unfortunately, such methods cost money, sometimes considerable sums. Nevertheless, seen in the context of the entire marketing budget, such research is actually a small fraction of the project costs and should be considered an essential part of the overall cost of launching a new product.

27.3. CONSUMER RESPONSE MODELS

Validity, speed of reading, and actionable diagnostics are key criteria for postlaunch measurement.

The key to obtaining a quick, yet predictive measure of a new product's performance after launch is understanding the consumer adoption process, or *consumer response model,* at work in the marketer's category. As a very valuable exercise, the marketer should diagram or lay out the sequence of events that will occur when the product is launched and which will contribute to the product's sales performance.

27.3.1. Packaged Goods

The typical model for packaged goods is the awareness–trial–repeat model (Figure 27.1). It assumes that the adoption process for such products follows these steps. First, consumers are made aware of the new product (usually via advertising). Next, some proportion of those aware of the brand decide to try it (i.e., buy it the first time). Then some of those triers will decide to buy the product again, and eventually adopt it into their buying repertory. The marketer can use this model to set specific performance goals of awareness, trial, and repeat purchase prior to launch. He or she can then measure these variables (e.g., in a telephone tracking study; see Section 27.5.1) and can begin to pinpoint the product's strong and weak areas. For instance, if awareness is below expectations or goals (see Section 27.5.1), the marketer can examine those aspects of the program designed to generate awareness: the advertising, the packaging visibility, public relations, and so on. If trial given awareness is below expectations, the marketer

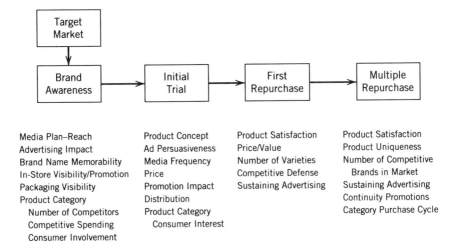

FIGURE 27.1 Typical awareness-trial-repeat model for packaged goods.

should reexamine the selling proposition, pricing, promotion effectiveness, and so on.

27.3.2. Consumer Services

A different model might apply to services; Figure 27.2 shows one formulation of an adoption model of new items offered in fast-food or quick-service restaurants. In some ways the model resembles the packaged goods model, in that at-home media such as TV and print advertising are assumed to generate consumer awareness of the new menu item. However, the impact of that awareness is potentially both on the choice of restaurant to visit (i.e., "I'll go to McDonald's to try that new sandwich") and on the decision of which item to buy once the consumer is in the store (i.e., "Hmmm, instead of my usual Big Mac, I will try this new sandwich"). The whole in-store environment is assumed to be more important as well in this case, as consumers scan the menu boards to make their decisions and see others buying or not buying the new item. And finally, in this case, the consistency of quality of product delivery becomes a particularly crucial variable toward ultimate consumer acceptance. If the new item's sales are initially sluggish, it may lead to a deterioration of the quality of delivery of that service to those who do try it (i.e., because the service staff do not get a sufficient quantity of experience in preparing the new product to learn to "do it well," and because

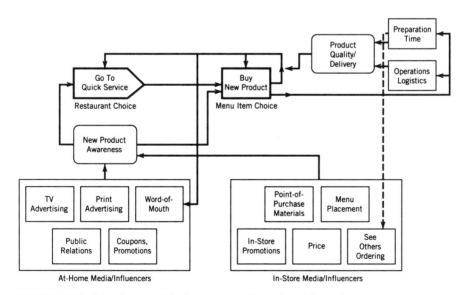

FIGURE 27.2 Adoption model of new menu item at quick-service restaurant.

the sandwiches may sit for a long time in the heating bins, leading to a reduction in quality). This feedback loop thus becomes a very important aspect of evaluating a new menu item early on; ongoing quality control monitoring is essential in this case to flag this potential problem.

Other services will have a different configuration of how the adoption process works; the specific model must be tailored to the individual situation.

27.3.3. Durables

Yet another model applies, obviously, to durables where repeat purchase or replacement sales are not important to early sales performance. In these cases the role of the salesperson, the impact of direct marketing, the effect of special-interest-group word of mouth, and the influence of publicity (e.g., reviews in specialized trade magazines) all play an important role in the new product's eventual sales performance. Models of durable adoption developed by Frank Bass and his colleagues serve as a good starting point in constructing a launch model for durables. As with services, a detailed model specific to the type of durable goods needs to be developed, to provide a yardstick against which the new product should be measured after it is introduced.

Different response models need to be developed for different types of launches.

27.3.4. Consumer Response Models: Summary

Even if it seems difficult or impossible to define *specific* measures of acceptance that are likely precursors of sales, it is still a very worthwhile exercise to try to lay out that adoption model. It provides guidance on where the marketer might look in trying to understand shortfalls in sales performance after launch, even if the process is more based on judgment and guesswork than on hard data. Setting performance criteria on these measures should be done, to the extent possible, based on past corporate or competitive performance:

- What was the average trade acceptance of the past five launches we have made?
- How many special-interest magazines reviewed our product, and how many were positive reviews?
- What levels of consumer awareness, trial, and repurchase have been associated with successful, versus unsuccessful, launches in the past?

If it has not already been done, a historical analysis of past launches, both corporate and competitive, should be undertaken to provide these sorts of benchmarks. This provides a very valuable framework, then, for assessing the new product's performance.

27.4. TEST MARKETING VERSUS NATIONAL LAUNCHES

> *Use past history to set reasonable target objectives on key measures.*

The marketer must decide whether he or she will want to introduce the product in a limited area, rather than immediately launching it nationally. The benefits of test marketing are ones of lower cost; reducing risk exposure (e.g., of possibly sullying the company's name or image among consumers or trade customers, etc.); obtaining a "success story" to use to obtain favorable trade acceptance in expansion areas; gaining early operational and logistical experience in manufacturing, distributing, and commercializing the new product or service; and permitting assessment of specific marketing elements to modify prior to full national launch. The drawbacks of test marketing are ones of opportunity cost, competitive exposure, and possible unreliability of reading performance (e.g., if competitors try to make the test unreadable by heavy defensive promotions, etc.). In addition, of course, test marketing may simply not be possible for some products (e.g., automobiles). Industrial and business-to-business products typically call for a very different approach, using pilot or prototype testing followed by beta testing [5].

At one time, for major manufacturers, test marketing was almost standard operating procedure (in those situations where it was feasible). In recent years, indications are that the popularity of test marketing has been declining [1]. One factor is the high costs of test marketing these days, due to factors such as the imposition of slotting fees by retailers, the high fixed costs of advertising (e.g., commercial production), and the costs of limited production runs. In addition, there are increased pressures from corporate management to launch products nationally to meet stockholder expectations or annual volume goals and to prevent competitive preemption [4]. Nevertheless, for many new products, test marketing remains an important and valuable step in the product's evaluation.

27.4.1. Selecting Test Markets

It can be said that there are two ways to go about selecting sites for the test market: the scientific, "right" way; and the way it tends to be done in practice. In the scientific way, cities would be chosen to be representative of the country as a whole (as a rule of thumb, normally those cities should represent from 0.5

to 1.5 percent of the country's population). The key matching criteria usually are, in order of importance, *category* sales development (CDI), *brand* or *corporate* sales development (BDI), and demographics (additional matching criteria might include regional dispersion, channel issues, media issues, and others). If this "scientific" approach were employed, the new product's sales performance in the test market might be expected to approximate its performance if launched nationally, subject to some likely chronic overstatement (see Section 27.4.2).

Unfortunately, in the real world, far more often test markets are selected for reasons of expediency. Very often, a company's "best" markets are chosen because they are more likely to achieve good distribution in those markets. In these cases it can be expected that the new product's performance will be considerably stronger than it is likely to be nationally. (Of course, if the purpose of the test market is more to gain early operational and logistical experience or to develop a "success story" to use with the trade in expansion markets than to obtain a true gauge of the product's national sales potential, it makes complete sense to conduct those tests in the company's best markets.) All of these issues need to be kept in mind when test market results are being evaluated [6].

> *Test markets chosen for expediency overstate the product's true sales potential.*

27.4.2. Adjustments of Test Market Results

It has been demonstrated that test market sales performance is almost always higher than subsequent national sales performance. *As a rule of thumb, test market sales should be reduced 15 percent even if the markets are chosen to be representative of the country as a whole.* This inflation is due to the unusual attention that test markets tend to receive by the company (e.g., trade support and other means to merchandise the product). If the markets are not reflective of the country as a whole but are strong areas for the manufacturer, sales must obviously be further discounted. (The unadjusted, inflated sales figures can and should, of course, be used for the purpose of trying to convince retailers in expansion markets to stock the new item!) Sophisticated statistical modeling of test market sales results can be done to yield a better prediction of the product's true probable sales performance if launched nationally.

27.4.3. Types of Test Markets

There are basically two choices in test marketing for a manufacturer whose products are sold through distribution channels not controlled by the manufacturer (e.g., as is the case for most packaged goods). In *traditional test marketing*, the new product is sold to trade accounts using the company's regular sales force, and advertised and promoted as if it were a national launch. In *controlled store testing,* outside companies are hired by the manufacturer to handle the product's distribution and merchandising, with no reliance on the company's sales force. The latter approach ensures good distribution for the product and that it is well displayed and always in stock. These companies may also coordinate local or marketwide merchandising programs. In addition, it is possible to set up special tests of alternative advertising, pricing, promotions, and so on, which are administered by the controlled-store-testing companies. In short, controlled store testing provides a "best case" scenario for the new product (which may not, and indeed probably *will not,* be matched by the company's own sales force).

Electronic or Scanner Test Markets

> Marketers can use traditional or controlled store testing in test marketing.

In some cases, test market areas have been established (by Nielsen and IRI) that permit highly sophisticated testing of new products and their marketing programs in supermarkets [2]. These areas use scanner panels (records of individual household buying patterns obtained via scanning of Universal Product Code symbols on packages), and one (IRI's BehaviorScan service) further links into local cable systems to permit testing of alternative television campaigns These provide the ultimate in in-depth assessment of the new product in a limited geographical area, as a precursor to a national expansion.

27.4.4. Other Limited Geography Sales Tests

Mention should be made of other types of tests that can be conducted, particularly for manufacturers whose sales and distribution process do not involve retail partners. If the product is a catalog item or is marketed via direct response and fulfilled directly by the manufacturer, new items can be tested in limited runs of catalogs to gauge consumer acceptance. On an informal level, products can be tested in individual sites, among a limited set of key prospects. More formally, clusters of individual stores can be used together with local advertising to conducted real-world tests at much less cost than traditional test marketing [3]. The "information superhighway" may permit testing opportunities not yet developed (e.g., home shopping via modem).

27.4.5. Test Marketing: Summary

Test marketing should be strongly considered prior to launching a new brand nationally. Although expensive, it is still far less expensive than a national launch.

With the right evaluation program in place, extremely valuable learning can be obtained on how to improve a new product's performance before it is launched nationally; instead, if a brand is launched nationally with a defective marketing program, it is very difficult to rectify the problems on the fly in the heat of pressure from top management, from the field force, and from trade customers to "fix it—and *fast!*"

At the same time, ways to accelerate learning from test marketing and guide modifications to the marketing program constantly need to be sought. Too often, corporate management—correctly—sees test markets as inconclusive and likely to delay the whole process. The key is finding ways to measure test market performance quickly and accurately. In the next section we discuss some of these assessment methods.

27.5. ASSESSMENT METHODOLOGIES

In this section we outline some of the ways to measure postlaunch performance, whether the product is being test marketed or has been launched nationally.

27.5.1. Sales

Obviously, the first measure everyone will be interested in is the product's initial sales level. Increasingly, such information is available quickly, even within a matter of a week or so, via improvements in information technology. However, while actual sales is doubtless an important metric, it can frequently be misleading. Factory shipments may be a poor indicator of actual consumer takeaway, due to "pipeline inventory." Initial consumer sales will reflect primarily early consumer trial of the new product (if it is a packaged good type of product); these can be artificially hyped by short-term consumer or trade promotions and thus make things appear rosier than they really should.

In addition, for most packaged goods, the sales velocity inevitably peaks in the first couple of months and then falls off (Figure 27.3) as trial flattens. Many companies read sales the first month or so and then extrapolate it erroneously, assuming that it can but only grow in subsequent months. Understanding the month-by-month sales growth and decline curves is essential to projecting sales accurately.

For nonpackaged goods or services, reading early sales as a means to gauge future success can be equally or even more treacherous. The initial sales will probably come from "early adopters" or innovators, whose reaction to the product may not be reflective of later adopters or laggards.

The company should examine the past period-by-period sales growth industry for similar launches as a way to gauge the new launch's likely future sales

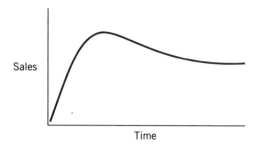

FIGURE 27.3 Sales as a function of time for new brand launches.

performance based on results to date. It is likely that it will require at least six months to produce an accurate estimate of the new product's first-year sales performance if sales alone is the barometer. This ability to read and forecast performance improves if other information is obtained during the first few months following launch, as discussed in the next section.

27.5.2. Sales Surrogates or "Leading Indicators"

Consumer research can be conducted to ascertain the magnitude of consumer response to the launch in the initial months following launch. This information can be used as input into sales forecasting models, which can provide very accurate estimates in most cases of eventual long-term (or at least first-year) sales. It also provides key diagnostic learning about the product's areas of strength and weakness.

Consumer Tracking

These surveys, typically conducted via telephone in the test market or nationally, obtain measures of consumer awareness, advertising awareness, trial, reasons for buying or not buying, repurchase (if applicable), repeat intentions, product likes and dislikes, and so on. Based on these early reads, the measures can be extrapolated and used as inputs into sales forecasting models to project sales. Equally or even more important, these data can be used to identify performance strengths and weaknesses. Table 27.2 outlines some typical measures and how to interpret results.

Figure 27.4 provides information gathered by the author's company over a period of years, relating brand awareness measures to advertising spending [gross rating points (GRPs)]. It can be used as a means to gauge whether the new product is attaining satisfactory brand awareness. If it is not, other measures in the tracking questionnaire can be examined to identify the most likely causes of

TABLE 27.2 New Product Tracking Study Questionnaire

Question Wording	Guidelines for Interpreting Results
Screener	
"In the past x months, have you bought (category)?"	• Base analysis on category buyers
"Are you aged 21–55?" (or other demographic controls)	• Analyze by demographic groups
Category usage, awareness, etc.	
"In the past x months, how many times have you bought (category)?"	• Analyze by heavy vs. light buyers
"What brands of (category) have you ever heard of?"	• Unaided awareness: usually very low for new brands
"Have you ever heard of (brand)?" (ask for 4 to 6 brands)	• Plot vs. GRPs or past launches (Figure 27.4)
"Have you ever bought (brand)?" (ask for 4 to 6 brands)	• Plot vs. awareness or past launches (Figure 27.5)
"In the past x months, which brands of (category) have you bought?"	• Past month penetration
"About how many (packages, times, etc.) have you bought (brand) in the past x months?"	• Calculate share of market for new brand
"On which of the following occasions do you use (category)?"; "Which members of your household use (category)?"; etc.	• Analyze trial, repeat of new brand by usage segments
Ad awareness	
"Do you recall seeing any advertising for (brand)?" (Ask for brands respondent is aware of)	• Norm: ad awareness = 67% of brand awareness
"Please describe to me the advertising for (brand)." (Record verbatim)	• Norm: proven awareness = 50% of claimed
"Do you recall seeing any (coupons, other promotions) for (brand)?"	• Norm: coupon awareness = 20% of brand awareness
"Where did you see the advertising for (brand)?"	• Norm: 70 to 80% on TV for TV launches
Ever bought	
IF YES:	
"Why did you first try (brand)?" (Record verbatim)	• Look for specific reasons, even if fairly small in percentage
"When did you first buy (brand)?"	• Analyze repurchase by time of first purchase
"How many times have you bought (brand)?"	• Norm: 50% repeat among earlier triers
"How likely are you to buy (brand) again?" (Definitely to Definitely will not buy—5-point scale)	• Take 100% of "Definitely's" and 50% of "Probably's"— norm = 50%
"What do you like about (brand)? What do you dislike?	• Look for specific likes and dislikes, even if small percentage
"What do you think of the price of (brand)?"	• Norm: 30% fair to poor value
"Did you use (coupons, other promotions) to buy (brand)?"	• Norm: 25% of trial from promotions
"How would you rate (brand) on (attributes)?"	• Analyze specific attributes
IF NO:	
"Did you look for the product in the store? Did you find it?"	• Norm: "Found" = two-thirds of "Looked for"
"Why didn't you try (product)?"	• Look for specific reasons, even if small percentage
"How likely are you to try (brand) in the future?" (5-point scale)	• Norm: 10 to 15% Definitely will try
	• Profiles of buyers vs. non buyers

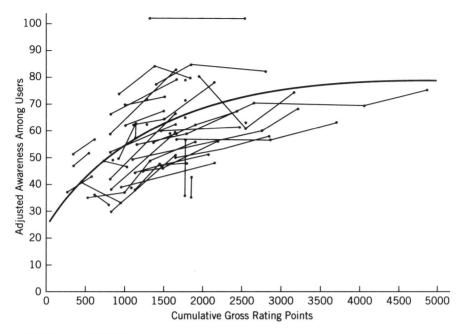

FIGURE 27.4 TV GRPs versus aided brand awareness.

the low brand awareness (e.g., by examining advertising awareness, product visibility in the store, etc.). A similar collection of data shows typical trial levels at given levels of awareness (Figure 27.5). Again, a shortfall in trial should lead the investigator to examine tracking study measures of price satisfaction, reasons for not trying, ability to locate the product in the store, and so on.

In this way, tracking data can show where the problems really are and give the marketer a focus for efforts to strengthen the program. Although not inexpensive (such tracking studies may cost from $10,000 to $50,000 and above), they can provide invaluable learning. Strong consideration should be given to building the cost of such studies into the launch program for the new product.

Panels

As discussed earlier, in some cases it is possible to obtain individual household purchase data, either from a scanner-based panel (Nielsen or IRI) or from a paper-and-pencil diary. These can be very expensive but generally provide better data than telephone tracking studies (which rely on self-reported purchase behavior). On the other hand, these panels do not provide the attitudinal data (e.g., reasons for buying or not buying) that the tracking studies provide. If panels are

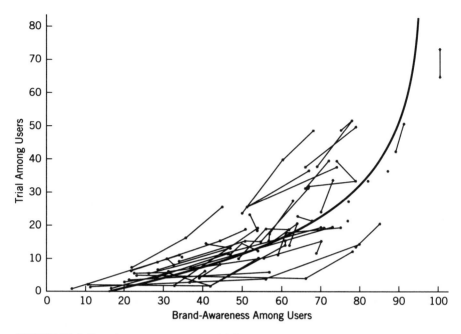

FIGURE 27.5 Brand awareness versus trial.

used, some additional research is needed to flesh out the problems and point the way to corrective actions.

27.5.3. Other Performance Measures

In addition to tracking studies or panels, which can provide data that can be used to project sales performance, other measures are very useful in gaining insight into why a new product is performing as it is. These include: customer inserts with mail-back questionnaires; monitoring of 1-800 customer complaints or comments; and interviews, formally or informally, with field force reps and trade customers. Also, very typically, qualitative research (usually focus groups) is conducted among buyers and nonbuyers to try to identify barriers to success. Such research, while useful to generate theories about possible problems, should not be relied on to identify the magnitude of problems; more quantitative data (e.g., from tracking) are called for. Table 27.3 is a summary of some of these measurement methods, how they are conducted, how they are used, and their primary drawbacks.

TABLE 27.3 Methods to Read Marketplace Performance

Measure	Source	Use	Drawbacks
Straight factory sales	Accounting department	Short-term financial results	Misleading early-on
Trial and repeat purchase	Tracking studies/ diary or scanner panels	Forecasting and projection, user characteristics	Expensive, forecasting error/ limitations
Awareness, attitudes, reasons for buying or not buying	Tracking studies, ad hoc surveys, mail-back consumer insert cards, 1-800 calls	Diagnosis of problems, focus on areas for improvement	Expensive to collect, errors in interpretation
Strengths and weaknesses of specific marketing elements	Focus groups, one-on-one interviews with consumers or customers	Hypothesis generation, definition of problems, evaluation of potential solutions	Errors in interpretation, nonprojectability of findings

27.6. CASE HISTORY AND CONCLUSIONS

In some cases, smart, insightful postlaunch research has been used to pinpoint potentially fatal problems with the launch, to provide guidance on how to overcome those problems, and to turn would-be failures into successes. In one case, a number of years ago a major food manufacturer launched a new brand into test market. It achieved an unsatisfactory share—only about half of its minimum acceptable share—and might easily have been abandoned. However, in-market tracking showed the sales problem to be due almost entirely to a very low awareness performance among consumers. Further postlaunch detective work suggested two areas for improvement: (1) the advertising, which was not clearly communicating the product proposition (despite prelaunch copy research which indicated the advertising to be very strong); and (2) the media plan, which was not providing the broad reach necessary for strong awareness. New advertising was developed, and radio was added to the media mix to broaden reach. Another test market was opened six months later, and to the client and agency's great satisfaction, the new product achieved much higher awareness, which translated into stronger trial and sales—and the product achieved its sales goals in this second market. It was launched nationally about nine months later, and continues to be a strong brand 17 years later!

The sales generated by this product in the 17 years since its national launch total well over $500 million, a rather nice return on a total postlaunch research investigation which perhaps cost the equivalent of $60,000 in today's dollars. Obviously, not every launch merits or can afford such a postlaunch budget. However, even more modest research programs can provide the sort of essential information on performance which marketers can use to pinpoint and fix problems quickly. Or, they can show that the product's poor sales are inherent in the launch and not easily remedied, in which case the product can be abandoned. The new product marketer should plan, before the product is launched, how he or she is going to obtain the crucial learning, early on, to help guide his or her decisions about how to address problems out in the market. Such money can be among the very best spent in the entire launch budget.

REFERENCES

1. Anonymous. Test marketing a new product: when it's a good idea and how to do it. *Profit-Building Strategies for Business Owners*, p. 14 (March 1993).
2. Maturi, Richard J. How to improve the odds for new product debuts. *Investor's Daily*, April 24, 1990, p. 8.
3. Needel, Stephen. Leveraging store-level scanner data for test marketing. Presentation at the 3rd Annual ARF Behavioral/Scanner Data Workshop, Advertising Research Foundation, New York, June 5–6, 1991.
4. Power, Christopher. Will it sell in Podunk? Hard to say. *Business Week*, August 10, 1992, p. 46.
5. Stern, Aimee L. Testing goes industrial. *Sales and Marketing Management*, p. 30 (March 1991).
6. Weinblatt, Ira. Beware of macho testing. *New Product News*, January 8, 1995, p. 12.

David W. Olson
Leo Burnett Company

David heads the New Product Planning Group, an internal consulting group for such companies as Procter and Gamble, Kellogg's, Pillsbury, and McDonald's. The group helps clients develop new product ideas, plan marketing programs, design consumer research, and evaluate sales potential using a proprietary expert system forecasting method. In his 23-year career he has also worked in the agency's London office as Director of New Product Planning for Europe. He is a graduate of Harvard University, and is a frequent speaker at new product conferences. He is a trustee of the Marketing Science Institute, and is a board member of PDMA.

28 PRODUCT DISCONTINUATION
Patricia A. Katzfey

28.1. INTRODUCTION

Products of all kinds (tangible or service; consumer or industrial) all progress through the product life cycle phases: *introduction, growth, maturity,* and *decline.* It is the final stage, product decline or discontinuation, which marks the natural and anticipated end of the product development process.

To illustrate the rate in which product decline occurs, consider two very unique industries, personal computers and factory process equipment. First, personal computers enter the commercial market, grow, mature, and decline at a phenomenal rate (12 months or less). On the other hand, factory process equipment, generally enjoys a longer product life—five to seven years, or more. Factory process equipment tends to, as a rule, sustain longer demand because high-dollar-capital equipment is often expensive to replace and can sometimes be upgraded (component hardware or software) to *nearly* match current generation product equivalents.

These life-extending options are often sought to avoid or deter a product's discontinuation, if technically or financially feasible. Other such life-prolonging alternatives may include price adjustments, value-added promotions, new market development, expanded distribution, line extensions, product upgrades, or significant new product innovation [5]. In the end, when product life extension or rejuvenation efforts no longer work, it is then time to consider the final planning stage: product discontinuation. Understanding and managing the product discontinuation stage is especially important as the continued trend toward shortened product life cycles continue.

As a guide to understanding and managing product discontinuation, this chapter is written to explain the nature of and methods in planning for product discontinuation. Practical information is discussed regarding the product discontinuation process, organizational commitment, channel management, legal considerations, support requirements, and final revenue opportunities. Now explore the critical steps of the product discontinuation process.

28.2. PRODUCT DISCONTINUATION DEFINED

Product discontinuation is by all accounts a complex subject. Surprisingly, very little practical information is available (articles or books) about real issues surrounding the planning and management of product discontinuation.

> *You must plan for product discontinuation, the timing of which depends on market and competitive factors.*

Generally, though, product discontinuation can occur as a planned market withdrawal of a product or service that no longer provides economic (sales, profit, growth) or strategic importance (competitive advantage, market share) for an organization. Products can also face rapid decline or discontinuation as a result of competitive new product entrants or market changes affecting product demand. Signals that product discontinuation is imminent may include shrinking sales, reduced profit margins, declining market share, or all three. Let's now take a detailed look at the fundamental causes of product decline.

28.3. NATURE OF PRODUCT DISCONTINUATION

Product decline is generally attributed to changes in the marketplace, affecting product demand. Many factors contribute to product decline; these are described in Table 28.1.

28.4. ORGANIZATIONAL ROLE IN PRODUCT DISCONTINUATION

The organization (executive management, functional departments, product teams, and product management) have three key objectives in managing the

TABLE 28.1 Key Reasons for Product Discontinuation

Why Products Decline	Explanation	Examples
Obsolete technology or mature service	Technology advancements create rapid product obsolescence.	386 microprocessor (replaced by 486 technology)
Product cannibalism	New generation product solutions cannibalize current product demand.	Windows operating system (replaced by Windows 95)
Reduced demand	User demand has shifted from current product or alternative solutions have been found.	Slide rule 8-Track tape player Typewriters
No profit margin	Global competition force prices down or operational costs increase over time, or both.	Inner-city hospitals New-car sales
Poor fit with strategic focus	A nontraditional or noncore product category is sold or spun off as separate business entity because it no longer fits the primary business objectives.	Sears (spinoff of Allstate, Dean Witter) Coca-cola (sold Columbia Pictures)
Poor fit with other products or product groups	Products that are unique in nature or not part of product groups or categories are divested or discontinued.	Kraft Foods (sold Entemann's Bakeries) General Mills (spin-off of Olive Gardens, Red Lobster)
Vendor supply has changed	Key components, licensing rights, or service components are no longer available through suppliers, which shortens the product life cycle.	Raw paper and lumber supplies Restrictions on commercial fishing (U.S. salmon supply)
Too difficult to support or maintain	Unique or complex technologies employed may strain current operations, divert resources, or require too much time to support the product.	AT&T (withdrawal from PC business)
Heavy competition	Increased global competition may offer better, cheaper, or more effective distribution (direct, telemarketing, distributor, catalog) than the current product.	Airlines Home Electronics (TV sets, microwaves)
Hazardous situation	Toxic or hazardous condition or use is discovered after product is commercially available.	Asbestos Ford Pinto Breast implants
Funding withdrawal or reallocation of funds	Internal resources may be reallocated or redistributed based on other new product developments or opportunities.	Jaguar's consolidation of new car models New Coke

product discontinuation process. These critical objectives in planning for and implementing product discontinuation include:

1. Determine the decision process.
2. Plan internal functional response to the external market message (reduced product demand).
3. Use information from the product discontinuation experience to enhance future product development projects.

28.4.1. Decision Process

The product discontinuation decision may be made by executive management alone or by a product review committee, product management group, sales, or some combination of all these. The decision to discontinue a product cannot be done in a vacuum but made as a result of factual market information combined with collective internal participation. An organization works to deliver the best market-oriented decision to pull a product from the market, ensuring the most minimal negative channel or user impact. The best collective management decision on product discontinuation ultimately times the market withdrawal at the right point—not too soon or too late.

> *Improper discontinuation can alienate users and prospective future customers.*

28.4.2. Response Plan for Product Discontinuation

As discussed in Section 28.5, here the organization comes together to define critical steps in the discontinuation process, departments involved, and deadlines. By defining time-line needs, as a documented process, the organization has a written and formalized plan to follow. Here the organization commits formally to the planning process and is therefore creating a lasting tool to follow as future product discontinuation decisions are made. Also, a formalized discontinuation plan moves the organization along the same critical path in completing the desired objective—removing the product from the market.

28.4.3. Learning Experience

Finally, as an organization, planning and implementing a product discontinuation plan means managing and attempting to control all the elements that must take place. Here the organization as a whole experiences the planned and unplanned activities in product discontinuation and can apply these events to the new product development process (steps). Once the discontinuation process is through, now it is time to audit the activities, measure the results, and improve, as an organization, how these steps can be improved in the future. These are experiences that can and should improve the organization's ability to become more customer focused and market oriented [4].

28.5. PLANNING THE PRODUCT DISCONTINUATION TIME LINE

The product discontinuation plan allows enough time to implement the market withdrawal. However, products can be withdrawn immediately (hazardous or liable conditions) up to an average period of one year following the announcement. The time line in Table 28.2 establishes key milestones of the discontinuation process. Relevant internal and external events are identified, completion dates set, and departmental responsibilities are assigned. (*Note*: Phases of the plan are defined in this example by calendar quarters; however, the actual time frame to complete these activities are based on any number of product variables.) A comprehensive discontinuation time line aids in achieving a seamless product transition. Also, a well-planned and implemented discontinuation plan can effectively support channel partners and users as they transition to other products offered by the organization.

Note on Developing the Plan

Test channel and user sensitivity of product demand. Quantify the customer base, survey impact on channel partners, and test for potentially negative channel or market response. Do these steps early in the time line, for this information may provide ways to transition users and channel partners as painlessly as possible. Internally, conduct interviews with functional departments to determine the steps involved, assign responsibilities, and set deadlines to ensure organizational commitment and focus. Ensure that all necessary individuals, functional developments, and, of course, executive management are on-board with the plan's objectives. Benchmark the discontinuation plan against other non-competitive companies in the industry or local organizations. A phone call or personal visit to companies that have experienced the challenges of product discontinuation is time well spent. This valuable step may prevent unforeseen problems or unexpected disasters.

28.6. POSTDISCONTINUATION PRODUCT SUPPORT

Product support, in the discontinuation and postdiscontinuation periods, is an extremely critical element for most high-technology or service-oriented products.

TABLE 28.2 Product Discontinuation Time-line Chart

Product Discontinuation Activities	Pre-Plan	Phase 1	Phase 2	Phase 3	Phase 4
1. New product development process projects estimated product life expectancy	×				
2. Utilize customer satisfaction, customer value analysis, installation audits, field service reports, market data to assess product viability	×				
3. Product review by executive management, product review committee, cross-functional team, divisional management, or product management whether to discontinue the product or service	×				
4. Impact analysis (sales, cost to support, final business opportunities, installed customer base, survey channels)	×				
5. Decision to discontinue product		×			
6. Discontinuation plan developed		×			
7. Interview functional department involved in discontinuation process (engineering, manufacturing, materials planning, purchasing, sales, service, marketing, customer service, legal, warehouse, MIS, finance, accounting		×			
8. Plan product support (either in-house or outsourced and costs associated with both options; see Section 29.6)		×			
9. Obtain from channels final unit, product, and supplies forecast for the discontinued product		×			
10. Plan final product schedules for discontinued product		×			
11. Take inventory of current product, parts, and supplies stock		×			
12. Formally announce the discontinuation (internally, channels, endusers, industry)		×	×		
13. Consider or plan inventory buy-back program for channel partners			×		
14. MIS advise on maintaining obsolete part numbers, costs, and price information system			×		
15. Security planning for obsolete sales history, part numbers, pricing, and so on			×		
16. Customer service training in fielding channel and enduser questions about the discontinued product			×		
17. Financial analysis (sales history, sales for forecasts, product costs)			×		
18. Decision to support engineering drawings			×		
19. Notify key component, parts, and supply vendors			×		
20. Plan of action in the event of a competitive response			×		
21. Marketing communications internal and external public relations activities (as required)				×	
22. Legal review	×	×	×	×	×
23. Ongoing functional team reviews and status reports		×	×	×	×
24. Final orders shipped		×	×	×	×
25. Product is formally discontinued					×
26. Postdiscontinuation support in place					×
27. Documentation of activities and link to new product development process					×

Product support, as shown in Table 28.3, helps differentiate a product and is often used to sustain a higher level of customer satisfaction. Product support is even more important to the discontinued product because loyal and long-standing customers will rely on the postsupport services to keep their product applications operating for an indefinite period of time [2].

To avoid or reduce the high cost of product support (work force and parts inventories), an organization may outsource some or all product support services to third-party service organizations. Customers, manufacturers, and third-party service organizations will win: Service continues for customers, and manufacturers transfer support to experienced and specialized service support organizations [3]. As an example, the computer and computer peripheral industries heavily

TABLE 28.3 Support Considerations for Discontinued Products

Menu of Product Support Services	Explanation	Retained or Outsourced
Spare or replacement parts or assemblies	Stock inventories of most commonly used and ordered parts, components, and key assemblies.	Easily and frequently outsourced
Technical service support	Technical telephone assistance, on-line services, electronic bulletin boards, or other assistance programs.	May be outsourced
On-site service	Available on-site repair services supporting trouble situations, preventive maintenance, and other warranty-related problems.	Easily and frequently outsourced
Technical publications	Technical manuals, videos, and audio tapes are stocked and maintained for the product for a limited period of time.	Generally managed by company in-house
Engineering design and drawings	Technical drawings, blueprints, and schematics are maintained for a period of time following product discontinuation announcement.	Generally managed by company in-house
Vendor or supplier support	Vendors are asked to provide continued support for their respective parts and key components associated with the product for a specified period of time.	Generally managed by company in-house
Customer service	Customer service personnel are instructed on how to support active users of the discontinued product.	Generally managed by company in-house
Customer training	Customer training programs may be continued support during the postdiscontinuation period.	May be outsourced

outsource much of their product support services (parts and on-site support) for many of their discontinued product lines. Outsourcing of resource-intensive product support is a standardized practice between these and most other high-technology industries where rapid product obsolescence occurs.

A company can transfer product support to another company.	**28.7. PRODUCT DISCONTINUATION CHANNEL ISSUES**

With any product, whether sold directly or through a distribution system, channel issues should be raised, addressed, and acted upon. Specifically, all sales channels, especially international channel partners, must be given a reasonable period of time to prepare their response to the product discontinuation.

Channel partners may require one or more of the following considerations:

- Time to assess the impact of the product discontinuation on the current or active installed base of users or potential product users. (Especially important for international markets where products are in use in remote or sparsely populated areas—example Australia's outback, Arizona's desert.)
- Alternative product solutions for current product users.
- Order time frame to stock or evaluate necessary spare parts and related supply inventories.
- Return program for excess product stock or parts inventories that will no longer have market demand.
- Technical product and service support for current product users until the users convert to alternative product solutions.

Examining the legal impact of product discontinuation on distribution channels is important. In any written distribution agreement, most suppliers provide the right to discontinue products at their discretion. It is wise to check for and comply with any legally binding contractual terms regarding product discontinuation. Beyond contractual terms, professional and ethical courtesy should be extended to distribution partners. Assess how and when the organization is obliged to support and maintain these important channel relationships. (Courtesy note: Consider all orders pending for the discontinued product, master contracts with key accounts where the product is involved, and distributor's inventory of the product, parts, or supplies associated.)

28.8. LEGAL CONSIDERATIONS OF PRODUCT DISCONTINUATION

> *The impact of discontinuation on your company's channels must be understood and accommodated.*

Presently, there are no laws of general applicability regarding product discontinuation, so the legal implications for the supplying company, other channel members, and endusers are generally considered on a case-by-case basis. The few laws that address the issue tend to be narrow (e.g., Texas requires that state vendors maintain a three-year parts supply after discontinuation), so the focus usually falls on the presence or absence of contract language and the covenant of good faith and fair dealing implicit in most agreements.

Suppliers generally have a good deal of leeway, but particularly troublesome areas could include situations where a supplier insists that its distributors invest in expensive, new facilities, although it expects to withdraw the relevant product shortly or where a supplier fails to discontinue or remedy a persistently sick product while hiding the truth by claiming the problems are limited or temporary. These acts demonstrate the sort of bad faith that may result in liability or at the very least a serious trade relations problem. As a rule, the best approach is to take advantage of all that the law allows, but to do so in a reasonable fashion. Even after considering these legal points, there still may be areas of uncertainty where legal counsel should be consulted. This cautionary step may prove especially beneficial when specialized or critical (life-supporting) products are discontinued from the market (Eugene F. Zelek, Jr., personal communication).

28.9. REVENUE OPPORTUNITIES FOR DISCONTINUED PRODUCTS

Throughout the life of any product, the objectives are to (1) create optimum customer value; (2) generate corporate revenue, growth, and market share; and (3) create a sustained opportunity for the organization. As the product matures, it too, has opportunities that may be optimized. Such opportunities may include:

- Sell the product or product line.
- Sell the formulation or product blueprints.
- Sell the brand name or brand name rights.
- Sell the licensing, manufacturing process, or distribution of the product, spare parts, or support for current installed products.
- Sell the core subassemblies or technology employed.

- Sell the operation, business units, or business entity that has been established for the sole purpose of producing the product.

Entrepreneurial firms, investment groups, or individuals may find value in purchasing discontinued products. For a smaller operation or investment group, the expected revenue minus the cost to manufacture, support, and sell a mature product may provide a level of profit great enough to extend a product's useful life. Selling a part or the whole product entity may provide significant revenue, which might have been overlooked. In the end this may be the single most important reason to take time to analyze a product's *final* market potential.

> *A product your company wishes to discontinue may have sufficient value to another firm so that you can sell the rights to it.*

As an example, Kraft, Inc. several years ago purchased the rights to Nabisco cereal products. By adding the Nabisco products to Kraft's existing Post cereal line, production economies were optimized, product breadth expanded, and overall market presence was heightened. Mutually beneficial results were realized for both companies.

28.10. STRATEGIC QUESTIONS TO CONSIDER

In assessing the decision to discontinue a product or service, use every effort to play out all possible scenarios and use good judgment in considering the situation. Managerial questions asked when making the decision to discontinue a product or service are:

1. What will the product discontinuation mean to the organization?
2. What is the correct process for planning and approving the discontinued product?
3. How much time is allowed before the product is discontinued? Three, six, or 12 months—or longer?
4. As a result of the product discontinuation, is there a way to measure if customers will adopt a new generation product or will customers defect to the competition?
5. Has there been an impact assessment of current users and channel partners regarding the discontinued product?
6. What functional departments will be involved in the product discontinuation process?
7. What type and duration of product support will be required?

8. What are the costs to extend the product support services?
9. Will these services be free, fee-based, by contract, or another method?
10. Will the outsourcing of support services work, and what considerations should be given when selecting a third-party service provider?
11. Will key parts, component, or supplies vendors continue to support the organization once the product has been discontinued?
12. How long will engineering drawings be maintained?
13. How will the drawings be archived?
14. Will critical or proprietary drawings be made available to channel partners or users?
15. What is the organization's policy on good-faith practices with channel partners regarding the discontinued product?
16. What revenue opportunities remain for the declining product?
17. Does the organization plan to replace the discontinued product with a new one, and if so, will the launch be timed with the product discontinuation?
18. Will the competition respond to the product discontinuation, and what is the organization's response?
19. Is management in agreement with the product discontinuation decision, or are there issues to be resolved?
20. What are the true costs of staging the product discontinuation?
21. Are there enough internal resources to pull off the product discontinuation?
22. How will this experience be documented and used as a template for future product development projects? [1]

28.11. SUMMARY

There is no escaping rapid changes (technology, international competition) in this global economy. The demand and availability of a wide range of products and services, of varying technological degrees, is forcing increased product obsolescence and compressing the product development process. Embracing and implementing product discontinuation should lead customers to adopt an organization's new-generation products. Even more, product discontinuation helps lift the drain on corporate resources and redirects organizational activity toward more profitable product opportunities. As it goes, the cycle of birth, growth, maturity, and aging affects all shining stars in any organization's product portfolio. The key is to manage the stages, anticipate change, and be ready to implement action.

Planning for a product's discontinuation is one of the most important learning experiences for any organization, product development team, and product management professional. There is much to be remembered and applied as the product life cycle winds down. Transferring this knowledge and practical experiences toward future product development projects is what it is all about—that's what makes for product success.

REFERENCES

1. Katzfey, Patricia A. Dealing with product discontinuation, *Product Management Insights,* p. 8 (January–February 1995).
2. Oliver, Philip M. Planning for the discontinued product. *American Field Service Management International* 16(10):69–73 (May 1992).
3. Rothmeier, Craig. "Outsourcing end-of-life service and support. *Service and Support Management* 11(10):18–20 (October 1995).
4. Slater, Stanley F. and Narver, John C. Market orientation and the learning organization. *Journal of Marketing* 59:63–74 (July 1995).
5. Urban, Glen L. and Hauser, John R. *Design and Marketing of New Products,* 2nd ed. Englewood Cliffs, NJ: Prentice-Hall, 1993.

Patricia A. Katzfey
Advanced Business Concepts, Inc.

Patricia A. Katzfey is principal of Advanced Business Concepts, Inc., a Chicago-based product marketing consulting firm. She has over 15 years of product development, market, channel, and price management experience. Ms. Katzfey has led multimillion-dollar high-technology development projects in a number of industries. Her expertise in both new product development and product line support has led to numerous successful product launches. In addition, she has published a newsletter entitled Product Management Insights. *Ms. Katzfey also conducts executive management seminars for the University of Wisconsin, Milwaukee. She has been a member of PDMA since 1994.*

29 PROCESS OWNERSHIP
Karen Graziano

29.1. INTRODUCTION

A successful, vital new product development (NPD) process has a technical and marketing side as well as an organizational side. The process owner has an important role in NPD, focusing primarily on the organizational side. This includes the way the organization views NPD, as well as providing the support to the people working in the new product development process. The process owner focuses on the process itself, from design through implementation and continuous improvement by working together with senior management as champions of NPD. This role is a unique opportunity for a person to work with multiple functions and levels in a business and influence NPD practices.

There are several dimensions to the topic of process ownership, beginning with the business's decision as to whether or not to identify a process owner. When to identify the process owner and how to prepare this person effectively for the role are additional considerations. It will be important to choose the right person, prepare him or her for the role, and understand how a process owner functions within an organization. The duration of the role of process owner will depend on the person's own judgment and the business's needs, but will probably last longer than expected.

29.2. To Have or Not to Have: An Identified Process Owner

Once the design of the NPD process is complete, the question of process ownership will arise. In general, identifying a process owner facilitates a smooth launch, maintenance, and continuous improvement of the NPD process. Many companies with a successful NPD process have a full-time process owner. Procter & Gamble, Polaroid, Exxon, Corning, and Rohm & Haas all have (or have had) full-time process owners (also known as process managers) [3, p. 285].

> *If new product development is a major effort in your company and you are serious about launching the process effectively, consider having a full-time, dedicated process owner.*

29.2.1. What Does Process Ownership Mean?

Process ownership is defined simply as having the responsibility for implementing and maintaining a successful NPD process in a business unit or company. Note that this definition indicates an *active* role. The process owner is dedicated full time to the process, acts as a champion, and is measured by the successful launch of the process within the company.

Often, this role is interchanged with that of the NPD sponsor, who typically is a senior executive. The decision to implement a NPD process is often made by the senior executive(s) in a company, but the task of making it work is often that of the process owner. It is important for the process owner and sponsor to work together closely and remain aligned with the goals. The process owner may become absorbed in the details of the NPD process and lose sight of the original goals in establishing the process. Similarly, senior management may focus on the daily tactical business decisions and assume that their participation is not needed. The process owner and senior management should overlap responsibilities and support one another through launch and well into implementation. This is best accomplished by meeting frequently, reviewing the NPD process objective, and modifying the objectives as the process matures. Senior management will have a different perspective on the NPD process than that of the process owner or project teams. The process owner needs to integrate all these points of view and provide a balanced perspective.

29.2.2. Benefits

The primary benefit of identifying a process owner is to ensure a smooth launch and continuous maintenance of the NPD process. The process owner focuses on process, and the multifunctional teams focus on the projects. Implementing a NPD process usually takes longer than originally estimated, as most of these processes involve organizational change. Clearly identifying a person as the owner indicates a higher level of commitment and raises the importance of NPD to the organization. As an example, one of the Rohm & Haas business units attempted to implement a stage-gate process without an identified process owner. This responsibility was added to the existing responsibilities of the line managers. The process was not fully implemented or used routinely. Realizing that little was changing, the process was rejuvenated and a process owner identified raising the visible commitment. Buy-in throughout the business increased significantly due primarily to the active participation by the process owner, who had as a primary objective launching and implementing the NPD process.

An identified process owner fully dedicated to the process can effectively nurture the practitioners by addressing the barriers and the preconceptions that people have. Common views are, first, that a new product development process is unnecessarily bureaucratic, and second, that it will lengthen the time needed to develop and launch new products. Every effort must be made to minimize bureaucracy and to speed products to market [2]. The process owner has a big responsibility here.

Constancy of purpose, effective communications, and continuous improvement are all clear benefits of having a process owner. A recent benchmarking survey from a variety of industries indicates that 60 percent of high-performance companies (with respect to time to market, innovativeness, new product success rate, and revenue contribution) designate process owners accountable for process improvement [1]. Comparatively, only 45 percent of low-performance companies designate a process owner accountable for process improvement. In this same survey, a wider gap exists between high- and low-performance companies (65 percent versus 35 percent) with respect to tracking process performance across projects (e.g., cycle time, cost, rework). Process improvements by tracking NPD process metrics is an ongoing, vital responsibility of the process owner to support the business. Continuous improvement can be an underestimated role as it requires constant attention to the way new products are developed, not only to the bottom line. The process owner will continue to contribute to the business by developing with the role as the emphasis moves away from implementing the NPD process.

29.2.3. Drawbacks

One drawback is that identifying a process owner might indicate a higher degree of bureaucracy than intended. Multifunctional teams complain that many companies focus an inordinate amount of energy on processes and not enough on product development itself—"enough process, just do it!" An identified process owner may put too much emphasis on process. This is a significant commitment to a staff position when many organizations are downsizing this function.

The most apparent drawback to identifying a process owner is that it may decrease the perceived need for top management's visible participation. Once a process owner is identified, senior management may feel that their role is complete. The opposite is true—senior management must continue to be a visible and committed champion of the process. As mentioned previously, senior management works side by side with the process owner and provides steadfast leadership of the NPD process. It is critical to maintain visible leadership and this should not become the process owner's sole responsibility at any time. Similarly, the NPD process cannot be effectively led by one function. Balanced, multifunctional commitment and leadership is desirable.

The process owner can lead the NPD process implementation but is often not in a position to establish and maintain performance expectations for all the business members. Performance evaluations usually are the functional managers' responsibilities, and the process owner might occasionally have input. If senior management does not set the performance expectations to follow the NPD process, the process will become unimportant, viewed as a nonessential business practice, and circumvented. The business members will assess continually if senior managers are genuinely committed to the NPD process.

29.2.4. When to Establish the Role and How Long You Need One

The process owner has an important role in the NPD, from design through process maintenance. The advantage to identifying a process owner early in the NPD design is to provide an in-depth knowledge of the process and the rationale behind the details. Expert knowledge of and buy-in to the process is an important attribute most easily gained through participating in the NPD process design. Teams chartered to design the NPD process may sometimes include senior managers as well as members from different functions and levels in the company. The partnership that develops between the process owner and the process designers is the beginning of a successful implementation. The process owner needs time to establish an effective working relationship with all levels and functions in the organization to be most effective in this role. Implementing an NPD process is easiest if there are champions and owners throughout the business, with the process owner providing leadership and maintaining the common link. Establishing this link early is beneficial.

The process owner's role will probably last longer than expected and it will be up to the organization and the process owner to determine when the role is obsolete. Plan on at least one year full-time. Rohm & Haas has had two full-time process owners in two separate business units for two years now without a clear end in sight. Responsibilities will change over the years from a focus on launch and organizational change, to maintenance, metrics, and continuous improvement. The time spent on the process may be reduced from full time to half-time if the organization grasps the concepts fully and learns to manage the process itself. Eventually, you want the teams and the entire organization to own the process. Without a dedicated person with specific responsibility to improve the process as the business climate changes, little will happen.

29.3. THE ROLE

29.3.1. Background, Skills, and Interests

The process owner's background is important. There is no formula for success. It depends on the person's commitment to the NPD process, the ability to affect change, and familiarity with the organization's people and projects.

Background

Rohm & Haas has process owners in the business units whose backgrounds range from quality consultant, market manager and senior scientist to midlevel research manager. All are effective in different ways, depending on their previous responsibilities in the functions. The common thread in effectiveness is a familiarity with the people and the types of new product development projects in their business units. Most often the business unit identifies a process owner who is already a member of that business unit. Many of these process owners have total quality management (TQM) backgrounds, and in fact, one is a joint process owner/quality manager for his business unit. Cooper, in fact, recommends positioning the NPD process as part of the corporation's overall TQM program [3, page 273]. The process owner ideally should have enough experience and responsibility to make change happen and have had some experience leading change. Below is a list of competences defined by Rohm & Haas.

- Knowledge of the new product development process
- Awareness of Rohm & Haas strategic intent
- Influence and interpersonal skills and team building
- Process facilitation
- Communication skills: listening, presentation, writing
- Group facilitation: running meetings, processing group dynamics
- Knowledge of TQM philosophy and principles

- Technical awareness
- Basic computing skills
- Customer focus and orientation

Skills and Interests

The process owner should have facilitation skills and an interest in organizational development and change. In fact, this person should like change and express an outward commitment to continuous improvement.

> *Implementing and managing the NPD process is a large, complex responsibility requiring a high degree of organization, patience, and tenacity.*

It is essential for the process owner to be a good communicator, an effective listener, and a negotiator. The process owner will work the organizational boundaries between levels and functions, which will require a nonpartisan viewpoint. Negotiation often involves actively listening to many sides of an issue without solving the problem for the parties involved. The process owner can assist in resolving issues between levels and functions by offering an objective point of view and facilitating open discussion. This can be a difficult and sometimes intimidating responsibility if the process owner does not have the skills or experience. Familiarity with the people throughout the business makes negotiation easier, and it is important for the process owner to establish these working relationships.

29.3.2. Where in the Organization?

The business unit's senior management or organization as a whole must sponsor the NPD process. The process owner does not need to be a midlevel or senior manager from a particular function, although leadership experience is helpful. If the process owner is not a senior manager, the process owner should report to the senior manager leading the new product development effort. The process owner may need to enlist the support of other functional, midlevel managers to implement the process effectively. This task is somewhat easier if the process owner and senior management work together closely toward the objectives.

29.3.3. Key Links Within and Outside the Organization

Links Within the Organization

Many companies have a group of quality consultants who focus on organizational development, team building skills, and total quality principles. This is an important internal link that the process owner should make early and nurture. There is an entire body of knowledge on both total quality and organizational development with which this group can help, particularly with respect to change management.

Large corporations often have several business units, each with a separate, dedicated process owner. These process owners might want to establish a process owners group to establish a link to each other. The process owners group meets frequently and shares experiences, best practices and observations, and the members support one another through the maturing of the NPD process. This group serves as a corporate resource for effective internal practices for new product development.

Links Outside the Organization

The NPD field is dynamic and global. Best practices are developing and changing rapidly, and it is nearly impossible to stay current by reading all the literature. One of the key responsibilities of the process owner (as well as other NPD professionals) is to bring in best practices and benchmark leading firms. One of the easiest ways to stay current in the field of NPD is to join and attend Product Development and Management Association (PDMA) meetings. There are local chapter, national, and international meetings and Frontier Dialogues which explore a topic similar to that of the Gordon Conferences. This organization provides a tremendous network of NPD professionals from all different industries.

29.4. CHANGING RESPONSIBILITIES AS THE NEW PRODUCT DEVELOPMENT PROCESS MATURES

29.4.1. The Role During NPD Design and Implementation

The process owner's role during the first phase is critical to the success of the NPD process. The goal is to establish the process firmly with the group and set the tone; this is the way that NPD work gets done. The process owner is the expert and an identifiable champion. It is important that the process owner be firmly committed to the principles outlined in the process and have tireless enthusiasm. A key responsibility in this first critical phase is a training program that involves everyone working in or associated with NPD. The process owner should work closely with the training department if there is one, or engage consultants to design an effective training program. The process owner should also deliver some of the training along with the sponsors and the professional training staff.

One aspect of the training and launch of the NPD process that has been used successfully in Rohm & Haas is the concept of pilot gate meetings. This is a form of on-the-job training where project teams and gatekeepers get together for a meeting to test the design of the process. The process owner acts as the facilitator and coach. In some instances, other members of the business unit have been invited to the meetings as observers. In a typical stage-gate process, gate meetings are decision points in the life of a project. The objective of the gate meeting is for the gatekeepers (resource allocators) and the project team to reach consensus on the fate of a project and the level of staffing for the next stage. Pilot gate meetings are similar to gate meetings in every way except that the objective is to test the process design, familiarize a team with the process, and determine what stage is most appropriate for a project. The decision at a pilot gate meeting is nonbinding unless the project team wants it to be. The project team is free to hold another gate meeting at which the objective will be to determine the fate of the project. These pilot gate meetings are a good way to give the teams and gatekeepers some hands-on experience with the process in an informal meeting.

The process owner uses the information and observations from the pilot gate meetings to improve the initial design and format of the NPD process. As an example, the launch of a stage-gate process in the Rohm & Haas corporate exploratory research group included pilot gate meetings on all active projects. A large part of these meetings included a critique of the process. After all the pilot gate meetings had been completed, three teams, facilitated by the process owner, looked at the feedback and modified the process accordingly. Including the teams and gatekeepers in the initial improvement process increased ownership, buy-in, and understanding of the NPD process.

29.4.2. The First Year: The Pains of Change

The difficulties encountered during the first year of using a defined NPD process require endless patience. There usually is a tendency to slip back to the old way of doing things, and some in the group will never embrace the NPD process. The process owner (and senior management) must maintain the integrity of the process as designed and continue to be champions and coaches to the teams and gatekeepers.

The process owner continues to play an active role in helping the teams and gatekeepers prepare for the gate meetings and also continues to facilitate most NPD gate meetings. The process owner acts as a coach and sounding board to the teams and managers working closely to resolve conflicts and facilitate an effective NPD process. Additional training may be needed for newly formed teams and gatekeepers. At this point, the process owner may want to introduce additional training in team skills, project management, planning and scheduling techniques, and other organizational skills training. It will take some time for the

NPD process to become routine in the business. The project teams and gate-keepers may not recognize additional skills training they need until they have used the process for even a year or more. A yearly training needs assessment as part of the annual process improvement survey is useful to consider. Complaints about the NPD process may be requests for a better understanding of how to fulfill the process expectations.

29.4.3. Maintaining the Process: Staying the Course

When, with time, the organization grows familiar with the NPD process and responsibility seems to diminish, the process owner may wonder if the role has become unnecessary. In fact, it might appear that the process could really run itself, which in many ways is true; it might run itself back to the former ineffective NPD practices! The process owner's role continues to be very important at this point, but it is less visible. It is still important to maintain the process integrity by facilitating the gate meetings and talking regularly with the practitioners. Continuous improvement is by definition an ongoing process. It will not happen without someone specifically responsible for it. The process owner actively solicits feedback from all users, acts on suggestions, and constantly looks for improvement opportunities. An example of a user satisfaction survey composed by a process owner in a Rohm & Haas business unit is included as an example in Table 29.1. The process owner might also publish a periodic newsletter updating the status of NPD projects, commercialization success, suggestions for improvement and a description of some of the ideas for new products. This keeps the process visible and user-friendly.

29.5. QUALITY PRINCIPLES AND NPD PROCESS

The successful NPD process is part of an organization's overall quality program. The process owner's skills should include an in-depth understanding of TQM, especially with respect to customer focus, continuous improvement, and measurement (metrics). It is particularly beneficial for the process owner to have been involved in quality improvement teams. There are many new programs that corporations have embraced, including TQM, stage-gate, empowerment, and teamwork. Some of the best initiatives have not had the impact or longevity expected. The more the initiatives overlap and support one another visibly, the greater the chance of sustainable, positive results. TQM tools should be used in training, gate meetings, team meetings, or whenever appropriate to create the interconnections.

**TABLE 29.1   New Product Development Process User Satisfaction
Survey Results from a Rohm & Haas Business Unit**

NPD SURVEY RESULTS
Current Versus 8/93

(5/94 results are derived from the 21 respondents who were or are members of NPD teams.)

Rating code: 1 Strongly Agree
2 Agree
3 No opinion
4 Disagree
5 Strongly disagree

	8/93 Results	5/94 Results
1. The NPD system is too bureaucratic.	3.3	3.4
2. The NPD system is too rigid.	3.4	3.4
3. The gate meetings are "inquisitions."	3.8	4.1
4. The NPD system is or will be circumvented.	2.4	2.8
5. It takes too long to use the NPD system.	3.0	3.4
6. I am not "bought-in" to the NPD system.	3.9	4.2
7. I understand the NPD system.	1.7	1.8
8. I know how to use the NPD system.	2.0	1.9
9. The marketing and technical questions are understandable and pertinent.	1.9	2.6
10. The gate meetings are effective.	2.0	2.3

29.5.1. Internal and External Customer Focus

The NPD process will initially focus the process owner's efforts on the internal customers of the process. Their level of satisfaction and view of the process effectiveness is important. Although the project teams and the business continue to concentrate on developing products for external customers, the process owner will play an important role here by ensuring that the NPD process delivers on time products that meet the customers' needs.

29.5.2. Metrics and Continuous Improvement

Metrics play a key role in the continuous improvement process. It has been said repeatedly that "what gets measured gets improved." The process owner has the primary responsibility to develop NPD process and output metrics (such as those described in Chapter 32) with the management teams. Once these are agreed upon, the process owner and the management teams gather and analyze the data. Following the analysis and agreement on improvements, the process owner implements the suggestions. One of the reason why companies do not measure development success and failure is that there is no system in place to do so [4].

The process owner has an important role to implement a measurement system that monitors product development success and failure.

29.6. THE PROCESS OWNERS ROLE IN ASSOCIATED BUSINESS PROCESSES

Briefly, the process owner has a role in the overall business process within the organization or business unit. This includes, to varying degrees, idea generation and management, portfolio management, and database management. A vital part of any NPD process is a steady stream of ideas. The process owner may actively gather ideas from NPD professionals or act as the focal point for idea submissions. Idea screening meetings, focus groups, and brainstorming sessions that engage the business in NPD development will be useful.

Portfolio management is a critically important business process by which a business unit decides on the mix of active projects, staffing, and dollar budget allocated to each project. The process owner should participate in the portfolio management process because they participate in NPD gate meetings. It may even be appropriate for the process owner to take a leadership role in establishing a data-based portfolio management process if it does not exist. The data generated from the NPD project gate meetings is used in the portfolio management process; in most cases the process owner will maintain the database. The process owner's participation in the NPD gate meetings lends a unique perspective on the project mix and importance.

The process owner often works closely with the computer applications group to choose or develop appropriate software to gather, track, and report the metrics. This database usually tracks project criteria: project title, objective, start date, project number, team members, gatekeepers, gate or stage number, last gate meeting date and decision, next gate meeting date, and dollars spent to date. The idea database can include an interactive feature where anyone in the business can input an idea to which other business members can add their comments and suggestions for embellishments.

29.7. SUMMARY

A process owner is an important, diverse, and changing role in the successful NPD process.

There are many advantages to identifying a process owner to be a champion and assistant to the NPD practitioners and to play a vital role in the launch, development, and maintenance of a NPD process. Previous experience with the people and projects in the organization, appropriate skills, and interest in fulfilling this challenging role will be critical. The process owner can effectively nurture the connections between the various corporate initiatives and functions by coaching, leadership, and facilitation. This is a unique and exciting opportunity to learn a great deal about and to improve the business of new product development within an organization.

REFERENCES

1. Anonymous. *High Performance New Product Development,* Boston: Mercer Management Consulting Co., 1995.
2. Cooper, Robert G. Implementing the new product process: the industry experience, private communication to the Rohm & Haas Company, Philadelphia, 1992.
3. Cooper, Robert G. *Winning at New Products,* (2nd ed.) Reading, MA: Addison-Wesley, 1993.
4. Griffin, Abbie and Page, Albert L. An interim report on measuring product development success and failure. *Journal of Product Innovation Management* 10:291–308 (September 1993).

Karen Graziano
Rohm & Haas

Ms. Graziano has worked for the Rohm and Haas Company for the past twelve years. Her educational background includes a B.S. in Forestry and an M.S. in Plant Pathology from N.C. State University. Ms. Graziano joined Rohm and Haas in 1983 as a scientist in the Fungicides Discovery Group in the Agricultural Chemical Division. In 1987 she moved to Corporate New Ventures to develop advanced photoresist materials. Ms. Graziano became New Product Process Manager for Corporate Exploratory Research in 1992 to launch one of the first stage-gate processes at Rohm and Haas. She joined the Polymers and Resins business unit in 1994, again as a New Product Process Manager. Her current responsibilities include implementing a stage-gate process within this unit.

30 USING A CONCURRENT TEAM TO REENGINEER THE PRODUCT DEVELOPMENT PROCESS

Gary S. Tighe and
Bruce P. Kraemer

30.1. INTRODUCTION

In this chapter we describe how one company improved the innovation cycle of a traditional new product development (NPD) process. The innovation cycle is defined herein as the period of time between the identification of a need or opportunity and the approval of a development project to realize the solution. *Process reengineering* is a discipline to measure and modify organizational dynamics by optimizing the activities required to reach end goals or objectives. Process reengineering has been covered extensively by popular authors [7,11]. Our working definition, however, is more closely aligned with the philosophy expressed by Rummler-Brache [16]. Typical end goals are getting orders, building high-quality products, delivering on time, inventing, and innovating. Reengineering targets the activities needed to get a product or service to a customer rather than how to enhance functional skills. Improvements in functional skills such as design engineering, quality control, selling, and marketing are individual or department responsibilities. Improvements in getting orders, manufacturing high-quality products, delivering on time, inventing and innovating are cross-functional, process responsibilities. Process reengineering analyzes, documents, and compares an existing process to "best-in-class" practice, then implements process improvements or installs an entire new process.

NPD processes have been compared and contrasted in many well-written and extensively researched texts which served as valuable reference material for this project [1,2,4,6,8,14,17,20,21]. In this instance we shall use an abbreviated definition as follows. NPD includes a number of activities, usually performed in series, which include discovery, innovation, specification, design, manufacture, and launch. Specification, design, manufacture, and launch are understood, quantified, and documented by most organizations. However, many organizations and cultures do not count discovery and innovation as part of the NPD cycle. Others do not view discovery and innovation as a process. Since expenditure of capital, personnel, and cash assets are invisible in the early phases of discovery and innovation, they are often relegated to a nether-land between selling and R&D. It is common to see organizations spend millions of dollars to shave hours or minutes from production or design cycles, then neglect larger savings available in the early phases of product development. Organizations are beginning to recognize that the value of time and management in the early stages of NPD is equivalent to that in the later stages. Organizations need to manage and control the innovation cycle because time is money, and excess time represents an irretrievable loss whether spent in design, manufacturing, or innovating.

Organizations that measure time to market typically monitor that time between initiation of product design and product launch. This internal accounting ignores dynamic market factors where the real time to market is the time between the first perception of a need and the launch of a product that fills that need. In competitive industries, the difference between new product success and failure is often determined by what happens in the time perception and fulfillment. Some markets, such as consumer electronics, might measure this *realization gap* in weeks. Industries experiencing global competition find that extended realization gaps limit new product revenue because of missed market windows and abbreviated product life cycles.

Organizations that are slow in translating needs to end products are forever behind the learning curve and mystified how the competition arrives in the market slightly ahead of their best effort. Organizations adept at translating needs to end products and managing their innovation cycle are usually first or second in their market and ahead of their competitors by weeks or months. In the case we describe, the innovation improvement team understood this and recognized that the operating innovation process in their organization was costing time, money, and market share. It was time for a change.

30.2. PROCESS SUCCESS

Reengineering a process requires that many things occur successfully in a team environment [13]. Unfortunately, success is not automatic but rather, requires significant attention to detail. Some authors have apparently observed where theory and practice can depart and synthesized quick guidelines that capture the essence of common pitfalls [3]. Similarly, extensive and diverse experiences collected by the authors during eight years of reengineering work within industry guided the process described below.

30.3. MANAGEMENT SPONSORSHIP AND OWNERSHIP

Reengineering a process requires top management sponsorship and willingness to assume ownership of the new process. Substantial process improvements often involve long and painful culture changes. Culture changes cannot be implemented at the grass roots or midmanagement levels in most organizations. The culture in this case was characterized as an association of individual contributors and innovators, some of whom were effective champions, operating in an informal organization. No process documentation was available to clarify the early new product development stages. To make matters worse, implementation of formal rules or documentation was seen as bureaucratic and arbitrary by the culture and much of its managements. The need for change was first recognized by the engineering vice-president, who saw a need to streamline the innovation process to ensure survival. The vice-president selected a team leader who began the process of reengineering team selection and team building.

30.4. TEAM SELECTION AND BUILDING

This project required multifunctional teams that represented the entire organization. Our innovation process characterization team included representatives from legal, design, marketing, manufacturing, sales, and management personnel. The reason for cross functionally was threefold: (1) it is important that the functions responsible for making the process work be a part of the process development to ensure acceptance and buy-in at implementation; (2) rich cross-functional representation helps ensure a broad range of thought, which adds great value to the finished product; and (3) multifunctional representation helps avoid the construction of "over-the-transom hand offs," where engineering works in isolation to complete a design and then hands it to manufacturing with little or no warning.

Members were generally chosen from those who had demonstrated skill in navigating the innovation process and those who had previously expressed opinions about the need for change. Once members were identified, they were invited to meet and begin the process reengineering project. One of the foremost problems in converting a group of individuals into a team is convincing them that there is a meaningful, attainable goal to which each of them can contribute. All team members in this example were senior people. This meant that they had either been involved with or observed a variety of improvement projects in the past. Some projects were successful, others not. It also meant that they were valuable contributors to the daily process of defining and designing products, and each felt considerable pressure to manage their precious time, investing it in only the most valuable tasks.

Given the issues mentioned above, the first objective was to establish some "buy-in" and the team sponsor had to adopt the role of "project salesperson." The first two team meetings were led by the project sponsor. Conversation began with a presentation, from the sponsor's perspective, of the goal, its importance, and the acceptable time frame for achieving it. Subsequent meetings involved developing simple team agreements: get to meetings on time, appoint alternates, meeting times, rules of consensus, and other basic procedures to ensure order and progress. The topic of process mapping was also introduced by the team leadership.

30.5. PROCESS MAPPING

Process maps are an effective way to show how a process works. A process map consists of an X and a Y axis, which show process sequence (or time) and process participants, respectively. The horizontal X axis illustrates time in process and the individual process activities or gates. The Y axis shows the departments or functions participating in the process: engineering, marketing, manufacturing, sales, and so on. In a well-defined process like manufacturing, the process map tends to be a single line connecting serial activities and events.

Complex, social processes such as selling, or orders acquisition, exhibit multiple parallel activities and complex interconnections. Even complex processes under control move smoothly from left to right. Processes out of control will not. Processes that employ concurrent teams show repetitive or continuous involvement by the same functions, step after step. Processes with "hand-offs" show singular, short-term involvements by departments in single process steps only.

30.6. THE AS-IS MAP

At first, the team saw little value in constructing a map to show existing conditions. Some team members felt the exercise was an attempt to assign responsibility or blame, while others were simply anxious to forge ahead with improvements to the system. In the end, the team decided to invest the time to understand what was currently in operation. The first objective of this engineering, manufacturing, marketing, finance, and sales team was to develop a mutually acceptable understanding of the innovation process currently in operation.

The first "as-is" map (Figure 30.1) was a very rough approximation of what the team leaders believed represented the existing process. It was important to develop this "straw man" representation, even though inaccurate, because it was easier for team members to edit the straw man than to create a new map from the ground up. Participation increased steadily as the team engaged the analysis. New insights into the organization occurred at every team session. After four 2-hour work sessions, the team spent the fifth meeting reviewing and polishing the wall-sized map. After five weeks the team agreed that the map represented the existing process accurately.

The as-is map uncovered an intricate informal network of cliques, alliances, and partners engaged in moving new product innovations through the organi-

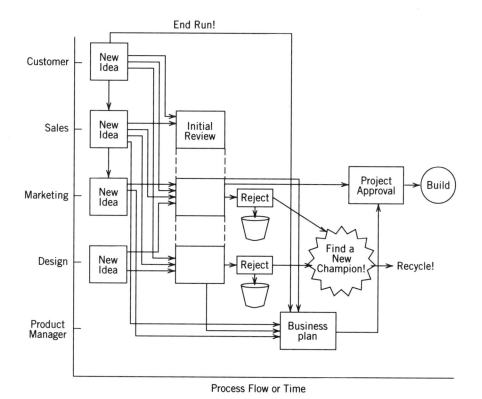

FIGURE 30.1 Innovation process "as-is" map.

---

zation. Strong emotional champions were effective in getting projects accepted, while projects lacking a champion died. Customers, especially large ones, were adept at finding individuals and groups within the organization most likely to support their projects. Shortcuts and end runs often permitted projects to be started with little regard for precious capital and design resources. Some projects were begun with no planning or management review. Others simply rode piggyback on existing projects. Projects were handled in a serial fashion, one at a time, with little regard to comparative merit. Worse, once started, projects were seldom reevaluated or canceled.

Had the team stopped here, the as-is map would be nothing but an object of unproductive criticism and possible mirth. The map of an existing process should serve as a benchmark against future activity, unless the existing process is perfect! Another value of the as-is map is as a selling tool to top management and the organization at large. The as-is map and its message continued to sell the work of the process reengineering team throughout the project and as additional people were briefed on the team's purpose and progress. Later, during the reengineering implementation phase, grass-roots employee support for change as depicted in the "should-be" map was easy to win when compared to the as-is map.

The as-is map also served as a constant reminder that the existing process was costing the company time to market, revenue, profitability, and market share. The graphic illustration of a broken process identified by an experienced, multifunctional management team is a powerful message that trouble is brewing. The next step required the team to check the existing innovation process against a known quantity. It was decided to benchmark companies known to be innovation leaders.

30.7. BENCHMARKING WORLD-CLASS LEADERS

Extensive discussion about characteristics of visionary companies have been documented in recent texts [5,10,19]. Leading innovators in high-technology industries are easy to identify. They rank first or second in the market share, profitability, growth, and shareholder performance. Thirty to fifty percent of their sales are from products introduced in the last three years, and everyone wants to benchmark them. Companies such as Hewlett-Packard, Motorola, Compaq Computer and Intel are most often cited as innovation leaders in the electronics industry.

Few companies are interested in sharing benchmarking information today unless there is something exchanged. Our company methodically engaged in quality, process improvement, qualification, and certification initiatives. Therefore, the team could cite company expertise in total quality management (TQM), quality function development (QFD), ISO 9000, and other areas to arouse interest in benchmarking partners wanting to exchange knowledge. Experience in benchmarking and characterizing the innovation process were additional areas of interest to benchmark partners. Once started, the flow of information was brisk.

Benchmarking direct competitors required literature research and collecting open market information. Annual reports, third-party experts, 10-Ks, trade journals, articles, company literature, trade shows, news items, and clipping services were sources of information. Direct contact was limited to former employees and a few personal contacts. Such information is valuable if it provides confidence in reaching conclusions and decisions.

Rather than contacting direct competitors, the team contacted companies with similar product and market profiles:

- Serves highly competitive, world market.
- Introduces hundreds of new products each year.
- Product price is a few cents or dollars each.
- Sales are primarily to other businesses.
- Product life is 5 to 15 years.

A company with a similar profile in a noncompeting industry was a manufacturer of electronic connectors and subsystems. The team had several conversations with this company's representatives and was able to share useful information on how an acknowledged leader in a similar business innovated

The benchmarking process soon revealed the difference between the world-class process and the process on the team's as-is map. Highlights of the leaders' processes included:

- Top management ownership of the process
- Early involvement of midmanagement in idea review
- A well-documented process with review gates
- A central collection point for new ideas
- Reward and recognition of idea contributors

Benchmarking disclosed many areas of improvement that would not otherwise have surfaced. The benchmarking data were also valuable in later discussions with management about what needed to be done to improve the existing process. Presentations to secure buy-in from management and employees responsible for implementation were more poignant when competitive and world-class companies were used as examples. After the team documented the benchmarking data and summarized the recommendations, work began to map out what the process should be (Figure 30.2).

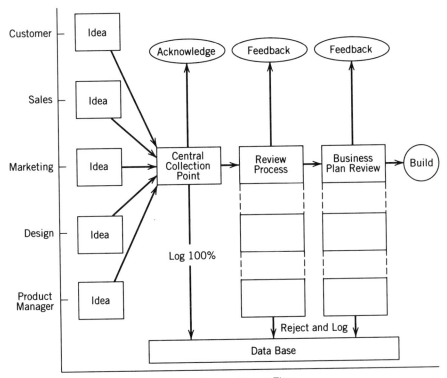

Process Flow or Time

FIGURE 30.2 Innovation process "should be" map.

   The axes and layout of a should-be map are identical to the as-is map in that functions are shown on the Y axis and process time or flow is shown on the X axis. As would be expected, the new process map was much cleaner and more linear than the as-is map. It presented a more logical and understandable process flow distinguished by an absence of multiple paths and reversals. It also showed a marked funneling process as the ideas and innovations flow through the process gates and undergo a selection process. All the needed new elements—earlier management involvement a central collection point, the need to compare ideas and projects, and the need for review gates—are incorporated in the new process map.
   The new should be map focuses management attention on the following areas:

   1. *Review gates and checkpoints.* A series of formal gates where projects either achieve rite of passage or die is crucial to a workable process. Like Gresham's law (bad money drives out good), marginal projects in the sys-

tem eventually clog the process and force the good projects to "go underground." Process gates become more rigorous as the investment levels increase. The goal is to eliminate marginal projects as early as possible where mistakes are relatively "cheap".

2. *Rewards and recognition.* These are as intrinsic to the innovation process as entrepreneurs are to capitalism. Every successful innovation process benchmarked had a reward and recognition program that kept innovators in the limelight. Successful programs are typically long on recognition and short on awards. This is in deference to keeping the process friendly, fun, and away from controversy [12,15,18]. The team addressed this by promoting innovation as an integral part of the business rather than a short-term "new deal." New ideas are seen as the lifeblood of the business and part of everyone's job. Therefore, innovators are well recognized but only nominally rewarded, which keeps the process lively and fun.

3. *Feedback.* This is critical to keep new ideas coming, especially for field sales and other personnel who are physically removed from the central idea evaluators. Lack of feedback quickly depletes enthusiasm among the idea originators and scuttles the best processes. Pollyana feedback has an equally deleterious effect because if all ideas are "good," the best innovators will see the process as lacking in credibility and worth. Feedback should both inspire and coach.

4. *Database and process metrics.* Data about the status of ideas are now collected. They serve two functions: (1) establish an ongoing market and customer database for future analysis, and (2) provide a method for tracking project status and process effectiveness.

5. *Idea merit index.* The "merit" of the ideas in the process can be measured in a number of ways. The team decided to focus on measuring the quality of "discards." The idea inventory can be considered a limited capacity holding area where ideas in the area are periodically evaluated, promoted, or discarded. When one starts discarding four-star ideas to make room, those remaining must be five-star or better. Another method of evaluating idea merit is to survey the end customers and the management team using the process output. Conventional gap analysis and survey techniques are used in this process.

6. *The innovation engine.* This is the catch phrase for the creative activity and people that actually think of new ideas. It represents the synthesis phase when someone first recognizes that customer and market opportunities can be translated into new product ideas. The innovation engine is the communal possession of the culture and is the end result of cultural nurturing (or starvation). It is the creative innovative activity versus the

activity of tracking and managing ideas through a process. It is an ongoing process that eventually defines the business.

7. *Other agendas.* The team also used the new process map to define and promote multifunctional, concurrent teams. The new map illustrates how concurrent teams formed early in a process are effectively utilized throughout the process. Since those functions most likely to participate on a concurrent team were present for the creation of the new map, they were able to understand and define their appropriate roles and ensure buy-in from their peer groups during implementation.

The should-be map is maintained throughout the implementation phase for presentations to management and to the people responsible for the work. Eventually, of course, the should-be map becomes the as-is map and is invaluable for reevaluating and renewing the process. The team promoted an understanding throughout the organization that the new process would always be a straw man, subject to editing by the organization in a spirit of continuous improvement.

30.8. IMPLEMENTING THE NEW PROCESS

Once the innovation process characterization team developed the should-be map, an implementation team was formed. An implementation team has different objectives from a process characterization team and may or may not use the same team members in its work. The implementation team seeks grass-roots support and involvement as it takes on the task of challenging and changing an entrenched process. The implementation team in this study continued to employ multifunctional team representation as a method to secure the best thinking across the organization and to ensure broad buy-in to the new process. The implementation team concentrated on establishing review gates, rewards, feedback, metrics, and a database as part of an ongoing process within the organization. The implementation of this new process will take at least as long as the three-month characterization process. It may possibly take twice as long as the theory is translated into robust, detailed, and practical reality and people begin to realize and comment on proposed changes that will affect their activities directly. (Therefore, it is important to form a team with a long-term outlook supported by a top management willing to invest the necessary time.)

1. *Changes continue.* At the early stage of implementation there was still ample opportunity for inputs and edits to the should-be map. In fact, it was vital to permit new team members and interested parties ample time to review and understand the proposed process, then make copious com-

ments and suggestions. If the organization is multinational, the world partners and team members should be included at this point. They add valuable perspective and insure buy-in if the process is to be adopted globally.

2. *Pilot testing and early adopters.* The team sought out early adopters in the organization who were willing to try out segments of the process in their organization. Early adopters are typically people not wedded to the existing process. These might include a new manager eager to experiment with new process tools, systems experts anxious to try new software, a sales office willing to supply new ideas for evaluation, and other experimenters. It is also advisable to expand the organizational support base beyond the project sponsor to develop additional management champions willing to promote the process throughout the organization.

A few beta sites were used in the pilot test and were valuable in providing an early warning of points overlooked during the process development. Beta sites were selected that had very low risk and a low profile and were friendly to the implementation team. They were also vocal critics of any process flaws, and since the team anticipated flaws, it was felt that this is the time and place to uncover them. Beta sites were initiated as soon as a process step was developed and documented.

3. *Training.* Training was used to install the process in the organization. This included "training the trainers," then training the people responsible for daily management of the process and the potential idea originators. The team designated two training team leaders. These team leaders were charged with training the U.S., European, and Asian organizations in the new process. Training began three weeks ahead of launching the new process worldwide to test the training and the trainers. This uncovered some flaws in the process, communication links, and other areas that would have been troublesome had the process launched without this pilot test.

4. *Documentation.* A key deliverable of a process reengineering team is a set of comprehensive documentation that describes the process and identifies those responsible for making the process work. Documentation is important to ensure a repeatable process and set a standard upon which improvements can be made later. During the early benchmarking, the world-class leaders were asked if their process was documented and all surveyed said "yes." However, some commented later that they were operating under a false assumption and that in the future they would develop documentation before their culture forgot what their successful process looked like.

30.9. THE NEW PROCESS OWNERS, MANAGERS, AND CHAMPIONS

A sustainable process needs managers, owners, and champions to perform daily operations and keep the process workable. The "old ways" of assigning operation or department heads to manage process segments are inadequate in process-driven organizations. The team established a process management structure as follows:

- The *process owner* in this case is the vice-president of engineering. The owner is responsible for the overall vitality and feasibility of the process. This includes process throughput, quality of output, and participation within the organization.
- The *process managers* are the product line managers. They are responsible for ensuring the orderly and timely flow of ideas and projects through the process. They eventually determine the makeup of the new product inventory, the selection of projects from the inventory, and the product mix of the organization.
- The *process champion* is the person responsible for the daily promotion and sale of the process throughout the organization and for the ongoing training, innovation input, and continuous improvement of the process.

30.10. SUMMARY

The team invested 10 months to review the existing process, benchmark world-class leaders, and create a new process. The implementation of the new process has been under way for a few months, and the results are gratifying. While a formal metric for cycle time has not yet been implemented [9], potential new revenues from the ideas received thus far exceed $10 million annually. The quality of new ideas received from employees are well directed toward the organization's end goals and are of good technical quality. The feedback to idea originators has been complimentary and supportive, while honest and constructive. The reward and recognition system has "forced" participation in some cases where a business unit was, at first, reluctant. This is acceptable. Top management response to the process has been one of willingness to support, sell, and promote the process. Midmanagement support has also been gratifying. Most of the process managers have adopted the process, and its language then modified it to fit best their respective business units. It is important to plan for and encourage this kind of customization, because in the final analysis, this is a process that people make work.

REFERENCES

1. Bacon, F. R., Jr. and Butler, T. W., Jr. *Planned Innovation*. Ann Arbor, MI: Institute of Science and Technology, University of Michigan, 1981.
2. Boznak, R. G. with Decker, A. K. *Competitive Product Development*. Milwaukee, WI: Quality Press, 1993.
3. Caluori, A. *10 Restructuring Don'ts*. Beyond Computing, p. 52 (September–October 1994).
4. Clark, K. B. and Wheelwright, S. C. *Managing New Product and Process Development*. New York: Free Press, 1993.
5. Collins, J. C., and Poras, J. I. *Built to Last*. New York: Harper, 1994.
6. Cooper, R. G. *Winning at New Products*, 2nd ed. Reading, MA: Addison-Wesley, 1993.
7. Davidson, W. H. Beyond Reengineering: The Three Phases of Business Transformation *IBM Systems Journal*, 32(1) (1993).
8. Erhorn, C. and Stark, J. *Competing by Design*. Essex Junction, VT: Oliver Wright Publications, 1994.
9. Griffin, A. Metrics for measuring product development cycle time. *Journal of Product Innovation Management* 10:112–125 (1993).
10. Hamel, G. and Prahalad, C. K. *Competing for the Future*. Cambridge, MA: Harvard Business School Press, 1994.
11. Hammer, M. and Champy, J. *Reengineering the Corporation*. New York: Harper, 1993.
12. Kriewell, T. J. *Rewarding Research*. In: *Management of R&D, Vol. 2, Robert Szakonyi (ed.)*. New York: Auerbach Publications, 1993.
13. Larson, C. E., and LaFasto, M. J. *TeamWork*. Newbury Park, CA: Sage Publications, 1989.
14. Patterson, M. L. *Accelerating Innovation*. New York: Van Nostrand Reinhold, 1993.
15. Rosenau, M. D., Jr. Rewards for new product development teams. *Journal of Product Innovation Management* 11:256–258 (1994).
16. Rummler, G. A. and Brache, A. P. *Improving Performance*. San Francisco: Jossey-Bass, 1990.
17. Smith, P. G. and Reinertsen, P. G. *Developing Products in Half the Time*. New York: Van Nostrand Reinhold, 1991.
18. Sykes, H. B. Incentive compensation for corporate venture personnel. *Journal of Business Venturing* pp. 253–265 (1992).
19. Treacy, M. and Wiersema, F. *The Discipline of Market Leaders*. Reading, MA: Addison-Wesley, 1995.
20. Vincent, G. *Managing New-Product Development*. New York: Van Nostrand Reinhold, 1989.
21. Wheelwright, S. C. and Clark, K. B. *Revolutionizing Product Development*. New York: Free Press, 1992.

Gary S. Tighe
Harris Semiconductor

Mr. Tighe has over 25 years' experience in guiding new product development and marketing in Fortune 100 corporations. His expertise is in formation and leadership of multifunction teams to implement innovation, design, manufacture, and marketing of high-technology products. Recently, he has focused on characterization and reengineering of the new product development process in high-technology businesses. This includes new product innovation, development, and launch. His work makes extensive use of benchmarking companies regarded as "best in class" in these fields.

Bruce P. Kraemer
Harris Semiconductor

Mr. Kraemer has over 15 years experience in new product development, marketing, business process improvement, and process reengineering at Foxboro Company and Harris Corporation. Within Harris he has been a Senior Manager and has worked with essentially all divisions leading teams in sales, marketing, engineering, accounting, and so on, through various reengineering projects. Most recently he is serving in Harris Semiconductor Strategic Marketing. His academic background includes a B.S. from MIT and an MBA from WPI.

31 MEASURING PRODUCT DEVELOPMENT SUCCESS AND FAILURE

A Framework Defining Success and Failure
Erik Jan Hultink and
Henry S. J. Robben

31.1. IMPORTANCE AND BENEFITS OF MEASURING NEW PRODUCT SUCCESS AND FAILURE

This chapter offers a guide on how and when to measure the performance of new products. In preceding chapters it has been shown that new products are important for a company's well-being. Every firm wants its finished products to become a success as quickly as possible after introduction. If a product is not successful immediately, companies need to adjust their new product strategies to make it successful eventually. Therefore, it is necessary to measure the performance of the new product in the market to figure out how well it is doing [1,2]. Measuring new product performance is valuable for several reasons. It facilitates organizational learning and process improvements and fulfills the need within companies and within new product teams for consensus on new product outcomes and determinants. In addition, measuring new product success and failure may lead to observable benefits such as improved cycle times, improved new product success rates, and an enhanced ability to assess new product process changes.

In this chapter we propose a framework that helps setting up a new product development (NPD) performance measurement system. Concerning new product success, how would you rate the following products?

- Philips Video 2000,
- 3M Post-it notes (TM),
- Ford Taurus

The answers are not straightforward. For example, the Philips Video 2000 system that was introduced in 1979–1980 was a technical success but failed in the marketplace. Philips sold only about 1.5 million units of the product in Europe and decided to withdraw the product in 1985, a mere five years after its market launch. On the other hand, the development of the glue on the Post-it notes (TM) was a technical failure, but its commercial and financial payoffs have been huge. Finally, the early models of the Ford Taurus are regarded as a technical and financial failure, requiring many years to pay off Ford's investments, but as a definite commercial success.

It is difficult to say whether a new product is successful. The difficulty of measuring new product success is the result of two problems:

- New product success has several dimensions (i.e., technical, financial, and commercial) [3,4].
- New product success is always judged against a yardstick.

The ultimate successful product is one that is successful on every dimension. This is very rare, so product developers are frequently forced to make trade-offs, sacrificing success in one dimension to achieve it in another. Different people may refer to different success dimensions when they talk about the same product, and thus come to different conclusions about its success.

> *New product project success has three dimensions: technical, financial, and commercial.*

The yardstick for judging success may be a plan, objective, expectation, goal, past product introduction, or competitors' new product performance. Different people may use different yardsticks and thus again reach different conclusions. For example, Philips managers compare the sales growth of the recently introduced CD-I (compact disc interactive) with that of previously introduced new-to-the-world products such as the CD and VCR. Similarly, one can evaluate the performance of Philips' digital compact cassette (DCC) against the performance of Sony's minidisc (MD). Using these yardsticks, both products appear successful on the commercial dimension of new product success. However, judging the commercial performance of both products against plan, objective, or expectation may have resulted in different conclusions.

So far, we have sketched the importance and difficulties associated with defining new product success and failure. We recommend being clear about the yardsticks companies use in measuring the success of new products. Being vague causes confusion. In addition, firms should decide up front which of the success dimensions is most important for success. Given that new product success has multiple dimensions, projects should be managed to optimize success over those dimensions. In Section 31.2 we offer a solution for when and how to measure new product success.

31.2. FRAMEWORK FOR MEASURING NEW PRODUCT SUCCESS

Be clear about the dimensions and yardsticks that you use in measuring the success of your new product. Being vague causes confusion.

The framework for measuring new product success consists of three dimensions: (1) level of measurement, (2) time perspective, and (3) dimensions of success (discussed above). The framework combined these three dimensions in Table 31.1. The first column in the table presents 12 *core indicators* of new product success. All indicators are relevant for assessing how well you have done [5]. They separate into a single firm-level

TABLE 31.1 Instrument for Choosing the Appropriate Performance Indicator for the Appropriate Time Perspective

Measurement Level and Performance Indicator	Time Perspective	
	Short Term	Long Term
Firm		
Percent of sales by new products	×	×
Market acceptance		
Customer acceptance	×	×
Customer satisfaction	×	×
Met revenue goals		×
Met market share goals		×
Met unit sales goals		×
Product Level		
Launched on time	×	
Product performance level	×	×
Met quality guidelines	×	×
Financial		
Attain margin goals		×
Attain profitability goals		×
IRR/ROI		×

indicator and three groups of project-level indicators: market acceptance, product level, and financial performance indicators.

To get a complete view of the performance of the total NPD project, it is necessary to measure inputs in the NPD process as well as outputs. Inputs are, for example, internal personnel and out-of-pocket expenses by phase and function. Outputs are the technical, market, and financial performance of the new product in the marketplace. In this chapter we focus on the performance of the new product after market launch and therefore deal only with the outputs of the NPD process.

The four categories (market acceptance, product level, financial, and firm level) measure different aspects of the new product's performance. The project level measures refer to the performance of a single development project. For example, market acceptance measures reflect current market position, product image, sales force and trade acceptance, and sales performance compared with competitors. Product-level indicators show how customers evaluate the product's quality, performance, and user friendliness. They provide information on how well the product follows market standards and firm specifications, and whether updates or extensions are necessary. Measuring the financial performance of a new product provides information on the project's profitability. Finally, firm-level measures reflect how proficient the firm as a whole is in NPD. An example of a firm-level measure is the percentage of the company's sales and profits generated by new products introduced in the last five years.

The second dimension in this framework is time perspective [5]. Although "the earlier you measure, the more you are in control," companies should use different measures in the short term than in the long term. For example, return on investment (ROI) is more important to measure in the long term because it usually takes several years to recover the development and market introduction costs. On the other hand, speed to market and development costs are more important in the short term. The following examples illustrate the importance of distinguishing short- and long-term new product success. Kodak's instant pictures were a commercial success for about two years. Because of patent violations, its market share of 33 percent dropped to zero. Ford's Taurus had a long break-even time (a short-term financial failure) but was a commercial success (in terms of share and volume) from its introduction onward.

The crosses in Table 31.1 show that some indicators are important to measure in both the short and long term: customer acceptance and satisfaction, product performance, and meeting quality guidelines. Others are more important to measure in the short term only (i.e., launched on time) or in the long term (i.e., revenue, market share, unit sales, margin, profitability, and ROI) [5].

No single measure is entirely satisfactory for a complete view of a new product's performance: Multiple measures are needed for both the short and long term. There is a trade-off involved: It is inefficient to follow all indicators continuously, and capitalizing on a single indicator is unsatisfactory because much relevant information is left out. To get a complete picture of a new product's performance, companies should regularly measure two customer acceptance measures and one measure from each of the other three groups in Table 31.1 [1].

Which specific customer acceptance measures to choose depends on the type of project developed and on the firm's innovation strategy [2]. For example, new-to-the-world and cost-reduction projects can best be assessed by using customer satisfaction and customer acceptance measures, whereas the performance of new-to-the-company projects and additions to existing lines can best be evaluated through their market share.

31.3. HOW TO IMPLEMENT AN NPD PERFORMANCE MEASUREMENT SYSTEM

> *There is no single measure that is entirely satisfactory. Monitor regularly, two customer acceptance measures and at least one measure from the other three groups in Table 31.1 to get a complete picture of a new product's performance for the short and long terms.*

Several considerations guide the implementation of an NPD performance measurement system: data availability, the costs in terms of time and money of collecting the necessary data, and the frequency of measuring. Chapter 32 offers a more complete description of these issues.

Reliable data are paramount for your measurement system. Data may be available within the firm, be purchased, or be collected. For example, the finance department usually provides revenue and profitability statistics. Market research agencies such as Nielsen, AGB, and Europanel sell market-share data. However, customer satisfaction data usually need to be collected through primary market research. Customer feedback sessions, complaints management, the sales force, dealer rounds, user clubs, interviews, surveys, and customer report cards all serve this purpose. It is usually more expensive and more troublesome for firms to collect external information themselves than to hire a market research agency to do it for them.

Costs of data vary with sample size, monitoring frequency, and research effort, in terms of instruments, analysis, and data col-

> *NPD performance data may be available within the firm, be purchased, or be collected.*

lection methods. For example, a nationwide representative mail questionnaire is useful for getting information such as purchase frequency and general satisfaction level. In contrast, firms employ focus groups with customers or dealers or in-depth interviews to try to uncover motives behind purchase behavior. Although multiple measurements of the same indicator are more expensive in absolute terms, per piece they may be cheaper than a single isolated measurement. However, some indicators are more useful to measure regularly than others. Calculating the ROI of a new product project is most useful on an annual basis, but customer acceptance and customer satisfaction benefit from regular monitoring.

After having measured the most appropriate success indicators, it is necessary to compare the actual results with the objectives. Management should interpret deviations from the plan and take action where deemed appropriate.

> *To make a reliable trade-off in terms of cost of collecting data and making proper NPD management decisions, follow developments in information technology closely.*

31.4. THE FUTURE OF MEASURING NEW PRODUCT SUCCESS AND FAILURE

Measuring new product performance is and will continue to be very important. Several developments in information technology could simplify the task of collecting relevant performance data. For example, scanner data equipment and procedures will increasingly find applications. Market research agencies will probably serve more customers through the Internet. For a reliable trade-off of costs of collecting data and making proper NPD management decisions, these developments should be followed closely.

REFERENCES

1. Griffin, Abbie and Page, Albert L. An interim report on measuring product development success and failure. *Journal of Product Innovation Management* 10(4):291–308 (1993).
2. Griffin, Abbie and Page, Albert L. Developing products and service: how do you know how well you've done? Presentation at the 18th Annual PDMA International Conference, Boston, November 1994.
3. Hart, Susan. Dimensions of success in new product development: an exploratory investigation. *Journal of Marketing Management* 9:23–41 (1993).
4. Hart, Susan and Craig, Angie. Dimensions of success in new-product development. In: *Perspectives on Marketing Management*, Vol. 3, M.J. Baker (ed). New York: Wiley, 1993, pp. 207–243.
5. Hultink, Erik Jan and Robben, Henry S.J. Measuring new product success: the difference that time perspective makes. *Journal of Product Innovation Management*, 12(5): 392–405 (1995).

Erik Jan Hultink
Delft University of Technology

Erik Jan Hultink is Assistant Professor of Marketing with the faculty of Industrial Design Engineering. He received his M.Sc. in economics from the University of Amsterdam. His Ph.D. research concentrates on launch strategies and new product success measures. He has published on both topics in the Journal of Product Innovation Management and the Journal of High Technology Management Research.

Henry S. J. Robben
Delft University of Technology

Henry S. J. Robben is Associate Professor of Marketing with the faculty of Industrial Design Engineering. He received his B.Sc. in psychology and his M.Sc. in economic psychology from Tilburg University, and his Ph.D. in psychology from Erasmus University. He has published on business management simulations, new product success and failure, and on the field of effectiveness of marketing communications in such journals as the Journal of Product Innovation Management and the Journal of Economic Psychology.

32 METRICS: A PRACTICAL EXAMPLE
Leland R. Beaumont

32.1. INTRODUCTION

A measurements program translates corporate goals and objectives into action. It makes progress toward goals visible, allowing for clear communication, objective analysis, and fact-based decision making. Analyzing measurements information helps satisfactory results continue and identifies opportunities for improving results.

32.2. WHY MEASURE?

Before measuring the new product development (NPD) process, it is important to decide why the measurements are being made. A measurement is one way to understand how well a process is working and what a process is doing. This includes the process design; the selection, qualification, and motivation of the people who carry out the work; and the tools, materials, and information systems that are used. As the underlying process is changed, the measured result may reflect that change. Changing a measured outcome requires a change in the design or operation of the underlying process.

Measurements can also identify problems or show progress toward goals. Making measurements visible and understood by the people who contribute to the result being measured can motivate change in an organization. Measurements provide the most useful basis for decision making.

32.3. DECIDING WHAT TO MEASURE

32.3.1. Selecting the Measurements

Before deciding what to measure, ask yourself this question: If the measurement goals are achieved, will you be satisfied? This makes it clear that goals and objectives for the organization must be set before measurement planning can begin. Typical objectives might include increasing short- or long-term profit, market share, customer satisfaction, reliability or effectiveness, decreasing cycle time, defects, rework, costs, or waste. How do you decide where to start and where to focus?

What gets measured gets done, so be careful what you choose to measure—you are liable to get it!

It is now well accepted that increasing market share increases long-term profit, and increasing customer value increases market share [4,19]. How, then, do you increase customer value? Figure 32.1 illustrates an example of elements that typically contribute to customer value. To establish an effective measurements program, understand this *customer value tree* in detail for your product in your markets.

32.3.2. Creating the Customer Value Tree Structure

Use Figure 32.1 as a starting point to create a detailed customer value tree specific to your products in your markets. Decide first on the products and markets to be addressed by the tree. Then determine what your target customers value in choosing products and services. To do this, gather a team of experts, drawing from marketing, sales, service, engineering, product planning, manufacturing, finance, and end customers to add elements (attributes of customer value) to the tree that are pertinent to your business. As each element is added to the tree, ask:

- Does this element contribute to its "parent" element?
- Does the parent element require this element to be described completely?
- Is there anything else at this level that contributes to the parent element?

A completed tree may contain as many as several hundred elements.

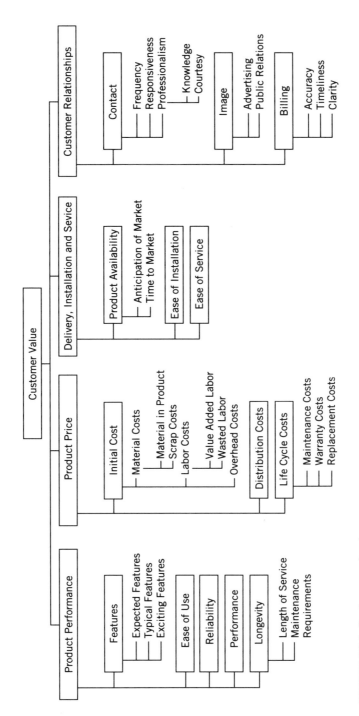

FIGURE 32.1 Customer value tree.

32.3.3. Establishing Priorities

With the detailed tree structure completed, the next step is to identify the vital few attributes that will contribute the most to the overall customer value. The overall priority of each attribute is a combination of its importance and the gap that exists between the current performance and the performance goal. It can be established using the following relationships:

$$\text{priority} = \text{importance} \times \text{performance gap}$$
$$\text{performance gap} = \text{desired level of performance}$$
$$\div \text{ current level of performance}$$

The *importance* is the degree to which a change in this attribute will influence the customers' perceived value of the product. It is often expressed as a percentage of the entire customer value. The *current level of performance* is how well your product is performing now with respect to that attribute. The *desired level of performance* reflects your business priorities and can be set by "shooting ahead of the competition" or by adopting improvement goals that each contributing unit commits to attain.

As an example, suppose that a survey has determined that customers attribute the following importance weights for your product in making purchase decisions:

- Product performance 40 percent
- Product price 30 percent
- Delivery, installation and service 20 percent
- Customer relationships 10 percent

The research also shows that your products are priced the same as your competitors, but your product performance is not as good. Your product performance is rated a 3 and your competitors' products performance is rated a 4 each on a 5-point scale. Considering this analysis, you decide to maintain parity pricing, but to set a goal of 5 for product performance.

$$\text{Product performance priority} = 40\% \times \frac{5}{3} = 67\%$$
$$\text{Product price priority} = 30\% \times 1 = 30\%$$

So in this example it is more important to work on increasing product performance than to reduce price.

Use priority estimates to identify a manageable set of attributes to form the basis for the measurements plan. The number of attributes that are manageable by the organization will depend greatly on the maturity of the information systems available to the organization. If the data are collected manually, only a handful of attributes will be manageable. If sophisticated automated data collection systems are in place, as many as several hundred attributes will soon be manageable. It is preferable to act on a few measurements than to be overwhelmed by too large a set. So start with a small set and use them as the basis for initial decision making.

32.3.4. Translating Customer Value Attributes into Metrics and Measurements

> *It is better to effect change as a result of acting on a few well-chosen metrics than to collect data and do nothing more than chart a large set of metrics.*

The customer value analysis may have identified reliability as critically important for your products, but how can it be measured? A translation is required between each customer value attribute and the actual measurement to be taken. Define this translation by consulting people who understand the products and how they are used by the customer. Measurement surrogates for "reliability" might include:

- Mean time between failures (MTBF) or mean time to repair (MTTR)
- System downtime
- Customer-reported problems, repair service call rate, or warranty repair rates
- Surveys of customers' perceptions of product reliability

> *The "goal, question, metric" approach may be helpful here. Begin by stating your goal: "Increase reliability." Then ask some more specific questions related to that goal, such as "How often does product A fail?" or "How often do customers complain about the reliability of product A?" or "What behavior from the development team will lead to increase reliability?" Then use these questions to suggest specific metrics, such as "mean time between failures for product A" or "customer-reported problems with product A" or "level of training of the development team on 'designing for high reliability' practices."*

The final choice of measurement will depend on how easily the information can be obtained, and most important, on how accurately the indicator reflects the customer value.

A good metric [8,12] must be accurate, informative, and objective. It must be easily communicated and understood by those who need to act on it. It must provide an agreed basis for decision making at the intended organizational level. It must apply to a broad range of applications to allow for useful comparisons of results. It must allow for uniform interpretation and be repeatable and independent of the observer—applied consistently by those who record and analyze it. The value it provides must be understood by the people who collect the data and the people who must act as a result of the data. It must reinforce desired behavior, reflect process performance, highlight opportunities for action, and be cost-effective to collect, analyze, and report.

32.3.5. Creating a Measurements Plan

A measurement plan must specify what is measured, the source of the data, the frequency of data collection and reporting, and the party responsible for collecting and reporting the data. A simple example might look like Table 32.1. When creating the measurement plan, you may be forced to strike a balance between those measures that are important to the customer and the business, and those that you are able to collect and act on. At each stage in your measurements program, always choose the most important measures that are actionable by the organization. A measurement is important if it is tied to strategic corporate goals and is broad in scope. A measure is actionable if it is (1) defined, (2) the data can be collected, (3) the results can be assigned to a person or organization that can take action to improve the result, (4) the improvement team

TABLE 32.1   Measurements Plan for the XYZ Product in the ABC Market[a]

Attribute	Measure	Data Source	Collection Interval	Collector
Reliability	Count of repair service incidents	Service department: count of service tickets	Weekly	Smith
	Number of designers completing "design for reliability" training	Team training records	Before beginning the "design" stage	Skinner
Performance	Top speed	Engineering lab tests	Each new release	Edison
Material costs	Component costs + procurement costs + inventory costs	Procurement department: activity-based costing system	Each new release	Maddona
Product availability	New product development cycle time	Program manager for each new product or new release	Each new release	Whitney

[a]All data are reported by Jones on the tenth calendar day of each month.

understands the data, (5) the data identify performance gaps, (6) the data support further analysis to identify the contributing causes of performance gaps.

Normalize metrics if your goal is to compare the efficiency of operations. Use the raw (unnormalized) metric if the goal is to improve the effectiveness of a result. For example, if the goal is to identify the most reliable product, use a normalized metric such as mean time between failures. If the goal is to improve customer satisfaction, use a raw metric such as the count of customer-requested service incidents.

Aggregating measures increases their importance. Decomposing measures makes them more actionable. For example, reporting an aggregate number representing all repair service incidents for all products offered by the organization increases the scope of this measure and makes it very important. Such an aggregate measure, however, is typically not actionable by any single group. To begin the analysis that will allow problems to be solved, the aggregate measure has to be broken down into components. For example, it can be reported by product type or by service call type or by geographic region or any combination of factors until the information is granular enough to allow a small team to take specific action.

32.3.6. Rounding out the Measurements Plan

> *Aggregate (roll up) measurements to summarize trends, to increase the scope of the analysis, and to identify the highest-priority opportunities. These summary metrics help answer "What is happening?" Decompose (drill down) measurements to gain detailed understanding of the causes of measurement behavior and to take action. These low-level metrics help answer why it is happening."*

The measurement example in Table 32.1 includes only "outcome" or "results" type of measurements. Although these are the most important and bear directly on the product that the customer receives, they may not be directly actionable and they may not provide the earliest opportunity to prevent problems. It is important to supplement the list with "input" and "in-process" measures.

Keeping the Program on Track

As the development program is under way, it is the responsibility of the program team to keep the schedule, feature content, and costs consistent with the current plan. One very powerful way to illustrate the plan is with a "return map" [6], as

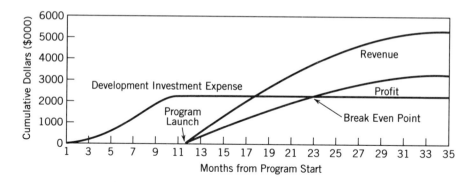

FIGURE 32.2 Program XYZ return map.

shown in Figure 32.2. This one-page summary of the program can be used initially as a plan, and again throughout the life of the program to track development expense, schedule outlook, sales revenue (including sales price and volume forecasts), profit and profit margin (including unit cost), and break-even time.

To track schedule outlook more closely, use a "slip chart" or "bull's-eye" chart like the one in Figure 32.3. A data point is added to this chart at each weekly program status meeting. It shows at a glance how the actual program is progressing with respect to the current plan and can be used to focus discussions on improving the NPD work. Similar charts can be used to track product cost outlook, sales volume outlook, feature content, and any other parameter key to achieving the plan described by the return map.

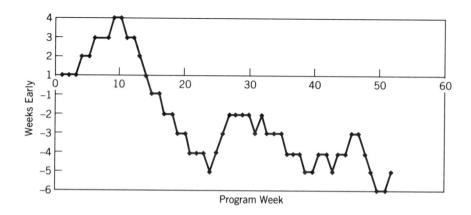

FIGURE 32.3 Program XYZ weeks early.

Learning from Existing Products

Other input or in-process measures can be derived by a drill down and analysis of the outcome measurement results from existing products. For example, suppose that a particular product required a large number of repair service calls. The analysis might uncover a particular component of the product that is failing, causing a large fraction of the repair calls. To reduce the number of service incidents, it may be most economical to subject this component to a more rigorous incoming inspection process. On a different product, it might be found that the large number of service calls are required because the service staff lack specific skills needed to install and repair the device. In this case it may be best to measure the number of staff that have completed in-depth training on this product or to plan for training the service staff on the new product.

Other Candidate Measures

To be complete, a measurements plan will contain some number of measurements directed toward direct financial contribution, employee satisfaction, growth, innovation, learning, process control, and other topics. A list is provided in Table 32.2 [5,10,11,13,16,18] to stimulate your thinking. In addition to choosing the topics of each metric, the scope of the measurement (firm-wide, department-wide, product-line-wide, product-wide, product-instance-only, subcomponent-only, or process-wide) the time frame (past results, current performance, future outlook), and the audience (executives, middle managers (e.g., project managers, engineering managers), specific work groups (or individuals, shareholders, current customers, future customers, suppliers, or others) must be decided.

Although there are too many options to be able to make a recommendation for any particular project or organization, here are a few metrics that can provide rich information and powerful results:

- NPD cycle time: time to develop new products (overall and by stage or subprocess); time to react to the market
- New product schedule, market size, and unit cost prediction accuracy

> The level of quality system maturity of an organization influences the practices that are most effective [3]. Similarly, the quality system maturity will heavily influence the metrics that are most valuable. For an organization just beginning to use process management and metrics, it is best to focus on measurements of activity, inputs, conformance, deployment, and process control. For a more mature organization, integrated measures of results with goals leading to breakthroughs in performance are appropriate.

TABLE 32.2 Possible Metrics

Financial performance
- Short-term revenue, profit, growth
- Long-term revenue, profit, growth
- Return on investment, economic value added, break-even time
- Development cost, product cost, service cost, warranty cost
- Financial risk

Customer satisfaction
- Customer satisfaction survey
- Product functionality, usability, reliability, performance, serviceability, ergonomics, and aesthetics
- Timeliness of product availability
- Product return rates, customer complaint levels
- Capture and loss of new customers, contracts and markets, customer loyalty

Employee satisfaction
- Satisfaction survey, by employee group or job classification
- Recruitment rates, turnover rates, employee complaints, and employee suggestions

Growth, innovation, and learning
- Revenue, profit, growth from new products
- Growth in market share, revenue, profitability
- Patents, copyrights, licenses, proprietary products
- Learning, teaching, innovation activity levels, and results
- Rate of progress in cycle-time reduction, defect reduction, cost reduction, process capability prediction, and customer satisfaction.

Process capability prediction
- Accuracy of cost, development schedule, manufacturing schedule, product reliability, product performance, and sales forecasts
- Variation from program to program and quarter to quarter.

Productivity and resource consumption
- Indicators of effective use of staffing, materials, energy, capital, and equipment
- Waste creation levels
- Expense/revenue ratios by function and by product
- Staffing levels, task volumes, equipment use

Process control [17]
- Manufacturing yields, scrap rates, line rejects, defects, rework levels, cycle times, order intervals, inventory levels, inventory turnover, and assets
- Design change activity rates
- Sales order cycle time, on-time delivery, and defects
- Supplier performance
- Speed of customer call answer and response
- Billing speed, accuracy, and problem resolution
- Service call response times, effectiveness
- Financial reporting accuracy, timeliness, usability
- Advertising activity levels and response rates
- Information systems availability, capacity, and response times
- Safety, absenteeism, turnover, sickness, and accident rates

- Defect removal efficiency [7]: the number of defects found in the present development stage as a fraction of all defects found in the entire product life cycle
- Percent (revenue, profit, model numbers) from new (e.g., newer than three years old) products
- Economic value added [15]
- Customer value-added ratio
- Market share
- Product service activity rates
- Break-even time for new products, derived from the return map [6]
- Lost customers

Learning from a Repeatable Process

> Select the vital few metrics that best help to deploy your corporate strategy. Always use the most important metrics that are actionable at this time.

One of the difficulties in predicting performance and improving the NPD process is that program development takes a long time to carry out. Furthermore, the NPD process seems to change each time a new program is developed. This makes it difficult to use measurements of other programs to help manage the present program.

Increased use of the ISO 9001 standard [1] and adoption of best practice make it typical for the NPD process to be both defined and repeatable. A defined and repeatable process allows measures from other programs to help manage the current program. Also, many measures can be analyzed in the process domain as well as in the product domain. For example, it may be possible to determine in which stage of the NPD process the most product defects are introduced (or not detected). To do so, assign each repair service incident, regardless of what product it occurs on, to NPD stages as follows:

1. Assign it to the stage in which the product problem was introduced (e.g., the specification stage or the design stage)
2. Assigned it again to the stage that had the last opportunity to detect the problem (e.g., the system testing stage or the customer validation stage)

Such an analysis can uncover deficiencies in the processes used in that stage, pertinent to all products that are developed using that process.

32.4. ESTABLISHING THE MEASUREMENTS PROGRAM

To make it effective, integrate the measurements plan into the organization. Because both measurement plans and organization structures are often hierarchies, a simple mapping from each aggregated measurement to the organization responsible for taking action on the results can often be made.

32.4.1. Defining Each Metric

The goal in defining each metric is to communicate to the organization both its definition and its importance. Choose a short descriptive name for the measurement. Describe the importance and intent of the measurement, mapping it back to customer value whenever possible, and describing the reasons it was chosen. Provide a clear and accurate mathematical definition of the metric, specifying what it includes and what it excludes. Finally, assign and communicate the responsibilities for defining, collecting, reporting, analyzing and acting on the data. For example:

- *Name*: Requests for Repair Service
- *Importance*: Surveys of our target customers have shown them to consider product reliability to be very important when choosing and using products like our ABC line. When asked to define product reliability, customers use phrases like "The product never breaks," "It works when I need it," "It never needs service," and "I want to install it and forget it." Studies have shown that our product reliability is inferior when compared to our competitors, especially Rockworx, the industry leader in reliability. A count of customer requests for service calls is a good translation of this customer need into something our organization can measure within our existing systems and act on for both current and future products.
- *Definition*: A raw count of customer requests for repair service of any of our products worldwide, aggregated and reported on a calendar-month basis. This includes requests for product repair or replacement, including incidents where the problem was resolved over the phone. It excludes requests for initial product installation.
- *Responsibilities*: Ed Jordan, of the Quality Office, is responsible for the definition of this metric.

32.4.2. Setting Goals for Measurement Results

To maintain current performance or to improve beyond the current performance requires that goals be set for each measured quantity. In setting goals, each of the following factors must be considered:

- Is the measurement being taken to improve performance? If so, an improvement goal must be set. Otherwise, if the measurement is taken to maintain the current level of performance, it is satisfactory to set a conservative "alarm threshold" below which no action is required.

- What is the current level of performance? If it is satisfactory, only a modest improvement goal needs to be set. If current performance is poor, set aggressive improvement goals. Consider your performance relative to the competition's performance or other relevant benchmarks when making these decisions. Keep in mind that the competition will continue to improve and a breakthrough can occur at any time.
- How difficult will it be to achieve an improvement? If large gains are possible, it makes sense to achieve them. If it is very difficult to make progress, a more modest goal can be set.
- What resources are available to achieve the goal? Setting a goal that requires more resources than have been made available to address the improvement will only frustrate the people in the organization.
- What goal are the people who must do the work willing to support? If the goal is set out of reach or the metric is not seen as relevant to the business, the people in the organization become disconnected from the goal. When this happens, no one is working to achieve the goal, and failure is assured.

Responsibility for goal setting has to be shared between the top executives responsible for overall organizational performance and the people at all levels of the organization who must do the work required to meet the goals that are set. During these negotiations (often called "catchball") it is important to understand and respect the difficulties that each group faces in meeting or not meeting a suggested target. Take care to communicate not only the goal, but why and how it was set. For example:

- *Goal for the Requests for Repair Service Metric*: Considering the importance of product reliability to our customers, and our lagging posi-

Thresholds and goals have different definitions and purposes. A threshold *establishes a performance standard and is used for process control, keeping the process working as well today as it worked yesterday. If a measurement crosses an established threshold, a specifically prescribed fix in the process operation must take place* to restore *the process operation to the acceptable level that it has maintained in the past. A* goal *is used for process improvement, making the process work better today than it has in the past. A plan for achieving the goal is carried out, with the purpose of* changing *the process operation to be able to achieve the stated goal. A comprehensive measurements plan will include both thresholds and goals.*

tion on reliability with respect to our competition, we have set an aggressive improvement goal for this metric. The managers of service, installation, manufacturing, and engineering, with the support of the people in their departments, have agreed to achieve an improvement of 20 percent over last year's average performance. The goal for this year is to receive no more than 4529 service requests in total, across the corporation. This goal has been further allocated to individual products according to the attached table. Note that some highly reliable products need only maintain the same level of performance that they achieved last year. Other less reliable products must meet aggressive improvement targets. Also note that products planned for introduction later this year will be expected to have a reliability substantially better than our current average. Staffing, expense, and capital equipment budgets include items needed by each department to carry out these improvement plans.

32.4.3. Collecting the Data

The definition of the metric starts to specify how it is collected. What remains is to clarify who collects the information, what systems they use, and who receives the data. Whenever possible, look for a place in the organization where the required information comes together. These "data funnels" occur where a large number of operations within the organization come together in a single place. For the "requests for repair service" metric, a natural data funnel is the repair service call dispatch center. They may already have an automated information system that collects this information. If not, each operator can be trained to keep a stroke count or other log of calls for repair service. To allow for further analysis, this log may need to include information such as the product model number and the nature of the repair requested.

32.4.4. Reporting The Measurement

To effect change, the measurements data must be reported to the people who have to act on it. Furthermore, they must be able to understand the data clearly, including its current level, recent trends, the goal for the measure, and whether an improvement is indicated by an increase or decrease in this measurement. Begin by deciding who must understand the results. If it is a small group, the data are easily shared. If it is a larger group, consider choosing some combination of the following methods:

- Use mail, group meetings, bulletin boards, the company newsletter, staff meeting discussions, and e-mail messages to communicate results.

- Have the people responsible for achieving the results report out at a "town meeting."
- Keep the data in a shared electronic database that interested people can interrogate at will.
- Post the results using a hyperlinked set of Internet World Wide Web pages (behind a corporate firewall that provides security for the information). Use a separate page for each measurement, maintained by those responsible for the results.

Use easily read graphs to display the data. Use a run chart showing the recent trend history, the goal, and an arrow labeled "good" pointing either up or down to show the direction of improvement. Include the definition of the metric along with names and organization of the various people who are responsible for collecting, reporting, analyzing, and acting on the information shown (see Figure 32.4 for an example). To show the current performance of a product along many dimensions, use a "radar chart" (see Figure 32.5 for an example). To assess the clarity of the presentation, ask a new or inexperienced employee to explain the chart to you. If they have any trouble, improve the presentation of the data.

32.4.5. Analyzing the Data

The data must be analyzed before they can be acted on intelligently. Begin by stratifying the data into rational subsets. Next, identify the largest performance gap, and finally, determine the causes of that gap. Here are the details.

32.4.6. Stratification

For discrete (counted) data such as a count of requests for repair service, create a Pareto chart [2]. The categories used to create the Pareto might be model number, geographic region, service call type, or some other dimension that aggregates data according to a similar characteristic. The result may look as shown in Figure 32.6. For continuous (measured) data such as mean time to repair, use a histogram [9] to identify outliners: items that are significantly (e.g., one or two standard deviations) beyond the mean. The result may look as shown in Figure 32.7.

32.4.7. Identify the Largest Performance Gap

Address the largest opportunity for improvement first. In the example in Figure 32.6, begin by investigating the repair call requests for model A. In the example in Figure 32.7, investigate the calls that have a repair time of more than 2.5

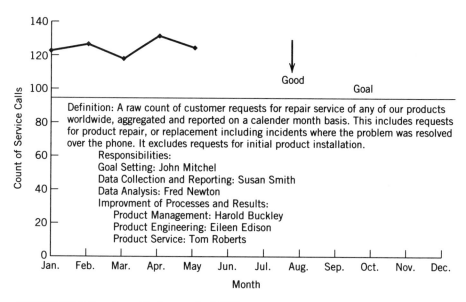

Definition: A raw count of customer requests for repair service of any of our products worldwide, aggregated and reported on a calender month basis. This includes requests for product repair, or replacement including incidents where the problem was resolved over the phone. It excludes requests for initial product installation.

Responsibilities:
Goal Setting: John Mitchel
Data Collection and Reporting: Susan Smith
Data Analysis: Fred Newton
Improvment of Processes and Results:
    Product Management: Harold Buckley
    Product Engineering: Eileen Edison
    Product Service: Tom Roberts

FIGURE 32.4 Service calls for product XYZ.

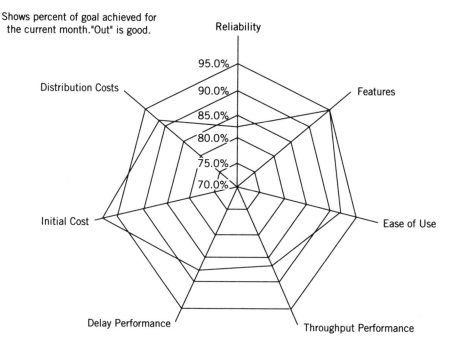

FIGURE 32.5 Product XYZ summary.

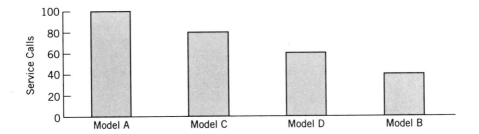

FIGURE 32.6 Pareto chart of service calls.

hours. At this stage it is best to turn the analysis over to a team who is expert in the operation of model A. This team of subject matter experts may need a facilitator skilled in the use of cause–effect diagrams to conduct an efficient and complete analysis.

32.4.8. Enumerate the causes for the Performance Gap

Use a fishbone (also called cause–effect diagram [14] or Ishikawa diagram) to enumerate the suspected causes of the performance gap. Refer to the example shown in Figure 32.8. Begin by stating the performance gap to be analyzed (model A had 100 service calls) at the head of the fish. Then list major causes contributing to the repair requests, each on a major "bone." The major causes in this example are "Other," "Misuse," "Compatibility Problems," and "Equipment Failure." For each of these major causes, add bones showing their contributing causes. For example, both hardware failure and software failure

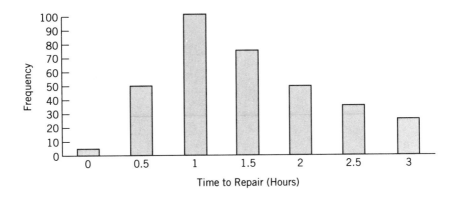

FIGURE 32.7 Histogram of repair time.

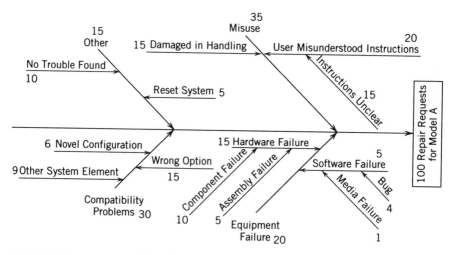

FIGURE 32.8 Causes contributing to 100 repair requests for model A.

contributed to equipment failure. Continue the analysis to the limit of the team's understanding. Then "weight the bones" by allocating the full gap (100 repair requests) across all the bones. In this example 35 requests were due to "misuse," and of those, 20 were due to the user misunderstanding instructions.

The team now chooses a few causes to prevent. Choose causes that have high weights or are easy to remedy. In this example the team has chosen to prevent unclear instructions (because of its high weight and relative ease of remedy) and component failures (because eight of the ten were due to a single component that has recently been eliminated from similar product designs).

32.4.9. Acting on the Measurement

Having identified the few causes that represent the best opportunity for improvement, the team identifies remedies that will prevent their occurrence in the future.

> *The team that is best able to collect and report the data may be different from the team that is best able to analyze the data and take action to improve based on that analysis. It is usually best to assign improvement responsibilities to those who carry out the process.*

Continuing with the example, to remedy the unclear instructions, the improvement team has decided to interview 10 of the 15 users who misread the instructions. Considering their findings, they will rewrite the unclear sections of the instructions and distribute a revised version of the instruction manual. The team has agreed to complete all of this work in the next six weeks. To remedy the component failure, the design will be changed to use a more reliable alternative part. The team has agreed to have the new part in production four weeks from today.

32.4.10. Avoiding the Trouble Spots

Designing and deploying a measurements program is a difficult task. You can expect difficulties at each stage. Here are some tips that may make the job easier.

> *Analysis precedes action. Analysis without action is wasteful because no change occurs and no result is accomplished. Action without analysis (often called tampering) is wasteful because the action is unlikely to be responsive to the underlying cause of the problem.*

Improve the Process: the Results Will Follow

Be clear that the goal is to achieve improved processes that result in better value to the customer. The measurements are only a tool, and no measurement is without its harmful side effects. Deal quickly and decisively with any attempt to improve the measured result without improving the underlying processes or adding value. For example, efforts to make it more difficult for customers to report problems may show an improvement in this reliability measurement. Such deliberate efforts are nothing short of sabotage and should be dealt with as such. Clarify or redefine any measurements that are having significant adverse effects.

Data and Reporting Integrity

Because the data will be used as the basis for decision making, insist on honest and accurate data collection and reporting. At the same time, allow the team to estimate information they do not yet know. For example, in allocating weights on a fishbone diagram, the team may have to rely on its collective judgment rather than on hard data. Encourage this when it speeds progress. Remind the teams that they should clearly identify any estimates they have made.

Motivating Positive Behavior

Being clear about what gets measured sends a strong signal throughout the organization defining what executive management views as important. At the same time, basing decision on measurements data shifts the center of power and control in the organization. Measurements empower people at all levels in the organization by giving them the information they need to make decisions based on facts. Imagine how the director of service operations might *really* feel about the goal to reduce service calls. What effect will a smaller service organization have on his or her career goals? How does each person react when measurements are reported that highlight problems in their area of responsibility? Are they truly pleased to see problems identified and solved, or are they defensive about the performance of their work group?

> ***Problems must be identified before they can be solved. Encourage reporting the defects; don't shoot the messenger, especially when the message contains bad news.***

To overcome these problems, first the executives, then the middle managers, and finally everyone must lead a cultural change in both word and action. They must hold steadfastly to the goal of improved customer value and long-term business results. They must encourage reports of problems, especially when opportunities for improvement are clearly identified. They must establish meaningful incentives based on measurement goals that are sufficient to overcome local discomfort with the changes taking place. The organization must learn over months and years from its experience in managing the business by the metrics.

Trial New Metrics

Before basing critical decisions on a newly defined metric, consider using it first during a trial period. This trial period provides an opportunity to examine several alternative definitions of the metric and determine which definition gives the most useful information. The stability of the metric from one measurement period to the next can be examined. A history of the metric's values can be obtained to provide a baseline reference for analyzing data in the future. Finally, people who may be skeptical about the usefulness of the metric will have an opportunity to observe its behavior before it is used to run the business. This is analogous to the demonstration sports included in each running of the Olympic games.

Correlate Measurements Results with Goals Achievement

Measurements at best can only be surrogates for the attainment of the true goals of the organization. To evaluate the effectiveness of the measurements program, examine the correlation between the measurements results and the goal attainment. As the reliability measurements improve, does a requisite improvement in customer satisfaction, market share, profitability, and growth occur? If they do, then you have an excellent and effective measurements program. If they do not, the current measurement set may not be an accurate surrogate for the goals you set out to achieve. Investigate to determine where the analysis has broken down. Revise the measurements plan to better reflect the goals.

34.2.11. Reviewing, Evaluating, and Improving the Measurements program

As the organization's quality system and information systems mature, the organization will be able to take action on increasingly important metrics. The annual planning cycle is a good time to revisit the overall measurements plan and to move to a more important set of measures. At that time the measurements set can be aligned with the latest corporate goals. The nature of the current performance gaps can be reassessed. Measures originally introduced to identify process improvements can now be used to sustain process control. Measures that will allow for still greater process improvements can be introduced. Opportunities to transform the NPD process may be identified by looking across measurements that identify chronic and systematic process problems. Also, the resources needed to carry out the measurements plan, including implementing improvements identified by analyzing the measurements, can be planned for at this time.

32.5. SUMMARY

A complete measurements program consists of an annual planning cycle and a more frequent periodic measurements information review cycle, including the major tasks shown here:

- Clarify business goals and objectives.
- Establish priorities.
- Translate objectives into metrics.
- Create and communicate the measurements plan.
- Set improvement goals.
- Collect measurements data.
- Report measurements results.
- Analyze measurements information.
- Identify improvement opportunities.
- Carry out improvement actions.
- Review and improve the measurements program.

REFERENCES

1. Beaumont, Leland R. *ISO 9001: The Standard Interpretation.* Middletown NJ: ISO Easy, January 1995.
2. Burr, John T. The tools of quality, Part VI: Pareto charts. *Quality Progress*, pp. 59–62 (November 1990).
3. Ernst & Young. *International Quality Study, Best Practices Report.* Milwaukee, WI: American Society for Quality Control, 1994.

4. Gale, Bradley T. *Managing Customer Value, Creating Quality and Service That Customers Can See.* New York: Free Press, 1994.

5. Griffin, Abbie, Developing products and services: how do you known how well you've done? Presentation at the 2nd Annual Program on Improving the New Product Development Process: Lessons from Experts, Houston, TX, 1995.

6. House, Charles H. and Price, Raymond L. The return map: tracking product teams. *Harvard Business Review* (January–February 1991).

7. Jones, Capers. *Applied Software Measurement, Assuring Productivity and Quality.* New York: McGraw-Hill, 1991.

8. Juran, Joseph M. *Juran on Planning for Quality.* New York: Free Press, 1988.

9. Juran Institute. The tools of quality, Part IV: Histograms. *Quality Progress,* pp. 75–78 (September 1990).

10. Kaplan, Robert S., and Norton, David P. The balanced scorecard: measures that drive performance. *Harvard Business Review* (January–February 1992).

11. Kaplan, Robert S. and Norton, David P. Putting the balanced scorecard to work. *Harvard Business Review* (September–October 1993).

12. Möller, K. H. and Paulish, D. J. *Software Metrics: A Practitioner's Guide to Improved Product Development.* Piscataway, NJ: IEEE Press, 1993.

13. Roseanu, Milton D. *International Benchmarking Clearinghouse Benchmarking Consortium Study, New Product Development Final Report.* Houston, TX. American Productivity and Quality Center, 1995.

14. Sarazen, J. Stephen. The tools of quality, Part II: Cause-and-effect diagrams. *Quality Progress,* pp. 59ff (July 1990).

15. Tully, Shawn. The real key to creating wealth. *Fortune,* September 20, 1993, pp. 38–50.

16. U.S. Department of Commerce, Technology Administration, National Institute of Standards and Technology. Malcolm Baldrige National Quality Award, 1995 Award Criteria.

17. Utah State University. Shingo Prize for Excellence in Manufacturing, 1995–1996 Application Guidelines. Logan, UT: College of Business, Utah State University, 1995.

18. Walrad, C. and Moses, E. Measurement: the key to application development quality. *IBM System Journal* 32(3):445–460 (1993).

19. Whiteley, Richard C. *The Customer Driven Company: Moving from Talk to Action.* Reading, MA: Addison-Wesley, 1991.

Leland R. Beaumont
AT&T Bell Laboratories

Author of the book ISO 9001, The Standard Interpretation, *he has developed new data communications products at AT&T Bell Laboratories since 1973. Currently he is Head of product realization process improvement at AT&T Paradyne and is responsible for defining, measuring, and improving their New Product Development process. He holds a Bachelor of Science Degree in Electrical Engineering from Lehigh University and Master of Science Degree in Electrical Engineering from Purdue University. He is a member of the American Society for Quality Control and the Institute of Electrical and Electronics Engineers. He lives with his wife and two children in Middletown, NJ.*

PART FIVE

PDMA'S BEST PRACTICES RESEARCH

REVIEWING CURRENT PRACTICES IN INNOVATION MANAGEMENT AND A SUMMARY OF SELECTED BEST PRACTICES

33

Thomas P. Hustad

33.1. INTRODUCTION

Innovation is one of the most complex of all business practices. For success it requires robust relationships inside the firm and between the firm and its customers and suppliers. Businesses grow and improve their performance by enhancing their productivity (increasing market share and enhancing efficiency), expanding their market coverage (extending distribution, serving new segments or markets with current products and extending existing product lines), and innovating (adding new products to their business portfolios). As firms try to do more with fewer resources, the first two sets of initiatives have become familiar business strategies.

The need for innovation becomes evident whenever a firm's performance goals exceed the values that can be supported by its existing businesses. Without this recognition it is not particularly surprising that productivity and expansion programs dominate the thinking of many managers, for they frequently represent tangible changes. Innovation, on the other hand, requires adding something new. It presents tough management challenges, since everything is based on unknown outcomes. Do we know our customer well enough? Can we build the technical competencies we require? How will the customer react? Is the need real? Can we compete? Can we sustain production? What about costs? Is there profit here? Will our business be incremental to the company or will it cannibalize existing products? When will competition enter the market? What about the cost of not pursuing the opportunity?

Increasingly, we must strive to create customer delight, and this sometimes involves knowing our customers' needs better than they know them themselves. Seldom can a customer describe a new product for us. We have to understand their problems and develop effective solutions.

We now have an especially rich opportunity to study how various companies approach the challenges of effective innovation management. A series of current best practices has emerged, and these practices have been identified in a number of research studies, including two major projects sponsored by the Product Development and Management Association and led, respectively, by Albert Page and Abbie Griffin. These data also allow us to establish a number of interesting benchmarks to gauge current practices.

Innovation is a handmaiden to success, as can be observed in Figure 33.1. Does new product success lead to industry leadership, or do only leaders have the resources to invest in the development of new products? These data, taken from PDMA's 1990 study, do not help us untangle the cause from the effect, yet it is difficult to fathom how a firm could lead an industry if it did not offer the products that helped define the basis for competitive success. Which comes first matters not, for sustained leadership must be aligned with innovation. The greater risk is not in developing new products, but in failing to innovate at a pace that matches changing customer needs.

How great is the risk of introducing new products? Actually, the level of new product failure is often overestimated, sometimes greatly so. The popular

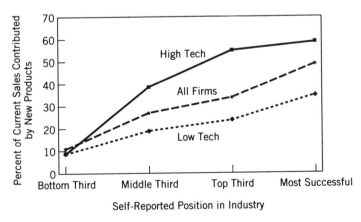

FIGURE 33.1 Percentage of current sales contributed by new products developed in the last five years by the company's self-reported rank in its industry.

press delights in telling us that most new products fail. They don't, at least not when they come from companies that take their new product work seriously. Companies are discovering that they have more control over the failure level than they realize. If the cost of a failure is high, management can tighten control. Such would be the case for a new, large, commercial jet airliner. If large commercial airlines felt that most new airplanes failed, they would refuse to buy. Even cne crash would be a severe deterrent to early commercial success. On the other hand, when development costs are low and failure has little effect on sales of other products made by the company, the need for tight control is lessened. Herein lies a subtle message. While we can learn certain best practices from other companies, we often need to tune and customize those lessons to meet the requirements of our own situation.

For instance, project abandonment and failure rates are displayed in Figure 33.2 for both the 1990 and 1995 PDMA studies. Failure is reserved for commercial failure—the failure of a product that has been launched into the market to meet its objectives. Project abandonment reflects the decision to cease development and is a desirable outcome for projects that are unlikely to succeed in the marketplace. These data show that on average about three of every four products introduced into the market were deemed a success by management, a far cry from the myth we often hear. In fact, if 80% of new products really failed, it might be impossible to show an economic return from innovation. Clearly, an informed management can obtain superior results managing new products, and presumptions about high failure rates should not be a barrier to learning critical skills. Our learning falls into four categories: process, organization, tools, and performance. We explore each in turn.

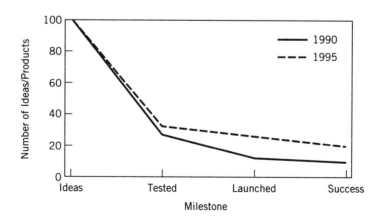

FIGURE 33.2 New product idea mortality curve for PDMA member firms in 1990 and 1995.

33.2. PROCESS

Organizations report many different approaches to new product development. Typically, one of the first steps that a company undertakes once it decides to increase the emphasis placed on new products is to examine its current practices. Sometimes this can reveal numerous opportunities for improvements, since duplication of tasks is quite common in complex, cross-functional processes such as new product development. The larger the company, the more important it becomes to have a defined process that is broadly understood by employees. Without documentation of a process, there is little opportunity for performance improvement and organizational learning. Furthermore, people have a harder time understanding their roles and contributions, making the process more abstract and mysterious than it should appear. Yet, recent PDMA data suggest that nearly 20% of reporting companies either have no formal process or one that is only informally understood (but not documented) within the company. Lack of process hampers involvement and participation and contributes to the poor understanding of effective new product development practices found in some companies. Figure 33.3 shows the frequency with which various forms of stage-gate processes are employed by reporting companies. Nearly three-fourths of responding companies report reliance on some variation of stage-gate systems: Traditional stage-gate processes implemented by a cross-functional team represent nearly 40% of these mentions; the addition of an assigned "process-owning" facilitator and advanced implementations allowing for overlapping review gates divide the remaining 60%. Although it is too early to detect a trend, more complex projects may be better served by the latter two variations.

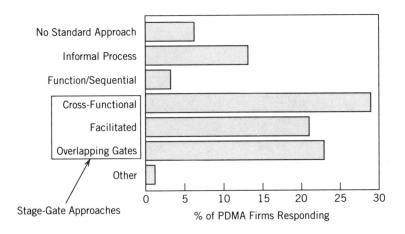

FIGURE 33.3 Nature of product development process reported by PDMA member firms, 1995.

Companies with formal product development processes report that, on average, they have been following them for four to five years. Since many of the working relationships are complex, the process places a heavy burden on cross-functional communication and dialogue with the customer. Success is not immediate, and there are many opportunities to refine the process with experience. Within formal processes are a number of tasks that must be performed. These tasks do not correspond to gates in a stage-gate system, since the gate typically involves a number of activities pertaining to a certain stage of the development process. Figure 33.4 indicates the frequencies of incorporation of general tasks in formally defined processes (firms with informal or no defined process are not included in this summary). Since some tasks may be omitted in certain projects, this figure also shows the percentage of projects that complete each listed task. Clearly, there is lots of variation across projects. The tasks themselves are described in Table 33.1. This table also includes the average number of weeks for each task reported by responding PDMA firms.

33.3. ORGANIZATION

As companies seek to improve new product performance, they have experimented with organization more than any other variable. Whereas new products were frequently controlled by a single function, there are many signs that cross-functional teams are becoming a very popular choice. When new products are recognized as special projects, the likelihood of success increases. That is not to say that each project requires a dedicated team, for not all projects are equally complex or strategically important. Benchmarking data can be very useful during times of change, when new approaches are being tried.

Figure 33.5 displays a series of approaches to new product organization, ranging from the traditional options of functional approach to new product groups. First, notice the wide variety in approaches reported by single companies. Organizations are experimenting and adopting approaches to the nature of their projects. Yet, when asked to note the dominant organizational approach, companies do not hesitate to list a most frequent choice. Perhaps the use of process owners is the newest change to emerge. New product skills become resident in the hands of professionals who install them in teams as demanded by the nature of the work. When new products are controlled by a particular function, engineering, R&D, and marketing are the dominant choices. The choice typically depends on the nature of the industry.

Leadership of new product projects is still overwhelmingly provided by project managers and champions. Process owners and leaderless teams are used

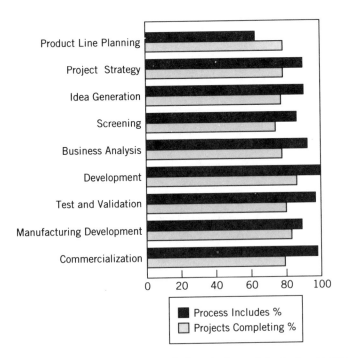

FIGURE 33.4 Percentage of processes that include certain tasks as reported by PDMA member firms and the percentage of projects that incorporate these tasks.

much less frequently. These results are displayed in Figure 33.6. The selection of team leaders is handled by management in most cases, as shown in Figure 33.7. In a number of firms, leadership is provided by functional experts who rotate at appropriate phases of the project. Nearly 10 percent of firms have experimented with team- and peer-selected leaders.

As the use of formally assigned teams becomes less novel, organizations have focused their use on new-to-the-world and new-to-the-firm projects, followed by major revisions to existing products (Figure 33.8). Teams are employed less frequently for repositioning efforts and minor improvements. It is possible that the use of teams will decline in time for such projects, since their cost may not be justifiable compared to the nature of these tasks.

Table 33.2 also shows the range of financial and nonfinancial incentives being used in responding companies. Clearly, the use of nonfinancial incentives dwarfs the use of financial ones. Although not yet among the most frequent mentions, nonfinancial incentives selected by the team members themselves may be an area to watch. Whenever financial compensation is used, firms distinguish between team leaders and team members as shown in Figure 33.9. Team leaders

TABLE 33.1   Specific Tasks Commonly Incorporated in Formally Defined Product Development Processes

Task	Scope	Average Number of Weeks Reported
Product line planning	Analyze the firm's current portfolio vis-à-vis the competitive arena	7
Project strategy development	Delineate the target market, determine market need, attractiveness	8
Idea/concept generation	Identify opportunities and initial generation of possible solutions	8
Idea screening	Sort and rank solutions, eliminate unsuitable and unattractive options	6
Business analysis	Evaluate the concept financially, write business case, prepare protocol/development contract	7
Development	Convert concept into a working product	32
Test and validation	Product use, field, market, and regulatory testing with customers	21
Manufacturing development	Developing and piloting the manufacturing processes	19
Commercialization	Launching the new product or service into full-scale production and sales	18

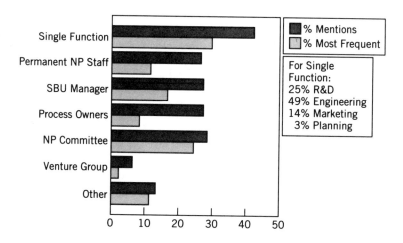

FIGURE 33.5 New product organizations reported by PDMA member firms.

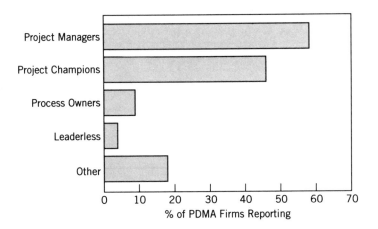

FIGURE 33.6 Who leads NPD projects?

are much more likely to participate in profit-sharing arrangements than are team members. This is the only sharp distinction between leader and member incentives reported in the data.

33.4. TOOLS

There has been considerable growth in the variety and power of tools available for support of new product development projects. The survey asked about the

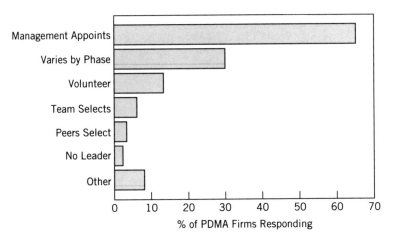

FIGURE 33.7 How is the team leader selected?

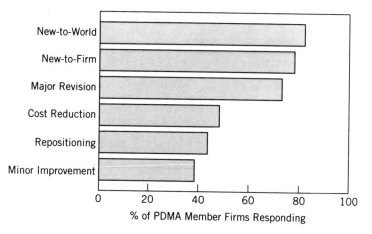

FIGURE 33.8 Percentage of projects using multifunctional teams by nature of project.

TABLE 33.2 Percent of PDMA Member Firms Using Various Incentives for Team Leaders and Team Members

Type of Incentive	Percentage of Companies Using
Financial compensation	
Project-based profit sharing	4
Project-based stock or stock options	2
Other financial rewards	25
Nonfinancial compensation	
Compensation time	15
Recognition in organization newsletters	54
Recognition at award dinners	31
Plaques, pins, project photographs	43
Project completion celebration lunches, dinners	54
Nonfinancial rewards chosen by the team (e.g., trips, family dinners)	13
Other nonfinancial awards	6

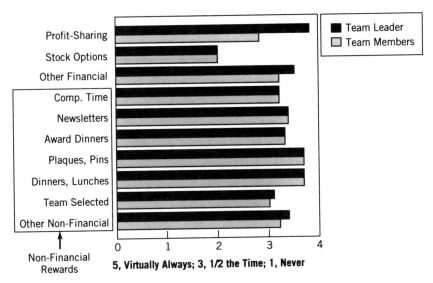

FIGURE 33.9 Frequency of incentive use for team leaders and members.

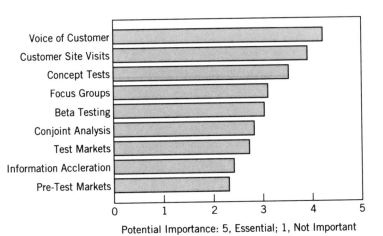

FIGURE 33.10 Potential importance of marketing research techniques.

use and value of three sets of tools: marketing research, engineering design, and organizational development. In Figure 33.10, five marketing research techniques receive average ratings of "important" or higher: voice of the customer, customer site visits, concept tests, focus groups, and beta testing. The first four tend to involve predevelopment dialogue with customers, as innovators strive to understand customers' problems and requirements. Each of these methods is relatively straightforward in implementation and the results can lead to rich discussions of possibilities. Beta testing represents limited-use testing, to ascertain customers reactions to actual products. Perhaps broader field testing received lower evaluations, as did more sophisticated procedures.

Only the voice of the customer, customer site visits, and concept tests were employed on at least one-half of projects, on average. Yet this represents significant increases in the use of these techniques over the past ten years, since a number of earlier research articles reported that concept tests and formal site visits rarely were conducted (see Figure 33.11).

Among the engineering tools, only virtual reality/virtual design fails to receive an average assessment of "important." Highest potential importance goes to rapid prototyping, concurrent engineering, and design for manufacturing and assembly, followed by the specific tools of computer-aided design and computer-aided engineering. Figure 33.12 summarizes these results. Obviously, the engineering tools have developed stronger appeal for respondents than the marketing tools, overall. On the other hand, only computer-aided design, concurrent engineering, and design for manufacturing and assembly appear to be used in at least

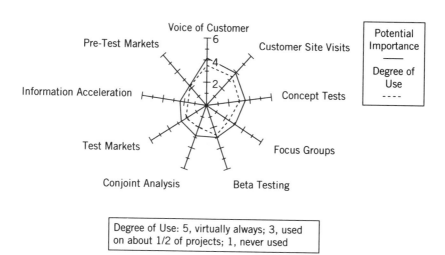

FIGURE 33.11 Potential importance of marketing research techniques contrasted with frequency of use.

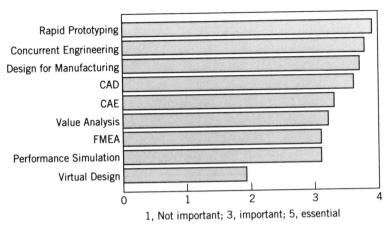

FIGURE 33.12 Potential importance of engineering design tools.

one-half of projects, on average (Figure 33.13). Virtual reality technology is not yet used on a regular basis. Perhaps in the future, the uses of virtual reality will be even more important in early dialogue with customers, since these techniques may become quite useful in communicating ideas and simulating product use prior to development.

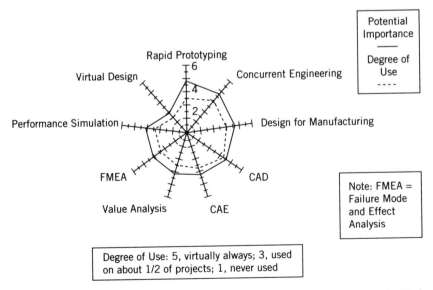

FIGURE 33.13 Potential importance of engineering design tools contrasted with frequency of use.

As with engineering tools, organized tools generally received high evaluations for potential importance (Figure 33.14). Only leaderless teams received low marks. The highest ratings are found for project scheduling tools and the development of champions, followed by team-building exercises and the training of process owners. Reported average frequency of use measures highlighted the use of project scheduling techniques in nearly 75 percent of projects, while process owners, champions, and matrix organizations reflected the high level of projectization being practiced in many firms today (Figure 33.15). The latter three tools were associated with at least half of projects overall. Perhaps surprising were the reported low use of QFD and co-location, given the frequency of discussion of these approaches. Clearly, co-location can be both inconvenient and expensive, no doubt greatly restricting use. Companies are sometimes experimenting to find the critical phases of projects where face-to-face contact with other team members has the greatest impact on project success.

Overall, the top five tools in average potential importance are the following:

- Voice of the customer (4.2)
- Customer site visits (3.9)
- Rapid prototyping (3.9)
- Project scheduling tools (3.9)
- Product champions (3.9)

While this is an arbitrary cutoff, it reflects balance among the three areas in the designation of "very important" tools. This balance is important, reflecting a

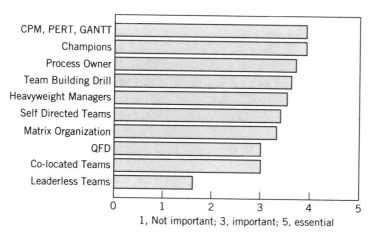

FIGURE 33.14 Potential importance of organizational approaches.

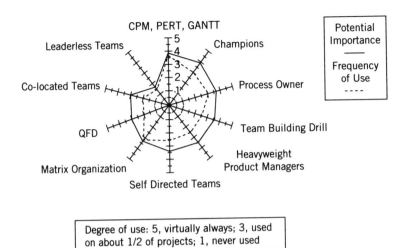

FIGURE 33.15 Potential importance of organizational approaches contrasted with frequency of use.

broad vision for the complexity of modern new product development practices, including customer focus, leadership, design, and effective project control.

On the other hand, the five tools scoring highest in frequency of use are the following:

- Project scheduling tools (3.7)
- Voice of the customer (3.6)
- Customer site visits (3.5)
- Computer-aided design (3.4)
- Matrix organizations (3.2)

These scores signify that the tools are used in between 75 percent (3.0) and virtually all (4.0) projects. They are the core of our toolkit. Again, we see high importance on market focus, project control, and productivity. Matrix organization reflects the complexity of approaching a level of projectization. It is an (unloved) necessity.

33.5. PERFORMANCE

Firms are about evenly divided between those that target a specific revenue goal for new products and those that do not. Those that have a target expect an average of 27 percent of sales to come from products commercialized within four years. Even those firms without a specific target realize the importance of new products, scoring an average of 7.7 on a 9-point scale in response to the following statement: "Our new product program is important to my organization's sales and profits." On the other hand, the average dropped to 5.6 for: "Overall, our new product program is a success." Clearly, we are working hard to improve our performance in an area of great strategic importance.

How is success measured? Criteria actually used by companies are many, but they can be divided into three categories: measures of customer acceptance, financial performance, and technical performance. Respondents were asked to allocate 100 possible points across these three categories five times, each time corresponding to a different type of new product. Average results are presented in Figure 33.16. Reliance on financial criteria increase markedly for incremental improvements and product repositioning. Customer acceptance remains high throughout, with somewhat lessened requirements for incremental improvements, while technical performance receives less support than does either other category.

How many products succeed? Of course, this question can be answered in many ways. Table 33.3 reports three possibilities. First, did the product meet the organization's definition of success? On average, 55.9 percent of new products launched did. A somewhat smaller number were successful strictly in terms of profitability. Yet given that they were launched, a resounding 74 percent remained on the market, making an overall contribution to the performance of the firm. These data are reviewed in Table 33.3.

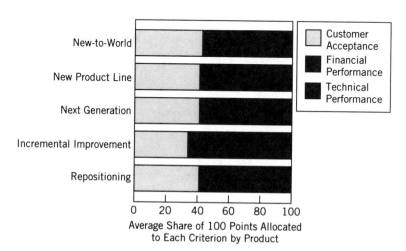

FIGURE 33.16 Relative importance of measures of success by level of innovativeness.

TABLE 33.3 New Product Success Rates

Criterion	Success Percentage
Based on your organization's definition of a successful new product, about what percentage of all the new products introduced into the market during the past five years were successful?	55.9
What percentage would you estimate were successful in terms of their profitability to the organization?	51.7
What percentage of the products that your organization commercialized during the past five years would you estimate are still on the market?	74.1

Table 33.4 shows the percentage of sales and profits contributed by new products during the preceding five years. Expectations for the future are sharply higher. Whether or not management will be able to deliver these results remains to be seen, but the escalation reflects the importance of innovation as a driver of corporate growth and performance. Table 33.5 shows average completion times for various types of new products. The range from modest repositioning to new-to-the-world products is substantial, with the latter taking nearly six times as long to prepare for market launch.

Figure 33.17 displays further information about development times now relative to typical performance five years ago. Note that while most firms report shorter development times, this is not universal. Not surprisingly, the greatest push for speed comes with incremental improvements and next-generation and major revision projects. These projects are the ones where user needs are most familiar to companies, since existing products and patterns of use can be studied

TABLE 33.4 Estimate of the Importance of New Product

Criterion	Percentage of New Product Sales to Total Sales Preceding Five Years	Percentage of New Product Sales to Total Sales Next Five Years
New product sales as a percentage of total sales	27.9	37.3
New product profits as a percentage of total sales	25.2	39.1

**TABLE 33.5   Average Reported Length of Product
Development Process**

Type of New Product	Average Development Time (months)
New-to-the-world	42
New product lines	29
Major revisions and next-generation products	18
Minor revisions/incremental improvements	8

in detail. Achieving speed without sacrificing quality becomes progressively difficult as the level of innovativeness increases.

The study also allows us to contrast the rates of new product introductions with the reported levels of expenditures (Figure 33.18). These results are grouped by product type. Consistent with levels of risk and uncertainty, spending on new-to-the-world products greatly exceeds the proportionate share of introductions When successful, these products can yield higher margins for longer periods of time. New product lines demonstrate this tendency as well, whenever firms select an attractive opportunity for development. The relationship is reversed, however, for incremental improvements, where success may be more a function of being able to create improvements (the process) repeatedly than with any single improvement itself.

Looking ahead five years, respondents forecast that more of their activity will, on average, be devoted to major innovations. These are tough challenges, and management will surely have to work to hone its skills if these results are to

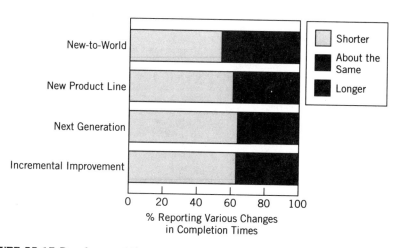

FIGURE 33.17 Development times now versus five years ago.

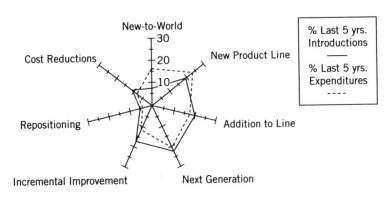

FIGURE 33.18 Comparison of last five years introductions by innovation level with allocation of expenditures.

be attained. Overall, Figure 33.19 reflects more emphasis on new products of all sorts. A more detailed look at the data will be required to see if some companies are becoming more ambitious (reducing work on modest projects, expanding it on more innovative programs) and other firms more conservative (downplaying really new products in favor of safer alternatives).

33.6. SUMMARY

These data show that product development practices are in a state of evolution. Managements are experimenting, trying new tools and approaches to improve

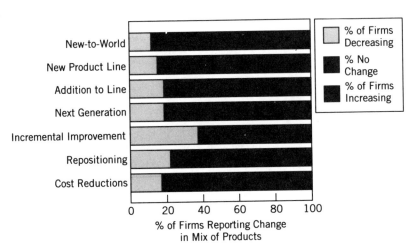

FIGURE 33.19 Projected changes in mix of new products in the next five years.

innovation performance. The tasks are becoming more challenging, with heightened corporate goals and expectations, probably in the face of resource constraints. Only time will tell if these forecasts will be realized. Yet several elements are clear. The great majority of firms employ stage-gate or related processes. They have learned the importance of developing a process, learning to use it effectively, and helping employees to understand their roles. The use of teams has increased, but organizations are becoming aware that teams are not a universal answer to all new product situations. We have not really decided how to develop incentives for new product work. While some companies are using financial incentives, many more believe that recognition and other nonmonetary rewards are sufficient. Although we are aware of many tools and are indeed involving the customer in our work (particularly the fuzzy front end) more than ever before, we remain disappointed that some tools do not answer more of our needs.

Looking beyond the snapshots, it is possible to begin to construct a list of important factors for success in new products. This list is not complete. The role of various items will change across industries. Yet some of these points touch on best practices as we know them today. A graphical summary of a process is shown in Figure 33.20.

1. Understand and document your process. Allow for customization by project. Prepare to run tasks in parallel, but try to define groups of tasks that represent critical decision points. If a decision is delayed, don't delay the team. Let it continue. But impress on the team the risk of continuing, especially if some of the tasks are delayed.

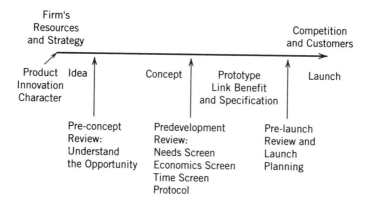

FIGURE 33.20 Evaluation continuum.

2. Open robust dialogue with your customers. Understand their problems. Envision the future scenarios in which they will operate. These will feed your pool of ideas. Build concepts and test them with your customers. Your ideas become familiar to you faster than they become familiar to your customers. They can help you translate their needs into your programs. Experiment with simulations. Graphics tools now product photo-like images of products that don't exist. Rapid prototyping can prepare tangible objects. Both of these tools provide customers with preproduct information that can help them make you more efficient in the development work ahead. Continue your testing once you have a product. Alpha tests, beta tests, and gamma tests can be made part of a systematic testing program. For many products, you will have to develop a convincing case that your new product creates an economic advantage for your end user. There is no time like these testing phases to gather these data and obtain customer endorsements.

3. Avoid the trap of being *somewhat* innovative. When you make an improved product you scale the costs to the earning potential. The same holds true for a new-to-the world product, but both expenses and earnings may be set at a higher level. In the middle, costs can be high for development, but customer delight may be absent. A product that fails to excite the customer but has been developed with the budget of a breakthrough leads to turnover in the new product department. Build the right product—for product superiority and uniqueness remain the most important predictors of new product success.

4. Use teams wisely. In ambitious projects they can be great. Members communicate and boost each other's enthusiasm, often at critical times. They trust and share. Face-to-face contact breeds respect, which is often absent when professionals seldom meet those from other functional departments. Yet some of the power of teams can be achieved in other ways, given improvement in communication. Some organizations report that teams increase development time. They can do so, particularly when the organization has not yet learned how to couple the team to an effective process. Pick your projects well and make certain that the lessons of teams shape your approach to next-generation projects.

5. Define your new products strategy—right down to the business and project levels. Organizations are far more successful in defining functional goals than project goals, and teams can lose valuable time when they fail to really understand their assignment. Try to focus on exploring projects that fit with company skills. If a new product requires success with an unfamiliar technology, don't start the product development team running until the technology becomes more certain. When possible, examine

trends in your markets and align your projects with the trends that are growing and increasing in a manner that support customers' interest in your product. When you grow by capturing new business, your path can be easier then when you have to displace an entrenched competitor. Be "on trend": It can help cover some imprecision in your demand forecast.

When you do these things, you will find that your team understands its role, gets excited by its insight into customers' needs, and sees how individual contributions can be combined into something really unique. This should lead to meaningful buy-in and participation. Momentum will follow. Capture learning of effective steps for the organization and consider installing it in the person of a process owner. Celebrate project milestones and successes frequently—don't wait for the end. If the project trajectory is not positive, you need a team strong enough to fire a nonperforming member, even the leader. Alternatively, if the people are performing, the team needs to assess the quality of the opportunity and make a timely and candid recommendation to the firm.

6. Recall that the project isn't complete until the goals are realized. Don't disband the team too soon, for they may be the only ones who know how to keep the project going in the face of unanticipated adversity.

If you don't have a process, your immediate challenge is to establish one with multiple stages. Include written evaluation criteria that you will use to judge progress and success. Make sure that the process is communicated, and that your organization understands it. Use it to define potential growth opportunities, develop insights into consumer needs and problems, and achieve shared focus on these options leading to commitment and participation. These are not easy steps, but they define a path to incredible excitement and professional satisfaction for all who become involved.

Innovation has been practiced since the start of commercial business. Yet the challenges facing innovation professionals are greater now than ever before. Increasingly, our experiences will translate into effective best practices. Right now we are engaged in a series of challenging experiments. Yet, unquestionably, we have begun to learn some very important lessons that are helping to reshape many of our organizations and work practices.

ACKNOWLEDGMENTS

This chapter relies on data gathered by Albert Page and Abbie Griffin, principal investigators for two best practices studies conducted by the Product Development and Management Association in 1990 and 1995, respectively. It is not our task here to discuss the research methodology employed in those studies. For that, the interested reader is referred to past and future articles in the *Journal of Product Innovation Management*. For the 1995 study, only data obtained from PDMA member firms is reported. In addition, I thank the many authors from *JPIM* who have contributed to my thinking over the years. These ideas have been presented to a variety of executive audiences that have help hone the ideas contained in this chapter. I wish to dedicate this chapter to C. Merle Crawford, who has been an inspirational leader in the new products field throughout his career. I can no longer separate my ideas from those he has given me.

Thomas P. Hustad
Indiana University School of Business

Hustad has served PDMA since its inception, notably as President in 1981, Secretary-Treasurer for many years, and the founder and editor of its Journal of Product Innovation Management. *He was named a Crawford Fellow and Kosin Professor in 1993. He has chaired Indiana University's MBA program, won a first-place dissertation award from the AMA, held an unsolicited Fulbright Award, and has frequently consulted to major corporations. He received the first Eli Lilly Teaching Excellence Award.* Business Week *cited him as a "Best Bet" teacher. He is listed in Marquis'* Who's Who of Emerging Leaders in America *and* Who's Who in the World.

APPENDIX A

Roles for Software
Greg Erman

A.1. INTRODUCTION

For the past 30 years software technology has helped people in numerous ways. The most common benefits are:

- Automating repetitive tasks
- Managing large amounts of information
- Executing transactions reliably
- Enforcing operating policies, rules, or methodologies
- Simulating or modeling business conditions
- Increasing user productivity
- Reducing operating costs

Why wouldn't the same benefits apply to people in the product development and management profession? They do apply! In particular, many software tools exist to help product managers improve productivity and reduce time to market. The purpose of this appendix is to summarize the roles and uses of software in the product development and management profession.

A.2. NEW PRODUCT MANAGEMENT STAGES

Since a large number of business applications exist, it is helpful to structure a classification to explain available software. This appendix employs Crawford's [1] five-stage new product management process: strategic planning, concept generation, screening, technical development, and commercialization.

A.3. SOFTWARE APPLICATIONS

A.3.1 Strategic Planning

Strategic planning refers to the stage where possibilities for new products are gathered, sorted, and screened. Strategic planning varies widely across industries, companies, and individuals. As a result, there is not much opportunity to automate repetitive tasks. However, strategic planning requires a large amount of information to support sorting and screening decisions. In addition, rules (which can be programmed) are usually employed to make these decisions.

Decision support software is available to help product managers forecast business conditions, understand trends, and analyze target markets. In addition, rules have been codified into software applications that can both analyze and generate complete business plans.

A.3.2. Concept Generation

Like the strategic planning stage, *concept generation* is a process that incorporates tremendous variability. Concept generation tends to be creative and spontaneous. Many software tools exist to *facilitate* this process. Databases of idea associations can help product managers trigger new features or ideas. Moreover, software tools can guide brainstorming sessions. These products are essentially "consultants in a box." They structure the formal ideation and problem solving methodology for the user. Users benefit from exploiting the best methodologies available, and problem solving or ideation sessions can be tracked and recorded for future use.

Market research can serve as a basis for concept generation. Surveys and focus groups can give product managers insights into new ideas. These studies typically require statistical analysis. Software is well suited to executing the complex calculations required for this type of analysis. In addition to statistical processing applications (to compute cross tabulations, for example), software is available to manage conjoint analysis, quality functional deployment, and market research surveys. These techniques help product managers identify optimal product features directly from the preferences of end users and customers.

Another class of software that enhances the process of concept generation is *groupware*, a class of products that help people communicate and share information. This information sharing occurs in many different ways. One example is posting notes on bulletin boards to which people can respond. Companies can hold virtual meetings or computer conferences using this technology. Participants do not need to be in the same room, nor do they even need to be "meeting" at the same time. For example, a sales representative could post a note discussing a customer need. The next day the marketing manager may see the note and post a reply stating that a study was done by another company about a market trend supporting this need. A week later an engineer may add that they know of a new technology that could enable the development of a product meeting this particular need. Groupware is widely available to companies throughout the world.

A.3.3. Screening

Screening refers to the process of testing whether concepts should be developed into products. Screening includes risk analysis, financial metrics, concept testing, portfolio analysis, and perhaps even market testing. A great deal of human judgment is required to screen new product concepts properly. Consequently, few standard software packages exist that actually screen concepts. On the other hand, software is available to support the *process* of screening.

The most common screening tool is the spreadsheet. Software spreadsheets store data and formulas (which process the data). Spreadsheets are used as a general screen to assess feasibility. Does the concept pass certain financial hurdles, for instance? Based on historical market data, spreadsheets can compute market size and market share to arrive at the return on investment (ROI) for the product. If this ROI is better than the corporate hurdle rate, the idea moves forward. Spreadsheets are also useful for graphically displaying data in order to gain insights into the quality of the concept or to uncover new concepts.

Screening metrics are useful for weeding out bad concepts, but they may not help in identifying optimal concepts. This task requires testing concepts with customers. Some concepts can be communicated directly to customers for testing. However, many concepts are too complex or may divulge competitive information prematurely. In these instances, purchasing behavior may be modeled. Software could then be utilized to simulate the purchasing process. This simulation can serve as a way to test new features because the basic purchasing pattern is understood. Simulation, however, may not be practical for new-to-the-world ideas that don't fit easily into any well-defined category.

A.3.4. Technical Development

Technical development tends to be clearly defined and relatively repetitive. The same general development process is used in a large company regardless of the specific product. Furthermore, the methodology is consistent. For example, the process of identifying tasks, assigning resources, understanding dependencies, calculating the critical path, and creating a project schedule is the same for most products. As a result, most development software focuses on the project management aspects of product management.

Software can be utilized to depict the product development process graphically using a computer-generated flowchart. Critical path schedules for specific projects, lists of key events or milestones, and resource utilization plans can all be prepared using project management software. In situations where a company's new product development projects are similar to each other, a master schedule template can be stored. If companies keep their project data up to date, this software can be an invaluable way to measure performance, identify potential opportunities and problems, communicate plans, and help complete projects on time and under budget.

A.3.5. Commercialization

Commercialization refers to all the activity from the time the product is developed to after market launch. Commercialization tasks tend to be marketing oriented. These activities help ensure that the product is communicated to the intended target audience in the optimal time, manner, and place. This process includes a large number of decisions that vary according to many variables. Unlike all other stages, commercialization requires an eclectic mix of software capabilities. Certain activities (such as sales forecasting) can be repetitive, benefiting from software automation, whereas other tasks (such as selecting the right channels or media mix) involve creative, spontaneous planning, which is more appropriate for decision support software.

Companies typically use software to help marketers predict revenue using mathematical forecasting algorithms, such as exponential smoothing. This software is also used to aggregate external data and the internal sales forecasts from many sales representatives across the corporation. These data can be combined and analyzed to identify optimal launch markets and venues. Software can also be used to assess market demographics. Mapping software contains extensive data (such as U.S. Census data) to help users identify target cities or even individuals that could be used for test marketing.

In addition to understanding target markets, commercialization includes planning many elements of the marketing mix. Decision support software provides product and marketing managers with information about their customers. This information comes from a variety of internal and external sources, and the decision support system formats the data to help the user identify trends and opportunities for exploitation. For example, planning the allocation of financial launch resources across direct sales, distributors, and consultative systems inte-

grators requires a vast amount of information including trends, channel performance, costs, and sales coverage. When this information is correlated in the right
manner, the optimal distribution of resources can become obvious.

A.4. SUMMARY

Software is available for all the classical stages of new product development and
management: strategic planning, concept generation, screening, technical development, and commercialization. The proliferation of low-cost, easy-to-use applications provides product managers with the opportunity to purchase software
directly. Product management will find that this software will help them improve
productivity and reduce time to market.

REFERENCE

1. Crawford, C. Merle. *New Products Management*, 4th ed. Burr Ridge, IL: Irwin, 1994.

Greg Erman
Waypoint Software Corporation

Waypoint develops software tools to help companies build catalogs on the Internet. Greg is President & CEO of Waypoint and was previously a Vice President and Director of Marketing at two successful software companies. Greg also spent eight years at Digital Equipment Corporation, where his most recent position was Channel Programs Director. He had served in a variety of managerial roles in the areas of sales, marketing, and product management at Digital. Greg has a BSEE with high honors and a Marketing MBA from Rutgers University

GLOSSARY

Accidental Discovery: New designs, ideas, and developments different from those originally hoped for from research.

Alpha Test: In-house testing of preproduction products to find and eliminate the most obvious design defects or deficiencies, either in a laboratory setting or in some part of the developing firm's regular operations. *See also* Beta Test.

Architecture: *See* Product Architecture.

As-Is-Map: A version of a process map depicting how an existing process actually operates. This may differ substantially from documented guidelines.

Awareness: A measure of the percentage of target customers who are aware of the new product's existence. Awareness is variously defined, including recall of brand, recognition of brand, recall of key features, or positioning.

Baton-Passing Process: *See* Relay-Race Process.

Benchmarking: A process of studying successful competitors (or organizations in general) and selecting the best of their actions or standards. In the new product program it means finding the best development process methods and the best process times to market and setting out to achieve them.

Benefit: A product attribute expressed in terms of what the user gets from the product rather than its physical characteristics or features. Benefits are often paired with specific features, but they need not be. They are perceived, not necessarily real.

Beta Test: An external test of preproduction products. The purpose is to test the product for all functions in a breadth of field situations to find those system faults that are more likely to show in actual use than in the firm's more controlled in-house tests before sale to the general market. *See also* Alpha Test.

Bill of Materials (BOM): A listing of all subassemblies, intermediate parts, and raw materials that go into a parent assembly, showing the quantity of each required to make an assembly.

Brainstorming: A group method of problem solving used in product concept generation. There are many modifications in format of use, each variation with its own name.

Brand: A name, term, design, symbol, or any other feature that identifies one seller's good or service as distinct from those of other sellers. The legal term for brand is *trademark*. A brand may identify one item, a family of items, or all items of that seller.

Brand Development Index (BDI): A measure of the relative strength of a brand's sales in a geographic area. Computationally, BDI is the percent of total national brand sales that occur in an area divided by the percent of U.S. households which reside in that area.

Breadboard: A proof-of-concept modeling technique that represents how a product will work but not how a product will look.

Business Analysis: An analysis of the business situation surrounding a proposed project. usually includes financial forecasts in terms of discounted cash flows, net present value, or internal rates of returns.

Business Case: The results of the business analysis, or up-front homework. Ideally defined just prior to the "go to development" decision (gate), the case defines the product and project, including the project justification and the action or business plan.

Business Management Team: Top functional managers and business unit head who work together throughout the design of the decision-flow component of a stage-gate process.

Business-to-Business: Nonconsumer purchasers such as manufacturers, resellers (e.g., distributors, wholesalers, jobbers, and retailers) institutional, professional, and governmental organizations. Often referred to in the past as "industrial" businesses.

Buyer: The purchaser of a product, whether or not the ultimate user. Especially in business-to-business markets, a purchasing agent may contract for the actual purchase of a good or service, yet never benefit from the function(s) purchased.

Buyer Concentration: The degree to which purchasing power is held by a relatively small percentage of the total number of buyers in the market.

Cannibalization: When the demand for a new product arises at least in part by eroding demand for (sales of) a current product the firm markets.

Capacity Planning: A forward-looking activity that monitors the skill sets and effective resource capacity of the organization.

Category Development Index (CDI): A measure of the relative strength of a category's sales in a geographic area. Computationally, it is the percent of total national category sales that occur in an area divided by the percent of U.S. households in that area.

Champion: A person who takes an inordinate interest in seeing that a particular process or product is fully developed and marketed. The role varies from situations calling for little more than stimulating awareness of the opportunity to extreme cases where the champion tries to force a project past the strongly entrenched internal resistance of company policy or that of objecting parties.

Change Equilibrium: A balance of organizational forces that either drives or impedes change.

Checklist: A memory-jogger list of items used to remind an analyst to think of all relevant aspects. It finds frequent use as a tool of creativity in concept generation, as a factor consideration list in concept screening, and to ensure that all appropriate tasks have been completed in any stage of the product development process.

Chunks: The building blocks of product architecture. They are made up of inseparable physical elements. Other terms for chunks may be modules or major subassemblies.

Classification: A systematic arrangement into groups or classes based on natural relationships.

Co-location: The physical locating of project personnel in one area, enabling more rapid and frequent communication among them.

Computer-Assisted Design (CAD): A technology that allows designers and engineers to use computers for their design work.

Computer-Enhanced Creativity: Using specially designed computer software that aid in the process of recording, recalling, and reconstructing ideas to speed up the new product development process.

Concept: A clearly written and possibly visual description of a new product idea, which includes its primary features and consumer benefits.

Concept Generation: The act by which new concepts, or product ideas, are generated. Also called *idea generation* or *ideation*.

Concept Optimization: A research approach that evaluates how specific product benefits or features contribute to a concept's overall appeal to consumers. Results are used to select from the options investigated to construct the most appealing concept from the consumer's perspective.

Concept Statement: A verbal or pictorial statement of a concept that is prepared for presentation to consumers to get their reaction prior to development.

Concept Study Activity: The set of product development tasks in which a concept is given enough examination to determine if there are substantial unknowns about the market, technology, or production process.

Concept Testing: The process by which a concept statement is presented to consumers for their reactions. These reactions can either be used to permit the developer to estimate the sales value of the concept or to make changes in the concept to enhance its potential sales value.

Concurrency: Carrying out separate stages of the product development process at the same time rather than sequentially.

Concurrent Engineering: When product design and manufacturing process development occur concurrently or simultaneously rather than sequentially. Also called *simultaneous engineering*.

Conjoint Analysis: A quantitative market research technique that determines how consumers make trade-offs among a small number of features or benefits.

Consumer: The most generic and all-encompassing term for a firm's targets. The term is used in either the business-to-business or household context and may refer to the firm's current customers, competitors' customers, or current nonpurchasers with similar needs or demographic characteristics. The term does not differentiate between whether the person is a buyer or a user target. Only a fraction of consumers will become customers.

Consumer Market: The purchasing of goods and services by individuals and for household use (rather than for use in business settings). Consumer purchases are generally made by individual decision makers either for themselves or for others in the family.

Consumer Need: A problem the consumer would like to have solved. What consumers would like a product to do for them.

Consumer Panels: Specially recruited groups of consumers whose longitudinal category purchases are recorded either by hand or via scanner technology.

Continuous Improvement: Review, analysis, and rework directed at improving practices and processes.

Continuous Learning Activity: The set of product development tasks involving an objective examination of how a product development project is progressing or how it was carried out to permit process changes to simplify its remaining steps or improve the product being developed or its schedule.

Contract Developer: An external provider of product development services.

Controlled Store Testing: A method of test marketing where specialized companies are employed to handle product distribution and auditing rather than a company's normal sales force.

Convergent Thinking: A technique generally performed in the initial phase of idea generation to help funnel the high volume of ideas created through divergent thinking into a small group or single idea on which more effort will be focused.

Coordination Matrix: A summary chart that identifies the key stages of a development project, their goals, and key activities within each stage.

Core Benefit Proposition (CBP): The central benefit or purpose for which a consumer buys a product. The CBP may come from the physical good or service performance, or it may come from the augmented dimensions of the product.

Cost of Goods Sole (COGS): The direct costs associated with producing a product.

Criteria: Statements of standards used by gatekeepers at each gate and related to all organizational functions. The criteria that must be achieved or surpassed for product development projects to continue in development. In the aggregate, these criteria reflect a business unit's new product strategy.

Critical Path Scheduling: A project management technique, frequently incorporated into various software programs, which puts all important steps of a given new product project into a sequential network based on task interdependencies.

Cross Sections: An explanation of a part that is referenced by slicing through the area that needs to be explained.

Crossing the Chasm: Making the transition to a mainstream market from an early market dominated by a few visionary customers.

Customer: One who purchases or uses your firm's products or services.

Customer-Based Success: The extent to which a new product is accepted by customers and the trade.

Customer Value-Added Ratio: The ratio of WWPF (worth what paid for) for your products to WWPF for your competitors' products. A ratio above 100% indicates superior value compared to that of the competitors.

Data: Measurements taken at the source of a business process.

Database: An electronic gathering of information organized in some way to make it easy to search, uncover, and manipulate.

Decline Stage: The fourth and last stage of the product life cycle. Entry into this stage is generally caused by technology advancements, consumer or user preference changes, global competition, or environmental or regulatory changes.

Deliverable: The completed end result or outcome of a series of tasks.

Delphi Processes: A technique that uses iterative rounds of consensus development across a group of experts to arrive at the most probable outcome for a future state.

Derivative Product: A new product based on changes to an existing product that modifies, refines, or improves some product features without affecting the basic product architecture or platform.

Development Change Order (DCO): A document used to implement changes during product development. It spells out the desired change, the reason for the change, and the consequences on time to market, development cost, and the cost of producing the final product.

Discounted Cash Flow Analysis: One method of providing an estimate of the current value of future incomes and expenses projected for a project.

Discrete Choice Experiment: A quantitative market research tool used to model and predict customer buying decisions.

Distribution: The method and partners used to get the product (or service) from where it is produced to where the end user can buy it.

Divergent Thinking: Technique performed early in the initial phase of idea generation which expands thinking processes to record and recall a high volume of new or interesting ideas.

Early Adopters: For new products, the customers who, relying on their own intuition and vision, buy into new product concepts very early in the life cycle. For new processes, these are organizations willing to try out new processes rather than simply maintaining the old.

Economic Value Added (EVA): The value added to or subtracted from shareholder value during the life of a project.

Engineering Design: A function in the product creation process where a good is configured and specific form is decided.

Engineering Model: The combination of hardware and software intended to demonstrate the simulated functioning of the intended product as currently designed.

Enhanced Product: A form of derivative product. Enhanced products include additional features not previously found on the base platform which provide increased value to consumers.

Entrance Requirement: The document(s) and reviews required before any phase of the development process can be started.

Event: Marks the point in time when a task is completed.

Event Map: A chart showing important events in the future which is used to map out potential responses to probable or certain future events.

Exit Requirement: The document(s) and reviews required to complete a stage of the development process.

Extrusion: A manufacturing process that utilizes a softened billet of material that is forced through a shape (or die) to allow for a continuous form, much like spaghetti.

Factory Cost: The cost of producing the product in the production location, including materials, labor, and overhead.

Failure Rate: The percentage of a firm's new products that make it to full market commercialization but fail to achieve the objectives set for them.

Feasibility Activity: The set of product development tasks in which major unknowns are examined to produce knowledge about how to resolve or overcome them or to clarify the nature of any limitations. Sometimes called *exploratory investigation.*

Feature: The solution to a consumer need or problem. Features are the way that benefits are provided to consumers. The handle is a feature that allows a laptop computer to be carried easily. Usually, any one of several different features may be chosen to meet a customer need. For example, shoulder straps on a laptop computer's carrying case allow the computer to be carried easily.

Field Testing: Product use testing with users from the target market.

Financial Success: The extent to which a new product meets its profit, margin, and return-on-investment goals.

Firm-Level Success: The aggregate impact of the firm's proficiency at developing and commercializing new products. Several different specific measures may be used to estimate performance.

First to Market: The first product that creates a new product category or a substantial subdivision of a category.

Flexible Gate: A permissive or permeable gate in a stage-gate process that is less rigid than the traditional "go–stop–recycle" gate. Flexible gates are useful in shortening time-to-market. A permissive gate is one where the next stage is authorized although some work in the almost-completed stage has not yet been finished. A permeable gate is one where some work in a subsequent stage is authorized before a substantial amount of work in the prior stage is completed.

Focus Groups: A qualitative market research technique where 8 to 12 market participants are gathered in one room for a discussion under the leadership of a trained moderator. Discussion focuses on a consumer problem, product or potential solution to a problem. The results of these discussions are not projectable to the general market.

Functional Elements: The individual operations that a product performs. These elements are often used to describe a product schematically.

Functional Pipeline Management: Optimizing the flow of projects through all functional areas in the context of the company's priorities.

Functional Schematic: A schematic drawing that is made up of all of the functional elements in a product. It shows the product's functions as well as how material, energy and signal flows through the product.

Functional Testing: Testing either an element of or the complete product to determine whether it will function as planned and as actually used when sold.

Fuzzy Front End: The messy "getting started" period of product development processes following the formation of a germ of an idea, but before a firm begins development.

Gantt Chart: A horizontal bar chart used in project scheduling that shows the start date, end date, and duration of tasks within the project. Sometimes used in conjunction with a network diagram.

Gap Analysis: The difference between projected outcomes and desired outcomes. In product development, the gap is frequently measured as the difference between expected and desired revenues or profits from currently planned new products if the corporation is to meet its objectives.

Garage Bill Scheduling: A scheduling tool that details every task, no matter how small, that must be completed to achieve a deliverable.

Gate: The decision point, often a meeting, at which a management decision is made to allow the product development project to proceed to the next stage, to recycle back into the current stage to better complete some of the tasks, or to terminate. The number of gates varies by company.

Gatekeepers: The group of managers who serve as advisors, decision makers, and resource allocators in a stage-gate process. They use established criteria to review product development projects at each gate. This multifunctional group is generally most visible at gate meetings.

Gross Rating Points (GRPs): A measure of the overall advertising exposure of consumer households.

Growth Stage: The second stage of the product life cycle. This stage is marked by a rapid surge in sales, market acceptance, and overall opportunity for the good or service.

Hurdle Rate: The minimum return on investment or internal rate of return percentage that a new product must meet or exceed as it goes through development.

Idea Exchange: A divergent thinking technique that provides a structure for building on different ideas in a quiet, nonjudgmental setting that encourages reflection.

Idea Generation: All the activities and processes that lead to creating new product or service ideas that may warrant development.

Idea Merit Index: An internal metric used to rank new product ideas impartially.

Implementation Team: A team that converts the concepts and good intentions of the "should-be" process into practical reality.

Incremental Improvement: A small change made to an existing product that serves to keep the product fresh in the eyes of customers.

Industrial Design (ID): The professional service of creating and developing concepts and specifications that optimize the function, value, and appearance of products and systems for the mutual benefit of both user and manufacturer (Industrial Design Society of America).

Information: Knowledge and insight, often gained by examining data.

Initial Screening: The first decision to spend resources (time or money) on a project. The project is born at this point. Sometimes called *idea screening*.

Injection Molding: A process that utilizes melted plastics injected into steel or aluminum molds which ultimately result in finished production parts.

Innovation: A new idea, method, or device. The act of creating a new product or process. The act includes invention as well as the work required to bring an idea or concept into final form.

Innovation Engine: The creative activity and people who actually think of new ideas. It represents the synthesis phase, when someone first recognizes that customer and market opportunities can be translated into new product ideas.

Innovative Problem Solving: Methods that combine rigorous problem definition, pattern-breaking generation of ideas, and action planning which results in new, unique, and unexpected solutions.

Integral Architecture: A product architecture in which most or all of the functional elements map into a single or very small number of chunks. It is difficult to subdivide an integrally designed product into partially functioning components.

Internal Rate of Return (IRR): The discount rate at which the present value of the future cash flows of an investment equals the cost of the investment. The discount rate with a new present value of zero.

Introduction Stage: The first stage of a product's commercial launch and the product life cycle. This stage is generally seen as the point of market entry, user trial, and product adoption.

ISO-9000: A set of five auditable standards of the International Standards Organization that establishes the role of a quality system in a company and which is used to assess whether the company can be certified as being compliant to the standards. ISO-9001 deals specifically with new products.

Launch: The process by which a new product is introduced into the market for initial sale.

Lead Users: Users for whom finding a solution to one of their consumer needs is so important that they have modified a current product or invented a new product to solve the need themselves because they have not found a supplier who can solve it for them. When these consumers' needs are portents of needs that the center of the market will have in the future, their solutions are new product opportunities.

Line Extension: A form of derivative product that adds or modifies features without changing the price significantly.

Long-Term Success: The new product's performance in the long run or at some large fraction of the product's life cycle.

M-Curve: An illustration of the volume of ideas generated over a given amount of time. The illustration often looks like two arches from the letter M.

Maintenance Activity: That set of product development tasks aimed at solving initial market and user problems with a new product or service.

Manufacturability: The extent to which a new product can be manufactured easily and effectively, at minimum cost and with maximum reliability.

Manufacturing Assembly Procedure: Procedural documents normally prepared by manufacturing personnel that describe how a component, subassembly, or system will be put together to create a final product.

Manufacturing Design: The process of determining the manufacturing process that will be used to make a new product.

Manufacturing Test Specification and Procedure: Documents prepared by development and manufacturing personnel that describe the performance specifications of a component, subassembly, or system that will be met during the manufacturing process, and that describe the procedure by which the specification will be assessed.

Market Conditions: The characteristics of the market into which a new product will be placed, including the number of competing products, level of competitiveness, and growth rate.

Market Development: Taking current products to new consumers or users. This effort may involve making some product modifications.

Market-Driven: Allowing the marketplace to direct a firm's product innovation efforts.

Market Segmentation: The act of dividing an overall market into groups of consumers with similar needs, where each group differs from others in the market in some way.

Market Share: A company's sales in a product area as a percent of the total market sales in that area.

Market Testing: The product development stage when the new product and its marketing plan are tested together. A market test simulates the eventual marketing mix and takes many different forms, only one of which bears the name *test market.*

Mating Part: A general reference to one of two parts that join together.

Matrix Converger: A convergent thinking tool that uses a matrix to help synthesize data into key concepts with numbered ratings.

Maturity Stage: The third stage of the product life cycle. This is the stage where sales begin to level due to heavy competition, alternative product options, or changing buyer or user preferences.

Metrics: A prescribed set of measurements to track product development and allow a firm to measure the impact of process improvements over time. These measures generally vary by firm, but may include measures characterizing both aspects of the process, such as time to market, and duration of particular process stages, as well as outcomes from product development such as the number of products commercialized per year and percentage of sales due to new products.

Modular Architecture: A product architecture in which each functional element maps into its own physical chunk. Different chunks perform different functions.

Monitoring Frequency: The frequency with which performance indicators are measured.

Multifunctional Team: A group of individuals brought together from more than one functional area of a business to work on a problem or process that requires the knowledge, training, and capabilities across the areas to complete the work successfully.

Needs Statement: Summary of consumer needs and wants, described in customer terms, to be addressed by a new product.

Net Present Value (NPV): Method used in comparably evaluating investments in very dissimilar projects by discounting the current and projected future cash inflows and outflows back to the present value based on the discount rate, or cost of capital, of the firm.

Network Diagram: A graphical diagram with boxes connected by lines that shows the sequence of development activities and the interrelationship of each task with another. Often used in conjunction with a Gantt chart.

New Product: A term of many opinions and practices, but most generally defined as a product (either a good or service)new to the firm marketing it. Excludes products that are only changed in promotion.

New Product Idea: A preliminary plan or purpose of action for formulating new products or services.

Nominal Group Process: A process that allows members of a group to participate in group discussion in writing instead of verbally.

Nonproduct Advantage: Elements of the marketing mix that create a competitive advantage other than the product itself. These elements can include marketing communications, distribution, company reputation, technical support, and associated services.

Operations: A term that includes manufacturing but is much broader, usually including procurement, physical distribution, and for services, management of the offices or other areas where the services are provided.

Operator's Manual: Written instructions to the users of a product or process. These may be intended for the ultimate customer or for the use of the manufacturing operation.

Pareto Chart: A bar graph with the bars sorted in descending order used to identify the largest opportunity for improvement. Pareto charts distinguish the "vital few" from the "useful many."

Payback: The time, usually in years, from some point in the development process until the commercialized product or service has recovered its costs of development and marketing. While some firms take the point of full-scale market introduction of a new product as the starting point, others begin the clock at the start of development expense.

Perceptual Mapping: A quantitative market research tool used to understand how customers think of current and future products.

Performance Indicators: Criteria with which the performance of a new product in the market can be evaluated.

Performance Measurement System: The system that enables the firm to monitor the relevant performance indicators of new products in the appropriate time frame.

Phase Review Process: See Relay-Race Process.

Physical Elements: The components that make up a product. These can be both components (or individual parts) in addition to minor subassemblies of components.

Pilot Gate Meeting: A trial, informal gate meeting usually held at the launch of a stage-gate process to test the design of the process and familiarize participants with the stage-gate process.

Pipeline Alignment: The balancing of project demand with resource supply.

Pipeline Inventory: Production of a new product that has not yet been sold to end consumers, but which exists within the distribution chain.

Pipeline Management: A process that integrates product strategy, project management, and functional management to optimize the cross-project management of all development-related activities on a continuing basis.

Pipeline Management Enabling Tools: The decision-assistance and data-handling tools that aid in managing the pipeline. The decision-assistance tools allow the pipeline team to perform systematic trade-offs without losing sight of priorities. The data-handling tools deal with the vast amount of information needed to analyze project priorities, understand resource and skillset loads, and perform pipeline analysis.

Pipeline Management Process: Consists of three elements: pipeline management teams, a structured methodology, and enabling tools.

Pipeline Management Teams: The teams of people at the strategic, project, and functional levels responsible for resolving pipeline issues.

Platform Product: The design and components that are shared by a set of products in a product family. From this platform, numerous derivative products can be designed.

Portfolio Criteria: The set of criteria against which the business judges proposed product development projects to create a balanced and diverse mix of ongoing efforts.

Portfolio Management: A business process by which a business unit decides on the mix of active projects, staffing, and dollar budget allocated to each project. *See also* pipeline management.

Preliminary Bill of Materials (PBOM): A forecasted listing of all the subassemblies, intermediate parts, raw materials, and engineering design, tool design, and customer inputs that are expected to go into a parent assembly showing the quantity of each required to make an assembly.

Preproduction Unit: A product that looks and acts like the intended final product but is made either by hand or in pilot facilities rather than by the final production process.

Process Champion: The person responsible for the daily promotion of and encouragement to use the process throughout the organization. They are also responsible for the ongoing training, innovation input, and continuous improvement of the process.

Process Managers: The operational managers responsible for ensuring the orderly and timely flow of ideas and projects through the process.

Process Map: A work-flow diagram that uses an x-axis for process time and a y-axis which shows participants and tasks.

Process Mapping: The General Electric term for "garage bill" scheduling.

Process Owner: The executive manager responsible for the strategic results of the process. This includes process throughput, quality of output, and participation within the organization.

Process Reengineering: A discipline to measure and modify organizational effectiveness by documenting, analyzing, and comparing an existing process to "best-in-class" practice, and then implementing process improvements or installing a whole new process.

Product: Term used to describe all goods and services sold. Products are bundles of attributes (features, functions, benefits, and uses) and can be either tangible, as in the case of physical goods, or intangibles, such as those associated with service benefits, or a combination of the two.

Product and Process Performance Success: The extent to which a new product meets its technical performance and product development process performance criteria.

Product Architecture: The way in which the functional elements are assigned to the physical chunks of a product and the way in which those physical chunks interact.

Product Definition: Defines the product, including the target market, product concept, benefits to be delivered, positioning strategy, price point, and even product requirements and design specifications.

Product Development: The overall process of strategy, organization, concept generation, product and marketing plan creation and evaluation, and commercialization of a new product.

Product Development & Management Association (PDMA): A not-for-profit professional organization whose purpose is to seek out, develop, organize, and disseminate leading-edge information on the theory and practice of product development and product development processes. The PDMA uses local, national, and international meetings and conferences, educational workshops, a quarterly newsletter (*Visions*), a bimonthly scholarly journal (*Journal of Product Innovation Management*), research proposal and dissertation proposal competitions, and this handbook to achieve its purposes.

Product Development Checklist: A predetermined list of activities and disciplines responsible for completing those activities used as a guideline to ensure that all the tasks of product development are considered prior commercialization.

Product Development Portfolio: The collection of new product concepts that are within the firm's ability to develop, are most attractive to the firm's customers, and deliver short- and long-term corporate objectives, spreading risk and diversifying investments.

Product Development Process: A disciplined and defined set of tasks and steps that describe the normal means by which a company repetitively converts embryonic ideas into salable products or services.

Product Development Strategy: The strategy that guides the product innovation program.

Product Development Team: A multifunctional group of people chartered to plan and execute a new product development project.

Product Discontinuation: A product or service that is withdrawn or removed from the market because it no longer provides an economic, strategic, or competitive advantage to include it in the firm's portfolio of offerings.

Product Discontinuation Time Line: The process and time frame in which a product is carefully withdrawn from the marketplace. The product may be discontinued immediately after the decision is made, or it may take a year or more to implement the discontinuation time line, depending on the nature and conditions of the market and product.

Product Failure: A product development project that does not meet the objective of its developers.

Product Family: The set of products that have been derived from a common product platform. Members of a product family normally have many common parts and assemblies.

Product Interfaces: Internal and external interfaces affecting the product development effort, including the nature of the interface, action required, and timing.

Product Life Cycle: The four stages that a new product is thought to go through from birth to death: introduction, growth, maturity, and decline. Controversy surrounds whether products go through this cycle in any predictable way.

Product Line: A group of products marketed by an organization to one general market. The products have some characteristics, customers, and uses in common and may also share technologies, distribution channels, prices, services, and other elements of the marketing mix.

Product Manager: The person assigned responsibility for overseeing all the various activities that concern a particular product. Sometimes called a brand manager in consumer packaged goods firms.

Product Plan: Detailed summary of all the key elements involved in a new product development effort, such as product description, schedule, resources, financial estimations, and interface management plan.

Product Platforms: Underlying structures or basic architectures that are common across a group of products or that will be the basis of a series of products commercialized over a number of years.

Product Rejuvenation: The process by which a mature or declining product is altered, updated, repackaged, or redesigned to lengthen the product life cycle and in turn extend sales demand.

Product Requirements Document: The contract between, at a minimum, marketing and development, describing completely and unambiguously the necessary attributes of the product to be developed.

Product Superiority: A product differentiated from those offered by competitors by offering consumers benefits and value for money above what other products offer. This is one of the critical success factors in commercializing new products.

Project Management: Both a process and a set of tools and techniques concerned with defining the project's goal, planning all the work to reach the goal, leading the project and support teams, monitoring progress, and seeing to it that the project is completed in a satisfactory way.

Project Pipeline Management: Fine-tuning resource deployment smoothly for projects during ramp up, ramp down, and midcourse adjustments.

Project Sponsor: The authorization and funding source of the project. The person who defines the project goals and to whom the final results are presented. Typically, a senior manger.

Protocol: A statement of the attributes (mainly benefits, features only when required) that a new product is expected to have. A protocol is prepared prior to assigning the project to the technical development team. The benefits statement is agreed to by all parties involved in the project.

Prototype: A physical model of the new product concept. Depending on the purpose, prototypes may be nonworking, functionally working, or both functionally and aesthetically complete.

Psychographics: Characteristics of consumers which, rather than purely demographic, measure their attitudes, interests, opinions, and lifestyles.

Q-Sorts: A process for sorting and ranking complex issues.

Qualitative Market Research: Consumer research conducted with a very small number of consumers, either in groups or individually. Results are not representative of consumers in general or projectable. Frequently used to gather initial consumer needs and obtain initial reactions to ideas and concepts.

Quality by Design: The process used to design quality into the product, service, or process from the inception of product development.

Quality Control Specification and Procedure: Documents that describe the specifications and the procedures by which they will be measured which a finished subassembly or system must meet before judged ready for shipment.

Quality Function Deployment (QFD): A structured method employing matrix analysis for linking what the market requires to how it will be accomplished in the development effort. This method is most valuable during the stage of development when a multifunctional team agrees on how customer needs relate to product specifications and features that deliver those. By explicit linking of these aspects of product design, QFD limits the chance of omitting important design characteristics or interactions across design characteristics. QFD is also an important mechanism in promoting multifunctional teamwork.

Quantitative Market Research: Consumer research, often surveys, conducted with a large enough sample of consumers to produce statistically reliable results that can be used to project outcomes to the general consumer population. Used to determine importance levels of different customer needs, performance ratings of and satisfaction with current products, probability of trial, repurchase rate, and product preferences. These techniques are used to reduce the uncertainty associated with many other aspects associated with product development.

Rapid Prototyping: Any of a variety of processes that avoid tooling time in producing prototypes or prototype parts and therefore allow (generally nonfuntioning) prototypes to be produced within hours or days rather than weeks. The prototypes are frequently used to quickly test the product product's technical feasibility or consumer interest.

Realization Gap: The time between first perception of a need and the launch of a product that fills that need.

Relay-Race Process: A staged product development process in which first one function completes a set of tasks, then passes the information they generated sequentially to another function, which in turn completes the next set of tasks and then passes everything along to the next function. Multifunctional teamwork is largely absent in these types of product development processes, which may also be called *phase review* or *baton-passing processes.*

Render: Process that industrial designers use to visualize their ideas by putting their thoughts on paper with any number of combinations of color markets, pencils, and highlighters.

Reposition: To change the product positioning, either on failure of the original positioning or to react to changes in the marketplace. Most frequently accomplished solely through changing the marketing mix.

Resource Matrix: An array that shows the percentage of each nonmanagerial person's time that is to be devoted to each of the current projects in the firm's portfolio.

Resource Plan: Detailed summary of all forms of resources required to complete product development, including personnel, equipment, time, and finances.

Responsibility Matrix: This matrix indicates the specific involvement of each functional department in each task or activity in each stage.

Return on Ideas: Reflects the potential value of an idea.

Return on Investment (ROI): A standard measure of project profitability, this is the discounted profits over the life of the project expressed as a percentage of initial investment.

Rigid Gate: A review point in a stage-gate process at which all the prior stage's work and deliverables must be complete before the next stage can begin.

Rugby Process: A product development process in which stages are partially or heavily overlapped rather than sequential with crisp demarcations between one stage and its successor.

Scanner Test Markets: Special test markets that provide supermarket scanner data from panels of consumers to help assess the product's performance.

Senior Management: That level of executive or operational management above the product development team which has approval authority or controls resources important to the development effort.

Services: Products, such as an airline flight or insurance policy, that are intangible or at least substantially so. If totally intangible, they are exchanged directly from producer to user, cannot be transported or stored, and are instantly perishable. Service delivery usually involves customer participation in some important way, cannot be sold in the sense of ownership transfer, and have no title.

Short-Term Success: The new product's performance shortly after launch, well within the first year of commercial sales.

Should-Be Map: A version of a process map depicting how a process will work in the future. A revised as-is process map. The result of the team's reengineering work.

Simulated Test Market: A form of quantitative market research and pretest marketing in which consumers are exposed to new products and to their claims in a staged advertising and purchase situation. Output of the test is an early forecast of expected sales or market share, based on mathematical forecasting models, management assumptions, and input of specific measurements from the simulation.

Slip Rate: Measures the accuracy of the planned project schedule according to the formula: Slip rate = [(actual schedule/planned schedule) − 1] × 100 percent.

Specification: A detailed description of the features and performance characteristics of a product. For example, a laptop computer's specification may read: 90-megahertz Pentium, with 16 megabytes of ram and 720 megabytes of hard disk space, 3.5 hours of battery life, weighing 4.5 pounds, with an active matrix 256-color screen.

Sponsor: An informal role in the product development project, usually a higher-ranking person in the firm who is not personally involved in the project (compared to the champion) but is ready to extend a helping hand if needed, or to provide a barrier to interference by others.

Stage: One group of concurrently accomplished tasks, with specified outcomes and deliverables, of the overall product development process.

Staged Product Development Activity: The set of product development tasks beginning when it is believed there are no major unknowns and that result in initial production of salable product, carried out in stages.

Stage-Gate Process: A widely employed product development process form managing product development that divides the effort into distinct time-sequenced stages separated by management decision gates. Multifunctional teams must complete successfully a prescribed set of related cross-functional tasks in each stage prior to obtaining management approval to proceed to the next stage of product development. The framework of the stage-gate process includes work-flow and decision-flow paths and defines the supporting systems and practices necessary to ensure the process's ongoing smooth operation.

Standard Cost: *See* Factory Cost.

Stoplight Voting: A convergent thinking technique by which participants vote their idea preferences using colored adhesive dots.

Strategic Balance: Balancing the portfolio of development projects along many dimensions, such as focus versus diversification, short versus long term, high versus low risk, extending platforms versus development of new platforms.

Strategic New Product Development (SNPD): A process that ties new product strategy to new product portfolio planning.

Strategic Pipeline Management: Focuses on achieving strategic balance, which entails setting priorities among the numerous opportunities and adjusting the organization's skill sets to deliver products.

Subassembly: A collection of components that can be put together as a single assembly to be inserted into a large assembly or final product. Often, the subassembly is tested for its ability to meet some set of explicit specifications before inclusion in the larger product.

Success Dimensions: Product development success has four dimensions. At the project level, there are three dimensions: financial, customer-based, and product and process performance. The fourth dimension of product development success is measured at the firm level.

Support Service: Any organizational function whose primary purpose is not product development but whose input is necessary to the successful completion of product development projects.

System Hierarchy Diagram: A diagram used to represent product architectures. This diagram illustrates how the product is broken into chunks.

Systems and Practices: Established methods, procedures, and activities that either drive or hinder product development. These may relate to the firm's day-to-day business or may be specific to product development.

Systems and Practices Team: Senior managers representing all functions who work together to identify and change those systems and practices hindering product development and who establish new tools, systems, and practices for improving product development.

Target Market: The group of consumers or potential customers selected for marketing. A market segment of consumers.

Task: The smallest describable unit of accomplishment in completing a deliverable.

Team: That group of persons who participate or manage the participation in the product development project. Frequently, each team member represents a function, department, or specialty, and together they provide the full set of capabilities needed to complete the project, in which case they are referred to as a *multifunctional team*.

Team Leader: The person leading the new product team. Responsible for ensuring that milestones and deliverables are achieved, even though they may not have any authority over project participants.

Technology-Driven: A new product or new product strategy based on the strength of a technical capability. Sometimes called *solutions in search of problems*.

Test Markets: The launching of a new product into one or more limited geographic regions in a very controlled manner, and measuring consumer response to the product and its launch. When multiple geographies are used in the test, different advertising or pricing policies may be tested and the results compared.

Think Links: Stimuli used in divergent thinking to help participants make new connections using seemingly unrelated concepts from a list of people, places, or things.

Think-Tank: Environments created by management to generate new ideas or approaches to solving organizational problems.

Thought Organizers: Tools that help categorize information associated with ideas such that the ideas can be placed into groups that can be more easily compared or evaluated.

Three R's: The fundamental steps of record, recall, and reconstruct that most creative minds go through when generating new product ideas.

Threshold Criteria: The minimum acceptable performance targets for any product development project being proposed or considered.

Thumbnail: The most minimal form of sketching, usually using pencils, to represent a product idea.

Time to Market: The length of time it takes to develop a new product from an early initial idea for a new product to initial market sales. Precise definitions of the start and end points vary from one company to another, and may vary from one project to another within the company.

Tone: The feeling, emotion, or attitude most associated with using a product. The appropriate tone is important to include in consumer new product concepts and advertising.

Total Quality Management (TQM): A comprehensive and continuous business improvement philosophy that involves all of an organization's functions in improvement activities.

Tracking Studies: Surveys of consumers (usually conducted by telephone) following the product's launch to measure consumer awareness, attitudes, trial, adoption, and repurchase rates.

User: Any person who uses a product or service to solve a problem or obtain a benefit, whether or not they purchase it. Users may consume a product, as in the case of a person using shampoo to clean hair, or eating a potato chip to assuage hunger between meals. Users may not consume a product directly, but may interact with it over a longer period of time, like a family owning a car with multiple family members using it for many purposes over a number of years. Products are also employed in the production of other products or services, where the users may be the manufacturing personnel who operate the equipment.

Utilities: The weights derived from conjoint analysis that measure how much a product feature contributes to purchase interest or preference.

Value-Added: The act or process by which tangible product features or intangible service attributes are bundled, combined, or packaged with other features and attributes to create a competitive advantage, reposition a product, or increase sales.

Visionary Companies: Leading innovators in their industries; they rank first or second in market share, profitability, growth, and shareholder performance. A substantial portion (e.g., 30% or more) of their sales are from products introduced in the last three years, and everyone wants to benchmark them.

Voice of the Customer (VOC): A process for eliciting needs from consumers, which uses structured in-depth interviews to lead interviewees through a series of situations in which they have experienced and found solutions to the set of problems being investigated. Needs are obtained through indirect questioning by coming to understand how the consumers found ways to meet their needs, and more important, why they chose the particular solutions they found.

Waste: Any activity that utilizes equipment, materials, parts, space, employee time, or other corporate resource beyond the minimum amount required for value-added operations to ensure manufacturability. These activities could include waiting, accumulating semiprocessed parts, reloading, passing materials from one hand to the other, and other nonproductive processes. The seven basic categories of waste that a business should strive to eliminate: overproduction, waiting for machines, transportation time, process time, excess inventory, excess motion, and defects.

Work-Flow Design Team: Functional contributors who work together to create and execute the work-flow component of a stage-gate system. They decide how the firm's stage-gate process will be structured, what tasks it will include, what decision points will be included, and who is involved at all points.

Worth What Paid For (WWPF): The quantitative evaluation by a person in your customer segment of the question: Considering the products and services that your vendor offers, are they worth what you paid for them?

ACKNOWLEDGMENT

A number of the definitions for terms in this glossary have been adopted from the glossary in *New Products Management*, 4th ed., by C. Merle Crawford (Burn Ridge, IL: Irving, 1994).

Contents of the *Journal of Product Innovation Management* (Through 1995) Cumulative Index of Articles

This index is organized by author and subject area and shows all articles published in the *Journal of Product Innovation Management* through the end of 1995. The final portion of each listing shows the *JPIM* volume number and page number. Please note that pages are numbered consecutively throughout each volume. This index was prepared by Thomas P. Hustad, JPIM Editor.

Subject Index

Creativity

Forecasting

An approach to assess the importance of brand equity in acquisition decisions (Vijay Mahajan, Vithala R. Rao, and Rajendra K. Srivastava), 11:221 (1994).

Are product life cycles really getting shorter? (Barry L. Bayus), 11:300 (1994).

A Brownian motion nodel for technology transfer: application to a machine maintenance expert system (Venkatesh Padmanabhan and William E. Souder), 11:119 (1994).

The co-diffusion of complementary innovations: supermarket scanners and UPC symbols (Louis P. Bucklin and Sanjit Sengupta), 10:148 (1993).

A conjoint-based product designing procedure incorporating price competition (S. Chan Choi and Wayne S. DeSarbo), 11:451 (1994).

A consumer-based approach to designing product line extensions (Paul E. Green and Abba M. Krieger), 4:21 (1987).

Cycle time in packaged software firms (Erran Carmel), 12:110 (1995).

Determinants of innovative durables' adoption: an empirical study with implications for early product screening (Susan L. Holak), 5:50 (1988).

Developing an effective testing program for consumer durables (Albert L. Page and Harold F. Rosenbaum), 9:267 (1992).

Developing and using forecasting models of consumer durables: the case of color television (Barry L Bayus, Saman Hong, and Russell P. Labe, Jr.), 6:5 (1989).

Diffusion at sub-national levels: a regional analysis of new product growth (William H. Redmond), 11:201 (1994).

An empirical comparison of sales forecasting models (Sanjay-kumar Rao), 2:232 (1985).

Enhancing concept test validity by using expert consumers (Jan P. L. Schoormans, Roland J. Ortt, and Cees J. P. M. de Bont), 12:153 (1995).

Estimating market growth for new products: an analogical diffusion model approach (Robert J. Thomas), 2:45 (1985).

Expert systems: an emerging technology for selecting new product winners (Sundaresan Ram and Sudha Ram), 6:89 (1989).

Explaining competitive reactions to new products: an empirical signalling study (Oliver P. Heil and Rockney G. Walters), 10:53 (1993).

Factors affecting new product forecasting accuracy in new firms (William B. Gartner and Robert J. Thomas), 10:35 (1993).

Five modern lessons from a 55 year old technological forecast (Steven P. Schnaars, Swee L. Chia, and Cesar M. Maloles III), 10:66 (1993).

Forecasting market size and market growth rates for new products (Brian C. Twiss), 1:19 (1984).

Forecasting new product market potential: combining multiple methods (Robert J. Thomas), 4:109 (1987).

Forecasting sales of new contingent products: an application to the compact disc market (Barry L. Bayus), 4:243 (1987).

Forecasting the market penetration of new technologies using a combination of economic cost and diffusion models (A. P. S. Teotia and P. S. Raju), 3:225 (1986).

From experience: benchmarking new product development funding (Kathleen A. Pierz), 12:43 (1995).

From experience: where does your new technology fit into the marketplace (Frank Lynn and Susan Heintz), 9:19 (1992).

Identifying key customers for novel industrial products (Richard N. Cardozo, David K. Smith, Jr., and Madhubalan Viswanathan), 5:102 (1988).

The impact of product aesthetics on the evaluation of industrial products (Mel Yamamoto and David R. Lambert), 11:309 (1994).

The impact of seasonality on the launch of infrequently purchased products (Marvin Berkowitz), 3:251 (1986).

Measuring technology incorporation/infusion (Robert W. Zmud and L. Eugene Apple), 9:148 (1992).

Metrics for measuring product development cycle time (Abbie Griffin), 10:112 (1993).

New product models: practice, short-comings and desired improvements (Vijay Mahajan and Jerry Wind), 9:128 (1992).

Opportunities for revitalizing stagnant markets: an analysis of household appliances (William A. V. Clark, Howard E. Freeman, and Dominique M. Hanssens), 1:242 (1984).

Perspective: The applicability of percolation theory to innovation (J. Mort), 8:32 (1991).

Perspective: barriers to innovation: intraorganizational dislocations (Roger A. More), 2:205 (1985).

Perspective: marketing hype: a new perspective for new product research and introduction (Jerry Wind and Vijay Mahajan), 4:43 (1987).

Pretest market models: a critical evaluation (Allen D. Shocker and William G. Hall), 3:86 (1986).

Problems in demand estimation for a new technology (Robert J. Thomas), 2:145 (1985).

Product design strategies for target-market positioning (Paul E. Green and Abba M. Krieger), 8:189 (1991).

Purchase intentions and dimensions of innovation: an exploratory model (Susan L. Holak and Donald R. Lehmann), 7:59 (1990).

Redesigning product lines with conjoint analysis: a comment (Dick R. Wittink), 6:289 (1989).

Redesigning product lines with conjoint analysis: a reply to Wittink (Albert L. Page and Harold F. Rosenbaum, 6:293 (1989).

Redesigning product lines with conjoint analysis: how Sunbeam does it (Albert L. Page and Harold F. Rosenbaum), 4:120 (1987).

Selecting winning new product projects: using the NewProd system (Robert G. Cooper), 2:34 (1985).

Significant issues for the future of product innovation (Members of the Editorial Board), 1:56 (1984).

Significant issues for the future of product innovation: issues in new product forecasting (Robert J. Thomas), 11:347 (1994).

Significant issues for the future: some additional perspectives (Members of the Editorial Board), 1: 129 (1984).

When technologies compete: the role of externalities in nonlinear market response (William H. Redmond), 8:170 (1991).

Industry Analysis

Accelerating the durable replacement cycle with marketing mix variables (Barry L. Bayus), 5:216 (1988).

Characteristics of innovative firms in the Brazilian computer industry (Angela da Rocha, Carl H. Christensen, and Newton A. Paim), 7:123 (1990).

Computing technology for the home: product strategies for the next generation (Alladi Venkatesh and Nicholas P. Vitalari), 3:171 (1986).

A cusp catastrophe model of the adoption of an industrial innovation (Paul A. Herbig), 8:127 (1991).

Cycle time in packaged software firms (Erran Carmel), 12:110 (1995).

The development of novel products through intra- and inter-organizational networks: the case of home automation (Joe Tidd), 12:307 (1995).

Entry strategies and market performance: causal modeling of a business simulation (Donna H. Green and Adrian B. Ryans), 7:45 (1990).

Expected development time reductions in the German mechanical engineering industry (Philipp A. Murmann), 11:236 (1994).

Exploring retail bank performance and new product development: a profile of industry practices (Eric R. Reidenbach and Donald L. Moak), 3:187 (1986).

Factors affecting the process of collaborative product development: a study of UK manufacturers of information and communications technology products (Dale Littler, Fiona Leverick, and Margaret Bruce), 12:16 (1995).

Factors influencing new product success and failure in small entrepreneurial high-technology electronics firms (Chee Meng Yap and William E. Souder), 11:418 (1994).

FDA regulation of product risk and its impact upon young biomedical firms (Oscar Hauptman and Edward B. Roberts), 4:138 (1987).

Forced adoption of innovations in organizations: consequences and implications (S. Ram and Hyung-Shik Jung), 8:117 (1991).

Forecasting sales of new contingent products: an application to the compact disc market (Barry L. Bayus), 4:243 (1987).

The harvesting of USAuto? From the gasoline crisis of 1973 to the imposition of "voluntary" import quotas in 1981 (Victor J. Cook and Robert R. Rothberg), 7:310 (1990).

The impact of product aesthetics on the evaluation of industrial products (Mel Yamamoto and David R. Lambert), 11:309 (1994).

Innovation in the systems business: dynamics of autonomy and cooperation (Glenn C. Bacon), 2:107 (1985).

Innovators, organization structure and management of the innovation process in the securities industry (Akira Iwamura and Vijay M. Jog), 8:104 (1991).

Integrating product innovation and market development to strengthen long-term planning, Bela Gold), 1:173 (1984).

Invention evaluation services: a review of the state of the art (Gerald G. Udell), 6:157 (1989).

Major new products: what distinguishes the winners in the chemical industry (Robert G. Cooper and Elko J. Kleinschmidt), 10:90 (1993).

Measuring technology incorporation/infusion (Robert W. Zmud and L. Eugene Apple), 9:148 (1992).

New product development for service companies (Christopher J. Easingwood), 3:264 (1986).

New product development in the pharmaceutical industry: pooling network resources (D. Jane Bower), 10:367 (1993).

New product management practices of small high technology firms (David A. Boag and Brenda L. Rinholm), 6:109 (1989).

New product strategy, structure, process and performance in the telecommunications industry (Gloria Barczak), 12:224 (1995).

New products and financial risk changes (Timothy M. Devinney), 9:222 (1992).

Opportunities for revitalizing stagnant markets: an analysis of household appliances (William A. V. Clark, Howard E. Freeman, and Dominique M. Hanssens), 1:242 (1984).

Organizational influences on the new product development process in financial services (Des Thwaites), 9:303 (1992).

Positioning of financial services for competitive advantage (Christopher J. Easingwood and Vijay Mahajan), 6:207 (1989).

Product development in the chemical industry: a description of a maturing business (Robert A. Linn), 1:116 (1984).

Product innovation by smaller high technology firms in Canada (Russell M. Knight), 3:195 (1986).

A profile of the new product professional (Laurence P. Feldman), 8:252 (1991).

Project team communication and cross-functional cooperation in new program development (Mary Beth Pinto and Jeffrey K. Pinto), 7:200 (1990).

R&D: Its relationship to company performance (Graham K. Morbey), 5:191 (1988).

R&D patterns in the video display terminal industry (Albert N. Linn and Robert W. Zmud), 1:106 (1984).

Redesigning product lines with conjoint analysis: a comment (Dick R. Wittink), 6:289 (1989).

Redesigning product lines with conjoint analysis: a reply to Wittink (Albert L. Page and Harold F. Rosenbaum), 6:293 (1989).

A retailer's view of industrial innovation: an interview with David Glass, President and CEO of Wal-Mart Stores Inc. (Gerald G. Udell and Linda S. Pettijohn), 8:231 (1991).

Rethink strategy or perish: technology lessons from telecommunications (Mariann Jelinek), 1:36 (1984).

Success and failure in new industrial services (Ulrike de Brentani), 6:239 (1989).

Technology strategy in a software products company (Marc H. Meyer and Luis Lopez), 12:294 (1995).

Technology transfer to the private sector: a field study of manufacturer buying behavior (David W. Large and Donald W. Barclay), 9:26 (1992).

Testing market segment acceptance of new designs of industrial services (Arch G. Woodside and William G. Pearce), 6:185 (1989).

What distinguishes the top performing new products in financial services (Robert G. Cooper, Christopher J. Easingwood, Scott Edgett, Elko J. Kleinschmidt, and Chris Storey), 11:281 (1994).

From experience: the customer's eye view of innovation (Donald V. Potter), 6:35 (1989).

From experience: developing new product concepts via the lead user method: a case study in a "low tech" field (Cornelius Herstatt and Eric von Hippel), 9:213 (1992).

From experience: The Role of Market Research in the Development of New Consumer Products (Robert E. Davis), 10:309 (1993).

From experience: The role of objective in vivo testing in the Product Development Process (Ronald Drozdenko and Sidney Weinstein), 3:120 (1986).

From experience: Where does your new technology fit into the marketplace (Frank Lynn and Susan Heintz), 9:19 (1992).

Identifying key customers for novel industrial products (Richard N. Cardozo, David K. Smith, Jr., and Madhubalan Viswanathan), 5:102 (1988).

Identifying new product success in China (Mark E. Parry and X. Michael Song), 11:15 (1994).

The impact of seasonality on the launch of infrequently purchased products (Marvin Berkowitz), 3:251 (1986).

Improving the organizational adoption rate for new high-technology industrial products (Roger A. More), 1:182 (1984).

The institutional domain of technology diffusion (N. Mohan Reddy, John D. Aram, and Leonard H. Lynn), 8:295 (1991).

Integrating customer requirements into product designs (Antonio J. Bailetti and Paul F. Litva), 12:3 (1995).

Invention evaluation services: a review of the state of the art (Gerald G. Udell), 6:157 (1989).

Maximizing the utility of customer product testing: Beta Test Design and Management (Robert J. Dolan and John M. Matthews), 10:318 (1993).

Measuring technology incorporation/infusion (Robert W. Zmud and L. Eugene Apple), 9:148 (1992).

New industrial financial services: what distinguishes the winners (Robert G. Cooper and Ulricke de Brentani), 8:75 (1991).

New industrial product design and evaluation using multiattribute value analysis (Ralph L. Keeney and Gary L. Lilien), 4:185 (1987).

New industrial product performance: the effects of market characteristics and strategy (Eunsang Yoon and Gary L. Lilien), 2:134 (1985).

New product models: practice, short-comings and desired improvements (Vijay Mahajan and Jerry Wind), 9:128 (1992).

New products over the business cycle (Timothy M. Devinney), 7:261 (1990).

Nine tested ways to mislead product planners (Robert J. Lavidge), 1:101 (1984).

Opportunities for revitalizing stagnant markets: an analysis of household appliances (William A. V. Clark, Howard E. Freeman, and Dominique M. Hanssens), 1:242 (1984).

Perspective: the applicability of percolation theory to innovation (J. Mort), 8:32 (1991).

Perspective: barriers to innovation: intraorganizational dislocations (Roger A. More), 2:205 (1985).

Perspective: market adaptation as a process in the product life cycle of radical innovations and high technology products (Shelby H. McIntyre), 5:140 (1988).

Perspective: marketing hype: a new perspective for new product research and introduction (Jerry Wind and Vijay Mahajan), 4:43 (1987).

Pretest market models: a critical evaluation (Allen D. Shocker and William G. Hall), 3:86 (1986).

Pricing augmented commercial services (Roberto Friedmann and Warren A. French), 4:33 (1987).

Problems in demand estimation for a new technology (Robert J. Thomas), 2:145 (1985).

Product design strategies for target-market positioning (Paul E. Green and Abba M. Krieger), 8:189 (1991).

Product growth strategies in young high-technology firms (Teresa M. Pavia), 7:297 (1990).

Product innovation management in Spain (Angel Martinez Sanchez and Luis Navarro Elola), 8:49 (1991).

Product shape as a design innovation srategy (Marvin Berkowitz), 4:274 (1987).

Psychological meaning of products and product positioning (Roberto Friedmann and V. Parker Lessig), 4:265 (1987).

New Product Planning

Developing an effective testing program for consumer durables (Albert L. Page and Harold F. Rosenbaum), 9:267 (1992).

Diffusing new ideas in-house (Sandra Vandermerwe), 4:256 (1987).

The dimensions of industrial new product success and failure in state enterprises in the People's Republic of China (X. Michael Song and Mark E. Parry), 11:105 (1994).

The dissemination and use of innovative knowledge (Neville Johnson and Warren B. Brown), 3:127 (1986).

Do new product development managers in large or high-market share firms perceive marketing–R&D Interface principles differently? (Ted Haggblom, Roger J. Calantone, and C. Anthony Di Benedetto), 12:323 (1995).

The early stages of new product development in entrepreneurial high-tech firms (Teresa M. Pavia), 8:18 (1991).

An ecological perspective on new product failure: the effects of competitive overcrowding (William H. Redmond), 12:200 (1995).

Emerging industries and the burnout of pioneers (Francisco-Javier Olleros), 3:5 (1986).

Evaluating QFD's use in U.S. firms as a process for developing products (Abbie Griffin), 9:171 (1992).

Expected development time reductions in the German mechanical engineering industry (Philipp A. Murmann), 11:236 (1994).

Expert systems: an emerging technology for selecting new product winners (Sundaresan Ram and Sudha Ram), 6:89 (1989).

An exploratory analysis of the impact of market orientation on new product performance (Kwaku Atuahene-Gima), 12:275 (1995).

Factors influencing new product success and failure in small entrepreneurial high-technology electronics firms (Chee Meng Yap and William E. Souder), 11:418 (1994).

Financial evaluation of the product line (Samuel Rabino and Arnold Wright), 2:56 (1985).

Five modern lessons from a 55 year old technological forecast (Steven P. Schnaars, Swee L. Chia, and Cesar M. Maloles III), 10:66 (1993).

From experience: balancing the product development process: achieving product and cycle-time excellence in high technology industries (Michael Anthony and Jonathan McKay), 9:140 (1992).

From experience: benchmarking new product development funding (Kathleen A. Pierz), 12:43 (1995).

From experience: creating brand names that work (Lorna Opatow), 2:254 (1985).

From experience Global Design (Robert Blaich), V (1988), 296.

From experience: how to increase the odds for successful brand extension (Chester L. Kane), 4:199 (1987).

From experience: implementing a stage-gate process: a multi-company perspective (Paul O'Connor), 11:183 (1994).

From experience: new idea enhancement at Amoco Chemical: an early report from a new system (Jeff D. Felberg and David A. DeMarco), 9:278 (1992).

From experience: the role of market research in the development of new consumer products (Robert E. Davis), 10:309 (1993).

From experience: schedule emphasis of new product development personnel (Milton D. Rosenau, Jr.), 6:185 (1989).

From experience: technical development and the innovation process (Harold C. Livesay, Marcia L. Rorke, and David S. Lux), 6:268 (1989).

From experience: time-driven development of software in manufactured goods (Tomlinson G. Rauscher and Preston G. Smith), 12:186 (1995).

From experience: where does your mew technology fit into the marketplace (Frank Lynn and Susan Heintz), 9:19 (1992).

Guidelines for corporate trademark licensing (Thomas A. Meyer, Cathie H. Tinney, and Terry J. Tinney), 2:196 (1985).

How involving more functional areas within a firm affects the new product process (Linda Rochford and William Rudelius), 9:287 (1992).

Identifying new product success in China (Mark E. Parry and X. Michael Song), 11:15 (1994).

Principles versus practice in new product planning (Laurence P. Feldman and Albert L. Page), 1:43 (1984).

Product development: an assessment of educational resources (L. Eugene Apple and Dinoo J. Vanier), 5:70 (1988).

Product development in the chemical industry: a description of a maturing business (Robert A. Linn), 1:116 (1984).

Product growth strategies in young high-technology firms (Teresa M. Pavia), 7:297 (1990).

Product innovation management in Spain (Angel Martinez Sanchez and Luis Navarro Elola), 8:49 (1991).

Product innovativeness and entry strategy: impact on cycle time and break-even time (Abdul Ali, Robert Krapfel, Jr., and Douglas LaBahn), 12:54 (1995).

Product/market innovations: a study of top management involvement among four cultures (W. Harvey Hegarty and Richard C. Hoffman), 7:186 (1990).

Product replacement: strategies for simultaneous product deletion and launch (John Saunders and David Jobber), 11:433 (1994).

Proficiency of new product process activities, project outcomes and organizational environment (Larry Dwyer and Robert Mellor), 8:39 (1991).

Project team communication and cross-functional cooperation in new program development (Mary Beth Pinto and Jeffrey K. Pinto), 7:200 (1990).

R&D marketing integration mechanisms, communication flows and innovation success (Rudy K. Moenaert, William E. Souder, Arnoud De Meyer, and Dirk Deschoolmeester), 11:31 (1994).

The risk pyramid for new product development: an application to complex aerospace hardware (William E. Souder and David Bethay), 10:181 (1993).

Significant issues for the future of product innovation: future issues in new product innovation management (Thomas D. Kuczmarski), 11:73 (1994).

Significant issues for the future of product innovation: third world niche players: way-chee for US new product developers (William E. Souder), 11:344 (1994).

Significant issues for the future of product innovation: we should be proud, but not satisfied (C. Merle Crawford), 11:253 (1994).

A strategic framework for assessing product line additions (Joseph Guiltinan), 10:136 (1993).

Success and failure in new industrial services (Ulrike de Brentani), 6:239 (1989).

Success factors in product innovation: a selective review of the literature (F. Axel Johne and Patricia A. Snelson), 5:114 (1988).

Success factors of high-tech SBUs: towards a conceptual model based on the Israeli electronics and computers industry (Dov Dvir and Aaron Shenhar), 7:288 (1990).

A survey of major approaches for accelerating new product development (Murray R. Millson, S. P. Raj, and David Wilemon), 9:53 (1992).

Team product reviews: a means of improving product quality and acceptance (Kenneth A. Kozar), 4:204 (1987).

Technology strategy in a software products company (Marc H. Meyer and Luis Lopez), 12:294 (1995).

Time-based management of the new product development process (Necmi Karagozoglu and Warren B. Brown), 10:204 (1993).

What distinguishes the top performing new products in financial services (Robert G. Cooper, Christopher J. Easingwood, Scott Edgett, Elko J. Kleinschmidt, and Chris Storey), 11:281 (1994).

When technologies compete: the role of externalities in nonlinear market response (William H. Redmond), 8:170 (1991).

Why put off until tomorrow what you can do today: incentives and the timing of new product introduction (William P. Putsis, Jr.), 10:195 (1993).

Organizing for Innovation

An analysis of the use of extrafunctional information by R&D and marketing personnel: review and model (Rudy K. Moenaert and William E. Souder), 7:213 (1990).

Improving the strategy–innovation link (Vasudevan Ramanujam and Gerhard O. Mensch), 2:213 (1985).

An information transfer model for integrating marketing and R&D personnel in new product development projects (Rudy K. Moenaert and William E. Souder), 7:91 (1990).

Innovation in the systems business: dynamics of autonomy and cooperation (Glenn C. Bacon), 2:107 (1985).

Innovators, organization structure and management of the innovation process in the securities industry (Akira Iwamura and Vijay M. Jog), 8:104 (1991).

Integrating customer requirements into product designs (Antonio J. Bailetti and Paul F. Litva), 12:3 (1995).

Issues for management thought and research (Members of the Editorial Board), 1:199 (1984).

Japanese and British companies compared: contributing factors to success and failure in NPD (Scott Edgett, David Shipley, and Giles Forbes), 9:3 (1992).

Leadership differences in new product development teams (Gloria Barczak and David Wilemon), 6:259 (1989).

Learning in new technology development teams (Patricia W. Meyers and David Wilemon), 6:79 (1989).

Managing relations between R&D and marketing in new product development projects (William E. Souder), 5:6 (1988).

Managing technologically innovative team efforts toward new product success (Hans J. Thamhain), 7:5 (1990).

Managing time efficiently to avoid product obsolescence: a survey of techniques (Rene Cordero), 8:283 (1991).

Marketing/R&D interaction in new product development: implications for new product success rates (Richard T. Hise, Larry O'Neal, A. Parasuraman, and James U. McNeal), 7:142 (1990).

The Marketing–R&D interface: do personality factors gave an impact (George H. Lucas, Jr., and Alan J. Bush), 5:257 (1988).

New product strategy, structure, process and performance in the telecommunications industry (Gloria Barczak), 12:224 (1995).

Organizational influences on the new product development process in financial services (Des Thwaites), 9:303 (1992).

An organizational learning approach to product innovation (Daryl McKee), 9:232 (1992).

Organizational obstacles to innovation: a formulation of the problem (Volney Stefflre), 2:3 (1985).

Organizing for product development projects (Erik W. Larson and David H. Gobeli), 5:180 (1988).

Perspective: cross-functional teams: good concept, poor implementation! (John W. Henke, Jr., A. Richard Krachenberg, and Thomas F. Lyons), 10:216 (1993).

Perspective: first things first (Colin Clipson), 7:135 (1990).

Perspective: get ready for innovation by invasion (Gerhard O. Mensch), 2:259 (1985).

Perspective: the Wal-Mart innovation network: an experiment in stimulating American innovation (Gerald G. Udell, Ronald Bottin, and David D. Glass), 10:23 (1993).

A profile of the new product professional (Laurence P. Feldman), 8:252 (1991).

R&D marketing integration mechanisms, communication flows and innovation success (Rudy K. Moenaert, William E. Souder, Arnoud De Meyer, and Dirk Deschoolmeester), 11:31 (1994).

The R&D–Marketing interface in high-technology firms (Ashok K. Gupta, S. P. Raj, and David Wilemon), 2:12 (1985).

The R&D–Marketing interface in Japanese high-technology firms (X. Michael Song and Mark E. Parry), 9:91 (1992).

The R&D/production interface: a case study of new product commercialization (Martin E. Ginn and Albert Rubenstein), 3:158 (1986).

Research notes: the need for a field of study of implementation innovations (C. A. Voss), 2:266 (1985).

Significant issues for the future of product innovation: from product innovation management to total innovation management (Chris Voss), 11:460 (1994).

Product Concept

From experience: developing new product concepts via the lead user method: a case study in a "low tech" field (Cornelius Herstatt and Eric von Hippel), 9:213 (1992).

From experience: how to increase the odds for successful brand extension (Chester L. Kane), 4:199 (1987).

From experience: new idea enhancement at Amoco Chemical: an early report from a new system (Jeff D. Felberg and David A. DeMarco), 9:278 (1992).

From experience: technical development and the innovation process (Harold C. Livesay, Marcia L. Rorke, and David S. Lux), 6:268 (1989).

Guidelines for corporate trademark licensing (Thomas A. Meyer, Cathie H. Tinney, and Terry J. Tinney), 2:196 (1985).

How concept knowledge affects concept evaluation (R. Eric Reidenbach and Sharon Grimes), 1:255 (1984).

Integrating customer requirements into product designs (Antonio J. Bailetti and Paul F. Litva), 12:3 (1995).

New industrial product design and evaluation using multiattribute value analysis (Ralph L. Keeney and Gary L. Lilien), 4:185 (1987).

A new positioning typology (C. Merle Crawford), 2:243 (1985).

A new way to create winning product ideas (Christian Wagner and Albert Hayashi), 11:146 (1994).

Perspective: marketing hype: a new perspective for new product research and introduction (Jerry Wind and Vijay Mahajan), 4:43 (1987).

Positioning of financial services for competitive advantage (Christopher J. Easingwood and Vijay Mahajan), 6:207 (1989).

Proficiency of new product process activities, project outcomes and organizational environment (Larry Dwyer and Robert Mellor), 8:39 (1991).

Protocol: new tool for product innovation (C. Merle Crawford), 1:85 (1984).

Psychological meaning of products and product positioning (Roberto Friedmann and V. Parker Lessig), 4:265 (1987).

Purchase intentions and the dimensions of innovation: an exploratory model (Susan L. Holak and Donald R. Lehmann), 7:59 (1990).

Redesigning product lines with conjoint analysis: a comment (Dick R. Wittink), 6:289 (1989).

Redesigning product lines with conjoint analysis: a reply to Wittink (Albert L. Page and Harold F. Rosenbaum), 6:293 (1989).

Redesigning product lines with conjoint analysis: how Sunbeam does it (Albert L. Page and Harold F. Rosenbaum), 4:120 (1987).

The risk pyramid for new product development: an application to complex aerospace hardware (William E. Souder and David Bethay), 10:181 (1993).

Sources of competitive advantage in new products (Michael W. Lawless and Robert J. Fisher), 7:35 (1990).

Speeding up new product development: the effects of leadership style and source of technology (Edward F. McDonough III and Gloria Barczak), 8:203 (1991).

What focus groups can and cannot do: a reply to Seymour (Edward F. McQuarrie and Shelby H. McIntyre), 4:55 (1987).

Product Development

Accelerating product development: a preliminary empirical test of a hierarchy of implementation (Ed J. Nijssen, Arthur R. L. Aarbouw, and Harry R. Commandeur), 12:99 (1995).

Accelerating the durable replacement cycle with marketing mix variables (Barry L. Bayus), 5:216 (1988).

An analysis of the use of extrafunctional information by R&D and marketing personnel: review and model (Rudy K. Moenaert and William E. Souder), 7:213 (1990).

Approaches to accelerating product and process development (Bela Gold), 4:81 (1987).

Are business incubators really creating new jobs by creating new businesses and new products? (Gerald G. Udell), 7:108 (1990).

Significant issues for the future of product innovation: from product innovation management to total innovation management (Chris Voss), 11:460 (1994).

Significant issues for the future of product innovation: a note contrasting approaches to strategic planning in U.S. and Japanese corporations (Bela Gold), 11:71 (1994).

Speeding up new product development: the effects of leadership style and source of technology (Edward F. McDonough III and Gloria Barczak), 8:203 (1991).

Strategic Control of R&D resource allocations in diversified businesses (Igal Ayal and Robert Rothberg), III (1986), 238.

Strategic mutual learning between producing and buying firms during product innovation (Patricia W. Meyers and Gerard A. Athaide), 8:155 (1991).

Success factors in product innovation: a selective review of the literature (F. Axel Johne and Patricia A. Snelson), 5:114 (1988).

A Survey of major approaches for accelerating new product development (Murray R. Millson, S. P. Raj, and David Wilemon), IX (1992), 53.

Team product reviews: a means of improving product quality and acceptance (Kenneth A. Kozar), 4: 204 (1987).

Technology strategy in a software products company (Marc H. Meyer and Luis Lopez), 12:294 (1995).

What distinguishes the top performing new products in financial services (Robert G. Cooper, Christopher J. Easingwood, Scott Edgett, Elko J. Kleinschmidt, and Chris Storey), 11:281 (1994).

Strategy

Adaptive responses by conservative and entrepreneurial firms (Necmi Karagozoglu and Warren B. Brown), 5:269 (1988).

Applying hedonic pricing models and factorial surveys at Parker Pen to enhance new product success (Chuck Tomkovick and Kathryn E. Dobie), 12:334 (1995).

An approach for determining optimal product sampling for the diffusion of a new product (Dipak Jain, Vijay Mahajan, and Eitan Muller), 12:124 (1995).

An approach to assess the importance of brand equity in acquisition decisions (Vijay Mahajan, Vithala R. Rao, and Rajendra K. Srivastava), 11:221 (1994).

Approaches to accelerating product and process development (Bela Gold), 4:81 (1987).

Are business incubators really creating new jobs by creating new businesses and new products? (Gerald G. Udell), 7:108 (1990).

Benchmarking the firm's critical success factors in new product development (Robert G. Cooper and Elko J. Kleinschmidt), 12:374 (1995).

Beyond the life cycle: organizational and technological design. I. an alternative perspective (Chris DeBresson and Joseph Lampel), 2:170 (1985).

Beyond the life cycle. II. an illustration (Chris DeBresson and Joseph Lampel), 2:188 (1985).

Characteristics of innovative firms in the Brazilian computer industry (Angela da Rocha, Carl H. Christensen, and Newton A. Paim), 7:123 (1990).

Characteristics of the industrial distributor's innovation activities: an exploratory study (Eunsang Yoon and Gary L. Lilien), 5:227 (1988).

The co-diffusion of complementary innovations: supermarket scanners and UPC symbols (Louis P. Bucklin and Sanjit Sengupta), 10:148 (1993).

Competitive advantage through product performance innovation in a competitive market (John H. Friar), 12:33 (1995).

Corporate innovation and entrepreneurship: a Canadian study (Russell M. Knight), 4:284 (1987).

Determinants of inward technology licensing intentions: an empirical analysis of australian engineering firms (Kwaku Atuahene-Gima), 10:230 (1993).

Determinants of technical success in product development when innovative radicalness is considered (Mushin Lee and Dohyeong Na), 11:62 (1994).

Developing a network R&D strategy (Hakan Hakansson and Jens Laage-Hellman), 1:224 (1984).

The development of novel products through intra- and inter-organizational networks: the case of home automation (Joe Tidd), 12:307 (1995).

It's still caveat, inventor (Gerald G. Udell), 7:230 (1990).

Japanese and British companies compared: contributing factors to success and failure in NPD (Scott Edgett, David Shipley, and Giles Forbes), 9:3 (1992).

Licensing as an alternative to foreign direct investment: an empirical investigation (Y. Adam, C. H. Ong, and A. W. Pearson), 5:32 (1988).

Major new products: what distinguishes the winners in the chemical industry (Robert G. Cooper and Elko J. Kleinschmidt), 10:90 (1993).

Managing design in small high growth companies (Peter Dickson, Wendy Schneier, Peter Lawrence, and Renee Hytry), 12:406 (1995).

Managing research and development for results (Peter R. Richardson), 2:75 (1985).

Managing time efficiently to avoid product obsolescence: a survey of techniques (Rene Cordero), 8: 283 (1991).

Measuring new product success: the difference that time perspective makes (Erik Jan Hultink and Henry S. J. Robben), 12:392 (1995).

A model for the development of small high-technology businesses based on case studies from an incubator (Alf Scherer and David W. McDonald), 5:282 (1988).

New industrial financial services: what distinguishes the winners (Robert G. Cooper and Ulricke de Brentani), 8:75 (1991).

New industrial product performance: the effects of market characteristics and strategy (Eunsang Yoon and Gary L. Lilien), 2:134 (1985).

New product development in the pharmaceutical industry: pooling network resources (D. Jane Bower), 10:367 (1993).

New product development practices of industrial marketers (William L. Moore), 4:6 (1987).

New product strategies: what distinguishes the top performers? (Robert G. Cooper), 1:151 (1984).

New product strategy, structure, process and performance in the telecommunications industry (Gloria Barczak), 12:224 (1995).

New products and financial risk changes (Timothy M. Devinney), 9:222 (1992).

New products over the business cycle (Timothy M. Devinney), 7:261 (1990).

New products: what separates winners from losers (R. G. Cooper and E. J. Kleinschmidt), 4:169 (1987).

Perspective: marketing hype: a new perspective for new product research and introduction (Jerry Wind and Vijay Mahajan), 4:43 (1987).

A philosophy for innovation (Carol J. Steiner), 12:431 (1995).

Pioneering versus incremental innovation: review and research propositions (Abdul Ali), 11:46 (1994).

Positioning of financial services for competitive advantage (Christopher J. Easingwood and Vijay Mahajan), 6:207 (1989).

Pricing augmented commercial services (Roberto Friedmann and Warren A. French), 4:33 (1987).

Product development strategy: an integration of technology and marketing (Harry Nystrom), 2:25 (1985).

Product growth strategies in young high-technology firms (Teresa M. Pavia), 7:297 (1990).

Product innovation by smaller high technology firms in Canada (Russell M. Knight), 3:195 (1986).

Product innovation management in Spain (Angel Martinez Sanchez and Luis Navarro Elola), 8:49 (1991).

Product innovativeness and entry strategy: impact on cycle time and break-even time (Abdul Ali, Robert Krapfel, Jr., and Douglas LaBahn), 12:54 (1995).

Product-market choices and growth of new businesses (Richard Cardozo, Karen McLaughlin, Brian Harmon, Paul Reynolds, and Brenda Miller), 10:331 (1993).

Product/market innovations: a study of top management involvement among four cultures (W. Harvey Hegarty and Richard C. Hoffman), 7:186 (1990).

Product replacement: strategies for simultaneous product deletion and launch (John Saunders and David Jobber), 11:433 (1994).

Proficiency of new product process activities, project outcomes and organizational environment (Larry Dwyer and Robert Mellor), 8:39 (1991).

Technological Innovation

Beyond the life cycle: organizational and technological design. I. an alternative perspective (Chris DeBresson and Joseph Lampel), 2:170 (1985).

Beyond the life cycle. II. an illustration (Chris DeBresson and Joseph Lampel), 2:188 (1985).

A Brownian motion model for technology transfer: application to a machine maintenance expert system (Venkatesh Padmanabhan and William E. Souder), 11:119 (1994).

The co-diffusion of complementary innovations: supermarket scanners and UPC symbols (Louis P. Bucklin and Sanjit Sengupta), 10:148 (1993).

Collapsing new product development times: six case studies (Vincent A. Mabert, John F. Muth, and Roger W. Schmenner), 9:200 (1992).

A comparison of approaches for setting standards for technological products (Barry Nathan Rosen, Steven P. Schnaars, and David Shani), 5:129 (1988).

Complementarity, compatibility and product change: breaking with the past (Anirudh Dhebar), 12: 136 (1995).

Computing technology for the home: product strategies for the next generation (Alladi Venkatesh and Nicholas P. Vitalari), 3:171 (1986).

Concurrent engineering practices in selected Swedish companies: a movement or an activity of the few? (Lars Trygg), 10:403 (1993).

A cusp catastrophe model of the adoption of an industrial innovation (Paul A. Herbig), 8:127 (1991).

Cycle time in packaged software firms (Erran Carmel), 12:110 (1995).

Designers' impressions of direct contact between product designers and champions of innovation (Antonio J. Bailetti and Paul D. Guild), 8:91 (1991).

Determinants of inward technology licensing intentions: an empirical analysis of Australian engineering firms (Kwaku Atuahene-Gima), 10:230 (1993).

Determinants of R&D–marketing integration in high-tech Japanese firms (Mark E. Parry and X. Michael Song), 10:4 (1993).

Determinants of technical success in product development when innovative radicalness is considered (Mushin Lee and Dohyeong Na), 11:62 (1994).

The development of novel products through intra- and inter-organizational networks: the case of home automation (Joe Tidd), 12:307 (1995).

A discussion of the link between one organization's style and structure and its connection with its market (Kathleen Bentley), 7:19 (1990).

The effects of cognitive problem solving orientation and technological familiarity on faster new product development (Edward F. McDonough III and Gloria Barczak), 9:44 (1992).

Emerging industries and the burnout of pioneers (Francisco-Javier Olleros), 3:5 (1986).

Evaluating QFD's use in U.S. firms as a process for developing products (Abbie Griffin), 9:171 (1992).

Evolving toward product and market orientation: the early years of technology-based firms (Edward B. Roberts), 7:274 (1990).

External technology and in-house R&D's facilitative role (Falguni Sen and A. H. Rubenstein), 6:123 (1989).

Factors affecting the process of collaborative product development: a study of UK manufacturers of information and communications technology products (Dale Littler, Fiona Leverick, and Margaret Bruce), 12:16 (1995).

Five modern lessons from a 55 year old technological forecast (Steven P. Schnaars, Swee L. Chia, and Cesar M. Maloles III), 10:66 (1993).

Forced adoption of innovations in organizations: consequences and implications (S. Ram and Hyung-Shik Jung), 8:117 (1991).

From experience: avoiding the best-of-the-best specification trap (Milton D. Rosenau, Jr.), 9:300 (1992).

From experience: balancing the product development process: achieving product and cycle-time excellence in high technology industries (Michael Anthony and Jonathan McKay), 9:140 (1992).

From experience: faster new product development (Milton D. Rosenau, Jr.), 5:150 (1988).

From experience: new idea enhancement at Amoco Chemical: an early report from a new system (Jeff D. Felberg and David A. DeMarco), 9:278 (1992).

Author Index

CUMULATIVE INDEX OF ABSTRACTS

The *Journal of Product Innovation Management* began publishing abstracts of important articles in the field of new products management in September 1986. This index is organized by subject area and shows the original source of each article. This cumulative index includes all abstracts published in the journal through the end of 1995. The final portion of each listing shows the *JPIM* volume number, the page number(s), and the issue month and year where the abstract appears in a particular issue. Please note that pages are numbered consecutively throughout each volume. Since its inception, the abstract section has been edited by C. Merle Crawford.

Creativity

Anderson, Joseph V. Creativity and play: a systematic approach to managing innovation. *Business Horizons*, pp. 80–85 (March–April 1994). [12:172 (March 1995)]

Badawy, Michael K. How to prevent creativity mismanagement. *Research Management*, pp. 28–35 (July–August 1986). [3:300–301 (December 1986)]

Bailetti, Antonio J. and Guild, Paul D. A method for projects seeking to merge technical advancements with potential markets. *R&D Management*, pp. 291–300 (October 1991). [9:178–179. (June 1992)]

Basadur, Min and Thompson, Ron. Usefulness of the ideation principle of extended effort in real world professional and managerial creative problem solving. *Journal of Creative Behavior*, pp. 23–34 (First Quarter 1986). [4:73 (March 1987)]

Bello, Daniel C. and Barczak, Gloria J. Using industrial trade shows to improve new product development. *Journal of Business and Industrial Marketing*, pp. 43–56 (Summer–Fall 1990). [8:58–59 (March 1991)]

Branscomb, Anne W. Who owns creativity? *Technology Review*, pp. 38–45 (May–June 1988). [6:69–70 (March 1989)]

Computers that talk and listen: has the time finally come? (unsigned article). *International Management*, pp. 34–35 [(October 1988). [6:227 (September 1989)]

Cooper, Eileen. A critique of six measures for assessing creativity. *Journal of Creative Behavior*, pp. 194–204 (Third Quarter 1991). [10:165 (March 1993)]

Cross, Nigel. The nature and nurture of design ability. *Design Studies*, (U.K.), pp. 127–140 (July 1990). [8:63–64 (March 1991)]

Dougherty, Elizabeth. Technology scouts. *Research and Development*, pp. 44–50 (October 1989). [7:163 (June 1990)]

Edwards, Mark R. Measuring creativity at work: seveloping a reward-for-creativity policy. *Journal of Creative Behavior*, pp. 26–37 (First Quarter 1989). [6:310 (December 1989)]

Ekvall, Göran. Creativity in project work: a longitudinal study of a product development project. *Creativity and Innovation Management*, pp. 17–26 (March 1993). [11:170–171 (March 1994)]

Gallupe, R. Brent and William H. Cooper. Brainstorming electronically. *Sloan Management Review*, pp. 27–36 (Fall 1993). [11:265–266 (June 1994)]

Gardner, Howard. Freud in three frames: a cognitive-scientific approach to creativity. *Daedalus*, pp. 105–134 (Summer 1986). [5:84–85 (March 1988)]

Gernand, Vivian L. Fantasies for sale: marketing products that do not yet exist. *Journal of Business and Industrial Marketing*, pp. 31–36 (GPL) (Summer–Fall 1991). [8:312–313 (December 1991)]

Gilad, Benny. Entrepreneurship: the issue of creativity in the market place. *Journal of Creative Behavior*, pp. 151–160 (Third Quarter 1984). [3:302–303 (December 1986)]

Gluck, Frederick W. "Big-bang" management: creative innovation. *The McKinsey Quarterly*, pp 49–59 (Spring 1985). [4:302 (December 1987)]

Goldsmith, Ronald E. and Kerr, John R. Entrepreneurship and adaption-innovation theory. *Technovation*, pp. 373–382 (September 1991). [9:252 September 1992)]

Hines, Terence. Left brain/right brain mythology and implications for management and training. *Academy of Management Review*, pp. 600–605 (October 1987). [5:172–173 (June 1988)]

Isaksen, Scott G., Puccio, Gerard J., and Treffinger, Donald J. An ecological approach to creativity research: profiling for creative problem solving. *Journal of Creative Behavior*, pp. 149–170 (Third Quarter 1993). [12:86–87 (January 1995)]

Kiely, Thomas. The idea makers. *Technology Review*, pp. 32–40 (January 1993). [11:82 (January 1994)]

Kiely, Tom. Innovation congregations. *Technology Review*, (April 1994, pp. 56–60). [12:84–85 (January 1995)]

Klein, Arthur R. Organizational barriers to creativity . . . and how to knock them down. *Journal of Consumer Marketing*, pp. 65–66 (Winter 1990). [7:324–325 (December 1990)]

Lammey, Glenn D. New product portfolio power. *Business Marketing*, pp. 64–70 (October 1987). [5:168 (June 1988)]

Mattimore, Bryan. Eureka: how to invent a new product. *The Futurist*, pp. 34–38 (March–April 1995). [12:451–452 (November 1995)]

Mellow, Craig. Successful products of the eighties. *Across the Board*, pp. 40–49 (November 1988). [6:145 (June 1989)]

Morse, David T. and Khatena, Joe. The relationship of creativity and life accomplishments. *Journal of Creative Behavior*, pp. 59–65 (First Quarter 1989). [6:302 (December 1989)]

Park, C. Wham and Smith, Daniel C. Product class competitors as sources of innovative marketing strategies. *Journal of Consumer Marketing*, pp. 27–37 (Spring 1990). [8:60–61 (March 1991)]

Perry, Tekla S. Designing a culture for creativity. *Research Technology Management*, pp. 14–17 (March–April 1995). [12:445–446 (November 1995)]

Promises, promises (unsigned article). *International Management*, pp. 34–35 (October 1988). [6:227 (September 1989)]

Richards, Tudor. Innovation and creativity: woods, trees and pathways. *R&D Management*, pp. 97–108 (April 1991). [8:309–310 (Decmeber 1991)]

Rosenberg, Michael S. and Thompson, Bruce M. Rooting out the causes of inefficient product creation. *Prism*, pp. 97–111 (Second Quarter 1993). [11: 262–263 (June 1994)]

Rosenman, Martin F. Serendipity and scientific discovery. *Journal of Creative Behavior*, pp. 132–138 (Second Quarter 1988). [6:231–232 (September 1989)]

Sapp, D. David. The point of creative frustration and the creative process: a new look at an old model. *Journal of Creative Behavior*, pp. 21–28 (First Quarter 1992). [10:85–86 (January 1993)]

Scott, Susanne G. and Bruce, Reginald A. Determinants of innovative behavior: a path model for individual innovation in the workplace. *Academy of Management Journal*, pp. 580–607 (June 1994). [12:83–84 (January 1995)]

Shalley, Christina E. Effects of productivity goals, creativity goals, and personal discretion on individual creativity. *Journal of Applied Psychology*, pp. 179–185 (April 1991). [8:318–319 (December 1991)]

Simon, Herbert A. How managers express their creativity. *Across the Board*, pp. 11–19 (March 1986). [4:236 (September 1987)]

Smith, Bruce L. Interpersonal behaviors that damage the productivity of creative problem solving groups. *Journal of Creative Behavior*, pp. 171–187 (Third Quarter 1993). [11:467–468 (November 1994)]

Stasch, Stanley F., Lonsdale, Ronald T., and LaVenka, Noel M. Developing a framework for sources of new-product ideas. *Journal of Consumer Marketing*, pp. 5–15 (GPL) (Spring 1992). [9:315–316 (December 1992)]

Van Andel, Pek. Serendipity: "expect also the unexpected". *Creativity and Innovation Management*, pp. 20–32 (March 1992). [10:256–257 (June 1993)]

Vantrappen, Herman and Collins John. Controlling the product creation process. *Prism*, pp. 59–73 (Second Quarter 1993). [11:266 (June 1994)]

Waitley, Denis E. and Tucker, Robert B. How to think like an innovator. *The Futurist*, pp. 9–15 (May–June 1987). [4:309–310 (December 1987)]

Wise, George. It's a myth that all inventions come from outside. *Research Technology Management*, pp. 7–8 (July–August 1989). [7:86 (March 1990)]

Wonder, Jacquelyn and Blake, Jeffery. Creativity east and west: intuition vs. logic. *Journal of Creative Behavior*, pp. 172–185 (Third Quarter 1992). [10:435–436 (November 1993)]

Forecasting

Brody, Herb. Great expectations: why predictions go awry. *Journal of Consumer Marketing*, 1:23–27 (1993). [11:84–85 (January 1994)]

Brody, Herb. It seemed like a good idea at the time. *High Technology Business,* pp. 38–41 (October 1988). [6:65 (March 1989)]

Brody, Herb. Sorry, wrong number. *High Technology Business,* pp. 24–28 (September 1988). [6:65 (March 1989)]

Choffray, Jean Marie and Lilien, Gary L. A decision-support system for evaluating sales prospects and launch strategies for new products. *Industrial Marketing Management,* pp. 75–85 (February 1986). [4:74–75 (March 1987)]

Duke, Charles R. Understanding customer abilities in product concept tests. *Journal of Product and Brand Management,* 1:48–57 (1994). [11:466–467 (November 1994)]

Fowler, Robert L. Confidence intervals for the cross-validated multiple correlation in predictive regression models. *Journal of Applied Psychology,* pp. 318–322 (1986). [3:298–299 (December 1986)]

Georgoff, David M. and Murdick, Robert G. Managers guide to forecasting. *Harvard Business Review,* pp. 110–120 (January 1986). [3:209–210 (September 1986)]

Martino, Joseph P. Technological forecasting. *The Futurist,* pp. 13–16 (July–August 1993). [11:172 (March 1994)]

Meyers-Levy, Joan and Peracchio, Laura A. Getting an angle in advertising: the effect of camera angle on product evaluations. *Journal of Marketing Research,* pp. 454–461 (November 1992). [10:357 (September 1993)]

Morwitz, Vicki G. and Schmittlein, David. Using segmentation to improve sales forecasts based on purchase intent: which "intenders" actually buy? *Journal of Marketing Research,* pp. 391–405 (November 1992). [10:359 (September 1993)]

Schnaars, Steven P. Where forecasters go wrong. *Across the Board,* pp. 38–45 (December 1989). [7:168 (June 1990)]

Shaw, Robin N. and Bodi, Anna. Diffusion of product code scanning. *Industrial Marketing Management,* pp. 225–235 (1986). [4:229 (September 1987)]

Traynor, Kenneth and Traynor, Susan C. Long-range scenario research as a factor in long-range consumer marketing planning. *Journal of Consumer Marketing,* pp. 5–14 (Winter 1990). [7:249–250 (September 1990)]

Tyebjee, Tyzoon T. Behavioral biases in new product forecasting. *International Journal of Forecasting,* 30:393–404 (1987). [5:247–248 (September 1988)]

Urban, Glen L., Hauser, John R., and Roberts, John H. Prelaunch forecasting of new automobiles. *Management Science,* pp. 401–421 (April 1990). [8:148–149 (June 1991)]

Wheeler, David R. and Shelley, Charles J. Toward more realistic forecasts for high-technology products. *Journal of Business and Industrial Marketing,* pp. 55–63 (Summer 1987). [6:142–143 (June 1989)]

Industry Analysis

Aaker, David A. Building a brand: the Saturn story. *California Management Review*, pp. 114–133 (Winter 1994). [12:166–167 (March 1995)]

Berry, Leonard L. and Cooper, Linda R. Competing with time-saving service. *Business*, pp. 3–7 (April–June 1990). [8:317–318 (December 1991)]

Bertrand, Kate. The channel challenge. *Business Marketing*, pp. 42–50 (May 1989). [7:162 (June 1990)]

Biemans, Wim G. User and third-party involvement in developing medical equipment innovations. *Technovation*, pp. 163–181 (April 1991). [9:76–77 (March 1992)]

Bloom, Paul N. and Reve, Torger. Transmitting signals to consumers for competitive advantage. *Business Horizons*, pp. 58–66 (July–August 1990). [8: 145–146 (June 1991)]

Bright, James R. Improving the industrial anticipation of current scientific activity. *Technological Forecasting and Social Change*, pp. 1–12 (February 1986). [4:155–156 (June 1987)]

Brody, Herb. It seemed like a good idea at the time. *High Technology Business*, pp. 38–41 (October 1988). [6:65 (March 1989)]

Brody, Herb. Sorry, wrong number. *High Technology Business*, pp. 24–28 (September 1988). [6:65 (March 1989)]

Brown, Stephen A. The prescription drug marketing act. *Food Drug and Cosmetic Law Journal*, 45:245–253 (1990). [8:71 (March 1991)]

Bruce, Margaret, Leverick, Fiona, Littler, Dale, and Wilson, Dominic. Success factors for collaborative product development: a study of suppliers of information and communication technology. *R&D Management*, pp. 33–44 (January 1995). [12:350–351 (September 1995)]

Chakrabarti, Alok K. and Weisenfeld, Ursula. An empirical analysis of innovation strategies of biotechnological firms in the U.S. *Journal of Engineering and Technology Management*, pp. 243–260 (December 1991). [10:168 (March 1993)]

Collinson, Simon. Managing product innovation at Sony: the development of the data discman. *Technology Analysis and Strategic Management*, 3:285–306 (1993). [11:467 (November 1994)]

Dankanyin, Robert J. Defense company diversification: what it takes to succeed. *Technology Management*, 1:11–16 (1994). [12:258 (June 1995)]

Day, Ralph L. and Herbig, Paul A. How the diffusion of industrial innovations is different from new retail products. *Industrial Marketing Management*, pp. 261–266 (August 1990). [8:68–69 (March 1991)]

Dholakia, Ruby Roy, Dholakia, Nikhilesh, and Della Bitta, Albert J. Acquisition of telecommunications products and services: an examination of inter-sector differences. *IEEE Transactions on Engineering Management*, pp. 327–335 (November 1991). [9:175–176 (June 1992)]

Eisenhardt, Kathleen M. Speed and strategic choice: how managers accelerate decision-making. *California Management Review*, pp. 39–54 (Spring 1990). [8:66–67 (March 1991)]

Florida, Richard L. and Kenney, Martin. Venture capital-financed innovation and technological change in the USA. *Research Policy*, pp. 119–137 (June 1988). [6:151–152 (June 1989)]

Floyd, Thomas H., Jr. Personalizing public transportation. *The Futurist*, pp. 29–34 (November–December 1990). [8:140 (June 1991)]

Fritz, Wolfgang. Determinants of product innovation activities. *European Journal of Marketing*, pp. 32–43 (1990). [8:223–224 (September 1991)]

Gibson, W. David. A maze for management: choosing the right technology. *Chemical Week*, pp. 74–78 (May 7, 1986). [4:237–238 (September 1987)]

Gobeli, David H. and Rudelius, William. Managing innovation: lessons from the cardiac-pacing industry. *Sloan Management Review*, pp. 29–41 (Summer 1985). [3:304–305 (December 1986)]

Holmes, Jerry D., Nelson, Gregory O., and Stump, David C. Improving the innovation process at Eastman Chemical. *Research Technology Management*, pp. 27–35 (May–June 1993). [12:172–173 (March 1995)]

Ivey, Mark, Pitzer, Mary J., Drayfack, Kenneth, and Vamos, Mark N. Home shopping: is it a revolution in retailing—just a fad? *Business Week*, December 15, 1986, pp. 62–69. [4:160 (June 1987)]

Katsuto, Uchihashi. Toward methodology innovation in industry. *Japan Quarterly*, pp. 2–7 (January–March 1987). [5:244–245 (September 1988)]

Klivans, Jane M. Launching a financial service. *Journal of Business Strategy*, pp. 8–11 (RKR), (September–October 1990). [8:310 (December 1991)]

Larson, Erik W. Project management in pharmaceutical R&D. *Product and Process Innovation*, pp. 20–27 (March–April 1991). [9:77–78 (March 1992)]

Lawton, Stephan E. Controversy under the orphan drug act: is resolution on the way? *Food Drug and Cosmetic Law Journal*, pp. 327–343 (March 1991). [9:82–83 (March 1992)]

Liswood, Laura A. A new system for rating service quality. *Journal of Business Strategy*, pp. 42–45 (July–August 1989). [7:246 (September 1990)]

Littler, Dale and Wilson, Dominic. Strategic alliancing in computerized business systems. *Technovation*, pp. 457–473 (1988 8). [9:322–323 (December 1992)]

Luke, Roice D., Begun, James W., and Pointer, Dennis D. Quasi firms: strategic interorganizational forms in the health care industry. *Academy of Management Review*, 1:–19 (1989). [7:81–82 (March 1990)]

Lysonski, Steven, Singer, Alan, and Wilemon, David. Coping with environmental uncertainty and boundary spanning in the product manager's role. *Journal of*

Business and Industrial Marketing, pp. 5–16 (Winter 1988). [6:73–74 (March 1989)]

Macdonald, Roderick J. and Wang Jinliang. Time, timeliness of innovation, and the emergence of industries. *Technovation*, pp. 37–53 (February 1994). [12: 78–79 (January 1995)]

MacMillan, Ian, McCaffery, Mary Lynn, and Van Wijk, Gilles. Competitors' responses to easily imitated new products: exploring commercial banking product introductions. *Strategic Management Journal*, pp. 75–86 (1985). [4:310 (December 1987)]

Mitchell, Graham R. Research and development for services. *Research Technology Management*, pp. 37–44 (November–December 1989). [7:257 (September 1990)]

Morrison, Thomas C. The false advertising of speciality medical products under the Lanham Act. *Food Drug and Cosmetic Law Journal*, pp. 265–271 (May 1989). [7:252–253 (September 1990)]

Morton, Peter D. and Tarrant, Crispian. A new dimension to financial product innovation research. *Marketing and Research Today*, pp. 173–179 (August 1994). [12:350 (September 1995)]

Pisano, Gary P. The governance of innovation: vertical integration and collaborative arrangements in the biotechnology industry. *Research Policy*, pp. 237–249 (June 1991). [10:78 (January 1993)]

Prasad, S. Benjamin. Technology transfer: the approach of a dutch multinational. *Technovation*, pp. 3–15 (1986). [4:65–66 (March 1987)]

Richins, Marsha L. and Bloch, Peter H. Post-purchase product satisfaction: incorporating the effects of involvement and time. *Journal of Business Research*, pp. 145–158 (1991). [9:178 (June 1992)]

Roberts, Edward B. and Hauptman, Oscar. The process of technology transfer to the new biomedical and pharmaceutical firm. *Research Policy*, pp. 107–120 (June 1986). [4:303–304 (December 1987)]

Romanelli, Elaine. New venture strategies in the minicomputer industry. *California Management Review*, pp. 160–175 (Fall 1987). [5:250 (September 1988)]

Sasaki, Toru. How the Japanese accelerated new car development. *Long Range Planning*, pp. 15–25 (January 1991). [8:313–314 (December 1991)]

Scheuing, Eberhard E. and Johnson, Eugene M. A proposed model for new service development. *Journal of Services Marketing*, pp. 25–34 (Spring 1989). [6:303–304 (December 1989)]

Shearman, Claire and Burrell, Gibson. The structures of industrial development. *Journal of Management Studies*, pp. 325–345 (July 1987). [5:173–174 (June 1988)]

Stern, Sydney Ladensohn and Schoenhaud, Ted. Toyland. *Across the Board*, pp. 24–31 (December 1990). [8:224–225 (September 1991)]

Teoh, Poh-Lin. Speed to global markets: an empirical prediction of new product success in the ethical pharmaceutical industry. *European Journal of Marketing*, pp. 11:29–49 (1994). [12:449–450 (November 1995)]

Terpstra, Vern. The Chinese look to world markets. *International Marketing Review*, pp. 7–19 (Summer 1988). [6:225–226 (September 1989)]

Ziemke, M. Carl and McCollum, James K. A message to Detroit: bridge the gap in mechanical innovation. *Sloan Management Review*, pp. 49–54 (Spring 1987). [4:306 (December 1987)]

Market Analysis

Adamian, Deborah M., McNamara, Pamela W., and Rubin, Marc D. Leveraging customer value. *Prism*, pp. 51–63 (*Third Quarter* 1994). [12:251–252 (June 1995).

Adams, David. Parallel market analysis: a technique for risk-averse brand innovation. *Journal of Brand Management*, 4:221–233 (1995). [12:449 (November 1995)]

Alberts, William W. The experience curve doctrine reconsidered. *Journal of Marketing*, pp. 36–49 (July 1989). [7:161–162 (June 1990)]

Alpert, Frank. Innovator buying behavior over time: the innovator buying cycle and the cumulative effects of innovation. *Journal of Product and Brand Management*, 8(2):50–62 (1994). [12:167–168 (March 1995)]

Arnold, Ulli and Barnard, Kenneth N. Just-In-time: some marketing issues raised by a popular concept in production and distribution. *Technovation*, pp. 401–431 (August 1989). [7:255–256 (September 1990)]

Asmus, David and John Griffin. Harnessing the power of your suppliers. *The McKinsey Quarterly*, 3:63–78. (1993). [11:469–470 (November 1994)]

Beaumont, William E. The new patent law of the People's Republic of China (PRC): evidence of a second Chinese "Renaissance"? *IDEA*, 1:39–65 (1986). [4:162 (June 1987)]

Bello, Daniel C. and Barczak, Gloria J. Using industrial trade shows to improve new product development. *Journal of Business and Industrial Marketing*, pp. 43–56 (Summer–Fall 1990). [8:58–59 (March 1991)]

Berry, Leonard L. and Cooper, Linda R. Competing with time-saving service. *Business*, pp. 3–7 (April–June 1990). [8:317–318 (December 1991)]

Bertrand, Kate. The channel challenge. *Business Marketing*, pp. 42–50 (May 1989). [7:162 (June 1990)]

Bloom, Paul N. and Reve, Torger. Transmitting signals to consumers for competitive advantage. *Business Horizons*, pp. 58–66 (July–August 1990). [8: 145–146 (June 1991)]

Bowe, Frank. Why seniors don't use technology. *Technology Review*, pp. 34–40 (August–September 1988). [6:144–145 (June 1989)]

Brown, Stephen A. The prescription drug marketing act. *Food Drug and Cosmetic Law Journal*, 45:245–253 (1990). [8:71 (March 1991)]

Bruno, Albert V. and Leidecker, Joel K. Causes of new venture failure: 1960s vs. 1980s. *Business Horizons*, pp. 51–56 (November–December 1988). [6: 224–225 (September 1989)]

Buday, Tom. Capitalizing on brand extensions. *Journal of Consumer Marketing*, pp. 27–30 (Fall 1989). [7:245–246 (September 1990)]

Carpenter, Gregory S. and Nakamoto, Kent. Consumer preference formation and pioneering advantage. *Journal of Marketing Research*, pp. 285–298 (August 1989). [7:158–159 (June 1990)]

Curry, David J. and Reisz, Peter C. Prices and price/quantity relationships: a longitudinal analysis. *Journal of Marketing*, pp. 36–51 (January 1988). [5:313 (December 1988)]

Day, Ralph L. and Herbig, Paul A. How the diffusion of industrial innovations is different from new retail products. *Industrial Marketing Management*, pp. 261–266 (August 1990). [8:68–69 (March 1991)]

de Brentani, Ulrike. New industrial service development: scenarios for success failure. *Journal of Business Research*, pp. 93–103 (February 1995). [12:447 (November 1995)]

Dholakia, Ruby Roy, Dholakia, Nikhilesh, and Della Bitta, Albert J. Acquisition of telecommunications products and services: an examination of inter-sector differences. *IEEE Transactions on Engineering Management*, pp. 327–335 (November 1991). [9:175–176 (June 1992)]

Duke, Charles R. Understanding customer abilities in product concept tests. *Journal of Product and Brand Management*, 1:48–57 (1994). [11:466–467 (November 1994)]

Dunn, Dan T., Jr. and Thomas, Claude A., Partnering with customers. *Journal of Business and Industrial Marketing*, 9(1):34–40 (1994). [12:258–259 (June 1995)]

Easingwood, Christopher J. and Storey, Christopher D. Marketplace success factors for new products. *Journal of Services Marketing*, 1:41–54 (1993). [11: 77–78 (January 1994)]

Evamy, Michael. Eco-friendly, but fern-free. *Design*, 30–32 (November 1990). [8:315 (December 1991)]

Gardner, Carl. Dealing from the bottom of the pack. *Design*, pp. 26–27 (November 1987). [5:319–320 (December 1988)]

Gernand, Vivian L. Fantasies for sale: marketing products that do not yet exist. *Journal of Business and Industrial Marketing*, pp. 31–36 (GPL) (Summer–Fall 1991). [8:312–313 (December 1991)]

Givon, Moshe. Taste tests: changing the rules to improve the game. *Marketing Science*, pp. 281–290 (Summer 1989). [7:254–255 (September 1990)]

Golder, Peter N. and Tellis, Gerard J. Pioneer advantage: marketing logic or marketing legend? *Journal of Marketing Research*, pp. 158–170 (May 1993). [11:80–81 (January 1994)]

Goldsmith, Ronald and Reinecke Flynn, Leisa. Identifying innovators in consumer product markets. *European Journal of Marketing*, 12:42–55 (1992). [10: 438 (November 1993)]

Goullart, Francis J. and Sturdivant, Frederick D. Spend a day in the life of your customers. *Harvard Business Review*, pp. 116–124 (January–February 1994). [11:468–469 (November 1994)]

Green, Paul E. and Srinivasan, V. Conjoint analysis in marketing research: new developments and directions. *Journal of Marketing*, pp. 3–19 (October 1990). [8:225 (September 1991)]

Hahn, Minhi, Park, Sehoon, Krishnamurthi, Lakshman, and Zoltners, Andris A. Analysis of new product diffusion using a four-segment trial-repeat model. *Management Science*, pp. 225–247 (Summer 1994). [12:351–352 (September 1995)]

Hastings, Hunter. Introducing new products without advertising. *Journal of Consumer Marketing*, pp. 19–25 (Summer 1990). [8:59–60 (March 1991)]

Heeter, Carrie and Greenberg, Bradley S. Profiling the zappers. *Journal of Advertising Research*, pp. 15–21 (April–May 1985). [4:230–231 (September 1987)]

Herbig, Paul A. and Kramer Hugh, The effect of information overload on the innovation choice process. *Journal of Consumer Marketing*, 2:45–54 (1994). [12:77–78 (January 1995)]

Higgins, Susan H. and Shanklin, William L. Seeking mass market acceptance for high-technology consumer products. *Journal of Consumer Marketing*, pp. 5–13 (GPL) (Winter 1992). [9:251–252 (September 1992)]

Kaplan, Barry M. Zapping: the real issue is communication. *Journal of Advertising Research*, pp. 9–15 (April–May 1985). [4:230 (September 1987)]

Kindel, Sharen. Selling by the book. *Sales and Marketing Management*, pp. 101–109 (October 1994). [12:255–256 (June 1995)]

King customer: at companies that listen hard and respond fast, bottom lines thrive (staff-written). *Business Week*, pp. 80–94 (March 12, 1990). [7:249 (September 1990)]

Kirkpatrick, David. Environmentalism: the new crusade. *Fortune*, pp. 44–54 (February 12, 1990). [7:332 (December 1990)]

Knowlton, Christopher. What America makes best. *Fortune*, pp. 40–53 (March 28, 1988). [5:252–253 (September 1988)]

Kroll, Alex. The most dynamic force on the blue planet. *Across the Board*, pp. 32–37 (December 1989). [8:63 (March 1991)]

Lambkin, Mary and Day, George. Evolutionary processes in competitive markets: beyond the product life cycle. *Journal of Marketing*, pp. 4–20 (July 1989). [7: 78–79 (March 1990)]

Lee, Chol. Determinants of national innovativeness and international market segmentation. *International Marketing Review*, pp. 39–49 (1990). [8:216–217 (September 1991)]

Letscher, Martin G. Fad or trend? How to distinguish them and capitalize on them. *Journal of Consumer Marketing*, pp. 21–26 (Spring 1990). [7:330 (December 1990)]

Liswood, Laura A. A new system for rating service quality. *Journal of Business Strategy*, pp. 42–45 (July–August 1989). [7:246 (September 1990)]

Lunsford, Dale A. and Burnett, Melissa S. Marketing product innovations to the elderly. *Journal of Consumer Marketing*, pp. 53–63 (GPL) (Fall 1992). [10: 431–432 (November 1993)]

Mellow, Craig. Successful products of the eighties. *Across the Board*, pp. 40–49 (November 1988). [6:145 (June 1989)]

Morgan, Fred W. Strict liability and the marketing of services vs. goods: a judicial review. *Journal of Public Policy and Marketing*, pp. 43–57 (1987). [5:174–175 (June 1988)]

Morrison, Thomas C. The false advertising of speciality medical products under the Lanham Act. *Food Drug and Cosmetic Law Journal*, pp. 265–271 (May 1989). [7:252–253 (September 1990)]

Moss, C. and Evans, A. Product liability-legal changes and marketing responses. *Marketing Intelligence and Planning*, pp. 57–64 (July 1986). [4:304–305 (December 1987)]

Narver, John C. and Slater, Stanley F. The effect of a market orientation on business profitability. *Journal of Marketing*, pp. 20–35 (October 1990). [8:223 (September 1991)]

Nelson-Horchler, Joani. Dodging the liability bullet. *Industry Week*, pp. 30–35 (April 6, 1987). [4:305–306 (December 1987)]

Nickolaus, Nicholas. Marketing new products with industrial distributors. *Industrial Marketing Management*, pp. 289–299 (1990). [8:146–147 (June 1991)]

Nine forces reshaping America (no author given). *The Futurist*, pp. 9–16 (July–August 1990). [8:69–70 (March 1991)]

Nishikawa, Tohru. New product development. *Journal of Advertising Research*, pp. 27–30 (April–May 1990). [8:64–65 (March 1991)]

Olesen, Douglas E. Six keys to commercialization. *Journal of Business Strategy*, pp. 43–47 (November–December 1990). [8:150 (June 1991)]

Omsen, Arne H. and Ekestrom, Swen. Implanting new organizational product ideas into operating companies. *Technovation*, pp. 23–37) (December 1987). [5:318–319 (December 1988)]

Park, C. Wham and Smith, Daniel C. Product class competitors as sources of innovative marketing strategies. *Journal of Consumer Marketing*, pp. 27–37 (Spring 1990). [8:60–61 (March 1991)]

Pine, B. Joseph II, Peppers, Don, and Rogers, Martha. Do you want to keep your customers forever? *Harvard Business Review*, pp. 103–114 (March–April 1995). [12:446 (November 1995)]

Pinto, Jeffrey K. and Mantel, Samuel J., Jr. The causes of project failure. *IEEE Transactions on Engineering Management*, pp. 269–276 (November 1990). [8: 214–215 (September 1991)]

Plummer, Joseph T. Outliving the myths. *Journal of Advertising Research*, pp. 26–28 (February–March 1990). [8:315–316 (December 1991)]

Quelch, John A. Marketing the premium product. *Business Horizons*, pp. 38–45 (May–June 1987). [5:167–168 (June 1988)]

Richins, Marsha L. and Bloch, Peter H. Post-purchase product satisfaction: incorporating the effects of involvement and time. *Journal of Business Research*, pp. 145–158 (1991). [9:178 (June 1992)]

Robertson, Kim. Strategically desirable brand name characteristics. *Journal of Consumer Marketing*, pp. 61–71 (Fall 1989). [7:326–327 (December 1990)]

Robertson, Thomas S. How to reduce market penetration cycle times. *Sloan Management Review*, pp. 87–95 (Fall 1993). [11:360–361 (September 1994)]

Rolfes, Rebecca. How green is your market basket. *Across the Board*, pp. 49–51 (January–February 1990). [7:332 (December 1990)]

Scheuing, Eberhard. Conducting customer service audits. *Journal of Services Marketing*, pp. 35–41 (Summer 1989). [7:248–249 (September 1990)]

Smith, Robert E. Integrating information from advertising and trial: processes and effects on consumer response to product information. *Journal of Marketing Research*, pp. 204–219 (May 1993). [11:167–168 (March 1994)]

Stalking the new consumer (no author given). *Business Week*, pp. 54–62 (August 28, 1989). [7:83–84 (March 1990)]

Teubal, Morris, Yinnon, Tamar, and Zuscovitch, Ehud. Networks and market creation. *Research Policy*, pp. 381–392 (1991). [9:250–251 (September 1992)]

Urban, Glen L., Hauser, John R., and Roberts, John H. Prelaunch forecasting of new automobiles. *Management Science*, pp. 401–421 (April 1990). [8:148–149 (June 1991)]

Wilcox, Stephen B., guest editor. High-octane fuel for ID's idealism: usability testing. *Innovation*, pp. 14–32 (Spring 1994). [12:168–169 (March 1995)]

Wittink, Dick R. and Cattin, Philippe. Commercial use of conjoint analysis: an update. *Journal of Marketing*, pp. 91–96 (July 1989). [7:159–160 (June 1990)]

Wittink, Dick R., Vriens, Marco, and Burhenne, Wim. Commercial use of conjoint analysis in Europe: results and critical reflections. *International Journal of Research in Marketing*, pp. 41–52 (January 1994). [11:742–473 (November 1994)]

Yorke, David A. and Kitchen, Philip J. Channel flickers and video speeders. *Journal of Advertising Research*, pp. 21–26 (April–May 1985). [4:231 (September 1987)]

New Product Planning

Aaker, David A. Building a brand: the Saturn story. *California Management Review*, pp. 114–133 (Winter 1994). [12:166–167 (March 1995)]

Alpert, Frank H., Kamins, Michael A., and Graham, John L. An examination of reseller buyer attitudes toward order of brand entry. *Journal of Marketing*, pp. 25–37 (July 1992). [10:262–263 (June 1993)]

Andrews, Kirby. Communications imperatives for new products. *Journal of Advertising Research*, pp. 29–32 (October–November 1986). [4:156–157 (June 1987)]

Ayal, Igal and Raban, Joel. Developing hi-tech industrial products for world markets. *IEEE Transactions on Engineering Management*, pp. 177–183 (August 1990). [8:144–145 (June 1991)]

Bacon, Glenn, Beckman, Sara, Mowrey, David, and Wilson, Edith. Managing product definition in high-technology industries: a pilot study. *California Management Review*, pp. 32–56 (Spring 1994). [12:174–175 (March 1995)]

Baldwin, Carliss Y. How capital budgeting deters innovation—and what to do about it. *Research Technology Management*, pp. 39–45 (November–December 1991). [9:181 (June 1992)]

Bertrand, Kate. Betting the ranch on a new product. *Business Marketing*, pp. 29–34 (July 1991). [9:81 (March 1992)]

Biemans, Wim G. User and third-party involvement in developing medical equipment innovations. *Technovation*, pp. 163–181 (April 1991). [9:76–77 (March 1992)]

Bowman, Douglas and Gatignon, Hubert. Determinants of competitors' response time to a new product introduction. *Journal of Marketing Research*, pp. 42–53 (February 1995). [12:452 (November 1995)]

Brenner, Merrill S. Tracking new products: a practitioner's guide. *Research Technology Management*, pp. 36–40 (November–December 1994). [12:443–444 (November 1995)]

Brimm, J. Michael. Risky business: why sponsoring innovations may be hazardous to career health. *Organizational Dynamics*, pp. 28–41 (Winter 1988). [5:245 (September 1988)]

Buchanan, Bruce, Givon, Moshe, and Goldman, Arieh. Measurement of discrimination ability in taste tests: an empirical investigation. *Journal of Marketing Research*, pp. 154–163 (May 1987). [4:301–302 (December 1987)]

Capon, Noel, Farley, John U., Lehmann, Donald R., and Hulbert, James M. Profiles of product innovators among large U.S. manufacturers. *Management Science*, pp. 157–169 (February 1992). [10:80 (January 1993)]

Christensen, Karen S. Coping with uncertainty in planning. *Accountants Digest*, pp. 23–33 (September 1985). [3:305–306 (December 1986)]

Cohen, Dorothy. Trademark strategy revisited. *Journal of Marketing*, pp. 46–59 (July 1991). [9:80–81 (March 1992)]

Constantineau, Larry A. The 20 toughest questions for new product proposals. *Journal of Product and Brand Management*, 1:51–54 (1993). [11:83–84 (January 1994)]

Cooper, R. G. and Kleinschmidt, E. J. Resource allocation in the new product process. *Industrial Marketing Management*, pp. 249–262 (1988). [6:148–149 (June 1989)]

Cooper, R. G. and Kleinschmidt, E. J. Success factors in product innovation. *Industrial Marketing Management*, pp. 215–223 (1987). [5:248–249 (September 1988)]

Cooper, Robert G. and Kleinschmidt, Elko J. New product processes at leading industrial firms. *Industrial Marketing Management*, pp. 137–147 (1991). [10:163 (March 1993)]

Cooper, Robert G. Defining the new product strategy. *IEEE Transactions on Engineering Management*, pp. 184–193 (August 1987). [5:170–171 (June 1988)]

Cooper, Robert G. Industrial firms' new product strategies. *Journal of Business Research*, pp. 107–121 (1985). [4:160–161 (June 1987)]

Cordero, Rene. The measurement of innovation performance in the firm: an overview. *Research Policy*, pp. 185–192 (1990). [8:219–220 (September 1991)]

de Brentani, Ulrike. New industrial service development: scenarios for success or failure. *Journal of Business Research*, pp. 93–103 (February 1995). [12:447 (November 1995)]

de Brentani, Ulrike and Droge, Cornelia. Determinants of the new product screening decision: a structural model analysis. *International Journal of Research in Marketing*, 2:91–106 (1988). [7:77–78 (March 1990)]

Desarbo, Wayne and Rao, Vithala R. A constrained unfolding methodology for product positioning. *Marketing Science*, pp. 1–19 (Winter 1986). [4:72–73 (March 1987)]

Devinney, Timothy M. and Stewart, David W. Rethinking the product portfolio: a generalized investment model. *Management Science*, pp. 1080–1095 (September 1988). [6:302–303 (December 1989)]

Dreyfuss, Joel. What do you do for an encore? *Fortune*, December 19, 1988, pp. 111–119. [6:146–147 (June 1989)]

Durgee, Jeffrey. New product ideas from focus groups. *Journal of Consumer Marketing*, pp. 57–65 (Fall 1987). [5:251 (September 1988)]

Dwyer, Larry and Mellor, Robert. New product process activities and project outcomes. *R&D Management*, pp. 31–41 (January 1991). [8:306–307 (December 1991)]

Edgett, Scott. The traits of successful new service development. *Journal of Services Marketing*, 8(3):40–49 (1994). [12:173–174 (March 1995)]

Eliasberg, Jehoshua and Robertson, Thomas S. New product preannouncing behavior: a market signaling study. *Journal of Marketing Research*, pp. 282–292 (August 1988). [6:70–71 (March 1989)]

Foxall, Gordon and Haskins, Christopher G. Cognitive style and consumer innovativeness: an empirical test of Kirton's adaption-innovation theory in the context of food purchasing. *European Journal of Marketing*, 3–4:63–80 (1986). [4:233–234 (September 1987)]

Gatignon, Hubert and Robertson, Thomas S. A propositional inventory for new product diffusion research. *Journal of Consumer Research*, pp. 849–867 (March 1985). [3:294 (December 1986)]

Gemignani, Michael C. Potential liability for use of expert systems. *IDEA*, 29(2): 120–127 (1989). [6:301 (December 1989)]

Gobeli, David H. and Brown, Daniel J. Improving the process of product innovation. *Research Technology Management*, pp. 38–44 (March–April 1993). [12:169 (March 1995)]

Gupta, Ashok K., Raj, S. P., and Wilemon, David. Managing the R&D–marketing interface. *Research Management*, pp. 38–43 (March–April 1987). [5:312–313 (December 1988)]

Haggerty, Matthew K. and Vogel, Brian L. The business/design culture gap. *Innovation*, pp. 8–13 (Winter 1992). [9:258–259 (September 1992)]

Hanna, Nessim, Ayers, Douglas J., Ridnaur, Rick E., and Gordon, Geoffrey L. New product development practices in consumer versus business organizations. *Journal of Product and Brand Management*, 1:33–55 (1995). [12: 442–443 (November 1995)]

Hauser, Richard D., Jr., and Hebert, Frederick J. Managerial issues in expert system implementation. *SAM Advanced Management Journal*, pp. 10–15 (Winter 1992). [10:255–256 (June 1993)]

Hawk, Stephen R. and Dos Santos, Brian L. Successful systems development: the effect of situational factors on alternate user roles. *IEEE Transactions on Engineering Management*, pp. 316–327 (November 1991). [9:182 (June 1992)]

Holmes, Jerry D., Nelson, Gregory O., and Stump, David C. Improving the innovation process at Eastman Chemical. *Research Technology Management*, pp. 27–35 (May–June 1993). [12:172–173 (March 1995)]

House, Charles H. and Price, Raymond L. The return map: tracking product teams. *Harvard Business Review*, pp. 92–100 (January–February 1990). [8: 220–221 (September 1991)]

Houston, Paul. Lessons in new product launching. *Direct Marketing*, pp. 78ff (May 1989). [8:149–150 (June 1991)]

Jaccard, James, Brinberg, David, and Ackerman, Lee J. Assessing attribute importance: a comparison of six methods. *Journal of Consumer Research*, pp. 463–468 (March 1986). [4:156 (June 1987)]

Johne, Axel and Snelson, Patricia. Successful product innovation in UK and US firms. *European Journal of Marketing*, pp. 7–21 (1990). [8:213–214 (September 1991)]

Jones, Charles. Strategic issues in new-product introductions. *Journal of Advertising Research*, pp. RC11–RC13 (April 1985). [3:214–215 (September 1986)]

Karakaya, Fahri and Kobu, Bulent. New product development process: an investigation of success and failure in high-technology and non-high-technology firms. *Journal of Business Venturing*, 9:49–66 (1993). [11:362; (September 1994)]

Kleinschmidt, E. J. A comparative analysis of new product programmes: European versus North American companies. *European Journal of Marketing*, 28(7):5–29 (1994). [12:254–255 (June 1995)]

Langowitz, Nan S. Managing new product design and factory fit. *Business Horizons*, pp. 76–79 (May–June 1989). [7:77] (March 1990)

LaTour, Michael S. and Roberts, Scott D. Cultural anchoring and product diffusion. *Journal of Consumer Marketing*, pp. 29–34 (Fall, 1992). [11:78 (January 1994)]

Lee, Jinjoo and Kim, Hong-bumm. Determinants of new product outcome in a developing country: a longitudinal analysis. *International Journal of Research in Marketing*, 3:143–156 (1986). [4:308 (December 1987)]

Lilien, Gary L. and Yoon, Eunsang. Determinants of new industrial product performance: A strategic reexamination of the empirical literature. *IEEE Transactions on Engineering Management*, pp. 3–10 (February 1989). [6:308 (December 1989)]

Link, Peter L. Keys to new product success and failure. *Industrial Marketing Management*, pp. 109–118 (May 1987). [4:307 (December 1987)]

MacMillan, Ian, McCaffery, Mary Lynn, and Van Wijk, Gilles. Competitors' responses to easily imitated new products: exploring commercial banking product introductions. *Strategic Management Journal*, pp. 75–86 (1985). [4:310 (December 1987)]

McKenna, Regis. Why high-tech products fail? *Journal of High Tech Marketing*, pp. 1–10 (Summer 1987). [5:175–176 (June 1988)]

Meyerowitz, Steven A. Protection through patents: new power for an old remedy. *Business Marketing*, pp. 63–67 (July 1988). [6:71–72 (March 1989)]

Meyers, Marc H. and Roberts, Edward B. New product strategy in small technology-based firms: a pilot study. *Management Science*, pp. 806–820 (July 1986). [5:89 (March 1988)]

Meyers-Levy, Joan and Peracchio, Laura A. Getting an angle in advertising: the effect of camera angle on product evaluations. *Journal of Marketing Research*, pp. 454–461 (November 1992). [10:357 (September 1993)]

Miles, Gregory L. Information thieves are now corporate enemy no. 1. *Business Week*, pp. 120–125 (May 5, 1986). [3:294–295 (December 1986)]

Mitchell, Russell. Masters of innovation. *Business Week*, pp. 58–62 (April 10, 1989). [6:299–300 (December 1989)]

Morton, Peter D. and Tarrant, Crispian. A new dimension to financial product innovation research. *Marketing and Research Today*, pp. 173–179 (August 1994). [12:350 (September 1995)]

Myhre, Terje. Factors influencing success of new corporate ventures. Division of Organization and Work Science, the Norwegian Institute of Technology, Trondheim, Norway (summary of dissertation). [8:151–152 (June 1991)]

Nickolaus, Nicholas. Marketing new products with industrial distributors. *Industrial Marketing Management*, pp. 289–299 (1990). [8:146–147 (June 1991)]

Olesen, Douglas E. Six keys to commercialization. *Journal of Business Strategy*, pp. 43–47 (November–December 1990). [8:150 (June 1991)]

Olson, David. The characteristics of high-trial new-product advertising. *Journal of Advertising Research*, pp. 11–16 (October–November 1985). [4:157–158 (June 1987)]

Pinto, Jeffrey K. and Mantel, Samuel J., Jr. The causes of project failure. *IEEE Transactions on Engineering Management.*, pp. 269–276 (November 1990). [8:214–215 (September 1991)]

Power, Christopher et al. Flops: too many new products fail: here's why—and how to do better. *Business Week*, pp. 76–82 (August 16, 1993). [11:163 (March 1994)]

Rao, Vithala R. and Laughlinh, Edward W. Modeling the decision to add new products by channel intermediaries. *Journal of Marketing*, pp. 80–88 (January 1989). [6:230 (September 1989)]

Reinertsen, Donald G. and Smith, Preston G. The strategist's role in shortening product development. *Journal of Business Strategy*, pp. 18–22 (July–August 1991). [9:81–82 (March 1992)]

Rice, Tracey. Teaming strategic marketing with design. *Design Management Journal*, pp. 59–63 (Spring 1991). [10:78–79 (January 1993)]

Schanholz, Jay David. The validity of patents after market testing: a new and improved experimental use doctrine. *Columbia Law Review*, pp. 371–396 (March 1985). [4:69–70 (March 1987)]

Scheuing, Eberhard E. and Johnson, Eugene M. A proposed model for new service development. *Journal of Services Marketing*, pp. 25–34 (Spring 1989). [6:303–304 (December 1989)]

Schneider, Eric. The user in focus. *Innovation*, pp. 26–29 (Summer 1991). [10:164–165 (March 1993)]

Schopler, Janice H. Interorganizational groups: origins, structure, and outcomes. *Academy of Management Review*, pp. 702–713 (October 1987). [5:165–166 (June 1988)]

Shannon, Kristen. The new biology of genius: brain training for the information age. *Technological Forecasting and Social Change*, pp. 229–310 (July 1988). [6:227–228 (September 1989)]

Skelton, Terrance M. and Thamhain, Hans J. Concurrent project management: a tool for technology transfer. R&D-to-market. *Project Management Journal*, pp. 41–48 (December 1993). [11:261–262 (June 1994)]

Souder, William E. Improving productivity through technology push. *Research Technology Management*, pp. 19–24 (March–April 1989). [6:305–306 (December 1989)]

Souder, William E. and Mandakovic, Tomislav. R&D project selection models. *Research Management*, pp. 36–42 (July–August 1986). [3:300 (December 1986)]

Stewart, Thomas A. Reengineering: the hot new managing tool. *Fortune*, pp. 41–48 (August 23, 1993). [11:356 (September 1994)]

Talaysum, Adil T. Understanding the diffusion process for technology-intensive products. *Research Management*, pp. 22–26 (July–August 1985). [3:299 (December 1986)]

Tenaglia, Mason and Noonan, Patrick. Scenario-based strategic planning: a process for building top management consensus. *Planning Review*, pp. 13–19 (March–April 1992). [10:261 (June 1993)]

Teoh, Poh-Lin. Speed to global markets: an empirical prediction of new product success in the ethical pharmaceutical industry. *European Journal of Marketing*, 11:29–49 (1994). [12:449–450 (November 1995)]

Vantrappen, Herman. Creating customer value by streamlining business processes. *Long Range Planning*, pp. 53–62 (February 1992). [10:261–262 (June 1993)]

Vitiello, Jill. Reengineering: it's totally radical. *Journal of Business Strategy*, pp. 44–47 (November–December 1993). [11:356–357 (September 1994)]

von Hippel, Eric. Lead users: a source of novel product concepts. *Management Science*, pp. 791–805 (July 1986). [4:158 (June 1987)]

Welch, Joe L. Researching marketing problems and opportunities with focus groups. *Industrial Marketing Management*, pp. 245–253 (1985). [4:234 (September 1987)]

Wheelwright, Stephen C. and Sasser, W. Earl. The new product development map. *Harvard Business Review*, pp. 112–125 (May–June 1989). [7:79–80 (March 1990)]

Whiteley, Richard C. Why customer focus strategies often fail. *Journal of Business Strategy*, pp. 34–37 (September–October 1991). [10:162–163 (March 1993)]

Woudhuysen, James. Tailoring IT to the needs of customers. *Long Range Planning*, pp. 33–42 (June 1994). [12:165–166 (March 1995)]

Wrubel, Robert. Scorch, burn and plunder. *Financial World*, pp. 28–30 (February 16, 1993). [10:349–350 (September 1993)]

Zirger, Billie Jo and Maidique, Modesto A. A model of new product development: an empirical test. *Management Science*, pp. 867–883 (July 1990). [8:65–66 (March 1991)]

Organizing for Innovation

Abernathy, William J. and Clark, Kim B. Innovation: mapping the winds of creative destruction. *Research Policy*, pp. 3–22 (1985). [4:308–309 (December 1987)]

Adler, Paul S., Riggs, Henry E., and Wheelwright, Steven C. Product development know-how: trading tactics for strategy. *Sloan Management Review*, pp. 7–17 (Fall 1989). [7:160–161 (June 1990)]

Allio, Michael K. 3M's sophisticated formula for teamwork. *Planning Forum*, pp 19–21 (November–December 1993). [11:268 (June 1994)]

Ancona, Deborah Gladstein and Caldwell, David. Improving the performance of new product teams. *Research Technology Management*, pp. 25–29 (March–April 1990). [7:329 (December 1990)]

Anderson, James C. and Narus, James A. Partnering as focused market strategy. *California Management Review*, pp. 95–112 (Spring 1991). [8:310–312 (December 1991)]

Bachmann, A. E. J. A product/market project system. *Journal of Engineering Management International*, pp. 183–188 (May 1984). [3:296–297 (December 1986)]

Banner, David K. Self-managed work teams: an innovation whose time has come? *Creativity and Innovation Management*, pp. 27–36 (March 1993). [10:437–338 (November 1993)]

Barczak, Gloria and Wilemon, David. Communication patterns of new product development team leaders. *IEEE Transactions on Engineering Management*, pp. 101–109 (May 1991). [9:75–76 March 1992)]

Barczak, Gloria and Wilemon, David. Successful new product team leaders. *Industrial Marketing Management*, pp. 61–68 (February 1992). [9:257 (September 1992)]

Bartlett, Christopher A. and Ghoshal, Sumantra. Matrix management: not a structure, a frame of mind. *Harvard Business Review*, pp. 138–145 (July–August 1990). [8:67–68 (March 1991)]

Bell, Robert R. and Burnham, John M. The paradox of manufacturing productivity and innovation. *Business Horizons*, pp. 58–64 (September–October 1989). [7:246–247 (September 1990)]

Bidault, Francis and Cummings, Thomas. Innovating through alliances: expectations and limitations. *R&D Management*, pp. 33–45 (January 1994). [11:474–475 (November 1994)]

Branscomb, Anne W. Who owns creativity? *Technology Review*, pp. 38–45 (May–June 1988). [6:69–70 (March 1989)]

Brown, Buck. Business incubators suffer growing pains. *The Wall Street Journal*, June 16, 1989, p. B1. [7:164 (June 1990)]

Bruce, Margaret, Leverick Fiona, Littler, Dale, and Wilson, Dominic. Success factors for collaborative product development: a study of suppliers of infor-

Francis, Philip H. Putting quality into the R&D process. *Research Technology Management*, pp. 16–23 (July–August 1992). [10:254–255 (June 1993)]

Frey, Donald N. Junk your linear R&D. *Research Technology Management*, pp. 7–8 (May–June 1989). [7:88 (March 1990)]

Gandz, Jeffrey. The employee empowerment era. *Business Quarterly*, pp. 74–79 (Autumn 1990). [8:147–148 (June 1991)]

Gupta, Ashok K., Raj, S. P., and Wilemon, David. A model for studying R&D/ marketing interface in the product innovation process. *Journal of Marketing*, pp. 7–17 (April 1986). [3:297–298 (December 1986)]

Habib, Mohammed M. and Victor, Bart. Strategy, structure, and performance of U.S. manufacturing and service MNCs: a comparative analysis. *Strategic Management Journal*, pp. 589–606 (1991). [10:167–168 (March 1993)]

Hagedorn, Homer. High performance in product development: an agenda for senior management. *Prism*, pp 47–57 (First Quarter 1992). [10:77–78 (January 1993)]

Hardy, Cynthia. The nature of unobtrusive power. *Journal of Management Studies*, pp. 384–399 (July 1985). [3:210 (September 1986)]

Harrigan, Kathryn Rudie and Dalmia, Gaurav. Knowledge workers: the last bastion of competitive advantage. *Planning Review*, pp. 4–9ff (November–December 1991). [9:174–175 (June 1992)]

Harvey, Michael. A new way to combat product counterfeiting. *Business Horizons*, pp. 19–28 (July–August 1988). [6:63–64 (March 1989)]

Hill, Charles W. C. and Snell, Scott A. External control, corporate strategy, and firm performance in research-intensive industries. *Strategic Management Journal*, pp. 577–590 (1988). [6:150–151 (June 1989)]

Hirschhorn, Larry and Gilmore, Thomas. The new boundaries of the "boundaryless" company. *Harvard Business Review*, pp. 104–115 (May–June 1992). [10: 253–254 (June 1993)]

Julian, Scott D. and Keller, Robert T. Multinational R&D siting. *Columbia Journal of World Business*, pp. 47–57 (Fall 1991). [9:249–250 (September 1992)]

Kanter, Rosabeth Moss. The new managerial work. *Harvard Business Review*, pp. 85–92 (November–December 1989). [7:169–170 (June 1990)]

Kanter, Rosabeth Moss. Swimming in newstreams: mastering innovation dilemmas. *California Management Review*, pp. 45–69 (Summer 1989). [7:86–87 (March 1990)]

Katzenbach, Jon R. and Smith, Douglas K. The delicate balance of team leadership. *The McKinsey Quarterly*, 4:128–142 (1992). [10:431 (November 1993)]

Katzenbach, Jon R. and Smith, Douglas K. Why teams matter. *The McKinsey Quarterly*, pp. 3–25 (1992). [10:356–357 (September 1993)]

Kennedy, Marilyn Moats. Empowered or overpowered? *Across the Board*, pp. 11–12 (April 1994). [12:164–165 (March 1995)]

Meyer, Christopher. How the right measures help teams excel. *Harvard Business Review*, pp. 95–103 (May–June 1994). [12:80 (January 1995)]

Meyerowitz, Steven A. Protection through patents: new power for an Old Remedy. *Business Marketing*, pp. 63–67 (July 1988). [6:71–72 (March 1989)]

Miller, Alex, Spann, Mary S., and Lerner, Linda. Competitive advantages in new corporate ventures: the impact of resource sharing and reporting level. *Journal of Business Venturing*, pp. 335–350 (September 1991). [9:252–253 (September 1992)]

Mitchell, Graham R. and Hamilton, William F. Managing R&D as a strategic option. *Research Technology Management*, pp. 15–22 (May–June 1988). [6: 72–73 (March 1989)]

Mitchell, Russell. Masters of innovation. *Business Week*, pp. 58–62 (April 10, 1989). [6:299–300 (December 1989)]

Myhre, Terje. Factors influencing success of new corporate ventures. Division of Organization and Work Science, the Norwegian Institute of Technology, Trondheim, Norway (summary of dissertation). [8:151–152 (June 1991)]

Nevens, T. Michael, Summe, Gregory L., and Uttal, Bro. Commercializing technology: what the best companies do. *Harvard Business Review*, pp. 154–163 (May–June 1990). [7:327–328 (December 1990)]

Nuemo, Pedro and Oosterveld, Jan. Managing technology alliances. *Long Range Planning*, 3:1–18 (1988). [6:68 March 1989)]

O'Dell, Carla. Team play, team pay—new ways of keeping score. *Across the Board*, pp. 38–46 (November 1989). [7:253–254 (September 1990)]

Okamoto, Akira. Creative and innovative research at RICOH. *Long Range Planning*, pp. 9–16 (October 1991). [9:174 (June 1992)]

Osborne, Richard L. The dark side of the entrepreneur. *Long Range Planning*, pp. 26–31 (June 1991). [10:166–167 (March 1993)]

Ouchi, William G. and Bolton, Michele Kremen. The logic of joint research and development. *California Management Review*, pp. 9–33 (Spring 1988). [6: 67–68 (March 1989)]

Parsons, Andrew I. Building innovativeness in large U.S. corporations. *Journal of Services Management*, pp. 5–20 (GPL) (Fall, 1991). [9:173–174 (June 1992)]

Parsons, Andrew J. Building innovativeness in large U.S. corporations. *Journal of Consumer Marketing*, pp. 35–50 (GPL) (Spring 1992). [9:319–320 (December 1992)]

Pearson, Andrall E. Tough-minded ways to get innovative. *Harvard Business Review*, pp. 99–106 (May–June 1988). [5:321–322 (December 1988)]

Pearson, Gordon. The strategic discount-protecting new business projects against DCF. *Long Range Planning*, pp. 18–24 (February 1986). [3:214 (September 1986)]

Peters, Tom. Get innovative or get dead. *California Management Review*, pp. 9–26 (Fall 1990). [8:218–219 (September 1991)]

Pisano, Gary P. The governance of innovation: vertical integration and collaborative arrangements in the biotechnology industry. *Research Policy*, pp. 237–249 (June 1991). [10:78 (January 1993)]

Purser, Ronald E. Redesigning the knowledge-based product development organization: a case study of sociotechnical systems change. *Technovation*, pp. 403–415 (November 1991). [10:80–81 (January 1993)]

Rafii, Farshad. How important is physical collocation to product development success? *Business Horizons*, pp. 78–84 (January–February 1995). [12:354–355 (September 1995)]

Robertson, Thomas S. and Gatignon, Hubert. Competitive effects on technology. *Journal of Marketing*, pp. 1–12 (July 1986). [4:231–232 (September 1987)]

Rothstein, Lawrence R. The empowerment effort that came undone. *Harvard Business Review*, pp. 20–31 (January–February 1995). [12:347–348 (September 1995).

Rothwell, Roy. Public innovation policy: to have or to have not? *R&D Management*, (January 1986, pp.25–36). [3:295 December 1986)]

Rothwell, Roy and Gardiner, Paul. Re-innovation and robust designs: producer and user benefits. *Journal of Marketing Management*, pp. 372–387 (Spring 1988). [5:324 (December 1988)]

Saleh, Shoukry D. and Wang, Clement K. The management of innovation: strategy, structure, and organizational climate. *IEEE Transactions on Engineering Management*, pp. 14–21 (HJT) (February 1993). [10:430–431 (November 1993)]

Schaffhauser, Robert J. How a mature firm fosters entrepreneurs. *Planning Review*, pp. 6–11 (March 1986). [3:213–214 (September 1986)]

Schein, Edgar H. Reassessing the "divine rights" of managers. *Sloan Management Review*, pp. 63–68 (Winter 1989). [6:307–308 (December 1989)]

Shaw, Robin N. and Bodi, Anna. Diffusion of product code scanning. *Industrial Marketing Management*, pp. 225–235 (1986). [4:229 (September 1987)]

Simon, Herbert A. Strategy and organizational evolution. *Strategic Management Journal*, pp. 131–142 (Winter 1993). [12:887–88 (January 1995)]

Soderberg, Leif G. Facing up to the engineering gap. *The McKinsey Quarterly*, pp. 2–18 (Spring 1989). [7:84–85 (March 1990)]

Soderberg, Leif G. and O'Halloran, J. David. Heroic engineering takes more than heroes. *The McKinsey Quarterly*, 1:3–23 (1992). [9:318–319 (December 1992)]

Souder, William E. and Nassar, Suheil. Choosing an R&D consortium. *Research Technology Managment*, pp. 35–41 (March–April 1990). [8:61–63 (March 1991)]

Souder, William E. and Nassar, Suheil. Managing R&D consortia for success. *Research Technology Management*, pp. 44–50 (September–October 1990). [8:61–63 (March 1991)]

Spendolini, Michael J. How to build a benchmarking team. *Journal of Business Strategy*, pp. 53–57 (March–April 1993). [11:85 (January 1994)]

The stateless corporation (no author given). *Business Week*, pp. 98–106 (May 14, 1990). [7:325–326 (December 1990)]

Stumpf, Bill. Six enemies of empowering design. *Innovation*, pp. 29–31 (Spring 1992). [10:86 (January 1993)]

Sundbo, Jon. The tied entrepreneur: on the theory and practice of institutionalization of creativity and innovation in service firms. *Creativity and Innovation Management*, pp. 109–120 (September 1992). [10:352–353 (September 1993)]

Sykes, Hollister B. Incentive compensation for corporate venture personnel. *Journal of Business Venturing*, pp. 253–265 (1992). [10:171–172 (March 1993)]

Thorn, Dick. Problem solving for innovation in industry. *Journal of Creative Behavior*, pp. 92–108 (Second Quarter 1987). [5:320 (December 1988)]

Tushman, Michael and Nadler, David. Organizing for innovation. *California Management Review*, pp. 74–92 (Spring 1986). [5:81–82 (March 1988)]

Udwadia, Firdaus E. and Kumar, K. Ravi. Impact of customer coconstruction in product/service markets. *Technological Forecasting and Social Change*, pp. 261–272 (November 1991). [9:170–171 (June 1992)]

Verespej, Michael A. The R&D challenge: getting it out of the lab. *Industry Week*, May 4, 1987, pp. 33–36. [5:89–90 (March 1988)]

von Hippel, Eric. The sources of innovation. *The McKinsey Quarterly*, pp. 72–79 (Winter 1988). [5:254 (September 1988)]

Wagner, Harvey E. The open corporation. *California Management Review*, pp. 46–60 (Summer 1991). [9:177–178 (June 1992)]

Waitley, Denis E. and Tucker, Robert B. How to think like an innovator. *The Futurist*, pp. 9–15 (May–June 1987). [4:309–310 (December 1987)]

Weber, Joseph. Farewell fast track. *Business Week*, pp. 192–200 (December 10, 1990). [8:226–227 (September 1991)]

Winslow, Erik K. and Solomon, George T. Further development of a descriptive profile of entrepreneurs. *Journal of Creative Behavior*, pp. 149–161 (Third Quarter 1989). [7:256 (September 1990)]

Wissema, J. G. and Euser, L. Successful innovation through inter-company networks. *Long Range Planning*, pp. 33–39 (December 1991). [10:163–164 (March 1993)]

Wolff, Michael F. Creating high-performance teams. *Research technology management*, pp. 10–12 (November–December 1993). [12:253–254 (June 1995)]

Wolff, Michael F. Technology council helps square D company manage global R&D. *Research-Technology Management*, pp. 8–10 (March–April 1993). [10:439 (November 1993)]

Yeaple, Ronald N. Why are small R&D organizations more productive? *IEEE Transactions on Engineering Management*, pp. 332–346 (November 1992). [11:79–80 (January 1994)]

Yovovich, B. G. Vertical no more. *Business Marketing*, pp. 20–21 (January 1992). [9:257–258 (September 1992)]

Product Concept

Bacon, Glenn, Beckman, Sara, Mowrey, David, and Wilson, Edith. Managing product definition in high-technology industries: a pilot study. *California Management Review*, pp. 32–56 (Spring 1994). [12:174–175 (March 1995)]

Berenson, Conrad and Mohr-Jackson, Iris. Product rejuvenation: a less risky alternative to product innovation. *Business Horizons*, pp. 51–57 (November–December 1994). [12:450–451 (November 1995)]

Berry, Leonard L. and Cooper, Linda R. Competing with time-saving service. *Business*, pp. 3–7 (April–June 1990). [8:317–318 (December 1991)]

Blackett, Tom. Researching brand names. *Marketing Intelligence and planning*, 3:5–8 (1988). [6:74 (March 1989)]

Burall, Paul. Green-ness is good for you. *Design*, pp. 22–24 (April 1994). [12: 354 (September 1995).

Cassok, David. The extended product line. *Health industry today*, pp. 26–37 (July 1986). [4:153–154 (June 1987)]

Cohen, Allen M. Marketing battlegrounds: how to win in cash management services. *Bank Administration*, pp. 22–28 (February 1986). [4:153 (June 1987)]

Cornish, Edward. The disposable home: here today, junk tomorrow. *The Futurist*, p. 2+ (September–October 1987). [5:166–167 (June 1988)]

Dowlatshahi, Shad. A novel approach to product design and development in a concurrent engineering environment. *Technovation*, 3:161–176 (1993). [11: 87–88 (January 1994)]

Duke, Charles R. Understanding customer abilities in product concept tests. *Journal of Product and Brand Management*, 1:48–57 (1994). [11:466–467 (November 1994)]

Floyd, Thomas H., Jr. Personalizing public transportation. *The Futurist*, pp. 29–34 (November–December 1990). [8:140 (June 1991)]

French, Robert L. Cars that know where they're going. *The Futurist*, pp. 29–36 (May–June 1989). [6:300–301 (December 1989)]

Gernand, Vivian L. Fantasies for sale: marketing products that do not yet exist. *Journal of Business and Industrial Marketing*, pp. 31–36 (GPL) (Summer–Fall 1991). [8:312–313 (December 1991)]

Gorman, Tom. What will our customers think of this product idea? *Business Marketing*, pp. 76–80 (September 1987). [5:163–164 (June 1988)]

Green, Paul E. and Srinivasan, V. Conjoint analysis in marketing research: new developments and directions. *Journal of Marketing*, pp. 3–19 (October 1990). [8:225 (September 1991)]

Hahn, Minhi, Park, Sehoon, Krishnamurthi, Lakshman, and Zoltners, Andris A. Analysis of new product diffusion using a four-segment trial-repeat model. *Management Science*, pp. 225–247 (Summer 1994). [12:351–352 (September 1995)]

Hauser, John R. How puritan-bennett used the house of quality. *Sloan Management Review*, pp. 61–70 (Spring 1993). [11:271 (June 1994)]

Houlihan, John T. Switching the buyer to buying mode: how new technology is revolutionizing product design. *Creativity and Innovation Management*, pp. 63–68 (March 1993). [11:365–366 (September 1994)]

Kay, John. Value-added winners. *International management*, pp. 44–45 (April 1993). [11:82–83 (January 1994)]

Kleinschmidt, Elko J. and Cooper, Robert G. The performance impact of an international orientation on product innovation. *European Journal of Marketing*, pp. 56–70 (1988). [6:228–229 (September 1989)]

Lauglaug, Antonio S. Technical-Market Research—get customers to collaborate in developing products. *Long Range Planning*, pp. 78–82 (April 1993). [11: 86–87 (January 1994)]

Mattimore. Bryan. Eureka: how to invent a new product. *The Futurist*, pp. 34–38 (March–April, 1995). [12:451–452 (November 1995)]

Mazumbdar, Tridib. A value-based orientation to new product planning. *Journal of Consumer Marketing*, 10(3):28–41 (1993). [11:260–261 (June 1994)]

Midgley, David F. and Dowling, Grahame R. A longitudinal study of product form innovation: the interaction between predispositions and social messages. *Journal of Consumer Research*, pp. 611–625 (March 1993). [10:439 (November 1993)]

Miller, James B., Bruvold, Norman T., and Kernan, Jerome B. Does competitive-set information affect the results of concept tests? *Journal of Advertising Research*, pp. 16–24 (April–May 1987). [4:311–312 (December 1987)]

Morrison, Thomas C. The false advertising of speciality medical products under the Lanham Act. *Food Drug and Cosmetic Law Journal*, pp. 265–271 (May 1989). [7:252–253 (September 1990)]

Parasuraman, A., Zeithaml, Valarie A., and Berry, Leonard L. SERVQUAL: a multiple-item scale for measuring consumer perceptions of service quality. *Journal of Retailing*, pp. 13–40 (Spring 1988). [6:66–67 (March 1989)]

Plummer, Joseph T. Outliving the myths. *Journal of Advertising Research*, pp. 26–28 (February–March 1990). [8:315–316 (December 1991)]

Ram, S. and Sheth, Jagdish N. Consumer resistance to innovations: the marketing problem and its solutions. *Journal of Consumer Marketing*, pp. 5–14 (Spring 1989). [6:298–299 (December 1989)]

Richins, Marsha L. and Bloch, Peter H. After the new wears off: the temporal context of product involvement. *Journal of Consumer Research*, pp. 280–285 (September 1986). [4:161–162 (June 1987)]

Roberts, R. J. Is information property? *Intellectual Property Journal*, pp. 209–215 (June 1987). [5:249 (September 1988)]

Shostak, G. Lynn. Service positioning through structural change. *Journal of Marketing*, pp. 34–43 (January 1987). [4:304 December 1987)]

Smith, Robert E. Integrating information from advertising and trial: processes and effects on consumer response to product information. *Journal of Marketing Research*, pp. 204–219 (May 1993). [11:167–168 (March 1994)]

Ughanwa, Davidson Oyemeka. Better ways of managing design: the Queen's Award Winners' experience. *Technovation*, pp. 377–399 (1988). [7:80–81 (March 1990)]

Vantrappen, Herman and Collins, John. Controlling the product creation process. *Prism*, pp. 59–73 (Second Quarter 1993). [11:266 (June 1994)]

Weiner, Edith and Brown, Arnold. Human factors: the gap between humans and machines. *The Futurist*, pp. 9–11 (May–June 1989). [6:304 (December 1989)]

Wilding, David. The contribution of market research to the testing of new concepts. *Marketing Intelligence and Planning*, 2:4–12 (1986). [4:228–229 (September 1987)]

Wittink, Dick R. and Cattin, Philippe. Commercial use of conjoint analysis: an update. *Journal of Marketing*, pp. 91–96 (July 1989). [7:159–160 (June 1990)]

Wittink, Dick R., Vriens, Marco, and Burhenne, Wim. Commercial use of conjoint analysis in Europe: results and critical reflections. *International Journal of Research in Marketing*, pp. 41–52 (January 1994). [11:742–473 (November 1994)]

Yeager, Bob. The high road to solutions marketing. *Business Marketing*, pp. 66–84 (May 1987). [5:79–80 (March 1988)]

Product Development

Abetti, Pier A. and Stuart, Robert W. Evaluating new product risk. *Research Technology Management*, pp. 40–43 (May–June 1988). [5:322–323 (December 1988)]

Allen, Thomas J. Organizational structure, information technology, and R&D productivity. *IEEE Transactions on Engineering Management*, pp. 212–217 (November 1986). [4:159–160 (June 1987)]

Anderson, James C. and Narus, James A. Partnering as focused market strategy. *California Management Review*, pp. 95–112 (Spring 1991). [8:310–312 (December 1991)]

Anderson, Philip and Tushman, Michael L. Managing through cycles of technological change. *Research Technology Management*, pp. 26–31 (May–June 1991). [8:316–317 (December 1991)]

Avlonitis, George J. Linking different types of product elimination decisions to their performance outcome: "Project Dropstat." *International Journal of Research in Marketing*, 4:43–57 (1987). [5:173 (June 1988)]

Bailetti, Antonio J. and Guild, Paul D. A method for projects seeking to merge technical advancements with potential markets. *R&D Management*, pp. 291–300 (October 1991). [9:178–179 (June 1992)]

Bell, Chip. How to invent service. *Journal of Services Marketing*, pp. 37–39 (Winter 1992). [9:255–256 (September 1992)]

Bodensteiner, Wayne and Priest, John. Managing the technical risks of the development–production transition. *Industrial Management*, pp. 10–16 (January–February 1988). [6:65 (March 1989)]

Bonnet, Didier C. L. Integrating marketing variables in the early stages of the new product process to support the design and the development of technologically advanced new industrial products. *Quarterly Review of Marketing*, pp. 7–11 (Autumn 1985). [4:67–68 (March 1987)]

Brown, Rick. Managing the "S" curves of innovation. *Journal of Consumer Marketing*, pp. 61–72 (Winter, 1992). [9:247–248 (September 1992)]

Buday, Robert S. Reengineering one firm's product development and another's service delivery. *Planning Review*, pp. 14–17 (March–April 1993). [11:173–174 (March 1994)]

Burkart, Robert E. Reducing R&D cycle time. *Research-Technology Management*, pp. 27–32 (May–June 1994). [12:356–357 (September 1995)]

Capon, Noel, Farley, John U., Lehmann, Donald R. and Hulbert, James M. Profiles of product innovators among large U.S. Manufacturers. *Management Science*, pp. 157–169 (February 1992). [10:80 (January 1993)]

Cassok, David. The extended product line. *Health Industry Today*, pp. 26–37 (July 1986). [4:153–154 (June 1987)]

Child, Peter, Diedrichs, Raimund, Sanders, Falk-Hayo, and Wisniowski, Stefan. The management of complexity. *The McKinsey Quarterly*, 4:52–69 (1991). [9:254–255 (September 1992)]

Clark, Douglas W. Bugs are good: a problem-oriented approach to the management of design engineering. *Research Technology Management*, pp. 23–27 (May–June 1990). [8:68 (March 1991)]

Cohen, Allen M. Marketing battlegrounds: how to win in cash management services. *Bank Administration*, pp. 22–28 (February 1986). [4:153 (June 1987)]

Conley, Ned L. and Mirabel, Eric P. The expanding personal liability of corporate officers and directors for patent infringement. *IDEA*, 4:225–247 (1988). [6:149 (June 1989)]

Coolley, Ronald B. Illinois ownership laws: employers may not own inventions and confidential information. *Illinois Bar Journal*, pp. 390–396 (April 1986). [4:71–72 (March 1987)]

Cowell, Donald W. New service development. *Journal of Marketing Management*, pp. 296–312 (Spring 1988). [5:317 (December 1988)]

Cross, Nigel. The nature and nurture of design ability. *Design Studies* (U.K.), pp. 127–140 (July 1990). [8:63–64 (March 1991)]

Curry, David J. and Faulds, David J. Indexing product quality. *Journal of Consumer Research*, pp. 134–145 (June 1986). [4:70 (March 1987)]

Czinkota, Michael and Kotabe, Masaaki. Product development the Japanese way. *Journal of Business Strategy*, pp. 31–36 (November–December 1990). [9: 325–326 (December 1992)]

deBont, Cees J. P., Schoormans, Jan P. L. and Wessel, Marianne T. T. Consumer personality and the acceptance of product design. *Design Studies*, pp. 200–209 (April 1992). [9:320–321 (December 1992)]

Desarbo, Wayne and Rao, Vithala R. A constrained unfolding methodology for product positioning. *Marketing Science*, pp. 1–19 (Winter 1986). [4:72–73 (March 1987)]

Dixon, John R. and Duffey, Michael R. The neglect of engineering design. *California Management Review*, pp. 9–22 (Winter 1990). [7:326 (December 1990)]

Dorf, Richard C. and Worthington, Kirby K. F. Technology transfer: research to commercial product. *Engineering Management International*, pp. 185–191 (February 1989). [6:304–305 (December 1989)]

Dougherty, Deborah. Interpretative barriers to successful product innovation. *Marketing Science Institute Report* 89–114. [7:247–248 (September 1990)]

Dowlatshahi, Shad. A novel approach to product design and development in a concurrent engineering environment. *Technovation*, 3:161–176 (1993). [11: 87–88 (January 1994)]

Dumaine, Brian. Design that sells and sells and . . . . *Fortune*, pp. 86–94 (March 11, 1991). [9:71–72 (March 1992)]

Dworkin, Terry Morehead and Sheffett, Mary Jane. Product liability in the 80s. *Journal of Public Policy and Marketing*, 4:69–79 (1985). [3:215–216 (September 1986)]

Ealey, Lance and Soderberg, Leif. How Honda cures design amnesia. *The McKinsey Quarterly*, pp. 3–14 (Spring 1990). [8:70–71 (March 1991)]

Eisenhardt, Kathleen M. Speed and strategic choice: how managers accelerate decision-making. *California Management Review*, pp. 39–54 (Spring 1990). [8: 66–67 (March 1991)]

Enslow, Beth. The benchmarking bonanza. *Across the Board*, pp. 16–22 (April 1992). [9:323–324 (December 1992)]

Evamy, Michael. Call yourself a designer? *Design*, pp. 14–16 (March 1994). [12: 82–83 (January 1995)]

Fischer, William A., Hamilton, Willard, McLaughlin, Curtis P., and Zmud, Robert W. The elusive product champion. *Research Management*, pp. 13–16 (May 1986). [3:212–213 (September 1986)]

Foxall, G. and Johnson, B. Strategies of user-initiated product innovation. *Technovation*, pp. 77–102 (June 1987). [5:86–87 (March 1988)]

Franko, Lawrence G. Global Corporate Competition: Who's winning, who's losing, and the R&D factor as one reason why. *Strategic Management Journal*, pp. 449–474 (1989). [7:252 (September 1990)]

Frantz, Mark G. Buying influences for high technology products. *Journal of High Tech Marketing*, pp. 52–57 (Spring 1987). [5:168–169 (June 1988)]

Gemignani, Michael C. Potential liability for use of expert systems. *IDEA*, 29(2): 120–127). [6:301 (December 1989)]

Gomory, Ralph E. From the "ladder of science" to the product development cycle. *Harvard Business Review*, pp. 99–105 (November–December 1989). [7: 157–158 (June 1990)]

Goodrich, Kristina. The designs of the decade. *Across the Board*, pp. 40–49 (March 1990). [7:250–251 (September 1990)]

Grabowski, Henry and Vernon, John. Longer patents for lower imitation barriers: the 1984 Drug Act. *AEA Papers and Proceedings*, pp. 195–198 (May 1986). [4:235 (September 1987)]

Greising, David. Quality: how to make it pay? *Business Week*, pp. 54–59 (August 8, 1994). [12:169–170 (March 1995)]

Grossman, Steven J. Experimental use or fair use as a defense to patent infringement. *IDEA*, 30(4):243–264 (1990). [7:335 (December 1990)]

Gupta, Ashok K. and Rogers, Everett M. Internal marketing: integrating R&D and marketing within the organization. *Journal of Services Marketing*, pp. 55–68 (GPL) (Spring 1991). 8:307–308 (December 1991)]

Gupta, Ashok K. and Wilemon, David L. Accelerating the development of technology-based new products. *California Management Review*, pp. 24–44 (Winter 1990). [7:332–333 (December 1990)]

Haines, Daniel W., Chandran, Rajan, and Parkhe, Arvinde. Winning by being the first to market . . . Or second? *Journal of Consumer Marketing*, pp. 63–69 (Winter 1989). [6:222–223 (September 1989)]

Haskins, Robert and Petit, Thomas. Strategies for entrepreneurial manufacturing. *Journal of Business Strategy*, pp. 24–28 (November–December 1988). [6: 152–153 (June 1989)]

Hauser, John R. How Puritan-Bennett used the house of quality. *Sloan Management Review*, pp. 61–70 (Spring 1993). [11:271 (June 1994)]

Heskett, John. Teaching an old dog new tricks. *International Design*, pp. 52–61 (March–April 1992). [9:324–325 (December 1992)]

Hilton, William E. What sort of improper conduct constitutes misappropriation of a trade secret? *IDEA*, 30(4):287–308 (1990). [8:64 (March 1991)]

Holt, Knut. Does the engineer forget the user? *Design Studies*, pp. 163–168 (July 1989). [7:168–169 (June 1990)]

Houlihan, John T. Switching the buyer to buying mode: how new technology is revolutionizing product design. *Creativity and Innovation Management*, pp. 63–68 (March 1993). [11:365–366 (September 1994)]

House, Charles H. and Price, Raymond L. The return map: tracking product teams. *Harvard Business Review*, pp. 92–100 (January–February 1990). [8: 220–221 (September 1991)]

Houston, Paul. Lessons in new product launching. *Direct Marketing*, pp. 78ff (May 1989). [8:149–150 (June 1991)]

Hufker, Tim and Alpert, Frank. Patents: a managerial perspective. *Journal of Product and Brand Management*, 3(2):33–54 (1944). [12:252–253 (June 1995)]

I can't work this thing (no author given). *Business Week*, April 29, 1991, pp. 58–66. [9:72–73 (March 1992)]

Jacobson, Robert and Aaker, David. Is market share all that it's cracked up to be? *Journal of Marketing*, pp. 11–22 (Fall 1985). [3:206–207 (September 1986)]

Jones, Robert R. Top notch technology: the year's best R&D. *Research and Development*, pp. 54–101 (October 1989). [7:254 (September 1990)]

Julian, Scott D. and Keller, Robert T. Multinational R&D siting. *Columbia Journal of World Business*, pp. 47–57 (Fall 1991). [9:249–250 (September 1992)]

Kamath, Rajan R. and Liker, Jeffrey K. A second look at Japanese product development. *Harvard Business Review*, pp. 154–170 (November–December 1994). [12:253 (June 1995)]

Klimstra, Paul D. and Raphael, Ann T. Integrating R&D and business strategy. *Research Technology Management*, pp. 22–28 (January–February 1992). [9: 321–322 (December 1992)]

Knight, Russell M. Technological innovation in Canada: a comparison of independent entrepreneurs and corporate innovators. *Journal of Business Venturing*, pp. 281–288 (1988). [7:85–86 (March 1990)]

Krause, Irv and Liu, John. Benchmarking R&D productivity. *Planning Review*, pp. 16–21 (January–February 1993). [10:434–435 (November 1993)]

Langowitz, Nan S. Managing new product design and factory fit. *Business Horizons*, pp. 76–79 (May–June 1989). [7:77 (March 1990)]

Larson, Clint. Team tactics can cut product development costs. *Journal of Business Strategy*, pp. 22–25 (September–October 1988). [6:140–141 (June 1989)]

Lauglaug, Antonio S. Technical-market research—get customers to collaborate in developing products. *Long Range Planning*, pp. 78–82 (April 1993). [11: 86–87 (January 1994)]

Levin, Richard C. A new look at the patent system. *AEA Papers and Proceedings*, pp. 199–202 (May 1986). [4:235–236 (September 1987)]

Mandell, Mel and Murphy, Brian. Wake-up strategies for tired R&D projects. *High Technology Business*, pp. 22–25 (February 1989). [7:256–257 (September 1990)]

Mansfield, Edwin. The R&D tax credit and other technology policy issues. *AEA Papers and Proceedings*, pp. 190–193 (May 1986). [4:235 (September 1987)]

Mansfield, Edwin. Technological creativity: Japan and the United States. *Business Horizons*, pp. 48–53 (March–April 1989). [7:75–76 (March 1990)]

McKenna, Regis. Why high-tech products fail. *Journal of high tech marketing*, pp. 1–10 (Summer 1987). [5:175–176 (June 1988)]

McNulty, Terry and Whittington, Richard. Putting the marketing into R&D. *Marketing Intelligence and Planning*. [9:10–16 (1992). 10:358–359 (September 1993)]

Meldrum, M. J. and Millman, A. F. Ten risks in marketing high-technology products. *Industrial Marketing Management*, pp. 43–50 (1991). [8:217–218 (September 1991)]

Millman, A. F. Design and international product competitiveness. *Journal of Engineering Management International*, pp. 237–244 (January 1986). [3:295–296 (December 1986)]

Misrock, S. Leslie, Coggio, Brian D., and Dulak, Norman C. The exercise of patent rights through multiple exclusive field-of-use licensing. *Rutgers Computer and Technology Law Journal*, 2:383–406 (1985). [4:73–74 (March 1987)]

Mitchell, Graham R. Research and development for services. *Research Technology Management*, pp. 37–44 (November–December 1989). [7:257 (September 1990)]

Mitchell, Russell. Masters of innovation. *Business Week*, April 10, 1989, pp. 58–62. [6:299–300 (December 1989)]

Nevens, T. Michael, Summe, Gregory L. and Uttal, Bro. commercializing technology: what the best companies do. *Harvard Business Review*, pp. 154–163 (May–June 1990) [7:327–328 (December 1990)]

Nishikawa, Tohru. New product development. *Journal of Advertising Research*, pp. 27–30 (April–May 1990). [8:64–65 (March 1991)]

Nussbaum, Bruce. Hot products: smart design is the common thread. *Business Week*, pp. 54–57 (June 7, 1993). [11:78–79 (January 1994)]

Onkvisit, Sak and Shaw, John J. Competition and product management: can the product life cycle help? *Business Horizons*, pp. 51–62 (July–August 1986). [4: 154–155 (June 1987)]

Ouchi, William G. and Bolton, Michele Kremen. The logic of joint research and development. *California Management Review*, pp. 9–33 (Spring 1988). [6: 67–68 (March 1989)]

Paul, Ronald N. Improving the new product development process-making technology push work! *Journal of Business and Industrial Marketing*, pp. 59–61 (Fall 1987). [5:243–244 (September 1988)]

Petre, Peter. How GE bobbled the factory of the future. *Fortune*, 1985, pp. 52–63 (November 11). [3:216 (September 1986)]

Pine, B. Joseph, II. Making mass customization happen: strategies for the new competitive realities. *Planning Review*, pp. 23–24 (September–October 1993). [11:364 (September 1994)]

Pinto, Jeffrey K. and Slevin, Dennis P. Critical success factors across the project life cycle. *Project Management Journal*, pp. 67–75 (June 1988). [6:64–65 (March 1989)]

Port, Otis. Quality: small and midsize companies seize the challenge—not a moment too soon. *Business Week*, November 30, 1992, pp. 66–75 (DTV). [10: 252–253 (June 1993)]

Powell, Robert E., Graeff, Kathryn Grill and MacFarlane, Earl W. The sophisticated user defense and liability for defective design: the twain must meet. *Journal of Products Liability*, pp. 113–120 (1991). [9:83 (March 1992)]

Quelch, John A. Marketing the premium product. *Business Horizons*, pp. 38–45 (May–June 1987). [5:167–168 (June 1988)]

Rabino, Samuel. High-technology firms and factors influencing transfer of R&D facilities. *Journal of Business Research*, pp. 195–205 (May 1989). [6:309 (December 1989)]

Rayner, Bruce C. P. The rising price of technological leadership. *Electronic Business*, pp. 52–56 (March 18, 1991). [8:314–315 (December 1991)]

Richards, Tudor. Innovation and creativity: woods, trees and pathways. *R&D Management*, pp. 97–108 (April 1991). [8:309–310 (Decmeber 1991)]

Saidman, Perry J. The ten commandments of design patent protection. *Innovation*, pp. 21–23 (Fall 1990). [8:221–222 (September 1991)]

Sasaki, Toru. How the Japanese accelerated new car development. *Long Range Planning*, pp. 15–25 (January 1991). [8:313–314 (December 1991)]

Schmidheiny, Stephan. The business logic of sustainable development. *Columbia Journal of World Business*, pp. 18–24 (Fall–winter 1992). [10:433–434 (November 1993)]

Schneider, Eric. The user in focus. *Innovation*, pp. 26–29 (Summer 1991). [10: 164–165 (March 1993)]

Schultz, Randall L., Slevin, Dennis P., and Pinto, Jeffrey K. Strategy and tactics in a process model of project implementation. *Interfaces*, pp. 34–46 (May–June 1987). [5:316 (December 1988)]

Sears, Ronald J. Market value innovation: designing the experience. *Innovation*, pp. 2–8 (Fall 1986). [4:302–303 (December 1987)]

Seely Brown, John. Research that reinvents the corporation. *The McKinsey Quarterly*, 2:78–96 (1992). [10:259–260 (June 1993)]

Shenhar, Aaron J. From low- to high-tech project management. *R&D Management*, 23(3):199–214 (1993). [11:364–365 (September 1994)]

Sisodia, Rajendra S. Why companies kill their technologies. *Journal of Business Strategy*, pp. 42–48 (January–February 1992). [10:350 (September 1993)]

Soderberg, Leif G. Facing up to the engineering Ggp. *The McKinsey Quarterly*, pp. 2–18 (Spring 1989). [7:84–85 (March 1990)]

Soderberg, Leif G. and O'Halloran, J. David. Heroic engineering takes more than heroes. *The McKinsey Quarterly*, 1:3–23 (1992). [9:318–319 (December 1992)]

Souder, William E. Improving productivity through technology push. *Research Technology Management*, pp. 19–24 (March–April 1989). [6:305–306 (December 1989)]

Stalk, George, Jr. and Hout, Thomas M. Competing against time. *Research Technology Management*, pp. 19–24 (March–April 1990). [7:334–335 (December 1990)]

Starling, Grover. Project management as a language game. *Industrial Management and Data Systems*, 9(3):10–18 (1993). [11:358–359 (September 1994)]

Stern, Marilyn. Is national design dead? *Across the Board*, pp. 32–37 (September 1993). [11:268–269 (June 1994)]

Stewart, Thomas A. Brace for Japan's hot new strategy. *Fortune*, September 21, 1992, pp. 62–74. [10:169–170 (March 1993)]

Takeuchi, Hirotaka and Nonaka, Ikujiro. The new new product development game. *Harvard Business Review*, pp. 137–146 (January 1986). [3:205–206 (September 1986)]

Towner, Simon J. Four ways to accelerate new product development. *Long Range Planning*, pp. 57–65 (April 1994). [12:170–171 (March 1995)]

Ughanwa, Davidson Oyemeka. Better ways of managing design: the Queen's Award Winners' experience. *Technovation*, pp. 377–399 (1988), [7:80–81 (March 1990)]

Ursic, Michael. Product safety warnings: a legal review. *Journal of Public Policy and Marketing*, 4:80–90 (1985). [3:216–217 (September 1986)]

Valentin, E. K. Commentary: five lethal product development and diversification traps. *Journal of Product and Brand Management*, 2:48–58 (1993). [11: 361–362 (September 1994)]

Vandermerwe, Sandra. Quality in services: the "softer" side is "harder" (and smarter). *Long Range Planning*, pp. 45–56 (April 1994). [12:85–86 (January 1995)]

Vaver, David. Some agnostic observations on intellectual property. *Intellectual Property Journal*, pp. 125–153 (June 1991). [9:73–74 (March 1992)]

Vickers, Graham. All muscle, no fat. *Design*, pp. 26–28 (April 1994). [12:86 (January 1995)]

von Braun, Christoph-Friedrich. The acceleration trap. *Sloan Management Review*, pp. 49–58 (Fall 1990). [8:139–140 (June 1991)]

Walleigh, Richard. Product design for low-cost manufacturing. *Journal of Business Strategy*, pp. 37–41 (July–August 1989). [7:83 (March 1990)]

Weiner, Charles. Universities, professors, and patents: a continuing controversy. *Technology Review*, pp. 13–15 (February–March 1986). [4:158–159 (June 1987)]

Wheelwright, Stephen C. and Clark, Kim B. Creating project plans to focus product development. *Harvard Business Review*, pp. 70–82 (WJA) (March–April 1992). [9:316–317 (December 1992)]

White, Philip. Waste not. *International Design*, pp. 67–69 (May–June 1992). [9:319 (December 1992)]

Zirger, Billie Jo and Maidique, Modesto A. A model of new product development: an empirical test. *Management Science*, pp. 867–883 (July 1990). [8:65–66 (March 1991)]

Zurn, James T. Problem discovery function: a useful tool for assessing new product introduction. *IEEE Transactions on Engineering Management*, pp. 110–119 (May 1991). [9:79–80 (March 1992)]

Strategy

Adams, David. Parallel market analysis: a technique for risk-averse brand innovation. *Journal of Brand Management*, 4:221–233 (1995). [12:449 (November 1995)]

Allen, Thomas J. Organizational structure, information technology, and R&D productivity. *IEEE Transactions on Engineering Management*, pp. 212–217 (November 1986). [4:159–160 (June 1987)]

Alpert, Frank. Breadth of coverage for intellectual property Law. *Journal of Product and Brand Management*, 2:5–17 (1993). [11:470–471 (November 1994)]

Alpert, Frank H., Kamins, Michael A., and Graham, John L. An examination of reseller buyer attitudes toward order of brand entry. *Journal of Marketing*, pp. 25–37 (July 1992). [10:262–263 (June 1993)]

Bakker, Hans, Jones, Wynford, and Nichols, Michele. Using core competencies to develop new business. *Long Range Planning*, pp. 13–27 (December 1994). [12:348–349 (September 1995)]

Barczak, Gloria J., Bello, Daniel C., and Wallace, Everett S. The role of consumer shows in new product adoption. *Journal of Consumer Marketing*, pp. 55–67 (GPL) (Spring 1992). [10:76–77 (January 1993)]

Barker, Jeffrey, Tjosvold, Dean, and Andrews, I. Robert. Conflict approaches of effective and ineffective project managers: a field study in a matrix organization. *Journal of Management Studies*, pp. 167–178 (March 1988). [5:323–324 (December 1988)]

Bartlett, Christopher A. and Ghoshal, Sumantra. Tap your subsidiaries for global reach. *Harvard Business Review*, pp. 87–94 (November–December 1986). [5:80–81 (March 1988)]

Basadur, Min and Thompson, Ron. Usefulness of the ideation principle of extended effort in real world professional and managerial creative problem solving. *Journal of Creative Behavior*, pp. 23–34 (First Quarter 1986). [4:73 (March 1987)]

Bassin, Sue. Innovative packaging strategies. *Journal of Business Strategy*, pp. 28–31 (January–February 1988). [250–251 (September 1988)]

Beard, Charles and Easingwood, Chris. Sources of competitive advantage in the marketing of technology-intensive products and processes. *European Journal of Marketing*, 12:5–18 (1992). [10:351–352 (September 1993)]

Beaumont, William E. The new patent law of the People's Republic of China (PRC): evidence of a second Chinese "Renaissance"? *IDEA*, 1:39–65 (1986). [4:162 (June 1987)]

Berenson, Conrad and Mohr-Jackson, Iris. Product rejuvenation: a less risky alternative to product innovation. *Business Horizons*, pp. 51–57 (November–December 1994). [12:450–451 (November 1995)]

Berman, Evan, Vasconcellos, Eduardo, and Werther, William B., Jr. Executive levers for the strategic management of technology. *Business Horizons*, pp. 53–61 (January–February 1994). [11:471–472 (November 1994)]

Bertrand, Kate. New product marketing: Breaking the corporate mold. *Business Marketing*, pp. 44–58 (July 1987). [5:82–83 (March 1988)]

Besford, John. Designing a quality product. *Journal of Marketing Management*, pp. 133–144 (Winter 1987). [5:171 (June 1988)]

Bloch, Peter H. The product enthusiast: implications for marketing strategy. *Journal of Consumer Marketing*, pp. 51–62 (Summer 1986). [4:68–69 (March 1987)]

Bonnet, Didier C. L. Integrating marketing variables in the early stages of the new product process to support the design and the development of technologically advanced new industrial products. *Quarterly Review of Marketing*, pp. 7–11 (Autumn 1985). [4:67–68 (March 1987)]

Bright, James R. Improving the industrial anticipation of current scientific activity. *Technological Forecasting and Social Change*, pp. 1–12 (February 1986). [4:155–156 (June 1987)]

Brockhoff, Klaus and Chakrabarti, Alok K. R&D/marketing linkage and innovation strategy: some West German experience. *IEEE Transactions on Engineering Management*, pp. 167–174 (August 1988). [6:143–144 (June 1989)]

Brown, Rick. Making the product portfolio a basis for action. *Long Range Planning*, pp. 102–110 (February 1991). [9:78 (March 1992)]

Brown, Rick. Managing the "S" curves of innovation. *Journal of Consumer Marketing*, pp. 61–72 (Winter 1992). [9:247–248 (September 1992)]

Buchanan, Bruce, Givon, Moshe, and Goldman, Arieh. Measurement of discrimination ability in taste tests: an empirical investigation. *Journal of Marketing Research*, pp. 154–163 (May 1987). [4:301–302 (December 1987)]

Buday, Tom. Capitalizing on brand extensions. *Journal of Consumer Marketing*, pp. 27–30 (Fall 1989). [7:245–246 (September 1990)]

Burall, Paul. Green-ness is good for you. *Design*, pp. 22–24 (April 1994). [12:354 (September 1995).

Burgelman, Robert A. Managing corporate entrepreneurship: new structures for implementing technological innovation. *Technology in Society*, pp. 91–103 (1985). [4:150–151 (June 1987)]

Burger, Philip C. and Cann, Cynthia W. Post-purchase strategy. *Industrial Marketing Management*, 2:91–108 (1995). [12:357 (September 1995)]

Butler, Richard J. and Carney, Mick. Strategy and strategic choice: the case of telecommunications. *Strategic Management Journal*, pp. 161–177 (March–April 1986). [303–304 (December 1986)]

Cahill, Dennis J. and Warshawsky, Robert M. The marketing concept: a forgotten aid for marketing high technology products. *Journal of Consumer Marketing*, 10(3):17–22 1993). [11:165 (March 1994)]

Campbell, Andrew and Young, Sally. Creating a sense of mission. *Long Range Planning*, pp. 10–20 (August 1991). [10:84–85 (January 1993)]

Capon, Noel, Farley, John U., Lehmann, Donald R., and Hulbert, James M. Profiles of product innovators among large U.S. manufacturers. *Management Science*, pp. 157–169 (February 1992). [10:80] (January 1993)

Carey, John et al. Moving the lab closer to the marketplace: can the US again turn invention into innovation? Special bonus issue of *Business Week*, pp. 164–171 (DTV) (1992). [10:255 (June 1993)]

Carpenter, Gregory S. and Nakamoto, Kent. Consumer preference formation and pioneering advantage. *Journal of Marketing Research*, pp. 285–298 (August 1989), [7:158–159 (June 1990)]

Chakrabarti, Alok K. and Weisenfeld, Ursula. An empirical analysis of innovation strategies of biotechnological firms in the U.S. *Journal of Engineering and Technology Management*, pp. 243–260 (December 1991). [10:168 (March 1993)]

Chandler, Colby H. Corporate innovation and entrepreneurship. *Journal of Business Strategy*, pp. 5–8 (Summer 1986). [4:70–71 (March 1987)]

Chaney, Paul K., Devinney, Timothy M., and Winer, Russell S. The impact of new product introductions on the market value of firms. *Journal of Business*, pp. 573–610 (October 1991). [9:317–318 (December 1992)]

Choudhury, Nandan. Incentives for the divisional manager. *Accounting and Business Research*, pp. 11–21 (Winter 1985). [4:63–64 (March 1987)]

Chussil, Mark J. Does market share really matter? *Planning Review*, pp. 31–37 (September–October 1991). [10:165–166 (March 1993)]

Clancy, Kevin J. and Shulman, Robert S. Marketing with blinders on. *Across the Board*, pp. 33–38 (October 1993). [11:471 (November 1994)]

Clark, Kim B. and Fujimoto, Takahiro. The power of product integrity. *Harvard Business Review*, pp. 107–118 (November–December 1990). [8:222–223 (September 1991)]

Coolley, Ronald B. Illinois ownership laws: employers may not own inventions and confidential information. *Illinois Bar Journal*, pp. 390–396 (April 1986). [4:71–72 (March 1987)]

Covin, Jeffrey G. Entrepreneurial versus conservative firms: a comparison of strategies and performance. *Journal of Management Studies*, pp. 439–462 (September 1991). [10:82–83 (January 1993)]

Day, George S. The capabilities of market-driven organizations. *Journal of Marketing*, pp. 37–52 (October 1994). [12:257–258 (June 1995)]

Dell, Michael S. Making the right choices for the new consumer. *Planning Review*, pp. 20–22 (September–October 1993). [11:355 (September 1994)]

Del Veccho, Eugene. Generating marketing ideas when formal research is not available. *Journal of Services Marketing*, pp. 71–74 (Spring 1988). [5:313–314 (December 1988)]

Deschamps, Jean-Philippe and Nayak, P. Ranganath. Lessons from product juggernauts. *Prism*, pp. 5–23 (Second Quarter 1993). [11:164–165 (March 1994)]

Devinney, Timothy M. and Stewart, David W. Rethinking the product portfolio: a generalized investment model. *Management Science*, pp. 1080–1095 (September 1988). [6:302–303 (December 1989)]

Dougherty, Elizabeth. Technology scouts. *Research and Development*, pp. 44–50 (October 1989). [7:163 (June 1990)]

Douma, Sytse. Success and failure in new ventures. *Long Range Planning*, pp. 54–60 (April 1991). [8:309 (December 1991)]

Doz, Yves, Angelmar, Reinhard, and Prahalad, C. K. Technological innovation and interdependence, a challenge for the large, complex firm. *Technology in Society*, pp. 105–125 (1985). [4:151–152 (June 1987)]

Dreyfuss, Joel. What do you do for an encore? *Fortune*, December 19, 1988, pp. 111–119. [6:146–147 (June 1989)]

Drucker, Peter F. The coming of the new organization. *Harvard Business Review*, pp. 45–53 (January–February 1988). [5:317–318 (December 1988)]

Dumaine, Brian. How managers can succeed through speed. *Fortune*, February 13, 1989, pp. 54–59. [6:230–231 (September 1989)]

Dumaine, Brian. What the leaders of tomorrow see. *Fortune*, July 3, 1989, pp. 48–62. [7:82–83 (March 1990)]

Edson, Lee. Patent wars. *Across the Board*, pp. 24–31 (April 1993). [11:169–170 (March 1994)]

Eppen, Gary D., Hansom, Ward A., and Martin, R. Kipp. Bundling—new products, new markets, low risk. *Sloan Management Review*, pp. 7–14 (Summer 1991). [9:74–75 (March 1992)]

Eschenbach, T. G. and Geistauts, G. A. Strategically focused engineering: design and management. *IEEE Transactions on Engineering Management*, pp. 62–70 (May 1987). [5:87–88 (March 1988)]

Eynon, Philip J. Avoid the seven deadly sins of strategic risk analysis. *Journal of Business Strategy*, pp. 18–22 (November–December 1988). [6:226–227 (September 1989)]

Fannin, Rebecca. Molecule to the marketplace. *Marketing and Media Decisions*, pp. 70–75 (February 1986). [4:71 (March 1987)]

Farquhar, Peter. Strategic challenges for branding. *Marketing Management*, 2: 8–15 (1994). [12:352 (September 1995)]

Feeser, H. R. and Willard, G. E. Founding strategy and performance: a comparison of high and low growth high tech firms. *Strategic Management Journal*, pp. 87–98 (February 1990). [7:333–334 (December 1990)]

Ford, David. Develop your technology strategy. *Long Range Planning*, pp. 85–95 (October 1988). [6:145–146 (June 1989)]

Forrest, James E. Management aspects of strategic partnering. *Journal of General Management*, pp. 25–40 (Summer 1992). [10:260 (June 1993)]

Gable, Myron, Fairhurst, Ann, and Dickinson, Roger. The use of benchmarking to enhance marketing decision making. *Journal of Consumer Marketing*, 10: 52–60 (1993). [11:172–173 (March 1994)]

Gemignani, Michael C. Potential liability for use of expert systems. *IDEA*, 29(2): 120–127 (1989). [6:301 (December 1989)]

Gluck, Frederick W. "Big-bang" Management: creative innovation. *The McKinsey Quarterly*, pp 49–59 (Spring 1985). [4:302 (December 1987)]

Goans, Judy Winegar. Intellectual property abroad. *Business America*, October 27, 1986, pp. 2–7. [5:81 (March 1988)]

Gobeli, David H. and Larson, Erik W. Matrix management: more than a fad. *Engineering Management International*, 4:71–76 (1986). [4:236–237 (September 1987)]

Goodspeed, Jonathan. HP's Alberding: hanging tough in Palo Alto. *High Technology Marketing*, pp. 11–14 (March 1987). [5:86 (March 1988)]

Gordon, Ian. Ten ways. *Business Quarterly*, pp. 69–75 (Autumn 1994). [12:259–260 (June 1995)]

Gross, Irwin. The perils of customer satisfaction. *Across the Board*, pp. 56–57 (April 1994). [11:473 (November 1994)]

Habib, Mohammed M. and Victor, Bart. Strategy, structure, and performance of U.S. manufacturing and service MNCs: a comparative analysis. *Strategic Management Journal*, pp. 589–606 (1991). [10:167–168 (March 1993)]

Halal, William E. Let's turn organizations into markets. *The Futurist*, pp. 9–14 (May–June 1994). [12:171–172 (March 1995)]

Hall, Richard. The strategic analysis of intangible resources. *Strategic Management Journal*, pp. 135–144 (1992). [10:83–84 (January 1993)]

Hardy, Cynthia. The nature of unobtrusive power. *Journal of Management Studies*, pp. 384–399 (July 1985). [3:210 (September 1986)]

Harvey, Michael. A new way to combat product counterfeiting. *Business Horizons*, pp. 19–28 (July–August 1988). [6:63–64 (March 1989)]

Hauser, John R. and Clausing, Don. The house of quality. *Harvard Business Review*, pp. 63–73 (May–June 1988). [6:68–69 (March 1989)]

Higgins, Susan H. and Shanklin, William L. Seeking mass market acceptance for high-technology consumer products. *Journal of Consumer Marketing*, pp. 5–13 (GPL) (Winter 1992). [9:251–252 (September 1992)]

Hill, Charles W. C. and Snell, Scott A. External control, corporate strategy, and firm performance in research-intensive industries. *Strategic Management Journal*, pp. 577–590 (1988). [6:150–151 (June 1989)]

Hisrich, Robert D. The need for marketing in entrepreneurship. *Journal of Business and Industrial Marketing*, pp. 55–60 (GPL) (Summer 1992). [10:79 (January 1993)]

Huey, John. Nothing is impossible. *Fortune*, September 23, 1991, pp. 135–140. [9:169–170 (June 1992)]

Irwin, Robert A. and Michaels, Edward G., III. Core skills: doing the right things right. *The McKinsey Quarterly*, pp. 4–19 (Summer 1989). [7:163–164 (June 1990)]

Jarillo, J. Carlos. On strategic networks. *Strategic Management Journal*, pp. 31–41 (January–February 1988). [5:251–252 (September 1988)]

Kanter, Rosabeth M. Supporting innovation and venture development in established companies. *Journal of Business Venturing*, pp. 47–60 (Winter 1985). [4: 152–153 (June 1987)]

Kaplan, Barry M. Zapping—the real issue is communication. *Journal of Advertising Research*, pp. 9–15) (April–May 1985. [4:230 (September 1987)]

Kekre, Sunder and Srinivasan, Kannan. Broader product line: a necessity to achieve success? *Management Science*, pp. 1216–1231 (October 1990). [9: 179–180 (June 1992)]

King, Stephan. Brand-building in the 1990s. *Journal of Consumer Marketing*, pp. 43–52 (GPL) (Fall 1991). [9:171–172 (June 1992)]

Kirkpatrick, David. Environmentalism: the new crusade. *Fortune*, February 12, 1990, pp. 44–54. [7:332 (December 1990)]

Klimstra, Paul D. and Raphael, Ann T. Integrating R&D and business strategy. *Research Technology Management*, pp. 22–28 (January–February 1992). [9: 321–322 (December 1992)]

Kokubo, Atsuro. Core-technology-based management: the next Japanese challenge. *Prism*, pp. 13–21 (First Quarter 1993). [11:166–167 (March 1994)]

Krogh, Lester C. Measuring and improving laboratory productivity/quality. *Research Management*, pp. 22–24 (November–December 1987). [5:249–250 (September 1988)]

Lambkin, Mary and Day, George. Evolutionary processes in competitive markets: beyond the product life cycle. *Journal of Marketing*, pp. 4–20 (July 1989). [7: 78–79 (March 1990)]

Lammey, Glenn D. New product portfolio power. *Business Marketing*, pp. 64–70 (October 1987). [5:168 (June 1988)]

Lawton, Stephan E. Controversy under the Orphan Drug Act: is resolution on the way?. *Food Drug and Cosmetic Law Journal*, pp. 327–343 (March 1991). [9:82–83 (March 1992)]

Lee, Moonkyu and Ulgado, Francis M. Service extension strategy: a viable basis for growth? *Journal of Services Marketing*, 7(2):24–35 (1993). [11:168–169 (March 1994)]

Letscher, Martin G. Fad or trend? How to distinguish them and capitalize on them. *Journal of Consumer Marketing*, pp. 21–26 (Spring 1990). [7:330 (December 1990)]

Levine, Jonathan B. and Byrne, John A. Corporate odd couples. *Business Week*, July 21, 1986, pp. 100–105. [3:297 (December 1986)]

Lilien, Gary L. and Yoon, Eunsang. Determinants of new industrial product performance: a strategic reexamination of the empirical literature. *IEEE Transactions on Engineering Management*, pp. 3–10 (February 1989). [6:308 (December 1989)]

Lipnack, Jessica and Stamps, Jeffrey. A network model. *The Futurist*, pp. 23–25 (July–August 1987). [5:83–84 (March 1988)]

Macdonald, Roderick J. and Wang Jinliang. Time, timeliness of innovation, and the emergence of industries. *Technovation*, pp. 37–53 (February 1994). [12:78–79 (January 1995)]

Magrath, Allan J. and Kenneth G. Hardy. Building customer partnerships. *Business Horizons*, pp. 24–28 (January–February 1994). [11:363–364 (September 1994)]

Maier, Gregory J. Software protection-integrating patent, copyright, and trade secret kaw. *IDEA*, 1:13–28 (1987). [5:171–172 (June 1988)]

Mansfield, Edwin. Technological creativity: Japan and the United States. *Business Horizons*, pp. 48–53 (March–April 1989). [7:75–76 (March 1990)]

Marshall, Michael and Siegler, Frank. Selecting the right rep firm. *Sales and Marketing Management*, pp. 46–49ff (January 1993). [10:350–351 (September 1993)]

Martin, Judy. Urgent memo! *Sales and Marketing management*, pp. 71–73 (March 1993). [11:85–86 (January 1994)]

Maru File, Karen; Judd, Benn B. and Prince, Russ Alan. Interactive marketing: the influence of participation on positive word-of-mouth and referrals. *Journal of Services Marketing*, pp. 5–14 (Fall 1992). [10:436–437 (November 1993)]

Mazumbdar, Tridib. A value-based orientation to new product planning. *Journal of Consumer Marketing*, 10(3):28–41 (1993). [11:260–261 (June 1994)]

McClelland, Sam. The consultative style of management. *Industrial Management*, pp. 12–13 (January–February 1987). [5:88–89 (March 1988)]

McGrath, Allan J. Six pathways to marketing innovation. *Planning Review*, pp. 12–17ff (November–December 1992). [10:354–355 (September 1993)]

McKee, Daryl O. and Konell, Sid. Product adaptability: assessment and strategy. *Journal of Product and Brand Management*, 2(2):33–47 (1993). [11:266–268 (June 1994)]

McKee, Daryl O., Varadarajan, P. R. and Pride, William M. Strategic adaptability and firm performance: a market-contingent perspective. *Journal of Marketing*, pp. 21–35 (July 1989). [7:76 (March 1990)]

Meyerowitz, Steven A. A legal feel to "look and feel" suits?. *Business Marketing*, pp. 49–51 (December 1988). [6:223–224 (September 1989)]

Meyers, Marc H. and Roberts, Edward B. New product strategy in small technology-based firms: a pilot study. *Management Science*, pp. 806–820 (July 1986). [5:89 (March 1988)]

Miller, Alex, Spann, Mary S., and Lerner, Linda. Competitive advantages in new corporate ventures: the impact of resource sharing and reporting level. *Journal of Business Venturing*, pp. 335–350 (September 1991). [9:252–253 (September 1992)]

Miller, Nancy A. Trade marks for services—the Kraft decision. *Intellectual Property Journal*, pp. 133–141 (November 1985). [4:229–230 (September 1987)]

Millman, A. F. Design and international product competitiveness. *Journal of Engineering Management International*, pp. 237–244 (January 1986). [3:295–296 (December 1986)]

Misrock, S. Leslie, Coggio, Brian D., and Dulak, Norman C. The exercise of patent rights through multiple exclusive field-of-use licensing. *Rutgers Computer and Technology Law Journal*, 2:383–406 (1985). [4:73–74 (March 1987)]

Mitchell, Graham R. New approaches for the strategic management of technology. *Technology in Society*, pp. 227–239 (1985). [4:300 (December 1987)]

Mitchell, Graham R. and Hamilton, William F. Managing R&D as a strategic option. *Research Technology Management*, pp. 15–22 (May–June 1988). [6:72–73 (March 1989)]

Mitchell, Russell. Masters of innovation. *Business Week*, April 10, 1989, pp. 58–62. [6:299–300 (December 1989)]

Narver, John C. and Slater, Stanley F. The effect of a market orientation on business profitability. *Journal of Marketing*, pp. 20–35 (October 1990). [8:223 (September 1991)]

Nelson-Horchler, Joani. Dodging the liability bullet. *Industry Week*, April 6, 1987, pp. 30–35. [4:305–306 (December 1987)]

Norris, Donald G. Ingredient branding: a strategy option with multiple beneficiaries. *Journal of Consumer Marketing*, pp. 19–32 (GPL) (Summer 1992). [10:81–82 (January 1993)]

Nye, David. Trust is a well-drawn employment contract. *Across the Board*, pp. 22–41 (October 1988). [6:144 (June 1989)]

Odioso, Raymond C. An R&D executive looks at marketing. *Research Management*, pp. 20–25 (September–October 1987). [5:169–170 (June 1988)]

Onkvisit, Sak and Shaw, John J. The international dimension of branding: strategic considerations and decisions. *International Marketing Review*, 3:22–34 (1989). [7:87–88 (March 1990)]

Osborne, Richard L. The dark side of the entrepreneur. *Long Range Planning*, pp. 26–31 (June 1991). [10:166–167 (March 1993)]

Park, C. Wham and Smith, Daniel C. Product class competitors as sources of innovative marketing strategies. *Journal of Consumer Marketing*, pp. 27–37 (Spring 1990). [8:60–61 (March 1991)]

Parsons, Andrew I. Building innovativeness in large U.S. corporations. *Journal of Services Management*, pp. 5–20 (GPL) (Fall 1991). [9:173–174 (June 1992)]

Parsons, Andrew J. Building innovativeness in large U.S. corporations. *Journal of Consumer Marketing*, pp. 35–50 (GPL) (Spring 1992). [9:319–320 (December 1992)]

Pascale, Richard Tanner. The renewal factor: constructive contention. *Planning Review*, pp. 4ff (July–August 1990). [8:143–144 (June 1991)]

Pavia, Teresa M. and Costa, Janeen Arnold. The winning number: consumer perceptions of alpha-numeric brand names. *Journal of Marketing*, pp. 85–98 (July 1993). [11:166 (March 1994)]

Pearson, Gordon. The strategic discount-protecting new business projects against DCF. *Long Range Planning*, pp. 18–24 (February 1986). [3:214 (September 1986)]

Pennings, Johannes M. and Harianto, Farid. The diffusion of technological innovation in the commercial banking industry. *Strategic Management Journal*, pp. 29–46 (1992). [10:433 (November 1993)]

Peters, Tom. The German economic miracle nobody knows. *Across the Board*, pp. 16–23 (April 1990). [7:330–331 (December 1990)]

Peters, Tom. Get innovative or get dead. *California Management Review*, pp. 9–26 (Fall 1990). [8:218–219 (September 1991)]

Petre, Peter. How GE bobbled the factory of the future. *Fortune*, November 11, 1985, pp. 52–63. [3:216 (September 1986)]

Pierc, Nigel F. and Morgan, Neil A. Mission analysis: an operational approach.. *Journal of General Management*, pp. 1–19 (Spring 1994). [12:80–81 (January 1995)]

Pine, B. Joseph, II. Mass customizing products and services. *Planning Review*, pp. 6–13ff (July–August 1993). [11:270 (June 1994)]

Pine, B. Joseph, II, Peppers, Don, and Rogers, Martha. Do you want to keep your customers forever? *Harvard Business Review*, pp. 103–114 (March–April 1995). [12:446–447 (November 1995)]

Pinto, Jeffrey K. and Kharbanda, Om P. Lessons for an Accidental Profession. *Business Horizons*, pp. 41–50 (March–April 1995). [12:444–445 (November 1995)]

Porter, Michael. Changing patterns of international competition. *California Management Review*, pp. 9–40 (Winter 1986). [3:208 (September 1986)]

Posner, Barry. What's all the fighting about? Conflicts in project management. *IEEE Transactions on Engineering Management*, November 1986, pp. 207–211. [4:226–227 (September 1987)]

Powell, Robert E., Graeff, Kathryn Grill, and MacFarlane, Earl W. The sophisticated user defense and liability for defective design: the twain must meet. *Journal of Products Liability* (1991), pp. 113–120. [9:83 (March 1992)]

Prasad, S. Benjamin. Technology transfer: the approach of a Dutch multinational. *Technovation*, pp. 3–15 (1986). [4:65–66 (March 1987)]

The quality imperative (no author given). *Business Week* (special bonus issue, October 21, 1991), 216 pages (DTV). [9:172–173 (June 1992)]

Quelch, John A. and Kenny, David. Extend profits, not product lines. *Harvard Business Review*, pp. 153–160 (September–October 1994). [12:249–250 (June 1995)]

Rabino, Samuel. High-technology firms and factors influencing transfer of R&D facilities. *Journal of Business Research* (May 1989, pp. 195–205). [6:309 (December 1989)]

Ram, S. and Sheth, Jagdish N. Consumer resistance to innovations: the marketing problem and its solutions. *Journal of Consumer Marketing*, pp. 5–14 (Spring 1989). [6:298–299 (December 1989)]

Rangan, V. Kasturi, Menezes, Melvyn A. J. and Maier, E. P. Channel selection for new industrial products: a framework, method, and application. *Journal of Marketing*, pp. 69–82 (July 1992). [10:170–171 (March 1993)]

Reddy, Srinivas K., Holak, Susan L., and Bhat, Subodh. To extend or not to extend: success determinants of line extensions. *Journal of Marketing Research*, pp. 243–262 (May 1994). [12:81–82 (January 1995)]

Reich, Robert B. Who is them? *Harvard Business Review*, pp. 77–88 (March–April 1991). [9:180–181 (June 1992)]

Rice, Tracey. Teaming strategic marketing with design. *Design Management Journal*, pp. 59–63 (Spring 1991). [10:78–79 (January 1993)]

Robertson, Thomas S. and Gatignon, Hubert. Competitive effects on technology. *Journal of Marketing*, pp. 1–12 (July 1986). [4:231–232 (September 1987)]

Robertson, Thomas S. and Gatignon, Hubert. How innovators thwart new entrants into their market. *Planning Review*, pp. 5–11ff (September–October 1991). [9:256–257 (September 1992)]

Rolfes, Rebecca. How green is your market basket. *Across the Board*, pp. 49–51 (January–February 1990). [7:332 (December 1990)]

Saleh, Shoukry D. and Wang, Clement K. The management of innovation: strategy, structure, and organizational climate. *IEEE Transactions on Engineering Management*, pp. 14–21 (HJT) (February 1993). [10:430 (November 1993)]

Schaars, Steven P. When entering growth markets, are pioneers better than poachers? *Business Horizons*, pp. 27–36 (March–April 1986). [4:227–228 (September 1987)]

Schmidheiny, Stephan. The business logic of sustainable development. *Columbia Journal of World Business*, pp. 18–24 (Fall–Winter 1992). [10:433–434 (November 1993)]

Schneebaum, Steven M. Products liability in the European community: what does it mean for U.S. companies? *Food Drug and Cosmetic Law Journal*, pp. 283–289 (May 1989). [6:308–309 (December 1989)]

Schoemaker, Paul J. H. Scenario planning: a tool for strategic thinking. *Sloan Management Review*, pp. 25–40 (Winter 1995). [12:355–356 (September 1995)]

Schopler, Janice H. Interorganizational groups: origins, structure, and outcomes. *Academy of Management Review*, pp. 702–713 (October 1987). [5:165–166 (June 1988)]

Sellers, Patricia. Winning over the new consumer. *Fortune*, July 29, 1991, pp. 116–125. [9:78–79 (March 1992)]

Serwer, Andrew E. How to escape a price war. *Fortune*, June 13, 1994, pp. 82–88. [11:465 (November 1994)]

Sharp, Byron M. Managing brand extension. *Journal of Consumer Marketing*, 10(3):11–17 (1993). [11:357–358 (September 1994)]

Sharp, Byron M. The marketing value of brand extension. *Marketing Intelligence and Planning*, 7:9–13 (1991). [10:168–169 (March 1993)]

Shipley, David and Howard, Paul. Brand-naming industrial products. *Industrial Marketing Management*, pp. 59–66 (1993). [10:353–354 (September 1993)]

Siegel, Robin, Siegel, Eric, and Macmillan, Ian C. Characteristics distinguishing high-growth ventures. *Journal of Business Venturing*, pp. 169–180 (March 1993). [10:435 (November 1993)]

Simon, Herbert A. Strategy and organizational evolution. *Strategic Management Journal*, pp. 131–142 (Winter 1993). [12:887–88 (January 1995)]

Slater, Stanley F. and Narver, John C. Product-market strategy and performance. *European Journal of Marketing*, 27(10)33–51 (1993). [11:359–360 (September 1994)]

Slywotzky, Adrian J. and Shapiro, Benson P. Leveraging to best the odds: the new marketing mind-set. *Harvard Business Review*, pp. 97–107 (September–October 1993). [11:264–265 (June 1994)]

Souder, William E. and Nassar, Suheil. Choosing an R&D consortium. *Research Technology Managment*, pp. 35–41 (March–April 1990). [8:61–63 (March 1991)]

Souder, William E. and Nassar, Suheil. Managing R&D consortia for Success. *Research Technology Management*, pp. 44–50 (September–October 1990). [8:61–63 (March 1991)]

Spencer, William J. and Triant, Deborah H. Strengthening the link between R&D and corporate strategy. *Journal of Business Strategy*, pp. 38–42 (January–February 1989). [6:229–230 (September 1989)]

Stalking the new consumer (no author given). *Business Week*, August 28, 1989, pp. 54–62. [7:83–84 (March 1990)]

The stateless corporation (no author given). *Business Week*, May 14, 1990, pp. 98–106. [7:325–326 (December 1990)]

Stewart, Thomas A. Brace for Japan's hot new strategy. *Fortune*, September 21, 1992, pp. 62–74. [10:169–170 (March 1993)]

Sykes, Hollister B. Lessons from a new ventures program. *Harvard Business Review*, pp. 69–74 (May–June 1986). [3:301–302 (December 1986)]

Tang, Victor and Collar, Emilio. IBM AS/400 new product launch process ensures satisfaction. *Long Range Planning*, pp. 22–27 (February 1992). [9:324 (December 1992)]

Taylor, Charles R. Prospering in the 90s. *Across the Board*, pp. 43–46 (January–February 1992). [9:253–254 (September 1992)]

Tenaglia, Mason and Noonan, Patrick. Scenario-based strategic planning: a process for building top management consensus. *Planning Review*, pp. 13–19 (March–April 1992). [10:261 (June 1993)]

Teresko, John. Be customer-driven, not function-driven. *Industry Week*, pp. 20–25 (August 2, 1993). [11:171–172 (March 1994)]

Teubal, Morris, Yinnon, Tamar, and Zuscovitch, Ehud. Networks and market creation. *Research Policy*, pp. 381–392 (1991). [9:250–251 (September 1992)]

Tichey, Noel M. and DeVanna, Mary Anne. The transformational leader. *Training and Development Journal*, pp. 27–32 (July 1986). [4:66–67 (March 1987)]

Tolle, Ernest F. Management team building: yes but! *Engineering Management International*, pp. 277–285 (1988). [5:253–254 (September 1988)]

Traynor, Kenneth and Traynor, Susan. The efficacy of strategic and promotional factors on the sales growth of high-tech Firms. *IEEE Transactions on Engineering Management*, pp. 126–134 (May 1994). [12:79–80 (January 1995)]

Udell, Gerald G. Strategies for stimulating home-grown technology-based economic development. *Business Horizons*, pp. 60–64 (November–December 1988). [6:221–222 (September 1989)]

Value marketing: quality, service, and fair pricing are the keys to selling in the 90s (no author given). *Business Week*, November 11, 1991, pp. 132–140 (DTV). [9:176–177 (June 1992)]

Varadarajan, P. R. and Rajaratnam, Daniel. Symbiotic marketing revisited. *Journal of Marketing*, pp. 7–17 (January 1986). [3:207–208 (September 1986)]

Verba, Stephen M. Commentary: strategic execution process for launching new products. *Journal of Product and Brand Management*, 2(2):18–32 (1993). [11:263–264 (June 1994)]

Voss, Bristol. Quality's second coming. *Journal of Business Strategy*, pp. 42–46 (March–April 1994). [11:473–474 (November 1994)]

Wagner, Harvey E. The open corporation. *California Management Review*, pp. 46–60 (Summer 1991). [9:177–178 (June 1992)]

Wall, Toby D., Kemp, Nigel J., Jackson, Paul R., and Clegg, Chris W. Outcomes of autonomous workgroups: a long-term field experiment. *Academy of Management Journal*, pp. 280–304 (1986). [3:304 (December 1986)]

Waterman, Robert H., Jr. The renewal factor. *Business Week*, September 14, 1987, pp. 100–120. [5:164–165 (June 1988)]

Weiner, Charles. Universities, professors, and patents: a continuing controversy. *Technology Review*, pp. 13–15 (February–March 1986). [4:158–159 (June 1987)]

Welch, Joe L. Researching marketing problems and opportunities with focus groups. *Industrial Marketing Management*, pp. 245–253 (1985). [4:234 (September 1987)]

Wheelwright, Stephen C. and Sasser, W. Earl. The new product development map. *Harvard Business Review*, pp. 112–125 (May–June 1989). [7:79–80 (March 1990)]

White, Philip. Waste not. *International Design*, pp. 67–69 (May–June 1992). [9:319 (December 1992)]

Whiteley, Richard C. Why customer focus strategies often fail. *Journal of Business Strategy*, pp. 34–37 (September–October 1991). [10:162–163 (March 1993)]

Williams, Jeffrey R. How sustainable is your competitive advantage? *California Management Review*, pp. 29–51 (Spring 1992). [10:258–259 (June 1993)]

Wise, George. It's a myth that all inventions come from outside. *Research Technology Management*, pp. 7–8 (July–August 1989). [7:86 (March 1990)]

Wrubel, Robert. Scorch, burn and plunder. *Financial World*, February 16, 1993, pp. 28–30. [10:349–350 (September 1993)]

Zhivago, Kristin. Timing is everything in a product rollout. *Business Marketing*, p. 36 (March 1994). [11:474 (November 1994)]

Zollers, Frances E. and Cook, Ronald G. Product liability reform: what happened to the crisis? *Business Horizons*, pp. 47–52 (September–October 1990). [8:142–143 (June 1991)]

Technological Innovation

Adler, Paul. New Technologies, New skills. *California Management Review*, 1:9–28 (1986). [4:232–233 (September 1987)]

Adler, Paul S., Riggs, Henry E., and Wheelwright, Steven C. Product development know-how: trading tactics for strategy. *Sloan Management Review*, pp. 7–17 (Fall 1989). [7:160–161 (June 1990)]

Anderson, Philip and Tushman, Michael L. Managing through cycles of technological change. *Research Technology Management*, pp. 26–31 (May–June 1991). [8:316–317 (December 1991)]

Ayal, Igal and Raban, Joel. Developing hi-tech industrial products for world markets. *IEEE Transactions on Engineering Management*, pp. 177–183 (August 1990). [8:144–145 (June 1991)]

Bacon, Glenn, Beckman, Sara, Mowrey, David, and Wilson, Edith. Managing product definition in high-technology industries: a pilot study. *California Management Review*, pp. 32–56 (Spring 1994). [12:174–175 (March 1995)]

Beard, Charles and Easingwood, Chris. Sources of competitive advantage in the marketing of technology-intensive products and processes. *European Journal of Marketing*, 12:5–18 (1992). [10:351–352 (September 1993)]

Berman, Evan, Vasconcellos, Eduardo, and Werther, William B., Jr. Executive levers for the strategic management of technology. *Business Horizons*, pp. 53–61 (January–February 1994). [11:471–472 (November 1994)]

Bertrand, Kate. More Than one way to set a standard. *Business Marketing*, pp. 38–46 (June 1988). [5:315–316 (December 1988)]

Bowe, Frank. Why seniors don't use technology. *Technology Review*, pp. 34–40 (August–September 1988). [6:144–145 (June 1989)]

Brandt, Richard and Port, Otis. How automation could save the day. *Business Week*, March 3, 1986, pp. 72–74. [3:208–209 (September 1986)]

Brown, Buck. Business incubators suffer growing pains. *The Wall Street Journal*, June 16, 1989, p. B1. [7:164 (June 1990)]

Brown, Rick. Managing the "S" curves of innovation. *Journal of Consumer Marketing*, pp. 61–72 (Winter 1992). [9:247–248 (September 1992)]

Burgelman, Robert A. Managing corporate entrepreneurship: new structures for implementing technological innovation. *Technology in Society*, pp. 91–103 (1985). [4:150–151 (June 1987)]

Burkart, Robert E. Reducing R&D cycle time. *Research Technology Management* (May–June 1994, pp. 27–32). [12 (September 1995):356–357]

Capon, Noel and Glazer, Rashi. Marketing and technology: a strategic coalignment. *Journal of Marketing*, pp. 1–14 (July 1987). [5:242–243 (September 1988)]

Carlsson, Matts H. Integration of technical functions for increased efficiency in the product development process. Department of Industrial Management and Economics, Chalmers University of Technology, Goteborg, Sweden (summary of dissertation). [8:150–151 (June 1991)]

Chandler, Colby H. Corporate innovation and entrepreneurship. *Journal of Business Strategy*, pp. 5–8 (Summer 1986). [4:70–71 (March 1987)]

Collinson, Simon. Managing product innovation at Sony: the development of the data discman. *Technology Analysis and Strategic Management*, 3:285–306 (1993). [11:467 (November 1994)]

Conley, Ned L. and Mirabel, Eric P. The expanding personal liability of corporate officers and directors for patent infringement. *IDEA*, 4:225–247 (1988). [6: 149 (June 1989)]

Conniff, Richard. Superchicken: whose life is it anyway? *Discover*, pp. 32–41 (June 1988). [5:320–321 (December 1988)]

Cordero, Rene. The measurement of innovation performance in the firm: an overview. *Research Policy*, pp. 185–192 (1990). [8:219–220 (September 1991)]

Dankanyin, Robert J. Defense company diversification: what it takes to succeed. *Technology Management*, 1:11–16 (1994). [12:258 (June 1995)]

Dorf, Richard C. and Worthington, Kirby K. F. Technology transfer: research to commercial product. *Engineering Management International*, pp. 185–191 (February 1989). [6:304–305 (December 1989)]

Dougherty, Elizabeth. Technology scouts. *Research and Development*, pp. 44–50 (October 1989). [7:163 (June 1990)]

Doz, Yves, Angelmar, Reinhard, and Prahalad, C. K. Technological innovation and interdependence, a challenge for the large, complex firm. *Technology in Society*, pp. 105–125 (1985). [4:151–152 (June 1987)]

Eisenhardt, Kathleen M. Speed and strategic choice: how managers accelerate decision-making. *California Management Review*, pp. 39–54 (Spring 1990). [8: 66–67 (March 1991)]

Engstrom, Therese. Little Silicon Valleys. *High Technology*, pp. 24–32 (January 1987). [4:231 (September 1987)]

French, Robert L. Cars that know where they're going. *The Futurist*, pp. 29–36 (May–June 1989). [6:300–301 (December 1989)]

Frey, Donald N. Junk your linear R&D. *Research Technology Management*, pp. 7–8 (May–June 1989). [7:88 (March 1990)]

Gomory, Ralph E. From the "ladder of dcience" to the product development cycle. *Harvard Business Review*, pp. 99–105 (November–December 1989). [7: 157–158 (June 1990)]

Gomory, Ralph E. and Schmitt, Roland W. Step-by-step innovation. *Across the Board*, pp. 52–56 (November 1988). [6:232–233 (September 1989)]

Hamilton, William F. Corporate strategies for managing emerging technologies. *Technology in Society*, pp. 197–212 (1985). [4:311 (December 1987)]

Hauser, John R. How Puritan-Bennett used the house of quality. *Sloan Management Review*, pp. 61–70 (Spring 1993). [11:271 (June 1994)]

Hayden, Michael A. What is technological literacy? *Bulletin of Science, Technology and Society*, 4:228–233 (1989). [7:331–332 (December 1990)]

Hilton, William E. What sort of improper conduct constitutes misappropriation of a trade secret? *IDEA*, 30(4):287–308 (1990). [8:64 (March 1991)]

Holt, Knut. Does the engineer forget the user? *Design Studies*, pp. 163–168 (July 1989). [7:168–169 (June 1990)]

Karakaya, Fahri and Kobu, Bulent. New product development process: an investigation of success and failure in high-technology and mon-high-technology firms. *Journal of Business Venturing*, 9:49–66 (1993). [11:362 (September 1994)]

Kelley, Robert and Caplan, Janet. How Bell Labs creates star performers. *Harvard Business Review* (July–August 1993, pp. 128–139). [11:269–270 (June 1994)]

Kodama, Fumio. Technology fusion and the new R&D. *Harvard Business Review*, pp. 70–78 (July–August 1992). [10:353–354 (September 1993)]

Kozlov, Alex. Rethinking artificial intelligence. *High Technology Business*, pp. 18–25 (May 1988). [5:314 (December 1988)]

Kupfer, Andrew. America's fastest growing company. *Fortune*, August 13, 1990, pp. 54–58. [8:141–142 (June 1991)]

Langowitz, Nan S. Managing new product design and factory fit. *Business Horizons*, pp. 76–79 (May–June 1989). [7:77 (March 1990)]

Luke, Roice D., Begun, James W., and Pointer, Dennis D. Quasi firms: strategic interorganizational forms in the health care industry. *Academy of Management Review*, 1:9–19 (1989). [7:81–82 (March 1990)]

Mandell, Mel and Murphy, Brian. Wake-up strategies for tired R&D projects. *High Technology Business*, pp. 22–25 (February 1989). [7:256–257 (September 1990)]

McDonald, David W. and Leahey, Harry S. Licensing has a role in technology strategic planning. *Research Management*, pp. 35–40 (January 1985). [3:211–212 (September 1986)]

McNulty, Terry and Whittington, Richard. Putting the marketing into R&D. *Marketing Intelligence and Planning* (1992 n 9), pp. 10–16. [10 (September 1993): 358–359]

Meldrum, M. J. and Millman, A. F. Ten risks in marketing high-technology products. *Industrial Marketing Management*, pp. 43–50 (1991). [8:217–218 (September 1991)]

Micromachines (unsigned article). *The Futurist*, p. 54 (September–October 1988). [6:65 (March 1989)]

Mitchell, Graham R. New approaches for the strategic management of technology. *Technology in Society*, pp. 227–239 (1985). [4:300 (December 1987)]

Nelson, R. U.S. technological leadership: where did it come from and where did it go? *Research Policy*, pp. 117–132 (1990). [8:215–216 (September 1991)]

Nuemo, Pedro and Oosterveld, Jan. Managing technology alliances. *Long Range Planning*, 3:11–18 (1988). [6:68 (March 1989)]

Perritt, Henry H., Jr. Government information goes on-line. *Technology Review*, pp. 60–67 (November–December 1989). [7:167–168 (June 1990)]

Pine, B. Joseph, II. Making mass customization happen: strategies for the new competitive realities. *Planning Review*, pp. 23–24 (September–October 1993). [11:364 (September 1994)]

Pine, B. Joseph, II. Mass customizing products and services. *Planning Review*, pp. 6–13ff (July–August 1993). [11:270 (June 1994)]

Purser, Ronald E. Redesigning the knowledge-based product development organization: a case study of sociotechnical systems change. *Technovation*, pp. 403–415 (November 1991). [10:80–81 (January 1993)]

Quinn, John J. How companies keep abreast of technological change. *Long Range Planning*, pp. 69–76 (April 1985). [5:85–86 (March 1988)]

Rabino, Samuel. High-technology firms and factors influencing transfer of R&D facilities. *Journal of Business Research*, pp. 195–205 (May 1989). [6:309 (December 1989)]

Ram, S. and Sheth, Jagdish N. Clearing the hurdles to technological innovation. *Product and Process Innovation*, pp. 10–19 (March–April 1991). [9:84 (March 1992)]

Ram, S. and Sheth, Jagdish N. Consumer resistance to innovations: the marketing problem and its solutions. *Journal of Consumer Marketing*, pp. 5–14 (Spring 1989). [6:298–299 (December 1989)]

Ransley, Derek L. Do's and don'ts of R&D benchmarking. *Research Technology Management*, pp. 50–56 (September–October 1993). [12:250–251 (June 1995)]

Rayner, Bruce C.P. The rising price of technological leadership. *Electronic Business*, March 18, 1991, pp. 52–56. [8:314–315 (December 1991)]

Rothwell, Roy and Wissema, Hans. Technology, culture and public policy. *Technovation*, pp. 91–115 (1986). [4:62–63 (March 1987)]

Seely Brown, John. Research that reinvents the corporation. *McKinsey Quarterly*, 2:78–96 (1992). [10:259–260 (June 1993)]

Shenhar, Aaron J. From low- to high-tech project management. *R&D Management*, 23(3):199–214 (1993). [11:364–365 (September 1994)]

Sisodia, Rajendra S. Why companies kill their technologies. *Journal of Business Strategy*, pp. 42–48 (January–February 1992). [10:350 (September 1993)]

Skiadas, Christos. Two simple models for the early and middle stage prediction of innovation diffusion. *IEEE Transactions on Engineering Management*, pp. 79–84 (May 1987). [4:306 (December 1987)]

The smart house (unsigned article). *The Futurist*, pp. 52–53 (September–October 1987). [5:164 (June 1988)]

Souder, William E. Improving productivity through technology fush. *Research Technology Management*, pp. 19–24 (March–April 1989). [6:305–306 (December 1989)]

Souder, William E. and Padmanabhan, Venkatesh. Transferring new technologies from R&D to manufacturing. *Research Technology Management*, pp. 38–43 (September–October 1989). [7:165–166 (June 1990)]

Spero, Donald M. Patent protection or piracy — a CEO views Japan. *Harvard Business Review*, pp. 58–67 (September–October 1990). [8:140–141 (June 1991)]

Taylor, Charles R. Prospering in the 90s. *Across the Board*, pp. 43–46 (January–February 1992). [9:253–254 (September 1992)]

Teece, David J. Profiting from technological innovation: implications for integration, collaboration, and public policy. *Research Policy*, pp. 285–305 (1986). [5: 78 (March 1988)]

Traynor, Kenneth and Traynor, Susan. The efficacy of strategic and promotional factors on the sales growth of high-tech firms. *IEEE Transactions on Engineering Management*, pp. 126–134 (May 1994). [12:79–80 (January 1995)]

Waltz, David L. The prospects for building truly intelligent machines. *Daedalus*, pp. 191–212 (Winter 1988). [5:315 (December 1988)]

Warner, Edward. Expert systems and the law. *High Technology Business*, pp. 32–35 (October 1988). [6:233 (September 1989)]

Weiner, Edith and Brown, Arnold. Human factors: the gap between humans and machines. *The Futurist*, pp. 9–11 (May–June 1989). [6:304 (December 1989)]

Westney, D. Eleanor and Sakakibara, Kiyonori. Designing the designers. *Technology Review*, pp. 24–31 (April 1986). [4:64–65 (March 1987)]

Wheelwright, Stephen C. and Sasser, W. Earl. The new product development map. *Harvard Business Review*, pp. 112–125 (May–June 1989). [7:79–80 (March 1990)]

Wrubel, Robert. Scorch, burn and plunder. *Financial World*, February 16, 1993, pp. 28–30. [10:349–350 (September 1993)]

CUMULATIVE INDEX OF BOOK REVIEWS

The following list cites all book reviews published in *JPIM* through the end of 1995. Each entry is alphabetized by the last name of the first author and shows the title of the book and the journal volume, issue, and page number where you may find the review. Over the years, our book reviews have been edited by Robert Cooper, Milton Rosenau, Jr., and Robert Rothberg.

Archibald, Russell D. *Managing High-Technology Programs and Projects*, 2nd ed. [10:266–267 (June 1993)]

Barnard. William and Wallace, Thomas F. *The Innovative Edge: Creating Strategic Breakthroughs Using the Voice of the Customer.* [12:90–91 (January 1995)]

Beuamont, Leland R. *ISO 9001: The Standard Companion.* [12:181 (March 1995)]

Blattberg, Robert C., Glazer, Rashi, and Little, John D. C., eds. *The Marketing Revolution.* [12:269–270 (June 1995)]

Block, Zenas and MacMillan, Ian C. *Corporate Venturing: Creating New Business within the Firm.* [10:361–362 (September 1993)]

Bly, Robert W. *Business to Business Direct Marketing.* [10:443 (November 1993)]

Boothroyd, Geoffrey, Dewhurst, Peter, and Knight, Winston. *Product Design for Manufacturing and Assembly.* [12:369 (September 1995)]

Boznak, Rudolph G. with Kecker, Audrey K. *Competitive Product Development.* [11:273–274 (June 1994)]

Burns, Marshall. *Automated Fabrication: Improving Productivity in Manufacturing.* [11:277 (June 1994)]

Butman, John. Flying Fox. *A Business Adventure in Teams and Teamwork.* [11:89–90 (January 1994)]

Caris-McManus, Jeannemarie. *The New Product Development Planner.* [9:184–185 (June 1992)]

Carter, Donald E. and Baker, Barbara Stillwell. *Concurrent Engineering: The Product Development Environment for the 1990s.* [10:176–177 (March 1993)]

Choffray, J. M. and Lilien, G. L. *Marketing Planning for New Industrial Products.* [3:63–64 (March 1986)]

Clark, Kim B. and Fujimoto, Takahiro. *Product Development Performance: Strategy, Organization, and Management in the World Auto Industry.* [9:85–86 (March 1992)]

Clarke, Thomas E. and Reavley, Jean. *Science and Technology Management Bibliography '93.* [11:92 (January 1994)]

Clausing, Don. *Total Quality Development: A Step-by-Step Guide to World-Class Concurrent Engineering.* [12:179–180 (March 1995)]

Cooper, Robert G. *Winning at New Products.* [3:307–308 (December 1986)]

Cooper, Robert G. *Winning at New Products: Accelerating the Process from Idea to Launch*, 2nd ed. [11:369–370 (September 1994)]

Crawford, C. Merle. *New Products Management.* [2:66–67 (March 1985)]

Crawford, C. Merle. *New Products Management*, 4th ed. [11:367–369 (September 1994)]

Deschamps, Jean-Philippe and Nayak, P. Ranganath. *Product Juggernauts: How Companies Mobilize to Generate a Stream of Market Winners.* [12:360–361 (September 1995)]

Dimancescu, Dan. *The Seamless Enterprise: Making Cross-Functional Management Work.* [12:178–179 (March 1995)]

Dolan, Robert J. *Managing the New Product Development Process.* [12:93–94 (January 1995)]

Dunham, Andrea and Marcus, Barry. *Unique Value: The Secret of All Great Business Strategies.* [11:376–377 (September 1994)]

Egan, Gerald. *Working the Shadow Side: A Guide to Positive Behind-the-Scenes Management.* [12:366–368 (September 1995)]

Erhorn, Craig and Stark, John. *Competing by Design: Creating Value and Market Advantage in New Product Development.* [12:92–93 (January 1995)]

Fisher, Donald C. *Measuring Up to the Baldrige: A Quick & Easy Self-Assessment Guide for Organizations of All Sizes.* [12:458–459 (November 1995)]

Floyd, Thomas D., Levy, Stu, and Wolfman, Arnold B. *Winning the New Product Development Battle.* [11:478–479 (November 1994)]

Foster, Richard N. *Innovation: The Attacker's Advantage.* [4:239–240 (September 1987)]

Fragnos, Stephen J. with Bennett, Steven J. Team Zebra. *How 1500 Partners Revitalized Eastman Kodak's Black & White Film Making Flow.* [11:274–275 (June 1994)]

Gale, Bradley T. *Managing Customer Value: Creating Quality and Service That Customers Can See.* [12:457–458 (November 1995)]

Galsworth, Gwendolyn D. *Smart, Simple Design: Using Variety Effectiveness to Reduce Total Cost and Maximize Customer Selection.* [12:365–366 (September 1995)]

Gibb, J. M., ed. *Science Parks and Innovation Centers: Their Economic and Social Impact.* [5:91–92 (March 1988)]

Gibson, David V. and Rogers, Everett M. *R&D Collaboration on Trial.* [11:378 (September 1994)]

Gilad, Benjamin. *Business Blindspots.* [12:454–455 (November 1995)]

Goodman, Richard A. and Lawless, Michael W. *Technology and Strategy: Conceptual Models and Diagnostics.* [12:363 (September 1995)]

Lawrence, Margarte, ed. *Field Guide to Strategy.* [11:378 (September 1994)]

Lehmann, Donald R. and Winer, Russell S. *Product Management.* [12:270–271 (June 1995)]

Lipnack, Jessica and Stamps, Jeffrey. *The TeamNet Factor: Bringing the Power of Boundary Crossing into the Heart of Your Organization.* [11:178–179 (March 1994)]

Lovelock, Christopher. *Product Plus: How Product + Service = Competitive Advantage.* [12:91–92 (January 1995)]

Martin, Andre J. *Infopartnering: The Ultimate Strategy for Achieving Efficient Consumer Response.* [12:181 (March 1995)]

Martin, Michael J. C. *Managing Technological Innovation.* [3:64–65 (March 1986)]

McGrath, Jospeh E. and Hollingshead, Andrea B. *Groups Interacting with Technology.* [11:479–481 (November 1994)]

McGrath, Michael E. *Product Strategy for High-Technology Companies: How to Achieve Growth, Competitive Advantage, and Increased Profits.* [12:358–360 (September 1995)]

McGrath, Michael E., Anthony, Michael T., and Shapiro, Amram R. *Product Development: Success Through Product and Cycle-Time Excellence.* [10:264–265 (June 1993)]

McQuarrie, Edward F. *Customer Visits: Building a Better Market Focus.* [11:476–477 (November 1994)]

Mead, Richard. *Cross Cultural Management Communication.* [9:185–186 (June 1992)]

Meltzer, Robert J. *Biomedical and Clinical Instrumentation: Fast Tracking from Concept Through Production in a Regulated Environement.* [12:263–264 (June 1995)]

Meyer, Chrisopher. *Fast Cycle Time: How to Align Purpose, Strategy, and Speed.* [11:272–273 (June 1994)]

Moore, William L. and Pessemier, Edgar A. *Product Planning and Management: Designing and Delivering Value.* [11:373–374 (September 1994)]

Morone, Joseph G. *Winning in High-Tech Markets: The Role of the General Manager.* [10:362–363 (September 1993)]

Moskowitz, Howard R. *Food Concepts and Products: Just-in-Time Development.* [12:264–266 (June 1995)]

Mosley, Thomas E., Jr. *Marketing Your Invention.* [11:91–92 (January 1994)]

Nagle, Thomas T. and Holden, Reed K. *The Strategy and Tactics of Pricing: A Guide to Profitable Decision Making,* 2nd ed. [12: 455–457 (November 1995)]

Nelson, Bob. *1001 Ways to Reward Employees.* [12:180 (March 1995)]

Nelson, Richard R., ed. *National Innovation Systems: A Comparative Analysis.* [12:94–95 (January 1995)]

Susman, Gerard I., ed. *Integrating Design and Manufacturing for Competitive Advantage.* [10:441–442 (November 1993)]

Szakonyi, Robert. *Technology Management* (2). [11:276–277 (June 1994)]

Thomas, Robert J. *New Product Development: Managing and Forecasting for Strategic Success.* [12:368 (September 1995)]

Turino, Jon. *Managing Concurrent Engineering: Buying Time to Market.* [9:328–329 (December 1992)]

Tushman, Michael L. and Moore, William L. *Readings in the Management of Innovation.* [2:272–274 (December 1985)]

Ulrich. Karl T. and Eppinger, Steven D. *Product Design and Development.* [12:262 (June 1995)]

Urban, Glen and Hauser, John. *Design and Marketing of New Products,* (2nd Ed.). [11:481–482 (November 1994)]

Utterback, James M. *Mastering the Dynamics of Innovation: How Companies Can Seize Opportunities in the Face of Tech Change.* [12:89–90 (January 1995)]

Vandermerwe, Sandra. *From Tin Soldiers to Russian Dolls: Creating Added Value Through Service.* [11:175–177 (March 1994)]

Wellins, Richard S., Bhyan, William C., and Dixon, George R. *Inside Teams: How 20 World-Class Organizations Are Winning Through Teamwork.* [12:262 (June 1995)]

Wessner, John W., Hiatt, Jeffrey M., and Trimble, David C. *Winning with Quality: Applying Quality Principles in Product Development.* [12:268 (June 1995)]

Wheelwright, Steven C. and Clark, Kim B. *Leading Product Development: The Senior Manager's Guide to Creating and Shaping the Enterprise.* [12:361–362 (September 1995)]

Wheelwright, Steven C. and Clark, Kim B. *Revolutionizing Product Development: Quantum Leaps in Speed, Efficiency, and Quality.* [10:87–88 (January 1993)]

Whitaker, Ken. *Managing Software Maniacs: Finding, Managing, and Rewarding a Winning Development Team.* [12:262–263 (June 1995)]

Williamson, Alisir D., ed. *Field Guide to Marketing.* [11:378 (September 1994)]

Winchell, William. *Continuous Quality Improvement: A Manufacturing Professional's Guide.* [9:262–263 (September 1992)]

Wind, Y. J. *Product Policy: Concepts, Methods, and Strategy.* [2:67–69 (March 1985)]

Zangwell, Willard I. *Lightning Strategies for Innovation: How the World's Best Firms Compete.* [10:364 (September 1993)]

INDEX